ADHD: Symptoms, Treatment and Management

ADHD: Symptoms, Treatment and Management

Edited by Carl Booth

hayle medical

New York

Hayle Medical,
750 Third Avenue, 9th Floor,
New York, NY 10017, USA

Visit us on the World Wide Web at:
www.haylemedical.com

ISBN: 978-1-63241-481-6

The publisher's policy is to use permanent paper from mills that operate a sustainable forestry policy. Furthermore, the publisher ensures that the text paper and cover boards used have met acceptable environmental accreditation standards.

Printed in China.

Cataloging-in-Publication Data

ADHD : symptoms, treatment and management / edited by Carl Booth.
p. cm.
Includes bibliographical references and index.
ISBN 978-1-63241-481-6
1. Attention-deficit hyperactivity disorder. 2. Attention-deficit hyperactivity disorder--Diagnosis.
3. Attention-deficit hyperactivity disorder--Treatment. I. Booth, Carl.

RJ506.H9 A34 2018
618.928 589--dc23

Table of Contents

Preface

Attention deficit hyperactivity disorder is a disorder found in children between the age of six months to twelve years. It includes problems such as paying attention, hyperactivity, difficulty in controlling behavior, etc. Genetics and environmental factors play an important role in developing ADHD. This book provides significant information of this topic to help develop a good understanding of ADHD and related topics. A number of latest researches have been included to keep the readers up-to-date with the treatment and management strategies related to attention deficit hyperactivity disorder.

Various studies have approached the subject by analyzing it with a single perspective, but the present book provides diverse methodologies and techniques to address this field. This book contains theories and applications needed for understanding the subject from different perspectives. The aim is to keep the readers informed about the progresses in the field; therefore, the contributions were carefully examined to compile novel researches by specialists from across the globe.

Indeed, the job of the editor is the most crucial and challenging in compiling all chapters into a single book. In the end, I would extend my sincere thanks to the chapter authors for their profound work. I am also thankful for the support provided by my family and colleagues during the compilation of this book.

Editor

1

Shared Cognitive Impairments and Aetiology in ADHD Symptoms and Reading Difficulties

Celeste H. M. Cheung[1], Alexis C. Fazier-Wood[2], Philip Asherson[1], Fruhling Rijsdijk[1], Jonna Kuntsi[1]*

1 MRC Social, Genetic and Developmental Psychiatry Centre, Institute of Psychiatry, King's College London, London, United Kingdom, **2** Human Genetics Center, Division of Epidemiology, Human Genetics and Environmental Science, School of Public Health, University of Texas Health Sciences Center at Houston, Houston, Texas, United States of America

Abstract

Background: Twin studies indicate that the frequent co-occurrence of attention deficit hyperactivity disorder (ADHD) symptoms and reading difficulties (RD) is largely due to shared genetic influences. Both disorders are associated with multiple cognitive impairments, but it remains unclear which cognitive impairments share the aetiological pathway, underlying the co-occurrence of the symptoms. We address this question using a sample of twins aged 7–10 and a range of cognitive measures previously associated with ADHD symptoms or RD.

Methods: We performed multivariate structural equation modelling analyses on parent and teacher ratings on the ADHD symptom domains of inattention and hyperactivity, parent ratings on RD, and cognitive data on response inhibition (commission errors, CE), reaction time variability (RTV), verbal short-term memory (STM), working memory (WM) and choice impulsivity, from a population sample of 1312 twins aged 7–10 years.

Results: Three cognitive processes showed significant phenotypic and genetic associations with both inattention symptoms and RD: RTV, verbal WM and STM. While STM captured only 11% of the shared genetic risk between inattention and RD, the estimates increased somewhat for WM (21%) and RTV (28%); yet most of the genetic sharing between inattention and RD remained unaccounted for in each case.

Conclusion: While response inhibition and choice impulsivity did not emerge as important cognitive processes underlying the co-occurrence between ADHD symptoms and RD, RTV and verbal memory processes separately showed significant phenotypic and genetic associations with both inattention symptoms and RD. Future studies employing longitudinal designs will be required to investigate the developmental pathways and direction of causality further.

Editor: Michael A. Motes, Center for BrainHealth, University of Texas at Dallas, United States of America

Funding: The Study of Activity and Impulsivity Levels in children (SAIL) is funded by a project grant from the Wellcome Trust (GR070345MF). The funders had no role in study design, data collection and analysis, decision to publish, or preparation of the manuscript.

Competing Interests: Philip Asherson has acted in an advisory role for Shire, Janssen-Cilag, Eli Lilly and Flynn Pharma. He has received education or research grants from Shire, Janssen-Cilag and Eli-Lilly. He has given talks at educational events sponsored by the above companies. The other authors report no conflicts of interest.

* E-mail: jonna.kuntsi@kcl.ac.uk

Introduction

Attention deficit hyperactivity disorder (ADHD) and reading disability are strongly heritable, complex neurodevelopmental disorders that frequently co-occur [1–4]. Sibling and twin studies indicate that the phenotypic association between ADHD and reading difficulties (RD) is largely attributed to shared familial/genetic influences [1,3,5,6]. Of the two ADHD symptom domains of hyperactivity-impulsivity and inattentiveness, RD shows stronger phenotypic and genetic associations specifically with inattention symptoms, compared to hyperactivity-impulsivity symptoms [3,5–7].

Linking the familial risk factors in ADHD to cognitive impairments, we obtained evidence in sibling-pair analyses for two familial cognitive impairment factors in ADHD [8]. The first and larger familial factor captured familial influences on RT variability (RTV), and is separated from the second familial factor which captured familial influences on commission errors (CE) and omission errors (OE) on a Go/No-Go task. Applying the same analysis approach to an independent dataset of ADHD and control sibling pairs, with different cognitive and motor tasks, again two familial factors emerged where familial factor loading on 'intra-individual variability' was separate from those on working memory (WM) [9]. Overall, the findings from the sibling studies on children and adolescents with ADHD indicate two familial cognitive impairment factors in ADHD, the first capturing slow and high variable responses and the second capturing aspects of executive functioning, both of which largely separate from familial influences shared between ADHD and IQ.

By mapping the aetiological factors underlying ADHD-related cognitive impairments onto those of the two ADHD symptom domains separately using a population sample of twins, we further demonstrated that RTV and CE reflect different genetic relationships to the two ADHD symptom domains [10]. While

RTV showed substantial genetic overlap particularly with inattentiveness, CE showed little genetic overlap with either hyperactivity-impulsivity or inattentiveness.

Similar to ADHD, individuals with RD also show impairments in multiple domains of cognitive functions including verbal WM [11–16], RTV [11,17–19] and processing speed [16,20,21]. However, RTV and verbal working memory have been more extensively studied in ADHD. Findings on response inhibition have, however, been inconsistent [15,16,22]. A sibling study indicated significant shared familial influences on RD with executive functioning and motor vulnerabilities [23], and a twin study further indicated shared genetic influences on RD with verbal short-term memory (STM) and WM [24].

To our knowledge, only one study to date has examined the aetiological sharing between ADHD symptoms, RD and specific cognitive processes. Willcutt et al. studied a population sample of 457 twin pairs, aged 8–18, from the Colorado Learning Disabilities Research Centre study [4]. Genetic factors underlying slow processing speed (measured as MRT in symbol search and picture identification tasks) captured a substantial proportion of shared genetic risks between ADHD symptoms and RD, whereas a significant proportion of genetic influences on inhibition or WM were independent of the genetic covariance between reading and inattention symptoms [4]. These findings require replication and extension into further cognitive measures.

Using multivariate model-fitting analyses on a large population twin sample, with a tightly defined age range (7–10 years), this study aims to investigate which cognitive impairments previously linked to either ADHD or RD or both (specifically RTV, response inhibition, verbal STM and WM, and choice impulsivity [3]), independent of IQ effects, underlie the co-occurring symptoms. Specifically, we address three key questions: i) Which cognitive impairments are associated with both ADHD symptoms and RD? ii) To what extent do these cognitive measures (the identified cognitive variables, RD, and ADHD symptoms) share genetic influences? iii) To what extent does a shared cognitive impairment capture the shared genetic risk between ADHD symptoms and RD?

Materials and Methods

Ethics statement

The study was conducted in accordance with the Declaration of Helsinki and was approved by the Institute of Psychiatry Research Ethics Committee. Parents of all participants gave written consent to the study procedure before their participation.

Sample and Procedure

Participants are members of the Study of Activity and Impulsivity Levels in children (SAIL), a general population sample of twins aged between 7 and 10 years. They were recruited from the Twins' Early Development Study (TEDS; [25], a birth cohort study in which parents of all twins born in England and Wales during 1994–1996 were invited to enroll. TEDS families were invited to take part if they fulfilled SAIL project criteria, including White European ethnic origin (to reduce population heterogeneity for molecular genetic studies); no extreme pregnancy or perinatal difficulties, specific medical syndromes, chromosomal anomalies or epilepsy; and not on stimulant or other neuropsychiatric medications (see [26] for a full list of inclusion criteria).

Of the 1,230 suitable families contacted, 672 families (55%) agreed to participate. Thirty-two children were subsequently excluded due to: IQ <70, epilepsy, autism, obsessive-compulsive or other neurodevelopmental disorder, illness during testing or placement on stimulant medication for ADHD. The final sample consisted of 1312 individuals: 257 monozygotic (MZ) twin pairs, 181 same-sex dizygotic (DZ) and 206 opposite-sex DZ twin pairs, as well as 24 singletons coming from pairs with one of the twins excluded. Data for the 24 singleton twins were also used in the structural equation modeling [27].

The families visited the research centre for the assessments. Two testers assessed the twins simultaneously in separate testing rooms. The tasks were administered in a fixed order as part of a more extensive test session, which in total (including breaks) lasted approximately 2.5 hours. The mean age of the sample was 8.83 (SD = 0.67), and half of the sample were female (N = 663, 50.5%). Children's IQs ranged from 70 to 158 (M = 109.34, SD = 14.72).

Measures

ADHD Ratings. Parent and teachers were asked to complete the Long Versions of Conners' Parent Rating Scale [28] and the Long Version of Conners' Teacher Rating Scales [29]. To obtain a composite score for ADHD symptoms, ADHD inattention and hyperactivity-impulsivity symptoms were obtained using the summed parent and teacher ratings on the 9-item inattentive DISM-IV subscales and the 9-item hyperactivity-impulsivity DSM-IV subscales, respectively, consistent with our previous studies that examined cognitive measures in relation to ADHD traits in this sample [3,30–32]. Teacher ratings were missing for 151 individuals and parent ratings for two individuals.

Reading difficulties. Reading Difficulties Questionnaire (RDQ) is a subscale of the Colorado Learning Difficulties Questionnaire [33]. This six-item parent rating scale is part of an instrument screening for learning disorders. On a scale that ranges from 1 (never/not at all) to 5 (always/a great deal), parents reported the extent of their child's difficulties with spelling, learning letter names, sounding words out, and to what extent their child reads slowly, below expectancy level or has required extra help at school. The total score ranges from 5 to 30, with higher scores indicating greater difficulties with reading. This scale has been shown to have excellent internal consistency (mean Cronbach's $\alpha = 0.90$) and high inter-rater ($r = 0.83$) and one-year test-retest ($r = 0.81$) reliabilities [34]. RDQ has shown strong correlations with other objective reading and spelling measures (average $r = 0.64$), but low correlations with measures of other learning difficulties ($r = 0.07$ to 0.02), which attest to its good criterion and discriminant validity [34]. Moreover, RDQ scores have demonstrated moderate to high heritability ($h^2 = 53$ to 83%) and high genetic correlations (0.71 to 0.89) with a composite measure of reading performance [5,35].

Wechsler Intelligence Scales for Children, Third Edition (WISC-III; [36]). The vocabulary, similarities, picture completion and block design subtests from the WISC-III were used to obtain an estimate of the child's IQ (prorated following procedures described by [37]). The digit span subtest from the WISC-III was administered to obtain digit span forward (DSF) and digit span backward (DSB) [36], which measure verbal STM and WM, respectively.

The Go/No-Go task [38,39]. On each trial, one of two possible stimuli appeared for 300 ms in the middle of the computer screen. The participant was instructed to respond only to the 'go' stimuli and to react as quickly as possible, but to maintain a high level of accuracy. The proportion of 'go' stimuli to 'no-go' stimuli was 4:1. The participants performed the task under three conditions (slow, fast and incentive), matched for length of time on task. Herein we present data from the slow condition, which had an inter-stimulus interval (ISI) of 8 s and consisting of 72 trials, and the fast condition, with an inter-stimulus interval

(ISI) of 1 second and consisting of 462 trials. The order of presentation of the slow and fast conditions varied randomly across participants. We focus here on two variables obtained from the task: CE and RTV.

The Fast Task [40,41]. The baseline condition, with a foreperiod of 8 s and consisting of 72 trials, followed a standard warned four-choice RT task. A warning signal (four empty circles, arranged side by side) first appeared on the screen. At the end of the foreperiod (presentation interval for the warning signal), the circle designated as the target signal for that trial was filled (coloured) in. The participant was asked to make a compatible choice by pressing the response key that directly corresponded in position to the location of the target stimulus. Following a response, the stimuli disappeared from the screen and a fixed inter-trial interval of 2.5 s followed. Speed and accuracy were emphasised equally. If the child did not respond within 10 s, the trial terminated. A comparison condition with a fast event rate (1 second) and incentives followed the baseline condition [41]. Herein we focus on RTV, obtained from the baseline condition.

To limit the total number of variables and to create psychometrically robust variables that would enable direct comparisons to our previous findings using the same tasks in a clinically diagnosed sample [8], the summed unstandardized scores of RTV were obtained across the baseline conditions of the Go/No-Go and Fast tasks [30,40]. A composite measure of CE was obtained by summing the raw CE scores from both the baseline (slow) and the fast conditions of the Go/No-Go task [40].

The Maudsley Index of Childhood Delay Aversion [26,31]. Two conditions, each with 20 trials, were administered. In each trial, the child had a choice between a smaller-immediate reward (one point involving a 2-second pre-reward delay) and a larger-delayed reward (two points involving a 30-second pre-reward delay). In the no post-reward delay condition, choosing the small reward led immediately to the next trial, reducing the overall length of the condition. In the post-reward delay condition, choosing the small reward led to a delay period of 30 seconds, and choosing the large reward led to a delay period of 2 seconds before the next trial; therefore, the overall delay was constant and independent of choice made. The order of the two conditions was randomly chosen for each twin. Choice impulsivity (CI) was calculated as the number of times the smaller-immediate reward was selected in the no post-reward delay condition, controlling for total number of trials attempted.

Statistical analyses

Structural equation models. The structural equation modeling program Mx was used [27]. Models were fitted to IQ-, age- and sex-regressed unstandardized residual summed scores, which were transformed to minimize skewness using the optimized minimal skew command in Stata (version 10.0; StataCorp, 2007). All estimates are provided with 95% confidence intervals (the inclusion of zero indicates non- significance). The relative goodness of fit of the competing hierarchical (or nested) models was assessed using a likelihood ratio test. Mx handles missing data by using raw maximum likelihood estimation to calculate a likelihood statistic for each missing observation based on the observed variance/covariance matrix. Therefore, participants with missing data were included in the analysis.

Univariate genetic models. Univariate genetic analyses use twin-pair correlations for a trait and, on the basis that MZ twins share 100% of their segregating alleles and DZ twins share 50% of additive genetic influences as well as 25% non-additive genetic influences, partition the phenotypic variance of the measures into additive genetic (A), dominance (D) or shared environmental (C), and non-shared environmental (E) effects. Any possible measurement error is subsumed under the E effects [42]. Greater phenotypic similarity between MZ twins, compared to DZ twins, suggests genetic influences on trait variance. If the phenotypic similarity of MZ twins is more than twice that of DZ twins, this suggests the presence of D, otherwise only A is suggested. DZ twin correlations greater than half the MZ twin correlations suggest the presence of C. The extent to which MZ twins are not 100% concordant for a trait reflects E [42]. As multivariate models have increased power over univariate models [43], we do not present parameter estimates from univariate models. Univariate modeling was used to inform the choice of parameters for the multivariate models (e.g. the choice of C or D parameters) and to test for sex effects.

Sex effects. Scalar differences for reading difficulties and inattention were observed. Scalar sex differences are found where only unstandardized A, C/D and E estimates differ (but standardized estimates are the same), due to variance differences in the trait distribution between males and females. Therefore, in the multivariate modeling, male phenotypic variances for these traits were pre- and post- multiplied by a scaling factor. As there are no significant qualitative or quantitative differences in variance components between the sexes, MZ and DZ correlations are not presented for each sex. However, given the scalar differences between the sexes, means and standard deviations are broken down into sex- and zygosity- specific groups (Table S1).

Parameter selection for the multivariate models. In the univariate analyses, an AE model provided the best fit for DSF, DSB and RTV, while ADE models (with scalar sex differences) fitted best for inattention and RD (as we would predict from the MZ: DZ ratios of cross-twin correlations for these traits; Table S1). In this study, as we lacked sufficient power to distinguish between A and D effects, we model broad-sense genetic (G) influences that combines both A and D effects. As there were no qualitative or quantitative sex differences in the univariate analyses beyond scalar differences, and due to the computational intensity of modeling sex effects and additional power issues [27], only scalar differences between males and females were allowed in the multivariate models.

Multivariate genetic models. Multivariate genetic analyses use the power given by the MZ: DZ ratio of cross-twin cross-trait correlations to decompose the covariation between traits into G and E influences [42]. A Cholesky decomposition was fitted to the data; and to estimate the extent to which the genetic (G) and environmental (E) factors overlap (i.e. the genetic (r_g) and environmental (r_e) correlations), the standardized (correlated factors) solution of the Cholesky was used to avoid giving precedence to any one latent variable where the ordering of measured variables was arbitrary [44]. The total covariance model is than given by $G{*}r_g{*}G' + E{*}r_e{*}E'$. In the Cholesky, a triangular decomposition is used to decompose the variance in each phenotype and covariance between the phenotypes into broad sense genetic (G1-G3; Figures 1–3) and unique environmental (E1–E3) influences. Since Cholesky decompositions require an a priori justification of variable order where they contain more than three variables (based on, for example, temporality within longitudinal data), and our data were cross-sectional, we ran three separate Cholesky models to determine the extent to which the covariation between ADHD symptoms and RD is independent of cognitive measures of RTV, verbal STM and WM. RTV/STM/WM (i.e. the objectively measured cognitive process) was entered as the first variable in the Cholesky model, with the rating scale data (RD and inattention) as second and third variables.

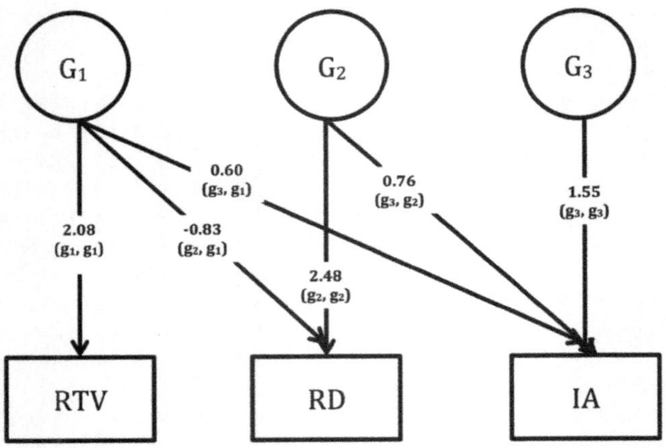

Figure 1. Unstandardised parameter estimates (G1–G3) from the Cholesky decomposition across reaction time variability (RTV), reading difficulties (RD) and inattention (IA).

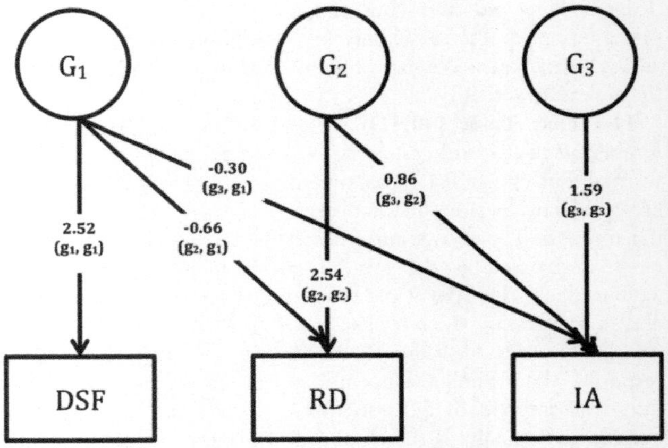

Figure 2. Unstandardised parameter estimates (G1–G3) from the Cholesky decomposition across digit span forward (DSF), reading difficulties (RD) and inattention (IA).

We regressed IQ from all cognitive variables and reading difficulties to ensure that we controlled for any mediating effects of IQ that were not the focus of the present analyses, consistent with our previously adopted approach [8]. Our previous analyses on the current [30] and a separate [8] sample have indicated that the majority of genetic influences shared between ADHD and cognitive variables are independent of those shared with IQ [30,45].

Results

Which cognitive impairments are associated with both ADHD symptoms and RD?

The maximum-likelihood correlations adjusting for familial structure indicated that a correlation between inattention and reading difficulties (RD) of 0.48 (Table 1). Intra-class partial correlations from STATA (which used the 'cluster command to control for the family structure) indicated that this dropped to $r = 0.39$, $r = 0.42$ and $r = 0.41$ when controlling for RTV, digit span forward (DSF) and digit span backward (DSB), respectively. RTV, DSF and DSB were significantly associated with both ADHD inattention symptoms and RD (Table 1). CE and choice impulsivity (CI) were not associated with RD, and only RTV and CE showed significant correlations with hyperactivity-impulsivity. Therefore, we only included RTV, DSF, DSB, inattention and RD in further genetic analyses.

To what extent do inattention, RD, RTV, verbal STM and WM share genetic /unique environmental influences?

Genetic factors accounted for around 60%, 30% and 40% of the variances on DSF, DSB and RTV, respectively (Table 2). All cognitive variables showed significant genetic correlations (r_g) with inattention symptoms and RD. The unique environmental correlations (which also includes measuring error) (r_e) were not significant between any cognitive variables and RD (all r_es <0.05). Inattention showed significant r_e only with RTV but not with DSF or DSB. There was substantial genetic overlap between DSB and DSF ($r_g = 0.63$), but the genetic overlap between DSB and RTV was not significant (indicated by confidence intervals overlapping zero).

To what extent does a shared cognitive impairment capture the shared genetic risk between ADHD symptoms and RD?

Using the Cholesky decomposition, we calculated the sum of genetic (G) influences underlying the G covariance between inattention and RD that were not shared with RTV ($G_{2,2}$ x $G_{3,2}$ in Figure 1) as a percentage of the total genetic covariance between inattention and RD ($G_{2,1}$ x $G_{3,1}$ + $G_{2,2}$ x $G_{3,2}$). This led us to deduce that 72% of the genetic overlap between inattention and RD was driven by shared genetic influences that are independent of those underlying RTV. Using the same method, we found that 89% and 79% of the genetic covariance between inattention and RD was independent of the genetic influences underlying DSF and DSB, respectively (Figure 2 and Figure 3). Since there was no significant overlap in unique environmental influences between RD and any of the cognitive variables, we did not interpret the E findings from the Cholesky decomposition.

Discussion

In genetic model fitting analyses on a population sample of twins aged 7–10, we identified three cognitive processes – reaction

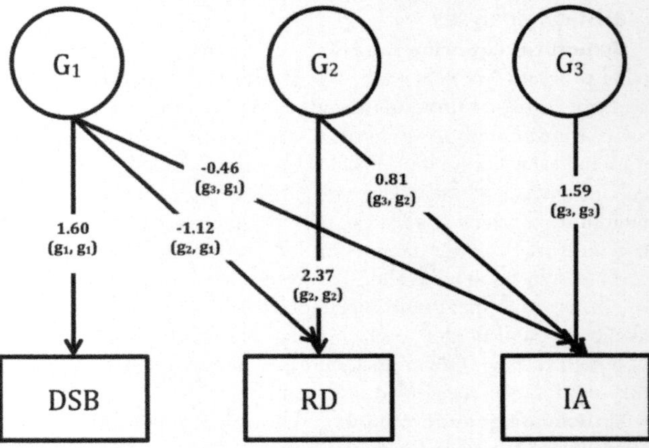

Figure 3. Unstandardised parameter estimates (G1–G3) from the Cholesky decomposition across digit span backward (DSB), reading difficulties (RD) and inattention (IA).

Table 1. Phenotypic correlations across inattention (IA), hyperactivity-impulsivity (H-I), reading difficulties (RD), reaction time variability (RTV), commission errors (CE), choice impulsivity (CI), digit span forward (DSF) and digit span backward (DSB).

	IA	H-I	RD	RTV	CE	CI	DSF
H-I	.59*						
RD	.48*	.17*					
RTV	.26*	.16*	.18*				
CE	.13*	.09*	.06	.12*			
CI	.14*	.08	.04	.08*	.06		
DSF	−.11*	−.06	−.15*	−.06	.01	−.06	
DSB	−.15*	−.05	−.18*	−.14*	−.05	−.09*	.29*

*p<0.01.

time variability (RTV), verbal working memory (WM) and verbal short-term memory (STM) – that showed significant phenotypic and genetic associations with both inattention symptoms and reading difficulties (RD). As the genetic influences on RTV separated from those on the memory measures, we further examined, for each cognitive variable in turn, the extent to which it captured the shared genetic risk between inattention and RD. While STM captured only 11% of the shared genetic risk between inattention and RD, the estimates increased somewhat for WM (21%) and RTV (28%); yet most of the genetic sharing between inattention and RD remained unaccounted for in each case.

Response inhibition (CE) and choice impulsivity (stronger preference for smaller-immediate rewards) were not significantly associated with RD, and therefore did not emerge as important cognitive processes that underlie the co-occurrence between ADHD symptoms and RD. Of the two ADHD symptom domains, the associations were largely limited to inattention, with only RTV and CE showing significant, though low, correlations with hyperactivity-impulsivity; the association between hyperactivity-impulsivity and RD was also low (0.17), though significant. Overall, the pattern of results further supports the partial etiological separation of the two ADHD symptom domains [46,47].

We observed no phenotypic association between STM and RTV. Despite some evidence of a phenotypic association between WM and RTV ($r_{ph} = 0.14$), there was no significant genetic overlap between them. These findings of the genetic risk factors underlying verbal memory processes separating from the genes that increase the susceptibility for increased RTV are consistent with the aetiological separation between top-down executive functioning in working memory (WM) and measures of intra-individual variability previously reported in a clinical ADHD and control sibling-pair sample [9].

The strengths of studying twin pairs from the general population lie in the ability to examine the two ADHD symptom domains separately and free from potential referral effects [48]. A limitation of the present study is that, despite a large sample of over 1300 twins, we lacked sufficient power to distinguish between additive (A) and dominance (D) genetic effects in the present multivariate analyses on this set of variables where univariate analyses suggested D effects for only two of them [49]. We therefore modelled 'broad sense heritability' (A+D influences) only. Future replication of these findings in larger samples is therefore important. Another limitation of this study is the inclusion of only parent ratings of RD; future studies should replicate these findings using examiner-administered measures of reading.

In this study we did not have a measure of processing speed, which has previously been identified as important for the association between RD and ADHD [4]. While processing speed measured in previous studies [2,4] may capture some elements of mean reaction time (MRT), the aetiology of these two measures cognitive processes are likely to be different. Compared to MRT and RTV obtained from simple RT tasks, where the underlying genetic influences shared with ADHD largely separate from those ADHD shares with IQ [30,45], processing speed measures are derived from IQ measures and capture higher cognitive processes such as matching and ordering objects; thus, our findings are not directly comparable with those in the previous study [4]; the associations between processing speed, MRT and RTV remain for future studies to explore further. As executive functions continue to develop throughout childhood and adolescence, their overlap with ADHD and RD should also be examined in future research from a developmental perspective across a wide age range.

Table 2. Standardised parameter estimates (with 95% confidence intervals) from the correlated factor model across digit span forward (DSF), digit span backward (DSB), reaction time variability (RTV), reading difficulties (RD) and inattention (IA).

	DSF	DSB	RTV	RD	IA
Genetic influences					
DSF	**0.59 (0.51, 0.66)**	*0.25 (86%)*	*	*−0.15 (97%)*	*−0.09 (91%)*
DSB	0.63 (0.46, 0.80)	**0.27 (0.17, 0.36)**	*−0.06 (43%)*	*−0.19 (97%)*	*−0.09 (56%)*
RTV	*	−0.17 (−0.37, 0.05)	**0.42 (0.33, 0.51)**	*0.16 (89%)*	*0.15 (63%)*
RD	−0.24 (−0.36, −0.12)	−0.46 (−0.50, −0.28)	0.32 (0.18, 0.46)	**0.63 (0.55, 0.69)**	*0.67 (0.50, 0.82)*
IA	−0.17 (−0.31, −0.03)	−0.24 (−0.44, −0.03)	0.32 (0.18, 0.46)	0.52 (0.46, 0.60)	**0.52 (0.40, 0.62)**
Unique environmental influences					
DSF	**0.41 (0.34, 0.49)**	*0.04 (14%)*	*	−0.004 (3%)	−0.009 (9%)
DSB	0.08 (−0.02, 0.19)	**0.73 (0.64, 0.83)**	*−0.08 (57%)*	*−0.005 (3%)*	*−0.07 (44%)*
RTV	0.13 (0.02, 0.24)	−0.12 (−0.22, −0.02)	**0.58 (0.49, 0.67)**	*0.02 (11%)*	*0.09 (37%)*
RD	−0.01 (−0.13, 0.12)	−0.01 (−0.12, 0.10)	0.04 (−0.07, 0.15)	**0.37 (0.31, 0.45)**	*0.33 (0.18, 0.50)*
IA	−0.02 (−0.13, 0.12)	−0.11 (−0.22, 0.01)	0.18 (0.06, 0.29)	0.34 (0.21, 0.46)	**0.48 (0.38, 0.59)**

The heritability (g^2) and unique environmental variances (e^2) are indicated as bold along the diagonal. The genetic and unique environmental correlations (and 95% confidence intervals) between pairs of variables are given below the diagonal. The contributions of genetic and unique environmental influences to the phenotypic correlations between variables are given above the diagonal (and the percentage of the phenotypic correlations due to each aetiological factor).
*Not interpreted due to a lack of phenotypic associatio.

In this study, we examined the aetiological relationship between ADHD and reading difficulties beyond general cognitive ability (IQ) to specific cognitive impairments associated with ADHD. We identified three cognitive processes (RTV, STM and WM) that share significant genetic influences with both inattention and reading difficulties. These findings inform and guide future research on the partly shared pathways from genetic influences to cognitive processes that underlie the observed association between ADHD and RD. Future studies should extend the investigation into additional cognitive measures, as well as further objective measures of reading. Longitudinal studies will be essential to investigate the developmental pathways and direction of causality.

Supporting Information

Table S1 Twin correlations, means and standard deviations across inattention (IA), reading difficulties (RD), reaction time variability (RTV), digit span forward (DSF) and digit span backward (DSB).

Acknowledgments

We thank all the families who kindly participated in this research. We also thank R. Gibbs, H. Rogers, E. Salih, G. Swinard, K. Lievesley, K. O'Flynn, S. Marquis and R. Whittemore; and everyone on the TEDS team.

Author Contributions

Conceived and designed the experiments: JK PA. Performed the experiments: JK PA. Analyzed the data: CC AF-W JK FR. Contributed reagents/materials/analysis tools: CC AF-W JK FR PA. Wrote the paper: CC AF-W JK FR PA.

References

1. Cheung CH, Wood AC, Paloyelis Y, Arias-Vasquez A, Buitelaar JK, et al. (2012) Aetiology for the covariation between combined type ADHD and reading difficulties in a family study: the role of IQ. J Child Psychol Psychiatry 53: 864–873.
2. McGrath LM, Pennington BF, Shanahan MA, Santerre-Lemmon LE, Barnard HD, et al. (2011) A multiple deficit model of reading disability and attention-deficit/hyperactivity disorder: searching for shared cognitive deficits. J Child Psychol Psychiatry 52: 547–557.
3. Paloyelis Y, Rijsdijk F, Wood AC, Asherson P, Kuntsi J (2010) The genetic association between ADHD symptoms and reading difficulties: the role of inattentiveness and IQ. J Abnorm Child Psychol 38: 1083–1095.
4. Willcutt EG, Betjemann RS, McGrath LM, Chhabildas NA, Olson RK, et al. (2010) Etiology and neuropsychology of comorbidity between RD and ADHD: the case for multiple-deficit models. Cortex 46: 1345–1361.
5. Martin NC, Levy F, Pieka J, Hay D (2006) A genetic study of Attention Deficit Hyperactivity Disorder, Conduct Disorder, Oppositional Defiant Disorder and Reading Disability: Aetiological overlaps and implications. International Journal of Disability, Development and Education 53: 21–34.
6. Willcutt EG, Pennington BF, Olson RK, DeFries JC (2007) Understanding comorbidity: a twin study of reading disability and attention-deficit/hyperactivity disorder. Am J Med Genet B Neuropsychiatr Genet 144B: 709–714.
7. Greven CU, Harlaar N, Dale PS, Plomin R (2011) Genetic Overlap between ADHD Symptoms and Reading is largely Driven by Inattentiveness rather than Hyperactivity-Impulsivity. J Can Acad Child Adolesc Psychiatry 20: 6–14.
8. Kuntsi J, Wood AC, Rijsdijk F, Johnson KA, Andreou P, et al. (2010) Separation of cognitive impairments in attention-deficit/hyperactivity disorder into 2 familial factors. Arch Gen Psychiatry 67: 1159–1167.
9. Frazier-Wood AC, Bralten J, Arias-Vasquez A, Luman M, Ooterlaan J, et al. (2012) Neuropsychological intra-individual variability explains unique genetic variance of ADHD and shows suggestive linkage to chromosomes 12, 13, and 17. Am J Med Genet B Neuropsychiatr Genet 159B: 131–140.
10. Kuntsi J, Pinto R, Price TS, van der Meere JJ, Frazier-Wood AC, et al. (2013) The Separation of ADHD Inattention and Hyperactivity-Impulsivity Symptoms: Pathways from Genetic Effects to Cognitive Impairments and Symptoms. J Abnorm Child Psychol.
11. Rucklidge JJ, Tannock R (2002) Neuropsychological profiles of adolescents with ADHD: effects of reading difficulties and gender. J Child Psychol Psychiatry 43: 988–1003.
12. Swanson HL, O'Connor R (2009) The role of working memory and fluency practice on the reading comprehension of students who are dysfluent readers. J Learn Disabil 42: 548–575.
13. Swanson HL, Xinhua Z, Jerman O (2009) Working memory, short-term memory, and reading disabilities: a selective meta-analysis of the literature. J Learn Disabil 42: 260–287.

14. Wang S, Gathercole SE (2013) Working memory deficits in children with reading difficulties: memory span and dual task coordination. J Exp Child Psychol 115: 188–197.
15. Willcutt EG, Pennington BF, Boada R, Ogline JS, Tunick RA, et al. (2001) A comparison of the cognitive deficits in reading disability and attention-deficit/ hyperactivity disorder. J Abnorm Psychol 110: 157–172.
16. Willcutt EG, Pennington BF, Olson RK, Chhabildas N, Hulslander J (2005) Neuropsychological analyses of comorbidity between reading disability and attention deficit hyperactivity disorder: in search of the common deficit. Dev Neuropsychol 27: 35–78.
17. Jacobson LA, Ryan M, Denckla MB, Mostofsky SH, Mahone EM (2013) Performance lapses in children with attention-deficit/hyperactivity disorder contribute to poor reading fluency. Arch Clin Neuropsychol 28: 672–683.
18. Li JJ, Cutting LE, Ryan M, Zilioli M, Denckla MB, et al. (2009) Response variability in rapid automatized naming predicts reading comprehension. J Clin Exp Neuropsychol 31: 877–888.
19. Tamm L, Epstein JN, Denton CA, Vaughn AJ, Peugh J, et al. (2014) Reaction time variability associated with reading skills in poor readers with ADHD. J Int Neuropsychol Soc 20: 292–301.
20. Catts HW, Gillispie M, Leonard LB, Kail RV, Miller CA (2002) The role of speed of processing, rapid naming, and phonological awareness in reading achievement. J Learn Disabil 35: 509–524.
21. Shanahan MA, Pennington BF, Yerys BE, Scott A, Boada R, et al. (2006) Processing speed deficits in attention deficit/hyperactivity disorder and reading disability. J Abnorm Child Psychol 34: 585–602.
22. Willcutt EG, Sonuga-Barke E, Nigg JT, Sergeant J (2008) Recent developments in neuropsychological models of childhood disorders. Advances in Biological Psychiatry 24: 195–226.
23. Rommelse NN, Altink ME, Fliers EA, Martin NC, Buschgens CJ, et al. (2009) Comorbid problems in ADHD: degree of association, shared endophenotypes, and formation of distinct subtypes. Implications for a future DSM. J Abnorm Child Psychol 37: 793–804.
24. van Leeuwen M, van den Berg SM, Peper JS, Hulshoff Pol HE, Boomsma DI (2009) Genetic covariance structure of reading, intelligence and memory in children. Behav Genet 39: 245–254.
25. Trouton A, Spinath FM, Plomin R (2002) Twins early development study (TEDS): a multivariate, longitudinal genetic investigation of language, cognition and behavior problems in childhood. Twin Res 5: 444–448.
26. Kuntsi J, Neale BM, Chen W, Faraone SV, Asherson P (2006) The IMAGE project: methodological issues for the molecular genetic analysis of ADHD. Behav Brain Funct 2: 27.
27. Neale MC, Roysamb E, Jacobson K (2006) Multivariate genetic analysis of sex limitation and G x E interaction. Twin Res Hum Genet 9: 481–489.
28. Conners CK, Sitarenios G, Parker JD, Epstein JN (1998) The revised Conners' Parent Rating Scale (CPRS-R): factor structure, reliability, and criterion validity. J Abnorm Child Psychol 26: 257–268.
29. Conners CK, Sitarenios G, Parker JD, Epstein JN (1998) Revision and restandardization of the Conners Teacher Rating Scale (CTRS-R): factor structure, reliability, and criterion validity. J Abnorm Child Psychol 26: 279–291.
30. Wood AC, Asherson P, van der Meere JJ, Kuntsi J (2010) Separation of genetic influences on attention deficit hyperactivity disorder symptoms and reaction time performance from those on IQ. Psychol Med 40: 1027–1037.
31. Paloyelis Y, Asherson P, Kuntsi J (2009) Are ADHD symptoms associated with delay aversion or choice impulsivity? A general population study. J Am Acad Child Adolesc Psychiatry 48: 837–846.
32. Kuntsi J, Pinto R, Price TS, van der Meere JJ, Frazier-Wood AC, et al. (2014) The separation of ADHD inattention and hyperactivity-impulsivity symptoms: pathways from genetic effects to cognitive impairments and symptoms. J Abnorm Child Psychol 42: 127–136.
33. Willcutt EG, Boada R, Riddle MW, Chhabildas N, DeFries JC, et al. (2011) Colorado Learning Difficulties Questionnaire: validation of a parent-report screening measure. Psychol Assess 23: 778–791.
34. Willcutt EG, Boada R, Riddle M, Chhabildas N, DeFries JC, et al. (2011) Colorado Learning Difficulties Questionnaire: Validation of a parent-report screening measure. (Under review).
35. Astrom R, DeFries JC, Pennington B, Wadsworth SJ, Willcutt E (2009) Etiology of covariation between a parent-report screening measure and reading performance. Behaviour Genetics 39: 634.
36. Wechsler D (1991) Wechler Intelligence Scale for Children (3rd ed.) London: The Psychological Corporation.
37. Sattler JM (1992) Assessment of Childhren: WISC-III and WPPSI-R Supplement. San Diego: Jerome M. Sattler.
38. Borger N, van der Meere J (2000) Motor control and state regulation in children with ADHD: a cardiac response study. Biol Psychol 51: 247–267.
39. Kuntsi J, Andreou P, Ma J, Borger NA, van der Meere JJ (2005) Testing assumptions for endophenotype studies in ADHD: reliability and validity of tasks in a general population sample. BMC Psychiatry 5: 40.
40. Kuntsi J, Rogers H, Swinard G, Borger N, van der Meere J, et al. (2006) Reaction time, inhibition, working memory and 'delay aversion' performance: genetic influences and their interpretation. Psychol Med 36: 1613–1624.
41. Andreou P, Neale BM, Chen W, Christiansen H, Gabriels I, et al. (2007) Reaction time performance in ADHD: improvement under fast-incentive condition and familial effects. Psychol Med 37: 1703–1715.
42. Rijsdijk FV, Sham PC (2002) Analytic approaches to twin data using structural equation models. Brief Bioinform 3: 119–133.
43. Schmitz S, Cherny SS, Fulker DW (1998) Increase in power through multivariate analyses. Behav Genet 28: 357–363.
44. Loehlin JC (1996) The Cholesky Approach: a cautionary note. Behavior Genetics 26: 65–69.
45. Wood AC, Rijsdijk F, Johnson KA, Andreou P, Albrecht B, et al. (2011) The relationship between ADHD and key cognitive phenotypes is not mediated by shared familial effects with IQ. Psychol Med 41: 861–871.
46. Greven CU, Rijsdijk FV, Plomin R (2011) A twin study of ADHD symptoms in early adolescence: hyperactivity-impulsivity and inattentiveness show substantial genetic overlap but also genetic specificity. J Abnorm Child Psychol 39: 265–275.
47. McLoughlin G, Ronald A, Kuntsi J, Asherson P, Plomin R (2007) Genetic support for the dual nature of attention deficit hyperactivity disorder: substantial genetic overlap between the inattentive and hyperactive-impulsive components. J Abnorm Child Psychol 35: 999–1008.
48. Rutter M, Macdonald H, Le Couteur A, Harrington R, Bolton P, et al. (1990) Genetic factors in child psychiatric disorders—II. Empirical findings. J Child Psychol Psychiatry 31: 39–83.
49. Rietveld MJ, Posthuma l D, Dolan CV, Boomsma DI (2003) ADHD: sibling interaction or dominance: an evaluation of statistical power. Behav Genet 33: 247–255.

2

Atomoxetine Effects on Executive Function as Measured by the BRIEF-A in Young Adults with ADHD: A Randomized, Double-Blind, Placebo-Controlled Study

Lenard A. Adler[1], David B. Clemow[2]*, David W. Williams[3], Todd M. Durell[2]

1 Departments of Psychiatry and Child and Adolescent Psychiatry, New York University, New York, New York, United States of America, **2** Lilly USA, LLC, Indianapolis, Indiana, United States of America, **3** inVentiv Health Clinical, Indianapolis, Indiana, United States of America

Abstract

Objective: To evaluate the effect of atomoxetine treatment on executive functions in young adults with attention-deficit/ hyperactivity disorder (ADHD).

Methods: In this Phase 4, multi-center, double-blind, placebo-controlled trial, young adults (18–30 years) with ADHD were randomized to receive atomoxetine (20–50 mg BID, N = 220) or placebo (N = 225) for 12 weeks. The Behavior Rating Inventory of Executive Function-Adult (BRIEF-A) consists of 75 self-report items within 9 nonoverlapping clinical scales measuring various aspects of executive functioning. Mean changes from baseline to 12-week endpoint on the BRIEF-A were analyzed using an ANCOVA model (terms: baseline score, treatment, and investigator).

Results: At baseline, there were no significant treatment group differences in the percentage of patients with BRIEF-A composite or index T-scores ≥60 (p>.5), with over 92% of patients having composite scores ≥60 (≥60 deemed clinically meaningful for these analyses). At endpoint, statistically significantly greater mean reductions were seen in the atomoxetine versus placebo group for the BRIEF-A Global Executive Composite (GEC), Behavioral Regulation Index (BRI), and Metacognitive Index (MI) scores, as well as the Inhibit, Self-Monitor, Working Memory, Plan/Organize and Task Monitor subscale scores (p<.05), with decreases in scores signifying improvements in executive functioning. Changes in the BRIEF-A Initiate (p = .051), Organization of Materials (p = .051), Shift (p = .090), and Emotional Control (p = .219) subscale scores were not statistically significant. In addition, the validity scales: Inconsistency (p = .644), Infrequency (p = .097), and Negativity (p = .456) were not statistically significant, showing scale validity.

Conclusion: Statistically significantly greater improvement in executive function was observed in young adults with ADHD in the atomoxetine versus placebo group as measured by changes in the BRIEF-A scales.

Trial Registration: ClinicalTrials.gov NCT00510276

Editor: Mark Bellgrove, Monash University, Australia

Funding: This research was funded by Lilly USA, LLC, who contributed to study design, data collection and analysis, decision to publish, and manuscript preparation (http://www.lilly.com).

Competing Interests: The authors have read the journal's policy and have the following conflicts: Dr. Adler has received research funding from Bristol-Myers Squibb, Chelsea Therapeutics, Eli Lilly and Company and/or one of its subsidiaries, National Institute of Drug Abuse, Pfizer, Shire; served on advisory boards or as a consultant for Astra Zeneca Pharmaceuticals, Eli Lilly and Company and/or one of its subsidiaries, i3 Research, Major League Baseball, Mindsite, Shire; served as a consultant for Epi-Q, INC Research, Otsuka Pharmaceuticals, and United Biosource; and has received royalty payments (as inventor) from NYU for license of adult ADHD scales and training materials. Drs. Clemow and Durell are full-time employees and minor shareholders of Eli Lilly and Company and/or one of its subsidiaries (Eli Lilly USA, LLC). Mr. Williams is a full-time employee of PharmaNet/i3 (vendor provider of Eli Lilly), and he is a former employee of Eli Lilly. Eli Lilly USA, LLC was the commercial source that funded all aspects of the study described in this manuscript, and Eli Lilly is the patent holder and marketing sponsor of Strattera (atomoxetine).

* Email: davidclemow@lilly.com

Introduction

A growing body of evidence suggests that attention-deficit/ hyperactivity disorder (ADHD) consists of more than just its primary diagnostic symptoms of inattention, impulsiveness, and hyperactivity. Some researchers argue that symptoms of deficient executive functioning (EF) are also involved in ADHD symptomology and consider ADHD a disorder of executive functioning dysregulation [1], [2]. There are 2 ADHD dimensions believed to be important to executive functioning: the inattentive dimension (working memory, planning/problem-solving) and the hyperactive, impulsive dimension (behavioral inhibition, motor regulation) [3], [4]. One group of researchers has grouped executive functioning into 6 clusters, all of which relate to core ADHD symptoms: activation (organizing tasks and materials, prioritizing and starting tasks, and estimating time); focus (sustaining focus, shifting focus to different tasks); effort (regulating alertness, sustaining effort, and processing speed); emotion (managing/

controlling frustration and emotion); memory (utilizing working memory and accessing recall); and action (recognizing appropriate behavior in response to a situation, self-regulating action, and impulsivity) [4], [5].

Executive functions become increasingly important as children mature and are expected to assume more responsibility for managing their behavior. Multiple studies have shown that children with ADHD are more likely to have executive function impairments that persist into adulthood [4], with neuropsychological studies consistently finding adults with ADHD to have impairments on measures of executive function [6]. Deficits in any one aspect of executive functioning might contribute to impairment, some of which could be associated with ADHD [3].

Response inhibition, working memory, and other executive functioning activities involve brain circuits that prioritize, integrate, and regulate other cognitive functions such as attention, motivation, and emotion. Many of these functions are controlled via regions of the brain that are known to have neurobiological differences in patients with ADHD compared to those without ADHD, and areas of the brain involved in executive function have neuronal projections that connect these different brain regions [7], [8], [9], [10]. The executive function areas of the brain and the circuits connecting them to the brainstem and other functional areas are heavily innervated with dopaminergic, serotonergic, noradrenergic, and cholinergic neurons. Dysregulation in these neurotransmitter signaling systems is believed to be involved in the manifestation of ADHD [7], [11], [12], [13].

Atomoxetine hydrochloride is a nonstimulant, selective norepinephrine reuptake inhibitor approved in the US as a treatment for ADHD in children, adolescents, and adults, as defined by the Diagnostic and Statistical Manual of Mental Disorders, Fourth Edition-Text Revision (DSM-IV-TR) [14]. Atomoxetine was approved for use in adults (age 18 and older) with ADHD based on 2 pivotal, randomized, placebo-controlled trials [15]. In these studies, the primary outcome measure was the Total ADHD Symptom Score, which is the sum of the Inattention and Hyperactivity/Impulsivity subscales of the investigator-rated Conners' Adult Attention Rating Scale (CAARS). For the CAARS, each of the 18 items of the subscales corresponds to one of the 18 DSM-IV-TR symptoms for ADHD.

In a phase 4 study that focused on prospectively assessing the efficacy and safety of atomoxetine in young adults, atomoxetine was observed to reduce ADHD symptoms and improve quality of life in young adults compared with placebo [16]. In the original publication that presents the primary efficacy measure results (CAARS), an *a priori* secondary analysis of Behavior Rating Inventory of Executive Function-Adult (BRIEF-A) data was also noted: after 12-weeks, atomoxetine-treated patients had statistically significantly greater mean reductions from baseline in BRIEF-A Global Executive Composite (GEC) score than placebo-treated patients [16]. However, additional BRIEF-A results were not provided. Therefore, the purpose of this paper is to fully examine the BRIEF-A data and present the BRIEF-A results from this ADHD study, including results from all of the subscales, examining the effect of atomoxetine on executive functioning in young adult ADHD patients.

Materials and Methods

The protocol for this trial and supporting CONSORT checklist are available as supporting information; see Checklist S1 and Protocol S1. The study procedures have been described previously in detail [16] and thus are summarized within this paper. This study was a phase 4, multicenter, 12-week, randomized, placebo-controlled, double-blind trial conducted at 32 sites in the United States and Puerto Rico between August 2007 and February 2009. Participants completing the double-blind portion of the trial were eligible to enter an optional 12-week, open-label, extension period. This paper reports the results of an *a priori* secondary analysis of BRIEF-A data from the 12-week double-blind acute period.

Ethics Statement

Before initiation of any study procedures, site investigators provided participants with thorough verbal and written descriptions of protocol requirements, and participants gave written consent under procedures approved by each participating site's institutional review board, which included: New England Institutional Review Board (IRB), University of Kentucky IRB, Western IRB, New York University School of Medicine Institutional Board of Research Associates, University of Nebraska Medical Center IRB, University of Cincinnati Medical Center IRB, McLean Hospital IRB, and Copernicus Group IRB. The study was conducted in accordance with the ethical principles originating from the Declaration of Helsinki and consistent with Good Clinical Practices.

Participant Population

Young adults (18–30 years of age) with ADHD were randomized 1:1 to the atomoxetine or placebo group for 12 weeks. Figure 1 details patient flow through the study. Participants met DSM-IV-TR criteria for ADHD, as determined by a clinical interview and as assessed by the Adult ADHD Clinical Diagnostic Scale (ACDS) version 1.2. The ACDS v1.2 is a validated, structured diagnostic scale for adult ADHD, containing separate modules of assessment of childhood and adulthood ADHD symptoms and impairments, which establishes whether a DSM-IV-TR diagnosis of adult ADHD is present or not [17]. Details of patient enrollment, allocation, and follow-up have been described previously in detail [16]. Of the 584 participants screened, 445 were randomized to treatment (220 atomoxetine; 225 placebo), and 385 received at least 1 dose of study drug. For this paper, which is focused on BRIEF-A results, only patients with baseline and at least one postbaseline BRIEF-A measurement were included in analyses: atomoxetine (N = 161) and placebo (N = 167). For each analysis, table footnotes provide details of the number of patients included for each analysis.

Participants with concomitant current (if diagnosed greater than 6 months immediately prior to Visit 1) or lifetime diagnoses of specific phobias, generalized anxiety disorder, or social anxiety disorder were allowed in the trial, as were participants with a current (if diagnosed greater than 2 years immediately prior to Visit 1) or lifetime history of dysthymia. Potential participants were excluded from the trial if they had current major depression, panic disorder, post-traumatic stress disorder, an eating disorder, or substance abuse or dependence, as well as current or lifetime obsessive-compulsive disorder, bipolar disorder, or psychosis. Concomitant medications such as anxiolytics and antidepressants with primarily central nervous system activity were not allowed, with few exceptions (e.g., acute analgesics). The incidence of prior stimulant medication use was approximately 35–38% and similar between treatment groups (Table 1).

Study Period I (5 to 28 day screening period, Visit 1–2)

After providing privacy statement consent, potential participants completed an internet-based, nonidentifiable Adult ADHD Self-Report Scale-V1.1 (ASRS-V1.1) Screener. Those with an ASRS-V1.1 Screener raw score of ≥14 were given the option to electronically sign an additional online informed consent. Partic-

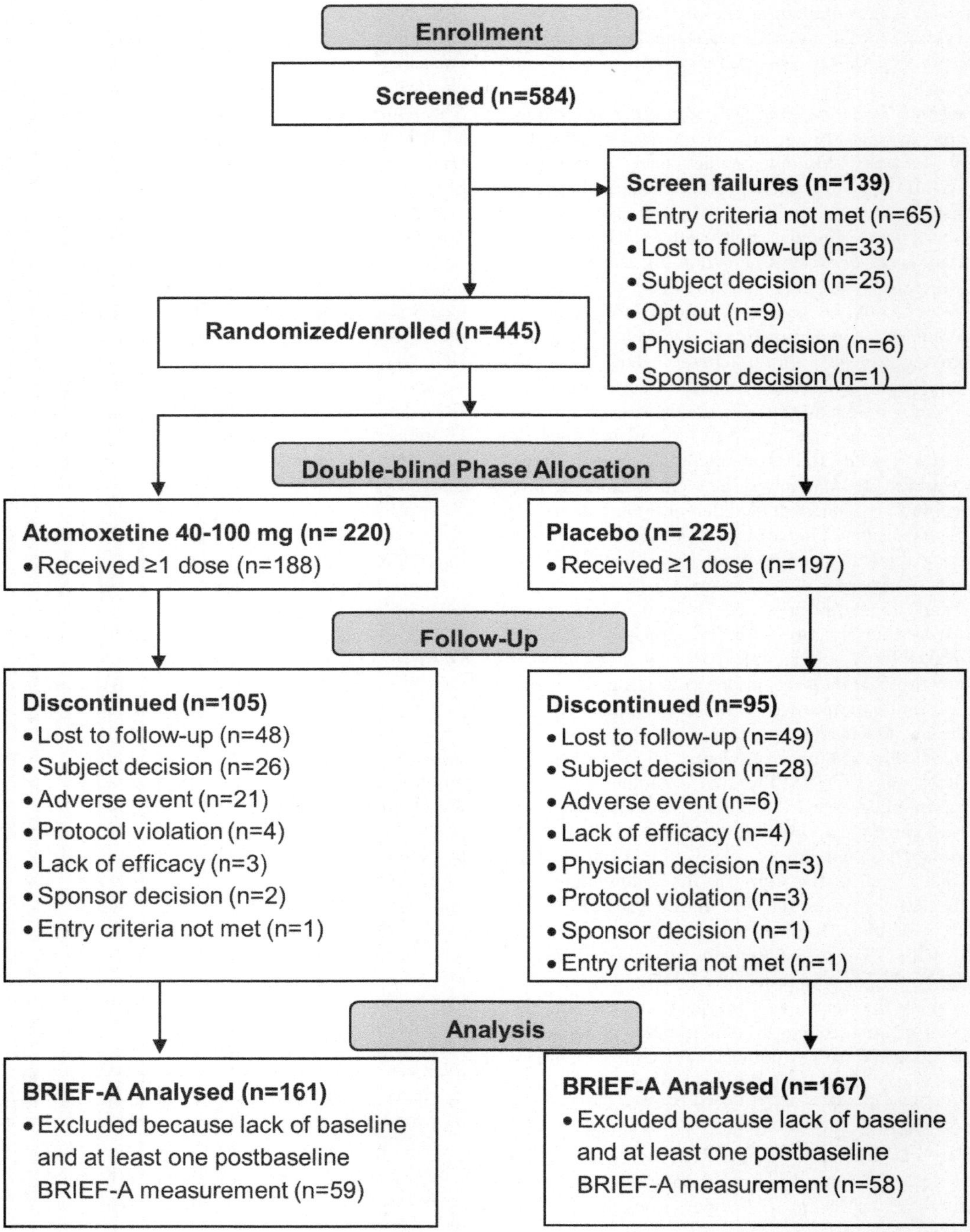

Figure 1. Participant disposition flow diagram.

ipants opting-in then answered additional inclusion/exclusion criteria questions via the study website. Those who met inclusion/exclusion criteria for the trial and who lived near an available investigative site were scheduled a live screening visit to confirm that the participant fully met all study inclusion/exclusion criteria. Site personnel obtained informed consent for the study from participants before conducting any study procedures. Participants underwent laboratory tests, an electrocardiogram (ECG) evaluation, a psychiatric evaluation, and a physical examination. Participants underwent a washout period if they had been taking medications excluded by the study protocol.

Study Period II (12-week double-blind acute treatment phase, Visit 2–6)

Participants were assessed 2 weeks after Visit 2, then every 3 weeks until Visit 5, and then after 4 weeks, which was Visit 6 (end of the double-blind phase of the study). This study employed a double-blind, sham placebo lead-in period, which blinded investigators and participants to the initiation of active therapy.

Table 1. Patient Baseline Characteristics.

	Atomoxetine	Placebo	*P*-value
Number of participants (N)[a]	220	225	
Age, years (mean ± SD)	24.7±3.4	24.7±3.5	.922[b]
Gender, n (%)			.774[c]
Female	92 (41.8)	98 (43.6)	
Male	128 (58.2)	127 (56.4)	
Height, cm (mean ± SD)[b]	171.9±9.6	172.5±9.9	.514[b]
Weight, kg (mean ± SD)[b]	79.6±22.6	81.6±21.5	.351[b]
Ethnicity, n (%)			.052[c]
African descent	12 (5.5)	26 (11.6)	
White	169 (76.8)	166 (73.8)	
East Asian	8 (3.6)	7 (3.1)	
Hispanic	27 (12.3)	25 (11.1)	
Native American	0 (0.0)	1 (0.4)	
West Asian	4 (1.8)	0 (0.0)	
DSM-IV-TR ADHD subtype, n (%)			.909[c]
Combined	173 (78.6)	174 (77.3)	
Hyperactive/Impulsive	1 (0.5)	1 (0.4)	
Inattentive	46 (20.9)	50 (22.2)	
Prior stimulant use, n (%)	83 (37.7)	79 (35.1)	.622[c]

[a]N includes all randomized patients.
[b]Analysis of variance (ANOVA) model: baseline = treatment (Type III sums of squares).
[c]Treatment comparison was analyzed using Fisher's exact test.
Abbreviations: ADHD = attention-deficit/hyperactivity disorder; DSM-IV-TR = Diagnostic and Statistical Manual of Mental Disorders, Fourth Edition-Text Revision; N = total number of participants; n = number of participants in the specified category; SD = standard deviation.

Participants were randomized 1:1 to either the atomoxetine or placebo group at the site level in a double-blinded manner, determined by a computer-generated random sequence using an interactive voice response system. Investigators were informed that all participants might receive placebo during a lead-in period between Visit 2 and Visit 4, prior to randomization. Investigators did not know that the randomization of all participants actually occurred at Visit 2.

Dosing

Atomoxetine-treated patients were dosed 40 mg/day (20 mg BID) for a minimum of 7 days. Following the last dose, the participants were dosed 80 mg/day (40 mg BID) for a minimum of 7 days. At or after Visit 5, the dose could be increased to the maximum of 100 mg/day (50 mg BID) based upon investigator judgment. One unscheduled dose change was allowed if needed for tolerability or safety. Participants unable to tolerate 40 mg/day were discontinued. Dosing was consistent with atomoxetine US label recommendations [18].

Assessments

The BRIEF-A is a standardized measure consisting of 75 items within 9 nonoverlapping clinical scales that measure various aspects of adult executive functioning and self-regulation in the person's everyday environment [19]. The BRIEF-A yields an overall score, the Global Executive Composite (GEC), which is a composite of 2 index scores: Behavioral Regulation Index (BRI) and Metacognitive Index (MI). The BRI is comprised of 4 subscales (Inhibit, Shift, Emotional Control, and Self-Monitor) and the MI is comprised of 5 subscales (Initiate, Working Memory, Plan/Organize, Task Monitor, and Organization of Materials). Patients rated behavior for each of the 75 items on a 3-point Likert scale (1 = behavior is never observed to 3 = behavior is often observed). GEC is a summary score that incorporates all of the clinical subscales of the BRIEF-A. Higher BRIEF-A scores indicate greater executive functioning impairment. Raw scores can be transformed (T-scores) based upon standardized population samples, with scores ≥65 having been considered to be clinically significant [20]. For assessment of treatment groups at baseline in these analyses, T-scores ≥60 were considered to be representative of clinical impairment. The percentage of patients with GEC, BRI, or MI T-scores ≥60 was measured at baseline.

The BRIEF-A also includes 3 built-in validity scales: Inconsistency, Infrequency, and Negativity, which check whether answers are provided in an inconsistent, atypical, or negative fashion, respectively, relative to normative and clinical samples.

Per the protocol, BRIEF-A assessments were collected at Visits 2 (baseline), 4 (5 weeks), and 6 (12 weeks, end of acute study period).

Safety analyses included treatment-emergent adverse events, weight, and vitals collected at every visit. Laboratory and ECG measures were collected study Visit 1 and 6. Although not the focus of this paper, safety findings were consistent with labeling, and have been described previously [16].

Statistical Analyses

Sample size was selected to allow for more than 80% power on the primary efficacy measure (CAARS) rather than secondary measures. This was based upon results from previous atomoxetine trials. Assignment to treatment groups was determined by a computer-generated random sequence using an interactive voice response system at the site level in a double-blind fashion. Details have been described previously [16].

Age, weight, and height treatment group differences were assessed with analysis of variance (ANOVA), with baseline equal to treatment (Type III sums of squares). Other demographic treatment comparisons were assessed with Fisher's exact test.

Mean changes from baseline to 12-week endpoint on the BRIEF-A were analyzed using a pre-specified analysis of covariance (ANCOVA) model with terms for baseline score, treatment, and investigator. Missing data were handled using last observation carried forward (LOCF) methodology. Hochberg's p-value adjustment method was used to control for potential multiplicity issues when analyzing the four component scores of the Behavioral Regulation Index and the five component scores of the Metacognitive Index. Additionally, a post-hoc mixed model repeated measures (MMRM) analysis on the GEC score with terms for baseline score, treatment, investigator, visit, treatment-by-visit interaction (time-by-treatment), and baseline-score-by-visit interaction was performed as a sensitivity analysis. MMRM utilizes modeling based upon included terms to handle missing data. The LOCF and MMRM analyses are based upon raw scores rather than T-scores.

Effect sizes were calculated as mean change in atomoxetine group scores minus mean change in placebo group scores divided by the pooled standard deviation of the changes.

Results

There were no statistically significant treatment group differences for any demographic parameter, including ADHD subtype, a majority of which was the combined type (Table 1). At baseline, there were no statistically significant differences in the percentage of patients with GEC, BRI, or MI T-scores ≥60. At baseline, 93.6% and 92.4% of the atomoxetine and placebo groups, respectively, had GEC T-scores ≥60, with 60 being 2 standard deviations away from the standardized mean (Table 2).

As published previously [16], the least squares mean change (± standard error) from baseline to end point in GEC score was statistically significantly greater for the atomoxetine group (−22.4±1.9) compared with the placebo group (−14.8±1.9; −12.37 to −2.78 95% confidence interval, $p = .002$). The mean ± standard deviation baseline and end point GEC scores for atomoxetine versus placebo were as follows: 155.0±21.5 to 135.2±28.4 (N = 161) versus 156.1±21.5 to 142.6±26.6 (N = 167). There was a statistically significantly greater decrease in mean change (± standard deviation) from baseline to last observation demonstrated in the atomoxetine group compared with the placebo group not only for the BRIEF-A overall GEC score but also the BRI and MI scores (Table 3).

Based upon the difference between the effect of atomoxetine versus placebo on GEC scores (change from baseline to end point), the atomoxetine treatment effect size was −0.32, indicating a clinically relevant small to moderate effect [21]. The effect size is negative since lower scores are better than higher scores and the atomoxetine group had the lower (improved) scores.

While there were significant decreases in BRIEF-A scores for both atomoxetine- and placebo-treated patients, there was also a statistically significantly greater decrease in mean change from baseline to last observation observed in the atomoxetine compared with the placebo group for the following BRIEF-A subscales: Inhibit, Self-Monitor, Working Memory, Plan/Organize, and Task Monitor (Table 3). Mean changes in BRIEF-A Shift, Organization of Materials, Initiate, and Emotional Control subscale scores were not statistically significantly different between treatment groups.

Mean baseline validity scores for both treatment groups were similar, low, and within the acceptable range for scale validity. Changes from baseline in the BRIEF-A validity scale scores were not statistically significantly different between treatment groups: Inconsistency ($p = .644$), Infrequency ($p = .097$), and Negativity ($p = .456$). These data demonstrate patient scoring validity for the study.

Repeated measures analyses of GEC score change from baseline to each post-baseline visit (when BRIEF-A assessments were captured) showed statistically significant separation between the atomoxetine and placebo groups at Week 5 (Visit 4) and Week 12 (Visit 6) (Table 4). The overall treatment effect was also statistically significant ($p < .001$) for BRIEF-A GEC score change from baseline using repeated measures analysis.

Discussion

In the currently described ADHD study, statistically significantly greater mean reductions were observed for the atomoxetine- versus placebo-treated patients for the BRIEF-A Global Executive Composite (GEC), Behavioral Regulation Index (BRI), and Metacognitive Index (MI) scores, as well as the Inhibit, Self-Monitor, Working Memory, Plan/Organize, and Task Monitor subscale scores. Thus, greater improvement in executive function was observed in young adults with ADHD in the atomoxetine

Table 2. BRIEF-A Baseline Subscale T-Scores.

	Atomoxetine (N = 219[a])	Placebo (N = 224[a])	
	n (%)	n (%)	*P*-value
GEC T-score ≥60 at baseline	205 (93.61)	207 (92.41)	.711
GEC T-score <60 at baseline	14 (6.39)	17 (7.59)	
BRI T-score ≥60 at baseline	162 (73.97)	166 (74.11)	1.0
BRI T-score <60 at baseline	57 (26.03)	58 (25.89)	
MI T-score ≥60 at baseline	204 (93.15)	212 (94.64)	.556
MI T-score <60 at baseline	15 (6.85)	12 (5.36)	

[a]n includes all randomized patients with a valid BRIEF-A score at baseline.
Abbreviations: BRI = Behavioral Regulation Index; GEC = Global Executive Composite; MI = Metacognitive Index; N = number of participants; n = number of participants in the specified category.

Table 3. BRIEF-A Mean Change from Baseline to Last Observation for All Randomized Patients.

	Change to Last Observation		
	Atomoxetine (n = 161[a])	Placebo (n = 167[a])	
Index/Scale	Mean ± SD	Mean ± SD	*P*-value[b]
Global Executive Composite	−19.78±25.59	−13.41±21.76	.002
Behavioral Regulation Index	−7.22±11.77	−4.47±10.05	.007
Inhibit	−2.33±3.17	−1.44±2.71	.005
Shift	−1.32±2.69	−0.93±2.57	.090
Emotional Control	−1.67±4.97	−1.18±4.48	.219
Self-Monitor	−1.91±2.89	−0.92±2.51	.005
Metacognitive Index	−12.55±15.14	−8.93±13.35	.003
Initiate	−2.11±3.42	−1.71±3.11	.051
Working Memory	−3.08±3.65	−1.98±3.02	<.001
Plan/Organize	−3.22±4.52	−2.14±3.92	.010
Task Monitor	−1.96±2.46	−1.46±2.61	.023
Organization of Materials	−2.19±3.24	−1.66±3.09	.051

[a]n includes all randomized patients who also had a baseline score and at least one post-baseline score on the BRIEF-A scale.
[b]All *p*-values were statistically significant ($p \leq .05$) except for Shift, Emotional Control, Initiative, and Organization of Materials; 9 component score p-values adjusted with Hochberg's Method to control for potential multiplicity.
Abbreviations: n = number of participants; SD = standard deviation.

versus placebo group as measured by changes in the BRIEF-A scales.

ADHD is known to be a neurological behavioral disorder. Multiple studies have shown that there are size, structural, and signaling differences in several regions and structures in the brains of patients with ADHD compared with normal controls. These differences are thought to be connected to the development of ADHD and its associated symptoms [7], [8], [9], [10], [11], [22]. One area of focus for ADHD is the prefrontal cortex that is involved in attention and executive functioning; more specifically, the dorsal anterior cingulate cortex and dorsolateral prefrontal cortex involved in inattention, the prefrontal motor cortex involved in hyperactivity, and the orbital frontal cortex involved in impulsivity [11]. An important function of catecholamines such as norepinephrine in these brain areas may be to facilitate or inhibit behavior [7], [12], [13], and medications that modulate this signaling may have effects on executive functioning [23]. The precise mechanism by which atomoxetine produces its therapeutic effects in ADHD is unknown, but it is thought to be related to selective inhibition of the pre-synaptic norepinephrine transporter, as determined in ex vivo uptake and neurotransmitter depletion studies [24]. Thus, atomoxetine may affect executive functioning via its actions on norepinephrine levels in the central nervous system. Additionally, while atomoxetine is selective for norepinephrine transporters, microdialysis studies suggest that atomoxetine may selectively increase dopamine levels in the prefrontal cortex, via the norepinephrine transporter or perhaps via a secondary signaling mechanism [23]. This could also play a role in signaling that affects executive function.

Interpretation of the currently presented BRIEF-A results should be tempered by the absence of neuropsychological assessments of executive function. However, neuropsychological tests have not been shown to reliably predict functional impairment in adult ADHD, while clinical ratings such as the BRIEF have been successful in this regard [25], [26]. Moreover, Biederman and colleagues [27] found only a modest overlap between psychometric and self-reported measures of executive function impairment among ADHD patients. Neuropsychological testing was largely found to identify patients with lower IQ and achievement testing, while behavioral questionnaire assessment chiefly identified patients with higher levels of ADHD symptoms, psychiatric comorbidity, and interpersonal deficits. As measured by the BRIEF-A at the end of 5 weeks and at the end of 12 weeks of treatment, atomoxetine treatment significantly improved

Table 4. BRIEF-A Mean Change from Baseline to Postbaseline Visits for All Randomized Patients – Repeated Measures Analysis for Global Executive Composite Scores.

Week	Treatment	n[a]	LSMean Change ± SE	Difference	*P*-value	95% CI
5	Atomoxetine	157	−18.02±1.69	−7.11	.002	−11.49 to −2.73
	Placebo	166	−10.91±1.67			
12	Atomoxetine	115	−22.53±2.07	−7.78	.005	−13.19 to −2.36
	Placebo	128	−14.75±2.00			

[a]n includes all randomized patients who also had a BRIEF-A baseline score and a postbaseline score at Visit 4 (Week 5) and/or Visit 6 (Week 12), as applicable.
Abbreviations: CI = confidence interval; LS = least squares; n = number of participants; SE = standard error.

executive functioning in young adults with ADHD compared with placebo. This is reflected in changes in the overall composite score, two index scores, and scores for seven of the nine BRIEF-A subscales (all but emotion control and organization). Over 90% of patients in this study had a GEC T-score ≥60 which shows an impairment of greater than 2 standard deviations from the mean, suggesting an ADHD population with deficits in executive functioning. Additionally, results from the three validity scales built into the BRIEF-A suggest valid self-reporting when completing the BRIEF-A assessment and provide strength to the merit of the atomoxetine versus placebo results. These results demonstrate that atomoxetine reduces symptoms of ADHD believed to be associated with deficits in executive functioning in young adults compared with placebo. These results are also consistent with findings from another recent double-blind, placebo-controlled trial of adults with ADHD, where atomoxetine was associated with significant improvement in executive function as measured by the Brown Attention-Deficit Disorder Scale (BADDS), which measures executive functioning across 5 clusters of daily activity functioning [4]. Statistically significant differences in score mean change over a 6-month period were observed for BADDS total score and all 5 cluster scores.

Similar findings (score reductions across all BRIEF-A scales) to those presented here were observed in a recent randomized, double-blind, placebo-controlled, adult study evaluating the efficacy of lisdexamfetamine dimesylate (prodrug of dextroamphetamine) for executive function deficits in adults with ADHD as measured by the self-reported BRIEF-A [28]. Amphetamines are believed to block the reuptake of norepinephrine and dopamine into the presynaptic neuron and increase the release of these monoamines into the extraneuronal space [29]. This could be a mechanism by which lisdexamfetamine dimesylate affected executive functioning. Other stimulant ADHD medications that affect norepinephrine and dopamine levels, such as methylphenidate, have also shown efficacy for improving deficits in some executive functioning categories but not others [30], [31]. Additionally, some aspects of executive functioning in patients with neurocognitive deficits caused by diseases other than ADHD have been shown to improve with administration of stimulants [32], [33].

Of note in the current study is that there were no statistically significant treatment group differences for the Shift ($p = .090$), Organization of Materials ($p = .051$), Initiate ($p = .051$), and the Emotional Control ($p = .219$) subscale scores, with $p \leq .05$ denoting significance after Hochberg's p-value adjustment was used to control for potential multiplicity. Similar to this study, in the lisdexamfetamine study, the effect of lisdexamfetamine on BRIEF-A subscale scores was least pronounced for the emotional control score compared with any of the other subscale scores [28]. This may indicate that emotional regulation may track separately from other executive function domains for ADHD patients. Low baseline scores for emotional control compared to the other index groups could have been a factor in the results for these studies. However, in comparison, in the atomoxetine study using the BADDS to assess executive functioning, the emotion domain had the lowest baseline BADDS cluster score and the lowest mean change from baseline score; but, in this case, the effect of atomoxetine on reducing the emotion cluster score was statistically significantly greater than placebo [4].

Potential limitations of the current results are that limited adjustments for multiple comparisons were made that included an overall gatekeeper analysis [16] and use of Hochberg's p-value adjustment for analysis of BRIEF-A component scores. Although not commonly used in adult ADHD trials [34], there was an absence of formal informant ADHD ratings. There was also an overrepresentation of white participants relative to African Americans and Hispanics compared with the overall US demographics. Additionally, this study had a higher-than-expected drop out rate, which could have reduced the power of the study. The BRIEF-A assessments were only conducted at baseline, Week 5, and Week 12. For the BRIEF-A analyses, only those patients with both a baseline and post-baseline measurement were included. The drop-out rate and the large window before the first assessment accounts for the decrease in patient number between baseline demographics and the BRIEF-A analyses.

These data, combined with the fact that the BRIEF-A subscales cover 75 items within 9 nonoverlapping clinical scales measuring various aspects of executive functioning (inhibition, shifting, emotion, self-monitoring, initiation, memory, planning/organizing, monitoring, and organization), support the utility of the BRIEF-A scale in measuring responses to atomoxetine of young adults with ADHD. Moreover, these results provide evidence that executive functioning impairments exist beyond the core symptoms of ADHD noted as diagnostic criteria in the DSM-IV-TR. The BRIEF-A has advantages as a behavioral rather than neuropsychological assessment of executive functioning in that it relies on ratings of real-world life activities [26]. Use of an executive function assessment such as the BRIEF-A may be an important tool for clinicians in diagnosing and monitoring ADHD symptomology relevant to patient real-world functioning outcomes and/or at least for managing a cognitive comorbidity often associated with ADHD [35].

Supporting Information

Checklist S1 CONSORT checklist of information to include when reporting a randomized trial.

Protocol S1 A double-blind study of atomoxetine hydrochloride versus placebo for the treatment of ADHD in young adults with an assessment of associated functional outcomes.

Acknowledgments

The authors thank the principal investigators and their research staffs, as well as the many participants who generously agreed to participate in the clinical trial.

Author Contributions

Conceived and designed the experiments: LAA DWW TMD. Performed the experiments: LAA. Analyzed the data: LAA DBC DWW TMD. Contributed reagents/materials/analysis tools: DBC DWW TMD. Wrote the paper: LAA DBC DWW TMD.

References

1. Brown TE (2009) ADD/ADHD and impaired executive function in clinical practice. Current Attention Disorder Reports 1: 37–41.
2. Saylor KE, Buermeyer CM, Spencer TJ, Barkley RA (2002) Adaptive changes related to medication treatment of ADHD: listening to parents of children in clinical trials of a novel nonstimulant medication. J Clin Psychiatry 63(S12): 23–28.
3. Barkley RA (2006) Attention deficit hyperactivity disorder: a handbook for diagnosis and treatment. 3rd Edition. New York, NY: The Guildford Press.

4. Brown TE, Holdnack J, Saylor K, Adler L, Spencer T, et al (2011) Effect of atomoxetine on executive function impairments in adults with ADHD. J Atten Disord 15(2): 130–138.
5. Brown TE (2001) Brown Attention-Deficit Disorder Scales for Children and Adolescents. San Antonio, TX: Psychological Corp; 5–7.
6. Faraone SV, Biederman J, Spencer T, Wilens T, Seidman LJ, et al (2000) Attention-deficit/hyperactivity disorder in adults: an overview. Biol Psychiatry 48: 9–20.
7. Makris N, Biederman J, Valera EM, Bush G, Kaiser J, et al (2007) Cortical thinning of the attention and executive function networks in adults with attention-deficit/hyperactivity disorder. Cerebral Cortex 17(6): 1364–1375.
8. Krain AL, Castellanos FX (2006) Brain development and ADHD. Clin Psychol Rev 26(4): 433–444.
9. Del Campo N, Chamberlain SR, Sahakian BJ, Robbins TW (2011) The roles of dopamine and noradrenaline in the pathophysiology and treatment of attention-deficit/hyperactivity disorder. Biol Psychiatry 69(12): e145–157.
10. Arnsten AFT, Rubia K (2012) Neurobiological circuits regulating attention, cognitive control, motivation, and emotion: disruptions in neurodevelopmental psychiatric disorders. J Am Acad Child Adolesc Psychiatry 51(4): 356–367.
11. Stahl SM (2008) Essential Psychopharmacology: Neuroscientific Basis and Practical Application. 3rd edition. New York (NY): Cambridge University Press.
12. Rogeness GA, Javors MA, Pliszka SR (1992) Neurochemistry and child and adolescent psychiatry. J Am Acad Child Adolesc Psychiatry 31(5): 765–781.
13. Yudofsky SC, Hales RE (2002) Textbook of Neuropsychiatry and Clinical Neurosciences. 4th ed. Washington, DC: American Psychiatric Publishing 71–113.
14. American Psychiatric Association (2000) Diagnostic and statistical manual of mental disorders. 4th ed. Text revised. Washington, DC: American Psychiatric Association.
15. Michelson D, Adler L, Spencer T, Reimherr FW, West SA, et al (2003) Atomoxetine in adults with ADHD: two randomized, placebo-controlled studies. Biol Psychiatry 53(2): 112–120.
16. Durell TM, Adler LA, Williams DW, Deldar A, McGough JJ, et al (2013) Atomoxetine treatment of attention-deficit/hyperactivity disorder in young adults with assessment of functional outcomes: a randomized, double-blind, placebo-controlled clinical trial. J Clin Psychopharmacol 33(1): 45–54.
17. Adler LA, Cohen J (2004) Diagnosis and evaluation of adults with attention-deficit/hyperactivity disorder. Psychiatr Clin N Am 27(2): 187–201.
18. Strattera (atomoxetine) (2013) package insert Indianapolis, IN: Eli Lilly and Company.
19. Roth RM, Isquith PK, Gioia GA (2005) Behavior Rating Inventory of Executive Function–Adult Version (BRIEF-A). Lutz, FL: Psychological Assessment Resources.
20. Isquith PK, Roth RM, Gioia GA, PAR Staff (2006) Behavior Rating Inventory of Executive Function – Adult Version (BRIEF-A) Interpretive Report. Lutz, FL: Psychological Assessment Resources.
21. Ferguson CJ (2009) An effect size primer: a guide for clinicians and researchers. Professional Psychol Res Pract 40(5): 532–538.
22. Qiu A, Crocetti D, Adler M, Mahone EM, Denckla MB, et al (2009) Basal ganglia volume and shape in children with attention deficit hyperactivity disorder. Am J Psychiatry 166(1): 74–82.
23. Arnsten AFT (2011) Catecholamine influences on dorsolateral prefrontal cortical networks. Biol Psychiatry 69(12): e89–e99.
24. Bymaster FP, Katner JS, Nelson DL, Hemrick-Luecke SK, Threlkeld PG, et al (2002) Atomoxetine increases extracellular levels of norepinephrine and dopamine in the prefrontal cortex of rat: a potential mechanism for efficacy in attention deficit/hyperactivity disorder. Neuropsychopharmacol 27: 699–711.
25. Barkley RA, Murphy KR (2010) Impairment in occupational functioning and adult ADHD: the predictive utility of executive function (EF) ratings versus EF tests. Arch Clin Neuropsychol 25(3): 157–73.
26. Barkley RA, Fischer M (2011) Predicting impairment in major life activities and occupational functioning in hyperactive children as adults: self-reported executive function (EF) deficits versus EF tests. Dev Neuropsychol 36(2): 137–161.
27. Biederman J, Petty CR, Fried R, Black S, Faneuil A, et al (2008) Discordance between psychometric testing and questionnaire-based definitions of executive function deficits in individuals with ADHD. J Attention Disorders 12(1): 92–102.
28. Adler LA, Dirks B, Deas PF, Raychaudhuri A, Dauphin MR, et al (2013) Lisdexamfetamine dimesylate in adults with attention-deficit/hyperactivity disorder who report clinically significant impairment in executive function: results from a randomized, double-blind, placebo-controlled study. J Clin Psychiatry 74(7): 694–702.
29. Vyvanse (2012) [package insert]. Wayne, PA: Shire US.
30. Biederman J, Seidman LJ, Petty CR, Fried R, Doyle AE, et al (2008) Effects of stimulant medication on neuropsychological functioning in young adults with attention-deficit/hyperactivity disorder. J Clin Psychiatry 69(7): 1150–1156.
31. Biederman J, Mick E, Fried R, Wilner N, Spencer TJ, et al (2011) Are stimulants effective in the treatment of executive function deficits? Results from a randomized double blind study of OROS-methylphenidate in adults with ADHD. Eur Neuropsychopharmacol 21(7): 508–515.
32. Morrow SA, Smerbeck A, Patrick K, Cookfair D, Weinstock-Guttman B, et al (2013) Lisdexamfetamine dimesylate improves processing speed and memory in cognitively impaired MS patients: a phase II study. J Neurol 260(2): 489–497.
33. Gehring K, Patwardhan SY, Collins R, Groves MD, Etzel CJ, et al (2012) A randomized trial on the efficacy of methylphenidate and modafinil for improving cognitive functioning and symptoms in patients with a primary brain tumor. J Neurooncol 107(1): 165–174.
34. Adler LA, Faraone SV, Spencer TJ, Michelson D, Reimherr FW, et al (2008) The reliability and validity of self- and investigator ratings of ADHD in adults. J Attention Disorders 11(6): 711–719.
35. Biederman J, Petty C, Fried R, Fontanella J, Doyle AE, et al (2006) Impact of psychometrically defined deficits of executive functioning in adults with attention deficit hyperactivity disorder. Am J Psychiatry 163: 1730–1738.

3

Visual Processing of Biological Motion in Children and Adolescents with Attention-Deficit/Hyperactivity Disorder: An Event Related Potential-Study

Anne Kröger[1]*, Katharina Hof[1], Christoph Krick[2], Michael Siniatchkin[1], Tomasz Jarczok[1], Christine M. Freitag[1], Stephan Bender[1]

1 Department of Child and Adolescent Psychiatry, Psychosomatics, and Psychotherapy, Goethe University Hospital Frankfurt, Frankfurt am Main, Germany, **2** Department of Neuroradiology, Saarland University Hospital, Homburg an der Saar, Germany

Abstract

Attention-deficit/hyperactivity disorder (ADHD) is often accompanied by problems in social behaviour, which are sometimes similar to some symptoms of autism-spectrum disorders (ASD). However, neuronal mechanisms of ASD-like deficits in ADHD have rarely been studied. The processing of biological motion–recently discussed as a marker of social cognition–was found to be disrupted in ASD in several studies. Thus in the present study we tested if biological motion processing is disrupted in ADHD. We used 64-channel EEG and spatio-temporal source analysis to assess event-related potentials associated with human motion processing in 21 children and adolescents with ADHD and 21 matched typically developing controls. On the behavioural level, all subjects were able to differentiate between human and scrambled motion. But in response to both scrambled and biological motion, the N200 amplitude was decreased in subjects with ADHD. After a spatio-temporal dipole analysis, a human motion specific activation was observable in occipital-temporal regions with a reduced and more diffuse activation in ADHD subjects. These results point towards neuronal determined alterations in the processing of biological motion in ADHD.

Editor: Marina Pavlova, University of Tuebingen Medical School, Germany

Funding: There were no industrial funders. This work was supported by the foundation of Marie Christine Held and Erika Hecker to AK, the German Research foundation "Deutsche Forschungsgemeinschaft" to CMF (FR2069/2-1), and by the LOEWE-Program "Neuronal Coordination Research Focus Frankfurt" (NeFF) to CMF and SB. The funders had no role in study design, data collection and analysis, decision to publish, or preparation of the manuscript.

Competing Interests: The authors have declared that no competing interests exist.

* E-mail: Anne.Kroeger@kgu.de

Introduction

Attention-deficit/hyperactivity disorder (ADHD) is one of the most common disorders in child and adolescent psychiatry and shows a prevalence of about 5% in the general population [1,2]. In addition to symptoms of inattention, hyperactivity and impulsivity, core symptoms of autism-spectrum disorders (ASD) including social communication and interaction deficits are frequently described in children and adolescents with a primary diagnosis of ADHD even though these symptoms are still below the cut-off for an ASD diagnosis [3–7]. Others only found elevated communication and social interaction deficits but no elevated repetitive behaviors [8]. However, these ASD-like symptoms seem to be a marker of a more strongly affected ADHD group with higher rates of comorbid disruptive behavior (including conduct and oppositional defiant disorder), other developmental disorders [5] and a higher co-occurrence of motor problems [9]. Furthermore these symptoms are clinically highly relevant for children with ADHD because especially deficits in the social domain are associated with a poor prognosis and higher risk for the development of other psychiatric problems, including mood disorders, anxiety, disruptive behavior disorders and substance abuse [10]. With regard to etiology and also with regard to specific therapeutic approaches, it is important to study if the clinically observed social interaction difficulties in ADHD might be associated with neural processing abnormalities.

Up to date, only a few experimental studies about social cognition deficits in ADHD can be found (for a review see [11]). Those few found e.g. disruptions in prosody perception and facial affect recognition. Reports about deficits in more complex tasks including theory of mind or empathy are more heterogeneous. Neuroimaging or neurophysiological studies about social cognition deficits in ADHD are even rarer. There is one neurophysiological study [12] which found several neural processes of emotional face processing to be disrupted in children with ADHD, including a reduced neuronal activation during early perceptual analysis (amplitude of the P120), elevated activity during processes associated with perceptual analysis of emotional expression (N170 amplitude), followed by a reduced activation in the P300, a marker for context processing. However these processes were partly normalized after treatment with methylphenidate.

Processing of biological motion, including human motion patterns (often presented in point-light displays), has recently been discussed as a marker of social cognition [13]. Indeed recognition of biological motion, such as eye movements and body gestures, is crucial for the development of adequate social interaction and adaptive responses, and usually emerges early in development [14,15]. In addition, one recent study [16] found correlations between measures of social perception (empathy, emotion recognition and theory of mind) and the individual ability in using form cues in biological motion processing in typically developing controls. The ability to detect emotions in point-light displays of a walking human correlates furthermore with the ability to discriminate biological from scrambled motion patterns [17]. A similar pattern was found in a sample of subjects with ASD [18]. In functional magnetic resonance imaging (fMRI) studies, neuronal structures in the right posterior temporal cortex were identified to be involved in the processing biological motion, especially the posterior superior temporal sulcus (pSTS) [13,19]. These structures are furthermore also important for the processing of socially relevant visual information e.g. emotions expressed by whole body movements and intentions of others revealed by actions and movement [20,21]. Especially in ASD, abnormal brain activation patterns to biological motion stimuli have been found, predominantly by fMRI studies (for a review see [22]).

Biological motion processing can also be studied with electroencephalography (EEG). In contrast to fMRI, EEG can differentiate time related sub-processes of visual processing. Regarding biological motion, first, a positive component 100 ms after stimulus onset can be observed at occipital electrodes, especially in the right hemisphere [23,24]. This P100 component is thought to evolve from the visual areas V1 and V2 [25] and to reflect stimulus feature extraction, including contrast, luminance, motion detection [26,27], and pattern processing [28,29]. After this first component, a negative deflection peaking around 200 ms is frequently described [23,30–32]. As the source of the N200 is close to MT+/V5, it seems to reflect, more specifically, motion processing [32] including detection of motion direction [27]. Using high-density electrical mapping and source-analysis on difference waves (biological – scrambled motion), Krakowski et al. described a dipolar activity after approximately 300 ms. Its source was located in posterior middle temporal regions, near the pSTS [24], a neuronal region especially involved in the processing of human motion [19] and also social information [33]. Finally, a positive deflection at centro-parietal electrodes starting approximately after 400 ms was described, with greater amplitudes during human motion processing when the human motion aspect of the stimuli was actively attended [24]. This component is thought to be a marker of top-down cognitive processes involved in active decoding of stimulus content and could be a sub-component of the so-called late positive complex (LPC). A particularly late and broadly distributed LPC around 500–600 ms was also observed in other studies, when object parts are poorly specified by the available contours and thus difficult to identify [34].

In the present study, we tested if biological motion processing is disturbed in children and adolescents with ADHD. To our knowledge there are no studies about biological motion processing or perception in ADHD. Therefore we assessed event-related potentials (ERPs) elicited by biological and scrambled motion to test if biological-motion processing is abnormal in these participants. More elevated ASD-symptoms and thus more social deficits were previously found in children with ADHD and comorbid disruptive behaviour disorders [5]. Therefore we compared ADHD patients with and without conduct disorder (CD) or oppositional defiant disorder (ODD) to assess the effects of a comorbid diagnosis of CD/ODD. We additionally tested for correlations between ADHD- and ASD-symptoms with brain activity related to disturbed biological motion processing to further test if such deficits are more related to ADHD or subclinical ASD symptoms.

Methods

Participants and recruitment

We included 48 children and adolescents in our study. Two participants had to be excluded because they showed too few responses during the experiment (one typically developing control and one ADHD participant), and four because of muscle artefacts in the EEG data (two in each group). The remaining 21 typically developing controls and 21 children and adolescents with ADHD were 7 to 15 years old (see Table 1). Only male and right-handed children with normal or corrected-to-normal vision were included. Handedness was validated using the Edinburgh Handedness Inventory [35].

ADHD out-patients were diagnosed according to ICD-10 (F90.0; [36]) at the Department of Child and Adolescent Psychiatry of the Goethe University of Frankfurt (Germany) by experienced clinicians. The ICD-10 diagnosis F90.0 correspondents to the ADHD combined subtype as described in DSM-IV TR (314.01; [2]), but hyperactive-impulsive symptoms were rated according to ICD-10. Before participating in the study, ADHD and comorbid diagnoses were verified with a semi-structured interview according to ICD-10 criteria (Kinder-DIPS; [37]). Thirteen subjects diagnosed with ADHD were treated with the psycho-stimulant methylphenidate. Methylphenidate inhibits the reuptake of dopamine and norepinephrine into the presynaptic neuron following their release. Thus, it increases levels or prolongs availability of these neurotransmitters in the synapses to exert its effects on postsynaptic neurons (e.g. [38–40]). Nine subjects received extended release methylphenidate, which was stopped at least 48 hours prior to participation. Four subjects were medicated with immediate release methylphenidate, which had not been taken for at least 24 hours before participation. Last application of medication varied between 24–252 hours (immediate release methylphenidate) and 48–228 hours (extended release methylphenidate).

Typically developing controls were recruited from local schools and screened with the German version of the Child Behaviour Checklist [41] for any clinically relevant symptoms. Participants with T-scores>60 on the second order scales or >70 on any first order subscales, respectively, were excluded.

Exclusion criteria for both groups were as follows: intellectual disability according to a standardized IQ assessment (percentile rank<2 corresponding to IQ<70 respectively; for details see below), any neurological disorders (including epilepsy), preterm birth with low birth weight (<2000 g), and dyslexia. In children with ADHD, comorbid psychiatric disorders (e.g. ASD, anxiety disorders) were excluded with the exception of oppositional defiant disorder (ODD) and conduct disorder (CD). Nine boys with ADHD and comorbid ODD or CD (ICD-10: F90.1) were included.

Subjects received a small fee for their participation. All participants and parents signed informed consent. The study was approved by the Ethics Committee of the Goethe University Frankfurt (Germany) in accordance with the Declaration of Helsinki.

Psychological assessment

IQ was assessed using the standard (over 11.5 years) or coloured (under 11.5 years) progressive matrices [42,43]. The matrices test is a non-verbal, multiple-choice IQ assessment tool which measures deductive reasoning. Raw scores are transformed into percentiles corresponding to the respective age group.

Autistic symptoms were assessed by the German version of the Social Communication Questionnaire (SCQ; [44]) in all partici-

Table 1. Descriptive data for typically developing controls (TC) and ADHD subjects.

Mean (±SD) Range (min–max)	TC (N = 21)	ADHD (N = 21)	statistics
Age	11.64 (±2.42)	11.94 (±1.75)	t(36.4)<1; *p* = *0.6*
	7.67–15.27	8.76–14.81	
Handedness	0.84 (±0.14)	0.79 (±0.18)	z<1; *p* = *0.4*
	0.54–1	0.50–1	
Raven Percentile	59.10 (±38.16)	71.19 (±29.19)	z<1; *p* = *0.5*
	3–100	3–100	
SCQ score	(N = 19*) 4.11 (±3.07)	(N = 20*) 7.45 (±4.78)	t(32.6) = −2.1; *p* = *0.014*
	0–12	1–16	
Correct responses walker condition	84.81 (±6.78)	85.29 (±6.15)	
	66–90	64–89	
Correct responses scramble condition	83.57 (±4.28)	82.24 (±9.68)	Group: F(1,39)<1; *p* = *0.77*
	61–90	59–89	
Reaction time walker condition in sec	1.35 (±0.29)	1.43 (±0.21)	
	0.76–1.89	0.82–1.66	
Reaction time scramble condition in sec	1.42 (±0.28)	1.51 (±0.24)	Group: F(1,39)<1; *p* = *0.35*
	0.79–1.75	0.83–1.75	

*different sample sizes because of missing questionnaires.

pants. This questionnaire was developed as a companion tool to the ADI-R [45] and shows good psychometric properties. The SCQ consists of 40 yes/no questions answered by the participants' main caregivers. To differentiate ASD from typically developing controls a cut-off = 17 was suggested in a German sample [46].

In ADHD subjects, ADHD symptoms were assessed with a parent rating scale taken from a German diagnostic system for mental disorders in children and adolescents (DISYPS-II; [47]). In this questionnaire, each DSM-IV TR derived symptom is rated on a scale between 0–3, with a score of 3 indicating the most severe problems. Parents from the ADHD group were asked to rate the behaviour of their child without medication. A total score and sub-scores for attention problems (9 items) and hyperactive/impulsive behavior (11 items) were calculated.

The SCQ and the ADHD symptom checklist were used to assess the level of these traits/symptoms in both groups and to be able to test if brain activity related to disturbed biological motion processing is related with ADHD or subclinical ASD symptoms.

Both questionnaires were not returned by all participants. The SCQ was missing in two typically developing controls and in one ADHD subject. The ADHD symptoms rating scale was missing in one ADHD subject. Those subjects were excluded from calculations regarding the respective questionnaire.

Experimental design, procedure and stimulus presentation

A 30×37.5 cm flat-screen was placed 80 cm in front of the head of the participant. In order to keep this distance constant and to minimise head movement, the participants had to place their chins on a 'chin-rest' fixed to the table. The room was dark during the entire experiment.

The biological motion stimuli ('walker' condition) consisted of moving point-light displays without contours. Fifteen female and 15 male walkers were used; each was marked by 15 white dots at the joints, tracking movements at the joints of the limps displayed against a black background. This was created using Labview version 6 (http//www.ni.com/labview). The walkers were shown in a frontal view walking with a speed of approximately two steps per second. Stimuli were based on motion capture data as previously described [48]. The 'scrambled' (i.e. control-) display was derived from these walkers by spatial scrambling. Thus the spatial position of the 15 dots was permutated while leaving the shape of each trajectory for each individual dot intact. This manipulation retains the individual frequency and acceleration profile of each dot, but masks the global acceleration profile indicative for biological motion. In sum, 30 different walkers and 30 scrambled motion stimuli were shown. Due to different starting points, dots were not strictly symmetrically organised. For the scrambled condition, dots were placed similar to the walker condition to cover the same visual field. Stimuli covered a visual field of about 12.5°×5.0° (height × width). Selected frames depicting both stimuli conditions are shown in Figure 1. Each individual stimulus was shown for 1 s, in a randomised order once per block. This block was repeated three times, thus each stimulus-class was presented 90 times. All stimuli were presented centrally on the screen. Between the stimuli, a white fixation-cross was presented for 2 s. In order to separate biological motion recognition and motor response, participants were instructed to react when the fixation cross (fixation period) appeared after the presentation of the stimulus. They were instructed to press the left mouse button if they had seen a walking person before and the right mouse button if they recognised a scrambled motion pattern (forced-choice). Correctness was emphasized over speed.

Children were allowed two breaks. The break duration was regulated by the participant. The experimenter continued the presentation after the participant's indication.

The stimulus sequence was controlled by PresentationTM software (http://www.neurobs.com/).

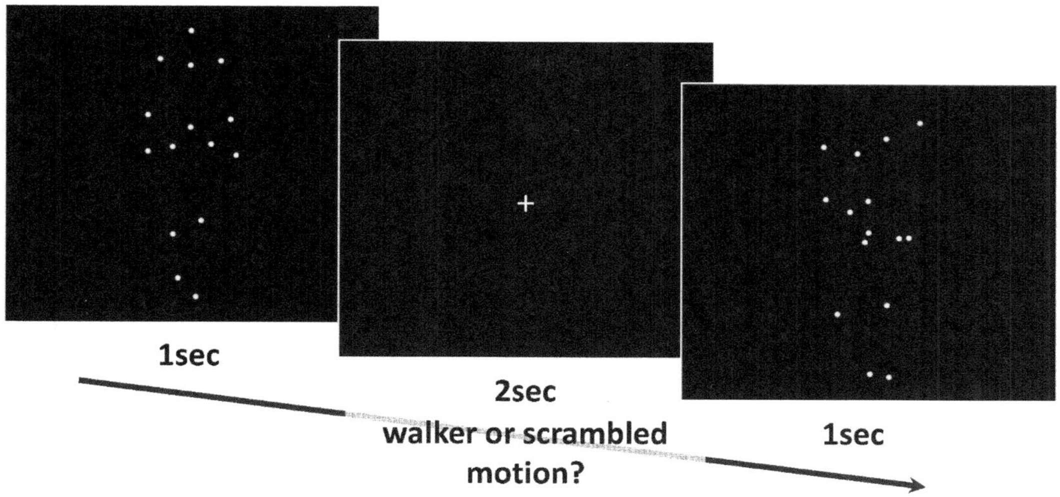

Figure 1. Example of experimental stimuli and stimuli presentation.

Electrophysiological assessment

Continuous direct current EEG (DC-EEG) from 64 channels at a sampling rate of 500 Hz was recorded against a reference at Fpz using BrainVision MR-Plus amplifiers and Brain Vision Recorder software (Brain Products GmbH, Munich, Germany). An anti-aliasing low-pass filter with 250 Hz high cut-off was applied online. Sixty-four sintered Ag–AgCl electrodes (impedances<10 kΩ) were fixed by equidistant electrode caps (Easycap GmbH, Herrsching, Germany). Vertical and horizontal electro-oculograms (VEOG and HEOG) were recorded from electrodes placed 1 cm above and below the left eye and lateral to the outer canthi.

Signal pre-processing

EEG-data was analysed using the Brain Vision-Analyzer 2 (Brain Products, Munich, Germany). Offline, raw EEG was high-pass filtered to 40 Hz (high cut-off) and recordings were transformed to an average reference. Continuous recordings were segmented into epochs of 3.5 s (starting 500 ms before stimulus onset until 3 s after onset). The first 500 ms of this epoch served as baseline. Only trials with correct responses were included in the analysis. The recordings were corrected automatically for eye movements and blinks by the algorithm of Gratton and Coles (Brain Vision Analyzer). Because no slow DC potentials were observable, no linear regressions to eliminate such trends were required. Artefacts were rejected automatically if the signal amplitude exceeded 150 μV (individual channel mode). This step was controlled by visual inspection, and remaining artefacts were removed by an experienced EEG technician who was blind to the study hypotheses. Electrodes with poor impedance or too many artefacts (in more than one third of all segments) were interpolated by nearest neighbours. The number of available artefact-free trials was compared between both groups. There were no differences between both typically developing controls (82.1±7.1) and ADHD (81.6±7.8) in the biological motion condition ($t(40)=0.23$; $p=0.82$), nor in the scrambled condition (typically developing controls: 80.9±9.7; ADHD: 78.8±10.7; $t(40)=0.68$; $p=0.5$).

ERP analysis

Scalp regions and time windows of interest were defined according to previous studies and visual inspection of group grand averages of our data [23,24,31]: we determined the first positive peak (P100) between 100–200 ms at O1 (left hemisphere) and O2 (right hemisphere) and the first negative peak (N200) between 170–280 ms at P9 (left hemisphere) and P10 (right hemisphere) in each data set (see Figure 2 for topographical scalp maps). The latencies (ms) and amplitudes (μV) were exported for further analysis.

In some studies, a second negative component was observed [23,31,32,49], but in our data, this second component was not observable on the scalp surface. For the slow positive deflection starting after 400 ms (P400+), mean activity at pooled centro-parietal leads (Pz, CPz, PO1, PO2, P1, P2) was assessed between 400–800 ms. Broader and later time windows for peak detection and mean activity calculations were chosen because the activity, especially in the late positive deflection, became prominent later in our data. This might be due to maturation differences in children and adolescents [50,51].

Analysis of dipole sources – biological motion specific activation

In order to further elucidate the cortical areas implicated in biological motion processing, we performed a spatio-temporal dipole source analysis using BESA research 5.1.8, Brain Electrical Source Analysis (BESA GmbH, Munich, Germany) according to Krakowski et al. (2011). First, we calculated the difference waveforms between the human motion and the scrambled stimuli in order to eliminate basic motion from biological motion processing.

In typically developing children, the difference waveforms indicated a stable topography with an occipito-temporal negativity and a central/centro-parietal positivity (see Figure 2) in good agreement with the topography described in adults for attended biological motion during the time-interval of 400–500 ms (Krakowski *et al.*, 2011). In contrast to Krakowski et al., the activation on our data peaked approximately 50–100 ms later. Therefore, we fitted two bilaterally symmetrical dipoles on the time interval 450–550 ms on the grand average of typically developing children, because of the better signal-to-noise ratio in grand averages compared to individual subject averages. Later time windows were not chosen, so as to minimize an overlap between the specific human motion activation and the P400+.

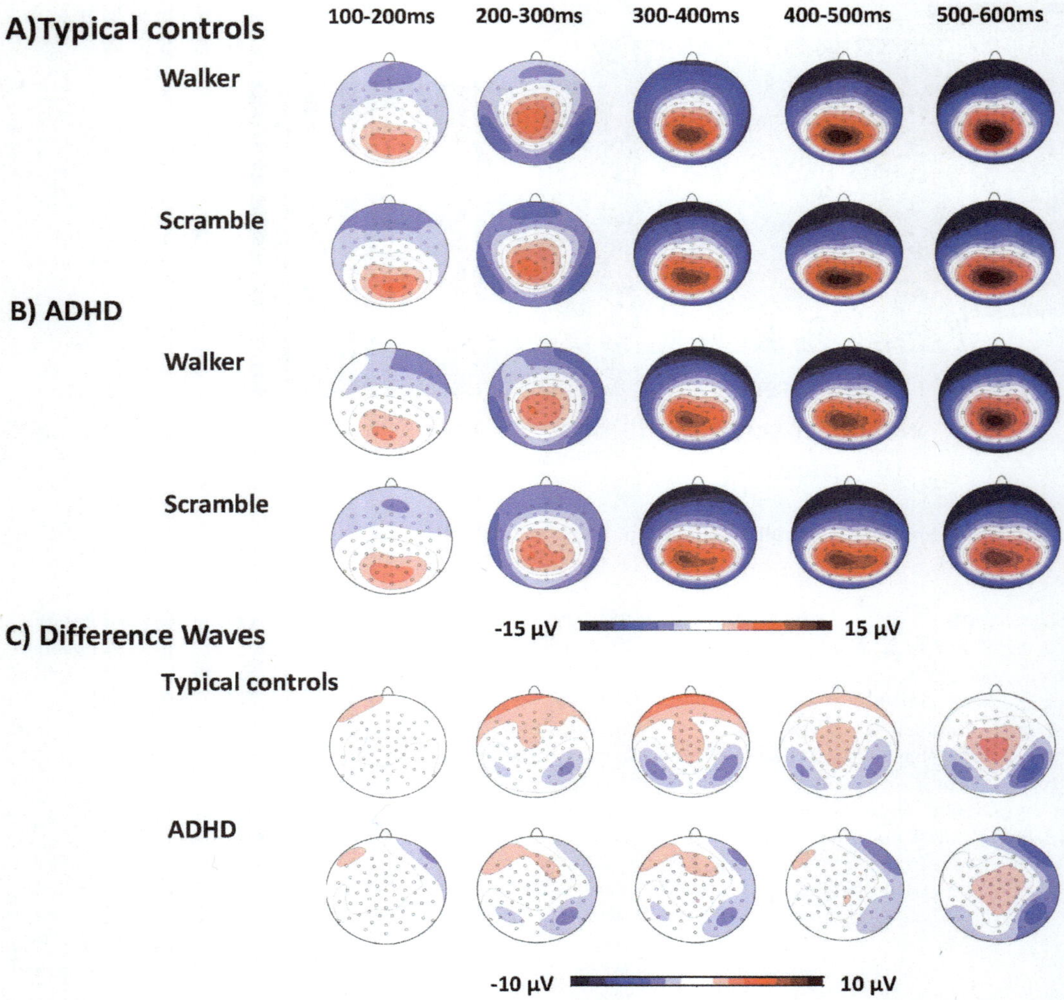

Figure 2. Topographic scalp maps. A) Maps for typically developing controls and B) for children and adolescents with ADHD in both experimental conditions and C) difference maps (walker – scramble) for both groups respectively.

Residual variance and dipole energy were minimized. Because the introduction of further dipoles did not further improve the model, the two-dipole solution was maintained.

Subjects with ADHD showed a more diffuse surface topography than typically developing subjects and lower amplitudes (see results section). Because of these low amplitudes, no reliable explanation of the surface topography was possible in the ADHD, as there were very high residual variances. Thus, no different source model was used for the ADHD group, but the source model fitted on typically developing children was applied to each individual subject. The fit procedure of the source model on the group grand average of typically developing children helped to minimize error variance that might distort dipole localization and/or orientation.

The dipole activations during the window of 450–550 ms after stimulus onset were exported for further statistical analysis in order to quantify the difference in the strength of the dipolar pattern reflected by the source model between groups.

In an additional, complementary approach to describe the more diffuse brain activity in ADHD, we also compared the amount of variance of the surface potential explained by the dipole model between groups. Accordingly, dipole orientations were refited for each individual subject's average and the explained variance (100%–residual variance) was exported for statistical analysis.

Statistical data analyses

Statistical tests and correlation-coefficients were chosen according to the distribution of the dependent variables of interests. To test for group differences in percentiles of Raven matrices and handedness non-parametrical tests (Mann-Witney-U tests) were performed. Age, SCQ score and ADHD symptoms were compared between typically developing controls and ADHD by using a t-test. Group differences in number of correct responses and reaction times were tested with an ANCOVA with the within-factor MOTION TYPE ('human-'/'scrambled motion'), between-factor GROUP, and age as covariate. Differences in ERP amplitudes and latencies were analysed by repeated-measures ANCOVAs with the within-factors MOTION TYPE and HEMISPHERE (right, left), the between-subjects factor GROUP, and AGE as a covariate. The P400+ was analysed by a repeated-measures ANCOVA with the within-factor MOTION TYPE, between-subjects factor GROUP, and AGE as covariate. Dipole moments in the right and left hemisphere obtained by source analysis were analysed by ANCOVAs with the factor GROUP, and AGE as covariate. The amount of variance of the surface potential explained by the source model was compared between groups by an ANCOVA with the between-subject factor GROUP, and AGE as a covariate.

Additionally we tested for differences between ADHD subjects with (N = 9) and without (N = 12) comorbid disruptive behaviour disorder in the ERP components or dipoles using t-tests. Furthermore, to exclude potential confounding effects of disruptive behaviour disorders, analysis between ADHD and typically developing controls were repeated but without the nine subjects with ODD or CD. In both approaches we focused at components, which differed between ADHD and typically developing controls in the ANCOVA models (N200 amplitude and dipole activation; see results section).

We further calculated exploratory Pearson correlations between SCQ score (for ADHD and typically developing controls respectively) and ADHD-symptoms (only ADHD subjects) with the N200 amplitude (averaged for both hemispheres and conditions) and the dipole activation (averaged for both hemispheres).

Significance levels were set to $p = 0.05$. The statistical analysis was performed using SPSS version 20.

Results

Sample

Descriptive data regarding age, handedness, IQ and SCQ score are summarized in Table 1. There were no significant differences regarding age ($t(36.4) < 1$; $p = 0.65$), handedness ($z(41) < 1$; $p = 0.4$) or Raven IQ percentile ranks ($z < 1$; $p = 0.5$) between groups.

Similar to previous studies [4,5], the ADHD group showed elevated SCQ scores (7.5±4.8) compared to typically developing control children (4.1±3.1; $t(32.6) = -2.1$; $p = 0.01$). ADHD children with ODD or CD (6.9±4.0) did not differ from the ADHD children without comorbid disruptive disorders (7.8±5.4) in regard to SCQ scores ($t(18) < 1$; $p = 0.67$; see Table 1 for details). Also, both ADHD groups did not differ in ADHD attention deficits (ADHD with ODD/CD: 14.5±6.5; ADHD without ODD/CD: 16.3±5.1; $t(18) = 0.7$; $p = 0.49$) or hyperactive-impulsive symptoms (ADHD with ODD/CD: 19±11.5; ADHD without ODD/CD: 15.8±5.5; $t(18) = -0.83$; $p = 0.42$).

Behavioural results

In the human motion condition, typically developing controls showed 94.2% correct responses and subjects with ADHD showed 94.8%. In the scrambled motion condition, typically developing controls showed 92.9% and ADHD 91.4% correct responses. There were no significant differences in the number of correct responses between the two groups ($F(1,39) < 1$; $p = 0.77$) nor between both conditions ($F(1,39) < 1$; $p = 0.34$; see Table 1 for details). Reaction times in both conditions ('human motion' and 'scrambled motion') also did not differ between the two groups ($F(1,39) < 1$; $p = 0.35$) but all children reacted faster in the walker compared to the scrambled condition ($F(1,39) = 4.8$; $p = 0.03$).

ERP analysis

Regarding the P100 component, there was a negative association between age and P100 amplitude ($F(1,39) = 10.2$; $p = 0.003$; $r = -0.46$) as well as a trend for an interaction of HEMISPHERE*GROUP ($F(1,39) = 3.3$; $p = 0.08$). In typically developing controls, the amplitudes were slightly higher in the right hemisphere at O2, while in ADHD amplitudes were equally high at O1 and O2 (Figure 3). There were no significant effects regarding latency of the P100.

In respect to the N200 an effect of HEMISPHERE ($F(1,39) = 6.0$; $p = 0.02$) with higher amplitudes in the right hemisphere compared to the left, and an effect for GROUP ($F(1,39) = 6.5$; $p = 0.01$) with reduced amplitudes bilaterally in ADHD were observed. Furthermore, a trend for the interaction HEMISPHERE*AGE ($F(1,39) = 4.0$; $p = 0.05$) was also observable, however, neither the correlation between age and averaged activation in the right hemisphere ($r = 0.17$; $p = 0.28$) nor averaged activation in the left hemisphere ($r = -0.17$; $p = 0.29$) reached significance. There were also no significant effects regarding the latency of the N200 (Figure 3; all mean and standard deviations are presented in Table S1).

There were no significant differences in N200 amplitude ($t(19) = 1.0$; $p = 0.34$) between ADHD subjects with or without comorbid CD or ODD (see Table S2 for means and standard deviations). After excluding subjects with ODD or CD, N200 amplitude still differed by trend between ADHD (N = 12) and typically developing controls ($F(1,30) = 3.2$; $p = 0.08$).

With regard to the P400+, no influence of MOTION TYPE, GROUP or AGE (including the interaction terms) was found (Figure 4; mean amplitudes and latencies are presented in Table S1).

Analysis of human motion specific activation (human – scrambled motion)

The equivalent dipoles were located at the occipito-temporal junction, between the pSTS and MT+/V5. Both dipoles were located at a certain depth in the brain, indicating that they reflected the centre of gravity of larger active brain areas. Occipito-temporal negativity and mid-central/mid-centro-parietal positivity were explained by the same sources using volume conduction. The time-course of activity is shown in Figure 5.

There was a significant effect for GROUP ($F(1,39) = 4.3$; $p = 0.04$) and AGE ($F(1,39) = 7.3$; $p = 0.01$) with reduced activation in ADHD. The age effect mainly resulted from a negative correlation between age and the left dipole activation ($F(1,39) = 7.2$; $p = 0.01$; $r = -0.40$; see Table S1 for means and standard deviations).

The two-dipole model explained 88.5% of variance of the difference waves elicited by human vs. scrambled motion in typically developing controls, and 82.6% in ADHD. Also when dipole orientations were refit to single subject averages, the dipole model explained significantly less variance in the ADHD group (54.8±17) compared to typically developing controls (65.3±11.5; $F(1,39) = 5.3$; $p = 0.03$).

In addition, there were no differences between ADHD with or without comorbid CD or ODD in the left dipole activation ($t(19) = 0.9$; $p = 0.38$), nor in the explained variance of both dipoles ($t(19) = 0.6$; $p = 0.53$; see Table S2 for means and standard deviations). After excluding subjects with ODD or CD, dipole activation still differed between ADHD (N = 12) and typically developing controls ($F(1,30) = 4.3$; $p = 0.05$) and the group effect also remained significant ($F(1,30) = 5.6$; $p = 0.03$).

Correlation trends for ADHD- and ASD symptoms and disturbed motion processing

We found no significant correlation between N200 amplitude and attention deficits ($r = 0.22$; $p = 0.35$) or hyperactive/impulsive symptoms ($r = 0.18$; $p = 0.46$). There were trends (without correcting for multiple comparisons) for the correlation between the dipole activation and attention deficits ($r = -0.40$; $p = 0.08$) and hyperactive/impulsive symptoms ($r = -0.40$; $p = 0.08$).

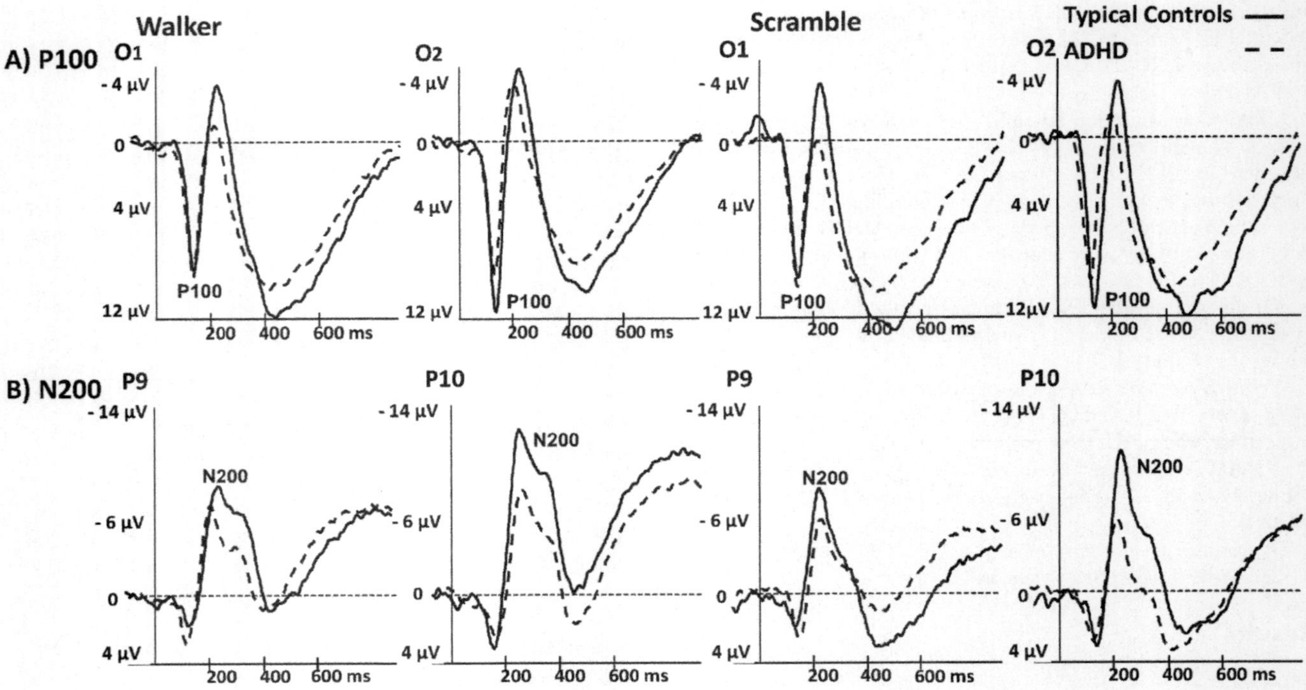

Figure 3. P100 and N200. A) P100 component at electrodes O1 and O2 and B) N200 at electrodes P9 and P10 for both conditions (walker, scramble) separately. Typically developing controls are indicated by solid lines and ADHD by dashed lines.

There were no correlations between the SCQ scores and neurophysiological parameters of human motion processing in typically developing controls (N200 amplitude: $r = 0.18$, $p = 0.45$; dipole activation: $r = 0.12$, $p = 0.63$) or in ADHD subjects (N200 amplitude: $r = -0.15$, $p = 0.53$; dipole activation: $r = 0.20$, $p = 0.40$).

Discussion

The main aim of this study was to clarify if processing of biological motion is disturbed in children and adolescents with ADHD. We observed reduced activity in motion sensitive components (N200), to both biological and scrambeld motion, as well as a reduced activation in dipole sources which is specific for biological motion processing. Differences on the behavioural level were not found. In the following paragraphs, the results will be discussed in detail.

ERPs

After about 100 ms a first positive deflection at occipital sites was observed. In typically developing controls, the amplitudes

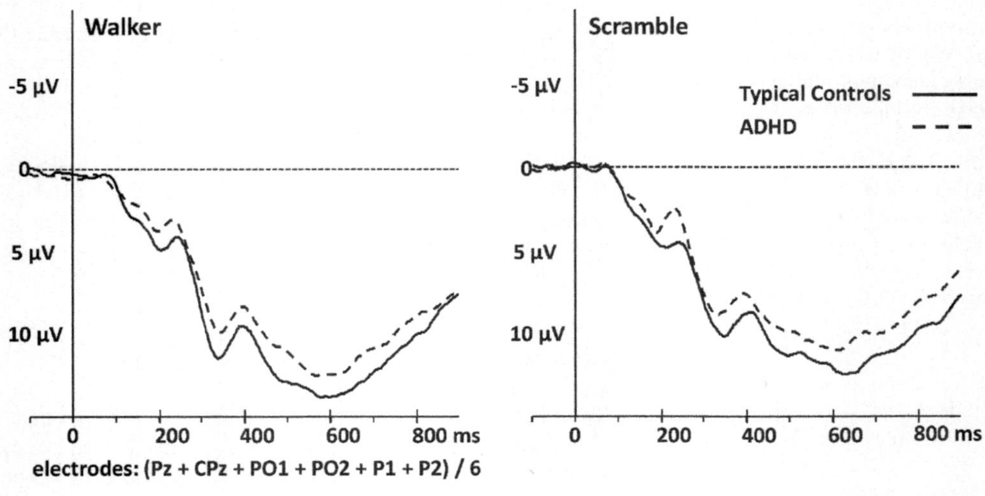

Figure 4. Late positive deflection. P400+ is shown at electrodes CPz, Pz, P1, P2, PO1 and PO2 (averaged) for the walker- and scrambled condition. Typically developing controls are indicated by solid lines and ADHD by dashed lines.

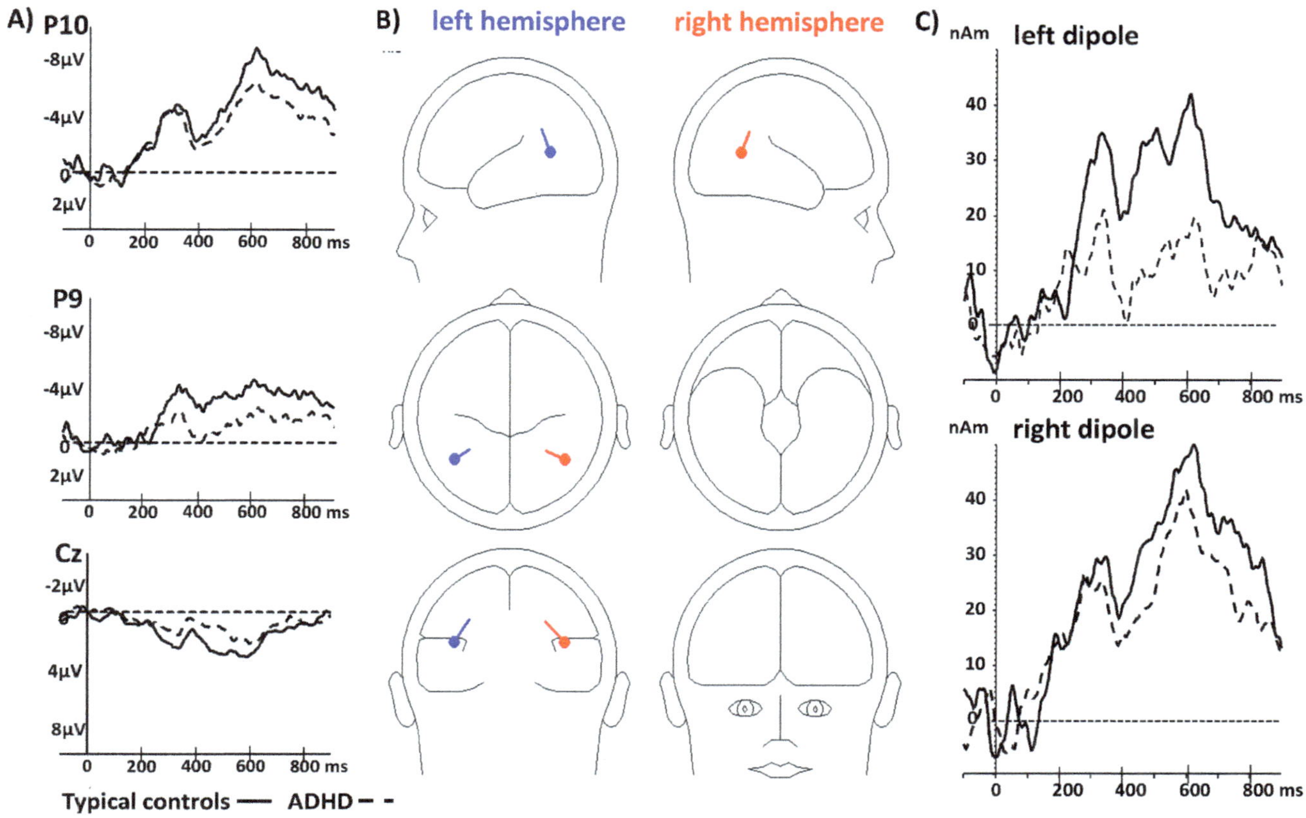

Figure 5. Dipole analysis. A) Difference waves at surface electrodes Cz, P10 (right hemisphere) and P9 (left hemisphere) in typically developing controls (solid line) and ADHD (dashed line); B) Dipole localisation in the left (blue) and right (red) hemisphere; C) Dipole waves, displaying activity in the left and right occipito-temporal junction in typically developing controls (solid line) and ADHD (dashed line).

were slightly higher in the right hemisphere, while in ADHD amplitudes were equal in both hemispheres. Indeed, biological motion has been found to be processed predominantly in the right visual cortex [23,24]. Thus a reduced lateralisation in ADHD could be an indicator of a reduced efficiency during visual processing of motion patterns. However, as this interaction only showed a trend, interpretations should be made cautiously. One previous study found clearly reduced occipital activation in ADHD during early perceptual analysis of facial expressions of anger and fear [12]. But in contrast to our stimuli, facial emotion expressions, especially of fear and anger, are also processed via the amygdala [52]. Thus, the reduced occipital activity in that study likely reflects a disruption of this early emotion-processing pathway between the amygdala and sensory areas and not deficits in visual processing in children with ADHD generally.

After 200 ms a negative deflection was observed at electrodes P10 and P9 – likely reflecting activity in MT+/V5 [27], with elevated amplitudes in the right hemisphere (P10). Our data clearly showed reduced activity of the temporal N200 in both hemispheres and in both conditions in ADHD. These reduced amplitudes might be due to attention related stimulus discrimination impairments, and deficits in stimulus evaluation which were described before in ADHD in an ERP study using an auditory oddball paradigm [53]. In contrast to the P100, during this second processing stage more attention might be needed to process all light-points and to detect motion coherence and motion direction. Furthermore, one study using magnetoencephalography showed that attention can affect these stages of biological motion processing in right temporal cortex [54]. Thus, children with ADHD might fail to allocate their attention focus properly at this stage of biological motion processing. On the other hand, we found no correlation between the N200 amplitude and attention deficits or hyperactive/impulsive symptoms, which might speak against such an association. But because we assessed those symptoms only via parent rating, it needs to be discussed whether a questionnaire is sufficient to assess such symptoms. Standardized behavioural tests might be better suited, to assess the real extent of attention deficits in a laboratory situation.

After 400 ms a slow and late positive deflection at parieto-central electrodes became evident. While earlier components reflect automatic processes, the P400+ is supposed to be a marker of a top-down, active cognitive process involved in decoding the stimulus content [24]. We did not find differences between ADHD and typically developing controls in this processing stage as both groups were equally capable in identifying the stimuli. This is likely due to a floor effect caused by the simple experimental task.

Dipole sources – biological motion specific activation

We analyzed the difference waves between both conditions ('human motion'–'scrambled motion') after 400 ms stimulus-onset by dipole source analysis. By comparing this difference, effects of non-biological motion processing are expected to be removed with the aim to investigate brain systems specifically involved in the detection of biological motion [31]. It is important to point out that those dipoles have to be interpreted as equivalent dipoles, i.e.

not indicating an exact anatomical localization of brain activation, but a centre of gravity. Its strength is the temporal resolution, which allows differentiating unspecific early processing and later specific biological motion processing stages. Our source analysis approach (fitting a source model to the grand average of typically developing subjects and applying this model to all individual subjects) has the disadvantage that remaining error variance in the typically developing group grand average can increase dipole strength in this group. However, group grand averages have good signal to noise ratios and the method can be used to examine whether two groups show similar or different topographical activation patterns. Furthermore, when dipole orientations were refit to individual subject average data, the two-dipole-model explained significantly less variance in subjects with ADHD. Therefore the activation pattern was indeed less focused in subjects with ADHD, and the increased dipole strength in typically developing children and adolescents cannot only be explained by the fitting procedure.

Specific activations to biological motion were previously described in fMRI studies in the posterior temporal cortex, including regions also important for the processing and perception of social stimuli [13,33]. Especially the right pSTS was found recently to be particularly sensitive for human motion compared to other biological motions, e.g. a walking animal [19]. Our dipole, approximately located in the occipital-temporal junction might therefore be centred in this region. The intraparietal sulcus which is located close to the dipole may also be indicated by the dipole, as it is involved in the detection of spatial relations [55,56] which is also important for biological motion detection.

The ADHD group showed a significantly reduced activity after 450 ms post stimulus-onset in both dipoles. In addition, the variance of the cortex activation explained by both dipoles was lower in the ADHD group compared to typically developing controls. Interestingly, reduced or atypical activation in temporal regions in response to biological motion was observed in ASD before [57–59]. Thus it can be discussed if there might be similar processing abnormalities regarding social cognition difficulties in ADHD and ASD, which could be causal for ASD-like symptoms in ADHD [3–7]. Consequently, social interaction problems may need to be addressed adequately in ADHD therapy, at least in a subgroup of patients even without a formal categorical diagnosis of a comorbid conduct disorder or oppositional defiant disorder. However, social skills trainings like those recommended for high functioning ASD [60,61] seem to have less effect on ADHD populations (see for a recent study [62] or review [63]). It also has to be mentioned at this point, that we found no correlation between ASD-like symptoms and the described processing deficits, although SCQ scores were increased in our ADHD sample, similar to previous studies [4,5]. Therefore, mechanisms underlying this processing deficit might be independent from ASD-like symptoms in ADHD. Processing abnormalities did start in the MT+/V5 after 200 ms in ADHD. Deficits in the processing of motion direction and coherence may affect the subsequent processing of spatial relations and detection of biological motion indicated by the dipoles. During this late processing stage, stimulus information needs to be combined which could be difficult for persons with ADHD as earlier processing steps are already disturbed. Therefore, a reduced activation during the processing of biological motion might be caused by a deficient top-down attention allocation. However, future studies need to clarify if this processing deficit simply results from attention problems or indicates disruptions in higher-ordered processing networks.

Behavioural data

Despite the observed differences on the neurological level we found no observable differences on the behavioural level – both groups were equally capable in identifying the stimuli. Such dissociations between neuronal activation and behavioural performance in biological motion perception were also found in ASD. For example in one fMRI study [64] subjects with ASD utilized different brain networks compared to typically developing controls but the behavioural performance was similar in both groups. Similarly, no differences in error rates were observed in another fMRI study [58] between ASD and typically developing controls despite differences on the level of neurological activation. Thus on the one hand it can be discussed that ADHD patients also use different networks to process these motion stimuli or that differences on the behavioural level can only be observed in more challenging tasks when the respective neuronal system breaks down. On the other hand ADHD children might simply need less "neuronal resources" to process biological motion because of excitability changes (see [65] for a discussion about the link between reduced brain activation and behavioural performance). Therefore it remains important to study the perception of biological motion in ADHD using different stimuli including distracters or noise to make these tasks more difficult or vary the level of intact and scrambled motion to identify different perception thresholds in children and adolescents with ADHD [64].

Another nice approach was adopted in one recent study [16]. Here, sensitivity in using global form or local motion cues for detecting facing or walking direction in point-light walkers was assessed. In this way it could be explored if subjects with ADHD may use different information sources to process biological motion. Interestingly only the ability to use form cues for biological motion processing was correlated with measures of social perception. Furthermore, we did not assess reaction times in our task in order to avoid artefacts in the EEG recordings. However, a longer reaction time could be an indicator of a higher cognitive effort to discriminate biological from scrambled motion [58] and should therefore be tested in further studies.

Differences between ADHD with and without a comorbid disruptive behaviour disorder

We found no further differences between ADHD subjects with and without a comorbid disruptive behaviour disorder in the N200 amplitude and dipole activation. Furthermore, even after the exclusion of nine subjects with CD/ODD, the effects regarding the N200 amplitude and dipole activation remained robust. This indicates a stronger relation between ADHD and social processing deficits in this population than with comorbid disruptive behaviour disorders. Alternatively the negative results might be due to small sub-sample size. In our study, only nine ADHD subjects were diagnosed with a comorbid disruptive disorder. Larger sample sizes are needed to test for differences between these subpopulations and exclude confounding effects of comorbid disruptive behaviour disorders.

Conclusion

In sum, for the first time we describe changes in biological motion processing in ADHD which starts 200 ms after stimuli onset in motion sensitive areas and continues at higher, more specialized processing stages. Thus our results suggest some alterations also in higher-ordered networks responsible for biological motion processing in ADHD. However, there are further open issues: first, we only included male participants, thus these results cannot be generalized to female populations. Secondly, the study sample size was still modest and the results need to be replicated in larger and also more heterogeneous samples (e.g. different comorbid disorders). Third, it needs to be addressed in future studies to which extend these disruptions are influenced by simple attention allocation deficits – and might therefore normalise in case of medication. Finally, it is important to point out, that as long as no deficits in the perception of biological motion stimuli are found it will remain unresolved whether the reduction of brain activity in ADHD really indicates a deficit in biological motion processing. Further studies need to address this question.

Supporting Information

Table S1 Mean amplitudes (μV) and latencies (ms) for all ERPs and mean dipole activation (nAm) separate for participants with ADHD and typically developing controls (TC).

Table S2 Differences between ADHD with CD/ODD (N = 9) and without (N = 12) regarding the N200 and dipole activation.

Acknowledgments

First, we thank all families who supported our work by participating in our study. We also thank Jennifer Böhm and Anke Bletsch for assistance with the data collection, Benjamin Teufert for dipole calculations, Christina Luckhardt for proofreading the manuscript and our colleagues for helping us with recruiting participants.

Author Contributions

Conceived and designed the experiments: AK CMF SB. Performed the experiments: AK KH TJ. Analyzed the data: AK KH MS SB. Contributed reagents/materials/analysis tools: CK CMF SB. Wrote the paper: AK KH CK TJ MS CMF SB.

References

1. Polanczyk G, de Lima MS, Horta BL, Biederman J, Rohde LA (2007) The worldwide prevalence of ADHD: A systematic review and metaregression analysis. Am J Psychiatry 164 (6): 942–948.
2. American Psychiatric Association, ed. (2000) DSM-IV-TR. Diagnostic and statistical manual of mental disorders. Washington DC: Amer. Psychiatric Ass.
3. Grzadzinski R, Di Martino A, Brady E, Angeles Mairena M, O'Neale M, et al. (2011) Examining autistic traits in children with ADHD: does the autism spectrum extend to ADHD. J Autism Dev Disord 41 (9): 1178–1191.
4. Kroeger A, Haenig S, Seitz C, Palmason H, Meyer J, et al. (2011) Risk factors of autistic symptoms in children with ADHD. Eur Child Adolesc Psychiatry 20 (11–12): 561–570.
5. Mulligan A, Anney RJL, O'Regan M, Chen W, Butler L, et al. (2009) Autism symptoms in attention-deficit/hyperactivity disorder: a familial trait which correlates with conduct, oppositional defiant, language and motor Disorders. J Autism Dev Disord 39 (2): 197–209.
6. Reiersen AM, Constantino JN, Volk HE, Todd RD (2007) Autistic traits in a population-based ADHD twin sample. J Child Psychol Psychiatry 48 (5): 464–472.
7. Santosh P, Mijovic A (2004) Social impairment in hyperkinetic disorder. Eur Child Adolesc Psychiatry 13 (3).
8. Kochhar P, Batty MJ, Liddle EB, Groom MJ, Scerif G, et al. (2011) Autistic spectrum disorder traits in children with attention deficit hyperactivity disorder. Child Care Health Dev 37 (1): 103–110.
9. Reiersen AM, Constantino JN, Todd RD (2008) Co-occurrence of motor problems and autistic symptoms in attention-deficit/hyperactivity disorder. J Am Acad Child Adolesc Psychiatry 47 47 (6): 662–672.
10. Greene RW, Biederman J, Faraone SV, Sienna M, GarciaJetton J (1997) Adolescent outcome of boys with attention-deficit/hyperactivity disorder and social disability: results from a 4-year longitudinal follow-up study. J Consult Clin Psychol 65 (5): 758–767.
11. Uekermann J, Kraemer M, Abdel-Hamid M, Schimmelmann BG, Hebebrand J, et al. (2010) Social cognition in attention-deficit hyperactivity disorder (ADHD). Neurosci Biobehav Rev 34 (5): 734–743.
12. Williams LM, Hermens DF, Palmer D, Kohn M, Clarke S, et al. (2008) Misinterpreting emotional expressions in attention-deficit/hyperactivity disorder: Evidence for a neural marker and stimulant effects. Biol Psychiatry (10): 917–926.
13. Pavlova MA (2012) Biological motion processing as a hallmark of social cognition. Cereb Cortex 22 (5): 981–995.
14. Grossmann T, Johnson MH (2007) The development of the social brain in human infancy. Eur J Neurosci 25 (4): 909–919.
15. Simion F, Regolin L, Bulf H (2008) A predisposition for biological motion in the newborn baby. Proc Natl Acad Sci USA 105 (2): 809–813.
16. Miller L, Saygin PE (2013) Individual differences in the perception of biological motion: Links to social cognition and motor imagery. Cognition 128 (2): 140–148.
17. Alaerts K, Nackaerts E, Meyns P, Swinnen SP, Wenderoth N, et al. (2011) Action and emotion recognition from point light displays: an investigation of gender differences. Plos One 6 (6): e20989.
18. Nackaerts E, Wagemans J, Helsen W, Swinnen SP, Wenderoth N, et al. (2012) Recognizing biological motion and emotions from point-light displays in autism spectrum disorders. Plos One 7 (9): e44473.
19. Kaiser MD, Shiffrar M, Pelphrey KA (2012) Socially tuned: Brain responses differentiating human and animal motion. Soc Neurosci 7 (3): 301–310.
20. Pelphrey KA, Morris JP, McCarthy G (2004) Grasping the intentions of others: the perceived intentionality of an action influences activity in the superior temporal sulcus during social perception. J Cogn Neurosci 16 (10): 1706–1716.
21. Kret ME, Pichon S, Grèzes J, de Gelder B (2011) Similarities and differences in perceiving threat from dynamic faces and bodies. An fMRI study. Neuroimage 54 (2): 1755–1762.
22. Kaiser MD, Pelphrey KA (2012) Disrupted action perception in autism: behavioral evidence, neuroendophenotypes, and diagnostic utility. Dev Cogn Neurosci 2 (1): 25–35.
23. Hirai M, Watanabe S, Honda Y, Kakigi R (2009) Developmental changes in point-light walker processing during developmental changes in point-light walker processing during childhood and adolescence: an event-related potential study. Neuroscience 161 (1): 311–325.
24. Krakowski AI, Ross LA, Snyder AC, Sehatpour P, Kelly SP, et al. (2011) The neurophysiology of human biological motion processing: a high-density electrical mapping study. Neuroimage 56 (1): 373–383.
25. Prieto EA, Barnikol UB, Soler EP, Dolan K, Hesselmann G, et al. (2007) Timing of V1/V2 and V5+ activations during coherent motion of dots: an MEG study. Neuroimage 37 (4): 1384–1395.
26. Allison T (1999) Electrophysiological studies of human face perception I: potentials generated in occipitotemporal cortex by face and non-face stimuli. Cereb Cortex 9 (5): 415–430.
27. Niedeggen M, Wist ER (1999) Characteristics of visual evoked potentials generated by motion coherence onset. Brain Res Cogn Brain Res 8 (2): 95–105.
28. Kubová Z, Kuba M, Spekreijse H, Blakemore C (1995) Contrast dependence of motion-onset and pattern-reversal evoked potentials. Vision Res 35 (2): 197–205.
29. Hoffmann M, Dorn TJ, Bach M (1999) Time course of motion adaptation: motion-onset visual evoked potentials and subjective estimates. Vision Res 39 (3): 437–444.
30. Hirai M, Fikushima H, Hiraki K (2003) An event-related potentials study of biological motion perception in humans. Neurosci Lett 344 (1): 41–44.
31. Jokisch D, Daum I, Suchan B, Troje NF (2005) Structural encoding and recognition of biological motion: evidence from event-related potentials and source analysis. Behav Brain Res 157 (2): 195–204.
32. Hirai M, Kakigi R (2008) Differential cortical processing of local and global motion information in biological motion: an event-related potential study. J Vis 8 (16) 2.1–17.
33. Hein G, Knight RT (2008) Superior temporal sulcus–it's my area: or is it. J Cogn Neurosci 20 (12): 2125–2136.
34. Schendan HE, Kutas M (2007) Neurophysiological evidence for the time course of activation of global shape, part, and local contour representations during visual object categorization and memory. J Cogn Neurosci 19 (5): 734–749.
35. Oldfield R (1971) The assessment and analysis of handedness: the Edinburgh inventory. Neuropsychologia 9 (1): 97–113.
36. World Health Organization (1992) The ICD-10 classification of mental and behavioural disorders. Clinical descriptions and diagnostic guidelines. Geneva.
37. Schneider S (2009) Kinder-DIPS. Diagnostisches Interview bei psychischen Störungen im Kindes- und Jugendalter. Heidelberg: Springer.
38. Urban KR, Gao W (2013) Methylphenidate and the juvenile brain: enhancement of attention at the expense of cortical plasticity. Med Hypotheses 81 (6): 988–994.
39. Berridge CW, Devilbiss DM (2011) Psychostimulants as cognitive enhancers: the prefrontal cortex, catecholamines, and attention-deficit/hyperactivity disorder. Biol Psychiatry 69 (12): e101.
40. Yano M, Steiner H (2007) Methylphenidate and cocaine: the same effects on gene regulation. Trends Pharmacol Sci 28 (11): 588–596.
41. Arbeitsgruppe Kinder Jugendlichen und Familiendiagnsotik (1998) CBCL/4-18 Elternfragebogen über das Verhalten von Kindern und Jugendlichen. Göttingen: Hogrefe.

42. Bulheller S, Häcker HO (2002) Coloured Progressive Matrices. Deutsche Bearbeitung und Normierung nach J.C. Raven. Frankfurt: Swets Test Services.
43. Bulheller S, Häcker H (2003) Ravens's Progressive Matrices and Vocabulary Scales. Deutsche Bearbeitung und Normierung nach J.C. Raven. Frankfurt: Swets Test Services.
44. Bölte S, Poustka F, Rutter M, Bailey A, Lord C (2006) Fragebogen zur sozialen Kommunikation. FSK; Autismus-Screening; deutsche Fassung des Social Communication Questionnaire (SCQ) von Michael Rutter, Anthony Bailey und Catherine Lord; Manual. Bern: Huber.
45. Bölte S, Rutter M, Le Couteur A, Lord C (2006) Diagnostisches Interview für Autismus - revidiert. ADI-R; deutsche Fassung des Autism Diagnostic Interview - Revised (ADI-R) von Michael Rutter, Ann Le Couteur und Catherine Lord; Manual. Bern, Göttingen: Huber; Hogrefe.
46. Bölte S, Crecelius K, Poustka F (2000) The Questionnaire on behaviour and social communication (VSK): an autism screening instrument for research and practice. Diagnostica 46 (3): 149–155.
47. Döpfner M, Görtz-Dorten A, Lehmkuhl G (2008) Diagnostik-System für psychische Störungen nach ICD-10 und DSM-IV für Kinder und Jugendliche-II. DISYPS-II. Bern: Huber.
48. Troje NF (2002) Decomposing biological motion: a framework for analysis and synthesis of human gait patterns. J Vis 2 (5): 2.
49. Hirai M, Hiraki K (2005) An event-related potentials study of biological motion perception in human infants. Brain Res Cogn Brain Res 22 (2): 301–304.
50. Taylor MJ, Smith ML (1995) Age-related ERP changes in verbal and nonverbal memory tasks. J Psychophysiol 9 (4): 283–297.
51. Taylor MJ, McCarthy G, Saliba E, Degiovanni E (1999) ERP evidence of developmental changes in processing of faces. Clin Neurophysiol 110 (5): 910–915.
52. Sergerie K, Chochol C, Armony JL (2008) The role of the amygdala in emotional processing: a quantitative meta-analysis of functional neuroimaging studies. Neurosci Biobehav Rev 32 (4): 811–830.
53. Senderecka M, Grabowska A, Gerc K, Szewczyk J, Chmylak R (2012) Event-related potentials in children with attention deficit hyperactivity disorder: An investigation using an auditory oddball task. Int J Psychophysiol 85 (1): 106–115.
54. Pavlova M (2004) Dissociable cortical processing of recognizable and non-recognizable biological movement: analysing gamma MEG activity. Cereb Cortex 14 (2): 181–188.
55. Grefkes C, Fink GR (2005) The functional organization of the intraparietal sulcus in humans and monkeys. J Anat 207 (1): 3–17.
56. Wandell BA, Dumoulin SO, Brewer AA (2007) Visual field maps in human cortex. Neuron 56 (2): 366–383.
57. Herrington JD, Baron-Cohen S, Wheelwright SJ, Singh KD, Bullmore ET, et al. (2007) The role of MT+/V5 during biological motion perception in Asperger Syndrome: an fMRI study. Research in Autism Spectrum Disorders 1 (1): 14–27.
58. Freitag CM, Konrad C, Häberlen M, Kleser C, von Gontard A, et al. (2008) Perception of biological motion in autism spectrum disorders. Neuropsychologia 46 (5): 1480–1494.
59. Kaiser MD, Hudac CM, Shultz S, Lee SM, Cheung C, et al. (2010) Neural signatures of autism. Proc Natl Acad Sci 107 (49): 21223–21228.
60. Tse J, Strulovitch J, Tagalakis V, Meng L, Fombonne E (2007) Social skills training for adolescents with Asperger syndrome and high-functioning autism. J Autism Dev Disord 37 (10): 1960–1968.
61. Freitag CM, Cholemkery H, Elsuni L, Kroeger AK, Bender S, et al. (2013) The group-based social skills training SOSTA-FRA in children and adolescents with high functioning autism spectrum disorder - study protocol of the randomised, multi-centre controlled SOSTA - net trial. Trials 14 (1): 6.
62. Storebo OJ, Gluud C, Winkel P, Simonsen E (2012) Social-skills and parental training plus standard treatment versus standard treatment for children with ADHD - the randomised SOSTRA trial. Plos One 7 (6): e37280.
63. Storebo OJ, Skoog M, Damm D, Thomsen PH, Simonsen E, et al. (2011) Social skills training for attention deficit hyperactivity disorder (ADHD) in children aged 5 to 18 years. Cochrane Database Syst Rev (12) CD008223.
64. McKay LS, Simmons DR, McAleer P, Marjoram D, Piggot J, et al. (2012) Do distinct atypical cortical networks process biological motion information in adults with autism spectrum disorders. Neuroimage 59 (2): 1524–1533.
65. Pavlova M, Bidet-Ildei C, Sokolov AN, Braun C, Krägeloh-Mann I (2009) Neuromagnetic response to body motion and brain connectivity. J Cogn Neurosc 21 (5): 837–846.

4

Prepulse Inhibition of the Acoustic Startle Reflex in High Functioning Autism

Sina Kohl[1], Carolin Wolters[1], Theo O. J. Gruendler[1,2,3], Kai Vogeley[1,4], Joachim Klosterkötter[1], Jens Kuhn[1]*

1 Department for Psychiatry and Psychotherapy, University Hospital of Cologne, Cologne, North Rhine-Westphalia, Germany, **2** Department of Economics, Otto-von-Guericke-University, Magdeburg, Saxony-Anhalt, Germany, **3** Center for Behavioral Brain Sciences, Magdeburg, Saxony-Anhalt, Germany, **4** Institute for Neuroscience and Medicine – Cognitive Neuroscience (INM3), Research Center Juelich, Juelich, North Rhine-Westphalia, Germany

Abstract

Background: High functioning autism is an autism spectrum disorder that is characterized by deficits in social interaction and communication as well as repetitive and restrictive behavior while intelligence and general cognitive functioning are preserved. According to the weak central coherence account, individuals with autism tend to process information detail-focused at the expense of global form. This processing bias might be reflected by deficits in sensorimotor gating, a mechanism that prevents overstimulation during the transformation of sensory input into motor action. Prepulse inhibition is an operational measure of sensorimotor gating, which indicates an extensive attenuation of the startle reflex that occurs when a startling pulse is preceded by a weaker stimulus, the prepulse.

Methods: In the present study, prepulse inhibition of acoustic startle was compared between 17 adults with high functioning autism and 17 sex-, age-, and intelligence-matched controls by means of electromyography.

Results: Results indicate that participants with high functioning autism exhibited significantly higher startle amplitudes than the control group. However, groups did not differ with regard to PPI or habituation of startle.

Discussion: These findings challenge the results of two previous studies that reported prepulse inhibition deficits in high-functioning autism and suggest that sensorimotor gating is only impaired in certain subgroups with autism spectrum disorder.

Editor: Harold A. Burgess, National Institutes of Health/NICHD, United States of America

Funding: The authors thank the Walter and Marga Boll Foundation, the German Research Foundation (KFO-219 grant), as well as the Center for Behavioral Brain Sciences for financial support. The funders had no role in study design, data collection and analysis, decision to publish, or preparation of the manuscript.

Competing Interests: The authors have declared that no competing interests exist.

* E-mail: jens.kuhn@uk-koeln.de

These authors contributed equally to this work.

Introduction

In Leo Kanner's [1] original description of autism, he made the following observation:

> "Another intrusion comes from loud noises and moving objects, which are therefore reacted to with horror. Tricycles, swings, elevators, vacuum cleaners, running water, gas burners, mechanical toys, egg beaters, even the wind could on occasions bring about a major panic. (...) Yet it is not the noise or motion itself that is dreaded. The disturbance comes from the noise or motion that intrudes itself, or threatens to intrude itself, upon the child's aloneness." (p. 245)

In fact, about 90% of children with an autism spectrum disorder (ASD) exhibit sensory abnormalities [2,3,4]. Many of those show auditory hypersensitivity [5,6,7]. It was suggested that hypersensitivity is associated with an exceptional attention to detail in autism [5]. The weak central coherence theory of autism hypothesizes that the detail-focused processing style in children and adults with autism leads to a failure of central processing, which involves difficulties to extract global form or meaning [8]. Research regarding acoustic stimulation suggests that persons suffering from ASD are less susceptible to interference from melodic structure in music processing and to interference from visual to auditory perception (i.e. the *McGurk effect*). In addition, persons with autism show superior pitch and loudness processing and less distinctive auditory filtering [9,10]. Behavioral experiments showed that persons with ASD require a higher signal-to-noise ratio in comparison to control subjects to perceive noise or speech [11,12,13]. In addition, individuals with ASD have difficulties ignoring distracting sounds in peripheral spatial locations [14] and segregating incoming sounds [15].

Abnormal sensory processing may lead to sensorimotor integration deficits [16], which have been shown across different sensory modalities in ASD [17]. Sensorimotor gating is an adaptive mechanism that prevents overstimulation within the transformation of sensory input into motor action [18]. Abnormalities of motor behavior are highly prevalent in autism and have a great impact on everyday life abilities [19]. However, the etiology of these symptoms remains unclear [20].

In the present study, prepulse inhibition (PPI) of the acoustic startle reflex is used as a proxy of sensorimotor gating. PPI indicates an extensive attenuation of the startle reflex that occurs when a startle eliciting stimulus, the pulse, is preceded by a weaker stimulus, the prepulse, within a timeframe of 30–500 ms [21]. More than 90% of healthy subjects show a reduction of 40–80% of the startle reflex, if a pulse is preceded by a prepulse that does not elicit a startle response itself [22]. The protection of processing hypothesis proposes that the processing of sensory stimuli is protected against interference through other irrelevant or distracting stimuli by preattentive mechanisms [21].

The present study aimed at exploring sensorimotor gating in high functioning autism (HFA), a subgroup of ASD that is characterized by social and communication deficits as well as repetitive, restrictive and stereotyped behavior, interests, and activities with preservation of intelligence and general cognitive functioning [23].

We could identify five studies that focused on PPI deficits in ASD patients. McAlonan and colleagues [24] as well as Perry and colleagues [25] found attenuated PPI in adults with high functioning autism and Asperger syndrome. In contrast, three other groups did not find any significant differences in PPI in samples that included children [26] or children as well as adolescents [27,28]. Motivated by the inconsistent literature and with the idea that repetitive thoughts, behavior and activities might be a product of malfunctioning inhibition, it seemed important to us to conduct a study of high methodological quality in order to examine processing of auditory startle stimuli in a clearly defined subgroup of ASD patients. Derived from the above mentioned considerations we hypothesize that: participants with HFA will exhibit higher amplitudes of the startle reflex accompanied by reduced PPI in comparison to healthy controls.

Materials and Methods

The study was approved by the local ethics committee of the Medical Faculty of the University of Cologne, and conducted in accordance with the declaration of Helsinki. The ethics committee was also involved in compiling the patient information and consent form. All subjects were informed in speech and writing about the purpose and procedure of the study and had to give their written informed consent in order to participate. Also approved by the local ethics committee, a very experienced psychiatrist and expert in the field of autism spectrum disorders (KV) gave the diagnosis and assessed the capacity of each participant to give his/her consent. As further support of the evaluation and for diagnostic purpose an intelligence test has been conducted with each participant (German multiple choice test *Wortschatztest* (WST)) to confirm ability to give consent. We did not obtain any surrogate consents.

Materials

Autistic traits were estimated using the self-assessment questionnaire autism quotient (AQ) as screening instrument [29]. Empathy was measured by the self-report questionnaire empathy quotient (EQ) [30], and the tendency to systemize was acquired using the self-report questionnaire systemizing quotient (SQ) [31]. The Beck Depression Inventory (BDI) [32] was completed by all participants in order to measure depressive symptomatology. Intelligence was measured using the German multiple choice test *Wortschatztest (WST)* [33], which provides a short and valid estimation of general intelligence [34]. In addition, participants were asked to fill out a questionnaire, which included questions about any regular intake of medication, and the frequency and last point of time they consumed caffeine, alcohol, cannabis, and other drugs.

Subjects

23 subjects with HFA and 23 normal control (NC) subjects (both groups: 7 women, 16 men) were assessed. The experimental group was diagnosed and recruited in the Autism Outpatient Clinic of the Department of Psychiatry, University of Cologne. The diagnosis was made by two experienced clinicians in two independent interviews (one of them KV) according to the International Classification of mental disorders [23] and supplemented by comprehensive neuropsychological assessment. Only individuals with the diagnosis of HFA (F84.5) were included into the sample. Formally, criteria of the DSM-IV [35] for HFA were met as well.

Control subjects were matched to sex, age, and intelligence scores of the experimental group. In our screening procedure, none of the control subjects had a BDI score above the clinically critical value of 17 [36] or an AQ above the cutoff score of 32 suggested by Baron-Cohen, Wheelwright, Skinner, Martin, and Clubley [37]. None of the control subjects showed any signs or symptoms of any possible psychiatric comorbid disorder. According to self disclosure, none of the participants suffered from any kind of hearing impairment. All of the subjects had an intelligence quotient (IQ) above 70 (see table 1).

Three of the subjects with HFA and three of the NC subjects had to be excluded from the data analysis because they did not exhibit sufficient startle responses and were thus classified as non-responders. One participant with HFA had to be excluded from further data analysis because he fell asleep during the test sessions, and one data set of an HFA subject was not usable due to technical malfunction. Additionally, one of the subjects with HFA and three of the NC subjects were excluded because visual inspection of the data indicated startle responses to the prepulses and PPI was therefore not reliably calculable.

Thus, $n = 17$ subjects with HFA and $n = 17$ NC subjects (each with 5 women, 12 men) remained in the sample (Table 1–3). There were no significant group differences regarding age, intelligence, and years of education. However, the HFA group showed significantly higher BDI scores than the control group. In addition, participants with HFA showed significantly higher AQ and SQ scores, and significantly lower EQ scores than NC participants.

Procedure

The startle reflex was measured in a quiet laboratory by means of an EMG of the musculus orbicularis oculi (EMG SR-HLAB, San Diego Instruments, San Diego, CA). To this end, two miniature electrodes were placed below and next to the participant's right eye, and a ground electrode was placed behind the right ear. Participants were briefed to sit quietly in an armchair and to fix their gaze on a spot. The stimulus material was presented binaurally through headphones (TDH-39-P, Maico, Minneapolis, MN). During the course of the measurement, background white noise of 70 dB was presented. Acoustic stimuli consisted of bursts of broadband white noise. Startle eliciting stimuli were presented for 40 ms at intensities of 110 dB with uncontrolled instant rise time, while prepulses were presented for 20 ms at 80 dB. Each PPI session started with a 5 min acclimation

Table 1. Participants' characteristics.

	HFA group		Control group		Statistical differences		
Variable	*M (SD)*	Range	*M (SD)*	Range	*T*	*df*	*p*
Age	40.2 (9.93)	23–53	43.4 (10.55)	26–56	.090	32	.373
Education	18.2 (5.48)	10–30	20.4 (3.35)	15–27	1.38	32	.178
IQ	116.4 (16.14)	89–143	119.2 (7.0)	101–133	.66	22	.515
BDI	11 (9.76)	0–34	5.1 (4.98)	0–15	2.24	24	.035*
AQ	41.1 (3.64)	34–45	15.9 (7.05)	5–29	13.09	24	<.001*
EQ	16.9 (7.82)	6–30	42.4 (12.83)	21–65	3.77	23	<.001*
SQ	37.3 (15.42)	11–67	21.7 (7.24)	11–36	7.01	32	<.001*

HFA = High functioning autism; Education = Years of education; IQ = Intelligence Quotient; BDI = Beck Depression Inventory; AQ = Autism Quotient; EQ = Empathy Quotient; SQ = Systemizing Quotient; *significant at an alpha level of .05.

period of white noise. The first and the last block of the measurement comprised 5 pulse-alone trials. Intermittently, 10 pulse-alone trials, 10 prepulse-alone trials, and 30 prepulse-pulse trials were presented in a pseudorandom order. Prepulse-pulse stimulus onset asynchronies (SOAs) varied between 60, 120, and 240 ms. Intertrial intervals were 10, 15, 20, or 25 sec. Each trial was preceded by a baseline period of 60 ms, starting 80 ms before the stimulus onset.

Data analyses

EMG data were analyzed using a *Matlab* program (MathWorks, Inc., Natick, MA) that was developed in our clinic in order to visually inspect and calculate PPI data. Recorded EMG activity was high-pass filtered at 30 Hz and low-pass filtered at 300 Hz using a 4th order butterworth filter, and a 50 Hz notch filter with a width of 6 Hz was used to reduce power line interference (hier bitte den van Boxtel Artikel zitieren). The EMG signal was then rectified and smoothed using a 10 point moving average. By means of visual inspection, any trial featuring excessive noise in the EMG signal or a spontaneous blink in the period immediately preceding the stimulus onset or the minimal response onset were excluded from further analyses. Based on these criteria, 9.44% of trials had to be excluded from data analysis. In addition, the first two pulse-alone trials of each PPI measure were excluded from the analysis, as it was assumed that these trials evoke unrepresentatively high startle amplitudes [38].

Criteria for qualifying the EMG signal as an actual startle response were defined in accordance with guidelines for human startle eye blink EMG studies [38]. The latency window was set at 20 to 150 ms after pulse onset, and the minimum response amplitude was set at 2 *SD* above baseline. The response peak was identified by a computerized algorithm. If visual inspection indicated that response onset was outside the latency window or the criteria for minimal response size was not met, the trial was classified as a zero response trial. These trials were not considered in the calculation of the specific values. Participants were identified as non-responders and therefore excluded if they exhibited startle responses in less than half of the pulse-alone trials. Participants for whom visual inspection of the prepulse-alone trials revealed distinct reactions to the prepulses in half or more of the trials were excluded as well.

Statistical analyses

A commercial software package was used for statistical analysis of the data (SPSS for windows, version 21, IBM Corp., Armonk, NY).

Startle amplitudes. Mean startle amplitudes were calculated by averaging the response peaks of all included trials, and compared between groups using an unpaired Student's *t*-test. Differences in startle amplitudes within the different trial conditions were compared by means of a one-way repeated-measure ANOVA. In addition to startle amplitudes we calculated the response probability, the probability that a valid startle response follows the startle eliciting pulse. The response probability is given in percent.

PPI. Percentage PPI values were calculated according to the following formula: 100 – [(mean amplitude prepulse trials/mean amplitude pulse alone trials) x 100]. Besides comparing PPI between the HFA and NC group, PPI group differences were assessed using three different one-way repeated measures ANOVAs, including the between-subjects factor of group (1. male/female; 2. smoker/non-smoker; 3. HFA/NC), and within-subjects repeated measures of PPI across the different trial types. Mean startle amplitude across all pulse-alone trials was included as a

Table 2. Comorbid psychiatric disorders.

Number of participants (group)	Psychiatric disorder
1 (HFA)	Bipolar disorder
1 (HFA)	Depression
1 (HFA)	Dysthymia
1 (HFA)	Anxiety Disorder
2 (HFA)	ADHD
1 (HFA)	ADD

HFA = High functioning autism; ADHD = attention deficit/hyperactivity disorder; ADD = attention deficit disorder.

covariate. Furthermore, PPI differences across all three types of trials were calculated using Student's *t*-tests.

Correlations between PPI and autistic traits. To assess the relationship between PPI and autistic traits, the AQ, EQ, and SQ scores of the HFA subjects were correlated with percentage PPI of the three trial types using the Pearson's correlation coefficient.

Habituation. Primarily, group differences in habituation of the startle response across all pulse-alone trials were calculated. To this end, the altogether 20 pulse-alone trials were split into four blocks of five trials each. A one-way repeated measures ANOVA was conducted, including the between-subjects factor of diagnosis (HFA/NC) and the within-subjects factor of mean startle amplitude of the four pulse-alone blocks. Additionally, the overall habituation rate was examined by calculating the percent decrease from mean startle amplitude in the first five pulse-alone trials to mean amplitude in the last five trials and compared between groups by means of an unpaired Student's *t*-test.

Before conducting the ANOVAs, the assumption of sphericity was tested for the data, and degrees of freedom were corrected using Greenhouse-Geisser estimates of sphericity, if necessary. Effect sizes for ANOVAs were calculated using $\eta^2_{partial}$, effect sizes for post-hoc pairwise comparisons were calculated using Cohen's *d*.

Results

Startle amplitudes

Analysis of startle amplitudes for pulse-alone trials revealed significantly higher startle amplitudes ($M = 179.1$, $SD = 146.93$) for HFA patients than control subjects ($M = 96.6$, $SD = 62.93$), $T(32) = 2.13$, $p = .041$. The mean response probability for a significant startle amplitude in pulse alone trials for the HFA group ($M = 93.66$ $SD = 9.04$) was significantly higher compared to the control group ($M = 80.52$, $SD = 18.81$), $T(32) = 2.6$, $p = .014$.

PPI

Examining PPI differences between the HFA and NC group, Mauchly's test of sphericity was not significant, $\chi^2 = .17$, $df = 2$, $p = .435$. There was a significant main effect of trial type (60/120/240 ms SOA), $F(2) = 3.35$, $p = .041$, $\eta^2_{partial} = .098$. Post-hoc pairwise comparisons indicated that PPI was significantly lower in trials with an SOA of 240 ms than in those with an SOA of 60 ms, $p = .015$, $d = .61$, and 120 ms, $p = .001$, $d = .63$ (*p*-values were Bonferroni adjusted).

However, there was no significant effect of mean startle amplitude across pulse-alone trials, $F(1) = .30$, $p = .590$, and no significant interaction of startle amplitude and trial type, $F(2) = .12$, $p = .887$. Equally, there was no significant main effect of diagnosis on PPI, $F(1) = .02$, $p = .879$, and no significant interaction of diagnosis and trial type, $F(2) = .13$, $p = .877$. Figure 1 shows the PPI values of HFA and NC subjects across the three different types of trials. Likewise, there were no differences in overall PPI between participants with HFA ($M = 32.5$, $SD = 31.11$) and control participants ($M = 36.8$, $SD = 22.11$), $T(32) = .46$, $p = .649$.

The response probabilities for the prepulse trials did not differ significantly between the HFA Group ($M = 84.18$, $SD = 18.73$) and the controls ($M = 72.66$, $SD = 24.18$), $T(32) = 1.55$, $p = .13$.

Correlations between autistic traits and PPI

There were no significant correlations between AQ, EQ, and SQ scores and PPI in the different trial types among HFA participants (all $p > .1$).

Table 3. Medication.

Number of participants	Medication
5 (HFA), 1 (NC)	Antidepressant drug (2× Sertraline, 2× Mirtazepine,
	1× Citalopram, 1× Moclobemid)
2 (HFA), 1 (NC)	Beta blocker (1× Bisoprolol, 1× Metahexal,
	1× Mesoprolol)
1 (HFA), 1 (NC)	Irbesartan
1 (NC)	Ramiprile
1 (HFA)	Lamotrigine

HFA = High functioning autism; NC = normal controls.

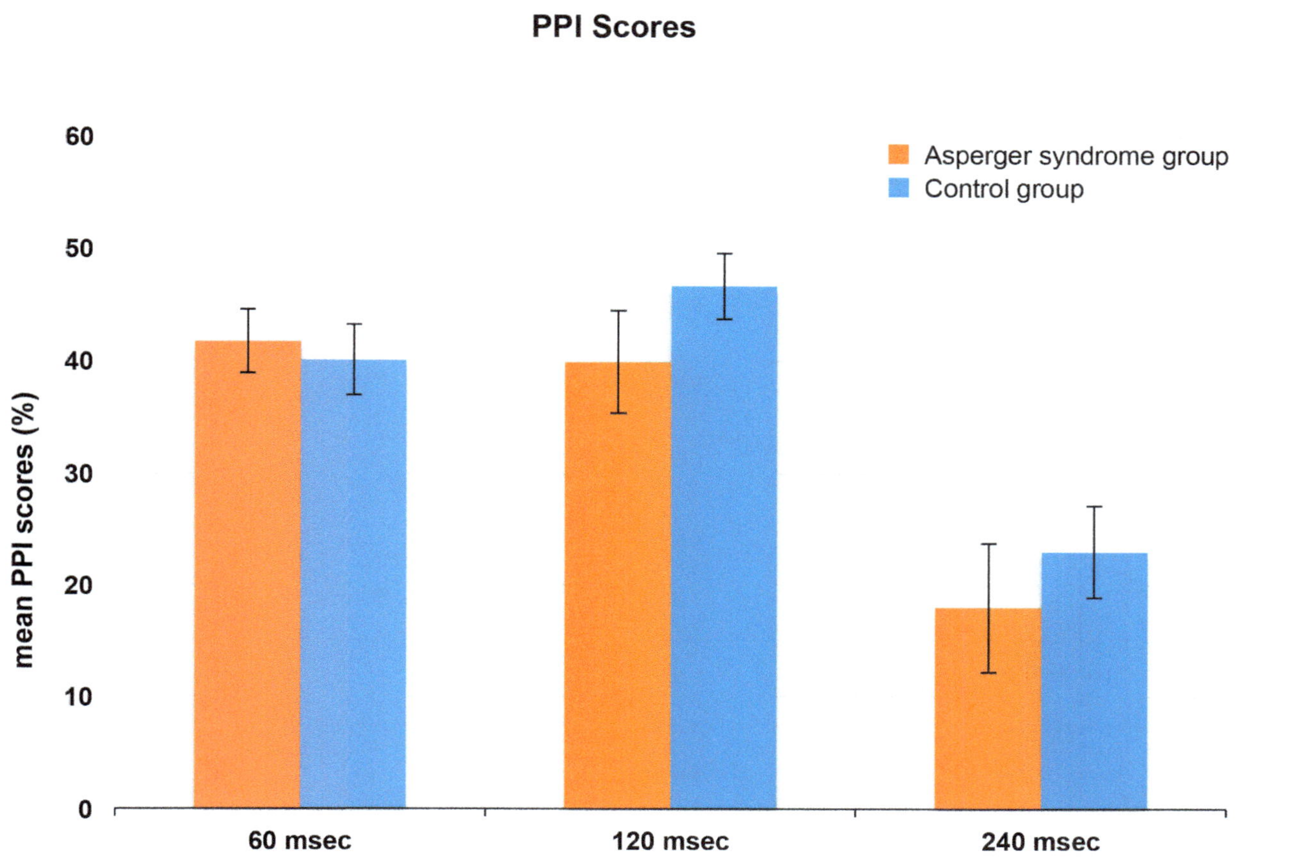

Figure 1. PPI scores. Mean PPI scores (± SEM) across the three trial conditions in subjects with high functioning autism (HFA) and normal control (NC) subjects.

Habituation

Mauchly's test indicated that the assumption of sphericity was not met for startle amplitude scores, $\chi^2 = 23.52$, $df = 5$, $p < .001$. Therefore, degrees of freedom were corrected using Greenhouse-Geisser estimates of sphericity. Results showed that the startle amplitude was significantly affected by block, $F(2) = 30.32$, $p < .001$, $\eta^2_{partial} = .486$, indicating habituation across the four blocks of pulse-alone trials. Pairwise comparisons determined that the mean startle amplitude decreased from the first block to the second, $p < .001$, $d = .47$, to the third, $p < .001$, $d = .67$, and to the fourth block, $p < .001$, $d = .75$. In addition, the startle amplitude significantly decreased from the second to the fourth block, $p < .001$, $d = .31$ (p-values were Bonferroni adjusted). Data analysis also revealed a significant main effect of diagnosis, $F(1) = 4.67$, $p = .038$, $\eta^2_{partial} = .127$, reflecting the differences in startle amplitude between HFA and NC participants. However, there was no significant block-by-group effect, $F(2) = .19$, $p = .834$. Visual inspection confirmed that the two groups had similar decreases in startle amplitude over the four blocks (see figure 2).

Analysis of overall percentage habituation from block 1 to block 4 did not show significant differences between HFA ($M = 48.0$, $SD = 26.31$) and NC participants ($M = 52.1$, $SD = 25.13$), $T(32) = .47$, $p = .641$.

Discussion

The present study assessed auditory sensorimotor gating by means of the acoustic startle reflex in subjects with HFA. Our results indicate significantly higher mean startle amplitudes in the HFA group and for the pulse alone condition significantly higher response probabilities compared to the control group. But groups did not differ significantly in terms of PPI, neither in the different SOA trial types, nor across all trials.

Startle amplitude

Increased startle amplitudes among HFA subjects may be caused by auditory hypersensitivity, which often occurs in autism [5]. Abnormalities in the processing of auditory information were also shown by neurophysiologic studies finding atypical neural activity in early auditory pathways in ASD [39]. Magnetoencephalography studies have linked auditory hypersensitivity to maturational abnormalities in the auditory cortex in autism, resulting in delayed responses of the auditory cortex to acoustic stimuli [40], and abnormalities in myelination processes, causing slower transmission rates in central auditory pathways [41,42]. In addition, reduced interneuron activity might lead to abnormal brain connectivity, which might in turn cause cortical hypersensitivity in the primary auditory cortex [43].

PPI

The other major hypothesis could not be proven by our results. Bearing in mind the weak central coherence theory of autism we hypothesized, subjects with HFA would show PPI deficits in comparison to the control group. But in accordance with three other studies [26,27,28] our results indicate that PPI does not

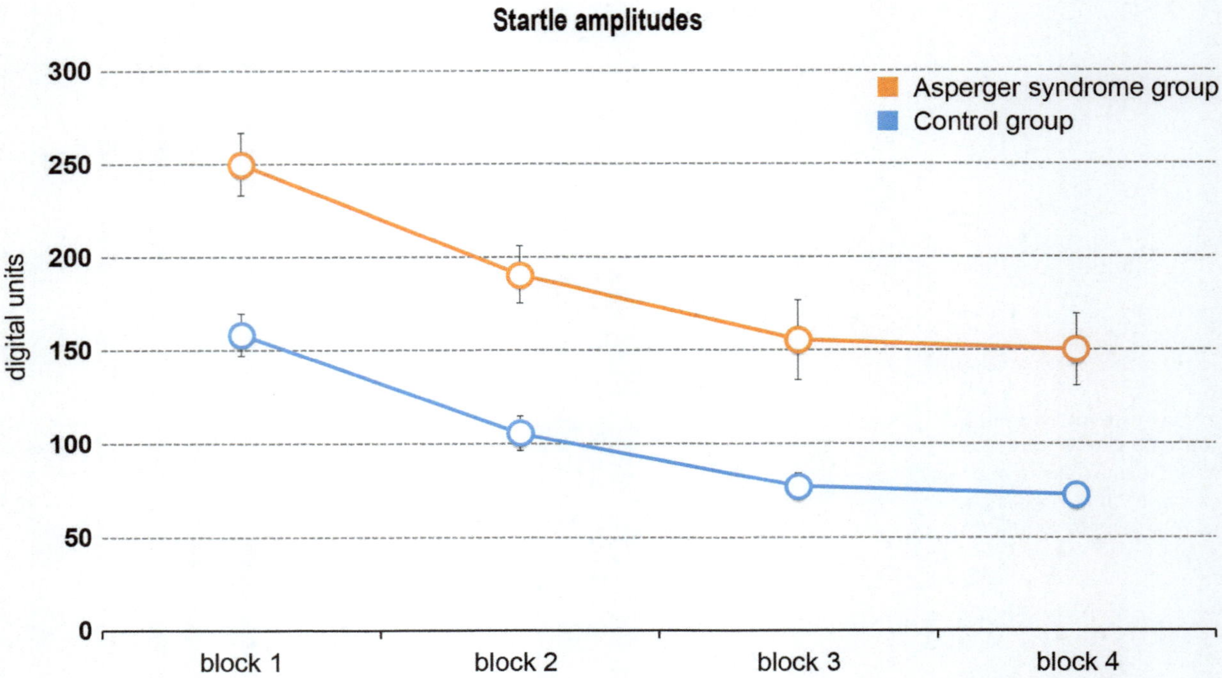

Figure 2. Startle amplitudes and habituation rates. Habituation rates across the four blocks of trials in the high functioning autism (HFA) and normal control (NC) group. Mean startle amplitudes (± SEM) of each five pulse-alone trials are shown. HFA participants showed significantly higher absolute startle amplitudes compared to NC participants, while habituation rates were similar.

differ between the HFA and the NC group. However, the aforementioned studies examined PPI in samples of children and young adults of different age on the autistic spectrum. As PPI is thought to mature with advancing age in childhood [44], PPI deficits might vary between children of different age groups, or may not be observable in children at all.

So far, only one study explicitly focused on adults with HFA [24]. The authors found significant PPI differences between subjects with HFA and the control group in only one condition (SOA 120 ms), while PPI in the HFA group was similar to or even higher than that of the control group in the other conditions (SOA 30 and 60 ms). In contrast, Perry et al. [25] found significantly reduced PPI in subjects with high-functioning autism in comparison to control subjects in the SOA 60 ms condition, but not in the SOA 30 and 120 ms conditions. However, these authors did not report the specific diagnoses of their participants. It must be emphasized that our cohort differs from the autism groups of previous studies in terms of age, sex, and IQ. These differences might have implications for our results. For example, our cohort has a higher mean IQ compared to previous studies, this might imply that our cohort is composed of pure HFA and not confounded by low intelligence or other cognitive dysfunctions.

Habituation

Even though individuals with HFA exhibited higher startle amplitudes than control subjects, habituation rates were similar in both groups. This finding is consistent with those of Ornitz et al. [27] and [24], who did not find any differences in habituation between subjects with ASD and control subjects. In contrast, Perry et al. [25] found that subjects with ASD show decelerated habituation, speculating that reduced habituation might lead to behavioral and cognitive deficits in autism. However, their sample comprised only male subjects with ASD, while the current study examined men and women with HFA. Then again, previous studies found reduced habituation to acoustic stimuli in children with autism [45] and at high risk for autism [46]. A cross-sectional questionnaire study found that less developmentally mature children with autism and other developmental disorders exhibited the highest rates of sensory processing difficulties [47]. Perhaps, habituation to sensory stimuli is associated with mental age, explaining normal habituation rates in normally intelligent adults with HFA.

Study limitations

Some factors might limit the degree to which the findings of the present study can be generalized. The determination of unimpaired hearing, potential psychiatric and neurological disorders as well as use of medication relied on self-report only. Therefore, information might be incomplete or unreliable. Seven HFA subjects reported an additional mental disorder. Studies consistently reported no alterations of PPI in depression and ADHD [48]. In bipolar disorder, PPI was found to be state dependent, while evidence regarding PPI deficits in anxiety disorders is still poor [48]. Although unlikely it can thus not completely be ruled out that comorbid disorders had an effect on sensorimotor gating. Drug intake of some participants in both groups might have influenced PPI, but here too an influence is more unlikely as animal and human studies showed that antidepressant drugs do not alter PPI [49]. However, evidence regarding the effects of other drugs, such as beta blockers, on PPI is still poor. In order to rule out such effects, subjects with comorbid psychiatric or neurological disorders and with drug intake should be excluded for less ambiguous results. Further, the mean PPI value of the healthy control group was relatively low compared to previous studies, which report PPI values between 40 to 80% in 90% of healthy adults [22]. Therefore there is a chance that comparison of control group and HFA group did not significantly differ due to relatively low PPI in controls.

Conclusions

While the results indicated no sensorimotor gating deficits, analysis of startle amplitudes revealed abnormalities in terms of exaggerated startle reaction in subjects with HFA. Individuals with HFA showed higher startle amplitudes than NC subjects, but exhibited similar rates of PPI and habituation of startle. These findings argue for functional pathophysiology on the level of the primary startle pathway, involving structures such as the caudal pontine reticular nucleus and ventrolateral tegmental nucleus in HFA. In contrast, the PPI circuit, including the pedunculopontine tegmental nucleus and inferior and superior colliculi, seems to be unimpaired.

Therefore, the extreme responses in individuals with autism to sensory stimulation that were already observed by Kanner in 1943 [1] are probably mainly due to a general hypersensitivity, but not difficulties in sensorimotor gating. Individuals with autism thus show unimpaired habituation of sensory stimuli and unimpaired transformation of these stimuli into motor action, while generally exhibiting more pronounced motor responses to sensory input in comparison to the healthy population.

The present study is the first to demonstrate normal PPI and habituation in a sample of adults with high-functioning autism. In consideration of previous studies, this finding suggests that sensorimotor gating deficits are not a distinctive feature of autism, but rather occur only in certain subgroups. For example, Yuhas et al. [28] found attenuated PPI in subjects with autism and Fragile-X-syndrome (FXS) in comparison to subjects with idiopathic autism and control subjects, indicating that FXS might be responsible for sensorimotor deficits in some individuals with autism. Therefore, future studies should focus on differential sample characteristics that might influence PPI, such as the occurrence of FXS. In order to minimize the possibility of type II errors, large sample sizes are needed. Future studies should particularly pay attention to careful sample selection and methodological aspects, as differences in methodology between the existing studies, such as reporting magnitude versus amplitude of the startle response, or different mean IQ or gender distributions, make a definite evaluation at this point in time impossible.

Moreover, it would be interesting to further explore the association between sensory processing and sensorimotor gating in autism. One possibility to explore sensory processing along with PPI is to measure gating of the auditory evoked potential by means of EEG [26]. Even though these authors did not find any significant differences between children and adolescents with and without autism, future research should examine possible associations between sensory gating and sensorimotor gating in higher-functioning adults.

Author Contributions

Conceived and designed the experiments: J. Kuhn SK CW. Performed the experiments: CW SK. Analyzed the data: TOJG CW SK J. Kuhn. Contributed reagents/materials/analysis tools: J. Kuhn J. Klosterkötter. Wrote the paper: SK CW TOJG KV J. Klosterkötter J. Kuhn. Diagnostics: KV.

References

1. Kanner L (1943) Autistic disturbances in affective contact. Nervous child 2: 217–250.
2. Kern JK, Trivedi MH, Garver CR, Grannemann BD, Andrews AA, et al. (2006) The pattern of sensory processing abnormalities in autism. Autism 10: 480–494.
3. Leekam SR, Neito C, Libby SJ, Wing L, Gould J (2001) Describing the sensory abnormalities of children and adults with autism. Journal of Autism Developmental Disorders 37: 894–910.
4. Tomchek SD, Dunn W (2007) Sensory processing in children with and without autism: a comparative study using the short sensory profile. Am J Occup Ther 61: 190–200.
5. Baron-Cohen S, Ashwin E, Ashwin C, Tavassoli T, Chakrabarti B (2009) Talent in autism: hyper-systemizing, hyper-attention to detail and sensory hypersensitivity. Philos Trans R Soc Lond B Biol Sci 364: 1377–1383.
6. Gomes E, Pedroso FS, Wagner MB (2008) Auditory hypersensitivity in the autistic spectrum disorder. Pro Fono 20: 279–284.
7. Hitoglou M, Ververi A, Antoniadis A, Zafeiriou DI (2010) Childhood autism and auditory system abnormalities. Pediatr Neurol 42: 309–314.
8. Frith U (1989) Autism: explaining the Enigma: Blackwell.
9. O'Connor K (2012) Auditory processing in autism spectrum disorder: a review. Neurosci Biobehav Rev 36: 836–854.
10. Ouimet T, Foster NE, Tryfon A, Hyde KL (2012) Auditory-musical processing in autism spectrum disorders: a review of behavioral and brain imaging studies. Ann N Y Acad Sci 1252: 325–331.
11. Alcantara JI, Weisblatt EJ, Moore BC, Bolton PF (2004) Speech-in-noise perception in high-functioning individuals with autism or Asperger's syndrome. J Child Psychol Psychiatry 45: 1107–1114.
12. DePape AM, Hall GB, Tillmann B, Trainor LJ (2012) Auditory processing in high-functioning adolescents with Autism Spectrum Disorder. PLoS One 7: e44084.
13. Groen WB, van Orsouw L, Huurne N, Swinkels S, van der Gaag RJ, et al. (2009) Intact spectral but abnormal temporal processing of auditory stimuli in autism. J Autism Dev Disord 39: 742–750.
14. Teder-Salejarvi WA, Pierce KL, Courchesne E, Hillyard SA (2005) Auditory spatial localization and attention deficits in autistic adults. Brain Res Cogn Brain Res 23: 221–234.
15. Lepisto T, Kuitunen A, Sussman E, Saalasti S, Jansson-Verkasalo E, et al. (2009) Auditory stream segregation in children with Asperger syndrome. Biol Psychol 82: 301–307.
16. Takarae Y, Luna B, Minshew NJ, Sweeney JA (2008) Patterns of visual sensory and sensorimotor abnormalities in autism vary in relation to history of early language delay. J Int Neuropsychol Soc 14: 980–989.
17. Fournier KA, Hass CJ, Naik SK, Lodha N, Cauraugh JH (2010) Motor coordination in autism spectrum disorders: a synthesis and meta-analysis. J Autism Dev Disord 40: 1227–1240.
18. Swerdlow NR, Braff DL, Geyer MA (2000) Animal models of deficient sensorimotor gating: what we know, what we think we know, and what we hope to know soon. Behav Pharmacol 11: 185–204.
19. Gowen E, Hamilton A (2013) Motor abilities in autism: a review using a computational context. J Autism Dev Disord 43: 323–344.
20. Miyahara M (2013) Meta review of systematic and meta analytic reviews on movement differences, effect of movement based interventions, and the underlying neural mechanisms in autism spectrum disorder. Front Integr Neurosci 7: 16.
21. Graham FK (1975) The More or Less Startling Effects of Weak Prestimulation. Psychophysiology 12: 238–248.
22. Filion DL, Dawson ME, Schell AM (1998) The psychological significance of human startle eyeblink modification: a review. Biol Psychol 47: 1–43.
23. Organization WH (1992) ICD-10 Classification of mental and behavioral disorders: Clinical descriptions and diagnostic guidelines. Geneva: World Helath Organization.
24. McAlonan GM, Daly E, Kumari V, Critchley HD, van Amelsvoort T, et al. (2002) Brain anatomy and sensorimotor gating in Asperger's syndrome. Brain 125: 1594–1606.
25. Perry W, Minassian A, Lopez B, Maron L, Lincoln A (2007) Sensorimotor gating deficits in adults with autism. Biol Psychiatry 61: 482–486.
26. Oranje B, Lahuis B, van Engeland H, Jan van der Gaag R, Kemner C (2013) Sensory and sensorimotor gating in children with multiple complex developmental disorders (MCDD) and autism. Psychiatry Res 206: 287–292.
27. Ornitz EM, Lane SJ, Sugiyama T, de Traversay J (1993) Startle modulation studies in autism. J Autism Dev Disord 23: 619–637.
28. Yuhas J, Cordeiro L, Tassone F, Ballinger E, Schneider A, et al. (2011) Brief report: Sensorimotor gating in idiopathic autism and autism associated with fragile X syndrome. J Autism Dev Disord 41: 248–253.
29. Baron-Cohen S, Hoekstra RA, Knickmeyer R, Wheelwright S (2006) The Autism-Spectrum Quotient (AQ)—adolescent version. J Autism Dev Disord 36: 343–350.
30. Baron-Cohen S, Wheelwright S (2004) The empathy quotient: an investigation of adults with Asperger syndrome or high functioning autism, and normal sex differences. J Autism Dev Disord 34: 163–175.
31. Baron-Cohen S, Richler J, Bisarya D, Gurunathan N, Wheelwright S (2003) The systemizing quotient: an investigation of adults with Asperger syndrome or high-functioning autism, and normal sex differences. Philos Trans R Soc Lond B Biol Sci 358: 361–374.

32. Hautzinger M, Bailer M, Worall H, Keller F (1995) Beck Depressions-Inventory (BDI). Bern: Huber.
33. Schmidt K-H, Metzler P (1992) Wortschatztest [Vocabulary test (WST)]. Weinheim: Beltz Test GmbH.
34. Lehrl S, Triebig G, Fischer B (1995) Multiple choice vocabulary test MWT as a valid and short test to estimate premorbid intelligence. Acta Neurol Scand 91: 335–345.
35. APA (2000) Diagnostic and Statistical Manual of Mental Disorders, foruth edition revised (DSM IV-TR). Washington, DC: American Psychiatric Association.
36. Beck AT, Ward C, Mendelson M (1961) Beck Depression Inventory (BDI). Archives of General Psychiatry 4: 561–571.
37. Baron-Cohen S, Wheelwright S, Skinner R, Martin J, Clubley E (2001) The autism-spectrum quotient (AQ): evidence from Asperger syndrome/high-functioning autism, males and females, scientists and mathematicians. J Autism Dev Disord 31: 5–17.
38. Blumenthal TD, Cuthbert BN, Filion DL, Hackley S, Lipp OV, et al. (2005) Committee report: Guidelines for human startle eyeblink electromyographic studies. Psychophysiology 42: 1–15.
39. Marco EJ, Hinkley LB, Hill SS, Nagarajan SS (2011) Sensory processing in autism: a review of neurophysiologic findings. Pediatr Res 69: 48R–54R.
40. Roberts TP, Khan SY, Rey M, Monroe JF, Cannon K, et al. (2010) MEG detection of delayed auditory evoked responses in autism spectrum disorders: towards an imaging biomarker for autism. Autism Res 3: 8–18.
41. Bruneau N, Roux S, Adrien JL, Barthelemy C (1999) Auditory associative cortex dysfunction in children with autism: evidence from late auditory evoked potentials (N1 wave-T complex). Clin Neurophysiol 110: 1927–1934.
42. Gage NM, Siegel B, Roberts TP (2003) Cortical auditory system maturational abnormalities in children with autism disorder: an MEG investigation. Brain Res Dev Brain Res 144: 201–209.
43. Matsuzaki J, Kagitani-Shimono K, Goto T, Sanefuji W, Yamamoto T, et al. (2012) Differential responses of primary auditory cortex in autistic spectrum disorder with auditory hypersensitivity. Neuroreport 23: 113–118.
44. Gebhardt J, Schulz-Juergensen S, Eggert P (2012) Maturation of prepulse inhibition (PPI) in childhood. Psychophysiology 49: 484–488.
45. Kemner C, Orange B, Verbaten MN, van Engeland H (2002) Normal P50 gating in children with autism. Journal of Clinical Psychiatry 63: 214–217.
46. Guiraud JA, Kushnerenko E, Tomalski P, Davies K, Ribeiro H, et al. (2011) Differential habituation to repeated sounds in infants at high risk for autism. Neuroreport 22: 845–849.
47. Baranek GT, David FJ, Poe MD, Stone WL, Watson LR (2006) Sensory Experiences Questionnaire: discriminating sensory features in young children with autism, developmental delays, and typical development. J Child Psychol Psychiatry 47: 591–601.
48. Kohl S, Heekeren K, Klosterkotter J, Kuhn J (2013) Prepulse inhibition in psychiatric disorders—apart from schizophrenia. J Psychiatr Res 47: 445–452.
49. Braff DL, Geyer MA, Swerdlow NR (2001) Human studies of prepulse inhibition of startle: normal subjects, patient groups, and pharmacological studies. Psychopharmacology (Berl) 156: 234–258.

Premarket Safety and Efficacy Studies for ADHD Medications in Children

Florence T. Bourgeois[1,2,3]*, Jeong Min Kim[4], Kenneth D. Mandl[1,2,3,5]

1 Division of Emergency Medicine, Boston Children's Hospital, Boston, Massachusetts, United States of America, **2** Department of Pediatrics, Harvard Medical School, Boston, Boston, Massachusetts, United States of America, **3** Children's Hospital Informatics Program at the Harvard-MIT Division of Health Sciences and Technology, Boston Children's Hospital, Boston, Massachusetts, United States of America, **4** Faculty of Arts and Sciences, Wellesley College, Wellesley, Massachusetts, United States of America, **5** Harvard Medical School Center for Biomedical Informatics, Boston, Massachusetts, United States of America

Abstract

Background: Attention-deficit hyperactivity disorder (ADHD) is a chronic condition and pharmacotherapy is the mainstay of treatment, with a variety of ADHD medications available to patients. However, it is unclear to what extent the long-term safety and efficacy of ADHD drugs have been evaluated prior to their market authorization. We aimed to quantify the number of participants studied and their length of exposure in ADHD drug trials prior to marketing.

Methods: We identified all ADHD medications approved by the Food and Drug Administration (FDA) and extracted data on clinical trials performed by the sponsor and used by the FDA to evaluate the drug's clinical efficacy and safety. For each ADHD medication, we measured the total number of participants studied and the length of participant exposure and identified any FDA requests for post-marketing trials.

Results: A total of 32 clinical trials were conducted for the approval of 20 ADHD drugs. The median number of participants studied per drug was 75 (IQR 0, 419). Eleven drugs (55%) were approved after <100 participants were studied and 14 (70%) after <300 participants. The median trial length prior to approval was 4 weeks (IQR 2, 9), with 5 (38%) drugs approved after participants were studied <4 weeks and 10 (77%) after <6 months. Six drugs were approved with requests for specific additional post-marketing trials, of which 2 were performed.

Conclusions: Clinical trials conducted for the approval of many ADHD drugs have not been designed to assess rare adverse events or long-term safety and efficacy. While post-marketing studies can fill in some of the gaps, better assurance is needed that the proper trials are conducted either before or after a new medication is approved.

Editor: Harriet de Wit, University of Chicago, United States of America

Funding: Drs. Bourgeois and Mandl were supported by a grant from the National Institute of Child Health and Human Development (1R21HD072382), National Institutes of Health. The funders had no role in study design, data collection and analysis, decision to publish, or preparation of the manuscript.

Competing Interests: The authors have declared that no competing interests exist.

* Email: florence.bourgeois@childrens.harvard.edu

Introduction

As many as 10% of children and adolescents in the United States carry a diagnosis of attention-deficit hyperactivity disorder (ADHD), making it one of the most common conditions of childhood. [1,2] The single most efficacious treatment for reducing symptoms of ADHD are medications and most children diagnosed with ADHD receive pharmacotherapy. [1,3,4] Clinicians and patients have a large therapeutic armamentarium to choose from, with over a dozen ADHD medications marketed in a wide array of formulations and delivery systems [5].

The short-term therapeutic response to ADHD medications is upwards of 70%, among the highest of psychiatric medications. [6,7] As a result, although ADHD typically requires long-term treatment, the short-term efficacy of ADHD drugs can be assessed after a brief treatment period, often on the order of days to weeks [6].

Since most trials focus on efficacy measures as primary endpoints, clinical trials testing ADHD medications may be relatively short, resulting in drugs with limited long-term safety or efficacy data. [8] Further, since studies are powered to measure efficacy endpoints, sample sizes may be inadequate to detect rare adverse events related to ADHD medications [7].

Guidelines for the safety and efficacy evaluation of drugs are provided by the International Conference on Harmonization of Technical Requirements for Registration of Pharmaceuticals for Human Use (ICH). [9] Though not binding, these requirements guide clinical trial practice by the United States Food and Drug Administration (FDA). [10] The ICH provides specific recommendations on the safety assessment of chronic drugs used in the treatment of non-life-threatening conditions, which includes ADHD. [11] The guideline states that since most adverse drug events first occur and are most frequent during the initial months of treatment, approximately 300 to 600 patients should be treated for at least 6 months prior to market availability. Some adverse events may increase in frequency or severity over time or may only occur after several months of treatment; therefore, at least 100 patients should be exposed to a drug for at least 12 months. And finally, the guidelines recommend that the total number of patients treated with a medicine prior to approval, including short-term exposure, should be about 1500.

To assess the extent to which rare adverse events and the long-term safety and efficacy of ADHD drugs have been evaluated prior to their market authorization, we sought to identify and evaluate all safety and efficacy trials submitted to the FDA for the approval of ADHD drugs and quantify the number of participants studied and their length of exposure prior to the market availability of each ADHD medicine. We hypothesized that the premarket study of many ADHD medications in children has been insufficient to adequately assess rare adverse events and long-term safety and efficacy.

Methods

Drugs Used in the Treatment of ADHD

We identified all drugs approved by the FDA for ADHD using information available on the FDA website as well as other online resources. [12,13] All products with a unique NDA number were selected. We recorded the drugs' FDA approval date for the indication of ADHD, the approved ages for treatment, the drug formulation, the pharmaceutical company sponsoring the application, and the current marketing status of the drug. When there was no FDA approval date for ADHD, we used the date of the first label on which ADHD was listed as an indication for the drug (N = 2).

Data Sources and Extraction

For each drug identified, we obtained the FDA Drug Approval Package, which includes the medical and statistical reviews, approval letters, drug labels, and any related administrative documents and correspondence. For newer agents, these documents are posted on the FDA website. [13] When the approval packages were not available, they were obtained from the FDA through a Freedom of Information Act request.

We reviewed the approval documents and identified the clinical trials performed by the sponsor and used by the FDA to evaluate the drug's clinical efficacy or safety in the review process. If the agent was not a New Molecular Entity (and thus prior trials and FDA review had been performed), we reviewed the clinical trials in the original FDA approval package in order to identify any pediatric patients who may have been studied in safety or efficacy assessments. Thus, for drugs representing new formulations or drugs repurposed for the indication of ADHD and for which the FDA approval process might be modified and possibly less stringent given the prior review, we analyzed all clinical trials that had been conducted for approval at any stage. Several drugs had FDA approvals that either recommended or required the conduct of additional, post-marketing clinical trials. When the approval packages did not include supplemental information on these trials, we searched the online trial registry ClinicalTrials.gov to determine whether additional trials had been performed. We also contacted the pharmaceutical companies who had sponsored the drug applications to inquire about clinical trials performed in response to the FDA requests.

For each medication we extracted the following information: number of clinical trials supporting the application, number of participants studied who received at least one dose of the study drug, participant age ranges, trial duration at dosage levels intended for clinical use (i.e. excluding open-label titration periods), and comparators (if any) employed. Trials were categorized as efficacy or safety trials, with safety trials defined as those explicitly labeled as safety by the sponsor.

The clinical trials related to the drug approvals were linked to publications in the medical literature with a search of PubMed. Trials and publications were matched on the drug name, trial design characteristics, number of participants, and trial duration [14].

Data Analysis

Descriptive statistics were used to report the total number of participants studied for less than 6 months, for at least 6 months, and for at least 12 months. Since many drugs used in the treatment of ADHD have been on the market for many years and the FDA approval process may have evolved over this period, we also calculated these values for the drugs approved in the last 10 years (since 2004).

Results

We identified 20 drugs approved by the FDA via a New Drug Application (NDA) for the treatment of ADHD in children (Table 1). These drugs represent 10 different active ingredients with the individual products differing based on the formulation and delivery systems. Most drugs were approved for children 6 years and older with two drugs approved for children as young as 3 years old. Only 3 of the drugs have been discontinued. Original drug approval packages were not available on the FDA website and therefore obtained via a Freedom of Information Act (FOIA) request for Ritalin, Ritalin SR, Desoxyn, Cylert, Dexedrine, Biphetamine, Adderall, and Adderall XR.

Characteristics of Clinical Trials

There were 32 clinical trials conducted by sponsors prior to the initial FDA approval of the ADHD drugs. Of these, 5 studies–representing 3 drugs–were safety studies. The minimum age of participants in all of the trials was 6 years. Six of the drugs were studied in efficacy trials that included an active comparator (5 included both an active comparator and placebo) while all others were approved based on comparison to placebo alone. Among the 10 most recently approved drugs, only 2 included comparison to one of the ADHD drugs already marketed. A total of 8 (25%) of the trials have been published in the medical literature.

Number of Participants and Length of Study

The median number of participants studied per drug was 75 (IQR 0, 419; range 0 to 660). Overall, 2756 (66%) participants were studied for less than 6 months, 746 (18%) for 6 to 11 months, and 688 (16%) for 12 or more months (Table 2).

Seven drugs were approved by the FDA for the treatment of ADHD without the submission of any clinical trial data by the sponsors. Of these, 5 were approved between 1943 and 1975, one (Adderall) in 1996 and another (Methylin) in 2003. Ritalin, the oldest drug approved for ADHD, was approved based on prior clinical experience, which was presented as a bibliography. Methylin was a new formulation of previously approved methylphenidate that underwent an NDA but without the submission of pediatric efficacy trials. [15] Desoxyn was originally approved in 1943 as an anorectic in the treatment of obesity but no clinical trials assessing its safety in children or its efficacy in the treatment of ADHD in children were identified in the original approval package. The indication for ADHD is first included on the drug label in 1965 without supporting clinical trials in the accompa-

Table 1. Medications approved by the FDA for the treatment of ADHD.

Active ingredient	Brand name[a]	FDA approval date[b]	Approved ages for use	Formulation and delivery system	Pharmaceutical company sponsoring application	Marketing status
Stimulants						
Methylphenidate hydrochloride	Ritalin	12/5/1955	6 years and older	Oral tablet	Novartis	Prescription
	Ritalin SR	3/30/1982	6 years and older	Oral extended-release tablet	Novartis	Prescription
	Concerta	8/1/2000	6 years and older	Oral extended-release tablet, OROS	Janssen Pharms	Prescription
	Metadate CD	4/3/2001	6 years and older	Oral extended-release capsule	UCB Inc.	Prescription
	Ritalin LA	6/5/2002	6 years and older	Oral extended-release capsule, SODAS	Novartis	Prescription
	Methylin	12/19/2002 4/15/2003	6 years and older	Oral solution Oral chewable tablet	Mallinckrodt	Prescription
	Daytrana	4/6/2006	6 years and older	Transdermal extended-release film	Noven Pharms	Prescription
	Quillivant XR	9/27/2012	6 to 17 years	Oral extended-release suspension	Nextwave Pharms	Prescription
Methamphetamine hydrochloride	Desoxyn	1965[c]	12 years and older	Oral tablet	Lundbeck	Prescription
Pemoline	Cylert	1/27/1975 1/30/1976	6 years and older	Oral tablet Oral chewable tablet	Abbott	Discontinued
Dextroamphetamine sulfate	Dexedrine	8/2/1976	3 years and older	Oral extended-release capsule	Amedra Pharms	Prescription
Amphetamine, dextroamphetamine mixed salts	Biphetamine	1979[c]	3 years and older	Oral extended-release capsule	UCB Inc.	Discontinued
	Adderall	02/13/1996	3 years and older	Oral tablet	Teva Womens	Discontinued
	Adderall XR	10/11/2001	6 years and older	Oral extended-release capsule	Shire	Prescription
Dexmethylphenidate hydrochloride	Focalin	11/13/2001	6 years and older	Oral Tablet	Novartis	Prescription
	Focalin XR	5/26/2005	6 years and older	Oral extended-release capsule, SODAS	Novartis	Prescription
Lisdexamfetamine dimesylate	Vyvanse	2/23/2007	6 to 12 years	Oral capsule	Shire	Prescription
Non-stimulants						
Atomoxetine hydrochloride	Strattera	11/26/2002	6 years and older	Oral capsule	Eli Lilly	Prescription
Guanfacine hydrochloride	Intuniv	9/2/2009	6 years and older	Oral extended-release tablet	Shire	Prescription
Clonidine hydrochloride	Kapvay	9/28/2010	6 years and older	Oral extended-release tablet	Shionogi Inc.	Prescription

[a]All drugs approved by the FDA under a New Drug Application (NDA).
[b]Approval date for treatment of ADHD.
[c]Date derived from first product labeling to include ADHD as an indication as the FDA approval package for biphetamine and desoxyn do not include ADHD as one of the drug indications.

nying documentation. The approval package for Cylert includes information on pre-clinical trials without mention of clinical trials conducted for any indication. Dexedrine was approved for the treatment of narcolepsy, obesity, and ADHD, but the approval package does not include trials enrolling children or studying efficacy for ADHD. Similarly, Biphetamine was previously approved as an anorectic in adults, but the original approval package does not include safety assessments in children and ADHD was added as an indication in product labels starting in 1979 without supporting clinical trials. Adderall was originally approved in 1960 as an anorectic under the trade name Obetrol before being marketed without FDA approval as Adderall for the treatment of ADHD. Approval was subsequently obtained without clinical trials assessing its safety in children or efficacy in ADHD [16].

Among the 13 drugs with clinical trials studying ADHD, a total of 4 drugs (31%) were approved after less than 100 participants had been studied while 7 drugs (54%) were approved after study in

Table 2. Clinical trials conducted for the FDA approval of ADHD drugs in children.

Brand name	Number and type of clinical trials	Participant age ranges	Number of participants studied and treated	Duration of trial and follow up	Comparator(s)	Trials published
Desoxyn	0					
Ritalin	0					
Ritalin SR	3 efficacy	unknown	48[a]	2 weeks	Ritalin	0
Concerta	3 efficacy	6 to 12 years	64	1 week	Placebo/Ritalin	0
			70	1 week		1[30]
			94	4 weeks		1[42]
	1 safety	6 to 13 years	432[b]	6 months	None	1[43]
Metadate CD	1 efficacy	6 years and older	158	3 weeks	Placebo	0
Ritalin LA	2 efficacy	6 to 12 years	34	2 weeks	Placebo	0
			63			
Methylin	0[c]					
Daytrana	2 efficacy	6 to 12 years	79	1 week	Placebo	0
			96	2 weeks	Placebo/Concerta	1[44]
	2 safety		127[b]	6 months	None	0
			327[b]	1 year		
Quillivant XR	1 efficacy	6 to 12 years	45	2 weeks	Placebo	0
Cylert	0[d]					
Dexedrine	0[e]					
Biphetamine	0[e]					
Adderall	0[f]					
Adderall XR	2 efficacy	6 to 12 years	360	3 weeks	Placebo	0
			51	1 week	Placebo/Adderall	
Focalin	2 efficacy	6 to 17 years	43	4 weeks	Placebo/Methylphenidate	0
			35	20 weeks	Placebo	
	2 safety		187[b]	6 months	None	0
			361[b]	1 year		
Focalin XR	1 efficacy	6 to 17 years	53	7 weeks	Placebo	0
Vyvanse	2 efficacy	6 to 12 years	50	1 week	Placebo/Adderall	1[45]
			213	4 weeks	Placebo	1[46]
Strattera	4 efficacy	6 years and older	213	8 weeks	Placebo	0
			85	6 weeks		
			65	9 weeks		
			64	9 weeks		
Intuniv	2 efficacy	6 to 17 years	259	8 weeks	Placebo	1[47]
			258	9 weeks		0
Kapvay	2 efficacy	6 to 17 years	154	8 weeks	Placebo	1[48]
			102			0

[a]Assumed equal distribution of randomized participants between the two study arms.
[b]Not all unique patients as some participants from efficacy trial subsequently enrolled in safety trial.
[c]Methylin was a new formulation of FDA-approved methylphenidate.
[d]FDA approval package includes information on pre-clinical trials only and there is no mention of the conduct of clinical trials.
[e]The FDA approval package included clinical trials of Dexedrine and Biphetamine for the treatment of obesity in adults, but no clinical trials assessing their use for the treatment of ADHD were identified.
[f]Adderall was originally approved in 1960 as an anorectic under the brand name Obetrol, but no clinical trials assessing their use for the treatment of ADHD were identified.

less than 300 participants. Efficacy trials ranged from 1 to 10 weeks and safety trials from 6 to 12 months in length. The median trial length prior to approval was 4 weeks (IQR 2, 9; range 1 to 52 weeks), with 5 (38%) drugs approved after participants were studied for less than 4 weeks, 7 (54%) after less than 8 weeks, and 10 (77%) after less than 6 months.

Focusing on the 6 drugs approved since 2004, the median number of participants studied per drug was 259 (IQR 53, 517; range 45 to 629) and there were 1309 (74%), 127 (7%), and 327

(18%), participants studied for less than 6 months, 6 to 11 months, and 12 or more months of study, respectively. The median trial length prior to approval was 8 weeks (IQR 2, 20; range 1 to 52 weeks).

Based on the ICH guidelines for safety assessments of chronic medications, none of the drugs met the recommendation for 1500 participants studied prior to drug approval (Table 3). Three of the drugs, Daytrana, Focalin, and Concerta (15% of all ADHD drugs), met requirements to have at least 300 participants total exposed to the drug for 6 months prior to marketing. Daytrana and Focalin (10% of all ADHD drugs) were also compliant with the recommendation to study at least 100 participants for 12 months.

Clinical Trials Requested by the FDA

FDA approval of 4 of the drugs included required submission of additional clinical trials by the sponsor and 2 drug approvals included recommendations for additional trials (Table 4). The basis for the required studies cited by the FDA included concerns over limited long-term safety data, limited study in the adolescent population, and insufficient information on specific potential adverse events [17–19].

The sponsors for Daytrana and Kapvay conducted the required studies, adhering to the timelines imposed by the FDA for study completion. None of the studies required for Vyvanse or Intuniv or any of the studies recommended for Ritalin or Focalin XR could be identified. The corresponding pharmaceutical companies in each of these cases were contacted and were also not able to provide us with information that these trials had been conducted.

Discussion

This is the first systematic assessment of patient exposure to ADHD medications prior to their approval and market availability. A total of 17 medications are currently available in the U.S. for the treatment of ADHD in children, 6 of which have been approved by the FDA in the last 10 years. These drugs are intended for chronic use in children, but the median trial length prior to approval is 4 weeks and only 3 of the drugs have been assessed in long-term safety trials. The number of exposed children prior to approval is also small, with 14 drugs approved after study in less than 300 participants. Concerta, Daytrana, and Focalin (15% of all ADHD drugs) are the only drugs that meet the ICH recommendations of at least 300 patients studied for 6 months prior to market availability.

Concerns over the lack of safety data–including adverse events and long-term safety issues–for ADHD drugs have been voiced by a number of entities, including the FDA, the NIH, and the European Committee for Medicinal Products for Human Use. [17,20,21] Known adverse effects vary for the different drugs and include growth retardation, decreased appetite, insomnia, and cardiovascular effects. [6,22–24] Post-marketing reports of adverse events prompted the FDA in 2007 to require manufacturers of drugs approved for the treatment of ADHD to develop Medication Guides with detailed information for clinicians and parents on possible adverse effects and precautions that can be taken to avoid them. [25,26] Package inserts of all stimulant drugs for the treatment of ADHD have also been amended to include warning language around specific risks. [7].

Because ADHD is a chronic condition, the long-term efficacy of ADHD drugs also warrants further consideration. [8,20] Long-term follow up studies of children treated with ADHD medications have not been designed to adequately assess the long-term benefits of medication therapy compared to behavioral interventions. [27], [28] One prospective 8-year follow-up study of children with ADHD who had been treated for at least 14 months with medication indicated there may be no advantage in academic performance or social functioning in children who received medication compared to those managed with behavioral interventions. [28] Additional long-term studies are needed assessing the impact of ADHD treatments into adolescence and of outcome measures beyond ADHD symptoms that capture effects on long-term functioning.

In order for drugs to become available in a timely fashion, large long-term randomized controlled trials may not always be feasible. Instead, post-marketing observational trials can provide additional information on rare adverse events and better delineate a drug's long-term safety and efficacy. [29] In the European Union, pharmaceutical companies seeking market authorization for a drug must submit a Risk Management Plan with detailed proposals for post-authorization pharmacovigilence activities and efficacy studies. [30,31] These management plans are considered continuous, evolving processes and can be modified at the request of regulatory agencies as new information–including safety concerns–become available [32,33].

In the U.S., the FDA historically relied on studies referred to as "post-marketing commitments" to obtain additional safety and efficacy data after a drug was approved. [34] These commitments were agreed upon by the FDA and the pharmaceutical companies at the time of approval and were often mandated as a condition for approval. However, the FDA lacked any avenues for enforcement, and reports showed that as many as two-thirds of requested studies were never started by the pharmaceutical companies. [35,36] The FDA Amendments Act of 2007 granted the FDA additional authority to require post-marketing studies–now referred to as "post-marketing requirements"–and also expanded the conditions under which the FDA could make the requests. [37] The FDA may now take enforcement action to ensure studies are conducted and recent reports have shown substantial improvement in compliance with study requests [38].

While we found poor compliance with post-marketing study requests for ADHD drugs, moving forward, these studies may represent an important tool for the detection of rare adverse events

Table 3. Compliance of pre-approval ADHD clinical drug trials with ICH guidelines overall and during past 10 years.

Time period	300 participants exposed for at least 6 months, N (%)	100 participants exposed for at least 12 months, N (%)	1500 participants exposed in total
Drugs approved pre-2004 (N = 14)	2 (14)	1 (7)	0
Drugs approved 2004 to 2013 (N = 6)	1 (17)	1 (17)	0
All drugs (N = 20)	3 (15)	2 (10)	0

Table 4. Clinical trials recommended or required by the FDA at the time of drug approval[a].

Brand name	Recommended or required	Details of recommended or required trials	Clinical trials conducted	Participant age range	Number of participants studied and treated	Duration of trial and follow-up	Trial publications
Ritalin	Recommended	Safety studies of Ritalin when administered to children for periods of 3, 6, 12, and 24 months, with specific reference to blood counts, including platelets, to possible causes of abdominal pain, cardiovascular function, and to growth	0				
Daytrana	Required	Safety study to investigate and characterize contact sensitization associated with the use of methylphenidate transdermal system, to be completed by April 2008	Double-blind, multi-center, parallel-group, dose optimization safety and efficacy trial completed in 2008	13 to 17 years	217	7 weeks	1[44]
		Study of Daytrana in the treatment of children 13–17 years old with ADHD, to be completed by April 2009	Open-label, extension safety study completed in 2009		162	6 months	1[49]
Focalin XR	Recommended	Safety and efficacy study in adolescents of at least 1 year duration	0[b]				
Vyvanse	Required	Clinical study in adolescents with ADHD, to be completed by February 2010	0[c]				
Intuniv	Required	Long-term maintenance study of efficacy and safety of guanfacine as monotherapy in children and adolescents to be completed by September 2012	0				
		Efficacy and safety study of guanfacine in adolescents to be completed by September 2012	0				
		Efficacy and safety study of guanfacine as adjunctive treatment with long-acting oral psychostimulants to be completed by June 2010	0				
Kapvay	Required	Longer-term randomized withdrawal maintenance study of efficacy and safety of clonidine hydrochloride extended-release tablets as monotherapy or, alternatively, as adjunctive therapy, in children and adolescents, to be completed by December 2013	Parallel-group, placebo-controlled, withdrawal efficacy study completed in 2012	6 to 17 years	68[d]	26 weeks	0

[a]All information on the trials obtained from ClinicalTrials.gov.
[b]Five trials were conducted by Novartis after the approval of Focalin XR, but all were <1 year in length (longest trial 5 weeks) and none focused on adolescents.
[c]Three phase 4 trials have been registered in ClinicalTrials.gov by Shire since the FDA approval of Vyvanse, including two trials focusing on adolescents. None are listed as completed (NCT01552915, NCT01552902, NCT01328756).
[d]Assuming 135 participants were equally distributed between active and placebo arms.

and the long-term safety and efficacy of medications. However, observational studies are not equivalent to randomized controlled trials powered to detect adverse events or specific efficacy endpoints, nor can they approximate the rigor of randomized trials in accounting for treatment selection bias and other design issues. [39] Instead, post-marketing observational studies should complement pre-approval clinical trials, designed to include sufficient patient exposure to reasonably assess specific long-term safety and efficacy measures. As such, it is critical that we re-evaluate current standards in pre-approval trials and the exposure of patients to a new drug prior to its approval [40].

Three-arm trials, including the experimental drug, an active reference treatment, and a placebo comparator, are recommended by the ICH and by the European Medicines Agency specifically for the clinical investigation of ADHD drugs. [20,41] Three-arm trials serve two main purposes. First, the placebo comparator provides internal trial validation and demonstrates superiority of both drugs to the placebo control. Secondly, comparison of the new drug to an acknowledged standard yields comparative data on the safety and efficacy profiles of new drugs to other agents already available. We identified only 6 ADHD drugs that had been studied in comparison to another drug, indicating that ADHD drugs are introduced to the market with very little comparative data to guide clinicians on the new drug's effectiveness in the context of all available options.

One of the limitations of this study is that, in some instances, the records from the FDA may have been incomplete. For each of the drugs, however, we were able to obtain the original approval packages. Given that many of these agents have been on the market for decades, there may be additional safety and efficacy information that has emerged in studies conducted after the original FDA approval. Nonetheless, our findings reflect the studies required in the FDA approval process, including the trials for a number of recently approved medications. Finally, our study was limited to ADHD drugs and additional study is needed to determine whether the FDA approval process is similar for other drug classes used in pediatric patients.

In conclusion, clinical trials conducted for the approval of many ADHD drugs have not been designed to assess rare adverse events or long-term safety and efficacy. Despite the large number of available drugs, comparative effectiveness trials are rare. While post-marketing studies can fill in some of the gaps, FDA enforcement is important to ensure that post-market surveillance studies are completed. An ambitious agenda to assess long-term outcomes in the millions of patients on these medications is warranted.

Author Contributions

Conceived and designed the experiments: FB KM. Analyzed the data: FB JK KM. Contributed to the writing of the manuscript: FB JK KM.

References

1. Visser SN, Danielson ML, Bitsko RH, Holbrook JR, Kogan MD, et al. (2014) Trends in the parent-report of health care provider-diagnosed and medicated attention-deficit/hyperactivity disorder: United States, 2003–2011. J Am Acad Child Adolesc Psychiatry 53: 34–46 e32.
2. Voort JLV, He J-P, Jameson ND, Merikangas KR (2014) Impact of the DSM-5 Attention-Deficit/Hyperactivity Disorder (ADHD) Age of Onset Criterion in the U.S. Adolescent Population. Journal of the AMerican Academy of Child & Adolescent Psychiatry In Press.
3. Visser SN, Lesesne CA, Perou R (2007) National estimates and factors associated with medication treatment for childhood attention-deficit/hyperactivity disorder. Pediatrics 119 Suppl 1: S99–106.
4. (1999) A 14-month randomized clinical trial of treatment strategies for attention-deficit/hyperactivity disorder. The MTA Cooperative Group. Multimodal Treatment Study of Children with ADHD. Arch Gen Psychiatry 56: 1073–1086.
5. Manos MJ, Tom-Revzon C, Bukstein OG, Crismon ML (2007) Changes and challenges: managing ADHD in a fast-paced world. J Manag Care Pharm 13: S2–S13; quiz S14–S16.
6. May DE, Kratochvil CJ (2010) Attention-deficit hyperactivity disorder: recent advances in paediatric pharmacotherapy. Drugs 70: 15–40.
7. Wigal SB (2009) Efficacy and safety limitations of attention-deficit hyperactivity disorder pharmacotherapy in children and adults. CNS Drugs 23 Suppl 1: 21–31.
8. Huang YS, Tsai MH (2011) Long-term outcomes with medications for attention-deficit hyperactivity disorder: current status of knowledge. CNS Drugs 25: 539–554.
9. International Conference on Harmonisation of Technical Requirements for Registration of Pharmaceuticals for Human Use. ICH Guidelines. Available: http://www.ich.org/products/guidelines. Accessed 2013 Oct 8.
10. U.S. Department of Health and Human Services. FDA Regulatory Information. Available: http://www.fda.gov/RegulatoryInformation/Guidances/ucm122049.htm. Accessed 2013 Oct 8.
11. International Conference on Harmonisation of Technical Requirements for Registration of Pharmaceuticals for Human Use (1994) ICH Harmonised Tripartite Guideline: The extent of population exposure to assess clincial safety for drugs intended for long-term treatment of non-life-threatening conditions–E1. Available: http://www.ich.org/fileadmin/Public_Web_Site/ICH_Products/Guidelines/Efficacy/E1/Step4/E1_Guideline.pdf. Accessed 2013 Oct 8.
12. National Institutes of Health (National Institute of Mental Health). Available: http://www.nimh.nih.gov. Accessed 2013 Oct 8.
13. U.S. Department of Health and Human Services Drugs@FDA. Available: http://www.accessdata.fda.gov.Accessed O2013 Oct 8.
14. Bourgeois FT, Murthy S, Mandl KD (2010) Outcome reporting among drug trials registered in ClinicalTrials.gov. Ann Intern Med 153: 158–166.
15. U.S. Food and Drug Administration: Center for drug evaluation and research (2002) Drug Approval Package: Methylin. Available: http://www.accessdata.fda.gov/drugsatfda_docs/nda/2002/21-419_Methylin.cfm. Accessed 2013 Dec 1.
16. U.S. Food and Drug Administration: Center for drug evaluation and research (1996) Approval letter: Adderall. Available: http://www.accessdata.fda.gov/drugsatfda_docs/nda/96/11522S010_Adderall.pdf. Accessed 2013 Dec 1.
17. U.S. Food and Drug Administration: Center for drug evaluation and research (2004) Medical Reveiw: Focalin XR. Available: http://www.accessdata.fda.gov/drugsatfda_docs/nda/2005/021802s000_MedR.pdf. Accessed 2013 Oct 8.
18. U.S. Food and Drug Administration: Center for drug evaluation and research (2007) Medical Review: Vyvanse. Available: http://www.accessdata.fda.gov/drugsatfda_docs/nda/2007/021977s000_MedR.pdf. Accessed 2013 Oct 8.
19. U.S. Food and Drug Administration: Center for drug evaluation and research (2010) Supplement Approval: Kapvay. Available: http://www.accessdata.fda.gov/drugsatfda_docs/appletter/2010/022331s001, s002ltr.pdf. Accessed 2013 Oct 8.
20. European Medicines Agency: Committee for Medicinal Products for Human use (2008) Guideline on the clinical investigation of medicinal products for the treatment of attention deficit hyperactivity disorder (ADHD). Available: http://www.ema.europa.eu/docs/en_GB/document_library/Scientific_guideline/2010/08/WC500095686.pdf. Accessed 2013 Oct 8.
21. NIH Consensus Development Program (1998) Diagnosis and treatment of attention deficit hyperactivity disorder. National Institutes of Health Consensus Development Conference Statement.
22. Dopheide JA, Pliszka SR (2009) Attention-deficit-hyperactivity disorder: an update. Pharmacotherapy 29: 656–679.
23. Swanson JM, Elliott GR, Greenhill LL, Wigal T, Arnold LE, et al. (2007) Effects of stimulant medication on growth rates across 3 years in the MTA follow-up. J Am Acad Child Adolesc Psychiatry 46: 1015–1027.
24. Warikoo N, Faraone SV (2013) Background, clinical features and treatment of attention deficit hyperactivity disorder in children. Expert Opin Pharmacother.
25. U.S. Food and Drug Administration. FDA Asks Attention-Deficit Hyperactivity Disorder (ADHD) Drug Manufacturers to Develop Patient Medication Guides. Available: http://www.fda.gov/drugs/drugsafety/postmarketdrugsafetyinformationforpatientsandproviders/ucm107918.htm. Accessed 2013 Oct 8.
26. U.S. Food and Drug Administration (2007) FDA Directs ADHD Drug Manufacturers to Notify Patients about Cardiovascular Adverse Events and Psychiatric Adverse Events. FDA News. Available: http://www.fda.gov/NewsEvents/Newsroom/PressAnnouncements/2007/ucm108849.htm. Accessed 2013 Oct 8.
27. Jensen PS, Arnold LE, Swanson JM, Vitiello B, Abikoff HB, et al. (2007) 3-year follow-up of the NIMH MTA study. J Am Acad Child Adolesc Psychiatry 46: 989–1002.
28. Molina BS, Hinshaw SP, Swanson JM, Arnold LE, Vitiello B, et al. (2009) The MTA at 8 years: prospective follow-up of children treated for combined-type ADHD in a multisite study. J Am Acad Child Adolesc Psychiatry 48: 484–500.

29. Golder S, Loke YK, Bland M (2011) Meta-analyses of adverse effects data derived from randomised controlled trials as compared to observational studies: methodological overview. PLoS Med 8: e1001026.
30. Pelham WE, Gnagy EM, Burrows-Maclean L, Williams A, Fabiano GA, et al. (2001) Once-a-day Concerta methylphenidate versus three-times-daily methylphenidate in laboratory and natural settings. Pediatrics 107: E105.
31. European Medicines Agency (2012) Guideline on good pharmacovigilance practices (GVP): Module V- Risk management systems. Available: http://www.ema.europa.eu/docs/en_GB/document_library/Scientific_guideline/2012/06/WC500129134.pdf. Accessed 2013 Oct 8.
32. International Conference on Harmonisation of Technical Requirements for Registration of Pharmaceuticals for Human Use (2004) Pharmacovigilence planning–E2E. Available: http://www.ich.org/fileadmin/Public_Web_Site/ICH_Products/Guidelines/Efficacy/E2E/Step4/E2E_Guideline.pdf. Accessed 2013 Oct 8.
33. Raine J, Wise L, Blackburn S, Eichler HG, Breckenridge A (2011) European perspective on risk management and drug safety. Clin Pharmacol Ther 89: 650–654.
34. U.S. Food and Drug Administration (2011) Guidance for Industry: Postmarketing studies and Clincial Trials–Implementation of section 505(o)(3) of the Federal Food, Drug, and Cosmetic Act. Available: http://www.fda.gov/downloads/Drugs/GuidanceComplianceRegulatoryInformation/Guidances/UCM172001.pdf. Accessed 2013 Oct 8.
35. Avorn J (2006) Evaluating drug effects in the post-Vioxx world: there must be a better way. Circulation 113: 2173–2176.
36. Avorn J (2007) Paying for drug approvals–who's using whom? N Engl J Med 356: 1697–1700.
37. U.S. Food and Drug Administration Amendments Act of 2007 (2007) Public Law No.105–185.
38. U.S. Food and Drug Administration (2012) Report on the Performance of Drug and Biologics Firms in Conducting Postmarketing Requirements and Commitments. Federal Register 77: 13339–13343.
39. Thomas L, Peterson ED (2012) The value of statistical analysis plans in observational research: defining high-quality research from the start. JAMA 308: 773–774.
40. Duijnhoven RG, Straus SM, Raine JM, de Boer A, Hoes AW, et al. (2013) Number of patients studied prior to approval of new medicines: a database analysis. PLoS Med 10: e1001407.
41. International Conference on Harmonisation of Technical Requirements for Registration of Pharmaceuticals for Human Use (2001) ICH Topic E10: Choice of control group in clinical trials. Available: http://www.ema.europa.eu/docs/en_GB/document_library/Scientific_guideline/2009/09/WC500002925.pdf. Accessed 2013 Oct 8.
42. Wolraich ML, Greenhill LL, Pelham W, Swanson J, Wilens T, et al. (2001) Randomized, controlled trial of oros methylphenidate once a day in children with attention-deficit/hyperactivity disorder. Pediatrics 108: 883–892.
43. Wilens T, McBurnett K, Stein M, Lerner M, Spencer T, et al. (2005) ADHD treatment with once-daily OROS methylphenidate: final results from a long-term open-label study. J Am Acad Child Adolesc Psychiatry 44: 1015–1023.
44. Findling RL, Turnbow J, Burnside J, Melmed R, Civil R, et al. (2010) A randomized, double-blind, multicenter, parallel-group, placebo-controlled, dose-optimization study of the methylphenidate transdermal system for the treatment of ADHD in adolescents. CNS Spectr 15: 419–430.
45. Biederman J, Boellner SW, Childress A, Lopez FA, Krishnan S, et al. (2007) Lisdexamfetamine dimesylate and mixed amphetamine salts extended-release in children with ADHD: a double-blind, placebo-controlled, crossover analog classroom study. Biol Psychiatry 62: 970–976.
46. Jain R, Babcock T, Burtea T, Dirks B, Adeyi B, et al. (2011) Efficacy of lisdexamfetamine dimesylate in children with attention-deficit/hyperactivity disorder previously treated with methylphenidate: a post hoc analysis. Child Adolesc Psychiatry Ment Health 5: 35.
47. Biederman J, Melmed RD, Patel A, McBurnett K, Konow J, et al. (2008) A randomized, double-blind, placebo-controlled study of guanfacine extended release in children and adolescents with attention-deficit/hyperactivity disorder. Pediatrics 121: e73–84.
48. Jain R, Segal S, Kollins SH, Khayrallah M (2011) Clonidine extended-release tablets for pediatric patients with attention-deficit/hyperactivity disorder. J Am Acad Child Adolesc Psychiatry 50: 171–179.
49. Findling RL, Katic A, Rubin R, Moon E, Civil R, et al. (2010) A 6-month, open-label, extension study of the tolerability and effectiveness of the methylphenidate transdermal system in adolescents diagnosed with attention-deficit/hyperactivity disorder. J Child Adolesc Psychopharmacol 20: 365–375.

6

Feedback-Related Negativity in Children with Two Subtypes of Attention Deficit Hyperactivity Disorder

Jingbo Gong[1,2], Jiajin Yuan[3], Suhong Wang[1,4], Lijuan Shi[1], Xilong Cui[1], Xuerong Luo[1]*

1 Mental Health Institute of The Second Xiangya Hospital, National Technology Institute of Psychiatry, Key Laboratory of Psychiatry and Mental Health of Hunan Province, Central South University, Changsha, Hunan, China, **2** Traditional Chinese Medicine University of Hunan, Changsha, Hunan, PR China, **3** School of Psychology, Southwest University, Chongqing, China, **4** Department of Neuroscience, the Third Affiliated Hospital of Soochow University, Changzhou, China

Abstract

Objective: The current model of ADHD suggests abnormal reward and punishment sensitivity, although differences in ADHD subgroups are unclear. This study aimed to investigate the effect of feedback valence (reward or punishment) and punishment magnitude (small or large) on Feedback-Related Negativity (FRN) and Late Positive Potential (LPP) in two subtypes of ADHD (ADHD-C and ADHD-I) compared to typically developing children (TD) during a children's gambling task.

Methods: Children with ADHD-C (n = 16), children with ADHD-I (n = 15) and typically developing children (n = 15) performed a children's gambling task under three feedback conditions: large losses, small losses and gains. FRN and LPP components in brain potentials were recorded and analyzed.

Results: In TD children and children with ADHD-C, large loss feedback evoked more negative FRN amplitudes than small loss feedback, suggesting that brain sensitivity to the punishment and its magnitude is not impaired in children with ADHD-C. In contrast to these two groups, the FRN effect was absent in children with ADHD-I. The LPP amplitudes were larger in children with ADHD-C in comparison with those with ADHD-I, regardless of feedback valence and magnitude.

Conclusion: Children with ADHD-C exhibit intact brain sensitivity to punishment similar to TD children. In contrast, children with ADHD-I are significantly impaired in neural sensitivity to the feedback stimuli and in particular, to punishment, compared to TD and ADHD-C children. Thus, FRN, rather than LPP, is a reliable index of the difference in reward and punishment sensitivity across different ADHD-subcategories.

Editor: Karen Lidzba, University Children's Hospital Tuebingen, Germany

Funding: This work was supported by grants from the Hunan Provincial Natural Science Foundation of China (No. 12JJ5066), the National Natural Science of Foundation of China (NSFC, No. 81101018; 31371042), and Changzhou Science and Technology Application Project (Nos. CJ20112009, CJ20130026). The funders had no role in study design, data collection and analysis, decision to publish, or preparation of the manuscript.

Competing Interests: The authors have declared that no competing interests exist.

* E-mail: luoxr@vip.sina.com

Introduction

Attention deficit hyperactivity disorder (ADHD), which is the most prevalent childhood neuropsychiatric disorder, is defined in the current Diagnostic and Statistical Manual of Mental Disorders (DSM-IV-TR) as developmentally inappropriate and impairing symptoms of inattention and/or hyperactivity-impulsivity [1]. ADHD affects 5.29% of school-age children worldwide [2], 7.8% in the USA [3] and 7.5% in Taiwan [4]. According to the DSM-IV, ADHD has three subtypes: predominantly inattentive type (ADHD-I), which accounts for 45% of all ADHD patients; predominantly hyperactive-impulsive (ADHD-H), which affects 21% of all patients; and combined-type (ADHD-C), which occurs in 34% of all patients [1,5].

Recent studies imply that ADHD is associated with an aberrant sensitivity to reinforcement [6–11], such as reward and punishment. Since reinforcement is highly associated with motivation, evidence suggests that an unusually low level of effort or intrinsic motivation accounts for the performance deficits in children with ADHD [12–15]. Behavioral studies have demonstrated that children with ADHD show an abnormal sensitivity to motivational cues. They have problems in maintaining optimal performance when they have to rely solely on their intrinsic motivation, i.e. without external motivators such as feedback or reward [16,17]. Furthermore, children with ADHD show an attention span that is very limited without supervision or when tasks are extremely boring [15], but benefit to a greater extent from reinforcement contingencies implemented in a task [18]. Motivational models of ADHD formulated several different predictions about reinforcement sensitivity (1) a preference for small immediate reward over larger delayed reward [19–21]; (2) reduced neurobiological sensitivity to reward [19,22] and reduced reward anticipation [20,21], and (3) reduced behavioral sensitivity to cues of aversive stimuli in general [23,24]. In addition, from a clinical perspective, reinforcement contingencies are found to normalize behaviors that characterize ADHD [25–27]. However, other studies have predicted that individuals with ADHD have increased sensitivity to punishment [28,29]. Recently, several event-related potential studies investigated how reward and punishment influences the monitoring of performance feedback in children with ADHD. van

Meel et al. [30] reported that the FRN amplitude to losses was more pronounced in the ADHD group, suggesting an enhanced sensitivity to unfavorable outcomes in children with ADHD. However, in another study by van Meel et al. [31], the FRN effect was found to be entirely absent in children with ADHD. The lack of modulation of the FRN by contingencies in ADHD suggests deficient detection of environmental cues as a function of their motivational significance. Interestingly, the finding is consistent with the report by Groen et al. [32] that the Methylphenidate-free (Mph-free) children with ADHD did not show an FRN effect in the loss condition. This may be indicative of either difficulties in computing reward prediction errors or more positive expectancies of their outcomes in the face of losses. These discrepancies arise, at least in part, from the fact that these studies did not classify ADHD children into different subtypes. However, this classification is important, because there are evidences that different subtypes of ADHD are associated with different reward or punishment processing [33,34]. To our knowledge, there are no reports describing differences among ADHD subgroups in the monitoring of performance feedback coupled with reward and punishment.

Emotional-motivational dysfunctions are likely to contribute to ADHD, especially to hyperactive and impulsive symptoms. Regarding subgroup differences, ADHD-C and ADHD-HI in particular should show emotional-motivational dysfunction, while ADHD-I is less likely to show differences. A reduced responsiveness of the reward system was found to be associated with hyperactive-impulsive symptoms but not with inattentiveness [33]. In ADHD-C, symptoms of inattentiveness may be a compensatory factor for blunted response to unpleasant stimuli, as these individuals are associated with internalizing behavior [35] marked by high reactivity to unpleasant stimuli. ADHD-C and ADHD-I differ in a variety of ways that could contribute to different patterns of motivational style. Children with ADHD-C are more likely to show comorbid externalizing and impulsive behavior. Moreover, the nature of the cognitive-attentional deficit appears to differ between subtypes, with the ADHD-C group characterized as distractible, sloppy and disorganized and the ADHD-I group characterized as drowsy, sluggish and less alert [36,37]. Carlson et al. [38] observed some motivational style differences between ADHD subtypes, with the ADHD-C group more motivated by competitiveness and a desire to be perceived as superior to others and the ADHD-I group less uncooperative and possibly more passive in their learning styles. In addition, a recent study [34] showed that healthy subjects exhibited startle response attenuation and potentiation by pleasant and unpleasant pictures, respectively. In ADHD with impulsive and hyperactive symptoms, the startle responses was not attenuated by pleasant and not potentiated by unpleasant stimuli. The startling response in ADHD-I was attenuated to a lesser degree by pleasant stimuli compared to the control group. These findings suggest that blunted emotional reactivity is especially pronounced in ADHD patients with symptoms of hyperactivity and impulsivity (ADHD-C, ADHD-HI). Recently, a fMRI study [39] compared neural activation in the ventral striatum and prefrontal regions during reward processing in ADHD subtypes and healthy adults. The result showed that, compared to ADHD-C and healthy subjects, ADHD-I subjects showed a bilateral ventral striatal deficit during reward anticipation. In contrast, ADHD-C subjects showed orbitofrontal hyporesponsiveness to reward feedback when compared with ADHD-I and healthy subjects.

The late positive potential (LPP) is a central-parietal positive slow ERP that reaches the largest amplitudes at 500–700 ms post-stimulus and lasts for several hundred milliseconds [40]. Specifically, many studies have revealed that the LPP is more pronounced for emotionally salient than for neutral stimuli [41–44]. LPP has been described to reflect increased levels of sustained attention to effective-motivational stimuli [45–47], its amplitude decreased with the reduction of experienced emotion arousal, and increased with enhancement of the arousal [40]. Making use of a time production task with visual performance feedback, van Meel demonstrated that children with ADHD showed a decreased late positivity (after 450 ms) to negative feedback stimuli indicating loss. This result has been interpreted as a deficit in the affective evaluation of feedback signals and altered evaluation of future consequences in children with ADHD. Furthermore, a study of Groen consistently reported aberrant late processing of non-reward and punishment (increased feedback LPP) in children with ADHD. However, another study by Groen [48] demonstrated a trend toward a reduced LPP in response to negative feedback stimuli in children with ADHD.

Numerous studies have reported that the human brain is especially sensitive to emotionally negative events, and that these events are preferentially processed relative to neutral and positive events [49–52]. Behavioral studies [53–55] have demonstrated that, relative to positive events, negative events recruit attentional resources more rapidly, or automatically. Moreover, the magnitude of the negative event is important, as extremely negative events typically represent a greater threat to survival than do moderately negative events [56,57]. Yuan et al. reported that humans are more sensitive to magnitude differences in negative stimuli, and these different magnitudes could be clearly differentiated in each step of information processing stream even when individuals are highly engaged in a non-emotional task [56,58]. In contrast, magnitude differences in positive events are often unattended to in daily life, as positive events typically bring no harm [56]. In our daily life, more negative stimuli are punishments or losses, not violence or traffic accidents. An issue that has yet to be investigated is whether children with ADHD are also sensitive to punishment and its magnitude, and how ADHD children with different symptoms may differ in this sensitivity.

Therefore, the present study investigated the monitoring of performance feedback coupled with score losses and gains in children with two subtypes of ADHD (ADHD-C and ADHD-I). In order to evaluate the effect of punishment on the monitoring of performance feedback, we manipulated the magnitude of punishment (−1, −4). Regarding the typically developing (TD) children, based on the outcomes of the study of van Meel and colleagues [31], we expected that they would show enhanced monitoring of feedback as reflected by an enhanced FRN to large losses compared with that to small losses and gains. Based on the study by Carlson [38], we predict that patients with ADHD-C, a group characterized by competitive motivation and the desire to be perceived as superior to others, would show more sensitivity to large punishment as reflected by an enhanced FRN to large losses compared with that to small losses. Regarding the children with ADHD-I, who have severe attention problems as the core symptom, we expected that they would show aberrant early feedback detection as reflected by a reduced or absent FRN under all conditions. As previous studies have demonstrated, the LPP may reflect the late processing of the affective value of feedback stimuli in the context of feedback processing [31,48,59]. Groen [32] speculated that the children with ADHD attached more value to the feedback stimuli than the TD children, because they are more dependent on external motivators to maintain their performance. Based on this speculation, we predict that children with ADHD-C show an enhanced feedback LPP to larger punishment. As the LPP has been described to reflect increased sustained attention to affective-motivational stimuli and the LPP amplitude depends on how the emotional stimuli are appraised and attended to, we predicted that children with ADHD-I with severe inattention problems would not show LPP effect during feedback processing.

Methods

Ethics Statement

This study was approved by the Ethics Committee of Xiangya Second Hospital. Written informed consent was obtained from all the children and their parents. All participants were informed of their right to withdraw from the study at any time.

Participants

The participants were 31 medication-free (stimulant-naive) children with ADHD (27 boys and 4 girls), aged 6–14 years, who were outpatients at the Clinic of Child Psychiatry of the Second Xiangya Hospital of Central South University. The inclusion criteria were as follows: meeting the DSM-IV-TR criteria and the Kiddie-Sads-Present and Lifetime Version (K-SADS-PL); no history of serious head injury, epilepsy, drug abuse or psychiatric disorders (e.g., schizophrenia, pervasive development disorder, mental retardation or mood disorder). The children with ADHD were classified into two subtypes: ADHD-I (n = 15), ADHD-C (n = 16). Fifteen TD children served as controls. The TD children were selected from local primary schools, and matched well with the ADHD group with respect to age and gender. The K-SADS-PL served to exclude TD children who displayed symptoms of ADHD. All participants reported normal or corrected-to-normal vision and were right-handed. Their full-scale IQ was above 80, according to the Wechsler Intelligence Scale for Children - Revised in China (C-WISC). Table 1 presents the demographic characteristics of the ADHD group and the TD group. There were no significant differences between the groups with respect to sex and mean age.

The Child Behavior Checklist (CBCL) [60,61] is a well-studied standardized instrument that asks parents to assess their child's competencies and behavioral and emotional problems on 118 specific items, using a 3-point scale (0 = "not true", 1 = "somewhat/sometimes true" and 2 = "very/often true"). The clinical scales of the CBCL contain a Total Problems score, two subscale scores (Internalizing and Externalizing Problems) and eight syndrome scales: Aggressive Behavior, Delinquent Behavior, Withdrawn, Somatic Complaints, Anxious/Depressed, Attention Problems, Social Problems and Thought Problems. The presence of psychopathology of TD children was checked by CBCL. None of the TD children scored within the clinical rage of subscales and the total problem scale of CBCL.

The symptoms at each ADHD cluster (inattention, hyperactivity/impulsivity and combined) were obtained from Swanson, Nolan, and Pelham Scale- version IV (SNAP-IV) [62], a widely used standandized measure of ADHD. The SNAP-IV scale has four subscale (Total Scores: 26 items; Inattention: 9 items, and Oppositional: 8 items). Each item is scored for severity on a 4-point scale (0 = "not at all," 1 = "just a little," 2 = "quite a bit" and 3 = "very much"). The scale was completed by the participants' parents. Individuals with 6 or more symptoms of inattention but fewer than 6 symptoms of hyper-impulsive were identified as inattentive type, participants with 6 or more hyper-impulsive symptoms and fewer than 6 symptoms of inattention were categorized as Hyper-Impulsive type, and individuals with 6 or more symptoms on both dimensions were identified as combined type.

Table 1. Group characteristics (ANOVA test statistics).

Group	TDs (n = 15)	ADHD-C (n = 16)	ADHD-I(n = 15)	F value (ANOVA)	p value (ANOVA)	p value (ADHD-I v.s. ADHD-C)	p value (ADHD-I v.s. TD)	p value (ADHD-C v.s. TD)
Gender (M/F)	11/4	13/3	14/1		ns(Fisher's exact test)			
Age (yrs)	10.47(2.53)	9.50(2.34)	8.87(1.51)	1.878	ns			
IQ score	119.07(12.72)	102.53(11.27)	104.50(15.23)	7.053	0.002	0.639	0.005	0.001
SNAP-IV								
Total score	14.64(2.65)	31.38(6.82)	20.07(3.67)	47.52	<0.001	<0.001	0.03	<0.001
Inattentionitem score	7.47(1.68)	16.56(4.27)	14.67(2.72)	46.83	<0.001	0.095	<0.001	<0.001
Hyperactivity/Impulsive item score	7.00(1.46)	14.81(3.39)	5.40(2.47)	59.20	<0.001	<0.001	0.098	<0.001
Child Behavior Checklist								
total problems	34.99(11.00)	63.22(22.57)	48.01(9.20)	12.66	<0.001	0.01	0.028	<0.001
Inattention item score	3.07(2.49)	8.31(3.55)	6.27(2.87)	11.84	<0.001	0.235	0.009	<0.001
internalizing problems	2.60(1.84)	8.31(5.77)	5.13(3.34)	7.78	0.001	0.034	0.093	<0.001
externalizing problems	3.47(2.70)	16.87(10.56)	10.07(8.90)	13.67	<0.001	0.091	0.001	<0.001

Note: TD = Typically developing, SNAP-IV = The Swanson, Nolan and Pelham Rating Scale; CBCL = The Child Behavior Checklist; IQ = Intelligence Quotient.

Children gambling paradigm

We modified the gambling task according to the children's cognitive characteristics. The experiment was programmed and executed with E-prime (Psychology Software Tools, Pittsburg, PA). The task was administered under three reinforcement-contingency conditions: reward, small punishment and large punishment, which were operationalized as score gains and losses. In each trial, the participants were presented with two "doors" side by side (3000 ms) in the center of a black screen, following a 600–1000 ms central fixation cue. Participants were told that there was a happy face behind one door and a sad face behind the other door. Participants used a response box to make their choices. After an 800 ms interval, the feedback was displayed on the screen (1500 ms) by a number that indicated what the participants gained or lost. The happy face was always "+2" (Reward, RD), while the sad face could be "−1" (Low-deduct, LD) or "-4" (High-deduct, HD). The RD:LD:HD ratio was 6:2:2. All stimuli were randomly presented. If the participants did not respond within the required time (3000 ms), while the doors were on the screen, the computer would choose one door at random.

The task took approximately 30 min and consisted of 10 blocks, with each block including 30 trials. The participants had a rest after each block. The children were told that they would be given the final reward according to the all rewards or punishments of the whole task. However, unknown to the children, happy faces and sad faces were randomly presented independent of their response. The children were simply told to "make as many scores as possible." All subjects were provided with the same amount of compensation, 50 yuan RBM.

EEG acquisition and analysis

The electroencephalography (EEG) measures were recorded continuously (−200 ms–0 ms; 500-Hz sampling rate; FCZ reference; AFZ ground; BrainAmp amplifiers) from 36 scalp sites using Ag/AgC1 electrodes mounted on an elastic cap, according to the 10–20 international system. The array included 7 midline sites (OZ, POZ, PZ, CPZ, CZ, FCZ, and FZ), 12 sites over each hemisphere (O1/O2, PO3/PO4, PO7/PO8, P3/P4, P7/P8, CP3/CP4, C3//C4, FC3/FC4, FT7/FT8, F3/F4, F7/F8 and FP1/FP2), the left and right mastoids (TP9, TP10), and the horizontal electrooculogram (EOG; FP1) and the vertical EOG (FP2) electrodes to monitor the EOG bipolarly. All electrode impedances were kept below 5 kΩ. The EOG was recorded for the purpose of artifact correction; eye movement and blink artifacts were corrected using the Gratton et al. [63] algorithm. Offline analysis was performed using Brain Vision Analyzer software 2.0 (Brain Products, Munich, Germany). All data were re-referenced to the average reference offline and digitally low-pass-filtered at 30 Hz. Epochs of 1200 ms were extracted from the continuous data file for analysis, commencing 200 ms before the feedback stimulus. Grand-average ERPs were obtained by averaging the data of individual participants according to each condition and feedback type. The average number of trials across the three feedback conditions was not significantly different across the TD, ADHD-I and ADHD-C groups [$F = 1.000$, $P = 0.371$]. The averaged number of trials was 84.49 for TD group,78.98 for ADHD-I group, 70.85 for ADHD-C group. Additionally, there was no significant interaction effect between group and feedback [$F = 1.943$, $P = 0.156$]. The average number of trials in the reward condition was 151.33 for TD group, 133.62 for ADHD-C group, 140.07 for ADHD-I group [$F = 1.670$, $P = 0.20$]. In addition, the averaged number of trials in the small loss condition was 55.80 for TD group,51.53 for ADHD-I group, 48.81 for ADHD-C group [$F = 2.64$, $P = 0.08$]. Lastly, the averaged number of trials during the large loss condition was 46.33 for TD group, 45.33 for ADHD-I group, 43.00 for ADHD-C group [$F = 0.64$, $P = 0.53$].

To assess the ERP waves elicited by feedback stimuli, we measured the average amplitude of FRN (250–350 ms) from Fz to Cz sites and the average amplitude of Lpp (400 ms–800 ms) from Pz site. A three-way ANOVA was conducted on the FRN component. ANOVA factors were feedback type (larger loss, smaller loss and gain feedback), electrode site (Fz, Cz) and group (TD, ADHD-C and ADHD-I participants). The same analysis was conducted for the LPP at Pz. The ERP data were analyzed using Brain Products Analyzer software. The degrees of freedom of the F-ratio were corrected according to the Greenhouse-Geisser method.

Results

The grand-average ERPs depicted in Figure 1. The topographical map of FRN in TD,ADHD-C and ADHD-I group was shown in Figure 2. The 3 (feedback type: large loss, small loss and gain feedback)×2 (electrode: Fz, Cz)×3 (group: TD, ADHD-C and ADHD-I participants) ANOVA revealed a significant effect of feedback type by group interaction effect during 250–350 ms [$F(4, 86) = 2.49$, $P = 0.049$]. When controlled for age and IQ score, the feedback type by group interaction effect was still marginally significant [$F(4, 86) = 2.43$, $P = 0.054$]. To further elucidate this interaction, we analyzed the feedback type effect in each group. In the TD group, the main effect of feedback type was significant [$F(2, 28) = 4.16$, $P = 0.032$], and large loss feedback elicited a larger negativity than did gain feedback [$F(1, 14) = 10.11$, $P = 0.007$] or small loss feedback [$F(1, 14) = 4.34$, $P = 0.056$], whereas no significant difference was observed between small loss and gain feedback [$F(1, 14) = 0.59$, $P = 0.46$]. In the ADHD-C group, the main effect of feedback type was significant [$F(2, 30) = 4.88$, $P = 0.023$], large loss feedback elicited a larger negativity than did small loss feedback [$F(1, 15) = 19.29$, $P = 0.001$]. However, no significant differences were observed between large loss and gain feedback [$F(1, 15) = 0.1$, $P = 0.33$], or between small loss and gain feedback [$F(1, 15) = 3.09$, $P = 0.1$]. In the ADHD-I group, no significant main effect of feedback type was observed [$F(2, 28) = 0.91$, $P = 0.41$]. In addition, we also broke down the feedback type by group interaction effect by analyzing the group effect during each feedback condition. No significant group effects observed during big loss feedback [$F(2, 43) = 2.05$, $P = 0.14$], small loss feedback [$F(2, 43) = 0.03$, $P = 0.97$], and gain feedback [$F(2, 43) = 0.47$, $P = 0.63$] conditions.

In order to analyze the large loss and small loss feedback effect, we further subtracted the gain feedback from large loss and small loss feedback. The 2 (feedback type: large loss vs gain, small loss vs gain)×2 (electrode: Fz, Cz)×3 (group: TD, ADHD-C and ADHD-I participants) ANOVA revealed a significant effect of feedback type by group interaction effect during 250–350 ms [$F(2, 43) = 6.17$, $P = 0.004$]. To break down this interaction, we further analyzed the feedback type effect in each group, respectively. In the TD group, the main effect of feedback type was significant, and the large loss feedback effect is larger than small loss feedback effect [$F(1, 14) = 10.11$, $P = 0.007$]. In the ADHD-C group, the main effect of feedback type was significant, and the large loss feedback effect is larger than small loss feedback effect [$F(1,14) = 19.29$, $P = 0.001$]. In the ADHD-I group, no significant main effect of feedback type was observed [$F(1, 14) = 0.34$, $P = 0.57$].

In addition, the LPP component was also measured at 100 ms intervals during the 400–800 ms intervals at the Pz electrode site. When controlled for age and IQ score, the main effect of feedback

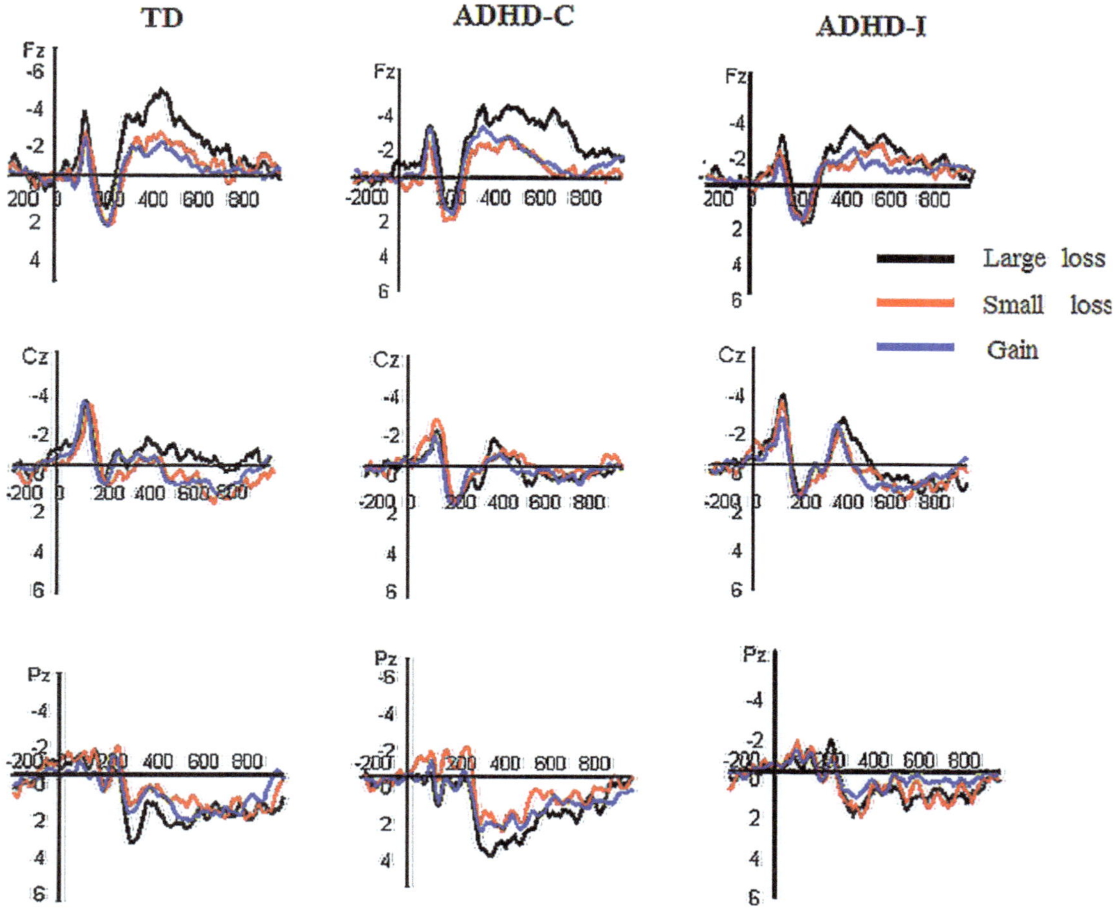

Figure 1. Grand-average of ERPs at Fz, Cz and Pz for the large loss (black lines), small loss (red lines) and gain (blue lines) feedback conditions in the TD, ADHD-C and ADHD-I groups.

type [$F(2, 82) = 0.21$, $P = 0.8$] and the feedback type by group interaction effect were not significant during 400–500 ms [$F(4, 82) = 1.37$, $P = 0.25$], but there was a significant main effect of group [$F(2, 41) = 4.15$, $P = 0.023$] during 400–500 ms. The LPP differences between the TD and ADHD-C [F (1, 27) = 2.69, $P = 0.11$], TD and ADHD-I [F (1, 26) = 0.39, $P = 0.54$] groups were not significant, but the LPP was larger in the ADHD-C group than in ADHD-I groups [F (1, 27) = 9.94, $P = 0.004$]. However, the main effect of feedback type [500–600 ms: $F(2, 82) = 1.27$, $P = 0.29$, 600–700 ms: $F(2, 82) = 0.34$, $P = 0.69$, 700–800 ms: $F(2, 82) = 0.39$, $P = 0.66$], group [500–600 ms: $F(2, 41) = 2.18$, $P = 0.13$, 600–700 ms: $F(2, 41) = 0.72$, $P = 0.49$, 700–800 ms: $F(2, 41) = 0.59$, $P = 0.56$] and the feedback type by group interaction effect [500–600 ms: $F(4, 82) = 1.2$, $P = 0.32$, 600–700 ms: $F(4, 82) = 1.31$, $P = 0.27$, 700–800 ms: $F(4, 82) = 1.35$, $P = 0.26$] were all non-significant during each 100 ms interval of the 500–800 ms intervals.

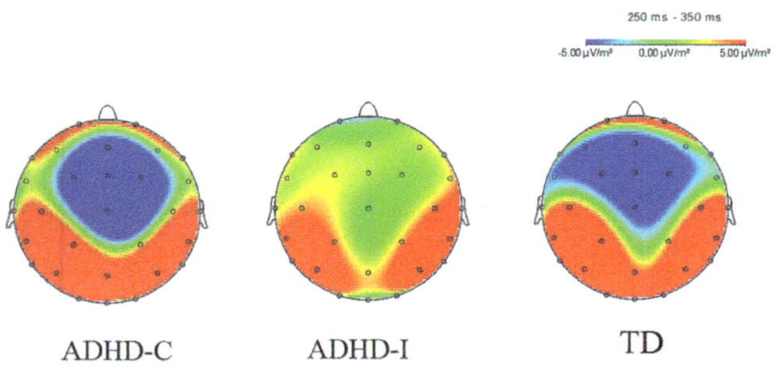

Figure 2. The topographical map of FRN in the TD,ADHD-C and ADHD-I groups in the phase of 250–350 ms.

Discussion

This is the first study to investigate the effect of feedback valence (reward or punishment) and punishment magnitude (small or large) on FRN and LPP in two subtypes of ADHD (ADHD-C and ADHD-I) compared to TD children during a children's gambling task. Analysis of the FRN interval revealed that TD children elicited a more negative FRN potential to large losses than to small losses or gains, which is consistent with previous studies showing larger FRN amplitudes to omitted gains and omitted losses in TD children [31], demonstrating that TD children exhibited enhanced monitoring of feedback when it was made more salient. These observations replicated prior findings that humans (including TD children) are especially sensitive to emotionally negative events, which are preferentially processed relative to neutral and positive events [49–51] and that humans are sensitive to magnitude differences in negative stimuli [56,58,64]. The children with ADHD-C also showed an enhanced FRN to large losses compared to that to small losses and gains, which is consistent with the finding of an enhanced sensitivity to unfavorable outcomes in children with ADHD [30], probably due to abnormalities in mesolimbic reward circuits. Affective evaluation and the assessment of future consequence of the feedback signal seems to be altered in ADHD. The children with ADHD-C did not differ in their feedback FRN amplitude from TD children, which suggests that children with ADHD are described as benefiting from renforcement contingencies from a clinical perspective. Reinforcement has proved to be highly effective in the treatment of ADHD [65] and that reinforcement contingencies are found to normalize behavior that characterizes ADHD [25]. Therefore, similar to TD children, children with ADHD-C are sensitive to punishment and magnitude differences in punishment. This finding may be explained by the fact that humans are equipped with a special sensitivity to negative stimuli as a result of evolutionary adaptation, as illustrated by the negative bias account [52,56]. Another plausible explanation is that the motivational style of children with ADHD-C is characterized by competitiveness and a desire to be perceived as superior to others, which might result in enhanced sensitivity to negative outcomes [40], therefore, children with ADHD-C paid more attention to the larger losses. However, the FRN effect was absent under all conditions in children with ADHD-I, even under the large punishment condition, which contradicted the bias for emotionally negative events in humans. The absence of the FRN effect in children with ADHD-I may be explained by their nature of the cognitive-attention deficit, which is characterized as drowsy, sluggish and less alert [36,37]. And compared to children with ADHD-C, the children with ADHD-I show different motivational style, possible less uncooperative and more passive in the learning style [38]. The FRN effect was elicited both in children with ADHD-C and in TD children, but not in children with ADHD-I, which may be attributed to the severe inattention problems, as the core symptom in children with ADHD-I, who suffer from a deficit detection of motivationally significant cues. However, one may question that both ADHD-C and ADHD-I showed similar symptoms of inattention, consequently this inattention explanation is probably unconvincing. It is worth note that ADHD-C children are characterized not only by inattention problems but also by competitiveness and perceived self-superiority. As discussed above, the latter characteristics are associated with enhanced sensitivity to negative outcomes which in turn enhances feedback negativity in brain potentials. This may constitute a compensating feature for ADHD-C children and explains why ADHD-C showed a robust FRN effect that was absent in ADHD-I, despite similar inattention problems in both groups. Also, this compensatory mechanism may explain why ADHD-C and TD children showed similar FRN effect, despite the inattention problems in the former group.

The present study observed an LPP component only in the early phase (400–500 ms) in children with ADHD-C, who showed an enhanced LPP amplitude to feedback indicating larger losses than TD children and children with ADHD-I. Furthermore, LPP has been reported to reach the largest amplitudes at 500–700 ms post-stimulus and to last for several hundred milliseconds [40]; In the current study, the LPP was larger in the ADHD-C group than in ADHD-I group [$F(1.27)=9.94$, $P=0.004$]. This was consistent with a prior study by Carlson and colleague [38] implying that individuals with ADHD-C were motivated by competitiveness and desired to be suprior to others which might contribute to greater sensitivity to larger losses. However, LPP emerged only in the 400–500 ms interval rather than in a longer time epoch. Thus, this observation should be considered as tentative and awaits future studies to be replicated.

There are some limitations to the interpretation of the current findings. First, of our study was the relatively small sample size, especially for female participants. There was only one girl in the ADHD-I group, three girls in the ADHD-C group and four girls in the TD group, which did not make it possible to examine the potential role of sex. Second, in our study we only recruited children with two subtypes of ADHD (ADHD-I and ADHD-C), and not the hyperactive/impulsive subtype (ADHD-H). Thus, we could assess only differences between the ADHD-I and ADHD-C subtypes. Finally, the children's gambling paradigm used in the present study was designed only for one reward condition (+2), and two different punishment conditions (−4 or −1). We probably should have designed two reward conditions. Future studies are needed to investigate whether the same results can be obtained when reward and punishment have an equal number of conditions.

In conclusion, this is the first study to investigate to the effect of feedback valence and punishment magnitude on feedback negative and LPP in two subtypes of ADHD (ADHD-C and ADHD-I). In TD children and children with ADHD-C, large loss feedbacks evoked more negative FRN amplitudes than small loss feedbacks, suggesting that children with ADHD-C may keep intact brain sensitivity to the punishment and its magnitude. In contrast with the above two groups, the above FRN effect was absent in children with ADHD-I, suggesting that children with ADHD-I are significantly impaired in neural sensitivity to the feedback stimuli and in particular, to punishment. Secondly, the Late positive potential amplitudes were larger in children with ADHD-C in comparison with those with ADHD-I, regardless of feedback valence and magnitude. Therefore, we speculate that FRN, rather than LPP, is a reliable index to detect this difference across different ADHD-subcategories.

Author Contributions

Conceived and designed the experiments: XL JG. Performed the experiments: LS. Analyzed the data: JY SW. Contributed reagents/materials/analysis tools: XC. Wrote the paper: JG JY.

References

1. American Psychiatric Association (2000) Diagnostic and statistical manual of mental disorders. 4th ed., revised. Washington, DC: Author.
2. Polanczyk G, de Lima MS, Horta BL, Biederman J, Rohde LA (2007) The worldwide prevalence of ADHD: A systematic review and metaregression analysis. Am J Psychiatry 164: 942–948
3. Centers for Disease Control, National Center for Prevention Services (US), Division of Tuberculosis Elimination, National Center for HIV (2001) Reported tuberculosis in the United States. US Department of Health and Human Services, Public Health Service, Centers for Disease Control and Prevention, National Center for Prevention Services, Division of Tuberculosis Elimination.
4. Gau SS, Chong MY, Chen TH, Cheng AT (2005) A 3-year panel study of mental disorders among adolescents in Taiwan. Am J Psychiatry 162: 1344–1350.
5. Woo BSC, Rey JM (2005) The validity of the DSM-IV subtypes of attention-deficit/hyperactivity disorder. Aust N Z J Psychiatry 39:344–353.
6. Douglas VI (1989) Can Skinnerian theory explain attention deficit disorder? A reply to Barkley. Attention deficit disorder: Current concepts and emerging trends in attentional and behavioral disorders of childhood 4: 235–254.
7. Haenlein M, Caul WF (1987) Attention deficit disorder with hyperactivity: a specific hypothesis of reward dysfunction.Journal of the American Academy of Child and Adolescent Psychiatry 26: 356–362.

8. Sagvolden T, Aase H, Zeiner P, Berger D (1998) Altered reinforcement mechanisms in attention-deficit/hyperactivity disorder. Behavioural Brain Research 94: 61–71.
9. Quay HC (1988) Attention deficit disorder and the behavioral inhibition system: The relevance of the neuropsychological theory of Jeffrey A. Gray. Attention deficit disorder: Criteria, cognition, intervention 117–125.
10. Quay HC (1988b) The behavioral reward and inhibition system in childhood behaviour disorder. In Bloomingdale LM (Ed.), Attention Deficit Disorder 3: 176–185.
11. Quay HC (1988c) Reward, inhibition, and attention deficit hyperactivity disorder. Journal of the American Academy of Child and Adolescent Psychiatry 27: 262–263.
12. August GJ (1987) Production deficiencies in free recall: A comparison of hyperactive, learning-disabled, and normal children. Journal of Abnormal Child Psychology 15: 429–440.
13. Barber MA, Milich R, Welsh R (1996) Effects of reinforcement schedule and task difficulty on the performance of attention deficit hyperactivity disordered and control boys. Journal of Clinical Child Psychology 25: 66–76.
14. Borcherding B, Thompson K, Kruesi M, Bartko J, Rapoport JL, et al. (1998) Automatic and effortful processing in attention deficit/hyperactivity disorder. Journal of Abnormal Child Psychology 16: 333–345.
15. Van der Meere J, Shalev R, Borger N, Gross-Tsur V (1995) Sustained attention, activation and MPH in ADHD: A research note. Journal of Child Psychology and Psychiatry 36: 697–703.
16. Douglas VI, Parry PA (1994) Effects of reward and nonreward on frustration and attention in attention-deficit disorder. J Abnorm Child Psychol 22: 281–302.
17. Sergeant JA (2000) The cognitive-energetic model: An empirical approach to attention-deficit hyperactivity disorder. Neurosci Biobehav Rev 24: 7–12.
18. Luman M, Oosterlaan J, Sergeant JA (2005) The impact of reinforcement contingencies on AD/HD: A review and theoretical appraisal. Clinical Psychology Review 25: 183–213.
19. Sagvolden T, Johansen EB, Aase H, Russell VA (2005) A dynamic developmental theory of attention-deficit/hyperactivity disorder (ADHD) predominantly hyperactive/impulsive and combined subtypes. Behav Brain Sci 28: 397–468.
20. Sonuga-Barke E (2003) The dual pathway model of AD/HD: An elaboration of neurodevelopmental characteristics. Neurosci Biobehav Rev 27: 593–604.
21. Tripp G, Wickens J (2008) Research review: Dopamine transfer deficit: A neurobiological theory of altered reinforcement mechanisms in ADHD. Journal of child psychology and psychiatry 49: 691–704.
22. Frank M, Santamaria A, O'Reilly R, Willcutt E (2007) Testing computational models of dopamine and noradrenaline dysfunction in attention deficit/ hyperactivity disorder. Neuropsychopharmacology 32: 1583–1599.
23. Nigg JT, Casey BJ (2005) An integrative theory of attention-deficit/hyperactivity disorder based on the cognitive and affective neurosciences. Dev Psychopathol 17: 785–806.
24. Patterson C, Newman J (1993) Reflectivity and learning from aversive events - toward a psychological mechanism for the syndromes of disinhibition. Psychol Rev 100: 716–736.
25. Hupp SD, Reitman D, Northup J, O'Callaghan P, LeBlanc M (2002) The effects of delayed rewards, tokens, and stimulant medication on sportsmanlike behavior with ADHD-diagnosed children. Behavior Modification 26: 148–162.
26. Kelly ML, McCain AP (1995) Promoting academic performance in inattentive children: The relative efficacy of school-home notes with and without response cost. Behavior Modification 19: 76–85.
27. Pelham PA, Carlson C, Sams SE, Vallano G, Dixon MJ, et al. (1993) Separate and combined effects of methylphenidate and behavior modification on boys with attention deficit–hyperactivity disorder in the classroom. Journal of Consulting and Clinical Psychology 61: 506–515.
28. Carlson CL, Mann M, Alexander DK (2000) Effects of reward and response cost on the performance and motivation of children with ADHD. Cognitive Therapy and Research 24: 87–98.
29. Carlson CL, Tamm L (2000) Responsiveness of children with attention deficithyperactivity disorder to reward and response cost: Differential impact on performance and motivation. J Consult Clin Psychol 68: 73–83.
30. van Meel CS, Oosterlaan J, Heslenfeld DJ, Sergeant JA (2005) Telling good from bad news: ADHD differentially affects processing of positive and negative feedback during guessing. Neuropsychologia 43:1946–1954.
31. van Meel CS, Heslenfeld DJ, Oosterlaan J, Luman M, Sergeant JA (2011) ERPs associated with monitoring and evaluation of monetary reward and punishment in children with ADHD. Journal of Child Psychology and Psychiatry 9: 942–953.
32. Groen Y, Tucha O, Wijers AA, Althaus M (2013) Processing of continuously provided punishment and reward in children with ADHD and the modulating effects of stimulant medication: an ERP study. PLOS ONE 8: e59240.
33. Scheres A, Milham MP, Knutson B, Castellanos FX (2007) Ventral striatal hyporesponsiveness during reward anticipation in attention- deficit/hyperactivity disorder. Biol Psychiatry 61: 720–724.
34. Conzelmann A, Mucha RF, Jacob CP, Romanos J, Gerdes AB, et al. (2009) Abnormal affevtive responsiveness in attention-deficit/hyperactivity disorder: subtype differences.Biol Psychiatry 65: 578–585.
35. Power TJ, Costigan TE, Eiraldi RB, Leff SS (2004) Variations in anxiety and depression as a function of ADHD subtypes defined by DSM-IV: Do subtype differences exist or not? J Abnorm Child Psychol 32:27–37.
36. Carlson CL, Tamm L (2000) Responsiveness of children with ADHD to rewardand response cost: Differentialim-pact on performance and motivation. Journal of Consulting and ClinicalPsychol-ogy 68: 73–83.
37. Lahey BB, Carlson CL, Frick PE (1997) Attention deficit disorder without hyperactivity. In I. A.Widiger, A.I. Frances, H.A.Pincus, R.Ross, M.B.First, &W.Davis (Eds.), DSM-IV source book (Vol. 3, pp. 163–188). Washington,DC: American Psychiatric Association.
38. Carlson CL, Booth JE, Shin M, Canu WH (2002) Parent-, teacher-, and self-rated motivational styles in ADHD subtypes. J Learn Disabil 35: 104–113.
39. Edel MA, Enzi B, Witthaus H, Tegenthoff M, Peters S, et al. (2013) Differential reward processing in subtypes of adult attention deficit hyperactivity disorder. J Psychiatr Res 47: 350–356.
40. Yuan JJ, Chen J, Yang JM, Ju E, Norman GJ, et al. (2014) Negative mood state enhanced the susceptibility to unpleasant events: neural correlate from a music-primed emotion classification task. PLOS ONE 9: E89844.
41. Foti D, Hajcak G (2008) Deconstructing reappraisal: Descriptions preceding arousing pictures modulate the subsequent neural response. J Cogn Neurosci 20: 977–988.
42. Krompinger JW, Moser JS, Simons RF (2008) Modulations of the electrophysiological response to pleasant stimuli by cognitive reappraisal. Emotion 8:132–137.
43. Moser JS, Hajcak G, Bukay E, Simons RF (2006) Intentional modulation of emotional responding to unpleasant pictures: an ERP study. Psychophysiology 43: 292–296.
44. Hajcak G, Nieuwenhuis S (2006) Reappraisal modulates the electrocortical response to unpleasant pictures. Cogn Affect Behav Neurosci 6:291–297.
45. Cuthbert BN, Schupp HT, Bradley MM, Birbaumer N, Lang PJ (2000) Brain potentials in affective picture processing: Covariation with autonomic arousal and affective report. Biological Psychology 52: 95–111.
46. Hajcak G, Moser JS, Simons RF (2006) Attending to affect: Appraisal strategies modulate the electrocortical response to arousing pictures. Emotion 6: 517–522.
47. Schupp HT, Cuthbert BN, Bradley MM, Cacioppo JT, Ito T, et al. (2000) Affective picture processing: The late positive potential is modulated by motivational relevance. Psychophysiology 37: 257–261.
48. Groen Y, Wijers A, Mulder L, Waggeveld B, Minderaa R, et al. (2008) Error and feedback processing in children with ADHD and children with autistic spectrum disorder: An EEG event-related potential study. Clinical neurophysiology 119: 2476–2493.
49. Cacioppo JT, Gardner WL (1999) Emotion. Annual Review of Psychology 50:191–214.
50. Delplanque S, Lavoie ME, Hot P, Silvert L, Sequeira H (2004) Modulation of cognitive processing by emotional valence studied through event-related potentials in humans. Neuroscience Letters 356:1–4.
51. Delplanque S, Silvert L, Hot P, Sequeira H (2005) Event-related P3a and P3b in response to unpredictable emotional stimuli. Biological Psychology 68:107–120.
52. Huang YX, Luo YJ (2006) Temporal course of emotional negativity bias: An ERP study. Neuroscience Letters 398: 91–96.
53. Hansen CH, Hansen RD (1988) Finding the face in the crowd: an anger superiority effect. Journal of Personality and Social Psychology 54:917–924.
54. Pratto F, Johu OP (1990) Automatic vigilance: The attention-grabbing power of negative social information. Journal of Personality and Social Psychology 61: 380–391.
55. Wentura D, Rothermund K, Bak P (2000) Automatic vigilance:The attention-grabbing power of approach- and avoidance-related social information. Journal of Personality and Social Psychology 78: 1024–1037.
56. Yuan JJ, Zhang QL, Chen A, Li H, Wang QH, et al. (2007) Are we sensitive to valence differences in emotionally negative stimuli? Electrophysiological evidence from an ERP study. Neuropsychologia 45: 2764–2771.
57. Yuan JJ, Lu H, Yang JM, Li H (2011) Do not neglect small troubles: moderately negative stimuli affect target processing more intensely than highly negative stimuli. Brain research 1415: 84–95.
58. Yuan JJ, Meng XX, Yang JM, Yao GH, Hu L, et al. (2012) The valence strength of unpleasant emotion modulates brain processing of behavioral inhibitory control: neural correlates. Biological Psychology 89: 240–251.
59. Althaus M, Groen Y, Wijers A, Minderaa R, Kema I, et al. (2010) Variants of the SLC6A3 (DAT1) polymorphism affect performance monitoring-related cortical evoked potentials that are associated with ADHD. Biol Psychol 85: 19–32.
60. Achenbach TM (1991). Integrative guide for the 1991 CBCL/4-18, YSR, and TRF profiles[M]. Burlington: Department of Psychiatry, University of Vermont.
61. Achenbach TM, Dumenci L, Rescorla LA (2003) DSM-oriented and empirically based approaches to constructing scales from the same item pools. J Clin Child Adolesc Psychol 32:328–340.
62. Swanson JM, Kraemer HC, Hinshaw SP, Arnold LE, Conners CK (2001) Clinical relevance of the primary findings of the MTA: success rates based on severity of ADHD and ODD symptoms at the end of treatment. J Am Acad Child Adolesc Psychiatry 40:168–179.
63. Gratton G, Coles MGH, Donchin E (1983) A new method for off-line removal of ocular artifact. Electroencephalogr Clin Neurophysiol 55: 468–484.
64. Yuan JJ, Yang JM, Meng XX, Yu FQ, Li H (2008) The valence strength of negative stimuli modulates visual novelty processing: electrophysiological evidence from an event-related potential study. Nueroscience 157: 524–531.
65. Barkley RA (2002) Psychosocial treatments for attention-deficit/hyperactivity disorder in children. Journal of Clinical Psychiatry 63: 36–43.

7

Impact of Early Life Adversity on Reward Processing in Young Adults: EEG-fMRI Results from a Prospective Study over 25 Years

Regina Boecker[1], Nathalie E. Holz[1], Arlette F. Buchmann[1], Dorothea Blomeyer[1], Michael M. Plichta[2], Isabella Wolf[1,3], Sarah Baumeister[1], Andreas Meyer-Lindenberg[2], Tobias Banaschewski[1], Daniel Brandeis[1,4,5,6]◑, Manfred Laucht[1,7]*◑

1 Department of Child and Adolescent Psychiatry and Psychotherapy, CIMH Medical Faculty Mannheim/Heidelberg University, Mannheim, Germany, **2** Department of Psychiatry and Psychotherapy, CIMH Medical Faculty Mannheim/Heidelberg University, Mannheim, Germany, **3** Department of Neuroimaging, CIMH Medical Faculty Mannheim/Heidelberg University, Mannheim, Germany, **4** Department of Child and Adolescent Psychiatry, University of Zurich, Zurich, Germany, **5** Center for Integrative Human Physiology, University of Zurich, Zurich, Germany, **6** Neuroscience Center Zurich, University of Zurich and ETH Zurich, Zurich, Germany, **7** Department of Psychology, University of Potsdam, Potsdam, Germany

Abstract

Several lines of evidence have implicated the mesolimbic dopamine reward pathway in altered brain function resulting from exposure to early adversity. The present study examined the impact of early life adversity on different stages of neuronal reward processing later in life and their association with a related behavioral phenotype, i.e. attention deficit/hyperactivity disorder (ADHD). 162 healthy young adults (mean age = 24.4 years; 58% female) from an epidemiological cohort study followed since birth participated in a simultaneous EEG-fMRI study using a monetary incentive delay task. Early life adversity according to an early family adversity index (EFA) and lifetime ADHD symptoms were assessed using standardized parent interviews conducted at the offspring's age of 3 months and between 2 and 15 years, respectively. fMRI region-of-interest analysis revealed a significant effect of EFA during reward anticipation in reward-related areas (i.e. ventral striatum, putamen, thalamus), indicating decreased activation when EFA increased. EEG analysis demonstrated a similar effect for the contingent negative variation (CNV), with the CNV decreasing with the level of EFA. In contrast, during reward delivery, activation of the bilateral insula, right pallidum and bilateral putamen increased with EFA. There was a significant association of lifetime ADHD symptoms with lower activation in the left ventral striatum during reward anticipation and higher activation in the right insula during reward delivery. The present findings indicate a differential long-term impact of early life adversity on reward processing, implicating hyporesponsiveness during reward anticipation and hyperresponsiveness when receiving a reward. Moreover, a similar activation pattern related to lifetime ADHD suggests that the impact of early life stress on ADHD may possibly be mediated by a dysfunctional reward pathway.

Editor: Andrea Antal, University Medical Center Goettingen, Germany

Funding: This work was supported by grants from the German Research Foundation (DFG LA 733/1-2) to ML, DB, TB, and AML. The funders had no role in study design, data collection and analysis, decision to publish, or preparation of the manuscript.

Competing Interests: Dr. Banaschewski served in an advisory or consultancy role for Hexal Pharma, Lilly, Medice, Novartis, Otsuka, Oxford outcomes, PCM scientific, Shire, and Viforpharma. He received conference attendance support and conference support or received speaker's fee by Lilly, Medice, Novartis, and Shire. He is/has been involved in clinical trials conducted by Lilly, Shire, and Viforpharma. The present work is unrelated to the above grants and relationships. Dr. Meyer-Lindenberg received consultant fees and travel expenses from AstraZeneca, Hoffmann-La Roche, Lundbeck Foundation, speaker's fees from Pfizer Pharma, Lilly Deutschland, Glaxo SmithKline, Janssen Cilag, Bristol-Myers Squibb, Lundbeck, and AstraZeneca. All other authors report no financial relationships with commercial interests.

* Email: manfred.laucht@zi-mannheim.de

◑ These authors contributed equally to this work.

Introduction

Accumulating evidence suggests that adversity in early childhood may impair human brain development and mental health later in life [1–3]. Moreover, clinical studies have highlighted striking effects of early life adversity on the development and persistence of mental disorders such as attention deficit/hyperactivity disorder (ADHD) [4–7]. Among the mechanisms mediating the detrimental impact of early adversity on psychopathology and brain development, alterations of the mesolimbic reward pathway have been suggested to play a major role [8–10]. Several functionally related brain regions have been implicated in the processing of rewards by a large body of functional magnetic resonance imaging (fMRI) findings and have been related to different stages of reward processing [11,12]. These findings emphasize a functional dissection of reward processing. While anticipation or "wanting" of a reward addresses the motivational aspect to receive a reward, reward delivery or "liking" has been interpreted as the hedonic impact of a reward producing the feeling of pleasure [13].

Common regions that are preferentially activated during the anticipation of rewards encompass the ventral striatum (VS), including the nucleus accumbens, ventral caudate nucleus and ventral putamen. Another region suggested to be involved in the delivery of rewards covers the medial orbitofrontal cortex, adjacent parts of the ventromedial prefrontal cortex, medial and dorsal caudate as well as putamen. With regard to ADHD, most studies have demonstrated a reduced activation of the VS during reward anticipation in patients compared to healthy controls [8,9,14–16], while for the delivery phase, an increased activation of the caudate nucleus was observed [15–17]. These effects are in line with the dopamine transfer deficit model, which postulates a diminished dopaminergic response shift from the actual reward to the anticipatory stimulus, but a remaining strong response during reward delivery [18,19].

In contrast to neuroimaging research, fewer studies have examined electrophysiological correlates of anticipatory reward processing. One anticipatory event-related potential (ERP) which has been investigated more systematically measuring an electroencephalogram (EEG) is the contingent negative variation (CNV) type activity, a slow negative potential shift before target or feedback stimuli, with a maximum over central sites, elicited by preparation and anticipation paradigms [20,21]. If feedback immediately follows the response, the CNV reflects reward anticipation along with motor and cognitive preparation or time estimation. If feedback is delayed, reward anticipation is also postponed and is mainly reflected by the feedback or stimulus-preceding negativity (SPN) following the CNV and the motor response [22]. So far, some findings have indicated higher CNV-like activity during reward anticipation [23–25], although other studies did not find an effect of reward anticipation on the target-preceding CNV in tests in which feedback was postponed or predictable [26,27]. In turn, several studies have shown a reduced CNV for children with ADHD or adults with a childhood diagnosis of ADHD, acting on a cued continuous performance test (CPT), investigating developmental effects of impaired cognitive brain functions [28–31].

Increasing evidence has implicated the neural circuitry of reward in altered brain function resulting from exposure to early life adversity. At the behavioral level, impaired responding to rewarding stimuli in maltreated individuals was reported [32]. These individuals exhibited faster reactions for risky options in a decision-making task than controls, but lacked the typical increase in response speed with the chance of winning. Further evidence for a reduced sensitivity to reward was provided in an fMRI study [10]. Young adults maltreated during childhood showed a blunted basal ganglia response (left putamen, left globus pallidus) and less positive ratings of reward cues during reward anticipation. Another study underscored these results by demonstrating a decreased activation in the VS to reward-predicting cues in Romanian adoptees who had experienced global early deprivation [33]. In these studies, no effect of early adversity on reward delivery was observed, suggesting that adversity might specifically affect responses to reward-predicting cues. However, a recent study by Kumar et al. [34] investigating the impact of acute stress found differential effects on phases of reward processing, with increased neuronal activation in the caudate and the amygdala during reward anticipation and decreased activation in the caudate and the putamen while receiving a reward. Hence, acute and early chronic stress seem to impact on the anticipatory and delivery stage of reward processing in specific ways, most likely mediated by alterations of the hypothalamus-pituitary-adrenal (HPA) axis [35].

In the present study, the impact of early adversity on reward processing was examined in a large sample of young adults from an epidemiological cohort study followed since birth. Using a monetary incentive delay (MID) task offering either money or verbal feedback, simultaneous EEG-fMRI was recorded in order to detect alterations at different stages of reward processing. Given the fact that the verbal feedback (control condition) of the MID represents a special reward characteristic, such as if receiving a social reward [36,37], modality-specific differences in rewarding quality will be examined. The use of EEG and fMRI provides both high spatial and temporal resolution of neuronal alterations during reward processing. Especially, the EEG enables a cue related analysis of time-resolved neurophysiological signatures within the anticipation phase as recently demonstrated by Plichta et al. [38]. First, we hypothesized that activation of reward-related areas induced by the anticipation of a monetary reward, especially the VS, would decrease with the level of early adversity. Second, we expected the same effect for the EEG, i.e. that the CNV, reflecting the motivational signature of reward anticipation, would decrease with increasing adversity. Third, in line with previous research, no adversity-specific alterations of the neuronal response to monetary reward outcome were predicted [10,33]. Fourth, we hypothesized that reward-related neuronal activation was related to lifetime ADHD symptoms, showing decreasing neuronal activity during reward anticipation and increasing activation during reward delivery with the level of ADHD [14,15,17].

Materials and Methods

Ethics statement

The current assessment was approved by the ethics committee of the University of Heidelberg. After complete description of the study to the participants, written informed consent was obtained. For assessments during childhood (age three months to 15 years) written informed consent was obtained from parents on behalf of the children.

Sample

This investigation was conducted in the framework of an epidemiological cohort study examining the long-term outcome of early risk factors from birth into adulthood. Detailed information about this study has been published elsewhere [39,40]. The initial sample consisted of 384 infants born between 1986 and 1988 of predominantly (>99%) European descent, who were consecutively recruited from two obstetric and six children's hospitals of the Rhine-Neckar Region of Germany. Only firstborn children with singleton births and German-speaking parents were enrolled in the study. Assessments were first conducted at the age of three months and subsequently at regular intervals throughout development, most recently in young adulthood. From the initial sample, 18 (4.7%) were excluded due to severe handicaps and 57 (14.8%) were dropouts, leaving a final sample of 309 for the current assessment. From these, 122 individuals had to be excluded due to usual contraindications for MRI and EEG, current psychopathology or psychotropic medication. This sample of N = 187 individuals participated in a simultaneous EEG-fMRI measurement. Another twenty-five participants were discarded due to movement artifacts (>3 mm) or insufficient EEG quality, leaving a final sample of N = 162 participants (mean age = 24.4 years; 58% female).

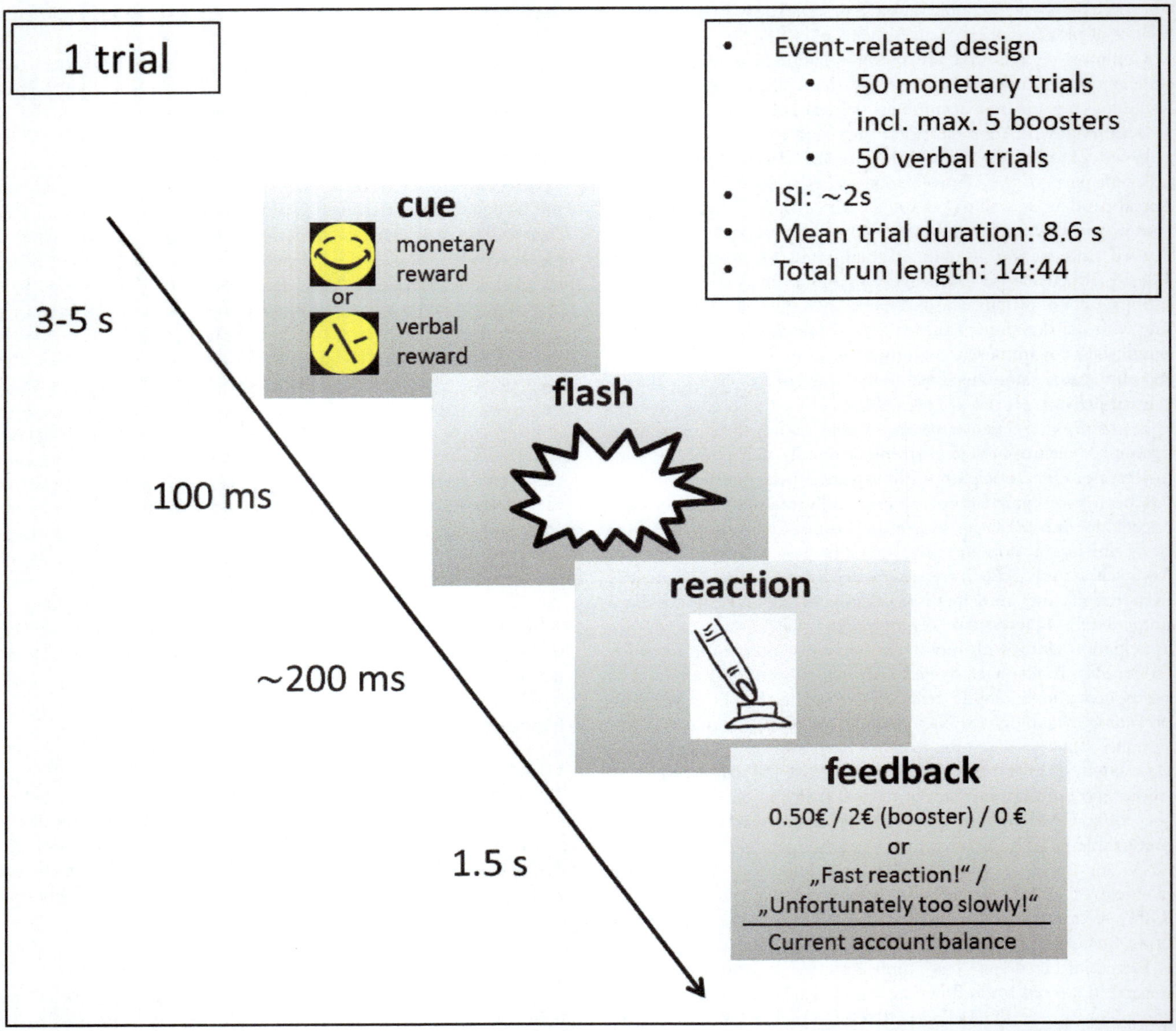

Figure 1. MID paradigm. The task requires a fast button press after a flash, indicated by either a laughing or a scrambled smiley, to receive either monetary or verbal feedback.

Psychological assessment

Early adversity was assessed using a standardized parent interview according to an 'enriched' family adversity index as proposed by Rutter and Quinton [41]. The interview comprised 11 items covering characteristics of the family environment (e.g., Overcrowding: More than 1.0 person per room or size of housing $\leq 50\ m^2$), the parents (e.g., Parental psychiatric disorder: Moderate to severe disorder according to DSM-III-R criteria) and their partnership (e.g., Unwanted pregnancy: An abortion was seriously considered) during a period of one year prior to the assessment (see Table S1). A total early family adversity (EFA) score was formed by counting the number of items present at the 3-month assessment [mean = 1.71±1.87; range: 0–7; Cronbach's alpha = .72]. The EFA index is a prospective and comprehensive measure of family adversity and does not exclusively focus on emotional and sexual abuse or neglect. Empirical evidence has largely confirmed the cumulative risk hypothesis that the likelihood of unfavorable child outcomes increases with the number of adversity factors [42]. Furthermore, a series of studies conducted in the context of the Mannheim Study of Children at Risk have provided evidence of the current validity of the family adversity measure [39,43,44]. The Structured Clinical Interview for DSM-IV (SCID-I German version) [45] was administered to measure young adults' psychiatric disorders. To examine current drug use, participants completed a substance use inventory [46]. Lifetime ADHD symptoms were assessed with the Mannheim Parent Interview (MEI) [47] at age 2, 4, 8 and 11 years and with the Schedule for Affective Disorders and Schizophrenia for School- Aged Children (K-SADS-PL) [48], German version [49] at age 15 years and sum scores were formed, indexing the severity and persistence of ADHD. The MEI is a highly structured interview adapted from Rutter's parent interviews to include all symptoms related to major DSM-IV diagnoses, and has been shown to be a sensitive measure of child disturbance [40,50,51]. With regard to ADHD, agreement with an independent child psychiatric examination was seen in 100% of cases. The K-SADS is a widely used structured diagnostic interview completed independently by parents and adolescents with established reliability and validity [52]. Information from different sources was combined by the logical operator OR.

Experimental paradigm

The fMRI paradigm (Figure 1) was a modified version of the MID task [53,54], probing reward anticipation and delivery which was adapted to simultaneous EEG-fMRI measurements. Previous results using this paradigm have shown reliable and robust activation of the VS [55]. The task requires a fast button press directly after a flash target following a reward anticipation cue to win a potential reward. Targets followed cues which consistently signaled different types of reward anticipation (unlike in reversal-learning paradigm): either a happy smiley signaling that responding fast enough would yield a monetary feedback (0.50 Euro), or a scrambled smiley indicating only verbal feedback ("Fast reaction!"; usually treated as the control condition). Smileys were used to further minimize learning effects. After every trial, the participants were informed about the current account balance. Boost trials with a monetary reward of 2 Euro instead of 0.50 Euro were given approximately every eighth win trial in order to improve the participants' motivational level. In total, 50 monetary and 50 verbal trials were presented in a pseudo-randomized order. The cue duration (and consequently trial length) was jittered (3-5sec) to cover the whole hemodynamic response function (HRF). The reaction time window (common for both reward conditions) was adaptively tailored to account for inter-individual differences and to yield comparable winnings across participants.

Data acquisition

1. EEG. The EEG was recorded inside the scanner using an MRI-compatible EEG system with 5 kHz sampling rate, 32 mV input range and 0.1–250 Hz band-pass filters. The signal was measured by equidistantly spaced silver/silver chloride (Ag/AgCl) scalp electrodes using EEG caps with twisted and fixed electrode cables (Easycap, Munich, Germany). The 60-channel EEG montage included most 10–10 system positions (for further information see Plichta et al. [55]). F1 served as recording reference, and F2 as the ground electrode. Four additional electrodes were placed to record the electro-oculogram (EOG) and the electrocardiogram (ECG). Via optic fibers, the signal was transmitted from two MRI-compatible amplifiers (Brain Products, Gilching, Germany) outside the scanner room. Electrode impedances were kept below 20 kΩ, except for ECG and EOG electrodes (<30 kΩ) as well as reference and ground (<10 kΩ). The EEG was monitored while scanning using online correction software (RecView Brain Products, Gilching, Germany).

2. fMRI. The fMRI data was recorded on a 3 Tesla whole-body scanner (Magnetom Trio, Siemens Erlangen, Germany). fMRI data were measured using a T2*-weighted EPI sequence with the following parameters: 400 volumes, 36 slices in ascending order and oriented 20° steeper than AC-PC-plane, 3mm slice thickness, TR/TE = 2210/28 ms, FOV = 220×220 mm, 64×64 matrix, Flip angle = 90°. A T1-weighted anatomical 3D sequence (MPRAGE) was acquired for each subject. The paradigm was created with Presentation software (Neurobehavioural Systems Inc., Albany, USA) and presented via video goggles (Resonance Technology Inc., Northridge, USA). Performance of participants was recorded using response pads (Current Designs, Philadelphia, USA & Presentation software).

Data analysis

1. Behavior. Reaction times (RT) were averaged across trials per condition (monetary, verbal) and the amount of win trials per condition was summed up. Condition differences were examined by means of paired t-tests, effects of EFA with linear regression analysis. The interaction between EFA and condition with regard to behavioral measures was obtained using repeated measures ANOVAs in SPSS Software package (Version 20, IBM Corp., Armonk, USA).

2. EEG. EEG data were corrected for MRI gradient [56] and cardioballistic artifacts [57] using standard template subtraction procedures as implemented in the Brain Vision Analyzer software 2.0 (Brain Products, Gilching, Germany). EEG data were digitally low-pass filtered (70 Hz) and down-sampled to 500 Hz. After exclusion of physical artifacts via raw data inspection, infomax independent component analysis (ICA) [6,58] was used to remove ocular (blinks, movements) and residual cardioballistic artifacts [59] related to gradient modulation. EEG data were re-referenced to the average reference, baseline-corrected to a 500 ms pre-stimulus interval and low-pass filtered with a cut-off of 30 Hz. Segmentation into ERP epochs of 3.5 seconds began 500 ms prior to cue onset. ERP averages for both conditions (monetary and verbal feedback) were calculated for each participant. The CNV at electrode Cz, commonly showing the highest amplitude and therefore the best signal-to-noise [29,38], was measured as the mean amplitude for the 2–3-second time window following cue onset.

3. fMRI. The fMRI data was analyzed using statistical parametric mapping (SPM8; Wellcome Trust Centre for Neuroimaging, London, UK). Preprocessing included slice-time correction, realignment (motion correction), spatial normalization into Montreal Neurological Institute space, resampling to 2×2×2 mm and spatial smoothing with an 8-mm full-width at half maximum (FWHM) Gaussian kernel. Spatial normalization was performed by coregistering the realigned mean image to the anatomical image, normalizing the anatomical image to the T1 template and applying these transformation parameters to the time series.

Individual first-level analysis was performed by linear regression analysis. A general linear model with eight regressors of interest (laughing and scrambled smiley, flash, response, monetary and verbal, win and no-win trials, respectively) was designed and convolved with the SPM hemodynamic response function (HRF). Six motion parameters were included in the design matrix and modeled as regressors of no interest. A high-pass filter with a cut-off frequency of 1/128 Hz was used to attenuate low-frequency components. All analyses were corrected for serially correlated errors by fitting a first-order autoregressive process (AR[1]) to the error term.

First-level contrasts were implemented in the second-level group analysis (monetary>verbal cue; win>no-win; monetary win> monetary no-win; verbal win>verbal no-win) with EFA embedded as a covariate of interest and controlling for gender. In a subsequent analysis, results were controlled for subclinical psychopathology as measured using the Young Adult Self-Report (YASR) [60] at the current assessment. A statistical threshold of

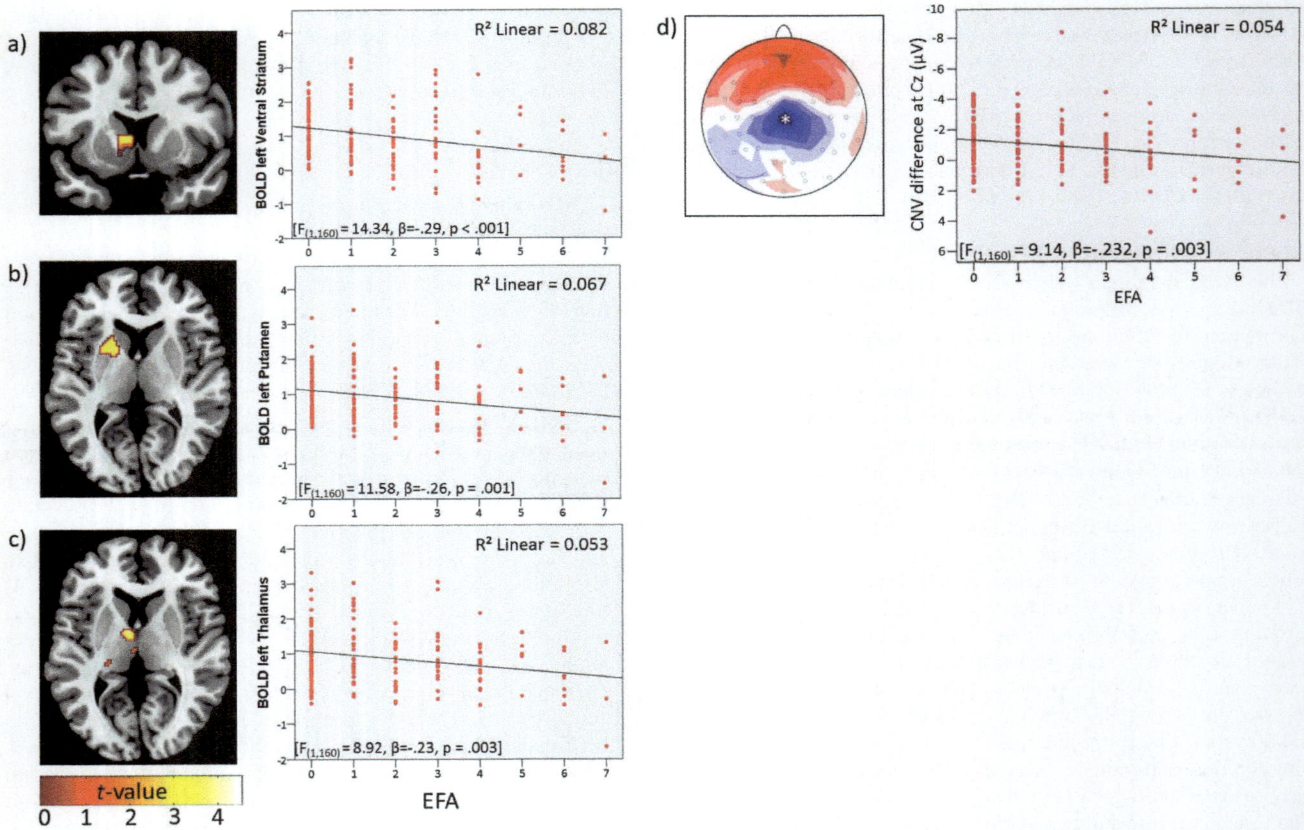

Figure 2. Left: neuronal activity ($p_{FWE}<.05$; ROI corr.) for the contrast monetary > verbal reward during reward anticipation by early family adversity (EFA) in **a)** left VS, **b)** left putamen and **c)** left thalamus; right: scatterplots of the correlations between the mean BOLD response of the respective regions and EFA; **d)** left: Scalp distribution of CNV difference (monetary > verbal condition; mean difference: 2–3 sec after stimulus presentation) dependent on EFA; right: scatterplot of the correlation between CNV difference at Cz (marked with an asterisk) and EFA [$F_{(1,160)}=9.14$, $p=.003$].

$p<.001$ (uncorrected) was applied in a whole-brain analysis and, a region of interest (ROI) analysis was performed. ROIs were anatomically labeled with WFU PickAtlas [61], determining putamen, pallidum, ACC, thalamus, insula, hippocampus and substantia nigra as ROIs of interest [11,12]. Results were thresholded at $p<.05$; family-wise error (FWE) corrected. The VS mask was defined according to Plichta et al. [38] as a fusion of the "caudate head" mask taken from the WFU-PickAtlas (human-atlas TD Brodmann areas+) and the "accumbens" mask from the Harvard–Oxford Subcortical Structural Atlas (implemented in FSLView 3.1.8; see http://www.cma.mgh.harvard.edu/fsl_atlas.html; probability threshold was set to 50%). The left and right VS were treated as separate ROIs. The hippocampus mask was divided along the y-axis in an anterior and a posterior part with MARINA [62] according to Poppenk et al. [63]. Mean beta values (across all voxels within ROIs) were imported into SPSS 20 for linear regression analysis. Post-hoc repeated measures ANOVAs, with *Phase* (Anticipation/Delivery) as the repeated factor and EFA as a covariate of interest were calculated for the left VS, right insula and left putamen ROIs. The same type of ANOVA was also conducted using the input of two different ROIs (left VS for reward anticipation/right insula for reward delivery), in order to directly examine the effects of phase in those regions which showed the highest activation in the separate ROI-analysis from each phase. In addition, a post-hoc factorial analysis provided a direct test of the interaction between condition (monetary vs. verbal) and outcome (win vs. no-win) during the delivery phase.

4. Association between early life stress, ADHD symptoms and neuronal activation. Pearson correlations were computed to establish the relationship of the significant cluster of neuronal activation with EFA and ADHD symptoms. A mediation analysis was conducted to assess whether a possible effect of EFA on ADHD symptoms is mediated by neuronal activation. Mediation was tested following previous work of our group [38] by means of the Sobel test [64] accompanied by a bootstrapping method with $N=5000$ samples [65] using SPSS 20.

Results

Behavior

Behavioral data analysis showed a performance advantage for RT and number of win trials when contrasting the monetary with the verbal condition. Participants responded faster after the presentation of a monetary relative to a verbal cue (monetary: 195.81±26.78 ms; verbal: 225.52±41.96 ms; $t_{(161)}=-10.56$; $p<.001$) and won a monetary trial more often than a verbal trial (monetary: 28.55±2.97; verbal: 21.52±3.19; $t_{(161)}=15.01$; $p<.001$). A significant effect of EFA on RT of monetary trials emerged ($F_{(1,160)}=9.22$, $p=.003$), with RT increasing with the level of adversity. A similar effect was observed for the verbal reward condition ($F_{(1,160)} = 6.45$, $p = .012$), after exclusion of one participant who exceeded the 3-fold interquartile range. No effect of EFA on the number of win trials (monetary: $F_{(1,160)} = .03$; $p = .863$; verbal: $F_{(1,160)} = .395$; $p = .531$) and no interaction between EFA and condition on RT ($F_{(7,154)} = .609$, $p = .748$) or number of win trials ($F_{(7,153)} = .076$, $p = .999$) was found. All participants gained money (mean: 21.91 €±2.02; range: 16.00–26.50 €). No effect of EFA on payoff emerged ($F_{(1,160)} = .040$; $p = .843$).

EEG

A task effect on the contingent negative variation (CNV) revealed that the anticipation of a monetary reward induced a higher CNV than the anticipation of a verbal reward [$t_{(161)} = -7.18$; $p < .001$; see Figure S3]. Furthermore, an effect of EFA indicated that the CNV (contrasting monetary to verbal reward) decreased when EFA increased (see Figure 2d).

fMRI

1. Effects on reward anticipation. Whole-brain analysis contrasting monetary to verbal reward anticipation revealed higher activation of reward-related regions (VS, supplementary motor area and anterior cingulate cortex, all $p_{FWE} < .0001$; see Figure S1a). Furthermore, a ROI-analysis revealed a significant effect of EFA on the contrast (monetary>verbal) in the VS, putamen, pallidum, left thalamus, left insula, left ACC and right anterior hippocampus ($p_{FWE} < .05$; ROI-corrected; see Table 1), indicating that activation in these regions decreased with the level of EFA. Figure 2a–c shows the respective activation maps together with corresponding extracted mean betas for the predefined ROIs, estimated by linear regression. Results remained constant or even improved (VS left: $t = 4.65$, $p < .001$; putamen left: $t = 4.36$, $p = .001$; pallidum left: $t = 4.37$, $p < .001$), when controlling for subclinical psychopathology at the current assessment.

2. Effects on reward delivery. Whole-brain analysis of the reward delivery phase induced similarly robust activation of reward-related areas (for the win>no-win contrast; task effect, pooling of monetary and verbal feedback), specifically the putamen, caudate, left inferior frontal gyrus, and right dorsolateral prefrontal cortex ($p_{FWE} < .0001$; see Figure S1b). In addition, a ROI-analysis indicated a significant effect of EFA on the former mentioned contrast, with increasing activation in the bilateral insula, right pallidum and bilateral putamen with the level of EFA ($p_{FWE} < .05$; ROI-corrected; see Table 2). Activation maps and extracted mean betas are displayed in Figure 3. Separate analysis for verbal outcome revealed that with increasing EFA, participants showed higher activation in the bilateral insula, pallidum, substantia nigra and right posterior hippocampus (contrasting verbal win>no-win; $p_{FWE} < .05$; ROI-corrected; see Table 3). Activation maps and extracted mean betas are displayed in Figure 4. In contrast, there was no significant EFA effect on activation in reward-related areas for monetary outcomes (regression analysis for left insula: $F_{(1,160)} = 1.41$, $p = .24$; right insula: $F_{(1,160)} = 1.47$, $p = .23$; left putamen: $F_{(1,160)} = 1.42$, $p = .24$; right putamen: $F_{(1,160)} = 2.7$, $p = .10$; right pallidum: $F_{(1,160)} = 2.73$, $p = .10$). Results for both contrasts (win>no-win, verbal win>no-win) were attenuated, when controlling for subclinical psychopathology at the current assessment, but still remained significant (win>no-win: putamen right: $t = 3.56$, $p = .021$, pallidum right: $t = 3.19$, $p = .021$, insula right: $t = 4.17$, $p = .005$; verbal win>no-win: pallidum right: $t = 3.43$, $p = .011$, posterior hippocampus right: $t = 3.97$, $p = .003$, insula right: $t = 4.15$, $p = .006$).The factorial interaction (directly testing increased EFA-related modulation of verbal>monetary wins) revealed overlapping activation with the verbal outcome in a hippocampal area, indicating that the difference between the EFA-related activation for win>no-win trials was higher for verbal than for monetary outcome.

Furthermore, a significant negative correlation between neuronal activation during reward anticipation and delivery emerged, indicating that activation of the left VS decreased during anticipation when activation of the right insula [$r = -.189$; $p = .016$] and right pallidum [$r = -.225$; $p = .004$] increased during delivery (see Figure S2).

3. Interaction between *Phase* (Anticipation/Delivery) and EFA. A significant interaction between Phase and EFA was obtained in all three ROIs (left VS: $F_{(1,160)} = 7.36$, $p = .007$; right insula: $F_{(1,160)} = 10.32$, $p = .002$; left putamen: $F_{(1,160)} = 10.75$, $p = .001$), when considering the same ROIs for both stages of reward processing. Post-hoc regression analysis revealed that the interaction effect in the left VS was driven by anticipation alone (anticipation: $F_{(1,160)} = 14.33$, $p < .001$; delivery: $F_{(1,160)} = 1.31$, $p = .255$), while, in the other ROIs, it was driven by both anticipation and delivery (right insula: anticipation: $F_{(1,160)} = 4.33$, $p = .039$; delivery: $F_{(1,160)} = 7.68$, $p = .006$; left putamen: anticipation: $F_{(1,160)} = 11.58$, $p = .001$; delivery: $F_{(1,160)} = 4.22$, $p = .042$). Additionally, a significant interaction between Phase and EFA emerged, when considering different ROIs for both reward processing stages (anticipation: left VS; delivery: right insula; $F_{(1,160)} = 17.72$, $p < .001$).

Correlation of fMRI activation with behavioral measures and CNV

Negative correlations between RT to monetary trials and neuronal activation (VS, putamen, thalamus) during reward anticipation, contrasting monetary over verbal reward, occurred in several regions (VS: $r = -.347$; $p < .01$; putamen: $r = -.367$; $p < .01$; thalamus: $r = -.345$; $p = < .01$). The analogous correlation emerged between RT and CNV contrasting monetary over verbal reward ($r = -.215$; $p < .01$). No significant correlation for RT of verbal trials was found. Furthermore, the number of monetary win trials was positively related to neuronal activation during reward anticipation contrasting monetary over verbal reward (VS: $r = -.321$; $p < .01$; putamen: $r = -.360$; $p < .01$; thalamus: $r = -.328$; $p = < .01$). A similar finding was obtained for the number of verbal win trials (VS: $r = -.198$; $p < .05$; putamen: $r = -.220$; $p < .01$; thalamus: $r = -.187$; $p = < .05$). There was no significant correlation between the number of win trials and CNV. A significant negative correlation of fMRI activation with the CNV during reward anticipation (contrasting monetary to verbal cues for both measures) emerged (VS: $r = -.215$; $p = .006$; putamen: $r = -.222$; $p = .004$; thalamus: $r = -.250$; $p = .001$), showing that the CNV decreased when fMRI activity increased.

Correlation of neuronal activity (fMRI/CNV) and EFA with lifetime ADHD

There was a significant correlation of fMRI activation contrasting monetary to verbal cues during reward anticipation in the left VS with ADHD symptoms, revealing decreasing activity with the number of ADHD symptoms ($r = -.160$; $p = .042$).

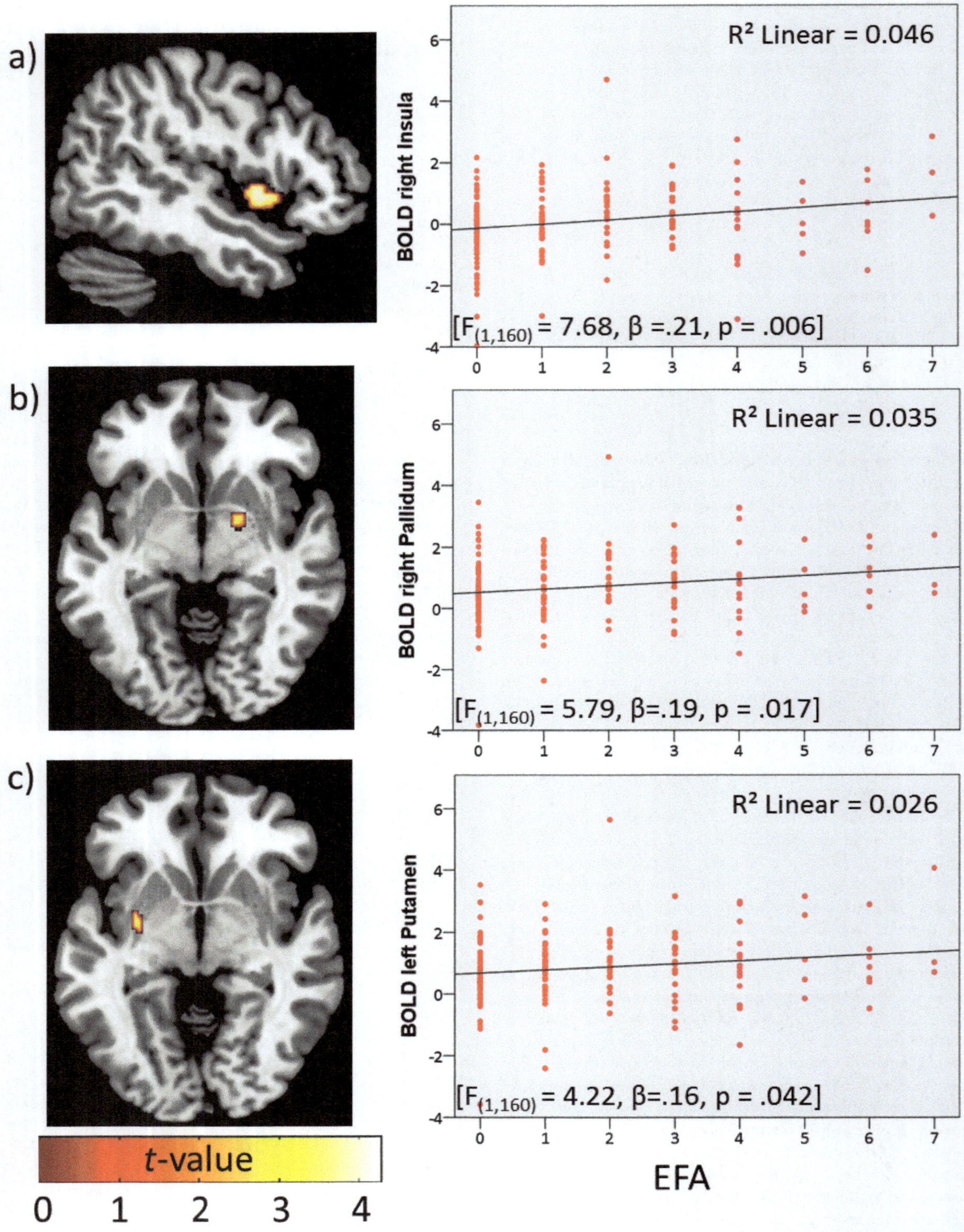

Figure 3. Left: neuronal activity (p_{FWE}<.05; ROI corr.) for the contrast win > no-win trials during reward delivery by EFA in **a**) right insula, **b**) right pallidum and **c**) left putamen; right: scatterplots of the correlations between the mean BOLD response of the respective regions and EFA.

Moreover, a significant correlation of fMRI activation contrasting win to no-win trials during reward delivery of the right insula with ADHD symptoms was obtained, showing increasing activity with the number of ADHD symptoms (r = .203; p = .01). In contrast, the CNV was found to be unrelated to ADHD symptoms (r = .10; p = .207). Furthermore, EFA correlated significantly with ADHD

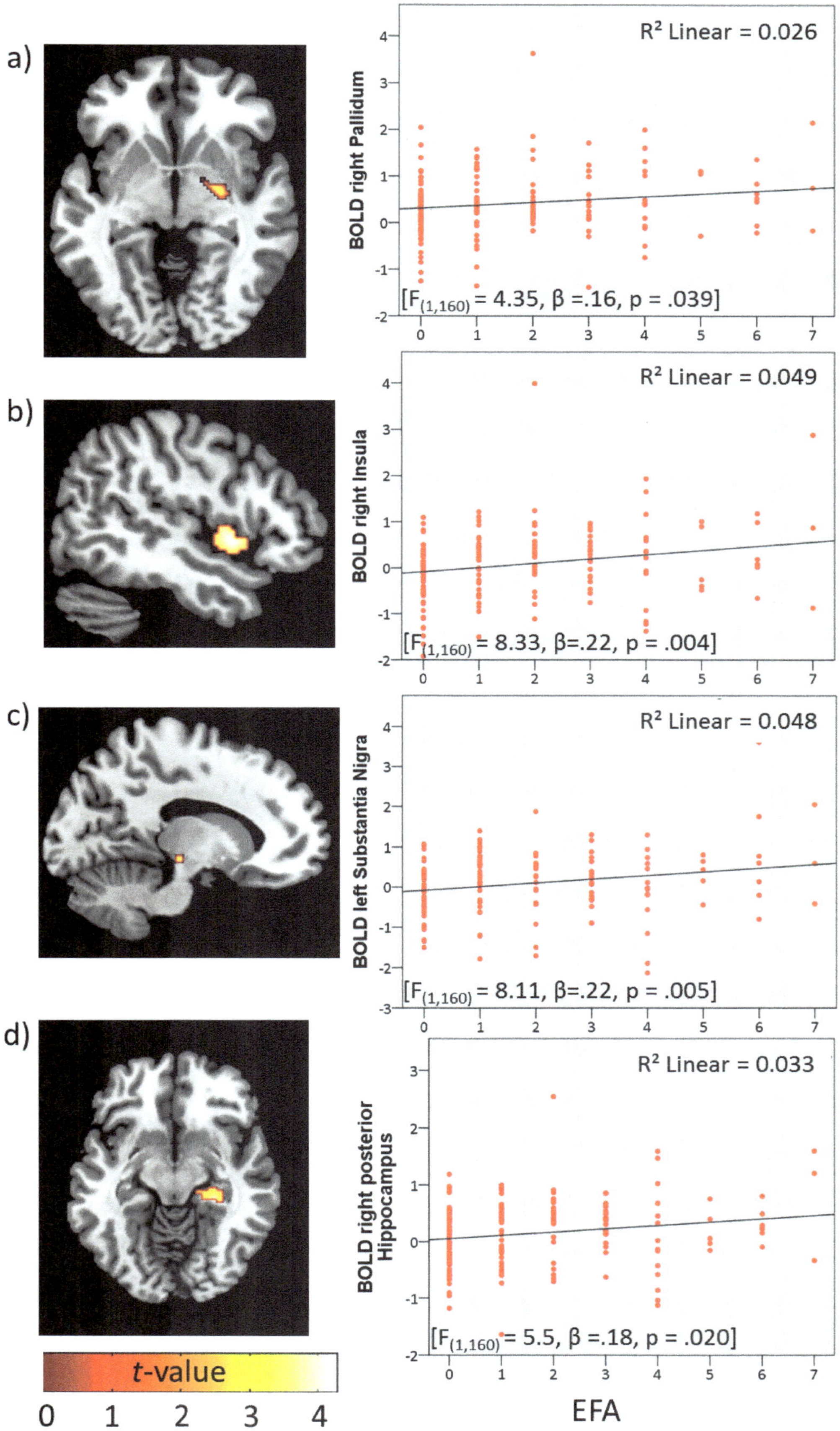
a)
b)
c)
d)
t-value
0 1 2 3 4
R² Linear = 0.026
BOLD right Pallidum
[F(1,160) = 4.35, β =.16, p = .039]
R² Linear = 0.049
BOLD right Insula
[F(1,160) = 8.33, β=.22, p = .004]
R² Linear = 0.048
BOLD left Substantia Nigra
[F(1,160) = 8.11, β=.22, p = .005]
R² Linear = 0.033
BOLD right posterior Hippocampus
[F(1,160) = 5.5, β =.18, p = .020]
EFA

Figure 4. Left: neuronal activity ($p_{FWE}<.05$; ROI corr.) for the contrast verbal win > no-win trials during reward delivery by EFA in **a**) right pallidum, **b**) right insula, **c**) left substantia nigra and **d**) right posterior hippocampus; right: scatterplots of the correlations between the mean BOLD response of the respective regions and EFA.

symptoms ($r=.285$; $p<.001$). The mediation analysis of the association between EFA and ADHD symptoms revealed no significant mediation by neuronal activation (left VS: $Z=1.01$, $p=.31$, 95% CI: −.019 □ .084; right insula: $Z=1.52$, $p=.13$, 95% CI: 0 □ .105).

Discussion

The current simultaneous EEG-fMRI study investigated the long-term impact of early life adversity on neuronal alterations of the reward system into adulthood. Using data of an epidemiological cohort study from birth onwards, the results presented above provided evidence of altered reward processing later in life following exposure to early adversity. Specifically, our findings demonstrated a differential impact of adversity on neural responding to distinct phases of reward processing, indicating that the activation of specific reward-related brain areas (VS, putamen, thalamus) decreased with the level of adversity during reward anticipation, while there was an increase in activity of other reward-related areas (pallidum, insula, substantia nigra, right posterior hippocampus) with the level of adversity during reward delivery. The fMRI finding during reward anticipation converged with EEG results showing a negative association between the CNV and adversity, matching the negative correlation of CNV with fMRI activation. Further analysis of the single reward conditions revealed striking effects of early adversity on the processing of verbal reward, which accounted for major parts of the total reward-related activity during the delivery phase.

Reward anticipation & early life stress

The results of the present study replicate recent findings with regard to reward anticipation [10,33], highlighting deficits in the reward processing circuitry associated with exposure to early adversity. While in these studies, small samples of individuals exposed to severe childhood adversity (maltreatment, deprivation) were investigated, the present study extends these findings to a substantially larger number of individuals from an epidemiological cohort study who experienced low to moderate levels of adversity. Moreover, in contrast to these studies, which included maltreated individuals with a current psychiatric disorder, the present analysis focused on currently healthy individuals only. The observed activation of the VS, the putamen and the thalamus is in accordance with previous research, supporting the assumption of a specific reward circuitry affected by stress in early life [11,12]. Interestingly, while Dillon et al. [10] reported less activation for maltreated individuals in the left pallidum and putamen, we replicated this effect for the putamen and, additionally, for the thalamus and the VS, the latter serving as the core region of reward processing. The prominent role of the thalamus in the reward circuit has recently been established by the demonstration of a strong direct link to the nucleus accumbens in studies measuring effective connectivity using dynamic causal modeling [38,66].

The finding of a negative association between the CNV and early adversity, which to our knowledge is new to the field, provides additional evidence to substantiate the hypothesis of an adversity-driven dysfunctional neuronal reward circuit, suggesting that reward processing is already impaired less than three seconds after cue onset. This result supports the notion of a reward-driven variability of the CNV-like activity preceding uncertain feedback, and is in accordance with previous findings of a relationship between CNV and reward anticipation [23–25]. Along the same lines, slower RTs with the level of EFA during reward anticipation were found to be linked with blunted neuronal activity and a reduced CNV.

Reward delivery & early life stress

The finding that neural activity in reward-related areas increased with the level of early adversity during reward delivery is in contrast to previous studies [10,33], which were unable to establish an effect of adversity on the processing of reward outcomes. Several reasons may account for this inconsistency: First, given our substantially larger sample, the present study had a considerably higher power to uncover effects of adversity. Second, a continuous, prospective measure of adversity such as applied in

Table 1. Regional BOLD changes to monetary > verbal reward by EFA.

Region	MNI coordinates	k cluster size	t value	p value*
VS left	−8 4 4	157	4.52	.000
VS right	14 14 6	49	3.18	.019
Putamen left	−18 6 12	434	4.10	.003
Putamen right	34 8 −2	394	3.75	.010
Pallidum left	−10 2 2	180	4.30	.006
Pallidum right	18 4 6	174	3.62	.006
ACC left	−14 36 20	110	4.24	.003
Thalamus left	−10 −2 6	44	4.13	.018
Insula left	−38 18 −6	41	3.81	.007
Anterior hippocampus right	18 −6 −12	15	3.56	.010

* FWE corrected at a threshold of .05, $k \geq 10$.

Table 2. Regional BOLD changes to win > no-win trials by EFA.

Region	MNI coordinates	k cluster size	t-value	p value*
Insula right	48 8 −2	78	4.25	.004
Insula left	−46 4 −4	13	3.84	.016
Putamen left	−32 −4 4	17	3.77	.011
Putamen right	32 2 4	24	3.63	.017
Pallidum right	18 0 −4	23	3.31	.015

* FWE corrected at a threshold of .05, k≥10.

this study may enable the detection of subtle adversity-modulated reward activation in contrast to a case-control design. Third, differences in the MID tasks used to assess reward processing may contribute to the discrepant findings. While in our study, monetary reward was contrasted with verbal reward as a control condition, others included a loss condition or used different intensities of monetary reward as contrasts [10,33]. This reduces the number of trials per condition and, in combination with small sample sizes, may lead to reduced effect sizes and less sensitivity to reward outcome.

The activation of the pallidum, insula, hippocampus and substantia nigra demonstrated here is in accordance with the assumption of the phasic transmission of reward information via dopaminergic projections from the midbrain to the VS [67]. The hippocampal area plays a prominent role in regulating the reward circuit [68,69] by showing afferent and efferent projections to the VS [70], regulating emotional, motivational and learning processes [71,72]. The observation of more pronounced EFA-related modulation following verbal reward may indicate a specific sensitivity for social reward appreciation in individuals exposed to high adversity in early childhood, which might be specifically represented by activation of the hippocampus. The VS directly projects to the pallidum, integrating reward information and driving action output [11,73]. Moreover, pallidum activation affected by early adversity, as previously found for reward anticipation [10], suggests a high involvement of the basal ganglia in reward processing, including both the anticipation and outcome phase. A specific activation of the medial orbitofrontal and ventromedial prefrontal cortex during reward delivery as proposed by Diekhof et al. [11] was not supported by the current study. This might be due to the absence of different magnitudes in monetary rewards in the present MID paradigm, which have been suggested to be processed by frontal activation.

Our finding that the impact of early adversity on reward outcome was only marked in the verbal reward control condition highlights the special reward quality of this condition, and may suggest that individuals exposed to early adversity are particularly prone to social rewards, such as verbal praise. This higher responsiveness to social rewards may result from the experience of poor parenting during childhood in individuals exposed to early family adversity [74–76], which may have increased the rewarding effect of social stimuli later in life. A retrospective cohort study by Baker and Hoerger [77] has implicated dysfunctional parenting, including low parental warmth or high rejection and control, in the development of difficulty delaying gratification. Such findings may support the hypothesis that poor parenting may lead to a reward deficiency syndrome [78], resulting in increased social reward retrieval.

Reward processing & acute vs. early life stress

In contrast to our results, Kumar et al. [34], when investigating the impact of acute stress on reward processing, reported an opposite activation pattern in regions (caudate [VS], putamen) partly overlapping with ours, indicating increased neuronal activation during reward anticipation and decreased activation while receiving a reward. These findings underpin the functional differences between the impact of acute stress vs. early life stress on reward processing. Specifically, it has been demonstrated that the stress (HPA axis) and the reward system show considerable overlap on both the structural and the functional level [35]. Acute stress leads to an up regulation of HPA axis activity, thereby increasing

Table 3. Regional BOLD changes to *verbal* win > no-win trials by EFA.

Region	MNI coordinates	k cluster size	t-value	p value*
Pallidum right	22 −8 −4	29	3.60	.006
Pallidum left	−24 −12 −4	15	3.41	.012
Posterior hippocampus right	28 −30 −10	61	4.12	.004
Insula left	−46 4 −4	54	4.44	.002
Insula right	48 8 −2	93	4.24	.004
Substantia nigra left	−12 −20 −10	15	3.59	.002
Substantia nigra right	10 −18 −12	14	3.02	.010

* FWE corrected at a threshold of .05, k≥10.

motivation and approach behaviors, but blunting reward responsiveness [79–82]. In contrast, early life stress may result in an adaptation of HPA axis activity with first increased cortisol release during stress exposure followed by later hypocortisolism [83,84] which might be linked to decreased dopamine transmission during reward anticipation but increased when receiving a reward.

Reward processing, early life stress & ADHD

Our findings provide additional insights into the relationship between altered reward processing in individuals exposed to early adversity and mental disorders related to dysfunction of the dopamine reward circuit, such as ADHD. The differential effect of early life stress on both stages of reward processing, characterized by hyporesponsiveness in individuals exposed to high early adversity when anticipating a monetary reward and hyperresponsiveness when receiving a reward, is in line with the literature on dysfunctional reward processing in ADHD [8,9,14–17]. Accordingly, there was a significant association between fMRI activation in reward-related regions and lifetime ADHD symptoms, showing the same differential effect on anticipatory and delivery phases as observed for early life stress. Given that the latter represents a major risk factor of ADHD [43], this might suggest an impact of EFA on ADHD via a dysfunctional reward pathway. Here, this pathway could not be confirmed by the mediation analysis. In contrast to fMRI, the CNV proved to be unrelated to ADHD. As the CNV has been identified as a stable ADHD marker for preparation deficits measured by cognitive paradigms such as the CPT [29,30], this result might be an effect of paradigm. Although there was a significant impact of EFA on the CNV, reward anticipation as part of an emotional paradigm might be less sensitive to ADHD effects than cognitive paradigms. However, given the significant correlation between CNV and fMRI activation, the different measures alone could not explain this differential effect.

Limitations

Several limitations have to be considered in the interpretation of our results. First, due to reduced data quality following the button press, it was not possible to analyze EEG feedback components such as the feedback-related negativity [26]. However, it would be most interesting to examine whether EEG feedback components would display a similar pattern of outcome-related EFA effects to that found for fMRI. Second, given the small effect size of EFA and the fact that several characteristics of EFA would not change during the individual's life course, the results cannot be attributed to early life stress alone but probably also reflects stress during later development [2]. Third, the present results do not provide evidence of the mechanisms mediating between exposure to EFA and altered reward processing in adulthood. Several mechanisms have been discussed as determining the transduction of environmental influences into changes in brain physiology and morphology. Among these, a major role has been attributed to epigenetic regulation [85,86]. Hence, the investigation of epigenetic signatures induced by exposure to EFA that persist into adulthood appears to be a promising research perspective. Fourth, current research has highlighted the differential susceptibility of individuals to EFA. Greater insight into the interplay between environmental and genetic factors that affect reward processing may further contribute to a better understanding of the underlying mechanisms. Genes that have been shown to exert remarkable effects on the reward circuit include, among others, the dopamine transporter gene (DAT) [87,88] and the catechol-O-methyltransferase gene (COMT) [6,89,90].

Conclusion

In sum, the present findings provide evidence of a differential long-term impact of early life adversity on two distinct phases of reward processing in adulthood, characterized by hyporesponsiveness during reward anticipation followed by hyperresponsiveness when receiving a reward. Moreover, a similar activation pattern related to lifetime ADHD may suggest that the impact of early life stress on ADHD may possibly be mediated by a dysfunctional reward pathway.

Supporting Information

Figure S1 Whole-brain task effects a) during the anticipation of monetary vs. verbal rewards, indicating significantly higher activation in the ventral striatum (VS), thalamus, anterior cingulate cortex, supplementary motor area, primary motor area and occipital cortex and b) during reward delivery (win vs. no-win), yielding significantly higher activation in the putamen, caudate, left inferior frontal gyrus, right dorsolateral prefrontal cortex, primary motor area, right medial frontal gyrus and occipital cortex (all $p_{FWE}<.0001$; $k\geq20$).

Figure S2 Significant negative correlation of activation in the left VS during reward anticipation with a) right insula activation (pooled reward) [$r=-.189$; $p=.016$] and b) right pallidum activation (verbal reward) [$r=-.225$; $p=.004$] during reward delivery.

Figure S3 Grand average ERPs showing the stronger contingent negative variation (CNV) developing at electrode Cz (marked with an asterisk) after the presentation of monetary (happy smiley, black curve) compared to verbal (scrambled smiley, red curve) reward cues; $p<.001$ in the analysis time window (blue, 2–3 sec following cue onset and preceding target onset on all trials).

Table S1 Definition of early family adversity (EFA) items.

Author Contributions

Conceived and designed the experiments: ML D. Brandeis TB AML. Performed the experiments: RB NEH SB. Analyzed the data: RB. Contributed reagents/materials/analysis tools: AFB D. Blomeyer MMP IW. Contributed to the writing of the manuscript: RB ML D. Brandeis.

References

1. Lupien SJ, McEwen BS, Gunnar MR, Heim C (2009) Effects of stress throughout the lifespan on the brain, behaviour and cognition. Nat Rev Neurosci 10: 434–445.
2. Heim C, Binder EB (2012) Current research trends in early life stress and depression: review of human studies on sensitive periods, gene-environment interactions, and epigenetics. Exp Neurol 233: 102–111.

3. McLaughlin KA, Greif GJ, Gruber MJ, Sampson NA, Zaslavsky AM, et al. (2012) Childhood adversities and first onset of psychiatric disorders in a national sample of US adolescents. Arch Gen Psychiatry 69: 1151–1160.
4. Pheula GF, Rohde LA, Schmitz M (2011) Are family variables associated with ADHD, inattentive type? A case-control study in schools. Eur Child Adolesc Psychiatry 20: 137–145.
5. Laucht M, Hohm E, Esser G, Schmidt MH, Becker K (2007) Association between ADHD and smoking in adolescence: shared genetic, environmental and psychopathological factors. J Neural Transm 114: 1097–1104.
6. Bates J, Bayles K, Bennet D, Ridge B, Brown M (1991) Origins of externalizing behavior problems at eight years of age. In: Pepler D, Rubin K, editors. The Development and Treatment of Childhood Aggression. Hillsdale, NJ: Lawrence Erlbaum.
7. Pressman LJ, Loo SK, Carpenter EM, Asarnow JR, Lynn D, et al. (2006) Relationship of family environment and parental psychiatric diagnosis to impairment in ADHD. J Am Acad Child Adolesc Psychiatry 45: 346–354.
8. Stark R, Bauer E, Merz CJ, Zimmermann M, Reuter M, et al. (2011) ADHD related behaviors are associated with brain activation in the reward system. Neuropsychologia 49: 426–434.
9. Scheres A, Lee A, Sumiya M (2008) Temporal reward discounting and ADHD: task and symptom specific effects. J Neural Transm 115: 221–226.
10. Dillon DG, Holmes AJ, Birk JL, Brooks N, Lyons-Ruth K, et al. (2009) Childhood adversity is associated with left basal ganglia dysfunction during reward anticipation in adulthood. Biol Psychiatry 66: 206–213.
11. Diekhof EK, Kaps L, Falkai P, Gruber O (2012) The role of the human ventral striatum and the medial orbitofrontal cortex in the representation of reward magnitude - an activation likelihood estimation meta-analysis of neuroimaging studies of passive reward expectancy and outcome processing. Neuropsychologia 50: 1252–1266.
12. Haber SN, Knutson B (2010) The reward circuit: linking primate anatomy and human imaging. Neuropsychopharmacology 35: 4–26.
13. Berridge KC, Robinson TE, Aldridge JW (2009) Dissecting components of reward: 'liking', 'wanting', and learning. Curr Opin Pharmacol 9: 65–73.
14. Plichta MM, Vasic N, Wolf RC, Lesch KP, Brummer D, et al. (2009) Neural hyporesponsiveness and hyperresponsiveness during immediate and delayed reward processing in adult attention-deficit/hyperactivity disorder. Biol Psychiatry 65: 7–14.
15. Strohle A, Stoy M, Wrase J, Schwarzer S, Schlagenhauf F, et al. (2008) Reward anticipation and outcomes in adult males with attention-deficit/hyperactivity disorder. Neuroimage 39: 966–972.
16. Furukawa E, Bado P, Tripp G, Mattos P, Wickens JR, et al. (2014) Abnormal Striatal BOLD Responses to Reward Anticipation and Reward Delivery in ADHD. PloS one 9: e89129.
17. Paloyelis Y, Mehta MA, Faraone SV, Asherson P, Kuntsi J (2012) Striatal sensitivity during reward processing in attention-deficit/hyperactivity disorder. J Am Acad Child Adolesc Psychiatry 51: 722–732.
18. Tripp G, Wickens JR (2008) Research review: dopamine transfer deficit: a neurobiological theory of altered reinforcement mechanisms in ADHD. J Child Psychol Psychiatry 49: 691–704.
19. Tripp G, Wickens JR (2009) Neurobiology of ADHD. Neuropharmacology 57: 579–589.
20. Walter WG, Cooper R, Aldridge VJ, McCallum WC, Winter AL (1964) Contingent negative variation: an electric sign of sensomotor association and expectancy in the human brain. Nature 203: 380–384.
21. Irwin DA, Knott JR, McAdam DW, Rebert CS (1966) Motivational determinants of the "contingent negative variation". Electroencephalogr Clin Neurophysiol 21: 538–543.
22. Brunia CH, Hackley SA, van Boxtel GJ, Kotani Y, Ohgami Y (2011) Waiting to perceive: reward or punishment? Clin Neurophysiol 122: 858–868.
23. Capa RL, Bouquet CA, Dreher JC, Dufour A (2013) Long-lasting effects of performance-contingent unconscious and conscious reward incentives during cued task-switching. Cortex 49: 1943–1954.
24. Kotani Y, Hiraku S, Suda K, Aihara Y (2001) Effect of positive and negative emotion on stimulus-preceding negativity prior to feedback stimuli. Psychophysiology 38: 873–878.
25. Pierson A, Ragot R, Ripoche A, Lesevre N (1987) Electrophysiological changes elicited by auditory stimuli given a positive or negative value: a study comparing anhedonic with hedonic subjects. Int J Psychophysiol 5: 107–123.
26. Broyd SJ, Richards HJ, Helps SK, Chronaki G, Bamford S, et al. (2012) An electrophysiological monetary incentive delay (e-MID) task: a way to decompose the different components of neural response to positive and negative monetary reinforcement. J Neurosci Methods 209: 40–49.
27. Goldstein RZ, Cottone LA, Jia Z, Maloney T, Volkow ND, et al. (2006) The effect of graded monetary reward on cognitive event-related potentials and behavior in young healthy adults. Int J Psychophysiol 62: 272–279.
28. Banaschewski T, Brandeis D, Heinrich H, Albrecht B, Brunner E, et al. (2003) Association of ADHD and conduct disorder–brain electrical evidence for the existence of a distinct subtype. J Child Psychol Psychiatry 44: 356–376.
29. Albrecht B, Brandeis D, Uebel H, Valko L, Heinrich H, et al. (2013) Familiality of neural preparation and response control in childhood attention deficit-hyperactivity disorder. Psychol Med 43: 1997–2011.
30. Doehnert M, Brandeis D, Schneider G, Drechsler R, Steinhausen HC (2013) A neurophysiological marker of impaired preparation in an 11-year follow-up study of attention-deficit/hyperactivity disorder (ADHD). J Child Psychol Psychiatry 54: 260–270.
31. van Leeuwen TH, Steinhausen HC, Overtoom CC, Pascual-Marqui RD, van't Klooster B, et al. (1998) The continuous performance test revisited with neuroelectric mapping: impaired orienting in children with attention deficits. Behav Brain Res 94: 97–110.
32. Guyer AE, Kaufman J, Hodgdon HB, Masten CL, Jazbec S, et al. (2006) Behavioral alterations in reward system function: the role of childhood maltreatment and psychopathology. J Am Acad Child Adolesc Psychiatry 45: 1059–1067.
33. Mehta MA, Gore-Langton E, Golembo N, Colvert E, Williams SC, et al. (2010) Hyporesponsive reward anticipation in the basal ganglia following severe institutional deprivation early in life. J Cogn Neurosci 22: 2316–2325.
34. Kumar P, Berghorst LH, Nickerson LD, Dutra SJ, Goer FK, et al. (2014) Differential effects of acute stress on anticipatory and consummatory phases of reward processing. Neuroscience 266C: 1–12.
35. Ulrich-Lai YM, Herman JP (2009) Neural regulation of endocrine and autonomic stress responses. Nat Rev Neurosci 10: 397–409.
36. Rademacher L, Krach S, Kohls G, Irmak A, Grunder G, et al. (2010) Dissociation of neural networks for anticipation and consumption of monetary and social rewards. Neuroimage 49: 3276–3285.
37. Delmonte S, Balsters JH, McGrath J, Fitzgerald J, Brennan S, et al. (2012) Social and monetary reward processing in autism spectrum disorders. Mol Autism 3: 7.
38. Plichta MM, Wolf I, Hohmann S, Baumeister S, Boecker R, et al. (2013) Simultaneous EEG and fMRI Reveals a Causally Connected Subcortical-Cortical Network during Reward Anticipation. J Neurosci 33: 14526–14533.
39. Laucht M, Esser G, Baving L, Gerhold M, Hoesch I, et al. (2000) Behavioral sequelae of perinatal insults and early family adversity at 8 years of age. J Am Acad Child and Adolesc Psychiatry 39: 1229–1237.
40. Laucht M, Esser G, Schmidt MH (1997) Developmental outcome of infants born with biological and psychosocial risks. J Child Psychol Psychiatry 38: 843–853.
41. Rutter M, Quinton D (1977) Psychiatric disorder - ecological factors and concepts of causation. In: McGurk M, editor. Ecological factors in human development. Amsterdam: North Holland. pp.173–187.
42. Evans GW, Li D, Whipple SS (2013) Cumulative risk and child development. Psychol Bull 139: 1342–1396.
43. Laucht M, Skowronek MH, Becker K, Schmidt MH, Esser G, et al. (2007) Interacting effects of the dopamine transporter gene and psychosocial adversity on attention-deficit/hyperactivity disorder symptoms among 15-year-olds from a high-risk community sample. Arch Gen Psychiatry 64: 585–590.
44. Laucht M, Treutlein J, Blomeyer D, Buchmann AF, Schmid B, et al. (2009) Interaction between the 5-HTTLPR serotonin transporter polymorphism and environmental adversity for mood and anxiety psychopathology: evidence from a high-risk community sample of young adults. Int J Neuropsychopharmacol 12: 737–747.
45. Wittchen HU, Zaudig M, Fydrich T (1997) [Structured clinical interview for DSM-IV Axis I and II - SCID]. Göttingen: Hogrefe.
46. Müller R, Abbet JP (1991) Changing trends in the consumption of legal and illegal drugs by 11-16-year-old adolescent pupils. Findings from a study conducted under the auspices of the WHO Europe. Lausanne: Swiss Professional Service for Alcohol Problems.
47. Esser G, Blanz B, Geisel B, Laucht M (1989) Mannheim Parent Interview - Structured interview for child psychiatric disorders. Weinheim: Beltz.
48. Kaufman J, Birmaher B, Brent D, Rao U, Ryan N (1996) Kiddie-Sads-Present and Lifetime Version (K-SADS_PL) [Internet]. Available: http://www.psychiatry.pitt.edu/node/8233.
49. Delmo C, Weiffenbach O, Gabriel M, Poustka F (2000) Kiddie-SADS-Present and Lifetime version (K-SADS-PL) 3. Auflage der deutschen Forschungsversion. Frankfurt. Available: http://www.adhs-essen.com/PDF/K-SADS_Fragebogen.pdf.
50. Laucht M, Esser G, Schmidt MH (2001) Differential development of infants at risk for psychopathology: the moderating role of early maternal responsivity. Dev Med Child Neurol 43: 292–300.
51. Holz NE, Boecker R, Baumeister S, Hohm E, Zohsel K, et al. (2014) Effect of Prenatal Exposure to Tobacco Smoke on Inhibitory Control: Neuroimaging Results From a 25-Year Prospective Study. JAMA Psychiatry.
52. Kaufman J, Birmaher B, Brent D, Rao U, Flynn C, et al. (1997) Schedule for Affective Disorders and Schizophrenia for School-Age Children-Present and Lifetime Version (K-SADS-PL): initial reliability and validity data. J Am Acad Child Adolesc Psychiatry 36: 980–988.
53. Kirsch P, Schienle A, Stark R, Sammer G, Blecker C, et al. (2003) Anticipation of reward in a nonaversive differential conditioning paradigm and the brain reward system: an event-related fMRI study. Neuroimage 20: 1086–1095.
54. Knutson B, Adams CM, Fong GW, Hommer D (2001) Anticipation of increasing monetary reward selectively recruits nucleus accumbens. J Neurosci 21: RC159.
55. Plichta MM, Wolf I, Hohmann S, Baumeister S, Boecker R, et al. (2013) Simultaneous EEG and fMRI reveals a causally connected subcortical-cortical network during reward anticipation. J Neurosci 33: 14526–14533.
56. Allen PJ, Josephs O, Turner R (2000) A method for removing imaging artifact from continuous EEG recorded during functional MRI. Neuroimage 12: 230–239.

57. Allen PJ, Polizzi G, Krakow K, Fish DR, Lemieux L (1998) Identification of EEG events in the MR scanner: the problem of pulse artifact and a method for its subtraction. Neuroimage 8: 229–239.
58. Makeig S, Bell AJ, Jung TP, Sejnowski TJ (1996) Independent component analysis of electroencephalographic data. Adv Neural Inf Process Syst 8: 145–151.
59. Debener S, Mullinger KJ, Niazy RK, Bowtell RW (2008) Properties of the ballistocardiogram artefact as revealed by EEG recordings at 1.5, 3 and 7 T static magnetic field strength. Int J Psychophysiol 67: 189–199.
60. Achenbach T (1997) Manual for the Young Adult Self-Report and Young Adult Behavior Checklist. Burlington, VT: Department of Psychiatry, University of Vermont
61. Maldjian JA, Laurienti PJ, Kraft RA, Burdette JH (2003) An automated method for neuroanatomic and cytoarchitectonic atlas-based interrogation of fMRI data sets. Neuroimage 19: 1233–1239.
62. Walter B, Blecker C, Kirsch P, Sammer G, Schienle A, et al. (2003) MARINA: An easy to use tool for the creation of MAsks for Region of INterest Analyses [abstract]. Presented at the 9th International Conference on Functional Mapping of the Human Brain, June 19–22, New York, NY. Neuroimage 19: Available on CD-Rom.
63. Poppenk J, Evensmoen HR, Moscovitch M, Nadel L (2013) Long-axis specialization of the human hippocampus. Trends Cogn Sci 17: 230–240.
64. Baron RM, Kenny DA (1986) The moderator-mediator variable distinction in social psychological research: conceptual, strategic, and statistical considerations. J Pers Soc Psychol 51: 1173–1182.
65. Preacher KJ, Hayes AF (2004) SPSS and SAS procedures for estimating indirect effects in simple mediation models. Behav Res Methods Instrum Comput 36: 717–731.
66. Cho YT, Fromm S, Guyer AE, Detloff A, Pine DS, et al. (2012) Nucleus accumbens, thalamus and insula connectivity during incentive anticipation in typical adults and adolescents. Neuroimage 66C: 508–521.
67. Schultz W (1998) Predictive reward signal of dopamine neurons. J Neurophysiol 80: 1–27.
68. Treadway MT, Buckholtz JW, Zald DH (2013) Perceived stress predicts altered reward and loss feedback processing in medial prefrontal cortex. Front Hum Neurosci 7: 180.
69. Knutson B, Bhanji JP, Cooney RE, Atlas LY, Gotlib IH (2008) Neural responses to monetary incentives in major depression. Biol Psychiatry 63: 686–692.
70. Friedman DP, Aggleton JP, Saunders RC (2002) Comparison of hippocampal, amygdala, and perirhinal projections to the nucleus accumbens: combined anterograde and retrograde tracing study in the Macaque brain. J Comp Neurol 450: 345–365.
71. Murty VP, Adcock RA (2013) Enriched Encoding: Reward Motivation Organizes Cortical Networks for Hippocampal Detection of Unexpected Events. Cereb Cortex.
72. Wise RA (2004) Dopamine, learning and motivation. Nat Rev Neurosci 5: 483–494.
73. Frank MJ, Claus ED (2006) Anatomy of a decision: striato-orbitofrontal interactions in reinforcement learning, decision making, and reversal. Psychol Rev 113: 300–326.
74. Schmid B, Blomeyer D, Buchmann AF, Trautmann-Villalba P, Zimmermann US, et al. (2011) Quality of early mother-child interaction associated with depressive psychopathology in the offspring: A prospective study from infancy to adulthood. J Psychiatr Res 45: 1387–1394.
75. Glascoe FP, Leew S (2010) Parenting behaviors, perceptions, and psychosocial risk: impacts on young children's development. Pediatrics 125: 313–319.
76. Burchinal M, Vernon-Feagans L, Cox M, Key Family Life Project I (2008) Cumulative Social Risk, Parenting, and Infant Development in Rural Low-Income Communities. Parenting, science and practice 8: 41–69.
77. Baker CN, Hoerger M (2012) Parental Child-Rearing Strategies Influence Self-Regulation, Socio-Emotional Adjustment, and Psychopathology in Early Adulthood: Evidence from a Retrospective Cohort Study. Pers Individ Dif 52: 800–805.
78. Blum K, Braverman ER, Holder JM, Lubar JF, Monastra VJ, et al. (2000) Reward deficiency syndrome: a biogenetic model for the diagnosis and treatment of impulsive, addictive, and compulsive behaviors. J Psychoactive Drugs 32: Suppl: i–iv, 1–112.
79. Berghorst LH, Bogdan R, Frank MJ, Pizzagalli DA (2013) Acute stress selectively reduces reward sensitivity. Front Hum Neurosci 7: 133.
80. Lupien SJ, Maheu F, Tu M, Fiocco A, Schramek TE (2007) The effects of stress and stress hormones on human cognition: Implications for the field of brain and cognition. Brain Cogn 65: 209–237.
81. Cabib S, Puglisi-Allegra S (1996) Stress, depression and the mesolimbic dopamine system. Psychopharmacology (Berl) 128: 331–342.
82. Bogdan R, Pizzagalli DA (2006) Acute stress reduces reward responsiveness: implications for depression. Biol Psychiatry 60: 1147–1154.
83. Fries E, Hesse J, Hellhammer J, Hellhammer DH (2005) A new view on hypocortisolism. Psychoneuroendocrinology 30: 1010–1016.
84. Heim C, Ehlert U, Hellhammer DH (2000) The potential role of hypocortisolism in the pathophysiology of stress-related bodily disorders. Psychoneuroendocrinology 25: 1–35.
85. Meaney MJ (2010) Epigenetics and the biological definition of gene x environment interactions. Child Dev 81: 41–79.
86. Roth TL, Sweatt JD (2011) Epigenetic marking of the BDNF gene by early-life adverse experiences. Horm Behav 59: 315–320.
87. Hahn T, Heinzel S, Dresler T, Plichta MM, Renner TJ, et al. (2011) Association between reward-related activation in the ventral striatum and trait reward sensitivity is moderated by dopamine transporter genotype. Hum Brain Mapp32: 1557–1565.
88. Dreher JC, Kohn P, Kolachana B, Weinberger DR, Berman KF (2009) Variation in dopamine genes influences responsivity of the human reward system. Proc Natl Acad Sci U S A 106: 617–622.
89. Camara E, Kramer UM, Cunillera T, Marco-Pallares J, Cucurell D, et al. (2010) The effects of COMT (Val108/158Met) and DRD4 (SNP -521) dopamine genotypes on brain activations related to valence and magnitude of rewards. Cereb Cortex 20: 1985–1996.
90. Yacubian J, Sommer T, Schroeder K, Glascher J, Kalisch R, et al. (2007) Gene-gene interaction associated with neural reward sensitivity. Proc Natl Acad Sci U S A 104: 8125–8130.

8

Fetal Exposure to Perfluorinated Compounds and Attention Deficit Hyperactivity Disorder in Childhood

Amanda Ode[1]*, Karin Källén[1], Peik Gustafsson[2], Lars Rylander[1], Bo A. G. Jönsson[1], Per Olofsson[3], Sten A. Ivarsson[4], Christian H. Lindh[1], Anna Rignell-Hydbom[1]

1 Division of Occupational and Environmental Medicine, Lund University, Lund, Sweden, **2** Child and Adolescent Psychiatry Unit, Department of Clinical Sciences, Lund University, Lund, Sweden, **3** Obstetrics and Gynecology Unit, Department of Clinical Sciences, Skåne University Hospital, Lund University, Malmö, Sweden, **4** Department of Clinical Sciences, Unit of Pediatric Endocrinology, Lund University/Clinical Research Centre (CRC), Malmö, Sweden

Abstract

Background: The association between exposure to perfluorinated compounds (PFCs) and attention deficit hyperactivity disorder (ADHD) diagnosis has been sparsely investigated in humans and the findings are inconsistent.

Objectives: A matched case-control study was conducted to investigate the association between fetal exposure to PFCs and ADHD diagnosis in childhood.

Methods: The study base comprised children born in Malmö, Sweden, between 1978 and 2000 that were followed up until 2005. Children with ADHD (n = 206) were identified at the Department of Child and Adolescent Psychiatry. Controls (n = 206) were selected from the study base and were matched for year of birth and maternal country of birth. PFC concentrations were measured in umbilical cord serum samples. The differences of the PFC concentrations between cases and controls were investigated using Wilcoxon's paired test. Possible threshold effects (above the upper quartile for perfluorooctane sulfonate (PFOS) and perfluorooctanoic acid (PFOA) and above limit of detection [LOD] for perfluorononanoic acid (PFNA)) were evaluated by conditional logistic regression.

Results: The median umbilical cord serum concentrations of PFOS were 6.92 ng/ml in the cases and 6.77 ng/ml in the controls. The corresponding concentrations of PFOA were 1.80 and 1.83 ng/ml. No associations between PFCs and ADHD were observed. Odds ratios adjusted for smoking status, parity, and gestational age were 0.81 (95% confidence interval [CI] 0.50 to 1.32) for PFOS, 1.07 (95% CI 0.67 to 1.7) for PFOA, and 1.1 (95% CI 0.75 to 1.7) for PFNA.

Conclusions: The current study revealed no support for an association between fetal exposure to PFOS, PFOA, or PFNA and ADHD.

Editor: Aimin Chen, University of Cincinnati, United States of America

Funding: The project was funded by the Swedish Research Council (via SIMSAM Early Life) (web page: www.vr.se/) and the Medical Faculty at Lund University (web page: www.med.lu.se). The funders had no role in study design, data collection and analysis, decision to publish, or preparation of the manuscript.

Competing Interests: The authors have declared that no competing interests exist.

* E-mail: amanda.ode@med.lu.se

Introduction

Emission of pollutants from densely populated areas and industries is a growing environmental problem. Contaminants present in the environment can have a negative impact on both human health and environment. Perfluorinated compounds (PFCs) are extremely stable and persistent man-made organic chemicals that have been identified as environmental pollutants. The unique properties of PFCs have made them highly useful in numerous industrial and consumer applications such as lubricants, firefighting foams, cleaning agents, and in surface coating for paper, food packaging, textiles, furniture, carpets and cookware [1–3].

PFCs, particularly perfluorooctane sulfonate (PFOS) and perfluorooctanic acid (PFOA) have been widely detected in the environment, wildlife, and humans [4–8]. Humans are exposed to PFCs through consumer products as well as contaminated air, water, and food [1]. In recent years, studies have revealed that PFCs cross the placenta and accumulate in the fetus [9–11]. The fetal brain is immature and is therefore susceptible to injury caused by toxic agents [12]. Animal data have indicated that PFCs accumulate in the brain both before and after the blood-brain barrier is formed [13–16].

Animal studies have shown that neonatal exposure to low doses of PFCs induced irreversible neurotoxic effects in adult mice and caused changes in behavior and habituation by altering the dopaminergic and cholinergic system [17,18]. PFCs also alter levels of neural proteins that are important for the formation and growth of the synapses [19]. Defects in the dopamine transporters and receptors have been suggested to be the most significant neurobiological problem in attention deficit hyperactivity disorder (ADHD) [20,21].

ADHD is a neurodevelopmental disorder defined by inattention, hyperactivity and impulsivity [22,23]. The disorder has its onset in childhood, and persists into adolescence and into adulthood in some cases [24,25]. The genetic factor is believed to play the major role in the development of ADHD [22,26,27]. In addition, exposure to environmental toxins, such as lead, mercury, and persistent chlorinated biphenyls, has also been related to ADHD [26,28,29].

Two cross-sectional studies based on parent-reported ADHD diagnosis have investigated the potential association between PFC levels in school-age children and ADHD [30,31]. The study by Hoffman et al. [30] found a positive relationship between ADHD and PFC levels in the blood of children between 12 and 15 years, whereas an association with only perfluorohexane sulfonate (PFHxS) was found in the study by Stein and Savitz [31]. In another cross-sectional study, PFC exposure was associated with impulsivity in children [32]. Other studies based on questionnaires investigated whether behavioral health and motor coordination as well as motor and mental developmental milestones were associated with maternal PFCs during pregnancy and found no such associations except for PFOS which was associated with delayed motor development in the first two years of life [33,34].

The frequency of children receiving an ADHD diagnosis has increased in recent years [35]. Improved diagnostic criteria might be responsible for the increased detection of ADHD cases. Increased exposure to environmental pollutants might also contribute to the high prevalence of ADHD. Since the human brain is susceptible to disturbance by environmental pollutants during the fetal period, it is of importance to investigate the association between exposure to these pollutants during the sensitive period of fetal development and ADHD.

The objective of this study is to investigate the association between fetal exposure to PFCs and ADHD diagnosis in childhood. Unlike previous studies, this case-control study is based on clinical ADHD diagnosis and PFCs are measured in umbilical cord serum samples which reflect the PFC concentrations in the fetus. The study is a part of the Fetal Environment and Neurodevelopment Disorders in Epidemiological Research project (the FENDER project).

Material and Methods

Participants

The selection procedure of the children with ADHD diagnosis has been previously described by Gustafsson and Kallen [36]. Briefly, at the Department of Child and Adolescent Psychiatry in the city of Malmö, 419 children born and living in Malmö between 1978 and 2000 with ADHD diagnosis were identified and were followed up until 2005. During the study period, the children with ADHD were diagnosed by one of ten experienced clinicians at the department using the Diagnostic and Statistical Manual of Mental Disorders (DSM). A child with suspected attention difficulties, hyperactivity and/or difficulties with impulse control is usually assessed to the child and adolescent psychiatry by a special teacher and a school psychologist or by the parents. The assessment begins with gathering information about the child's general medical health condition and the child's development from birth until the present time. The school psychologist or the psychologist at the psychiatric clinic performs a cognitive testing with the Wechsler Intelligence Scale (WISC). The parents and the teacher are asked to fill in questionnaires like SNAP-IV, Conner's questionnaire or the 5–15 questionnaire which all cover the symptoms of ADHD. Parents are usually asked to fill in the BRIEF-questionnaire concerning the child's executive functions in every-day life. Sometimes a member of the team at the clinic observes the child at school. The child's ability to concentrate is tested with TEA-Ch or with a computerized test of attention such as QB-Tech or IVA+. The child psychiatrist performs a paediatric examination with assessment of neurological soft-signs. The child's behaviour in different test situations and at the visits at the clinic is observed and registered. When all parts of the assessment have been performed, a team consisting of doctor, psychologist and sometimes a social worker meet and discuss the findings to come to a consensus decision concerning the diagnosis using DSM criteria. The DSM criteria DSM-III-R_{11} and DSM-IV_{12} were used before 1994 and from 1994 and onwards, respectively. Age at the time of diagnosis varied between 5 and 17 years, with most children being diagnosed between the ages of 8 and 12 years.

Using the personal identification numbers, children with ADHD were linked to the Swedish Medical Birth Register (SMBR) which contains demographic and obstetric information on nearly all (99%) the mothers and the infants in Sweden. Umbilical cord serum samples for children with ADHD were collected from the Malmö Maternity Unit Serum Biobank (MMUSB) using the personal identification numbers. Nearly all deliveries in Malmö take place at the Malmö University Hospital Maternity Unit, where blood samples from the mother and from the umbilical cord of the newborn have been collected at the time of delivery and stored at $-20°C$ at the MMUSB since 1969. Controls were selected into two phases. In the first phase, for each ADHD case with an available umbilical blood sample in the biobank, the next-baby-born with serum sample of the same sex was selected as a control. However, a new publication by Gustafsson and Kallen [36] revealed the impact of maternal country of birth on the diagnosis of ADHD. Thus, the benefit of matching for the maternal country of birth completely overrode that from matching for the infant's sex. Therefore, in the second phase, a pool of ten eligible controls per ADHD case were collected from the SMBR and were matched to the cases for year of birth (± 12 months) and country of birth of the mother. The sample of the next-baby-born from the first phase was used if no newborn in that eligible pool of controls had an available umbilical blood sample in the biobank. The selection procedure for cases and controls is presented in Figure 1.

Ethics statements

At the Maternity Unit, the women were informed that the umbilical cord serum sample collected could be used for research purposes in the future and those who accepted gave their verbal informed consent that was documented in the medical records. During the study period only verbal informed consent was obtained. The written informed consent has been implemented in 2005 and therefore could not be considered for the current study. The data were analysed anonymously. The study protocol followed the requirements of the Declaration of Helsinki and the study, together with the consent procedure, was approved by the Research Ethics Committee at Lund University, Sweden.

Analysis of perfluorinated compounds and cotinine in umbilical cord serum

The analyses of PFHxS, PFOS, PFOA, PFNA, perfluorodecanoic acid (PFDA), perfluoroundecanoic acid (PFUnDA), perfluorododecanoic acid (PFDoDA), and cotinine were performed as previously described [37]. Briefly, aliquots of 100 µL sera were added with isotopically labeled internal standards, the proteins were precipitated by acetonitrile and centrifugation, and analysis was then performed using a hybrid triple quadrupole linear ion-trap mass spectrometer (LC/MS/MS; UFLCXR, Shimadzu Corporation, Kyoto, Japan; QTRAP 5500; Sciex, Framingham, MA, USA). The limits of detections for the detected PFCs and

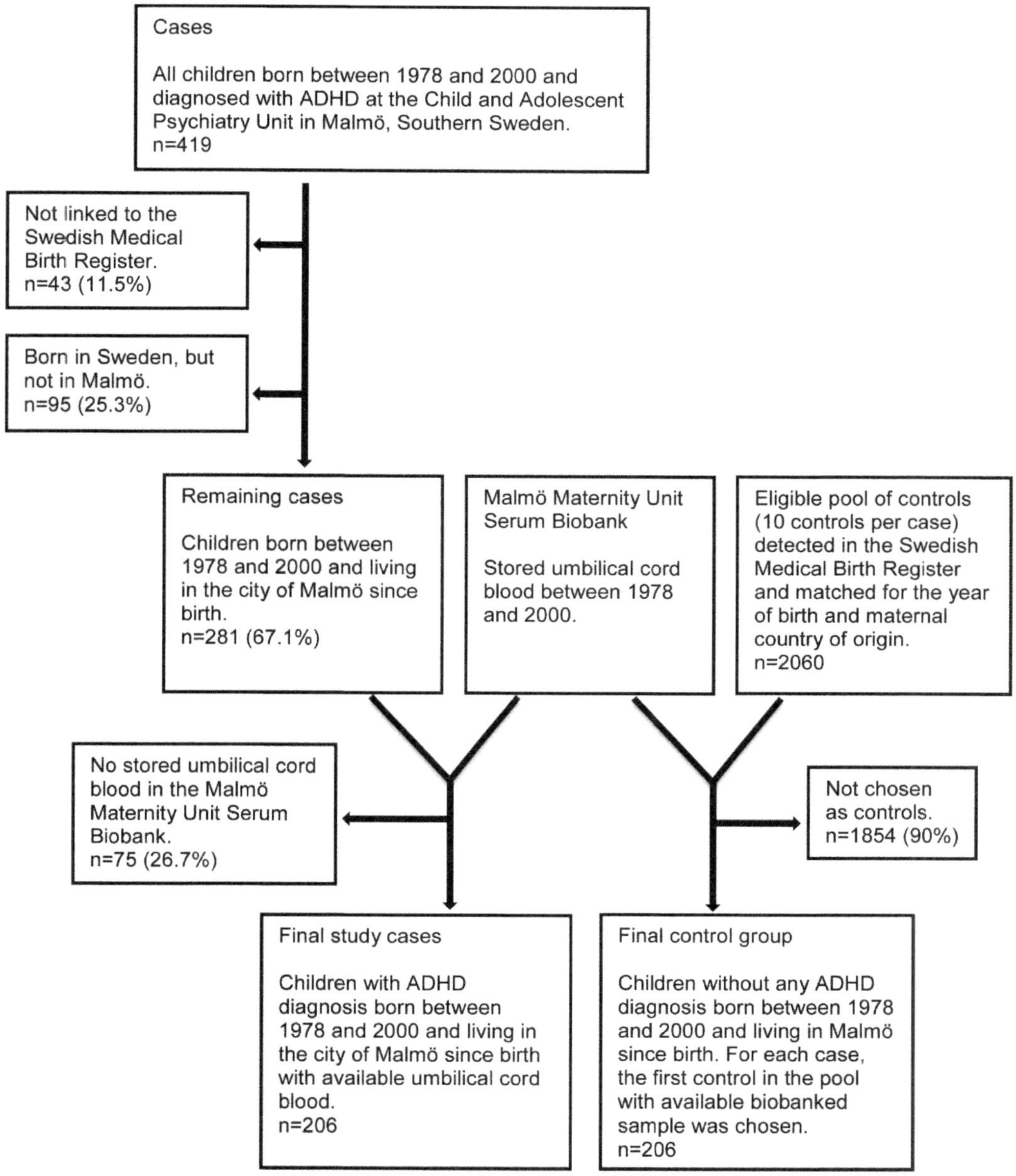

Figure 1. Flowchart for the selection procedure of the children with attention deficit hyperactivity disorder and controls.

cotinine were 0.2 ng/ml. To increase the accuracy, the result reported is the average of two measurements from the same sample worked up and analyzed on different days. In all sample batches, the quality of the measurements was controlled by analyzing chemical blanks and in-house quality control (QC) samples. The reproducibility, determined as the relative standard deviation, between measured duplicate samples was 11% for PFOS, 12% for PFOA, 12% for PFNA, and 9% for cotinine. The reproducibility in QC samples was 8% for PFOS, 11% for PFOA, 8% for PFNA, and 5% for cotinine. Usually we are able to analyze several more PFCs with the method but some factor, probably during the storage of the samples, resulted in a high background noise in the chromatograms making detection impossible. Thus, PFHxS, PFDA, PFUnDA, and PFDoDA could not be detected in the samples due to this effect. On the other hand, due to the high correlation between PFOS and other PFCs often only PFOS and PFOA are reported in studies of PFCs. Although contamination of samples during collection is believed to be minimal, field blanks could not be provided to control for eventual contamination of the samples with PFCs. The analyses of PFOS and PFOA are part of the round robin intercomparison program (Professor Dr. med. Hans Drexler, Institute and Outpatient Clinic for Occupational, Social and Environmental Medicine, University of Erlangen-Nuremberg, Germany) with results within the tolerance limits.

Statistical analyses

The Wilcoxon's paired test was used to compare the PFC concentrations between ADHD cases and controls. Conditional logistic regression analysis was used to assess the association between fetal exposure to PFCs and ADHD. The odds ratio was

Table 1. Median concentration (in nanograms/milliliters) of perfluorinated compounds by the maternal and infant demographic characteristics.

Characteristics	Children with ADHD			Control group		
	n (%)	PFOS	PFOA	n (%)	PFOS	PFOA
Group (cases/controls)	203 (49.8%)	6.92	1.80	205 (50.2%)	6.77	1.83
Year of delivery						
1978–1981	2 (1.0)	2.66	0.45	2 (1.0)	8.70	0.85
1982–1985	13 (6.4)	5.69	1.50	10 (4.9)	6.49	1.71
1986–1989	63 (31.0)	6.96	2.0	66 (32.2)	6.71	1.82
1990–1993	86 (42.4)	7.08	1.78	87 (42.4)	6.74	1.82
1994–1997	34 (16.7)	6.65	1.69	35 (17.1)	7.44	1.87
1998–2000	5 (2.5)	7.68	1.64	5 (2.4)	8.11	1.86
Maternal age (years)						
<20	8 (3.9)	6.67	1.57	6 (2.9)	8.65	2.16
20–34	172 (84.7)	6.94	1.81	171 (83.4)	6.74	1.82
≥35	23 (11.3)	6.34	1.64	28 (13.7)	7.05	1.81
Parity						
0 [nulliparous]	97 (47.8)	7.00	2.01	106 (51.7)	7.56	2.13
1	71 (35.0)	6.60	1.55	68 (33.2)	6.22	1.55
≥2	35 (17.2)	6.80	1.68	31 (15.1)	6.17	1.42
Maternal country of origin						
Sweden	168 (83.3)	7.02	1.85	170 (82.9)	7.06	1.89
Other Nordic countries[a]	7 (3.4)	4.28	2.13	7 (3.4)	6.18	1.69
Rest of Europe[b]	8 (3.9)	7.47	1.60	9 (4.4)	5.48	1.48
Sub-Saharan Africa	2 (1.0)	4.23	0.72	2 (1.0)	2.10	0.45
Middle East and North Africa	13 (6.4)	4.42	0.85	12 (5.9)	2.76	0.47
East Asia	1 (0.5)	6.83	1.71	2 (1.0)	9.36	1.43
South America	2 (1.0)	7.58	2.89	2 (1.0)	7.63	13.5
Unknown	1 (0.5)	2.96	0.46	1 (0.5)	2.60	1.70
Maternal body mass index (kg/m^2)[c]						
Not available	141 (69.5)	6.85	1.89	142 (69.3)	6.67	1.83
<18.5 (Underweight)	1 (0.5)	10.1	2.64	3 (1.5)	8.75	2.39
18.5–24.9 (Normal)	37 (18.2)	6.83	1.63	42 (20.5)	7.50	1.72
25–29.9 (Overweight)	16 (7.9)	7.27	1.36	14 (6.8)	7.58	2.02
≥30 (Obese)	8 (3.9)	6.06	2.09	4 (2.0)	6.40	2.31
Smoking during pregnancy[d]						
Non-smoker	65 (32.0)	6.54	1.83	85 (41.5)	6.82	1.86
Second-hand smoker	57 (28.1)	7.08	1.71	57 (27.8)	6.91	1.86
Active smoker	81 (39.9)	7.49	1.82	63 (30.7)	6.37	1.72
Infant sex						
Male	180 (88.7)	6.97	1.76	163 (79.5)	6.87	1.84
Female	23 (11.3)	6.32	1.99	42 (20.5)	6.51	1.64
Birth weight (grams)						
<1500	4 (2.0)	5.73	2.31	0		
<2500	9 (4.4)	4.85	1.44	5 (2.4)	6.37	1.84
2500–4000	166 (81.8)	7.12	1.84	152 (74.1)	6.63	1.82
>4000	24 (11.8)	6.41	1.67	48 (23.4)	7.25	1.94
Gestational age (weeks)						
<32	5 (2.5)	4.77	1.44	1 (0.5)	4.71	1.05
<37	6 (3.0)	4.36	1.09	6 (2.9)	4.74	1.97
37–42	176 (86.7)	7.12	1.88	178 (86.8)	6.73	1.82
>42	16 (7.9)	6.54	1.63	20 (9.8)	8.37	1.77

Table 1. Cont.

Characteristics	Children with ADHD			Control group		
	n (%)	PFOS	PFOA	n (%)	PFOS	PFOA
SD scores (for gestational age)						
<−2 (small for gestational age)	9 (4.4)	6.69	2.26	14 (6.8)	7.92	1.94
−2 to −1.1	37 (18.2)	6.60	1.53	29 (14.1)	6.56	1.94
−1.1 to 1	138 (68.0)	7.01	1.79	126 (61.5)	6.67	1.77
1.1 to 2	15 (7.4)	5.48	2.00	32 (15.6)	7.79	2.02
>2 (large for gestational age)	4 (2.0)	7.30	2.40	4 (2.0)	4.05	1.20
Apgar scores						
0–6	5 (2.5)	4.28	1.80	2 (1.0)	10.2	2.44
≥7	198 (97.5)	6.94	1.79	203 (99.0)	6.74	1.82

Abbreviations: ADHD, attention deficit hyperactivity disorder; PFOS, perfluorooctane sulfonate; PFOA, perfluorooctanoic acid; Parity, number of previous pregnancies.
[a]Finland, Denmark, and Norway.
[b]Western Europe and former Eastern Europe.
[c]Body mass index was classified according to the standard values of the World Health Organization.
[d]Maternal smoking is based on measured cotinine concentrations in the umbilical cord serum.

calculated for both 1 unit increase (nanogram per milliliter) in the concentrations of PFOS and PFOA and for comparisons between concentrations above and below the 75th percentile for the control group. For PFNA the concentrations above the limit of detection (LOD) were compared to those below LOD (0.2 ng/ml).

The potential confounding variables that were considered in the present study were smoking during pregnancy, parity, and gestational age at birth, since they have been found to be associated with both PFC exposure and ADHD [11,38–46].

Smoking during pregnancy was determined by cotinine levels in umbilical cord serum. Cotinine levels below the LOD (0.2 ng/ml) were related to nonsmoking pregnant women, cotinine levels higher than 15 ng/ml were related to active smokers and levels between 0.2 and 15 ng/ml were related to second-hand smokers [47]. Parity was divided into three groups according to number of previously born children (0 [i.e. nulliparous], 1, or ≥2 children). Gestational age was entered in the analyses as class variable divided into three groups; <37, 37–42, and >42 weeks of pregnancy.

The odds ratios were calculated in paired samples (n = 202) using Egret for Windows 2.0 (Cytel Software Corporation). The rest of the analyses were performed in IBM SPSS Statistics version 20 (IBM Corporation 1989, 2011).

The power calculation was based on 206 cases and matched controls. With the current setting, we had an 80% chance of detecting a difference in the levels of 0.20 standard deviations, with α value of 0.05, between cases and controls. For the analysis of the threshold effect, with α value of 0.05 and β value of 0.80, the lowest detectable odds ratio was 1.8.

Results

PFOS and PFOA concentrations were above the LOD in 98% of the samples, whereas for PFNA about 12% were above the LOD. PFOS and PFOA concentrations below the LOD in individual samples (n = 2 for each) were replaced with 0.2 ng/ml.

The demographic characteristics and the umbilical cord PFC concentrations of the study population are presented in Table 1.

Figure 2 shows the distribution of PFOS and PFOA levels in the ADHD cases and the controls. The median concentrations of PFNA above LOD for cases and controls were 0.31 and 0.28 ng/ml, respectively. Wilcoxon's paired test revealed no differences in cord serum PFC concentrations between children with ADHD diagnosis and controls ($p = 0.72$, 0.44, and 0.48 for PFOS, PFOA, and PFNA respectively).

Conditional logistic regression analyses revealed no significant associations between umbilical cord concentrations of PFCs and ADHD (Table 2). The result did not change after adjusting for smoking during pregnancy, parity, and gestational age at birth.

Discussion

The present study found no statistically significant associations between exposure to PFCs during pregnancy and ADHD diagnosis during childhood, although the measured umbilical cord concentrations of PFOS were among the highest in Europe [42,48,49] and even among the highest in the world [9,50–52]. For PFOA, the levels were higher than those measured in Norway and other non-European countries but lower than those in Danmark and Faraoe Islands [9,42,48,49].

Animal data revealed that neonatal mice that were exposed to high doses of PFOS and PFOA showed behavioral defects which ranged from slight effects at the anxiety level [53] to reduced habituation and hyperactivity in adult mice [17]. It has been suggested that PFOS and PFOA act as developmental neurotoxicants that mediate their effects on normal brain development, with consequences for cognitive and behavioral functions, through different mechanisms. Examples of those mechanisms are alteration in the dopaminergic system [17,18], elevated levels of proteins important for normal neuronal survival, growth and synaptogenesis, such as CaMKII, GAP-43, synaptophysin and tau, in the brain [19], and induction of apoptosis of neuronal cells [54]. Although most of these findings were obtained from experiments on mice or rat derived cell lines that were exposed to extremely high levels of PFOS and PFOA compared to the low levels measured in the present study, other studies found that PFCs were detrimental to neurodevelopment at levels comparable to those observed in humans [17,19].

Our study is primarily comparable to the study by Fei and Olsen [34] because both studies used measures of prenatal rather than postnatal exposure to PFCs. Fei and Olsen [32] found higher levels of PFOS and PFOA compared to those seen among

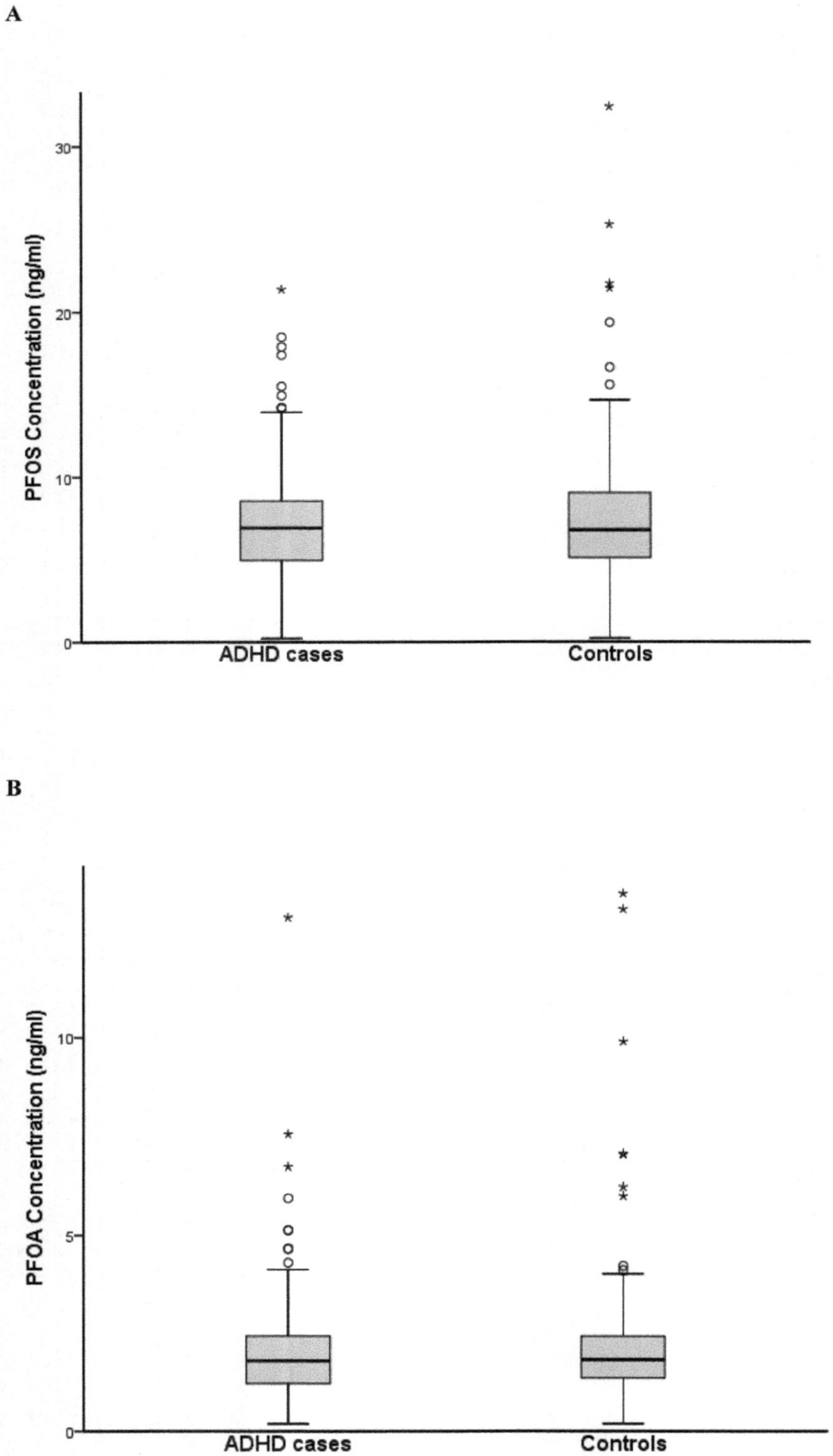

Figure 2. Boxplot of the umbilical cord concentrations of perfluorooctane sulfonate (PFOS) (a) and perfluorooctanoic acid (PFOA) (b) in cases having attention deficit hyperactivity disorder and controls. The extreme values of perfluorooctanoic acid for the ADHD cases, 48 and 36 ng/ml, and for the controls, 66, 49, 31, and 23 ng/ml, are not presented in the boxplot.

pregnant women in other countries including the Nordic countries [11,48]. Consistent with that study, our results provide further indication that fetal exposure to PFCs at the present levels do not play a major role in having ADHD diagnosis at later age. Hoffman et al. [30] found an association between PFC serum concentrations and ADHD in children aged 12 to 15 years. Another study

Table 2. The crude and adjusted odds ratio with 95% confidence interval of attention deficit hyperactivity disorder and exposure to perfluorinated compounds.

	ADHD Diagnosis	
	Crude	Adjusted[a]
PFOS[b]	0.98 (0.92–1.03)	0.98 (0.92–1.04)
PFOA[b]	0.98 (0.94–1.02)	0.98 (0.94–1.02)
PFOS[c]		
<75th percentile	1	1
≥75th percentile	0.82 (0.51–1.31)	0.81 (0.50–1.32)
PFOA[c]		
<75th percentile	1	1
≥75th percentile	1.03 (0.65–1.6)	1.07 (0.67–1.7)
PFNA[d]		
<LOD	1	1
≥LOD	1.1 (0.72–1.6)	1.1 (0.75–1.7)

Abbreviations: ADHD, attention deficit hyperactivity disorder; PFOS, perfluorooctane sulfonate; PFOA, perfluorooctanoic acid; PFNA, perfluorononanoic acid; LOD, limit of detection.

[a]Adjusted for maternal active smoking, parity, and gestational age at birth.

[b]Odds ratio is calculated for 1 ng/ml increase in umbilical cord serum concentration.

[c]Odds ratio is calculated for PFOS and PFOA concentrations at or above the 75th percentile (75th percentile for PFOS and PFOA were 9,1 ng/ml and 2,4 ng/ml, respectively).

[d]Odds ratio is calculated for PFNA concentrations at or above the LOD (0.2 ng/ml).

by Stein and Savitz [31] on the relationship between self-reported ADHD and PFC levels in children in the same age range as for those in the study of Hoffman et al. [30] showed an association with PFHxS but not with the other PFCs even though both ADHD prevalence and exposure levels for PFCs were higher in the study by Stein and Savitz. Exposure to PFCs tends to be higher among newborns, toddlers, and children due to high uptake via food consumption, hand-to-mouth transfer of the PFCs from carpets, and through ingestion of dust [55]. If the positive association between PFC exposure and self-reported ADHD found in the study by Hoffman et al. [30] was not due to a chance finding, that might indicate that postnatal exposure to PFCs, rather than prenatal exposure, is associated with ADHD.

The present study has some limitations. Unfortunately, while 419 children with ADHD diagnosis were identified at the Department of Child and Adolescent Psychiatry, there were significant losses to get to the final study sample. The study was restricted to children born in Malmö with available obstetric and demographic information from the SMBR and stored cord blood samples in the biobank. About 50% of the identified children met these two inclusion criteria and were included in the study. The second limitation of the current study is the small number of ADHD cases. Although we would be able to detect an odd ratio of 1.8 and a difference in PFC levels of at least 0.20 standard deviations between cases and controls, it should be emphasized that the statistical power was not high enough to detect some minor associations and we could not accordingly rule out small effects. In addition, we lack information about other exposures that are significant for ADHD, such as exposure to mercury and lead. The PFC levels measured here might also be too low to trigger undesirable effects on the brain development.

During our study period, the clinical diagnostic criteria for ADHD were changed from the definition in DSM-III-R to the definition in DSM-IV, where DSM-IV is regarded as more inclusive. Thus, DSM-IV criteria yield a higher prevalence of ADHD [56]. Most individuals (93%–97.5%) who fulfill a diagnosis of ADHD according to DSM-III-R also fulfill the diagnostic criteria according to DSM-IV [57-59]. Individuals with ADHD according to DSM-IV that also fulfilled diagnostic criteria according to DSM-III-R were 85% [57] and 60% [59]. Thus the overlap between ADHD diagnoses according to DSM-III-R and DSM-IV is considerable. The more inclusive diagnosis used in the latter part of the study probably includes some less severe cases which might slightly weaken possible statistical associations between exposure to PFCs and having an ADHD diagnosis.

The study has also several important strengths. First, unlike most of the previous studies on the associations between PFC levels and ADHD, our prospective study design is more reliable in the sense that it is based on clinical diagnosis of ADHD made at the Department of Child and Adolescent Psychiatry. Children were diagnosed at the same psychiatric clinic through the whole study period.

Second, the present study is based on analyzed blood samples from the fetal period, which we believe is the most susceptible exposure window, whereas in other studies, which were of a cross-sectional nature, blood samples were collected from school-age children [30,31].

Third, we were able to account for important covariates; smoking during pregnancy, parity, and gestational age at birth that have been found to be associated with both PFC levels in pregnant women or infants [11,38,42,46] and ADHD diagnosis or symptoms [39–41,43–45]. Epidemiological findings have shown that prevalence of ADHD is higher among males [20]. It has also previously been shown that infant sex has no effect on the concentrations of PFCs [11,42,60]. Thus, infant sex was not considered as a potential confounder in the current data set.

In a previous study, we found that fetuses of mothers originating from a country other than Sweden, especially those from Middle East and sub-Saharan Africa, had lower PFC levels in the cord blood than fetuses of native Swedish mothers [11]. Another study found higher odds of having an ADHD diagnosis for native Swedish children compared to children of mothers born outside Sweden [36]. Since the proportion of immigrants is relatively high in Malmö, no matching for the maternal country of birth might result in a false positive relationship between PFCs and ADHD.

Human serum PFC levels showed an increasing pattern from the early 1970s through the late 1990s, followed by leveling out and a decreasing trend right after the phase-out of the production of PFOS and PFOS related compounds in 2002 [8,61–64]. Diagnosis criteria for ADHD have been changed during the study period. We matched for the year of delivery to remove the effect of those differences in PFC levels and diagnosis on the results.

According to our findings, fetal exposure to PFOS, PFOA and PFNA was not associated with ADHD diagnosis in childhood.

Acknowledgments

We would like to thank the laboratory technicians Åsa Amilon and Agneta Kristensen for analyzing the samples.

Author Contributions

Conceived and designed the experiments: KK PG LR SAI PO ARH AO. Performed the experiments: BAGJ CHL. Analyzed the data: AO KK LR ARH. Contributed reagents/materials/analysis tools: BAGJ CHL. Wrote the paper: AO. Wrote the section about the laboratory analysis: BAGJ CHL. Reviewed the manuscript and made comments on it before submission: ARH LR KK PO PG SAI.

References

1. Fromme H, Tittlemier SA, Volkel W, Wilhelm M, Twardella D (2009) Perfluorinated compounds—exposure assessment for the general population in Western countries. Int J Hyg Environ Health 212: 239–270.
2. Kissa E (2001) Fluorinated Surfactants and Repellants. NY, USA: Marcel Dekker Inc.
3. Lemal DM (2004) Perspective on fluorocarbon chemistry. J Org Chem 69: 1–11.
4. Butt CM, Berger U, Bossi R, Tomy GT (2010) Levels and trends of poly- and perfluorinated compounds in the arctic environment. Sci Total Environ 408: 2936–2965.
5. Giesy JP, Kannan K (2001) Global distribution of perfluorooctane sulfonate in wildlife. Environ Sci Technol 35: 1339–1342.
6. Giesy JP, Kannan K (2002) Perfluorochemical surfactants in the environment. Environ Sci Technol 36: 146A–152A.
7. Kannan K, Corsolini S, Falandysz J, Fillmann G, Kumar KS, et al. (2004) Perfluorooctanesulfonate and Related Fluorochemicals in Human Blood from Several Countries. Environmental Science & Technology 38: 4489–4495.
8. Olsen GW, Huang H-Y, Helzlsouer KJ, Hansen KJ, Butenhoff JL, et al. (2005) Historical Comparison of Perfluorooctanesulfonate, Perfluorooctanoate, and Other Fluorochemicals in Human Blood. Environmental Health Perspectives 113: 539–545.
9. Beesoon S, Webster GM, Shoeib M, Harner T, Benskin JP, et al. (2011) Isomer profiles of perfluorochemicals in matched maternal, cord, and house dust samples: manufacturing sources and transplacental transfer. Environ Health Perspect 119: 1659–1664.
10. Inoue K, Okada F, Ito R, Kato S, Sasaki S, et al. (2004) Perfluorooctane Sulfonate (PFOS) and Related Perfluorinated Compounds in Human Maternal and Cord Blood Samples: Assessment of PFOS Exposure in a Susceptible Population during Pregnancy. Environmental Health Perspectives 112: 1204–1207.
11. Ode A, Rylander L, Lindh CH, Kallen K, Jonsson BA, et al. (2013) Determinants of maternal and fetal exposure and temporal trends of perfluorinated compounds. Environ Sci Pollut Res Int 20: 7970–7978.
12. Grandjean P, Landrigan PJ (2006) Developmental neurotoxicity of industrial chemicals. Lancet 368: 2167–2178.
13. Austin ME, Kasturi BS, Barber M, Kannan K, MohanKumar PS, et al. (2003) Neuroendocrine Effects of Perfluorooctane Sulfonate in Rats. Environmental Health Perspectives 111: 1485–1489.
14. Butenhoff JL, Ehresman DJ, Chang SC, Parker GA, Stump DG (2009) Gestational and lactational exposure to potassium perfluorooctanesulfonate (K+ PFOS) in rats: developmental neurotoxicity. Reprod Toxicol 27: 319–330.
15. Cui L, Zhou QF, Liao CY, Fu JJ, Jiang GB (2009) Studies on the toxicological effects of PFOA and PFOS on rats using histological observation and chemical analysis. Arch Environ Contam Toxicol 56: 338–349.
16. Greaves AK, Letcher RJ, Sonne C, Dietz R (2013) Brain region distribution and patterns of bioaccumulative perfluoroalkyl carboxylates and sulfonates in east greenland polar bears (Ursus maritimus). Environ Toxicol Chem 32: 713–722.
17. Johansson N, Fredriksson A, Eriksson P (2008) Neonatal exposure to perfluorooctane sulfonate (PFOS) and perfluorooctanoic acid (PFOA) causes neurobehavioural defects in adult mice. Neurotoxicology 29: 160–169.
18. Slotkin TA, MacKillop EA, Melnick RL, Thayer KA, Seidler FJ (2008) Developmental neurotoxicity of perfluorinated chemicals modeled in vitro. Environ Health Perspect 116: 716–722.
19. Johansson N, Eriksson P, Viberg H (2009) Neonatal exposure to PFOS and PFOA in mice results in changes in proteins which are important for neuronal growth and synaptogenesis in the developing brain. Toxicol Sci 108: 412–418.
20. Faraone SV, Perlis RH, Doyle AE, Smoller JW, Goralnick JJ, et al. (2005) Molecular Genetics of Attention-Deficit/Hyperactivity Disorder. Biological Psychiatry 57: 1313–1323.
21. Gizer IR, Ficks C, Waldman ID (2009) Candidate gene studies of ADHD: a meta-analytic review. Hum Genet 126: 51–90.
22. Faraone SV, Khan SA (2006) Candidate gene studies of attention-deficit/hyperactivity disorder. J Clin Psychiatry 67 Suppl 8: 13–20.
23. Gustafsson P, Thernlund G, Ryding E, Rosen I, Cederblad M (2000) Associations between cerebral blood-flow measured by single photon emission computed tomography (SPECT), electro-encephalogram (EEG), behaviour symptoms, cognition and neurological soft signs in children with attention-deficit hyperactivity disorder (ADHD). Acta Paediatr 89: 830–835.
24. Faraone SV, Biederman J, Mick E (2006) The age-dependent decline of attention deficit hyperactivity disorder: a meta-analysis of follow-up studies. Psychol Med 36: 159–165.
25. Lara C, Fayyad J, de Graaf R, Kessler RC, Aguilar-Gaxiola S, et al. (2009) Childhood predictors of adult attention-deficit/hyperactivity disorder: results from the World Health Organization World Mental Health Survey Initiative. Biol Psychiatry 65: 46–54.
26. Banerjee TD, Middleton F, Faraone SV (2007) Environmental risk factors for attention-deficit hyperactivity disorder. Acta Paediatr 96: 1269–1274.
27. Thapar A, Cooper M, Jefferies R, Stergiakouli E (2012) What causes attention deficit hyperactivity disorder? Arch Dis Child 97: 260–265.
28. Braun JM, Kahn RS, Froehlich T, Auinger P, Lanphear BP (2006) Exposures to environmental toxicants and attention deficit hyperactivity disorder in U.S. children. Environ Health Perspect 114: 1904–1909.
29. Eubig PA, Aguiar A, Schantz SL (2010) Lead and PCBs as risk factors for attention deficit/hyperactivity disorder. Environ Health Perspect 118: 1654–1667.
30. Hoffman K, Webster TF, Weisskopf MG, Weinberg J, Vieira VM (2010) Exposure to polyfluoroalkyl chemicals and attention deficit/hyperactivity disorder in U.S. children 12-15 years of age. Environ Health Perspect 118: 1762–1767.
31. Stein CR, Savitz DA (2011) Serum perfluorinated compound concentration and attention deficit/hyperactivity disorder in children 5–18 years of age. Environ Health Perspect 119: 1466–1471.
32. Gump BB, Wu Q, Dumas AK, Kannan K (2011) Perfluorochemical (PFC) exposure in children: associations with impaired response inhibition. Environ Sci Technol 45: 8151–8159.
33. Fei C, McLaughlin JK, Lipworth L, Olsen J (2008) Prenatal exposure to perfluorooctanoate (PFOA) and perfluorooctanesulfonate (PFOS) and maternally reported developmental milestones in infancy. Environ Health Perspect 116: 1391–1395.
34. Fei C, Olsen J (2011) Prenatal exposure to perfluorinated chemicals and behavioral or coordination problems at age 7 years. Environ Health Perspect 119: 573–578.
35. Pastor PN, Reuben CA (2008) Diagnosed attention deficit hyperactivity disorder and learning disability: United States, 2004–2006. Vital Health Stat 10: 1–14.
36. Gustafsson P, Kallen K (2011) Perinatal, maternal, and fetal characteristics of children diagnosed with attention-deficit-hyperactivity disorder: results from a population-based study utilizing the Swedish Medical Birth Register. Dev Med Child Neurol 53: 263–268.
37. Lindh CH, Rylander L, Toft G, Axmon A, Rignell-Hydbom A, et al. (2012) Blood serum concentrations of perfluorinated compounds in men from Greenlandic Inuit and European populations. Chemosphere 88: 1269–1275.
38. Apelberg BJ, Goldman LR, Calafat AM, Herbstman JB, Kuklenyik Z, et al. (2007) Determinants of fetal exposure to polyfluoroalkyl compounds in Baltimore, Maryland. Environ Sci Technol 41: 3891–3897.
39. Carballo JJ, Garcia-Nieto R, Alvarez-Garcia R, Caro-Canizares I, Lopez-Castroman J, et al. (2013) Sibship size, birth order, family structure and childhood mental disorders. Soc Psychiatry Psychiatr Epidemiol 48: 1327–1333.
40. Chu SM, Tsai MH, Hwang FM, Hsu JF, Huang HR, et al. (2012) The relationship between attention deficit hyperactivity disorder and premature infants in Taiwanese: a case control study. BMC Psychiatry 12: 85.
41. Desrosiers C, Boucher O, Forget-Dubois N, Dewailly E, Ayotte P, et al. (2013) Associations between prenatal cigarette smoke exposure and externalized behaviors at school age among Inuit children exposed to environmental contaminants. Neurotoxicol Teratol 39C: 84–90.

42. Fei C, McLaughlin JK, Tarone RE, Olsen J (2007) Perfluorinated chemicals and fetal growth: a study within the Danish National Birth Cohort. Environ Health Perspect 115: 1677–1682.
43. Kotimaa AJ, Moilanen I, Taanila A, Ebeling H, Smalley SL, et al. (2003) Maternal smoking and hyperactivity in 8-year-old children. J Am Acad Child Adolesc Psychiatry 42: 826–833.
44. Langley K, Holmans PA, van den Bree MB, Thapar A (2007) Effects of low birth weight, maternal smoking in pregnancy and social class on the phenotypic manifestation of Attention Deficit Hyperactivity Disorder and associated antisocial behaviour: investigation in a clinical sample. BMC Psychiatry 7: 26.
45. Perricone G, Morales MR, Anzalone G (2013) Neurodevelopmental outcomes of moderately preterm birth: precursors of attention deficit hyperactivity disorder at preschool age. Springerplus 2: 221.
46. Washino N, Saijo Y, Sasaki S, Kato S, Ban S, et al. (2009) Correlations between prenatal exposure to perfluorinated chemicals and reduced fetal growth. Environ Health Perspect 117: 660–667.
47. George L, Granath F, Johansson AL, Cnattingius S (2006) Self-reported nicotine exposure and plasma levels of cotinine in early and late pregnancy. Acta Obstet Gynecol Scand 85: 1331–1337.
48. Gutzkow KB, Haug LS, Thomsen C, Sabaredzovic A, Becher G, et al. (2012) Placental transfer of perfluorinated compounds is selective—a Norwegian Mother and Child sub-cohort study. Int J Hyg Environ Health 215: 216–219.
49. Needham LL, Grandjean P, Heinzow B, Jorgensen PJ, Nielsen F, et al. (2011) Partition of environmental chemicals between maternal and fetal blood and tissues. Environ Sci Technol 45: 1121–1126.
50. Kim S, Choi K, Ji K, Seo J, Kho Y, et al. (2011) Trans-placental transfer of thirteen perfluorinated compounds and relations with fetal thyroid hormones. Environ Sci Technol 45: 7465–7472.
51. Kim SK, Lee KT, Kang CS, Tao L, Kannan K, et al. (2011) Distribution of perfluorochemicals between sera and milk from the same mothers and implications for prenatal and postnatal exposures. Environ Pollut 159: 169–174.
52. Liu J, Li J, Liu Y, Chan HM, Zhao Y, et al. (2011) Comparison on gestation and lactation exposure of perfluorinated compounds for newborns. Environ Int 37: 1206–1212.
53. Fuentes S, Vicens P, Colomina MT, Domingo JL (2007) Behavioral effects in adult mice exposed to perfluorooctane sulfonate (PFOS). Toxicology 242: 123–129.
54. Lee HG, Lee YJ, Yang JH (2012) Perfluorooctane sulfonate induces apoptosis of cerebellar granule cells via a ROS-dependent protein kinase C signaling pathway. Neurotoxicology 33: 314–320.
55. Trudel D, Horowitz L, Wormuth M, Scheringer M, Cousins IT, et al. (2008) Estimating consumer exposure to PFOS and PFOA. Risk Anal 28: 251–269.
56. Skounti M, Philalithis A, Galanakis E (2007) Variations in prevalence of attention deficit hyperactivity disorder worldwide. Eur J Pediatr 166: 117–123.
57. Lahey BB, Applegate B, McBurnett K, Biederman J, Greenhill L, et al. (1994) DSM-IV field trials for attention deficit hyperactivity disorder in children and adolescents. Am J Psychiatry 151: 1673–1685.
58. Biederman J, Faraone SV, Weber W, Russell RL, Rater M, et al. (1997) Correspondence between DSM-III-R and DSM-IV attention-deficit/hyperactivity disorder. J Am Acad Child Adolesc Psychiatry 36: 1682–1687.
59. Baumgaertel A, Wolraich ML, Dietrich M (1995) Comparison of diagnostic criteria for attention deficit disorders in a German elementary school sample. J Am Acad Child Adolesc Psychiatry 34: 629–638.
60. Hamm MP, Cherry NM, Chan E, Martin JW, Burstyn I (2010) Maternal exposure to perfluorinated acids and fetal growth. J Expo Sci Environ Epidemiol 20: 589–597.
61. Calafat AM, Wong LY, Kuklenyik Z, Reidy JA, Needham LL (2007) Polyfluoroalkyl chemicals in the U.S. population: data from the National Health and Nutrition Examination Survey (NHANES) 2003–2004 and comparisons with NHANES 1999–2000. Environ Health Perspect 115: 1596–1602.
62. Harada K, Koizumi A, Saito N, Inoue K, Yoshinaga T, et al. (2007) Historical and geographical aspects of the increasing perfluorooctanoate and perfluorooctane sulfonate contamination in human serum in Japan. Chemosphere 66: 293–301.
63. Haug LS, Thomsen C, Becher G (2009) Time trends and the influence of age and gender on serum concentrations of perfluorinated compounds in archived human samples. Environ Sci Technol 43: 2131–2136.
64. Olsen GW, Ellefson ME, Mair DC, Church TR, Goldberg CL, et al. (2011) Analysis of a homologous series of perfluorocarboxylates from American Red Cross adult blood donors, 2000-2001 and 2006. Environ Sci Technol 45: 8022–8029.

9

Childhood ADHD and Risk for Substance Dependence in Adulthood: A Longitudinal, Population-Based Study

Sharon Levy[1], Slavica K. Katusic[2]*, Robert C. Colligan[3], Amy L. Weaver[2], Jill M. Killian[2], Robert G. Voigt[4], William J. Barbaresi[1]*

1 Division of Developmental Medicine, Boston Children's Hospital, Harvard Medical School, Boston, Massachusetts, United States of America, **2** Department of Health Sciences Research, Mayo Clinic, Rochester, Minnesota, United States of America, **3** Department of Psychiatry and Psychology, Mayo Clinic, Rochester, Minnesota, United States of America, **4** Department of Pediatrics, Texas Children's Hospital, Baylor College of Medicine, Houston, Texas, United States of America

Abstract

Background: Adolescents with attention-deficit/hyperactivity disorder (ADHD) are known to be at significantly greater risk for the development of substance use disorders (SUD) compared to peers. Impulsivity, which could lead to higher levels of drug use, is a known symptom of ADHD and likely accounts, in part, for this relationship. Other factors, such as a biologically increased susceptibility to substance dependence (addiction), may also play a role.

Objective: This report further examines the relationships between childhood ADHD, adolescent- onset SUD, and substance *abuse* and substance *dependence* in adulthood.

Method: Individuals with childhood ADHD and non-ADHD controls from the same population-based birth cohort were invited to participate in a prospective outcome study. Participants completed a structured neuropsychiatric interview with modules for SUD and a psychosocial questionnaire. Information on adolescent SUD was obtained retrospectively, in a previous study, from medical and school records. Associations were summarized using odds ratios (OR) and 95% CIs estimated from logistic regression models adjusted for age and gender.

Results: A total of 232 ADHD cases and 335 non-ADHD controls participated (mean age, 27.0 and 28.6 years, respectively). ADHD cases were more likely than controls to have a SUD diagnosed in adolescence and were more likely to have alcohol (adjusted OR 14.38, 95% CI 1.49–138.88) and drug (adjusted OR 3.48, 95% CI 1.38–8.79) dependence in adulthood. The subgroup of participating ADHD cases who did not have SUD during adolescence were no more likely than controls to develop new onset alcohol dependence as adults, although they were significantly more likely to develop new onset drug dependence.

Conclusions: Our study found preliminary evidence that adults with childhood ADHD are more susceptible than peers to developing *drug dependence*, a disorder associated with neurological changes in the brain. The relationship between ADHD and alcohol dependence appears to be more complex.

Editor: Efthimios M. C. Skoulakis, Alexander Fleming Biomedical Sciences Research Center, Greece

Funding: Supported by Public Health Service research grants MH076111, HD29745, and AG034676. Pilot work for the prospective portion of the project was funded by an investigator-initiated grant from McNeil Consumer and Specialty Pharmaceuticals. The funders had no role in study design, data collection and analyses, decision to publish, or preparation of the manuscript.

Competing Interests: Pilot work for the prospective portion of this project was provided through an investigator-initiated research grant from McNeil Consumer and Specialty Pharmaceuticals.

* Email: William.Barbaresi@childrens.harvard.edu (WB); Slavica.Katusic@mayo.edu (SK)

Introduction

Individuals with attention-deficit/hyperactivity disorder (ADHD) are known to be at significantly greater risk for the development of substance use disorders (SUD) compared to their non-ADHD peers. [1–3] The *Diagnostic and Statistical Manual of Mental Disorders, Fourth Edition-Text Revision* (DSM-IV-TR) had defined two types of SUDs: *substance abuse* (substance use that interferes with daily functioning or is associated with recurrent problems) and *substance dependence* (manifested by an intense desire for the drug of choice and loss of control over use). [4] (The nomenclature was changed to mild-, moderate- or severe- SUD in the Diagnostic and Statistical Manual of Mental Disorders, Fifth Edition (DSM-5), [5] with "substance abuse" roughly correlating to moderate SUD and "substance dependence" to severe SUD. In this manuscript we will use the terms "abuse" and "dependence" because we are reporting on data from a standardized neuropsychiatric interview that was validated based on DSM-IV terms and definitions.) Research over the past decade has revealed that substance dependence (addiction, or severe SUD) is a neurologically-based disorder resulting from disruption of neurons in the reward center of the brain. This disruption results from repeated exposure to a psychoactive substance. [6–8] While substance *abuse* and substance *dependence* are grouped together as "substance use disorders", they are clearly different: substance *dependence* involves a distinct pattern of neurological changes caused by repeated exposure to a psychoactive substance, while substance *abuse* does not.

Human brain development occurs in an orderly, rostral-caudal progression. Notably, the nucleus accumbens, sometimes referred to as the "reward center," is mature by mid-adolescence, while the maturation of the pre-frontal cortex continues until the mid-20's. [9] A body of epidemiologic data and analysis has established that the earlier an individual initiates psychoactive substance use, the more likely she or he is to ultimately develop substance dependence, with a near linear relationship. [10–13] In the population at large, by early adulthood, individuals seem to develop a relative resistance to substance dependence and the incidence falls dramatically. The declining incidence is thought to be related in part to maturation of the pre-frontal cortex [14,15] and attendant maturation of "executive functions."

Previously, we reported on the association between ADHD and SUD prior to 18 years of age among research-identified childhood ADHD cases and controls from a population-based birth cohort. [1] Our childhood ADHD cases were 6.2 times more likely (95% CI = 4.0–9.4; $p<0.001$) to have an alcohol/drug use disorder documented in their medical and/or school records than non-ADHD controls from the same birth cohort. Other investigators have also clearly demonstrated this relationship. [16–18] In our previous study, the association between ADHD case status and SUD was consistent for both boys and girls. Stimulant treatment tended to be protective, especially in boys, with significantly fewer stimulant-treated boys having a documented SUD during adolescence compared to boys with ADHD who were not treated with stimulants. [1].

The mechanisms underlying the relationship between ADHD and SUD are not fully understood, and previous research has not distinguished between substance *abuse* and substance *dependence* among individuals with ADHD. This distinction, however, may help to elucidate the complex relationship between the two disorders. This report examines the relationships between ADHD, substance abuse, and substance dependence among adults with research-identified childhood ADHD versus controls in order to explore whether individuals with ADHD are more susceptible to developing the neurological disorder of substance dependence in adulthood, after the typical period of heightened vulnerability in adolescence.

Methods

Study Setting

Rochester, Minnesota is geographically isolated in southeastern Minnesota and virtually all medical care for residents of Rochester is provided by Mayo Clinic, Olmsted Medical Center, and their 3 affiliated hospitals. The resources of the Rochester Epidemiology Project (REP) provide infrastructure for population-based research. [19,20] All medical diagnoses and surgical procedures are recorded and indexed for computerized retrieval. For this ADHD study, all 41 public and private schools in Minnesota Independent School District 535 (city of Rochester school system) participated in a contractual research agreement that gave us permission to access their cumulative educational records for every child from the 1976–1982 Rochester, MN birth cohort. Written informed consent was obtained from all participants in the prospective portion of this study. The study was approved by the Institutional Review Boards of Mayo Clinic and Olmsted Medical Center.

Retrospective Phase of the Study

Birth Cohort. This study employed a birth cohort consisting of all children born between January 1, 1976, and December 31, 1982, to mothers residing in the townships comprising Minnesota Independent School District 535, who continued to live in Rochester until at least age 5 years (N = 5718). Nineteen subjects with severe intellectual disability were subsequently excluded.

Identification of Childhood ADHD Cases and Controls. Our approach to identify ADHD incidence cases consisted of several steps, used multiple sources of information, and relied on recorded history of symptoms, individual test results (psychological assessments, including ADHD rating scales), and treatment documented in medical and school records that were available for all members of the birth cohort. Details of this process were previously reported. [21] Briefly, several steps were used to narrow the pool of potential ADHD incident cases, starting with cumulative school records of each child in the birth cohort (n = 5718). School records were searched for indications of concern about learning and/or behavior; 1961 children were identified with such concerns documented by teachers, parents, school psychologists, physicians, social workers, or/and school nurses. Next, we abstracted all descriptions of ADHD symptoms consistent with DSM-IV, results from teacher/parent ADHD questionnaires and clinical diagnoses of ADHD from school and medical records.

Identification of ADHD incident cases consisted of applying research criteria to these 1961 children. Subjects were defined as research-identified ADHD incident cases if their school/medical records included various combinations of three different categories of information: 1) met DSM-IV criteria for ADHD, 2) positive ADHD questionnaire results, 3) clinical diagnosis of ADHD. A total of 379 childhood ADHD incident cases were identified. Research diagnostic criteria were met at a mean age of 10.4 years. Non-ADHD controls were identified from the remaining members of the birth cohort who were in the community after 5 years of age, and who had *not* fulfilled research criteria for childhood ADHD.

Identification of Childhood Psychiatric Disorders among ADHD Cases and Controls. Details regarding the identification of co-occurring psychiatric disorders in childhood among ADHD cases and controls in this birth cohort are described elsewhere, [21] and consisted of a systematic, multistage process, utilizing detailed, routinely collected data as part of the Rochester Epidemiology Project. [19] This process included systematic abstraction of data from the medical records of ADHD cases and controls. To be classified with a psychiatric disorder in this study, we required documentation of (a) the initial diagnosis and (b) separate confirmation of the initial diagnosis prior to 18 years of age.

Identification of Adolescent Onset SUD's among ADHD Cases and Controls. Information about alcohol and/or drug abuse was available in school records (e.g., school psychologist notes, guidance counselor reports, summaries of school assessments, social workers' notes) and/or medical records (social worker, psychology and psychiatry records including correspondence regarding treatment for substance abuse provided by private treatment facilities). The school and medical records of each of the ADHD case and control subjects were reviewed by trained abstractors using a detailed protocol, for documentation of a clinical diagnosis of SUD. Additionally, the computerized Medical Diagnostic Index was also searched for any diagnosis related to or including "substance use disorder" among the 379 childhood ADHD cases under study and their matched controls. Adolescent onset "substance use disorder" required documentation of SUD in the medical and or school records prior to 18 years of age. [1].

Stimulant Medication Treatment. Medical and school records for every member of the birth cohort were reviewed and all documentation about treatment with stimulant medications was abstracted. We have previously described stimulant treatment among this cohort of ADHD cases, including age of onset, dosage, and duration of treatment throughout childhood. [22].

Prospective Phase of the Study

Recruitment for Prospective Study. Of the 379 subjects with research-identified childhood ADHD identified in our retrospective study, 362 provided continued permission to access their medical records for research and were invited to participate in the adult outcome study. To ensure enrollment of sufficient non-ADHD controls, a random sample of 801 adults from the same birth cohort was also invited to participate. Five control subjects in the prospective study stated they had received a diagnosis of childhood ADHD. We reviewed records from these 5 subjects and determined that they had fulfilled our research criteria for childhood ADHD, but had not been thus classified previously because they had moved from the community before receiving this diagnosis or because of the timing of the original data abstraction. These 5 subjects were therefore reclassified as childhood ADHD cases for all analyses presented in this paper.

Identification of Adult Psychiatric Disorders and SUDs among Childhood ADHD Cases and Controls. All participants in the prospective study were administered the Mini International Neuropsychiatric Interview (M.I.N.I), including the module for Adult ADHD. [23,24] The M.I.N.I. is a structured diagnostic interview for DSM-IV-TR and ICD-10 psychiatric disorders. Psychiatric disorders were determined by symptoms consistent with DSM-IV TR/ICD 10 as specified by the M.I.N.I.

The M.I.N.I. includes modules on "Alcohol Abuse and Dependence". Each subject was first asked, "In the past 12 months, have you had 3 or more alcoholic drinks within a 3 hour period on 3 or more occasions?" All subjects responding "yes" to this first item were then asked a series of questions to determine classification as *current* alcohol dependence or *current* alcohol abuse. For the purposes of this study, subjects who reported consuming 3 alcoholic drinks within a 3 hour period on 3 or more occasions, but who did not meet criteria for alcohol abuse or dependence, were defined as having *heavy alcohol use*. Alcohol *abuse* and alcohol *dependence* were defined as per the M.I.N.I. Because the M.I.N.I does not ask about lower levels of alcohol use, subjects who did not report "heavy drinking" were defined as *no heavy alcohol use*. The M.I.N.I. also includes modules for "Non-Alcohol Psychoactive Substance Use Disorders." The latter modules are completed for each psychoactive substance used in the past 12 months to "get high, to feel better, or to change your mood." According to the M.I.N.I. administration protocol, a diagnosis of "dependence" pre-empts a diagnosis of "abuse" for all substances. For the purposes of this study, we defined any illicit substance use that did not meet criteria for drug abuse or dependence as drug *use without a disorder*. Drug *abuse* and drug *dependence* were defined as per the M.I.N.I., and drug *exposure* was defined as drug *use*, drug *abuse*, or drug *dependence*.

SUD Treatment. All subjects completed an extensive psychosocial questionnaire that included specific questions about having participated in a treatment program for "alcohol or drinking problems", "marijuana use," or "other street drugs or hard drugs."

Statistical Methods. Characteristics were compared between participating and non-participating ADHD cases and between participating ADHD cases and participating non-ADHD controls using the two-sample t-test for age, the Fisher's exact test for race, and the chi-square test for all other categorical variables. Current SUD outcomes in young adulthood (as determined from the M.I.N.I.) were first compared overall between individuals with childhood ADHD and non-ADHD controls and then separately stratified by adolescent onset SUD. The association between the 4-level current drug exposure status (no use, drug use without a disorder, abuse, dependence) and ADHD case status was assessed based on fitting a generalized logits model. The association between current drug dependence and ADHD case status was assessed based on fitting a binary logistic regression model. All logistic regression models included gender and age at participation and all reported odds ratios (OR) are reported as ORs adjusted for age and gender unless otherwise noted. The same approach was used to analyze current alcohol exposure. The Sobel test was used to test whether the estimate of mediation for co-occurring childhood psychiatric diagnoses was statistically significant. [25] All calculated p-values were two-sided and p-values less than 0.05 were considered statistically significant. Analyses were performed using SAS version 9.2 software (SAS Institute, Inc.; Cary, NC; 2010).

Results

Description of Participants in the Prospective Phase of the Study

Participating adults with childhood ADHD ($n = 232$) were similar to non-participants ($n = 152$) in regard to gender, age, ethnicity, rates of co-occurring mental health disorders, and stimulant treatment history. Control subjects were slightly older at the time of follow-up participation, more likely to be female, and significantly less likely to have had a co-occurring mental health disorder during childhood as compared to ADHD cases (Table 1).

Substance Use Disorders in Adolescence and Adulthood Among ADHD Cases and Controls

ADHD cases were significantly more likely to have SUD diagnosed during adolescence compared to controls (23.7% vs. 4.5%; unadjusted OR 6.63, 95% CI 3.64–12.08; Table 1). Among the 55 ADHD cases with adolescent onset SUD, the median age of SUD documented in the medical and school records was 16.3 years (range 13.2–18.0), while among the 15 controls with adolescent onset SUD, median age of SUD was 16.9 years (range 15.4–17.8). ADHD cases were also more likely to meet criteria for drug dependence (10.8% vs. 2.7%; adjusted OR 4.42, 95% CI 1.95–9.99, $p<0.001$) and alcohol dependence (14.7% vs. 8.7%; adjusted OR 1.87, 95% CI 1.07–3.27, $p = 0.03$) in adulthood. Marijuana was the most common substance of dependence among participating cases and controls (Table 2).

Drug Use in Adulthood by Adolescent Onset SUD Status

Among the subgroup of participants who did not have adolescent onset SUD, rates of drug exposure in adulthood (i.e. drug use, drug abuse or drug dependence) were higher in adulthood among ADHD cases compared with controls (27.7% vs. 18.1%, Table 3). Notably rates of drug *use* and *abuse* were similar while ADHD cases were approximately 3.5 times more likely to develop drug dependence (vs. no drug use) compared to controls (adjusted OR 3.48, 95% CI 1.38–8.79, $p = 0.01$). Simply put, as ADHD cases grew into adults, they were both more likely to use drugs and more likely to develop new onset drug

Table 1. Comparison of demographic factors, co-occurring mental health disorders and stimulant treatment among participating ADHD cases, non-participating ADHD cases and controls.

Characteristic		ADHD cases		Participating Non-ADHD Controls (N = 335)	Participating ADHD cases vs. Non-participating ADHD cases,	Participating ADHD cases vs. Participating Non-ADHD controls, *P*
		Participating ADHD cases (N = 232)	Non-Participating ADHD cases (N = 152)			
Male, n (%)		167 (72.0)	121 (79.6)	210 (62.7)	0.09	0.02
Age at time of participation (years)	Mean (SD)	27.0 (2.6)	–	28.6 (2.2)	–	<0.001
	Range	21.7–33.5	–	24.3–33.8	–	
White, n (%)		231 (99.6)	150 (98.7)	329 (98.2)	0.57	0.25
Received stimulant treatment, n (%)		178 (76.7)	119 (78.3)	–	0.72	–
Psychiatric diagnosis prior to age 18, n (%)	Unknown, n	0	17†	0	0.92	<0.001
	No	101 (43.5)	58 (43.0)	281 (83.9)		
	Yes	131 (56.5)	77 (57.0)	54 (16.1)		
Substance use disorder (SUD) prior to age 18, n (%)	Unknown, n	0	17†	0	0.75	<0.001
	No	177 (76.3)	105 (77.8)	320 (95.5)		
	Yes	55 (23.7)	30 (22.2)	15 (4.5)		

†Seventeen of the non-participating ADHD cases had not authorized access to their medical records for research purposes at the time of the abstraction of these two parameters.

dependence than controls. The effect is mediated through co-occurring childhood psychiatric diagnoses, which accounts for 39.2% of the association (p = 0.014).

Among the individuals who did have adolescent onset SUD, rates of drug exposure in adulthood tended to be higher in ADHD cases as compared to controls (49.1% vs. 20.0%; Table 3). However, given the limited sample size, we were unable to identify significant differences in the rates of non-alcohol drug use, drug abuse, or drug dependence in adulthood between ADHD cases and controls who had adolescent onset SUD.

Alcohol Use in Adulthood by Adolescent Onset SUD Status

Among the subgroup of individuals with adolescent-onset SUD, those with ADHD were significantly more likely to have alcohol dependence (vs. no heavy alcohol use) as adults compared to controls (29.1% vs. 6.7%; adjusted OR 14.38, 95% CI 1.49–138.88, p = 0.02; Table 4). Our findings on alcohol dependence among the subgroup of adults who did not have a SUD in adolescence were distinctly different. In this group, ADHD cases were less likely to report heavy alcohol use (i.e. 3 or more drinks in a 3 hour period) (adjusted OR 0.56, 95% CI 0.36–0.88, p = 0.01) while there were no differences in the rates of alcohol abuse

Table 2. Subjects with drug dependence in adulthood, by substance†.

Substance	ADHD Cases N = 232	Controls N = 335
Marijuana	16	6
Cocaine	11	4
Stimulants	10	2
Narcotics‡	3	1
Tranquilizers*	3	0
Hallucinogens††	2	0

†Some subjects were found to be dependent on more than one substance. A total of 18 ADHD cases and 5 controls were dependent on substances other than marijuana.
‡Includes heroin, morphine, Dilaudid, opium, Demerol, methadone, codeine, Percodan, Darvon, OxyContin.
*Includes quaalude, Seconal ("reds"), Valium, Xanax, Librium, Ativan, Dalmane, Halcion, barbituates, Miltown.
††Includes LSD ("acid"), mescaline, peyote, PCP ("Angel dust", "peace pill"), psilocybin, STP, "mushrooms", ecstasy, MDA, MDMA.

Table 3. Current drug use, abuse and dependence among adults with versus without childhood ADHD, stratified by substance use disorder prior to 18 years of age.

Current Status	Adolescent Onset SUD = No			Adolescent Onset SUD = Yes		
	ADHD Cases (N = 177)	Non-ADHD (N = 320)	Adjusted OR‡ (95% CI), P	ADHD Cases (N = 55)	Non-ADHD (N = 15)	Adjusted OR‡ (95% CI), P
No drug use	128 (72.3%)	262 (81.9%)	Referent	28 (50.9%)	12 (80.0%)	Referent
Drug use without a disorder	28 (15.8%)	38 (11.9%)	1.11 (0.63–1.98), 0.72	10 (18.2%)	1 (6.7%)	5.17 (0.56–47.86), 0.15
Drug abuse	6 (3.4%)	12 (3.8%)	0.81 (0.28–2.36), 0.69	7 (12.7%)	1 (6.7%)	2.97 (0.30–29.24), 0.35
Drug dependence	15 (8.5%)	8 (2.5%)	3.48 (1.38–8.79), 0.01	10 (18.2%)	1 (6.7%)	5.97 (0.64–55.61), 0.12

OR, odds ratio; CI, confidence interval.
†Drug (non-alcohol) substances include the following: stimulants, cocaine, narcotics, hallucinogens, inhalants, marijuana, and tranquilizers. In order to create mutually exclusive categories, each individual's overall current non-alcohol substance use status was classified as the most severe status among all substances.
‡Adjusted for age and gender.
*Adjusted for age.

(adjusted OR 1.31, 95% CI 0.64–2.71, p = 0.46) or dependence (adjusted OR 0.94, 95% CI 0.47–1.89, p = 0.86).

Persistence of Alcohol and Non-Alcohol Substance Dependence from Adolescence to Adulthood

The complex relationship between childhood ADHD, adolescent- onset SUD, and adult SUD's are summarized in Figure 1. The overall rate of persistent SUD from adolescence into young adulthood was higher among childhood ADHD cases versus controls (19/232 or 8.2% versus 2/335 or 0.6%; $p<0.001$). Among the subgroup of subjects with adolescent-onset SUD, SUD persisted into adulthood for 34.6% for ADHD cases (19/55) versus 13.3% for controls (2/15). This finding was not statistically significant ($p = 0.20$) due to limited power, with only 15 controls having adolescent-onset SUD.

Impact of Stimulant Treatment in childhood on Substance Dependence in Adulthood

Our previous, retrospective review of records found that 178 of the 232 ADHD cases received stimulant treatment in childhood, and information about the age at which stimulants were started and duration of treatment was available for 167. [23] Subjects who were treated for 6 months or longer (n = 139) were considered "treated" for analyses of the association between stimulant treatment in childhood and substance dependence in adulthood. For analyses of the association between stimulant treatment and risk for adult drug or alcohol dependence, we dichotomized subjects into those who received any treatment after the age of 13 years (n = 114) versus those who only received treatment prior to age 13 years (n = 25). We found no association between timing of stimulant treatment during childhood and classification as adult drug or alcohol dependence when each of these outcomes were analyzed separately; however, the combined risk for *either* adult drug or alcohol dependence was higher among subjects who had received at least some stimulant treatment after age 13 years (Table 5). Furthermore, there was no association between age of initiation, dosage, or duration of stimulant treatment and risk for SUD (data not shown).

Impact of ADHD on treatment for substance dependence

We calculated the rates of substance dependence among ADHD cases and controls who had received any form of treatment for a SUD to examine whether ADHD moderated SUD treatment effects. Overall, we found that individuals with ADHD were more likely than controls to have received treatment for alcohol, marijuana, or other drug use disorders (26.7% vs. 9.3%; adjusted OR 3.37, 95% CI, 2.05–5.54, $p<0.001$). Forty-seven ADHD cases and 19 controls reported treatment for alcohol disorders. Among study participants who received treatment for an alcohol disorder, ADHD cases were more likely to have alcohol *dependence* in adulthood compared with controls (40.4% (19/47) vs. 15.6% (3/

Table 4. Current heavy alcohol use, abuse and dependence among adults with versus without childhood ADHD, stratified by substance use disorder prior to 18 years of age.

Current Status	Adolescent Onset SUD = No			Adolescent Onset SUD = Yes		
	ADHD Cases (N = 177)	Non-ADHD (N = 320)	Adjusted OR‡ (95% CI), P	ADHD Cases (N = 55)	Non-ADHD (N = 15)	Adjusted OR‡ (95% CI), P
No heavy alcohol use	77 (43.5%)	125 (39.1%)	Referent	14 (25.5%)	9 (60.0%)	Referent
Heavy alcohol use	60 (33.9%)	146 (45.6%)	0.56 (0.36–0.88), 0.01	20 (36.4%)	4 (26.7%)	3.12 (0.73–13.29), 0.12
Alcohol abuse	22 (12.4%)	21 (6.6%)	1.31 (0.64–2.71), 0.46	5 (9.1%)	1 (6.7%)	3.24 (0.29–36.65), 0.34
18 (10.2%)	18 (10.2%)	28 (8.8%)	0.94 (0.47–1.89), 0.86	16 (29.1%)	1 (6.7%)	14.38 (1.49–138.88), 0.02

OR, odds ratio; CI, confidence interval.
†Adjusted for age and gender.
*Adjusted for ag.

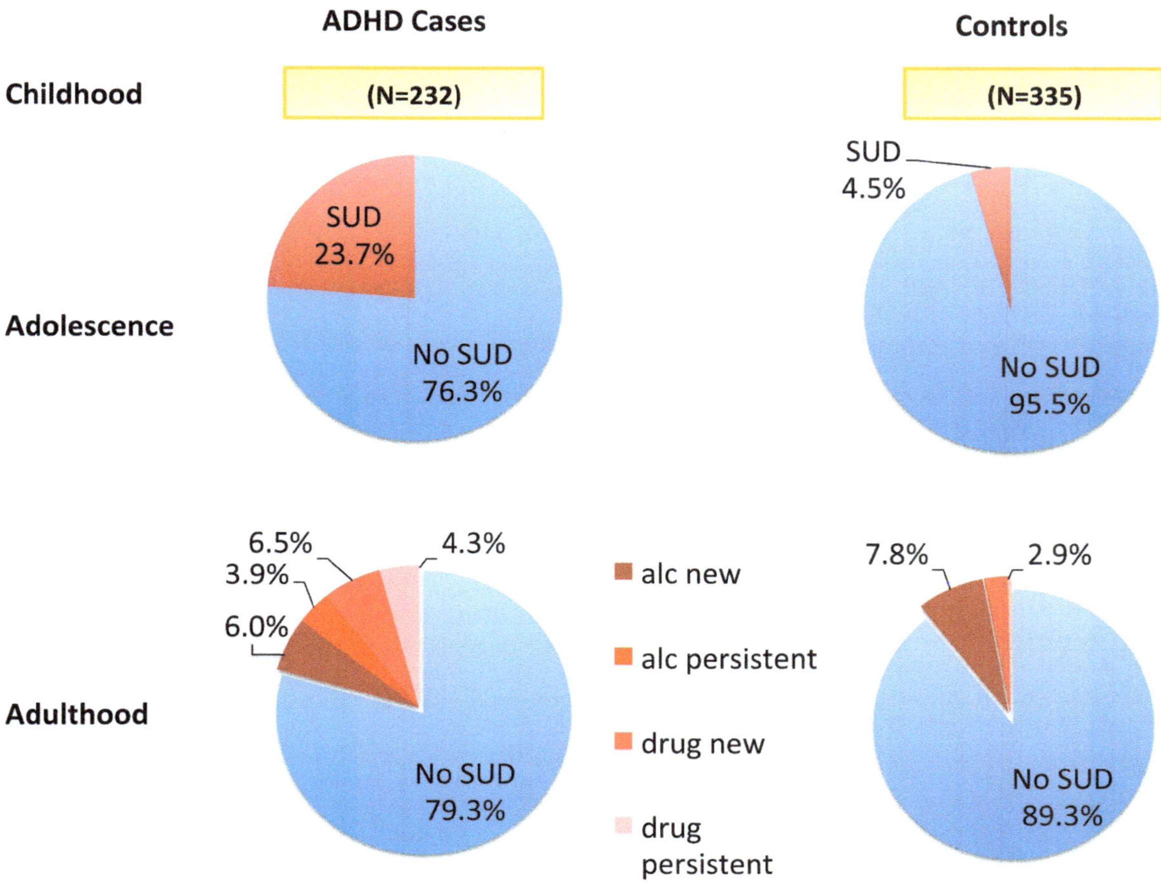

Figure 1. Adolescent SUD and adult substance dependence outcomes for childhood ADHD incident cases and controls. *Individuals with both "drug" dependence and alcohol dependence are coded as drug dependent in these figures. Individuals coded as alcohol dependent did not meet dependence criteria for any other substance.

19); adjusted OR 3.84, 95% CI 0.95–15.57, p = 0.06). Few participants had received treatment for marijuana or another drug disorder, and we did not find statistically significant effects for other substances.

Discussion

Our study provides initial evidence that individuals with childhood ADHD remain more susceptible than peers (without ADHD) to developing new onset drug dependence, a disorder associated with neurological changes in the brain, in adulthood. This finding suggests that early onset drug use, a factor known to increase the risk of developing substance dependence, does not fully account for the relationship between ADHD and SUD. Overall, the rate of drug exposure (i.e. drug use or drug abuse or drug dependence) was higher in adults with ADHD, suggesting that impulsivity and poor decision-making continue to play a role. However, among individuals who reported any drug use as adults, rates of new onset drug dependence was significantly higher among ADHD cases – suggesting that the relationship is multifactorial and not fully explained simply by a greater propensity to use drugs. Furthermore, our findings suggest that individuals with ADHD are more likely than their non-ADHD peers to have persistence of substance dependence in young adulthood. Our data did not allow us to evaluate the relationship between individual drugs and adult onset substance dependence because of small cell sizes, and it is possible that results vary depending on substance. We note that marijuana was the most frequently used drug by adult participants in this study. It is important to note that

Table 5. Impact of stimulant treatment in childhood on substance dependence in adulthood.

Substance Dependence Status	Stimulant treatment ended before age 13 (N = 25)	Stimulant treatment ended after age 13 (N = 114)	*P value*
Alcohol dependence	1 (4.0%)	19 (16.7%)	0.125
Substance dependence	1 (4.0%)	12 (10.5%)	0.463
Alcohol or substance dependence	1 (4.0%)	25 (21.9%)	0.046

"medical" marijuana was not recommended during the years when members of this birth cohort were children or adolescents, so these findings cannot be attributed to clinician recommendations. Most importantly, while some advocates for "medical" marijuana have suggested marijuana as a potential therapy for ADHD, our findings of heightened susceptibility to adult onset substance dependence give reason for pause.

The pre-frontal cortex is an area of the brain that has been implicated in ADHD, [26–28] and poor executive functioning is one of the core features of the disorder. [29–32] Perhaps not surprisingly, we found that adults with a history of childhood ADHD who did not have a SUD during adolescence were nevertheless significantly more likely than controls to develop drug dependence, a condition known to be associated with poor executive functioning during young adulthood. This finding is mediated by the presence of co-occurring mental health disorders, and we speculate that the maturation of executive functions might be further slowed in individuals with a mental health disorder, leaving them at very high risk for using drugs and developing drug dependence. This group should be counseled to avoid drugs and should be carefully monitored for SUDs beyond adolescence.

Our findings regarding alcohol use were different. Individuals with childhood ADHD and adolescent SUD were more likely to have *alcohol dependence* in adulthood. However, ADHD cases that did not develop a SUD in their teens were less likely than peers to drink heavily and they were *not* at increased risk for developing new onset *alcohol dependence*.

While all substances of abuse have action in the brain's "reward center," alcohol's mechanism of action is distinct. Unlike marijuana and most other illicit substances, alcohol freely crosses cell membranes and exerts its actions on a variety of targets, rather than via a specific receptor. Alcohol dependence is highly heritable, with some individuals particularly prone to developing alcohol use disorders and others relatively resistant. For example, specific alleles for genes that encode alcohol dehydrogenase appear to be protective against alcoholism. Animal studies have found that the neuronal sensitivity to alcohol induced excitation is lower in mice that are bred to be "heavy drinkers." [33].

We speculate that individuals with ADHD can be divided into two groups regarding liability for developing alcohol dependence. Individuals with a "high liability" develop alcohol use disorders in adolescence and have persistent alcohol dependence in adulthood. In other words, adolescents with ADHD may be less likely to "outgrow" an alcohol use disorder than their peers. As in reports from other authors, we found that treatment for SUD is less effective in this group. [34–39] On the other hand, individuals with ADHD who have a "lower liability" for alcohol problems may be *less* likely to drink heavily which may be protective from developing alcohol use disorders in both adolescence and adulthood. We cannot tell from our data whether this "liability" is inborn or present early in life, or the result of refraining from substance use during adolescence. Whatever the mediators, they seem to be specifically related to alcohol regulation and do not protect individuals from developing *drug dependence* as adults. While the causes remain unclear, it seems prudent to counsel adolescents with ADHD to avoid alcohol use. The National Institute on Alcohol Abuse and Alcoholism (NIAAA) has recommended alcohol screening and brief intervention for children as young as 9 years old, the age prior to initiation of alcohol use for most individuals. [40] Our findings highlight the importance of preventative alcohol counseling, particularly for individuals with ADHD.

In our previous retrospective study of the association between stimulant treatment and risk for SUD through adolescence in this cohort of childhood ADHD cases, we found that among boys who were treated, 21.8% had substance abuse compared to 36.4% for those not treated. [1] However, among girls who were treated (N = 10), 15.2% had substance abuse compared to 10.3% of those not treated, although the total number of girls with SUD in adolescence was small (n = 13). In the current, prospective study of SUD outcomes in adulthood, subjects who received stimulant treatment for at least 6 months, and who received some treatment after age 13 years, were at *greater* risk for adult drug or alcohol dependence than subjects who only received stimulant treatment prior to age 13 years. Given our finding of increased risk for SUD developing after adolescence among ADHD cases, it should not be surprising that stimulant treatment ending in mid-adolescence would be unlikely to continue to protect against the subsequent development of drug or alcohol dependence. Furthermore, although it cannot be determined from our dataset, subjects who continued to receive treatment after age 13 years may have had more severe ADHD symptoms and hence may have been at greater risk for development of SUD. Future studies that ensure continued stimulant treatment of ADHD through young adulthood may offer an opportunity to better understand the potential impact of stimulant treatment on risk for SUD into adulthood.

Our study has a number of strengths. Our data came from a large, population-based birth cohort and did not depend on a sample referred for ADHD treatment, which typically over represents individuals with the most challenging disorders. Our birth cohort was large, retrospective data was extensive, and our prospective data included a comprehensive, structured neuropsychiatric interview, making our data set unique among published studies of ADHD outcomes. We also note a number of limitations. Our retrospective data did not include age of initiation of substance use, which was not routinely noted in the medical record. Thus, we were unable to evaluate the relationship between age of initiation of substance use and outcomes. Retrospective data were not sufficiently detailed to distinguish between substance *abuse* and substance *dependence* during adolescence nor to determine which substances were used during adolescence. Our control group was well matched on demographic measures, though co-occurring mental health disorders were more common in ADHD cases than controls, and these disorders play a role in the relationship between ADHD and SUD. It is also possible that other, unmeasured factors may confound our findings. Although our initial cohort of ADHD cases was large, the number of subjects with adolescent-onset SUD followed into adulthood was smaller, contributing to relatively large confidence intervals around estimates of rates of adult SUD in this sub-group; hence, these specific results should be interpreted with caution.

Conclusions

This report is the first to utilize a population-based birth-cohort to examine the relationship between childhood ADHD and SUD during young adulthood and to describe differential rates of new onset substance dependence in adults with a history of childhood ADHD. Our findings make an important contribution in understanding the intersection between these two common disorders. Most importantly, our findings underscore the importance of continuous monitoring, prevention and early intervention for substance use among children, adolescents, and adults with ADHD to prevent the development of substance dependence. Further study is needed to determine the most effective mechanisms for achieving these goals.

Acknowledgments

We thank study coordinators Candice Klein and Ann Van Oosten for their efforts in subject recruitment and conduct of the study assessments, and Rosemary Ziemnik for assistance in preparing this manuscript.

Author Contributions

Conceived and designed the experiments: SL SK RC AW JK RV WB. Performed the experiments: SK RC RV WB. Analyzed the data: SL SK RC AW JK RV WB. Contributed to the writing of the manuscript: SL SK RC AW JK RV WB.

References

1. Katusic SK, Barbaresi WJ, Colligan RC, Weaver AL, Leibson CL, et al. (2005) Psychostimulant treatment and risk for substance abuse among young adults with a history of attention-deficit/hyperactivity disorder: a population-based, birth cohort study. J Child Adolesc Psychopharmacol 15: 764–776. Available: http://www.ncbi.nlm.nih.gov/entrez/query.fcgi?cmd = Retrieve&db = PubMed&dopt = Citation&list_uids = 16262593.
2. Upadhyaya HP, Rose K, Wang W, O'Rourke K, Sullivan B, et al. (2005) Attention-deficit/hyperactivity disorder, medication treatment, and substance use patterns among adolescents and young adults. J Child Adolesc Psychopharmacol 15: 799–809. Available: http://online.liebertpub.com.ezp-prod1.hul.harvard.edu/doi/abs/10.1089/cap.2005.15.799?journalCode = cap. Accessed 2014 February 6.
3. Groenman AP, Oosterlaan J, Rommelse N, Franke B, Roeyers H, et al. (2013) Substance use disorders in adolescents with attention deficit hyperactivity disorder: a 4-year follow-up study. Addiction 108: 1503–1511. Available: http://www.ncbi.nlm.nih.gov/pubmed/23506232. Accessed 2014 February 7.
4. American Psychiatric Association (1994) Diagnostic and Statistical Manual of Mental Disorders. Fourth Edi. Washington, DC: American Psychiatric Association.
5. American Psychiatric Association (2013) Diagnostic and Statistical Manual of Mental Disorders, Fifth Edition. Arlington, VA: American Psychiatric Association.
6. Nestler EJ (2001) Molecular basis of long-term plasticity underlying addiction. Nat Rev Neurosci 2: 119–128. Available: http://www.nature.com.ezp-prod1.hul.harvard.edu/nrn/journal/v2/n2/full/nrn0201_119a.html. Accessed 2014 February 6.
7. Volkow ND, Li T-K (2004) Drug addiction: the neurobiology of behaviour gone awry. Nat Rev Neurosci 5: 963–970. Available: http://www.nature.com.ezp-prod1.hul.harvard.edu/nrn/journal/v5/n12/full/nrn1539.html. Accessed 2014 February 6.
8. Everitt BJ, Belin D, Economidou D, Pelloux Y, Dalley JW, et al. (2008) Review. Neural mechanisms underlying the vulnerability to develop compulsive drug-seeking habits and addiction. Philos Trans R Soc Lond B Biol Sci 363: 3125–3135. Available: http://rstb.royalsocietypublishing.org.ezp-prod1.hul.harvard.edu/content/363/1507/3125.short. Accessed 2014 January 24.
9. Gogtay N, Giedd JN, Lusk L, Hayashi KM, Greenstein D, et al. (2004) Dynamic mapping of human cortical development during childhood through early adulthood. Proc Natl Acad Sci U S A 101: 8174–8179. Available: http://www.pubmedcentral.nih.gov/articlerender.fcgi?artid = 419576&tool = pmcentrez&rendertype = abstract. Accessed 2014 February 5.
10. Hingson RW, Heeren T, Winter MR (2006) Age at drinking onset and alcohol dependence: age at onset, duration, and severity. Arch Pediatr Adolesc Med 160: 739–746. Available: http://www.ncbi.nlm.nih.gov/entrez/query.fcgi?cmd = Retrieve&db = PubMed&dopt = Citation&list_uids = 16818840.
11. Grant BF, Dawson DA (1998) Age of onset of drug use and its association with DSM-IV drug abuse and dependence: results from the National Longitudinal Alcohol Epidemiologic Survey. J Subst Abuse 10: 163–173. Available: http://www.ncbi.nlm.nih.gov/pubmed/9854701. Accessed 2014 February 5.
12. Taioli E, Wynder EL (1991) Effect of the Age at Which Smoking Begins on Frequency of Smoking in Adulthood – NEJM. N Engl J Med 325: 968–969. Available: http://www.nejm.org.ezp-prod1.hul.harvard.edu/doi/full/10.1056/NEJM199109263251318. Accessed 2014 February 6.
13. Chen C-Y, Storr CL, Anthony JC (2009) Early-onset drug use and risk for drug dependence problems. Addict Behav 34: 319–322. Available: http://www.sciencedirect.com/science/article/pii/S0306460308003031. Accessed 2014 January 26.
14. Sowell ER, Thompson PM, Holmes CJ, Jernigan TL, Toga AW (1999) In vivo evidence for post-adolescent brain maturation in frontal and striatal regions. Nat Neurosci 2: 859–861. Available: http://www.nature.com.ezp-prod1.hul.harvard.edu/neuro/journal/v2/n10/full/nn1099_859.html. Accessed 2014 February 6.
15. Deas D, Riggs P, Langenbucher J, Goldman M, Brown S (2000) Adolescents are not adults: developmental considerations in alcohol users. Alcohol Clin Exp Res 24: 232–237.
16. Molina BSG, Pelham WE (2003) Childhood predictors of adolescent substance use in a longitudinal study of children with ADHD. J Abnorm Psychol 112: 497–507. Available: http://www.ncbi.nlm.nih.gov/pubmed/12943028. Accessed 2014 February 6.
17. Molina BS, Pelham WE (2001) Substance use, substance abuse, and LD among adolescents with a childhood history of ADHD. J Learn Disabil 34: 333–342, 351. Available: http://www.ncbi.nlm.nih.gov/pubmed/15503577. Accessed 2014 February 6.
18. Lee SS, Humphreys KL, Flory K, Liu R, Glass K (2011) Prospective association of childhood attention-deficit/hyperactivity disorder (ADHD) and substance use and abuse/dependence: a meta-analytic review. Clin Psychol Rev 31: 328–341. Available: http://www.ncbi.nlm.nih.gov/pubmed/21382538.
19. Melton LJ (1996) History of the Rochester Epidemiology Project. Mayo Clin Proc 71: 266–274. doi:10.4065/71.3.266.
20. Rocca WA, Yawn BP, St Sauver JL, Grossardt BR, Melton LJ (2012) History of the Rochester Epidemiology Project: Half a Century of Medical Records Linkage in a US Population. Mayo Clin Proc 87: 1202–1213. Available: http://www.ncbi.nlm.nih.gov/pubmed/23199802.
21. Yoshimasu K, Barbaresi WJ, Colligan RC, Voigt RG, Killian JM, et al. (2012) Childhood ADHD is strongly associated with a broad range of psychiatric disorders during adolescence: a population-based birth cohort study. J Child Psychol Psychiatry Allied Discip 53: 1036–1043. Available: http://www.ncbi.nlm.nih.gov/pubmed/22647074.
22. Barbaresi WJ, Katusic SK, Colligan RC, Weaver AL, Leibson CL, et al. (2006) Long-term stimulant medication treatment of attention-deficit/hyperactivity disorder: results from a population-based study. J Dev Behav Pediatr 27: 1–10. Available: http://www.ncbi.nlm.nih.gov/pubmed/16511362. Accessed 2014 February 5.
23. Sheehan D, Lecrubier Y, Harnett Sheehan K, Janavs J, Weiller E, et al. (1997) The validity of the Mini International Neuropsychiatric Interview (MINI) according to the SCID-P and its reliability. Eur Psychiatry 12: 232–241. doi:10.1016/S0924-9338(97)83297-X.
24. Sheehan DV, Lecrubier Y, Sheehan KH, Amorim P, Janavs J, et al. (1998) The Mini-International Neuropsychiatric Interview (M.I.N.I.): the development and validation of a structured diagnostic psychiatric interview for DSM-IV and ICD-10. J Clin Psychiatry 59 Suppl 2: 22–33;quiz 34–57. doi:10.1590/S1516-44462000000300003.
25. Jasti S, Dudley WN, Goldwater E (2008) SAS Macros for Testing Statistical Mediation in Data With Binary Mediators or Outcomes. Nurs Res 57. Available: http://journals.lww.com/nursingresearchonline/Fulltext/2008/03000/SAS_Macros_for_Testing_Statistical_Mediation_in.8.aspx.
26. Booth JR, Burman DD, Meyer JR, Lei Z, Trommer BL, et al. (2005) Larger deficits in brain networks for response inhibition than for visual selective attention in attention deficit hyperactivity disorder (ADHD). J Child Psychol Psychiatry 46: 94–111. Available: http://www.ncbi.nlm.nih.gov/pubmed/15660647. Accessed 2014 February 5.
27. Rubia K, Smith AB, Brammer MJ, Toone B, Taylor E (2005) Abnormal brain activation during inhibition and error detection in medication-naive adolescents with ADHD. Am J Psychiatry 162: 1067–1075. Available: http://www.ncbi.nlm.nih.gov/pubmed/15930054. Accessed 2014 February 6.
28. Vasic N, Plichta MM, Wolf RC, Fallgatter AJ, Sosic-Vasic Z, et al. (2012) Reduced Neural Error Signaling in Left Inferior Prefrontal Cortex in Young Adults With ADHD. J Atten Disord. Available: http://www.ncbi.nlm.nih.gov/pubmed/22660917. Accessed 2014 February 6.
29. Pennington BF, Ozonoff S (1996) Executive functions and developmental psychopathology. J Child Psychol Psychiatry 37: 51–87. Available: http://www.ncbi.nlm.nih.gov/pubmed/8655658. Accessed 2014 February 6.
30. Barkley RA (1997) Behavioral inhibition, sustained attention, and executive functions: constructing a unifying theory of ADHD. Psychol Bull 121: 65–94. Available: http://www.ncbi.nlm.nih.gov/pubmed/9000892. Accessed 2014 January 22.
31. Schachar R, Mota VL, Logan GD, Tannock R, Klim P (2000) Confirmation of an inhibitory control deficit in attention-deficit/hyperactivity disorder. J Abnorm Child Psychol 28: 227–235. Available: http://www.ncbi.nlm.nih.gov/pubmed/10885681. Accessed 2014 February 6.
32. Nigg JT, Stavro G, Ettenhofer M, Hambrick DZ, Miller T, et al. (2005) Executive functions and ADHD in adults: evidence for selective effects on ADHD symptom domains. J Abnorm Psychol 114: 706–717. Available: http://www.ncbi.nlm.nih.gov/pubmed/16351391. Accessed 2014 February 4.
33. Ries RK, David FA, Miller SC, Saitz R, editors (2009) Principles of Addiction Medicine. Fourth. Philadelphia PA: Lippincott Williams & Wilkins.
34. Wilens TE (2004) Impact of ADHD and its treatment on substance abuse in adults. J Clin Psychiatry 65 Suppl 3: 38–45. Available: http://www.ncbi.nlm.nih.gov/pubmed/15046534. Accessed 2014 February 7.
35. Mariani JJ, Levin FR (2007) Treatment strategies for co-occurring ADHD and substance use disorders. Am J Addict 16 Suppl 1: 45–54; quiz 55–6. Available: http://www.pubmedcentral.nih.gov/articlerender.fcgi?artid = 2676785&tool = pmcentrez&rendertype = abstract. Accessed 2014 February 7.
36. Wise BK, Cuffe SP, Fischer T (2001) Dual diagnosis and successful participation of adolescents in substance abuse treatment. J Subst Abuse Treat 21: 161–165.

Available: http://www.ncbi.nlm.nih.gov/pubmed/11728790. Accessed 2014 February 7.

37. Grella CE, Hser YI, Joshi V, Rounds-Bryant J (2001) Drug treatment outcomes for adolescents with comorbid mental and substance use disorders. J Nerv Ment Dis 189: 384–392. Available: http://www.ncbi.nlm.nih.gov/pubmed/11434639. Accessed 2014 February 7.
38. Wilens TE, Biederman J, Mick E (1998) Does ADHD Affect the Course of Substance Abuse?: Findings From a Sample of Adults With and Without ADHD. Am J Addict 7: 156–163. Available: http://doi.wiley.com/10.1111/j.1521-0391.1998.tb00330.x. Accessed 2014 February 6.
39. Molina BS, Hinshaw SP, Eugene Arnold L, Swanson JM, Pelham WE, et al. (2013) Adolescent substance use in the multimodal treatment study of Attention-Deficit/Hyperactivity Disorder (ADHD) (MTA) as a function of childhood ADHD, random assignment to childhood treatments, and subsequent medication. J Am Acad Child Adolesc Psychiatry 52: 250–263. Available: http://www.ncbi.nlm.nih.gov/pubmed/23452682.
40. National Institute on Alcohol Abuse and Alcoholism (2011) Alcohol Screening and Brief Intervention for Youth: A Practitioner's Guide. NIH Publication No.11–7805. Available: http://pubs.niaaa.nih.gov/publications/Practitioner/YouthGuide/YouthGuide.pdf.

10

Prevalence of and Associated Factors for Adult Attention Deficit Hyperactivity Disorder in Young Swiss Men

Natalia Estévez[1,2]*, Dominique Eich-Höchli[3], Michelle Dey[1], Gerhard Gmel[4], Joseph Studer[4], Meichun Mohler-Kuo[1]

1 Institute of Social and Preventive Medicine, Zurich, Switzerland, **2** Department of Neuroradiology, University Hospital Zurich, Zurich, Switzerland, **3** Psychiatric University Hospital Zurich, Zurich, Switzerland, **4** Alcohol Treatment Centre, Lausanne University Hospital CHUV, Lausanne, Switzerland

Abstract

Objective: The present study aimed to measure the prevalence of adult attention deficit hyperactivity disorder (ADHD) in a large, representative sample of young Swiss men and to assess factors associated with this disorder.

Methods: Our sample consisted of 5656 Swiss men (mean age 20 years) who participated in the Cohort Study on Substance Use Risk Factors (C-SURF). ADHD was assessed with the World Health Organization (WHO) adult ADHD Self Report Screener (ASRS). Logistic regression analyses were conducted to assess the association between ADHD and several socio-demographic, clinical and familial factors.

Results: The prevalence of ADHD was 4.0%, being higher in older and French-speaking conscripts. A higher prevalence also was identified among men whose mothers had completed primary or high school/university and those with a family history of alcohol or psychiatric problems. Additionally, adults with ADHD demonstrated impairment in their professional life, as well as considerable mental health impairment.

Conclusion: Our results demonstrate that ADHD is common among young Swiss men. The impairments in function and mental health we observed highlight the need for further support and interventions to reduce burden in affected individuals. Interventions that incorporate the whole family also seem crucial.

Editor: Efthimios M. C. Skoulakis, Alexander Fleming Biomedical Sciences Research Center, Greece

Funding: This study has been supported by the Swiss National Science Foundation [grant number: 33CS30_139467; website: www.snf.ch]. The funders had no role in study design, data collection and analysis, decision to publish, or preparation of the manuscript.

Competing Interests: The authors have declared that no competing interests exist.

* E-mail: natalia.estevez@ifspm.uzh.ch

Introduction

According to the DSM-IV-TR [1], Attention Deficit Hyperactivity Disorder (ADHD) is characterized by inattention and/or hyperactivity-impulsivity symptoms, which affect functioning considerably in several life domains. In contrast to an earlier assumption that ADHD only occurs during childhood and adolescence, more recent research has demonstrated that ADHD often persists into adulthood [2,3]. Adult ADHD is associated with functional impairment relating to professional achievements (e.g., lower levels of education; poorer socioeconomic outcomes) [3–9] as well as with more difficulties in relationships (e.g., higher rates of unsuccessful marriage; more family conflicts; more problems with peers) [3,5,6,10,11]. Moreover, in adults with ADHD, comorbidities with other psychiatric disorders - particularly with mood disorders, anxiety disorders, antisocial personality disorder and substance use disorder [2,6,8,9,12] - are common and can lead to further impairment.

The functional impairment and poor mental health that many experience can have a cumulative effect over the course of one's life [13], even in those who only exhibit a few ADHD symptoms and thereby fail to meet enough criteria for a clinical diagnosis [8,14]. Thus, achieving better insights into the prevalence of ADHD and its associated factors in young adults may be crucial to preventing negative consequences and reducing illness burdens during later phases of life.

To date, the prevalence of ADHD has mainly been investigated in children and adolescents. In the limited number of studies that have focused on adults, prevalence estimates for ADHD have varied considerably, ranging from 1.0 to 7.5% (For a review, see [15,16]), though even higher rates have been uncovered when more liberal diagnostic criteria were applied [4,14,16,17]. Most of these studies were potentially biased, however, due to their use of convenience samples, drawing from particular communities, families, or from student or patient populations [3,14,16–20] rather than enrolling samples more representative of the community [16]. Only a few studies have assessed prevalence within more representative samples [6,8–10,21,22]. However, some of these studies [6,10,21] utilized indirect methods (e.g., multiple imputation) by which prevalence was estimated only in a small subset of participants, and the attained estimates then extrapolated to the entire sample [16].

To date, no published epidemiological data on adult ADHD in Switzerland exist. In this country, prevalence estimates have been limited to children within the age range of 7 to 17 years. In that group, the prevalence was 5.2% (6.1% boys, 3.3% girls), meaning that it is one of the most common psychiatric disorders observed in this age group [23].

The aims of the present study were (1) to measure the prevalence of adult ADHD within a large, representative sample of young Swiss men; and (2) to identify factors associated with this disorder in this age-group. To our knowledge, this is the largest sample of young men used in a population-based study in Europe to estimate the prevalence of adult ADHD.

Materials and Methods

Study Design

The present study used data drawn from the *'Cohort Study on Substance Use Risk Factors' (C-SURF)*, a longitudinal study designed to assess substance use patterns within a cohort of young Swiss men. The study was approved by the Ethics Committee for Clinical Research at Lausanne University Medical School (protocol number 15/07) and informed written consent was obtained from the participants.

The sample was recruited between August 2010 and November 2011 at three of a total of six centres that recruit men for military service, covering 21 of 26 Swiss cantons (including all French-speaking cantons). Switzerland has a mandatory army recruitment process, such that all Swiss men must submit to a formal evaluation to determine their eligibility for military service, civil service, or no service at approximately age 19. Both those who were deemed eligible to serve in the army and those deemed ineligible for military service were eligible for enrolment in our study. As there is no pre-selection to army conscription, a representative sample of young Swiss men was thereby provided for the study. It is important to note that the army centres were used only to enrol participants into the study. Both the study itself and the men's decision to participate were entirely independent of the army. The present study used data collected during the baseline assessment only.

Participants

A total of 7,563 conscripts gave informed consent to participate in the study. Among them, 5,990 (79.2%) completed the baseline questionnaire. A further 334 conscripts were excluded from the analysis due to missing data, so that the final sample consisted of 5,656 (74.8%) subjects.

Assessment of ADHD

Adult ADHD was assessed using the Adult ADHD Self-Report Scale Screener (ASRS-v1.1), developed by the World Health Organization (WHO) [24,25]. This instrument includes six questions about ADHD symptoms, which are based upon DSM-IV diagnostic criteria for ADHD. For this study, all questions referred to the last 12 months. Each item was rated on a five-point scale, from "never" (0) to "very often" (4), with responses summed up to generate a summary score ranging from 0 to 24. The answers then were dichotomized into the variable "no ADHD" (scores 0–13) and "ADHD" (scores 14–24). In order to distinguish those with borderline scores from those with more extreme scores, a four-strata classification system [25] also was utilized, with subjects assigned to the four strata as follows: 0–9 "stratum I", 10–13 "stratum II", 14–17 "stratum III", and 18–24 "stratum IV".

Participants who failed to answer at least three questions from the ASRS Screener were excluded (n = 20, 0.4%). In contrast, when participants failed to answer only one or two questions, these missing responses were replaced by means of nearest-neighbour hot-deck imputation, using a random recursive partitioning (RRP) dissimilarity matrix. This method was implemented within the RRP package [26] running in version 2.15 of the R statistical environment (R Team Core Development, 17).

Assessment of Socio-demographic Variables and Childhood Factors

Socio-demographic variables included age ('younger than 20 years' vs. '20 years or older'), linguistic region ('German-' vs. 'French-speaking'), residence ('rural' vs. 'urban'), marital status ('in relationship' vs. 'single'), highest achieved education ('primary school' vs. 'secondary vocational school' vs. 'high school/university'), and degree of financial autonomy ('financial autonomy' vs. 'partial financial dependency' vs. 'financial dependency'). Additionally, several socio-demographic variables related to the subject's childhood were assessed, including maternal education ('primary school' vs. 'secondary vocational school' vs. 'high school/university'), family affluence ('above average' vs. 'average' vs. 'below average'), living arrangement before the age of 18 ('living with biological parents' vs. 'living with others'), and separation of parents before 18 years of age ('no' vs. 'yes').

Furthermore, family histories for alcohol abuse and psychiatric problems were assessed for the mother, father and siblings, as well as for paternal and maternal grandparents, uncles and aunts, based upon questions adopted from the Addiction Severity Index (ASI) [27]. Answers for family members on the mother's side were combined to generate two dichotomous variables, one for alcohol ('yes' vs. 'no') and one for psychiatric problems ('yes' vs. 'no'). The same procedure was applied to family members on the father's side and siblings. In order to reduce the number of predictors for logistic regression, answers for all family members were combined to generate two dichotomous variables for the whole family, one for alcohol ('yes' vs. 'no') and one for psychiatric problems ('yes' vs. 'no').

Assessment of Co-morbidity

Major depression. Major Depression (MD) was assessed using the Major Depressive Inventory (ICD-10) – WHO-MDI [28,29], which is a 10-item screening instrument that uses a 6-point scale for responses that range from "never" (1) to "all the time" (6). MDI items were first dichotomised to indicate the absence (0) or presence (1) of each symptom, and afterwards coded according to the DSM-IV criteria to generate a binary variable: "no MD" vs. "MD". In accordance with the DSM-IV, MD was defined as the presence of at least five MDI items, with either item 1 or item 2 required to be among those five items [28]. Scores were computed when at least 8 of the 10 questions were answered.

Anti-Social Personality Disorder (ASPD). Symptomatology of anti-social personality disorder was measured via the Mini International Neuropsychiatric Interview (MINI plus, [30]). Responses were recorded using a 6-point scale, ranging from "never" (1) to "20 times or more" (6). Afterwards, answers were dichotomised to indicate the absence (0) or presence (1) of each symptom and further coded to generate a binary variable: "no ASPD" vs. "ASPD". In accordance with the MINI plus, ASPD was defined as the presence of two symptoms, both before and after the age of 15. Cases were excluded when more than half of the questions were not answered for before and/or after the age of 15.

Alcohol abuse and dependence. Twelve-month diagnoses of alcohol abuse and dependence were assessed by questionnaires [31] based on DSM-IV diagnostic criteria. The questions were originally adapted from the Semi-Structured Assessment for the Genetics of Alcoholism (SSAGA) [32,33]. The presence of alcohol abuse was defined as a positive response to any one of the four abuse criteria and the absence of a dependence diagnosis. An alcohol dependence diagnosis was defined as a positive response to any three or more of seven dependence criteria [31].

Statistical Analysis

All statistical analyses were performed using the statistical package SPSS 20.0. We used contingency tables to present 12-month prevalence rates for adult ADHD, as well as for socio-demographic characteristics, childhood factors, and comorbidities. Variables relating to socio-demographic characteristics, family history, and co-morbidity were compared between participants with and without ADHD using Pearson chi-square analysis. Logistic regression analyses were conducted to examine the association between adult ADHD (dependent variable) and socio-demographic variables, including family history for the whole family. Unadjusted and adjusted odds ratios (OR) and 95% confidence intervals (95% CI) were calculated for all predictors. Adjusted values were assessed using all socio-demographic variables and family histories of alcohol and psychiatric problems for the whole family as covariates.

Results

Prevalence of ADHD

The socio-demographic characteristics of the study sample are summarized in Table 1 (columns 1 and 2).

The 12-month prevalence of ADHD was 4.0% (n = 226). Using the four-strata classification system, no ADHD was reported in 81.3% of participants, while 14.7%, 3.4%, 0.6% of the participants were classified within strata II, III and IV, respectively, representing possible through definite cases of ADHD (Table 2).

More than half (50.8 to 65.3%) of the sample reported at least one ADHD symptom "rarely", "sometimes", "often" or "very often". Symptoms of hyperactivity were reported slightly more frequently than the majority of inattention symptoms (56.0 to 65.3% and 50.8 to 61.4%, respectively). Symptoms of inattention were reported as occurring "often" or "very often" in 0.7 to 9.0% men and hyperactivity symptoms in 1.9 to 13.6%. The frequencies of each symptom are shown in Table 3.

Socio-demographic Variables and Childhood Factors

A positive association with ADHD was found for subject age, linguistic region, education level, and degree of financial autonomy. Older subjects and those from French-speaking regions were more likely to report ADHD symptoms than those who were younger or from German-speaking regions. For education, a trend ($p<0.10$) was observed, with a high school/university level education associated with a higher prevalence of ADHD than having completed primary school only; however, this association failed to achieve statistical significance after adjusting for all other variables. Additionally, compared to financial autonomy, ADHD was positively related to partial or complete financial dependency. However, when adjusting for all other variables, only complete financial dependency was significant. No significant difference between participants with and without ADHD was identified for residence or marital status.

For childhood factors, logistic regression analysis revealed that subjects whose mothers had completed high school/university or just primary school were more likely to report ADHD than those whose mothers completed secondary school. Frequencies for these two former education levels were similar. Reporting a family history of alcohol or psychiatric problems was significantly associated with a higher prevalence of ADHD than not having such a history. Family affluence, living arrangement before the age of 18, and separation of parents before 18 years of age did not differ between those with and without ADHD. Table 1 presents unadjusted and adjusted ORs and 95% CI for correlates of adult ADHD.

Co-morbid Conditions

Using the dichotomous classification ("no ADHD" vs. "ADHD") 13.7% of our subjects with ADHD reported MD, 36.3% ASPD, 38.9% alcohol abuse, and 20.8% alcohol dependence. Rates for all these disorders were significantly higher among those with than those without ADHD (MD: $X^2 = 114.94$, $p<.001$; ASPD: $X^2 = 67.99$, $p<.001$; alcohol abuse and dependence $X^2 = 58.90$, $p<.001$). Similarly, a higher percentage of men in strata II, III and IV reported the presence of MD, ASPD, alcohol abuse and dependence than men allocated to stratum I. The rate of having at least one of these psychiatric disorders systematically increased from strata I to IV (Figure 1), indicating that men with more ADHD symptoms are more likely to suffer from other psychiatric disorders as well. Rates for these co-morbid disorders, per stratum, are presented in Table 4.

Discussion

Prevalence of ADHD

The present study aimed to assess the prevalence of adult ADHD in a large, representative sample of young men living in Switzerland, and to examine factors associated with ADHD. In our sample, the prevalence of adult ADHD was 4.0%. This rate is midway between the rates of 1.0 to 7.5% reported in previous studies [15,16]. Although we assessed prevalence only by applying a self-report screening questionnaire, our rate was similar to the average rate of 4.2% that was reported for higher income countries in a WHO-orchestrated international survey [6]. In the WHO study, more accurate diagnostic assessments were performed at least for a small portion of the recruited US sample, and multiple imputations were applied to estimate prevalence across all other participating countries. Our results are also in line with the crude prevalence estimate of 4.7% reported recently for a representative sample of the German population [9], in a study in which a variety of self-report instruments were used. Relative to the only pre-existent prevalence estimates for Switzerland, specifically for youths between the ages of 7 and 17 (6.2%) [23], our rates are somewhat lower. However, the previous estimate only incorporated the city of Zurich.

Socio-demographic Variables

Contradicting earlier findings [6,9,16,20], the prevalence of ADHD increased with age in our sample. By analysing the rates of adult ADHD for each age separately, we noticed that they fluctuated from age to age among older subjects (≥20 years) (data not shown). For example, a higher rate of adult ADHD was found among those who were 20 years old (5.4%) than those who were 21 (3.7%). The latter rate was similar to the rates obtained for subjects aged 18 (3.1%) and 19 (3.8), who were assigned to the younger of our two dichotomized age groups (<20 years). One possible explanation for this result may be our use of self-reports to diagnose ADHD, as self-reports may be less reliable than informant/proxy reports (e.g. parents, teachers) because people with ADHD exhibit diminished self-appraisal/awareness and thereby tend to underreport their own symptoms [34,35]. Nevertheless, it is also possible that critical life periods may lead people with ADHD to increasingly having to confront their difficulties and, hence, be more likely to self-report symptoms. For

Table 1. Description of the study sample and correlates of adult ADHD; logistic regression analyses with ADHD as the outcome variable.

	Participants with characteristic	Prevalence of ADHD within characteristic	Unadjusted	Adjusted[a]
	% (n = 5656)	% (n = 226)	Odds ratio [95% CI]	Odds ratio [95% CI]
Age[b]				
<20	60.0	3.4	1.00	
≥20	40.0	4.9	1.45 [1.11, 1.89]*	1.35 [1.02, 1.80]*
Linguistic region				
German	45.2	2.7	1.00	
French	54.8	5.1	1.96 [1.47, 2.62]**	1.75 [1.27, 2.40]**
Residence				
rural	33.0	3.4	1.00	
urban	67.0	4.3	1.26 [0.94, 1.69]	1.00 [0.74, 1.36]
Marital status[c]				
in relationship	5.1	2.8		
single	94.9	4.1		
Education				
primary school	50.0	3.9	1.00	
secondary vocational school	28.5	3.2	0.82 [0.58, 1.14]	0.80 [0.56, 1.15]
high school/university	21.5	5.2	1.34 [0.98, 1.84]†	0.97 [0.69, 1.37]
Financial autonomy				
financial autonomy	23.5	2.7	1.00	
partial financial dependency	42.7	4.0	1.49 [1.01, 2.20]*	1.36 [0.91, 2.04]
financial dependency	33.8	4.9	1.86 [1.26, 2.75]*	1.78 [1.16, 2.72]*
Living arrangement[d]				
biological parents	78.1	3.8	1.00	
others	21.9	4.7	1.24 [0.91, 1.68]	1.02 [0.74, 1.41]
Separation of parents[c, d]				
no	74.5	3.8	1.00	
before birth	1.5	5.8	1.55 [0.62, 3.89]	
after birth	24.0	4.4	1.16 [0.86, 1.58]	
Mother's education				
primary school	13.5	5.4	1.00	
secondary vocational school	62.2	3.2	0.59 [0.41, 0.84]*	0.64 [0.44, 0.94]*
high school/university	24.3	5.2	0.98 [0.66, 1.45]	0.94 [0.61, 1.43]
Family affluence				
above average	44.5	3.7	1.00	
average	41.1	4.0	1.09 [0.81, 1.46]	1.06 [0.78, 1.45]
below average	14.4	4.7	1.26 [0.86, 1.85]	1.13 [0.75, 1.72]
Family history				
Problems with alcohol				
no	76.2	3.4	1.00	
yes	23.8	6.0	1.84 [1.39, 2.44]**	1.46 [1.09, 1.96]*
Psychiatric disease				
no	85.0	3.4	1.00	
yes	15.0	7.6	2.39 [1.77, 3.21]**	2.13 [1.56, 2.92]**

†p<.10,
*p<.05,
**p<.001;
[a]adjusted for all variables;
[b]age range: 17–28;
[c]no logistic regression analyses were performed due to the small number of participants in one of the variable's categories;
[d]before 18 years of age.

Table 2. 12-month prevalence of adult ADHD in young Swiss men.

	Prevalence	
ASRS CLASSIFICATION	n	%
Dichotomized Classification		
ADHD (score = 14–24)	226	4.0
no ADHD (score = 0–13)	5430	96.0
4-Strata Classification		
I (score = 0–9)	4599	81.3
II (score = 10–13)	831	14.7
III (score = 14–17)	192	3.4
IV (score = 18–24)	34	0.6

instance, at the age of 20 years, most Swiss people start university or their first job after training, which may be experienced as rather challenging, potentially contributing to the higher prevalence rates that we observed.

We noted no significant differences in the prevalence of ADHD between those with a rural versus urban residence. This result is consistent with some previous findings [10], but stands in contrast with other prior studies identifying higher rates in urban [4] or rural areas [9]. This inconsistency might be due to differences in how rural and urban were defined in the different studies, as well as to differences in the nature of the rural and urban areas themselves [36].

Linguistic region was associated with adult ADHD, in that a higher prevalence was discovered among French-speaking versus German-speaking conscripts. Differences in prevalence between countries with different cultures have already been reported [6,18], as well as between culturally-diverse populations within the same country [37]. These differences could be explained by differences in knowledge, understanding, and the assessment and management of ADHD symptoms between different countries and cultures. For example, a given symptom might be considered deviant in some cultures, while more accepted in others. This could affect the reports of informants [18,37,38]. Since how ADHD is understood, diagnosed and managed is similar throughout Switzerland, at least among health professionals and in schools, we suspect that cultural differences in response behaviours were primarily responsible for the linguistic effect we observed. French-speaking conscripts, for instance, seem to give more extreme responses than those who speak German, a pattern that was observed for every ADHD item (data not shown) as well as for other variables [39].

For our analysis, highest achieved education and financial autonomy were used as markers of professional achievement. Men with adult ADHD were more likely to have completed high school or attended university ($p<0.10$), although this association failed to achieve statistical significance after adjusting for all other variables. Our results are clearly contrary to most previous reports, which constantly revealed a positive association between ADHD and lower education level [3,6,7,9]. It is possible that enhanced identification and referral of cases with ADHD in Switzerland, as well as more accessible and effective treatment during childhood and adolescence, might have allowed affected individuals to achieve higher levels of education than in other countries. However, it must be emphasized that, consistent with the findings of others [7], in our sample adult ADHD was positively related to partial and, even more so, to complete financial dependency. The observed positive relationship between adult ADHD and financial dependency may suggest that adults with ADHD still are impaired in some aspects of their professional life, despite having achieved a similar education level as those without ADHD. Thus, they may need more support to manage tasks at work.

In contrast to previous studies, in which problems with personal relationships were reported [3,6,10], in our sample no significant difference was found in marital status between those with and without ADHD. This failure to identify any significant marital difficulties could be due to the definition of marital status we used: being in a relationship was defined as being married or living with a partner, and not just having a girlfriend. Due to the young age of our participants, only a small number of subjects fulfilled our requirement for 'marriage' (286/5656), meaning that the number of partnered subjects with ADHD (8/226) was too small to allow for meaningful analysis.

Table 3. Frequency of ADHD symptoms, as assessed with the ASRS Screener.

	Total		Often		Very often	
	N	%	n	%	n	%
Inattention symptoms						
How often do you have trouble wrapping up the fine details of a project, once the challenging parts have been done?	3068	54.2	216	3.8	41	0.7
How often do have difficulty getting things in order when you have to do a task that requires organization?	2875	50.8	216	3.8	41	0.7
How often do you have problems remembering appointments or obligations?	2880	50.9	201	3.6	46	0.8
When you have a task that requires a lot of thought, how often do you avoid or delay getting started?	3466	61.4	507	9.0	134	2.4
Hyperactivity symptoms						
How often do you fidget or squirm with your hands or your feet when you have to sit down for a long time?	3696	65.3	769	13.6	359	6.3
How often do you feel overly active and compelled to do things, like you were driven by a motor?	3169	56.0	383	6.8	106	1.9

Total: Total number of men experiencing symptoms "rarely", "sometimes", "often" or "very often".

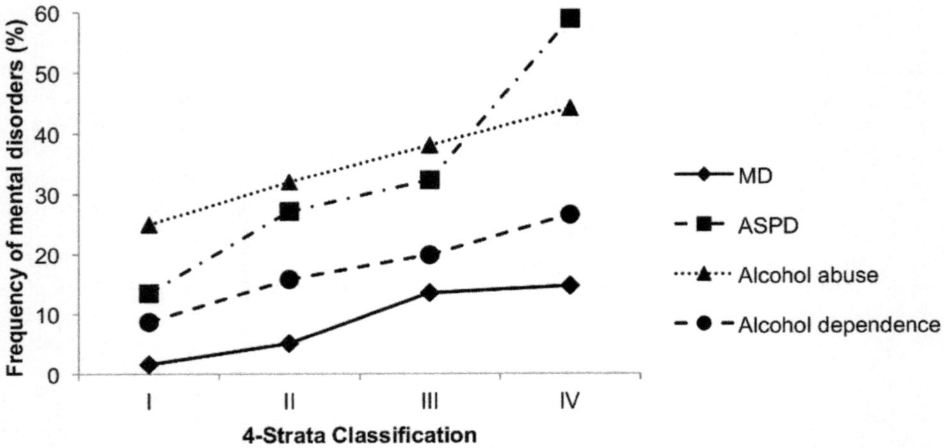

Figure 1. Relationship between ASRS strata and the presence of MD, ASPD, alcohol abuse and dependence.

Childhood Factors

We did find that both a subject's mother's level of education and a family history of alcohol or psychiatric problems differed between those with and without adult ADHD. Mothers of participants with adult ADHD were more likely to have either a primary school or high school/university level education, while those without ADHD more often had mothers who had completed secondary school but not beyond. The finding that a low level of maternal education was associated with a greater prevalence of adult ADHD is consistent with the results of other studies, in which a higher risk for ADHD in children was observed in those with less-educated parents [40,41]. In this context, it has been claimed that, due to its strong genetic component, parents of affected children may be more likely to have had ADHD themselves and, as a consequence, to have not been able to achieve higher education levels [41]. In contrast, the observation that a higher level of maternal education was associated with a greater prevalence of ADHD in offspring has not been reported before; but it is consistent with what Gau et al. [42] have found: a positive association between the number of psychiatric referrals and higher maternal education levels in children with ADHD. This, in turn, suggests that mothers of higher education may be more likely to be aware of their children's problematic behaviours and have more knowledge about ADHD. One could speculate that higher parental awareness of ADHD might help their offspring to better identify and report their own symptoms.

Family history of either alcohol or psychiatric problems also was positively associated with adult ADHD. In fact, a family history of psychiatric problems exhibited the highest odds ratio for ADHD of any variable, on logistic regression analysis. Once again, the strong genetic component of ADHD and the high comorbidity of ADHD with alcohol use disorders and other mental disorders could explain this association [2]. Additionally, the difficulties and stress inherent to raising a child with ADHD could affect family functioning and the well-being of family members (for a Review, see [43]). For instance, ADHD in adolescents is linked to more depressive symptoms in mothers [44] and to more alcohol use disorders in parents [44–46]. These findings are even stronger when parents of affected children have ADHD themselves [44,45]. Thus, a higher rate of family alcohol abuse and psychiatric problems may be induced by both genetic factors and challenges in the interactions of family members with the ADHD-affected individual. As such, further efforts should be undertaken to include all family members in the treatment of ADHD, and to provide special interventions for families with more than one ADHD-affected individual.

Table 4. Relationship between ADHD and the presence of MD, ASPD, alcohol abuse and dependence.

	I	II	III	IV	With ADHD
MD	1.6	5.1	13.5	14.7	13.7
ASPD	13.5	27.1	32.3	58.8	36.3
Alcohol abuse	24.9	32.0	38.0	44.1	38.9
Alcohol dependence	8.7	15.8	19.8	26.5	20.8

Co-morbid Conditions

Consistent with previously-published findings [2,6,8–10,12], a considerable proportion of our men with ADHD appeared to suffer from major depression, anti-social personality disorder, and either alcohol abuse or dependence. Additionally, men with more ADHD symptoms appear to be more likely to suffer from one of these psychiatric disorders [8]. In our sample, among those with the highest number of ADHD symptoms, the probability of having MD was nine times greater than among those in the lowest strata, in which any ADHD cases are expected. For ASPD, alcohol abuse and dependence, the rates were approximately four, two, and three times greater in the highest vs. lowest stratum, respectively. For all these psychiatric disorders, an elevated rate also was identified in those with few ADHD symptoms [8,14]. Our results, combined with previous findings, highlight the considerable impairments in mental health that young men with ADHD can experience, as well as the need for health care providers to offer appropriate interventions for this population to reduce further illness burdens.

Study Limitations

The following limitations must be considered relating to the currently-presented study. First, women were not included in our sample. Although some study results suggest that men and women experience ADHD in a similar way [8], inconsistent results in ADHD prevalence estimates have been reported comparing adult males and females. The reasons behind these inconsistent results remain unclear and must be clarified in future studies.

Second, the prevalence of ADHD was assessed in the context of a population-based study that was not initially intended or designed to address ADHD-related questions. Therefore, prevalence only was assessed by means of self-report using the ASRS Screener and did not further include any confirmatory diagnostic assessment. This also was true for the assessment of MD, ASPD, alcohol abuse and alcohol dependence, as well as for family histories of alcohol and psychiatric problems. However, the assessment instruments we used are all well validated. Thus, we feel that our study provides a reasonable approximation of the prevalence of ADHD among young Swiss men. Nevertheless, it is important to note that, despite excellent concordance between the ASRS Screener and a clinical diagnosis of ADHD [24,25], the ASRS is based upon the DSM-IV criteria originally developed for children and might not provide appropriate information for the diagnosis of adult ADHD. Indeed, some study results suggest that these criteria are too conservative for adults [4,20]. As a consequence, the true prevalence of ADHD might be slightly underestimated in our study.

Third, the medical history for ADHD, mental disorders and family histories of alcohol and psychiatric problems, was not assessed; consequently, we do not know the clinical status of our study participants or whether they had received or continued to receive any treatment.

Finally, since our data were collected at a single time point and not longitudinally, we cannot draw causal inferences.

In summary, we found that roughly 4.0% of young Swiss men have ADHD, and that associations exist with other mental disorders, like major depression and alcohol abuse, as well as with family histories of alcohol and psychiatric problems. ADHD adversely affects work, health and interpersonal relationships. As such, clinicians and school professionals should remain alert to its existence and consequences in young males.

Acknowledgments

We are grateful to Dr. Alois Tschopp and Prof. Alex Gamma for their methodological advice and to Charlotte Eidenbenz and Petra Dermota for their valuable input.

Author Contributions

Conceived and designed the experiments: MMK GG. Performed the experiments: MMK GG JS. Analyzed the data: NE MD JS. Contributed reagents/materials/analysis tools: MMK GG. Wrote the paper: NE. Interpretation of data: NE DEH. Revising manuscript: NE DEH MD JS GG MMK.

References

1. American Psychiatric Association (1994) Diagnostic and statistical manual of mental disorders (DSM-IV). 4th rev. ed. American Psychiatric Press, Washington, D.C.
2. Faraone SV, Biederman J, Spencer T, Wilens T, Seidman LJ, et al. (2000) Attention-deficit/hyperactivity disorder in adults: an overview. Biol Psychiatry 48: 9–20.
3. Ebejer JL, Medland SE, van der Werf J, Gondro C, Henders AK, et al. (2012) Attention deficit hyperactivity disorder in Australian adults: prevalence, persistence, conduct problems and disadvantage. PloS One 7: e47404.
4. Faraone SV, Biederman J (2005) What is the prevalence of adult ADHD? Results of a population screen of 966 adults. J Atten Disord 9: 384–391.
5. Biederman J, Faraone S (2006) The effects of attention-deficit/hyperactivity disorder on employment and household income. MedGenMed 8: 12.
6. Fayyad J, De Graaf R, Kessler R, Alonso J, Angermeyer M, et al. (2007) Cross-national prevalence and correlates of adult attention-deficit hyperactivity disorder. Br J Psychiatry 190: 402–409.
7. Biederman J, Petty CR, Woodworth KY, Lomedico A, Hyder LL, et al. (2012) Adult outcome of attention-deficit/hyperactivity disorder: A controlled 16-year follow-up study. J Clin Psychiat 73: 941–950.
8. Das D, Cherbuin N, Butterworth P, Anstey KJ, Easteal S (2012) A population-based study of attention deficit/hyperactivity disorder symptoms and associated impairment in middle-aged adults. PloS One 7: e31500.
9. de Zwaan M, Gruss B, Muller A, Graap H, Martin A, et al. (2012) The estimated prevalence and correlates of adult ADHD in a German community sample. Eur Arch Psychiatry Clin Neurosci 262: 79–86.
10. Kessler RC, Adler L, Barkley R, Biederman J, Conners CK, et al. (2006) The prevalence and correlates of adult ADHD in the United States: results from the National Comorbidity Survey Replication. Am J Psychiatry 163: 716–723.
11. Rosler M, Casas M, Konofal E, Buitelaar J (2010) Attention deficit hyperactivity disorder in adults. World J Biol Psychiatry 11: 684–698.
12. Moss SB, Nair R, Vallarino A, Wang S (2007) Attention deficit/hyperactivity disorder in adults. Prim Care Clin Office Pract 34: 445–473.
13. Brod M, Schmitt E, Goodwin M, Hodgkins P, Niebler G (2012) ADHD burden of illness in older adults: a life course perspective. Qual Life Res 21: 795–799.
14. Kooij JJ, Buitelaar JK, van den Oord EJ, Furer JW, Rijnders CA, et al. (2005) Internal and external validity of attention-deficit hyperactivity disorder in a population-based sample of adults. Psychol Med 35: 817–827.
15. Willcutt EG (2012) The prevalence of DSM-IV attention-deficit/hyperactivity disorder: a meta-analytic review. Neurotherapeutics 9: 490–499.
16. Simon V, Czobor P, Balint S, Meszaros A, Bitter I (2009) Prevalence and correlates of adult attention-deficit hyperactivity disorder: meta-analysis. British J Psychiatry 194: 204–211.
17. Heiligenstein E, Conyers LM, Berns AR, Miller MA (1998) Preliminary normative data on DSM-IV attention deficit hyperactivity disorder in college students. J Am Coll Health 46: 185–188.
18. DuPaul GJ, Schaughency EA, Weyandt LL, Tripp G, Kiesner J, et al. (2001) Self-report of ADHD symptoms in university students: cross-gender and cross-national prevalence. J Learn Disabil 34: 370–379.
19. Almeida Montes LG, Hernandez Garcia AO, Ricardo-Garcell J (2007) ADHD prevalence in adult outpatients with nonpsychotic psychiatric illnesses. J Atten Disord 11: 150–156.
20. Bitter I, Simon V, Balint S, Meszaros A, Czobor P (2010) How do different diagnostic criteria, age and gender affect the prevalence of attention deficit hyperactivity disorder in adults? An epidemiological study in a Hungarian community sample. Eur Arch Psychiatry Clin Neurosci 260: 287–296.
21. Medina-Mora ME, Borges G, Lara C, Benjet C, Blanco J, et al. (2005) Prevalence, service use, and demographic correlates of 12-month DSM-IV psychiatric disorders in Mexico: results from the Mexican National Comorbidity Survey. Psychol Med 35: 1773–1783.
22. Bernardi S, Faraone SV, Cortese S, Kerridge BT, Pallanti S, et al. (2012) The lifetime impact of attention deficit hyperactivity disorder: results from the National Epidemiologic Survey on Alcohol and Related Conditions (NESARC). Psychol Med 42: 875–887.
23. Steinhausen HC, Winkler C, Meier MM, Kannenberg R (1998) Prevalence of child and adolescent psychiatric disorders: the Zurich epidemiological study. Acta Psychiatr Scand 98: 262–271.
24. Kessler RC, Adler L, Ames M, Demler O, Faraone S, et al. (2005) The World Health Organization Adult ADHD Self-Report Scale (ASRS): a short screening scale for use in the general population. Psychol Med 35: 245–256.
25. Kessler RC, Adler LA, Gruber MJ, Sarawate CA, Spencer T, et al. (2007) Validity of the World Health Organization Adult ADHD Self-Report Scale (ASRS) Screener in a representative sample of health plan members. Int J Methods Psychiatr Res 16: 52–65.
26. Iacus SA, Porro G (2007) Missing data imputation, matching and other applications of random recursive partitioning. Computational Statistics & Data Analysis 52: 773–789.
27. Mclealen AT, Luborsky L, Cacciola J, Griffith J, Evans F, et al. (1985) New data from the Addiction Severity Index. Reliability and validity in three centers. J Nerv Ment Dis 173: 412–423.
28. Bech P, Rasmussen NA, Olsen LR, Noerholm V, Abildgaard W (2001) The sensitivity and specificity of the Major Depression Inventory, using the Present State Examination as the index of diagnostic validity. J Affect Disord 66: 159–164.
29. Olsen LR, Jensen DV, Noerholm V, Martiny K, Bech P (2003) The internal and external validity of the Major Depression Inventory in measuring severity of depressive states. Psychol Med 33: 351–356.
30. Lecrubier Y, Weiller E, Hergueta T, Amorim P, Bonora LI, et al. (1998) MINI Mini International Neuropsychiatric Interview. French version 5.00. Hopital de la Pitié Salpétriere, INSERM. Paris, France.
31. Knight JR, Wechsler H, Kuo M, Seibring M, Weitzman ER, et al. (2001) Alcohol abuse and dependence among U.S. college students. J Stud Alcohol 63: 263–270.
32. Bucholz KK, Cadoret R, Cloninger CR, Dinwiddie SH, Hesselbrock VM, et al. (1994) A new, semistructured psychiatric interview for use in genetic-linkage studies - a report on the reliability of the SSAGA. J Stud Alcohol 55: 149–158.

33. Hesselbrock M, Easton C, Bucholz KK, Schuckit M, Hesselbrock V (1999) A validity study of the SSAGA - a comparison with the SCAN. Addiction 94: 1361–1370.
34. Barkley RA, Fischer M, Smallish L, Fletcher K (2002) The persistence of attention-deficit/hyperactivity disorder into young adulthood as a function of reporting source and definition of disorder. J Abnorm Psychol 111: 279–289.
35. Sibley MH, Pelham WE, Molina BSG, Gnagy EM, Waxmonsky JG, et al. (2012) When diagnosing ADHD in young adults emphasize informant reports, DSM items, and impairment. J Consult Clin Psych 80: 1052–1061.
36. Peen J, Schoevers RA, Beekman AT, Dekker J (2010) The current status of urban-rural differences in psychiatric disorders. Acta Psychiatr Scand 121: 84–93.
37. Waite R, Ramsay JR (2010) Cultural proficiency: a Hispanic woman with ADHD - a case example. J Atten Disord 13: 424–432.
38. Skounti M, Philalithis A, Galanakis E (2007) Variations in prevalence of attention deficit hyperactivity disorder worldwide. Eur J Pediatr 166: 117–123.
39. Dey M, Gmel G, Mohler-Kuo (2013) Body mass index and health-related quality of life among young Swiss men. BMC Public Health 13:1028 doi:10.1186/1471-2458-13-1028.
40. Ezpeleta L, de la Osa N, Domenech JM (2013) Prevalence of DSM-IV disorders, comorbidity and impairment in 3-years-old Spanish preschoolers. Soc Psychiatry Psychiatr Epidemiol doi:10.1007/s00127-013-0683-1.
41. Cuffe SP, Moore CG, McKeown RE (2005) Prevalence and correlates of ADHD symptoms in the National Health Interview Survey. J Atten Disord 9: 392–401.
42. Gau SSF, Lin YJ, Shang CY, Liu SK, Chiu YN, et al. (2010) Emotional/behavioral problems and functional impairment in clinic- and community-based children with attention-deficit/hyperactivity disorder in Taiwan. J Abnorm Child Psychol 38: 521–532.
43. Harpin VA (2005) The effect of ADHD on the life of an individual, their family, and community from preschool to adult life. Arch Dis Child doi:10.1136/Adc.2004.059006.
44. Babinski DE, Pelham WE, Molina BS, Gnagy EM, Waschbusch DA, et al. (2012) Maternal ADHD, parenting, and psychopathology among mothers of adolescents with ADHD. J Atten Disord doi:10.1177/1087054712461688.
45. Minde K, Eakin L, Hechtman L, Ochs E, Bouffard R, et al. (2003) The psychosocial functioning of children and spouses of adults with ADHD. J Child Psychol Psyc 44: 637–646.
46. Pelham WE, Lang AR (1999) Can your children drive you to drink? Stress and parenting in adults interacting with children with ADHD. Alcohol Res Health 23: 292–298.

11

A Multi-Methodological MR Resting State Network Analysis to Assess the Changes in Brain Physiology of Children with ADHD

Benito de Celis Alonso[1]*, Silvia Hidalgo Tobón[2], Pilar Dies Suarez[2], Julio García Flores[3], Benito de Celis Carrillo[4], Eduardo Barragán Pérez[5]

1 Faculty of Physics and Mathematics, Benemérita Universidad Autónoma de Puebla (BUAP), Puebla, Mexico, **2** Imaging Department, Hospital Infantil de México Federico Gómez, México DF, Mexico, **3** Feinberg School of Medicine, Northwestern University, Chicago, Illinois, United States of America, **4** School of Industrial Engineering, Universidad de León, León, Castilla y León, Spain, **5** Neurology Department, Hospital Infantil de México Federico Gómez, México DF, Mexico

Abstract

The purpose of this work was to highlight the neurological differences between the MR resting state networks of a group of children with ADHD (pre-treatment) and an age-matched healthy group. Results were obtained using different image analysis techniques. A sample of n = 46 children with ages between 6 and 12 years were included in this study (23 per cohort). Resting state image analysis was performed using ReHo, ALFF and ICA techniques. ReHo and ICA represent connectivity analyses calculated with different mathematical approaches. ALFF represents an indirect measurement of brain activity. The ReHo and ICA analyses suggested differences between the two groups, while the ALFF analysis did not. The ReHo and ALFF analyses presented differences with respect to the results previously reported in the literature. ICA analysis showed that the same resting state networks that appear in healthy volunteers of adult age were obtained for both groups. In contrast, these networks were not identical when comparing the healthy and ADHD groups. These differences affected areas for all the networks except the Right Memory Function network. All techniques employed in this study were used to monitor different cerebral regions which participate in the phenomenological characterization of ADHD patients when compared to healthy controls. Results from our three analyses indicated that the cerebellum and mid-frontal lobe bilaterally for ReHo, the executive function regions in ICA, and the precuneus, cuneus and the clacarine fissure for ALFF, were the "hubs" in which the main *inter-group* differences were found. These results do not just help to explain the physiology underlying the disorder but open the door to future uses of these methodologies to monitor and evaluate patients with ADHD.

Editor: Oscar Arias-Carrion, Hospital General Dr. Manuel Gea González, Mexico

Funding: These authors have no support or funding to report.

Competing Interests: The authors have declared that no competing interests exist.

* Email: benileon@yahoo.com

Introduction

Attention deficit hyperactivity disorder (ADHD) is a common neuropsychiatric disorder in children and adolescents with a prevalence of 5.29% according to current meta-analysis studies [1]. Three main groups of symptomatologies have been found: Inattentiveness, Impulsivity-Hyperactivity and Combined. These symptoms are believed to change with age, driven by changes in brain structures and connectivity [2]. Unfortunately, an objective diagnostic tool useful to monitor this kind of patient is still lacking. It is therefore important to understand from a neurobiological angle the behavior of brain regions and their connections in these patients, allowing for information-based therapies. Brain resting state networks represent correlated slow fluctuations of the BOLD MR signal in different brain regions (frequencies between 0.01 and 0.1 Hz) [3,4]. They are characterized by comprising regions involved in similar tasks, even when distant in the brain (i.e. vision, motor cortex, etc.). They are very plastic [5] and change with age [6]; [7]. These networks are consistently found in healthy volunteers [8], but they are known to be affected by drug abuse [9] and almost every kind of neurodegenerative disorder [10]; [11].

There are several analytical approaches (i.e. ReHo, ALFF, fALFF, independent component analysis, AFNI, etc.), as well as computing platforms (i.e. FSL, SPM, RETROICOR, etc.) that can be used to study resting state networks. In this study three of these approaches were used: firstly, Regions of Homogeneity (ReHo). In this approach the BOLD time course of each voxel of the brain (excluding CSF and white matter) is filtered, retaining frequencies between 0.01 and 0.1 Hz. Kendall correlation coefficients (a non-parametric test for correlation) for each voxel are then calculated with respect to its closest 27 neighbors. These neighbors represent a cube in 3D around the given voxel [12]. The result of the p-value for this correlation is then plotted on top of an anatomical image. Unlike in independent component analysis, in which Bayesian statistics are used to find covariance trends between voxels, ReHo analysis is a "simple" correlation calculation which will show all resting state networks together in the brain under study. The connectivity showed by a region and calculated with this technique will be limited to its neighbor regions in the brain. ReHo analysis is a widely known method and has been used, for example, in connectivity studies of deaf patients [13], epilepsy [14] and sensorimotor cortex [15]. The second approach used was ALFF (amplitude of low frequency fluctuations). The ALFF measurement is an indirect biomarker of brain activity. It shows not a correlation between regions as with ReHo, but rather the amplitude of the BOLD contrast in a given area. It has been found that ALFF activations were larger in the right paracentral lobule when volunteers lay in the scanner with eyes closed, compared to open-eyed volunteers [16]. Mathematically it is obtained by calculating the power spectra of the low frequency BOLD fluctuations. ALFF is a technique which has started to become available for neuroscientists, and has been used in studies of schizophrenia [17], vision [18] and neurological disorders like apathy or depression [19]. Thirdly, independent component analysis (ICA) is a computational and statistical method used to separate linearly mixed signals without an a priori model. When used on fMRI data, there are two approaches that separate the signals based on time or space variances. The second is the most common and has been successfully used in multiple studies: some examples to date include Wolf et al. [20] on ADHD adult patients, and studies of schizophrenia [21]. A review of the technique was compiled by Robinson et al. [22]. One of the early limitations of this technique was that it worked well on individual subjects but did not allow for data grouping. Calhoun et al. [23] developed algorithms that included data compression, ICA and back-reconstruction steps, which now make it possible to extend these analyses to group studies.

Several reviews [24]; [25]; [26] of resting state networks in ADHD patients indicate that several brain regions are more active or inactive when compared to healthy groups: larger ReHo was found in ADHD patients, compared to healthy volunteers, bilaterally in the dorsal anterior cingulate cortex, cerebellum, thalamus, pons and insula [27]. Other cases of larger homogeneities were found in the occipital cortex [28] and sensory and sensory-related cortexes [29]. ALFF was found to be increased in young ADHD patients in the right anterior cingulate cortex, the left sensorimotor cortex and bilaterally in the brainstem [30]. In contrast, healthy volunteers presented ReHo correlations, which did not appear in the ADHD group, in the frontal striatal cerebellum [28]. ICA analysis has become to be a useful tool to differentiate ADHD patients from healthy controls, and therefore is becoming more of a diagnostic tool [31]. Nevertheless, work with pediatric patients using ICA is sparse. A study on children with ADHD that used different imaging techniques (voxel based morphometry, diffusion tensor imaging and magnetization transfer; [32] has found four fMRI components from their ICA analysis. These components were divided into two groups: positively correlated with a working memory paradigm, which included the parietal and frontal regions; and negatively correlated, connecting anterior and posterior cingulate cortex with the precuneus, as well as temporal regions. The latter were thought to be part of the Default network. Another study on adult patients [20] has found a functional network comprising lateral prefrontal (bilaterally), striatal, and cingulate regions. ADHD adults, when compared with healthy controls, had lower connectivity bilaterally for the VLPFC region, the superior parietal lobe, the anterior cingulate cortex and the cerebellum. Increased connectivity in ADHD adults was found in the left dorsal cingulate cortex, the right prefrontal regions and the left cuneus. Recently, the ADHD 200 global competition (http://fcon_1000.projects.nitrc.org/indi/adhd200/) has made available free resting state data sets of 747 volunteers (healthy and ADHD with ages between 7 and 16 years old). This project aims at differentially diagnosing ADHD patients (with their corresponding subtype) from healthy controls. It has been able to identify the illness with a maximum efficiency till now of 69.59% [33]. It has also helped showing the implication in ADHD of structures in the ventral default network region (precuneus, para-hippocampal, and posterior cingulate) ([34]) ([35]).

One of the pre-existing hypotheses for ADHD is that a malfunction or subnormal performance of the dopaminergic and norepinephrinergic systems is the main source of the disorder. These problems affect primarily the prefrontal cortex which is responsible, amongst other things, for: inhibition, concentration, executive functions, motivation, memory, organizing, planning and problem solving [36]. The dopaminergic system has an important role in the control of motion, arousal, motivation and reward, through its activity in the substantia nigra in the basal ganglia (motion), and the ventral tegmental area (VTA) in the limbic system (motion, motivation and decision making; [37]. The norepinephrinergic system, based in the lateral tegmental area as well as the locus coeruleus, reaches almost all of the CNS [38]. It controls the reward system, arousal and motivation.

Work on ADHD has been predominantly performed in young adults/adolescents (ages 10–17; see [24], for a complete review), but not on children specifically. In this study we compared medication-naïve children with ADHD (ages between 6 and 12 years) to age and sex matched healthy ones. We analysed the inter-group differences in MR resting states with different analytical approaches (ReHo, ALFF and ICA). We highlighted some of the physiological differences of the ADHD brain when compared to a healthy one.

Methods

Volunteers

All experiments were performed according to the international conventions for biomedical studies on humans. The ethical research committee of the Hospital Infantil de México, Federico Gómez (México DF, México) granted the necessary ethical approval for this study under the title "Técnicas avanzadas de Resonancia Magnética Funcional en población pediátrica con diagnóstico de TDAH" ("Advanced functional MR techniques applied on patients diagnosed with ADHD"). This permission was obtained in June 2012, six months prior to the start of experiments which were performed over the first 6 months of 2013. When enrolling a volunteer to this study, an information session was first held, in which the task was explained to the volunteer and their legal guardian, and they were told what to expect from the experimental protocol, as well as its dangers. Secondly, they were asked to read at home the information sheets which repeated all of the information provided in the oral session. The language level of the oral sessions as well as the written information sheet was intended to be accessible for non-scientific or medically trained people. Finally, consent forms were signed by the legal guardians and handed to scientists in charge of the study. Twenty-seven (n = 27) ADHD patients together with 24 healthy volunteers (H from now on) were included in this study. One ADHD volunteer was excluded from the study as he could not remain in the scanner for the whole length of the protocol. Another four volunteers (three in the ADHD group and one in the control) were excluded as their head motion exceeded the motion threshold for this study (described below). All ADHD volunteers were diagnosed with the disorder after an interview performed before initiating imaging. For a patient to be diagnosed with ADHD, he/she should fulfil the diagnostic criteria of the Diagnostic and Statistical Manual of Mental Disorders, Fifth Edition, (DSM-5). This was so for all the symptoms of inattentiveness, hyperactivity and impulsivity. On top of these requirements symptoms for ADHD infants were required to be present practically on each day of the week for the last six months. Also symptoms must have been inducing a dysfunction of the day to day normal activities. Finally, no other diagnosis should explain the symptoms. Once this was established in an interview two tests were always performed on patients: Conners and ADHD rating scales (ADHD-RS). In some occasions the Wechsler (WEISC, to indicate IQ in normal levels) and the TOVA were also applied (data not presented here). All ADHD volunteers had never received medication for this disorder. Only volunteers with ADHD of the Inattentive and the Impulsivity-Hyperactivity subtypes were considered for this study. Controls were completely healthy at the time of the study, with no history of any previous psychological or mental disorder and no prior neurological interventions. No intelligence matching between groups was performed.

The 46 infants finally involved in this study had an average age of 9.7±2.4 (6–12 years old), (mean ± standard deviation, (age range)), with the ADHD group (n = 23) being 9.3±2.8 (6–12 years old), and the H group (n = 23) 9.3±3.5 (6–11 years old) on average. There was a predominance of male subjects, as just 4 out of 46 volunteers were female (2 in the ADHD group and 2 in the H). ADHD patients of the inattentive subtype scored in the ADHD-RS scales 38.0±3.1 and in Conners 66.1±2.8. ADHD patients of the mixed subtype scored in the ADHD-RS scales 38.3±4.0 and in Conners 69.4±1.3. All patients were selected randomly from the population which checked in the Neurology department of the Hospital Infantil de México, Federico Gómez (Mexico). Due to the nature of the hospital being the public national reference in children care; volunteers belonged to all the social, economic and cultural backgrounds found in Mexican society. Nevertheless, no test or scale was used to support this fact.

Hardware

Experiments were performed on a 1.5 T Philips Intera-Achieva scanner (Philips, Inc., Netherlands), using an 8 channel SENSE head-coil. Gradient coils were NOVA (Copley 271 Dual, slew rate 80 mT/m/ms, peak amplitude 120 mT/m).

Protocol: Resting state scans were acquired immediately after standard setup of the scanner and patient, with the volunteer in a supine position with closed eyes (but always awake). The resting state sequence was the first one to be run on all patients and lasted for a period of 7 minutes 25 seconds. Following this sequence a fast anatomical image was acquired which lasted for 3 minutes 10 seconds. Once these sequences were acquired patients were extracted from the scanner.

MRI Sequences

Resting State: 150 whole brain volumes, comprising 35 axial slices covering the whole of the brain (including the cerebellum), were acquired with a fast-echo EPI sequence. TR = 2.9 s, TE = 50 ms, 90 degree flip angle, 64×64 matrix with a 3.6×3.6 mm *in-plane* resolution and 4 mm slice thickness (no gap between slices). Anatomical images were acquired with a T_1-weighted gradient echo sequence (TR = 307.81 ms, TE = 2.48 ms, 4 repetitions and 80 degree flip angle). Sequences covered the same FOV with a 640×640 matrix which gave a 0.36×0.36 mm *in-plane* resolution and 4 mm slice thickness (also no gap between slices).

Data Analysis

Resting state network data analysis was performed with: Data Processing Assistant for Resting State fMRI Advanced edition (DPARSFA_V2.2; [39]; http://www.restfmri.net), Resting-State fMRI Data Analysis Toolkit (REST1.8; [40]; http://www.restfmri.net) and Group ICA of fMRI Toolbox (GIFT; [23]; http://mialab.mrn.org/index.html). All software programs were run on a Statistical Parametric Mapping platform (SPM8; http://www.fil.ion.ucl.ac.uk/spm), based on the Matlab programming language (The Mathworks Inc., USA).

Image Analysis

Resting state network analysis began by converting all DICOM files obtained from the scanner into the ANALYZE format. In the process the first 7 volumes of functional data were discarded to avoid signal saturation problems (each subject had 143 useful sets of volumes). Slice timing correction followed on the 35 slices (ascending order, centered on the middle slice). It has been shown previously that spurious systematic correlations arise due to head motion during experimentation [41]. The DPARSFA realignment step was based on the correction used by SPM8 (a standard least squares approach using a rigid body approximation with six motion parameters). To this correction, a voxel-specific head motion calculation was added which performed frame-wise displacement measurements (FD) of head motion as introduced by Power et al. [42]. This was done at volume and at voxel levels (always relative to the previous time point). It has been demonstrated that when FD values of volumes were over 0.5, artifactual BOLD correlations appeared in the results. Therefore a threshold for head motion during this study was established at 3.5 mm and/or 3 degrees shift during the experiment together with the requirement that no volume in a subject was allowed to have an FD value over 0.5. To these thresholds of motion a data scrubbing step executed before image analysis (before Alff and ReHo) was performed to reduce even more significantly motion effects. In it, all volumes with FD voxel values over 0.5 were deleted from the analysis together with the previous and consecutive volumes. Finally a parallel study to this image analysis performed with the artifact detection tool (art, www.nitrc.org) showed that the number of volumes that should be eliminated due to motion at voxel level was 5.73±6.15 (mean ± standard deviation) for the control group and 9.32±8.25 for the ADHD group. As suspected the ADHD group had more movement than their control counterparts. Nevertheless this difference did not reach statistically significance ($p = -0.146$, t-test) limiting the effect that motion could have on results for this study. Motion values of each individual during scanning were incorporated to the analysis further on, in the regression of nuisance covariates step. Anatomical and functional images of each volunteer were co-registered using interpolation and DARTEL methods [43]. In this step the anterior commissure was considered as the reference point in the brain. The quality of the co-registration was assessed visually by a researcher in each case by overlaying anatomical and functional data in a display window for each volunteer. All the anatomical data was then combined together and used to segment white matter, grey matter and CSF. The CSF and white matter segmentation data were applied as masks to the functional data of each volunteer in a regression of nuisance covariates step, which eliminated these sources of noise. The use of global signal correction has been controversial in the field [44] and was not used in this analysis. Nuisance regression was done prior to filtering for low frequencies, to avoid the creation of artifacts due to these random sources remaining in the data. During this step, data was also detrended for linear and quadratic drifts. With the denoised data, DPARSFA software was used to wrap the masks of each individual into their own space. An ALFF (amplitude of low frequency fluctuations; [45]) calculation of the BOLD fluctuations between 0.01 and 0.1 Hz was then performed on each volunteer. These analyses gave an idea of the activity of different regions in the resting state network results. Regions of homogeneity (ReHo) or areas of correlated voxels were calculated using up to 27 neighbors for each voxel and employing the ReHo analysis toolkit of DPARSF (ReHo analysis; [12]). Once all of the functional analysis was completed for each volunteer, all individual data, masks and results were normalized to a standard Montreal Neurological Institute (MNI) brain template using the DARTEL approach. Finally, in order to reduce noise and compensate for anatomical differences when performing inter-subject averages all normalized data was smoothed with a [4,4,4] mm FWHM Gaussian kernel. Image presentation used the viewer option of the REST software application projecting data on the Open Ch2 brain template (also in MNI coordinates).

For ICA analysis, data was first preprocessed. All the data (H and ADHD groups) were analyzed together in these first steps. Slice time and motion correction of data was performed as in the resting state network analysis and was then normalized (estimated and written) to an EPI.nii template in MNI coordinates using SPM8 software. Normalization was performed with a tri-linear interpolation, a bounding box of -78-112-50 mm and voxel sizes of (2, 2, 2) mm. After this, data was filtered to retain frequencies between 0.01 and 0.1 Hz, and smoothed using a (4, 4, 4) mm kernel using DPARSFA software. To complete preprocessing, data was visually assessed using the "Check Registration" option in SPM8, and was fed to the GIFT software. At this point data was divided into three groups; one with ADHD subjects (description of ADHD with ICA), the other with the H volunteers (ICA results from the H group) and a mixed group (all data together to perform second-level statistics of the ICA results between groups). ICA analysis was performed for each of the three subgroups with the following parameters: regular analysis (analysis run only once) with the Infomax algorithm and with 40 components. The number of components selected for ICA analysis is always controversial. This value was selected based on the work of Damoiseaux et al. which found 12 components in healthy patients. This would give our analysis 28 components more to show the possible appearance of new networks. All the analysis steps that this software follows were completed (parameter initialization, group reduction, ICA calculation, back reconstruction, component calibration and group statistics). Finally each individual component (average of the same component for all the subjects) was displayed on top of the EPI.nii template image. A threshold of $Z>3.33$ was used to eliminate random results. All 40 components were visually assessed. 12 were regularly found in all groups and considered to be significant as they corresponded to networks reported by Damoiseaux et al. The other 28 components were considered to be noise (correlations in structures outside of the brain) or motion (correlations on the borders of brain structures like in brain ventricle walls or in the limit of imaged volumes), and were discarded.

Second-level analysis was used to compare the different components between the ADHD and H group. It was implemented using the statistical capabilities of SPM8, which were accessed through the utilities option in the GIFT software. Here, two sample Mann–Whitney U tests were performed between the same components of the ADHD and H mixed group. This way, component 9, for example, was the same for both the H and ADHD groups. Results of the comparison for each component were also thresholded at $Z>3.33$ and projected onto the EPI.nii template. For publication purposes, each significant component was displayed using the "View" option of the REST software (5×5 images with 7 mm separation between slices that covered the whole brain including cerebellum).

Statistics

All data studied failed normality tests; therefore non-parametric statistical tests were applied. When comparing voxel numbers and images, Mann–Whitney U tests were used with a threshold of $p<0.001$ ($Z>3.33$) corrected for multiple comparisons. For display purposes images were subject to a $p<0.01$ ($Z>2.58$) threshold (also corrected for multiple comparisons), with the added requirement of at least 4 responding voxels lying together to consider the activation as a positive result [46]. The requirement of 4 voxels lying together can increase five-fold the statistical power of a result in some cases [47]. Multiple comparison corrections were performed with family wise error methods (FWE) available in SPM8 and GIFT. The p threshold value selected was similar or stricter than those used in other publications in this field (i.e. [12], [30]).

Results

The first objective of this study was to perform a comparison between resting state networks of ADHD patients and age matched healthy controls using the ReHo methodology. Results (Figure 1, top row) showed similar networks for both groups. Values of Z score varied between 2.58 ($p=0.01$) and 4 ($p<0.0001$) in both cases. In the first row of this image the average image for ADHD patients showed a larger number of total voxels correlated when compared to the H group. This difference was 26% at the thresholds used. In order to quantify this effect, data from each subject of the two groups was studied. No statistically significant difference was found between the two groups in this analysis. Significant areas in both cases were: the occipital and frontal cortex almost completely, the inferior and medial temporal cortex, anterior and posterior cingulate cortex, as well as the cerebellum, cuneus, precuneus, motor cortex and insula. All the regions listed above presented $p<0.001$ after correction for multiple comparisons. In Figure 1 bottom row, results from a comparison between the two groups showed the presence of regions with significantly different correlation values. These values were greater for the H compared with the ADHD subjects in some regions (precuneus, cuneus, left mid-occipital cortex, right putamen, left lingual and ventral pallidum), and lower than ADHD subjects in others (cerebellum lobes 8 and 9 as well as the cerebral crus and the medial frontal cortex bilaterally). All the regions listed above were obtained as a result of a Mann–Whitney U test comparison, with p values under 0.001 after correction for multiple comparisons. In Figure 2, ICA networks obtained from the ADHD group of this study were compared with the resting state networks of healthy volunteers presented by Damoiseaux et al. [8]; ten healthy volunteers with ages of 22.8±2.3 years old). Values of the Z score varied between 2.58 ($p=0.01$) and 4 ($p<0.0001$). All the networks that were present in the Damoiseaux article appeared in this study. The Executive Function & Memory, Ventral Stream and Visual Cortex II networks did not show differences with respect to the control networks and could be clearly recognized. The Ventral Stream network showed new bilateral activations in the ADHD group, in a region that corresponded to frontal inferior orbital cortex. The Executive Function network in this study took up parts of the frontal cortex and did not reach the medial parts of it. ADHD's Visual Cortex II networks invaded medial structures in the occipital/parietal lobe. Finally, the default mode network was found here to have three components and not just two (Figure S1). In this image, calculated and presented in the same manner as Figure 2, there was a third component for the Default Mode network (named Default 3) which covered the cuneus and

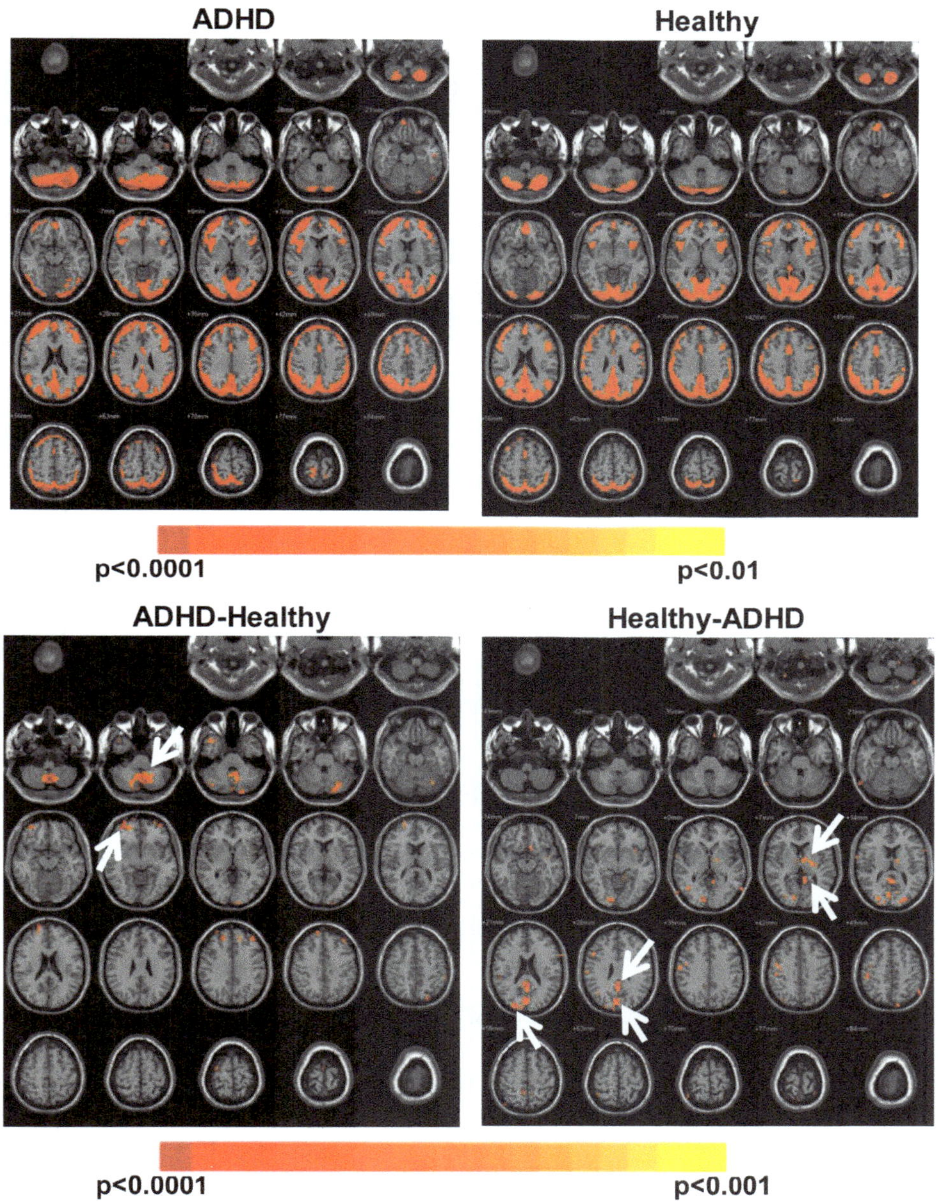

Figure 1. Region of Homogeneity (ReHo). ReHo results are presented in this image. The first row shows averaged data for the ADHD and H groups. Pseudo-colored images (red color scale) are threshold at $p<0.01$ (corrected for multiple comparisons). The second row presents Mann–Whitney U test comparisons between the images of the two groups, ADHD-H and H-ADHD. These images are threshold at $p<0.001$ (corrected for multiple comparisons). They show relevant regions of difference between the groups, with the most significant ones highlighted by white arrows.

precuneus regions as well as the angular and superior parietal cortex (bilaterally).

In order to assess the differences between the ICA studies of the ADHD and H groups, Mann–Whitney U tests comparing the different networks were performed. As before, p values were thresholded at 0.001 after correction for multiple comparisons. In Figure 3, examples of significant brain ROIs recruited differently for each group can be observed (i.e. Visual 1, Default, Somatosensory and Left Memory Function networks).

A list with the position in MNI coordinates, number of significant voxels as well as the names that correspond to these regions can be seen in Table 1. All the networks showed significant *inter-group* differences, except for the Right Memory Function network. In general the majority of these differences between networks were found in the frontal and temporal cortices, as well as cuneus, precuneus and the lingual regions.

In Figure 4 results from the ALFF study comparing, once again, the H and the ADHD group are presented. The difference between this analysis and those presented previously is that it can be considered as a measurement of function or activity of the different brain regions and not a correlation. In the only row of this figure the average results for both groups can be found. Data was thresholded to a Z value between 2.58 ($p = 0.01$) and 4 ($p< 0.0001$) in both cases. Significant amplitudes could be found in both cases in deep brain structures such as the pons and the medulla oblongata. Significant amplitudes were also found in both

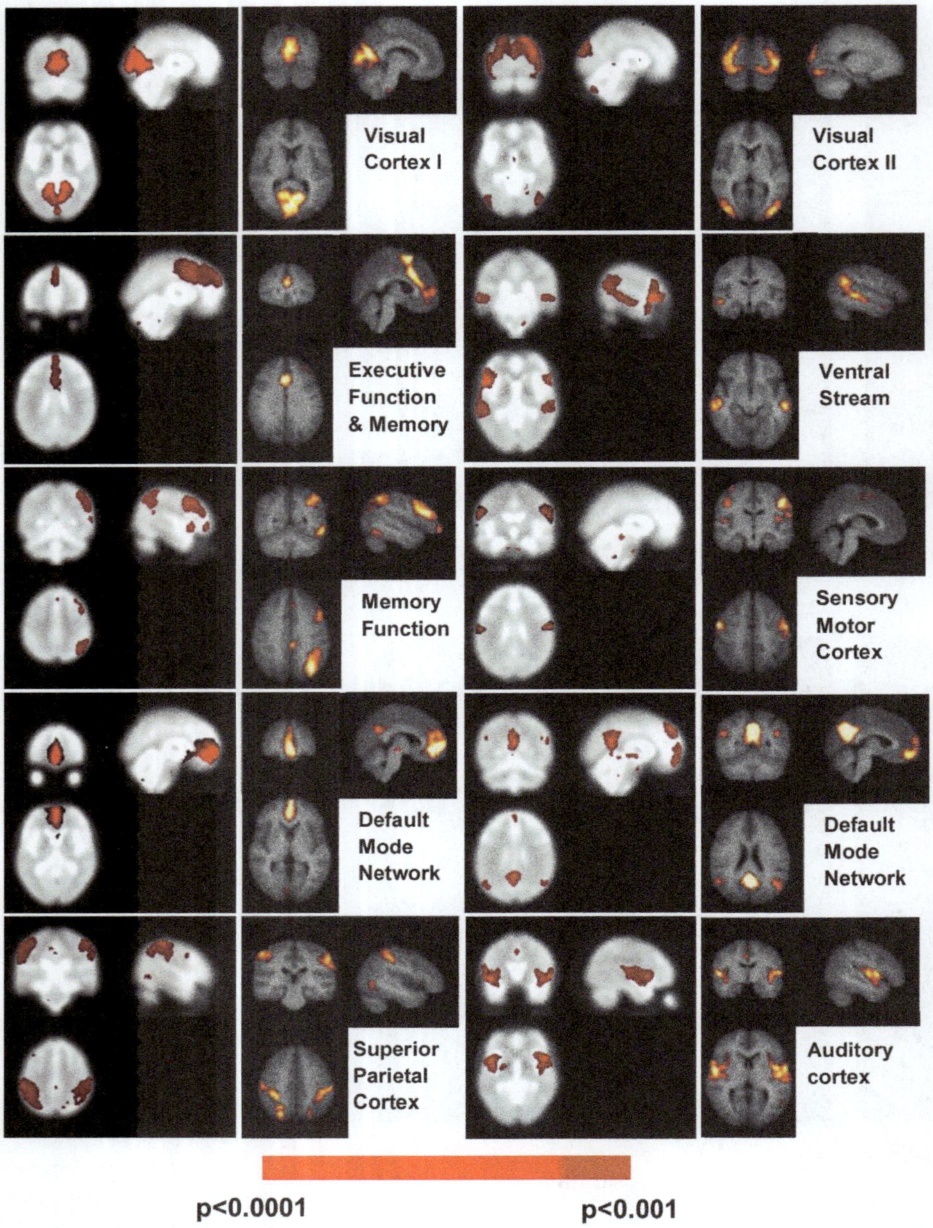

Figure 2. A comparison of ICA results between healthy adult subjects and the group of ADHD children. This figure presents the ten principal ICA networks found in healthy adult humans, as presented by Damoiseaux et al. It compares them with the results from our ICA analysis of the ADHD group. On the left of each panel the results for the ADHD group can be seen and compared with the right panel, where the network obtained by Damoiseaux appears with its corresponding name. Results were thresholded for the ADHD group at $Z>3.33$, corresponding to $p<0.001$. Only the Right Memory Function network is presented for simplicity, but a similar Left Memory Function network exists.

cases in the cerebellum (cerebellar crus 2 and vermis 1) together with the right calcarine fissure and the precuneus. All the regions listed above were significant at $p<0.001$ corrected. No differences with respect to areas and magnitude of amplitudes between the two groups were found (Mann–Whitney U test for comparison of images, data not presented).

Discussion

In this project the resting state networks of pre-treatment ADHD children (aged between 6 and 12 years old) and sex-matched controls were compared. The objective of this work was to highlight some of the physiological differences of the ADHD brain when compared to a healthy one. Different image analysis techniques were used for this study (ReHo, ICA and ALFF). The following major differences were found: ReHo and ICA analyses identified differences between the two groups while ALFF analysis did not. ReHo and ALFF analysis showed different regional recruitment in the ADHD group of this study when compared to previous work. ICA analysis showed that the same resting state networks that appear in healthy volunteers of adult age were obtained for both groups in this study. These networks were not

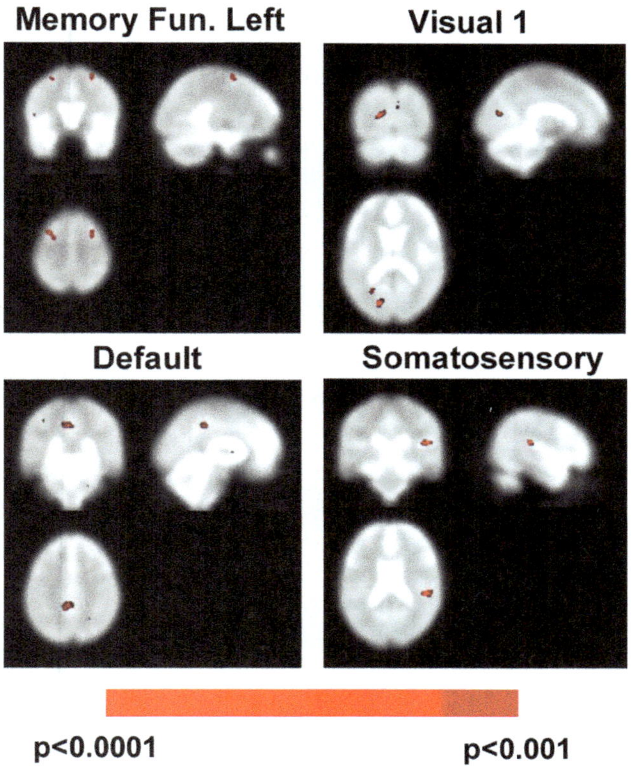

Figure 3. Second-level analysis comparing the ICA results of the H and ADHD groups. This figure presents four sample regions that were found to be statistically significant ($p<0.0001$, U-Mann Whitney tests) in the ICA analysis of the H group over the ADHD group. These regions are the left temporal superior lobe (72, 49,45, MNI coordinates) in the Somatosensory network, the right calcarine fissure (33, 33, 43) in the Principal Visual network, the mid-frontal lobe (33, 68, 68 and 54, 68 68) for the Left Memory Function network and the right middle cingulum (45, 45, 58) for the Default network.

identical and included changes such as the appearance of a third component of the Default network. When comparing healthy and ADHD groups, ICA analysis also showed differences in responding areas for all the networks except for the Right Memory Function network.

Differences between H and ADHD Groups Obtained with ReHo Analysis

When considering ReHo activations, which were greater for the H group compared to the ADHD patients, the following regions were statistically highlighted: cuneus, precuneus, occipital cortex, right putamen and right globus pallidus. The relevance of these findings is consistent with the difficulty that ADHD patients have to process visual and spatial inputs (precuneus), as well as to plan and organise movements (putamen & cerebellum). Also, the precuneus and cuneus are important nodes of the default mode network. The precuneus has been previously reported to have reduced connectivity for ADHD patients when compared to controls [48]. The cuneus is also affected by ADHD [49]. The results in our study corroborate all of these findings.

The putamen and globus pallidus, which form the lentiform nucleus with their high level of connectivity are involved in several functions such as reinforcement, learning, concept learning, motor function, etc. The globus pallidus controls, through its inhibitory function, the positive activity of the cerebellum in movement. It is also known that ADHD affects it as well as the putamen [50]. Probably this de-regulation of the inhibitory function of the lentiform nucleus is what is being observed in these results; thereby presenting a positive correlation in the globus pallidus of the healthy subjects which is not observed in ADHD patients. Recently the putamen has been involved in a new, specific ADHD resting state network involved in information integration and emotional control [51]. The globus pallidus, in contrast, has been known to present different degrees of centricity (number of connected voxels; see [52] but was never reported to have a different ReHo.

When considering which ReHo activations were greater for the ADHD patients when compared to the H, the following regions were statistically highlighted: cerebellum (crus and lobes 8 and 9) and mid-frontal cortex, bilaterally. The cerebellum is known to be involved in planning, organization and execution. It is also known to control the calibration of motor function and learning by inference. Both of these last two functions are altered in ADHD patients. The excess of coherence found in the cerebellum for the ADHD group indicates a neurological basis to this effect. This "dysfunction" of the cerebellum is accompanied by a reduction in its volume [53], especially in areas in which this study found large correlations for the ADHD group (lobes 8 to 10).

It is important to notice that ReHo correlations did appear in both groups in the same areas. Differences were driven exclusively by the strength or magnitude of the correlations, and not because of the lack or absence of a correlation in a given region.

Differences between Healthy Adult Volunteers and ADHD Patients Obtained with ICA Analysis

No new networks were found for the ICA analysis of ADHD patients when compared to healthy adult volunteers (Figure 2). Therefore no new resting state networks associated with the underlying neurobiological mechanisms of ADHD were found in this experiment. Nevertheless, almost all networks showed significant changes between groups.

The Visual Cortex II network invaded medial structures of the occipital lobe that corresponded mainly to parietal cortex and its function as a convergence point between vision and proprioception. It also showed lower correlations in areas like Brodmann 18 and 19, which are secondary and tertiary regions related to image association. The Ventral Stream network showed new bilateral activations in the ADHD group in a region that corresponded to the frontal inferior orbital cortex (Brodmann area 47). Both of these findings supported previous studies in which ADHD children showed impaired early visual processing [54].

The Executive Function network of ADHD patients took up areas of the frontal cortex but did not reach the medial parts of this lobe as it did for healthy subjects. This region, which did not show up in the ICA analysis for ADHD patients, would correspond to Brodmann area 10, or equivalently, the frontopolar prefrontal cortex. This is a meaningful result as this region is known to be involved specifically in executive function (as well as strategic processes and memory recall). The lack of connectivity to this region may account for the problems ADHD patients have in planning or using working memory, or with their task flexibility.

A new component for the Default network (Default 3) appeared in both healthy and ADHD groups. The regions involved (angular, cuneus, precuneus and superior parietal lobe) were areas which appeared in the two previous default networks found by Damoiseaux et al. Based on these two considerations it could be argued that this third component is just a manifestation of the

Table 1. Second-level analysis comparing the ICA results of the H and ADHD groups.

Network	ADHD>H	H>ADHD	Number of Voxels	Regions Name
Auditory	48, 85, 59		88	Superior medial Frontal R
		19, 71, 36	23	Superior Temporal R
Somat. Cortex	27, 86, 41		12	Inferior Frontal Tri R
	69, 56, 34		17	Mid-Temporal L
	40, 35, 64		32	Precuneus R
		72, 49, 45	62	Temporal Superior L
Executive Function	58, 30, 35		25	Lingual L
	47, 96, 46		22	Mid-Superior Frontal
	71, 54, 43		28	Temp Superior L
	42, 39, 74		19	Paracentral Lobule R
		71, 60, 37	40	Temp Superior L
		26, 76, 60	23	Mid-Frontal R
		50, 34, 39	15	Lingual L
Visual 1		40, 25, 44	102	Calcarine R
		74, 59, 60	15	Precentral L
		33, 33, 43	21	Calcarine R
		54, 27, 56	19	Cuneus L
Visual 2		35, 14, 42	22	Mid-Occipital R
Memory Fun. Left	77, 47, 38		17	Superior Temporal L
	27, 46, 59		14	Postcentral R
	60, 89, 56		19	Mid-Frontal L
		33, 68, 68	16	Mid-Frontal R
		62, 68, 68	16	Mid-Frontal L
		18, 77, 40	30	Inferior Frontal Tri R
Ventral Stream		72, 63, 66	46	Precentral L
		63, 73, 39	20	Insula L
		54, 60, 75	15	Precentral L
Sup. Parietal Cortex	23, 73, 58		25	Inferior Frontal Operculum R
		34, 45, 23	20	Cerebellum 4_5_R
Default 1	41, 95, 41		17	Mid-Superior-Frontal L
		71, 49, 61	77	Inferior Parietal L
		23, 30, 59	20	Angular R
		67, 93, 37	19	Mid-Orbito-Frontal L
		40, 97, 48	15	Mid-Frontal R
Default 2	69, 37, 63		34	Parietal Inferior L
	25, 36, 19		17	Cerebellum Crus 1_R
	45, 23, 58		13	Cuneus R
		55, 38, 13	22	Cerebellum_8_L
Default 3	63, 42, 31		18	Fusiform_L
	51, 82, 62		21	Frontal Superior Medial L
	18, 74, 49		30	Frontal Inferior Tri R
		45, 45, 58	90	Mid-cingulum R
		61, 32, 36	52	Lingual L
Memory Fun. Right	NONE	NONE		

This table presents the different regions found when performing a comparison between the ICA results of H and ADHD groups. After comparison ($p<0.0001$, Mann–Whitney U tests), the resulting regions are presented with the following information: ICA network name, ADHD>H or ADHD<H, position of maxima in MNI coordinates, voxel number, and finally region name.

different results obtained when using different image analysis methodologies (i.e. it is a mathematical and not a biological result).

It is nevertheless of interest to highlight the difference in connectivity of the medial cingulate cortex, which in H was larger

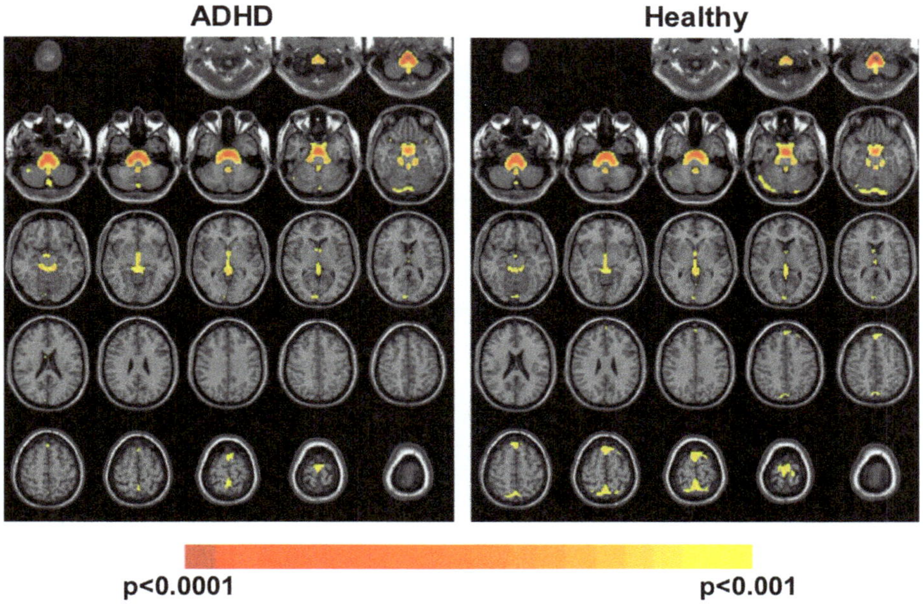

Figure 4. Amplitude at low frequency (ALFF). Here ALFF results with pseudo-colored images (red color scale) are presented. The first row shows averaged data for the ADHD and H groups. Images are threshold to $Z>2.58$ ($p<0.001$ corrected for multiple comparisons).

than in ADHD patients. It is known that damage to this region can induce mental disorders as well as affect information integration (cognitive and affective disorders), and our findings corroborate this.

Differences between H and ADHD Groups Obtained with ICA Analysis

Differences between the networks of the two groups were broad and statistically significant (with the exception of the right memory function network).

The visual networks (Vision I and II as well as the Ventral Stream) included eight regions which were involved in image processing in healthy subjects that did not appear for the ADHD patients. The most consistently observed regions amongst these eight were the calcarine sulcus, the precentral gyrus and areas in the occipital lobe. The calcarine sulcus is where primary visual cortex is located in the brain [55], and the occipital lobe is an association area for vision. These findings highlight the problems that ADHD patients show with visual information integration.

Lenz et al. [54] found that image processing inability for ADHD patients was associated with the lack of an early memory classification of problems. In the ICA analysis of this study, no changes were found in the Right Memory Function network between groups, but gross changes were found for the left network. From this, we might conclude that healthy subjects made primary use of the frontal lobe, while in ADHD patients a mixture of regions were involved, including the frontal and temporal lobes. In a study by Spinelli and colleagues [56], auditory cortex as well as the precentral gyrus were recruited by ADHD patients when solving problems before the appropriate regions for this task were involved. This could easily explain why the ICA activation on precentral gyrus appeared. We therefore argue that image processing is impaired in ADHD patients due to three factors. First, the lack of inputs from V1 as well as the malfunction of some association cortex areas. Second, the recruitment of regions which are not related to image processing, such as precentral gyrus and Brodmann 47 (as seen in Figure 2). Finally, an inappropriate mixture of recruited areas for memory tasks that exclude the frontal areas of the cortex.

Executive function is related to problem solving, planning, working memory, reasoning and task flexibility. When comparing controls to ADHD patients, the latter presented in ICA analysis a strong correlation in what would correspond to the paracentral lobule. This is a meaningful result as this region is known to have reduced connectivity in ADHD patients [27]. This result, combined with the fact that all the other statistically significant regions (lingual, frontal and temporal lobes, see Table 1) appeared in both groups, indicates that ADHD patients were unable to recruit this region for executive function processing.

Differences between H and ADHD Groups Obtained with ALFF Analysis

In this study no significant differences in ALFF activity was found between the two groups. This indicates that for the population of this study, ADHD did not affect the function of the different regions of the brain. This is in contrast with previous work comparing non-medicated ADHD patients to healthy ones, which showed larger activations for healthy in sensory motor cortex, frontal cortex and cerebellum [30]. It also showed larger activations for ADHD in brainstem, anterior cingulate cortex and cerebellum.

ALFF analysis did show that regions in the brainstem (pons and medulla oblongata), which had previously been mentioned in literature for ADHD patients, were also active here. In contrast, a group of regions not previously reported were found to be active for both groups. These were the precuneus, cuneus and the calcarine fissure. Except for the calcarine fissure, all the other regions were also found in the ReHo analysis and were found in both groups at a similar magnitude. These results could be an indication that ADHD does not affect drastically the function of a region. It could be argued that it is the inter-regional connectivity, as well as the areas recruited for a given function, which are altered by the disorder.

Differences with Respect to Previous Work

We believe that the main differences found between this study and previous work arise mainly because of the population used, and methodological issues.

Even if the patient sample used here is in general larger than those used in the past, there are plenty of biological factors that might affect the results and produce differences, such as age, medication, subtype of ADHD, IQ, emotional situation of the patient, genetic origin, etc. As mentioned before, patients in this study had ages between 6 and 12, while the majority of previous studies were performed on patients with ages between 11 and 18 years old. There is a large difference in brain physiology of children and adolescents [57], and some of the differences highlighted as different findings of the ReHo analysis could have this origin. The different subtype of ADHD studied is also a factor to be considered. To our knowledge all work that has been previously performed has considered ADHD patients as a homogeneous group without any subdivision into one of the three subtypes. Considering that ADHD patients from just two subgroups were used here, this could certainly account for some of the differences.

The methodological issues should also be considered (ICA vs. ReHo, ICA vs. ALFF, kind of platform used for analysis, etc.). These are complicated computational analyses in which several (if not hundreds) of parameters have to be set by the researchers. It is impossible for the methods section of an article to present all of this information. Therefore differences between studies will appear due to this factor.

Conclusions

In general, results from the three techniques indicated that the cerebellum and mid-frontal lobe bilaterally for ReHo, the executive function regions in ICA and the precuneus, cuneus and the clacarine fissure for ALFF, were the "hubs" through which ADHD affected brain function. Results from ReHo also showed that regions like the cuneus, precuneus, occipital cortex, right putamen and right globus pallidus were significantly important. In fact, ReHo correlations were always present for both groups in all regions and just presented different strengths, indicating different connectivity but not a complete malfunction of the region in question. ALFF results indicated that in general, function in every region was the same when comparing healthy controls and ADHD patients.

Based on our results, the techniques used in this study could be considered part of the spectrum of techniques employed in the assessment of attentional disorders. The combination of them has shown that they are complementary and provide different views of the problem. This opens a door to more objective studies for ADHD diagnosis and the understanding of its physiopathology. In the near future the methodology used here could represent a helpful diagnostic tool to monitor the neurobiological changes of this disorder over time and during drug treatments. It was of great interest to observe how connectivity and dysfunction of several brain regions changed. This supported a context in which ADHD was a neurodevelopment disorder, and shows how early-stage intervention could help balance these intricate compensatory neuronal networks.

Supporting Information

Figure S1 Default network components obtained from the ICA analysis of this study. In this image the three components into which the Default network was found to be divided in this study are presented. The first two are compared to the components obtained from Damoiseaux et al. (right panels), while the third stands alone. Data was thresholded between $p < 0.001$ and $p < 0.0001$, and a pseudo-colored bar indicates these differences.

Author Contributions

Conceived and designed the experiments: BCA SHT PDS JGF BCC EBP. Performed the experiments: BCA SHT PDS JGF BCC EBP. Analyzed the data: BCA SHT PDS JGF BCC EBP. Contributed reagents/materials/analysis tools: BCA SHT PDS JGF BCC EBP. Wrote the paper: BCA SHT PDS JGF BCC EBP.

References

1. Polanczyk G, de Lima MS, Horta BL, Biederman J, Rohde LA (2007) The worldwide prevalence of ADHD: a systematic review and metaregression analysis. Am J Psychiatry 164: 942–948.
2. Satterfield JH, Schell AM, Backs RW, Hidaka KC (1984) A cross-sectional and longitudinal study of age effects of electrophysiological measures in hyperactive and normal children. Biol Psychiatry 19: 973–990.
3. Biswal B, Yetkin FZ, Haughton VM, Hyde JS (1995) Functional connectivity in the motor cortex of resting human brain using echo-planar MRI. Magn Reson Med 34: 537–541.
4. Raichle ME, MacLeod AM, Snyder AZ, Powers WJ, Gusnard DA, et al. (2001) A default mode of brain function. Proc Natl Acad Sci U S A 98: 676–682.
5. Takeuchi H, Taki Y, Nouchi R, Hashizume H, Sekiguchi A, et al. (2012) Effects of working memory training on functional connectivity and cerebral blood flow during rest. Cortex.
6. Ferreira LK, Busatto GF (2013) Resting-state functional connectivity in normal brain aging. Neurosci Biobehav Rev 37: 384–400.
7. Hampson M, Tokoglu F, Shen X, Scheinost D, Papademetris X, et al. (2012) Intrinsic brain connectivity related to age in young and middle aged adults. PLoS One 7: e44067.
8. Damoiseaux JS, Rombouts SA, Barkhof F, Scheltens P, Stam CJ, et al. (2006) Consistent resting-state networks across healthy subjects. Proc Natl Acad Sci U S A 103: 13848–13853.
9. Li Q, Yang WC, Wang YR, Huang YF, Li W, et al. (2013) Abnormal function of the posterior cingulate cortex in heroin addicted users during resting-state and drug-cue stimulation task. Chin Med J (Engl) 126: 734–739.
10. Pievani M, de Haan W, Wu T, Seeley WW, Frisoni GB (2011) Functional network disruption in the degenerative dementias. Lancet Neurol 10: 829–843.
11. Cherkassky VL, Kana RK, Keller TA, Just MA (2006) Functional connectivity in a baseline resting-state network in autism. Neuroreport 17: 1687–1690.
12. Zang Y, Jiang T, Lu Y, He Y, Tian L (2004) Regional homogeneity approach to fMRI data analysis. Neuroimage 22: 394–400.
13. Li Y, Booth JR, Peng D, Zang Y, Li J, et al. (2013) Altered intra- and inter-regional synchronization of superior temporal cortex in deaf people. Cereb Cortex 23: 1988–1996.
14. Zeng H, Pizarro R, Nair VA, La C, Prabhakaran V (2013) Alterations in regional homogeneity of resting-state brain activity in mesial temporal lobe epilepsy. Epilepsia 54: 658–666.
15. Lv Y, Margulies DS, Villringer A, Zang YF (2013) Effects of finger tapping frequency on regional homogeneity of sensorimotor cortex. PLoS One 8: e64115.
16. Yang H, Long XY, Yang Y, Yan H, Zhu CZ, et al. (2007) Amplitude of low frequency fluctuation within visual areas revealed by resting-state functional MRI. Neuroimage 36: 144–152.
17. Turner JA, Chen H, Mathalon DH, Allen EA, Mayer AR, et al. (2012) Reliability of the amplitude of low-frequency fluctuations in resting state fMRI in chronic schizophrenia. Psychiatry Res 201: 253–255.
18. Li L, Liu J, Chen F, Feng L, Li H, et al. (2013) Resting state neural networks for visual Chinese word processing in Chinese adults and children. Neuropsychologia 51: 1571–1583.
19. Skidmore FM, Yang M, Baxter L, von Deneen K, Collingwood J, et al. (2013) Apathy, depression, and motor symptoms have distinct and separable resting activity patterns in idiopathic Parkinson disease. Neuroimage 81: 484–495.
20. Wolf RC, Plichta MM, Sambataro F, Fallgatter AJ, Jacob C, et al. (2009) Regional brain activation changes and abnormal functional connectivity of the

ventrolateral prefrontal cortex during working memory processing in adults with attention-deficit/hyperactivity disorder. Hum Brain Mapp 30: 2252–2266.
21. Tang J, Liao Y, Song M, Gao JH, Zhou B, et al. (2013) Aberrant default mode functional connectivity in early onset schizophrenia. PLoS One 8: e71061.
22. Robinson SD, Schopf V (2013) ICA of fMRI Studies: New Approaches and Cutting Edge Applications. Front Hum Neurosci 7: 724.
23. Calhoun VD, Adali T, Pekar JJ (2004) A method for comparing group fMRI data using independent component analysis: application to visual, motor and visuomotor tasks. Magn Reson Imaging 22: 1181–1191.
24. Konrad K, Eickhoff SB (2010) Is the ADHD brain wired differently? A review on structural and functional connectivity in attention deficit hyperactivity disorder. Hum Brain Mapp 31: 904–916.
25. Castellanos FX, Kelly C, Milham MP (2009) The restless brain: attention-deficit hyperactivity disorder, resting-state functional connectivity, and intrasubject variability. Can J Psychiatry 54: 665–672.
26. Castellanos FX, Proal E (2012) Large-scale brain systems in ADHD: beyond the prefrontal-striatal model. Trends Cogn Sci 16: 17–26.
27. Tian L, Jiang T, Wang Y, Zang Y, He Y, et al. (2006) Altered resting-state functional connectivity patterns of anterior cingulate cortex in adolescents with attention deficit hyperactivity disorder. Neurosci Lett 400: 39–43.
28. Cao Q, Zang Y, Sun L, Sui M, Long X, et al. (2006) Abnormal neural activity in children with attention deficit hyperactivity disorder: a resting-state functional magnetic resonance imaging study. Neuroreport 17: 1033–1036.
29. Tian L, Jiang T, Liang M, Zang Y, He Y, et al. (2008) Enhanced resting-state brain activities in ADHD patients: a fMRI study. Brain Dev 30: 342–348.
30. Zang YF, He Y, Zhu CZ, Cao QJ, Sui MQ, et al. (2007) Altered baseline brain activity in children with ADHD revealed by resting-state functional MRI. Brain Dev 29: 83–91.
31. Mueller A, Candrian G, Kropotov JD, Ponomarev VA, Baschera GM (2010) Classification of ADHD patients on the basis of independent ERP components using a machine learning system. Nonlinear Biomed Phys 4 Suppl 1: S1.
32. Kobel M, Bechtel N, Specht K, Klarhofer M, Weber P, et al. (2010) Structural and functional imaging approaches in attention deficit/hyperactivity disorder: does the temporal lobe play a key role? Psychiatry Res 183: 230–236.
33. Dey S, Rao AR, Shah M (2012) Exploiting the brain's network structure in identifying ADHD subjects. Front Syst Neurosci 6: 75.
34. Anderson A, Douglas PK, Kerr WT, Haynes VS, Yuille AL, et al. (2013) Non-negative matrix factorization of multimodal MRI, fMRI and phenotypic data reveals differential changes in default mode subnetworks in ADHD. Neuroimage.
35. Sripada C, Kessler D, Fang Y, Welsh RC, Prem Kumar K, et al. (2014) Disrupted network architecture of the resting brain in attention-deficit/hyperactivity disorder. Hum Brain Mapp.
36. Arnsten AF, Li BM (2005) Neurobiology of executive functions: catecholamine influences on prefrontal cortical functions. Biol Psychiatry 57: 1377–1384.
37. Rubia K, Halari R, Cubillo A, Smith AB, Mohammad AM, et al. (2011) Methylphenidate normalizes fronto-striatal underactivation during interference inhibition in medication-naive boys with attention-deficit hyperactivity disorder. Neuropsychopharmacology 36: 1575–1586.
38. Cubillo A, Smith AB, Barrett N, Giampietro V, Brammer MJ, et al. (2014) Shared and drug-specific effects of atomoxetine and methylphenidate on inhibitory brain dysfunction in medication-naive ADHD boys. Cereb Cortex 24: 174–185.
39. Chao-Gan Y, Yu-Feng Z (2010) DPARSF: A MATLAB Toolbox for "Pipeline" Data Analysis of Resting-State fMRI. Front Syst Neurosci 4: 13.
40. Song XW, Dong ZY, Long XY, Li SF, Zuo XN, et al. (2011) REST: a toolkit for resting-state functional magnetic resonance imaging data processing. PLoS One 6: e25031.
41. Power JD, Barnes KA, Snyder AZ, Schlaggar BL, Petersen SE (2012) Spurious but systematic correlations in functional connectivity MRI networks arise from subject motion. Neuroimage 59: 2142–2154.
42. Power JD, Barnes KA, Snyder AZ, Schlaggar BL, Petersen SE (2013) Steps toward optimizing motion artifact removal in functional connectivity MRI; a reply to Carp. Neuroimage 76: 439–441.
43. Ashburner J (2007) A fast diffeomorphic image registration algorithm. Neuroimage 38: 95–113.
44. He H, Liu TT (2012) A geometric view of global signal confounds in resting-state functional MRI. Neuroimage 59: 2339–2348.
45. Zou QH, Zhu CZ, Yang Y, Zuo XN, Long XY, et al. (2008) An improved approach to detection of amplitude of low-frequency fluctuation (ALFF) for resting-state fMRI: fractional ALFF. J Neurosci Methods 172: 137–141.
46. Alonso Bde C, Lowe AS, Dear JP, Lee KC, Williams SC, et al. (2008) Sensory inputs from whisking movements modify cortical whisker maps visualized with functional magnetic resonance imaging. Cereb Cortex 18: 1314–1325.
47. Forman SD, Cohen JD, Fitzgerald M, Eddy WF, Mintun MA, et al. (1995) Improved assessment of significant activation in functional magnetic resonance imaging (fMRI): use of a cluster-size threshold. Magn Reson Med 33: 636–647.
48. Uddin LQ, Kelly AM, Biswal BB, Margulies DS, Shehzad Z, et al. (2008) Network homogeneity reveals decreased integrity of default-mode network in ADHD. J Neurosci Methods 169: 249–254.
49. Cao QJ, Zang YF, Wang YF (2007) [Brain functions in attention deficit hyperactivity disorder combined and inattentive subtypes: A resting-state functional magnetic resonance imaging study]. Beijing Da Xue Xue Bao 39: 261–265.
50. Teicher MH, Anderson CM, Polcari A, Glod CA, Maas LC, et al. (2000) Functional deficits in basal ganglia of children with attention-deficit/hyperactivity disorder shown with functional magnetic resonance imaging relaxometry. Nat Med 6: 470–473.
51. Yu D (2013) Additional brain functional network in adults with attention-deficit/hyperactivity disorder: a phase synchrony analysis. PLoS One 8: e54516.
52. Di Martino A, Zuo XN, Kelly C, Grzadzinski R, Mennes M, et al. (2013) Shared and Distinct Intrinsic Functional Network Centrality in Autism and Attention-Deficit/Hyperactivity Disorder. Biol Psychiatry.
53. Berquin PC, Giedd JN, Jacobsen LK, Hamburger SD, Krain AL, et al. (1998) Cerebellum in attention-deficit hyperactivity disorder: a morphometric MRI study. Neurology 50: 1087–1093.
54. Lenz D, Krauel K, Flechtner HH, Schadow J, Hinrichs H, et al. (2010) Altered evoked gamma-band responses reveal impaired early visual processing in ADHD children. Neuropsychologia 48: 1985–1993.
55. Born P, Leth H, Miranda MJ, Rostrup E, Stensgaard A, et al. (1998) Visual activation in infants and young children studied by functional magnetic resonance imaging. Pediatr Res 44: 578–583.
56. Spinelli S, Vasa RA, Joel S, Nelson TE, Pekar JJ, et al. (2011) Variability in post-error behavioral adjustment is associated with functional abnormalities in the temporal cortex in children with ADHD. J Child Psychol Psychiatry 52: 808–816.
57. Lou H, Henriksen L, Greisen G, Schneider S (1990) Redistribution of cerebral activity during childhood. Brain Dev 12: 301–305.

12

Adults with Dyslexia Demonstrate Large Effects of Crowding and Detrimental Effects of Distractors in a Visual Tilt Discrimination Task

Rizan Cassim, Joel B. Talcott, Elisabeth Moores*

School of Life and Health Sciences, Aston University, Birmingham, West Midlands, United Kingdom

Abstract

Previous research has shown that adults with dyslexia (AwD) are disproportionately impacted by close spacing of stimuli and increased numbers of distractors in a visual search task compared to controls [1]. Using an orientation discrimination task, the present study extended these findings to show that even in conditions where target search was not required: (i) AwD had detrimental effects of both crowding and increased numbers of distractors; (ii) AwD had more pronounced difficulty with distractor exclusion in the left visual field and (iii) measures of crowding and distractor exclusion correlated significantly with literacy measures. Furthermore, such difficulties were not accounted for by the presence of covarying symptoms of ADHD in the participant groups. These findings provide further evidence to suggest that the ability to exclude distracting stimuli likely contributes to the reported visual attention difficulties in AwD and to the aetiology of literacy difficulties. The pattern of results is consistent with weaker and asymmetric attention in AwD.

Editor: Lawrence M. Ward, University of British Columbia, Canada

Funding: This work constitutes part of RC's PhD thesis for which he received a scholarship from Aston University. The funders had no role in study design, data collection and analysis, decision to publish, or preparation of the manuscript.

Competing Interests: The authors have declared that no competing interests exist.

* Email: e.j.moores@aston.ac.uk

Introduction

Although phonological difficulties are well-established as core features underlying literacy impairments [2–4], focus is being increasingly devoted to the role of visual attention difficulties in reading disorders, including developmental dyslexia. A variety of attention difficulties have been reported in dyslexia, including asymmetric attention distribution [5], reduced visual attention span [6], increased crowding effects [1,7–11], difficulty in using cues [12–14] and less effective mechanisms for noise exclusion [15,16]. Controversially, it has been argued that even core phonological language difficulties shown in dyslexia can be statistically accounted for by an underlying visual deficit [17]. The majority of research implicates a model of dyslexia based on multiple underlying deficits [18], with attention difficulties as an additional contributing factor to the genesis of reading impairments in some individuals. Moreover, the high comorbidity between dyslexia and attention deficit hyperactivity disorder (ADHD) [19] may also account for some of the covariance between deficits in visual attention and core reading skills. Here, we examined three specific aspects of visual attention: (i) visual crowding, (ii) the ability to exclude distractors and (iii) the distribution of attention across the visual field. We also investigated the relationship of these three aspects of attention with four different measures of literacy and with the presence of sub-clinical ADHD symptoms, in our sample.

1.1 Effects of visual crowding

Visual crowding occurs when stimuli become more difficult to either detect or discriminate when surrounded by other stimuli, compared to when they are presented in isolation. Crowding is a phenomenon that occurs in nearly every visual context. It can occur with simple stimuli - such as orientation gratings – and also with complex stimuli such as letters [20]. Efficient allocation and control of visual attention can ameliorate the negative effects of crowding [21,22], although Dakin, Bex, Cass and Watt [23] have argued that crowding does not specifically reflect a limitation in attention. He, Cavanagh and Intriligator have provided alternative evidence from an orientation adaptation and discrimination task that suggests that it is attention – rather than visual acuity – that ultimately limits spatial resolution under normal circumstances [24]. Several studies have suggested that persons with reading impairments such as dyslexia suffer more from crowding than do similarly aged control readers [1,7–11,25]. Research in this area, however, has mainly used letter or letter-like stimuli to investigate this hypothesis. Because dyslexia is also associated with deficits in recognition and processing of linguistic stimuli – including letters – it is difficult to adjudicate between effects linked to visual attention and those associated with processing the symbols of language in such tasks.

1.2 Noise (distractor) exclusion

In addition to evidence for increased crowding effects in dyslexia, other studies also identify difficulties in excluding distracting stimuli. Sperling *et al.* [15,16] showed that performance of adults in a visual motion detection task only correlated with their reading ability in conditions where the signal to noise ratio was low. Using a visual search paradigm, Roach and Hogben [26] measured psychophysical thresholds of adults with dyslexia (AwD) and controls for detection of a tilted target stimulus presented amongst vertical distractors. Although the set size effect of the control group, but not the AwD, was diminished when targets were cued, they provided evidence [13,14] to suggest that the difficulty of the AwD was one of ineffective noise exclusion, rather than problems detecting and localising the cue *per se*. Using a similar paradigm, Moores *et al.* [1] also reported that AwD could use pre-cues to modulate attention, but that they were less successful at using them to counter effects of increasing numbers of distractors on target detectability. A limitation of these studies, however, is that visual search paradigms were used, in which - for uncued conditions - the target location was not known. Therefore, any potential beneficial effects of cueing for either group could reflect reduced spatial uncertainty regarding target location, rather than the effects of enhanced attention or distractor exclusion. As an alternative, the current study presented the target stimulus at one of only two possible fixed locations in the left and right visual fields. This manipulation minimised the potential for eye movements towards a fixed stimulus location. Also, because previous research has shown an asymmetrical distribution of attention in dyslexia, it allowed us to replicate this effect here.

1.3 Distribution of attention

Facoetti, Paganoni and Lorusso [27] have previously reported that a group of children with dyslexia (CwD) showed more distributed or diffuse attentional focus, evidenced by a relatively flat profile of reaction times for stimulus detection with increasing retinal eccentricity. Facoetti and Molteni [28] demonstrated that this profile only occurred for stimuli presented in the right visual field, whereas responses of CwD in the left visual field were slower than those of controls overall, but were faster for stimuli presented at central compared to peripheral locations. They proposed that an attention disorder affecting the left visual field would explain the slower responses overall, with the lack of a performance gradient across eccentricity accounting for the over-distractibility associated with stimulus processing in the right visual field. Hari, Renvall and Tanskanen [29] also reported slower performance in AwD in the left visual field on two psychophysical tasks and from this evidence proposed a left-sided 'minineglect' in dyslexia. Consistent with this hypothesis, Waldie and Hausmann [30] reported a reversal of the normal leftward bias observed in a line bisection task in CwD and in children with ADHD (see also [31]). Further evidence for an asymmetry was provided by Facoetti and Turatto [5], who reported a reduced effect of flankers in the left visual field, and by Facoetti, Turatto, Lorusso and Mascetti [32], who showed slower reaction times to invalidly cued targets in the left compared to the right visual field. A body of psychophysical evidence therefore points toward an asymmetric and more diffuse distribution of attention in dyslexic readers.

1.4 Relationship between literacy and effects of crowding, set-size and visual field asymmetry

It is important to determine whether the differences in attention associated with dyslexia are related to measures of literacy, or more to third variables which also co-occur with dyslexia and other development disorders. Relationships between measures of visual attention and of literacy have previously been demonstrated. Sperling *et al.* [16] reported a moderate [33] correlation between reading ability and ability to detect visual coherent motion amongst noise in adults. Moores *et al.* [1] reported moderate to strong correlations between literacy measures and dependence on attentional cues, effects of crowding and the impact of a greater number of distractors. Facoetti *et al.* [34] reported a strong correlation in dyslexic readers between nonword reading accuracy and the extent of a deficit in attentional inhibition in the right visual field (i.e. the finding that when cued to the left visual field, targets in the right visual field are not inhibited). All these associations between reading and attention variables, however, might plausibly be related to the overlapping dimensions dyslexia shares with ADHD, rather than to literacy skills directly. In the present study, we examined the relationships between four measures of literacy (word reading accuracy, word spelling accuracy, real word reading efficiency and nonword reading efficiency) and our measures of crowding, distractor exclusion and attention asymmetry.

1.5 Associations with ADHD

Previous research has suggested that dyslexic readers suffer more from crowding, are less effective at excluding distractors, and have a different distribution of attention compared to controls. Furthermore, these difficulties correlate with literacy abilities. However, it has been estimated that upwards from 15% of children with dyslexia also have co-occurring attention deficit hyperactivity disorder (ADHD) and around 36% of children with ADHD are estimated to have dyslexia [19]. According to the Diagnostic and Statistical Manual of Mental Disorders 5th Edition [35] the primary symptoms of ADHD are 'inattention' (which includes poor sustained attention, forgetfulness and distractibility) and 'hyperactivity/ impulsivity'. Most contemporary theories of ADHD argue that the core deficits are associated with either poor inhibitory control [36] or aversion to delay [37]. However, an alternative explanation may be that reported 'attention' difficulties in dyslexia may be accounted for by concomitant ADHD symptoms. The dimensions of literacy and attention are continuous variables, with categories derived from rather arbitrary statistical cut-offs. Although many dyslexia studies investigating aspects of visual attention have excluded participants with actual diagnoses of ADHD from their studies, few have specifically investigated the potential role of sub-clinical ADHD symptoms by controlling statistically for their presence. It should be noted, however, that 'inattention' type symptoms as discussed in the context of ADHD may be conceptually different from the type of visual selective attention difficulties investigated in this study and other research in this area. A lack of sustained attention or a general distractibility would be expected to adversely affect performance across *all* conditions of any task, whereas research into visual attention difficulties in dyslexia invariably reports dissociated patterns of deficit which only present in particular conditions; for example only when a display is crowded, or only in the left visual field. Nonetheless, in a different context, it has been shown that ADHD symptoms can mediate the effects of differences in performance variables between groups of persons with dyslexia and controls [38], so in the current study it was important to assess the potential impact of sub-clinical ADHD effects as an alternative hypothesis.

1.6 Limitations, summary and overview

Moores *et al.* [1] showed that a greater dependence on pre-cues, larger effects of crowding and the impact of increased numbers of distractors all correlated strongly with measures of literacy skill. However, as discussed in *section 1.2*, this task was a visual search task in which the target location was not known (unless pre-cued). The advantage of pre-cueing in this task could therefore have been due to a reduced spatial uncertainty over target location as well as – or instead of – enhanced attention and/ or noise exclusion. In addition, crowding could have simply made the target more difficult to locate, rather than more difficult to discriminate *per se* [39]. Furthermore, our previous study did not investigate the potential role of ADHD symptomatology on task performance. With any potential effects of ADHD statistically removed, the present study therefore investigated whether: (i) AwD experienced increased crowding effects and difficulty excluding distractors even when target location was known, (ii) any increased difficulties in excluding distractors or in crowding showed any asymmetry in AwD and (iii) any difficulties with crowding, excluding distractors, or any asymmetry had any relationship with four different measures of literacy.

Materials and Methods

2.1 Participants

Participants provided informed written consent which conformed to the procedures approved by the Aston University's Ethics Committee on use of human participants. The study was approved by Aston University Ethics Committee. Sixteen control adults (7 males) and eighteen AwD (8 males) equated for age and full scale IQ took part in this study (Eleven control adults (7 males) and thireteen AwD (6 males) also took part in our previous study [1]). Participants were also asked to provide ratings of their behaviour across the dimensions of inattention and hyperactivity/ impulsivity on the Barkley Current Symptoms Scales [40]. Scores of greater than 6 on either measure, or exceeding 9 for the sum of inattention and hyperactivity scores, are indicative of dimensions in which further exploration toward a clinical diagnosis of ADHD is usually suggested [40]. The selection criteria required that each participant had a profile of enduring reading and spelling difficulties and/or previous clinical diagnosis, but no prior history of any other developmental disorder. The control group was required to have no previously reported problems in spelling or reading. All participants were required to have a minimum full scale IQ of 90, English as their first language and normal or corrected-to-normal vision. All participants also had completed at least some higher education (on average 12.8 years of schooling, SD = 0.49) and most of them (15 controls and 15 AwD) were either previously or currently enrolled in university degree programmes.

Participants from both groups were initially screened using a battery of assessments for cognitive skills and literacy achievement. All AwD provided a recent report from an educational psychologist at the time of testing, which provided the estimate of full-scale IQ used in the study (using the Wechsler Adult Intelligence Scale (WAIS) [41]). The IQ test for control participants was administered on the day of testing (using the Wechsler Abbreviated Scale of Intelligence (WASI) [42]), unless they had been previously assessed with either the Wechsler Adult Intelligence Scale or the Wechsler Abbreviated Scale of Intelligence. Reading and spelling achievement was measured using the Wechsler Individual Achievement Test (WIAT-II UK) reading and spelling subtests [43] unless these measures had already been administered within the previous 12 months. The Test of Word Reading Efficiency (TOWRE) [44] - a speeded reading test designed to measure word reading accuracy and fluency - was also conducted. The Sight Word Efficiency (SWE) test provided a fluency measure for real words, whilst the Phonemic Decoding Efficiency (PDE) test provided a decoding measure for accuracy and fluency of pronounceable non-words.

A comparison of demographic and psychometric data for both the controls and AwD is summarised in Table 1. Independent sample t-tests (with Levene's correction for unequal variances when appropriate) showed no significant differences between groups for age [$t\ (28.08) = 0.46$], level of education [$t\ (22.14) = 1.27$] or IQ [$t\ (31.98) = 2.51$]. The average performance of the AwD group was significantly lower than the controls for all measures of literacy: WIAT-II word reading [$t\ (31.53) = 9.54$, $p < .001$], WIAT-II spelling [$t\ (28.26) = 6.11$, $p < .001$], TOWRE SWE [$t\ (32.00) = 3.79$, $p < .001$] and TOWRE PDE [$t\ (28.06) = 19.46$, $p < .001$]. AwD also had higher scores on the ADHD measure [$t\ (29.62) = -3.87$, $p < .001$].

2.2 Stimuli and apparatus

The tilt discrimination experiment was developed using E-Prime Version 2-Professional [45] and conducted on a P4 Dell Optiplex GX 260 desktop computer displaying the output on a 19-inch CRT Vision Master Pro 510 monitor (1024×768-pixel screen resolution, 60-Hz refresh rate).

The stimuli consisted of five greyscale sine-phase Gabor patches generated using Matlab (MathWorks Ltd) comprising wavelength ($\lambda = 10$ pixels per cycle) and a Gaussian standard deviation ($\sigma = 10$). The target Gabors were tilted (θ) at different angles relative to the vertical distractors in two conditions which varied in difficulty: i) $\theta = \pm 5^\circ$ ('easy' condition) and, ii) $\theta = \pm 2^\circ$ ('difficult' condition).

The participants were asked to support their head within a chin rest while seated at a viewing distance of 57 cm in a dimly lit room. Participant responses were entered using specific key presses on a standard computer keyboard.

2.3 Design

The independent variables of interest were group (AwD or Control), display type (zero distractors, two-spaced distractors, two-crowded distractors, four distractors or eight distractors), task difficulty (easy or difficult tilt) and visual field (VF: left or right). The direction of tilt was also randomised. The dependent variable was percent correct for the detection of the correct orientation of the target stimulus.

Participants performed a two alternative forced choice task (see Figure 1) in which they were required to indicate the orientation (left or right tilt) of a single tilted target stimulus that was always presented in the centre of a variable length string of vertically oriented distractors. On a given trial, there was an equal probability of the target stimulus having a tilt of either $\pm 2^\circ$ (easy) or $\pm 5^\circ$ (difficult). The string was comprised of varying configurations presented with equal probability: zero distractors, two crowded distractors, two spread distractors, four distractors or eight distractors. The stimuli (target and distractors) were positioned either to the left-VF or right-VF (50% probability) of the display on the circumference of an imaginary semi-circle located 5° of visual angle peripheral to the central fixation point. In either VF, the target stimulus always appeared at a fixed central position (indicated by the arrow placeholder as in Figure 1) whilst the distractors were arranged symmetrically above and below it in the same hemifield. To evaluate the effect of distractors alone, crowding effects in the different array conditions were kept constant by separating the distractors closest to the target by an interstimulus distance of 3.5° visual angle from the target while the distance between distractors was constant throughout at 1.6° visual angle. The exception to this was in the two distractor crowded condition in which the effects of crowding were systematically manipulated by positioning the two distractors nearer to the target (target-distractor separation of 1.6° visual angle). Although our spacing manipulation led to unequal spacing of stimuli in four and eight distractor conditions, it enabled us to manipulate the number

Table 1. Demographic and psychometric group data.

	Control (n = 16)		AwD (n = 18)		p-value
	Mean	**SD**	**Mean**	**SD**	
Age (years)	26.69	5.65	25.89	4.35	ns
Education[a]	12.94	0.25	12.72	0.67	ns
Full-Scale IQ	124.19	6.53	118.11	7.58	ns
Spelling (WIAT-II UK)[b]	116.50	5.39	100.72	9.25	<.001
Reading (WIAT-II UK)[b]	110.31	3.18	98.44	4.06	<.001
TOWRE (SWE)[b]	107.69	6.09	99.28	6.86	<.001
TOWRE (PDE)[b]	116.63	3.44	95.94	2.65	<.001
ADHD	1.44	1.15	3.39	1.75	<.05

[a]The level of education represents years of schooling from year 1 (infant school) to year 13 (college/sixth form).
[b]The composite standard scores (SS). For the TOWRE these were calculated using the norms 17:0–24:11 (years: months).

of distractors presented in a single hemifield *without* varying the spacing between the central target and its nearest distractors (i.e. without varying the degree of crowding of the target). Stimuli were presented with consistent spacing in the two conditions where we specifically investigated crowding effects (since only two distractors were used in each case).

2.4 Procedure

Initiated by a single key press, each trial sequence commenced with an onset of a blank grey screen with a central fixation point (+) of 40 ms duration. Participants were instructed to visually fixate this position throughout the entire duration of each trial. A second fixation screen followed for 110 ms which had arrows on

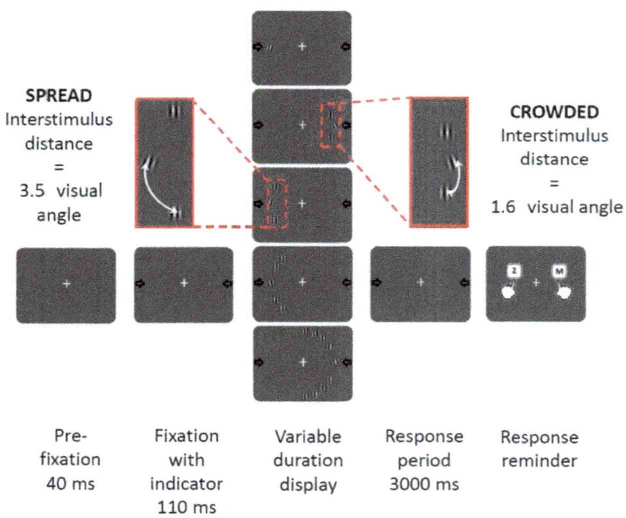

Figure 1. Schematic representation of the stimulus sequence for the tilt discrimination task. The two possible target locations (left and right sides of the screen) were indicated on the display screen with arrows. Targets could be presented either alone, or surrounded by two, four or eight distractors arranged symmetrically above and below the target. In conditions in which two distractors were presented they could be presented with an interstimulus distance of either 3.5 degrees (spread) or 1.6 degrees (crowded). Participants responded whether the target tilted left or right using the z and m keys on the computer keyboard.

each side of the display corresponding to the two specific locations at which the target could appear. This was followed by a variable duration display (containing any one of the five display types) and then by a further fixation screen until response (see Figure 1 for a visual schematic of the experimental set-up). If a response was not made a reminder screen followed after 3000 ms.

The display was of a variable duration titrated to achieve individual accuracy levels of between 60% and 90%. The experimental session had a total of 15 blocks with each block having 40 trials (total of 600 trials). In each block, two trials (one target tilting right and one left) of each of 20 conditions were conducted and the detection accuracy calculated for that block. When overall response accuracy either surpassed 90% or fell below 60% a 10 ms reduction or increase (respectively) was made to the stimulus duration. Before commencing the main experiment, the participants performed two blocks of practice and calibration sessions (20 trials each) to ensure that they were sufficiently familiar with the procedure and to establish an accuracy level within the 60%–90% range. The average display durations of the AwD and the control group did differ significantly (119 ms vs. 98 ms, $t(32) = 1.47$, $p < .05$).

Results

The results comprised the proportion of correct discriminations in each of the 20 conditions and are available in the Dataset S1. We first investigated effects of visual crowding using ADHD score as a covariate. Second, we investigated the effects of increasing distractor set size and visual field, again using ADHD as a covariate. Third, we examined the relationship between literacy measures and measures of crowding, distractor set-size and asymmetry of attention with statistical effects of ADHD partialled out from the correlations.

3.1 Effects of Crowding

To assess the potential effects of crowding, a four-way ANCOVA was conducted using the variables: group (controls, AwD); set-size-two display type (spread, crowded); task difficulty (easy, hard) and visual field (left, right). Analyses indicated a significant main effect of group ($F_{(1,31)} = 43.77$, $p < .001$, $\eta^2_p = .59$) with higher performance in controls. There were also significant main effects of display type ($F_{(1,31)} = 6.46$, $p < .05$, $\eta^2_p = .17$) and task difficulty ($F_{(1,31)} = 13.02$, $p < .001$, $\eta^2_p = .30$), showing inferior performance in crowded and difficult conditions. The effect of visual field was not significant ($F_{(1,31)} = 2.46$). ADHD was not a significant covariate ($F_{(1,31)} = 0.69$). Significant interactions between display type and group ($F_{(1,31)} = 8.67$, $p<.01$, $\eta^2_p = .22$) and task difficulty and group ($F_{(1,31)} = 10.66$, $p<.01$, $\eta^2_p = .26$) suggested a different pattern of performance by AwD when the discrimination task was difficult and the display was crowded. No other interactions reached statistical significance.

To investigate the significant interactions, analyses were conducted on each group separately with ADHD as a covariate. The descriptive statistics are summarised graphically in Figure 2. A significant effect of display type emerged for AwD ($F_{(1,16)} = 14.18$, $p<.001$, $\eta^2_p = .47$) but not for controls ($F_{(1,14)} = .108$). Both the control group ($F_{(1,14)} = 9.18$, $p<.05$, $\eta^2_p = .40$) and the AwD ($F_{(1,16)} = 6.97$, $p<.05$, $\eta^2_p = .30$) showed a significant effect of task difficulty. ADHD was not a significant covariate for either the controls ($F_{(1,14)} = .001$) or the AwD ($F_{(1,16)} = 1.05$). The main effect of visual field was not significant for either AwD or controls (Fs<1), although in controls there was a significant interaction between visual field and difficulty ($F_{(1,14)} = 4.97$, $p<.05$, $\eta^2_p = .26$) with similar performance across visual fields in the easy condition, but slightly lower performance in the left visual field in the difficult condition.

3.2 Effects of distractor set size and visual field

The effect of distractor set-size on target discrimination was investigated using a four-factor ANCOVA: group (controls, AwD), distractor set-size (zero, two-spread, four, eight), task difficulty (easy, hard) and visual field (left, right). The descriptive statistics are summarised graphically in Figure 3. Again, a significant main effect of group ($F_{(1,31)} = 39.40$, $p<.001$, $\eta^2_p = .56$) was demonstrated, with higher performance in controls. There were also significant main effects of set-size ($F_{(1,31)} = 15.56$, $p<.001$, $\eta^2_p = .33$), task difficulty ($F_{(1,31)} = 11.31$, $p<.001$, $\eta^2_p = .27$) and visual field ($F_{(1,31)} = 10.98$, $p<.001$, $\eta^2_p = .26$), demonstrating higher performance with fewer distractors, less difficult discriminations, and in the right visual field. ADHD was not a significant covariate (F<1).There were significant two-way group interactions between group and: set-size ($F_{(1,31)} = 13.81$, $p<.001$, $\eta^2_p = .31$), task difficulty ($F_{(1,31)} = 8.72$, $p<.05$, $\eta^2_p = .22$); and visual field ($F_{(1,31)} = 42.49$, $p<.001$, $\eta^2_p = .58$). Also significant were interactions between set-size and task difficulty ($F_{(1,31)} = 4.88$, $p<.05$, $\eta^2_p = .14$), set-size and visual field ($F_{(1,31)} = 10.54$, $p<.001$, $\eta^2_p = .25$), set-size, task difficulty and group ($F_{(1,31)} = 3.84$, $p<.05$, $\eta^2_p = .11$), set-size, visual field and group ($F_{(1,31)} = 30.04$, $p<.001$, $\eta^2_p = .49$)], and set-size, task difficulty, visual field and group ($F_{(3,93)} = 6.71$, $p<.001$, $\eta^2_p = .18$).

To aid interpretation, a three factor ANOVA (visual field×set-size×task difficulty) was conducted for each group separately. The control group showed no main effect of set-size ($F_{(1,42)} = 1.61$) or visual field ($F_{(1,14)} = 0.15$), although there was a significant main effect of task difficulty ($F_{(1,14)} = 8.36$, $p<.05$, $\eta^2_p = .37$) in the expected direction. ADHD did not act as a significant covariate ($F_{(1,14)} = 2.63$). The interactions between set-size and visual field ($F_{(1,14)} = 0.57$); task difficulty and visual field ($F_{(1,14)} = 0.19$); and set-size, task difficulty and visual field ($F_{(1,14)} = 0.16$) were not statistically significant. However, a significant set-size by task difficulty interaction ($F_{(1,14)} = 3.95$, $p<.05$, $\eta^2_p = .22$) suggested that larger set sizes negatively affected control performance when the orientation discrimination judgement was also difficult.

In contrast to controls, the AwD showed significant main effects of set-size ($F_{(1,16)} = 14.47$, $p<.001$, $\eta^2_p = .48$); task difficulty ($F_{(1,16)} = 5.35$, $p<.05$, $\eta^2_p = .25$); and visual field ($F_{(1,16)} = 11.53$, $p<.001$, $\eta^2_p = .42$). ADHD did not act as a significant covariate (F<1). There were significant interactions between set-size and task difficulty ($F_{(1,16)} = 3.57$, $p<.05$, $\eta^2_p = .24$); and set-size and visual field ($F_{(1,16)} = 12.29$, $p<.001$, $\eta^2_p = 0.43$). The interactions between task difficulty and visual field ($F_{(1,12)} = 0.76$), and set-size, task difficulty and visual field ($F_{(1,16)} = 1.36$) were not statistically significant. Unlike the controls, AwD were significantly affected by increasing numbers of distractors regardless of task difficulty and showed lower performance in the left compared to the right visual field. Similar to the controls, AwD were more affected by larger distractor set sizes when the discrimination was also difficult.

3.3 Relationship between literacy measures, crowding, visual field & set-size effects

First, to evaluate the potential predictive relationships for crowding, visual field asymmetry and set size effects on literacy measures three summary variables were created. By using comparisons across conditions for these measures - rather than absolute performance levels in any single condition - these

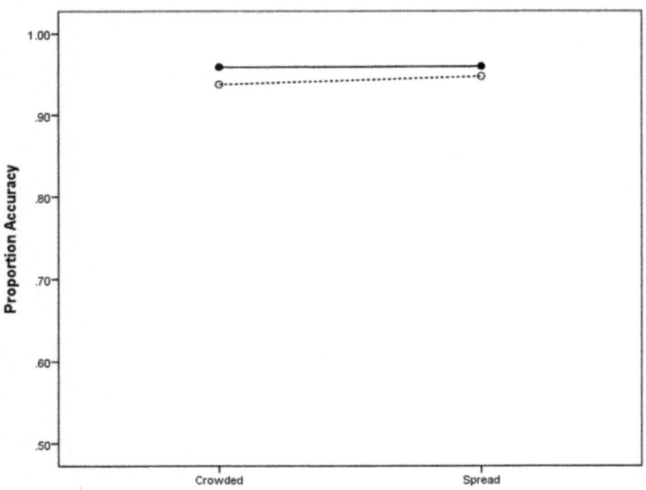

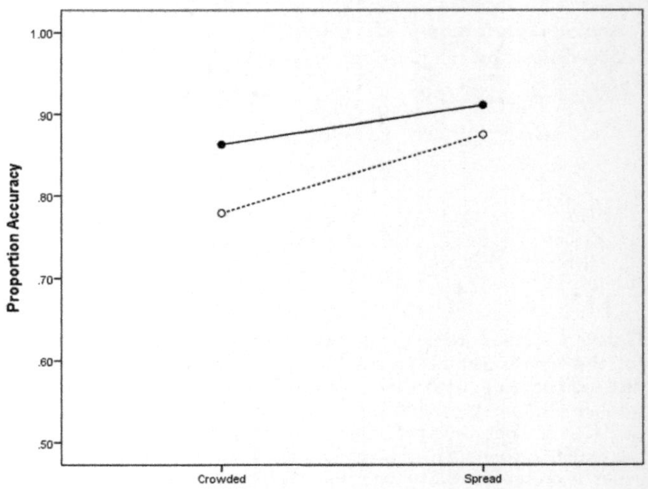

Figure 2. Interaction plots indicating performance accuracy for both controls (left panel) and AwD (right panel) plotted as a function of display type (crowded vs. spread) and task difficulty (solid lines - easy conditions and dotted lines - hard conditions).

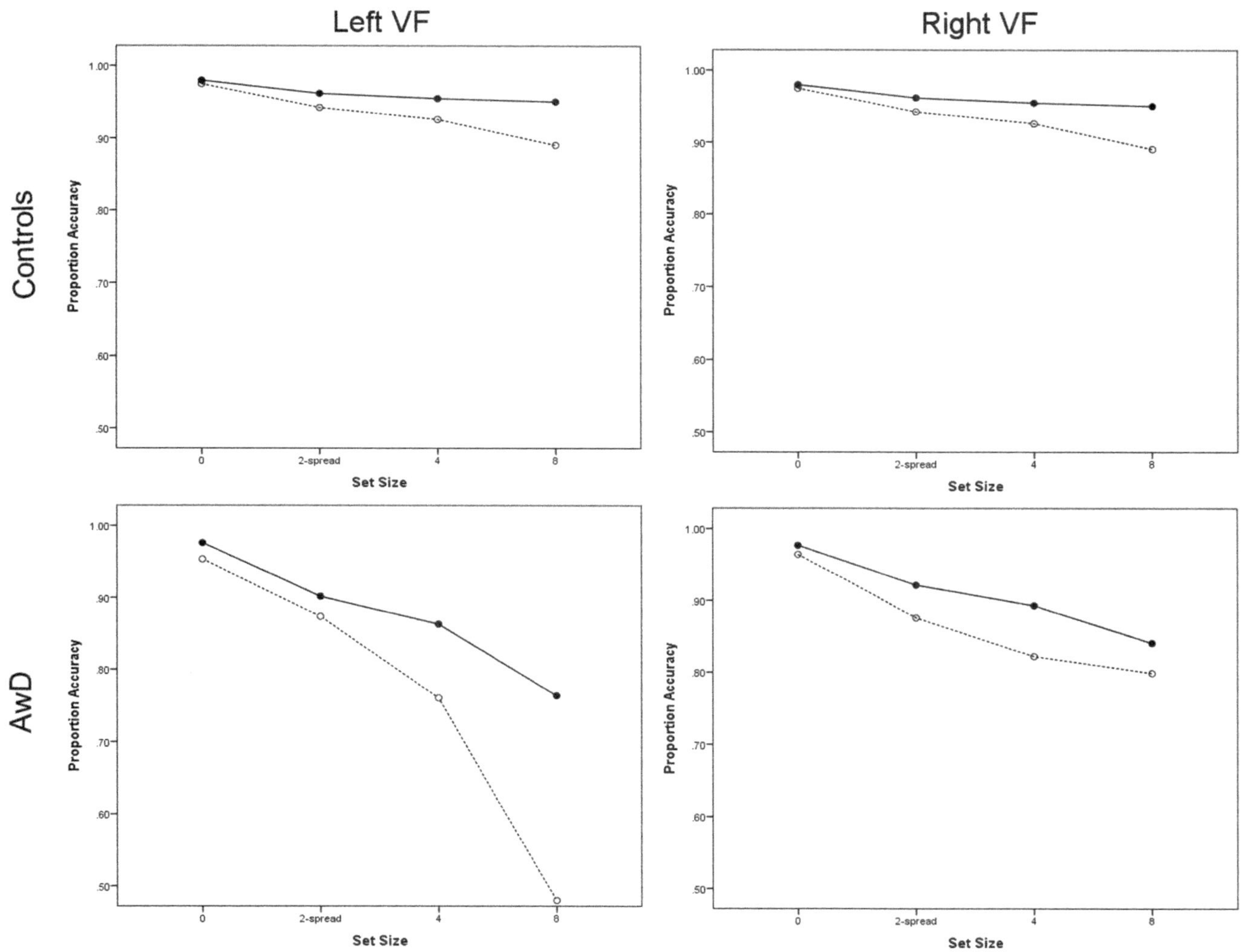

Figure 3. Descriptive statistics showing performance accuracy for both controls (top horizontal panel) and AwD (bottom horizontal panel) for the stimulus display side conditions (left vs. right-VF) plotted as a function of set-size and task difficulty (solid lines representing easy conditions and dotted lines representing hard conditions).

measures tapped crowding, asymmetry and set size effects independent of overall performance.

a) Crowding: The mean difference in accuracy between spread and crowded display types for set size 2
b) Set size: The mean difference in accuracy between set-size eight and set-size zero display types
c) Asymmetry: The mean set size effect (as calculated above in b) for the right visual field minus that for the left visual field

These variables were then entered in to a series of partial correlation analyses (ADHD scores statistically removed) with the literacy variables: WIAT-II spelling, WIAT-II reading, TOWRE-SWE and TOWRE-PDE ($n = 34$ in all cases, approximate critical value of r for a two-tailed 5% confidence level = 0.38). Figure 4 shows scatter plots of these relationships.

The crowding measure correlated significantly with WIAT-II reading ($r = -.54$, $p < .001$) and TOWRE-PDE ($r = -.50$, $p < .01$), suggesting that the larger the impact of crowding the lower the scores on these measures, but not with WIAT-II spelling ($r = -.19$) or TOWRE-SWE ($r = -.17$). The set size measure correlated significantly with WIAT-II spelling ($r = -.50$, $p < .001$), WIAT-II reading ($r = -.77$, $p < .001$) and TOWRE-PDE ($r = -.70$, $p < .001$) but not TOWRE-SWE ($r = -.16$). Again, the significant correlations suggested that the greater the impact of set size on performance, the lower were the scores on the literacy measures. The asymmetry measure correlated significantly with WIAT-II spelling ($r = -.47$, $p < .01$), WIAT-II reading ($r = -.57$, $p < .001$), TOWRE-SWE ($r = -.44$, $p < .01$) and TOWRE-PDE ($r = -.80$, $p < .001$). Here, the more rightward the asymmetry (i.e. better performance on the right vs. the left), the lower the scores on the literacy measures. In order to help clarify the meaning of these correlations, the same partial correlations were repeated, but split by group (AwD/ control). These analyses yielded only one significant correlation for the control group – a negative correlation between WIAT-II reading and set size ($r = -.52$, $p < .05$). For the AwD, there were two significant negative correlations between WIAT-II reading and set size ($r = -.50$, $p < .05$) and WIAT-II reading and crowding ($r = -.67$, $p < .01$).

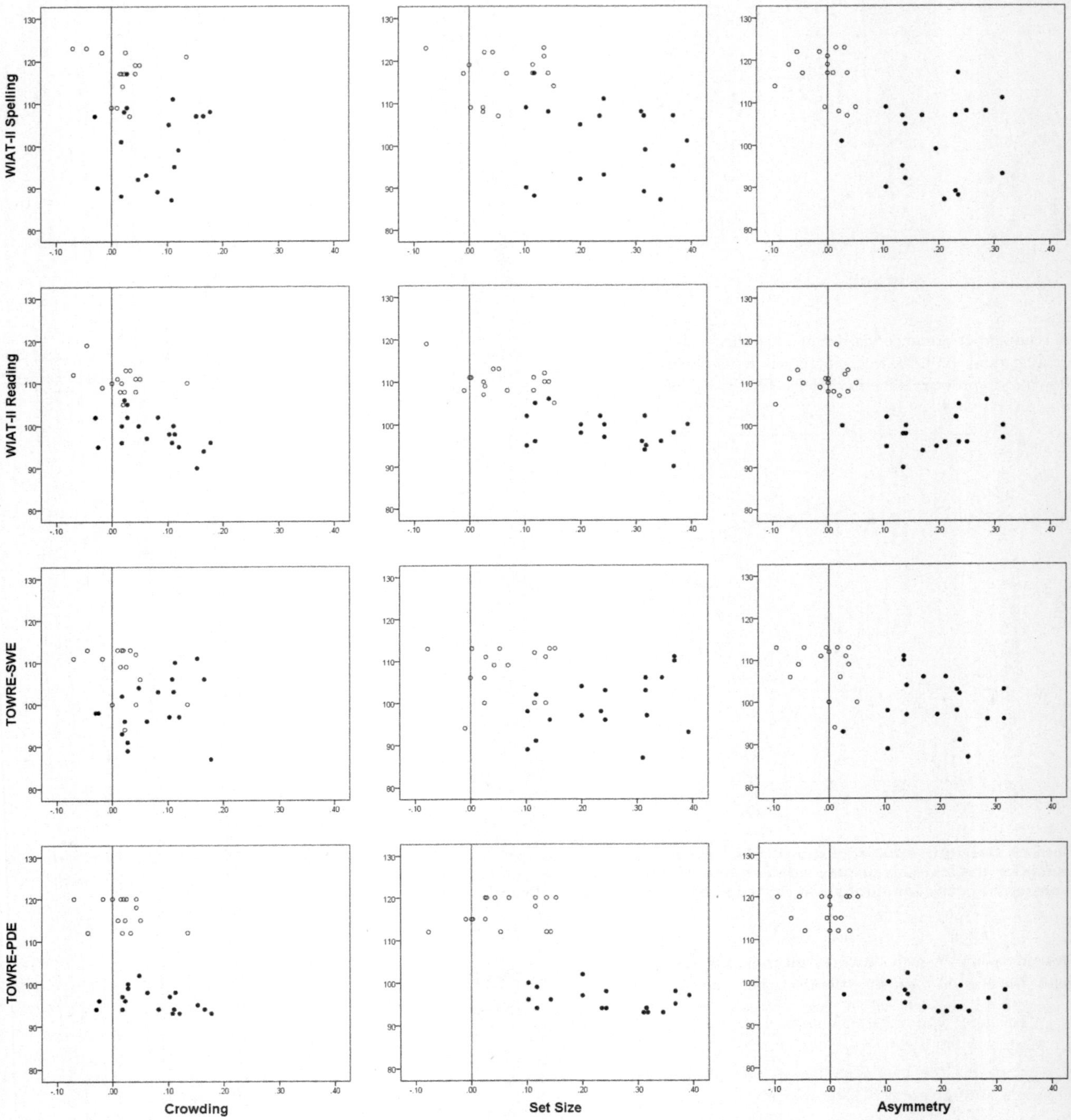

Figure 4. Scatter plots showing the relationships between measures of WIAT-II Spelling, WIAT-II Reading, TOWRE-PDE and TOWRE-SWE with measures of crowding, set size and asymmetry. Controls (empty dots). AwD (filled dots).

Discussion

This study compared adults with dyslexia and controls on a target orientation discrimination task with varying numbers of distractors presented at different spatial proximities to the target. We showed that AwD experienced detrimental effects of crowding and increased numbers of distractors even when the target location was known, and when effects of ADHD were statistically controlled. Difficulty with distractor exclusion in AwD was more pronounced in the left visual field and this asymmetry was also not explained by the magnitude of ADHD symptoms. In AwD, measures of crowding and distractor exclusion correlated significantly with the WIAT-II reading measure, even after removing any effects of co-occurring ADHD symptoms. This suggests that visual attention impacts upon literacy skill directly in dyslexia and not through third variables such as ADHD symptoms.

4.1. Effects of visual crowding

This study confirmed previous findings that AwD are more adversely affected by crowded displays than controls [1,7–11,25], but in a paradigm in which non-complex stimuli were used and in which target location was known. Moores *et al.* [1] demonstrated an effect of crowding in AwD in a visual search task, but performance was equivalent to that of controls when the target stimuli were pre-cued. In that study, the pre-cue may have helped participants to locate the target as well as to enable attentional enhancement of its properties. In the present study, the target was always in one of two possible locations (and was always located on the same side as the distracting stimuli). This result counters any explanation for this pattern of results involving target search, rather than attention enhancement or distractor exclusion. It is not difficult to envisage how crowding effects might impact negatively on reading performance via detrimental effects on letter or word identification [8,9]. Indeed, increased letter spacing has been shown to improve reading in dyslexia [9,46], although it does not provide complete remediation.

4.2. Noise (distractor) exclusion

This study confirmed previous findings that detection performance of AwD suffers more than that for controls from the presence of additional distractors in a display [1,13–16,26]. Moores *et al.* [1] demonstrated an increased impact of number of distractors in AwD whether or not the target was cued. Overall, it was clear that AwD did use information from cues, but employed it less successfully. The present study supports the conclusion that AwD have difficulty excluding distractors, because target discrimination was adversely impacted in displays with increased numbers of distractors even when target location was known. Inter-individual differences on a self-report ADHD measure were unable to account for these effects.

4.3. Distribution of attention

Our results demonstrate that difficulties with distractor exclusion in AwD are asymmetric across the right and left visual fields, with lower performance on the left. As discussed in *section 1.3*, there is increasing evidence for an asymmetric distribution of spatial attention of this type in dyslexia [29]. Whereas Facoetti and Turatto [5] reported a reduced effect of flankers in the left visual field, our data point towards a *difficulty with* distractor exclusion in the left visual field. However, in their paradigm the target was presented centrally with only the flanker presented in the left visual field, whereas in our study both target and distractors were presented in the left visual field. Facoetti and Molteni [28] suggested an inattention disorder in the left visual field (to explain the slower responses in their paradigm overall), but right visual field over-distractibility (to explain the lack of a performance gradient across the eccentricities). The results from all three studies can therefore be explained by weaker attention in the left visual field. Such an asymmetric distribution of attention can explain reduced performance levels overall in the left visual field (the present study and [28]), reduced left flanker effects for a *centrally* presented target [5] and difficulty excluding distractors from a target presented in the left visual field in the present study.

4.4 Relationship between literacy and effects of crowding, set-size and visual field asymmetry

Even when the potential mediating effects of ADHD symptoms were removed statistically, for both AwD and controls the effect of set-size correlated significantly with reading (see Figure 4). For the AwD the effect of crowding additionally correlated with WIAT-II reading. Correlation analyses across both groups suggested that, the effect of asymmetry correlated significantly with all four literacy measures used. However, the removal of this effect in the separate group analyses, suggested that these effects were better explained by asymmetry being an effective discriminator of AwD and control groups rather than there necessarily being any linear relationship between asymmetry and literacy *per se*. The relationships between reading, crowding and set size are consistent with previous research [1,16,34]. In addition, Facoetti *et al.* [34] reported correlations between nonword reading accuracy and the extent of a right attentional inhibition deficit in dyslexic readers. Interestingly, however, they only showed this deficit in dyslexic readers who had impaired non-word reading. On the basis of previous research into neglect dyslexia Facoetti *et al.* [34,47,48], argued that efficient focusing of visuo-spatial attention is crucial for the phonological reading route, but has little effect on lexical-semantic access. It should be noted, of course, that the presence of correlational (or other) effects shown in our study does not necessarily mean that these effects are the *cause* of any reading difficulties exhibited. However, other recent longitudinal research *has* provided evidence to implicate visual attention as a causal factor in dyslexia [49–51], with preschool performance predicting later difficulties.

Summary and Conclusions

These findings provide further evidence to suggest that distractor exclusion difficulties can explain the reported visual attention difficulties in AwD and that such difficulties are associated with literacy. The effects cannot be accounted for by ADHD. Furthermore, they cannot be accounted for by phonological difficulties alone; the task was purely visual and had identical cognitive requirements in all conditions. Weaker and asymmetric attention can explain the crowding and distractor exclusion deficits presented. Visual attention therefore plays an important role in the aetiology of dyslexia.

Supporting Information

Dataset S1 Data collected. This spreadsheet includes psychometric details of participants and their percentage accuracy in the different conditions of the experiment. Information on the different column headings are provided below the dataset.

Author Contributions

Conceived and designed the experiments: EM RC. Performed the experiments: RC. Analyzed the data: RC EM. Wrote the paper: EM JT RC.

References

1. Moores E, Cassim R, Talcott JB (2011) Adults with dyslexia exhibit large effects of crowding, increased dependence on cues, and detrimental effects of distractors in visual search tasks. Neuropsychologia 49: 3881–90.
2. Snowling M (1987) Dyslexia: A Cognitive Developmental Perspective. Blackwell, Oxford.
3. Stanovich KE (1988) Explaining the differences between the dyslexic and the garden variety poor reader: The phonological-core variable-difference model. J Learn Disabil 21: 590–612.
4. Vellutino FR (1979) Dyslexia: Theory and Research. Cambridge, MA: MIT Press.
5. Facoetti A, Turatto M (2000) Asymmetrical visual fields distribution of attention in dyslexic children: a neuropsychological study. Neurosci Lett 290: 216–218.

6. Bosse ML, Tainturier MJ, Valdois S (2007) Developmental dyslexia: the visual attention span hypothesis. Cognition 104: 198–230
7. Bouma H, Legein Ch P (1977) Foveal and parafoveal recognition of letters and words by dyslexics and by average readers. Neuropsychologia 15: 69–80.
8. Spinelli D, DeLuca M, Judica A, Zoccolotti P (2002) Crowding effects on word identification in developmental dyslexia. Cortex 38: 179–200.
9. Martelli M, DiFilippo G, Spinelli D, Zoccolotti P (2009) Crowding, reading, and developmental dyslexia. J Vis 9: 1–18.
10. Pernet C, Valdois S, Celsis P, Démonet JF (2006) Lateral masking, levels of processing and stimulus category: A comparative study between normal and dyslexic readers. Neuropsychologia 44: 2374–2385.
11. Callens M, Whitney C, Tops W, Brysbaert M (2013) No deficiency in left-to-right processing of words in dyslexia but evidence for enhanced visual crowding. Q J Exp Psychol 66: 1803–1817.
12. Facoetti A, Paganoni P, Turatto M, Marzola, Mascetti GG (2000) Visual-spatial attention in developmental dyslexia. Cortex 36: 109–123.
13. Roach NW, Hogben JH (2007) Impaired filtering of behaviourally irrelevant visual information in dyslexia. Brain 130: 771–785.
14. Roach NW, Hogben JH (2008) Spatial cueing deficits in dyslexia reflect generalised difficulties with attentional selection. Vision Res 48: 193–207.
15. Sperling AJ, Lu Z-L, Manis FR, Seidenberg MS (2005) Deficits in perceptual noise exclusion I developmental dyslexia. Nat Neurosci 8: 862–863.
16. Sperling AJ, Lu Z-L, Manis FR, Seidenberg MS (2006) Motion-Perception Deficits and Reading Impairment: It's the noise, not the motion. Psychol Sci 17: 1047–1053.
17. Vidyasagar TR, Pammer K (2010) Dyslexia: a deficit in visuo-spatial attention, not in phonological processing. Trends Cogn Sci 14: 57–63.
18. Pennington BF (2006) From single to multiple-deficit models of developmental disorders. Cognition 10: 385–413.
19. Shaywitz S E, Fletcher JM, Shaywitz BA (1994) Issues in the definition and classification of attention deficit disorder. Top Lang Disord 14: 1–25.
20. Whitney D, Levi DM (2011) Visual crowding: a fundamental limit on conscious perception and object recognition. Trends Cogn Sci 15: 160–168.
21. Yeshurun Y, Rashal E (2010) Precueing attention to the target location diminishes crowding and reduces the critical distance. J Vis 10: 1–12.
22. Freeman J Pelli DG (2007) An escape from crowding. J Vis 7: 1–14.
23. Dakin S, Bex PJ, Cass JR, Watt RJ (2009) Dissociable effects of attention and crowding on orientation averaging. J Vis 9: 1–16.
24. He S, Cavanagh P, Intriligator J (1996) Attentional resolution and the locus of visual awareness. Nature 383: 334–7
25. Pelli DG, Tillman KA, Freeman J, Su M, Berger TD et al. (2007) Crowding and eccentricity determine reading rate. J Vis 7: 1–36.
26. Roach NW, Hogben JH (2004) Attentional modulation of visual processing in adult dyslexia: a spatial cueing deficit. Psychol Sci 15: 650–654.
27. Facoetti A, Paganoni P, Lorusso ML (2000) The spatial distribution of visual attention in developmental dyslexia. Exp Brain Res 132: 531–538.
28. Facoetti A, Molteni M (2001) The gradient of visual attention in developmental dyslexia. Neuropsychologia 39: 352–357.
29. Hari R, Renvall H, Tanskanen T (2001) Left minineglect in dyslexic adults. Brain 124:1373–80.
30. Waldie KE, Hausmann M (2010) Right fronto-parietal dysfunction in children with ADHD and developmental dyslexia as determined by line bisection judgements. Neuropsychologia 48: 3650–3656.
31. Sireteanu R, Goertz R, Bachert I, Wandert T (2005) Children with developmental dyslexia show a left visual "mininеglect". Vision Res 45: 3075–3082.
32. Facoetti A, Turatto M, Lorusso ML, Mascetti GG (2001) Orienting of visual attention in dyslexia: evidence for asymmetric hemispheric control of attention. Exp Brain Res 138: 46–53.
33. Cohen J (1998) *Statistical Power Analysis for the Behavioral Sciences* (second ed.) Lawrence Erlbaum Associates.
34. Facoetti A, Zorzi M, Cestnick L, Lorusso ML, Molteni M et al. (2006) The relationship between visuo-spatial attention and nonword reading in developmental dyslexia. Cogn Neuropsychol 23: 841–855.
35. American Psychiatric Association (2013) Diagnostic and Statistical Manual of Mental Disorders (5th Edition).
36. Barkley RA (1997) Behavioral inhibition, sustained attention, and executive functions: constructing a unifying theory of ADHD. Psychol Bull 121: 65–94.
37. Sonuga-Barke EJS (2005) Causal models of attention-deficit/ hyperactivity disorder: from common simple deficits to multiple developmental pathways. Biol Psychiatry 57: 1231–1238.
38. Rochelle KSH, Witton C, Talcott JB (2008) Symptoms of hyperactivity and inattention can mediate deficits of postural stability in developmental dyslexia. Exp Brain Res 192: 627–633.
39. Cohen A, Ivry RB (1990) Density effects in conjunction search: Evidence for a coarse location mechanism of feature integration. J Exp Psychol: Hum Percept Perform 17: 891–901.
40. Barkley RA, Murphy KR (2006) Attention Deficit Hyperactivity Disorder: - A Clinical Workbook. New York: Guilford
41. Wechsler D (1999a) Wechsler Adult Intelligence Scale – Third UK edition. Pearson Assessment.
42. Wechsler D (1999b). Wechsler Abbreviated Scale of Intelligence. Pearson Assessment.
43. Wechsler D (2005) Wechsler Individual Achievement Test – Second UK edition. Pearson Assessment.
44. Torgesen J, Wagner R, Rashotte C (1999) Test of Word Reading Efficiency.
45. Schneider W, Eschmann A, Zuccolotto A (2002) E-Prime user's guide. Pittsburgh, PA: Psychology Software Tools.
46. Zorzi M, Barbiero C, Facoetti A, Lonciari I, Carozzi M et al. (2012) Extra-large letter spacing improves reading in dyslexia. ProcNatl AcadSci U S A 28: 11455–11459
47. Ladavas E, Shallice T, Zanella MT (1997) Preserved semantic access in neglect dyslexia. Neuropsychologia 35: 257–270.
48. Ladavas E, Umiltà C, Mapelli D (1997) Lexical and semantic processing in the absence of word reading: evidence from neglect dyslexia. Neuropsychologia 35: 1075–1085.
49. Plaza M, Cohen H (2007) The contribution of phonological awareness and visual attention in early reading and spelling. Dyslexia 13: 67–76.
50. Kevan A, Pammer K (2009) Predicting early reading skills from pre-reading measures of dorsal stream functioning. Neuropsychologia 47: 3174–3181.
51. Franceschini S, Gori S, Ruffino M, Pedrolli M, Facoetti A (2012) A causal link between visual spatial attention and reading acquisition. Curr Biol 22: 814–819.

13

Good Vibrations – Effects of Whole Body Vibration on Attention in Healthy Individuals and Individuals with ADHD

Anselm B. M. Fuermaier[1], Lara Tucha[1], Janneke Koerts[1], Marieke J. G. van Heuvelen[2], Eddy A. van der Zee[3], Klaus W. Lange[4]*, Oliver Tucha[1]

1 Department of Clinical and Developmental Neuropsychology, University of Groningen, Groningen, the Netherlands, **2** Center for Human Movement Sciences, University of Groningen, University Medical Center Groningen, Groningen, the Netherlands, **3** Center of Behaviour and Neuroscience, Department of Molecular Neurobiology, University of Groningen, Groningen, the Netherlands, **4** Department of Experimental Psychology, University of Regensburg, Regensburg, Germany

Abstract

Objectives: Most of the current treatment strategies of ADHD are associated with a number of disadvantages which strengthen the need for alternative or additional approaches for the treatment of ADHD. In this respect, *Whole Body Vibration* (WBV) might be interesting as it was found to have beneficial effects on a variety of physiological measures. The present study explored the effects of WBV on attention of healthy individuals and adults diagnosed with ADHD.

Methods: Eighty-three healthy individuals and seventeen adults diagnosed with ADHD participated in the study. WBV treatment was applied passively, while participants were sitting on a chair which was mounted on a vibrating platform. A repeated measure design was employed in order to explore potential effects of WBV treatment on attention within subjects. Attention (i.e. inhibitory control) was measured with a color-word interference paradigm.

Results: A period of two minutes of WBV treatment had significant beneficial effects of small to medium size on attention of both healthy individuals and adults with ADHD. The effect of WBV treatment on attention did not differ significantly between groups.

Conclusions: WBV was demonstrated to improve cognitive performance of healthy individuals as well as of individuals with ADHD. WBV treatment is relatively inexpensive and easy to apply and might therefore be of potential relevance for clinical use. The application of WBV treatment as a cognitive enhancement strategy and as a potential treatment of cognitive impairments is discussed.

Editor: Yu-Feng Zang, Hangzhou Normal University, China

Funding: The authors have no support or funding to report.

Competing Interests: The authors have declared that no competing interests exist.

* E-mail: klaus.lange@ur.de

Introduction

Attention deficit hyperactivity disorder (ADHD) is associated with a reduced quality of life [1]. Children and adults with ADHD frequently experience problems in social interaction, which can lead to social rejection, social isolation and discrimination [2–5]. Moreover, ADHD is associated with lower academic achievement which was shown to be directly linked to ADHD symptoms and cognitive deficits [6]. With regard to cognition of adults with ADHD, neuropsychological research revealed problems in attention and executive dysfunctions as core features of ADHD, including problems in working memory, inhibitory control, distractibility, vigilance, set-shifting, and task planning [7–13]. Accordingly, subjective experiences of inattention and executive dysfunctioning were shown in a considerable proportion of adults with ADHD by using self-report instruments [14].

Conventional behavioral and pharmacological treatment strategies of adults with ADHD include, beside others, cognitive behavioral therapy (CBT) and stimulant drug treatment (e.g. using methylphenidate). Both intervention strategies were shown to have beneficial effects on adults with ADHD, although the first-line choice of treatment strategies is often a stimulant drug therapy [15–18]. However, pharmacological treatment of ADHD is associated with several disadvantages for the individuals. For example, it was found that a pharmacological treatment may lead to unsatisfactory effects in a number of patients [17,19]. In particular, clinical side effects can occur together with stimulant medication, such as insomnia, dry mouth, decreased appetite, and headache [20]. Furthermore, it was demonstrated that methylphenidate improves cognitive functions of adults with ADHD, but does not normalize their level of performance [11,21]. Consequently, there is a need for alternative or additional treatment options which (1) can be given in addition to the effective treatments (e.g. no interaction with stimulant drug treatment), (2) are time and cost effective, (3) have no detrimental side effects and (4) are effective on symptoms that are most detrimental to the patients' functioning, such as problems related to attention [13,22]. To address this need for further treatment options, the present study explores whether *Whole Body Vibration* (WBV) can be a beneficial approach to the treatment of adult ADHD.

WBV can be described as a training method which exposures the whole body of an individual to low frequency environmental vibration. In contrast to the use of WBV in combination with dynamic exercises in the fields of sports and fitness, a passive application of WBV is realized by holding static poses (i.e. standing or sitting) during the time of exposure to vibration. Beneficial effects of WBV were found on various physiological measures, including balance, mobility, posture control, oxygen uptake, heart rate, blood pressure, blood flow and muscle strength [23–27]. Moreover, recent animal research provided evidence for a potential value of WBV in improving cognition, as indicated by improved maze learning and an enhanced neuronal activity in mice following the application of WBV treatment [28,29]. The effect of WBV on cognition in humans, however, was not examined in detail and therefore remains widely unsolved. Several studies applied WBV on healthy individuals and examined whether cognitive functioning was different when participants performed cognitive tasks *while* they received WBV. While some studies did not find any effect of WBV on cognition (i.e. on short-term memory and reasoning skills) [30,31], others revealed impaired short-term memory, long-term memory and arithmetic reasoning skills while WBV was applied [32–34]. A field study to predict the effects of WBV on professional drivers exposed participants to different levels of WBV by testing them in a van which was driving either on asphalt or cobblestone or when the van was halted. Participants had to perform a visual cognitive task and showed a decreased performance while being exposed to WBV compared to a condition of no WBV (van halted) [35]. In contrast to these detrimental effects of WBV on cognition, WBV has also been suggested as an alerting system for improving vigilance [36]. It was argued that particular bands of vibration frequencies cause individuals to increase muscle tension which might facilitate alertness [36]. A study conducted by Mueller and colleagues [37] showed positive effects of passive vibration (proprioceptive stimulation) of the forearm on both neuropsychological performance (as assessed with a computerized attention task) and neurophysiological measures (as assessed with event-related potentials) in patients with traumatic brain injury (TBI) as well as healthy individuals. In this study, proprioceptive stimulation was found to improve task performance of a collapsed group of patients with TBI and healthy individuals. Moreover, patients with TBI showed longer ERP latencies (P300) than healthy individuals. These P300 latencies were shortened by vibratory stimuli in patients with TBI, but not in healthy individuals. This study, therefore, demonstrated that passive vibration may have the potential to improve pathological cognitive processes in patients with neurological conditions and may thus be of relevance for the treatment of cognitive dysfunctions and the field of cognitive rehabilitation. So far, the majority of studies applied WBV at the same time as the cognitive tasks were performed whereas prolonged effects of WBV on subsequent cognitive functioning have not been examined. This is surprising (1) as it appears plausible that vibratory stimuli can cause distraction when they are performed during cognitive testing and (2) when considering that the prolonged effects of WBV are of particular clinical relevance.

Thus, the aim of the present study was to explore the effects of WBV on attention in a group of healthy individuals and in a clinical sample of individuals with cognitive dysfunctions, i.e. adults with ADHD. The potential value of WBV as a cognitive enhancement strategy and its application for the treatment of cognitive dysfunctions are discussed.

Methods

Participants

Participation in the study was announced to undergraduate students of the University of Groningen, the Netherlands. The description of the study objectives emphasized that the aim of the study was to examine cognition of typically developed students as well as of students with problems of attention. Therefore, a considerable number of students diagnosed with ADHD indicated their interest to participate in the study. In total, 83 healthy individuals and 17 individuals with ADHD took part in the experiment. All participants were undergraduate students from the University of Groningen, the Netherlands. Participation was voluntary and no monetary compensation was offered.

Healthy individuals (43 female, 40 male) had a mean age of 22.5 years (SD = 3.7 years), ranging from 18 to 31 years. The self-reported body height of individuals ranged from 163 cm to 205 cm (M = 179 cm, SD = 10 cm), with a body weight ranging from 50 kg to 105 kg across individuals (M = 72 kg; SD = 12 kg). Furthermore, the healthy individuals indicated to spend on average 3.8 hours per week on active exercise (SD = 3.6 hours), which ranged from no active exercise at all (0 hours) to 20 hours per week across individuals. None of the healthy individuals reported any history of neurological or psychiatric diseases and none were currently treated with medication known to affect the central nervous system. Furthermore, none of the healthy individuals indicated to suffer from red-green color deficiency which was a prerequisite to perform the Stroop Color-Word Interference task (see below). In addition, all healthy individuals successfully completed two plates of the Ishihara Color Test [38] in order to ensure unimpaired red-green color perception [39].

Individuals with ADHD (9 female, 8 male) had a mean age of 24.2 years (SD = 1.9 years), ranging from 21 to 28 years. According to self-reports, the body height ranged from 159 cm to 190 cm (M = 176 cm, SD = 8 cm) with a body weight ranging from 45 kg to 101 kg (M = 75 kg; SD = 17 kg) across individuals with ADHD. Furthermore, individuals with ADHD reported to spend in average 3.2 hours per week on active exercise (SD = 5.1 hours), ranging from no exercise at all (0 hours) to 20 hours per week across individuals. None of the individuals with ADHD indicated to suffer from red-green color deficiency which was again ensured by successful completion of two plates of the Ishihara Color Test [38,39]. Moreover, all individuals in the ADHD group reported that they had previously been diagnosed with ADHD by a qualified psychologist or physician. The diagnosis of ADHD was confirmed by a clinical psychiatric interview with an experienced psychologist belonging to the research group. The diagnostic interview involved a retrospective diagnosis of an ADHD in childhood and currently as devised by Barkley and Murphey [40]. In addition, individuals in the ADHD group qualified for inclusion on the basis of four self-report measures for ADHD symptoms. All patients completed the self-report ADHD Rating Scale (ARS, DSM-IV) for retrospective symptoms in childhood (patients fulfilled in average 6.1 criteria for inattention and 6.1 criteria for hyperactivity/impulsivity) and the self-report ADHD Rating Scale (ARS, DSM-IV) for current symptoms (patients fulfilled in average 6.8 criteria for inattention and 5.9 criteria for hyperactivity/impulsivity). Moreover, individuals with ADHD completed the short form of the Wender Utah Rating Scale for childhood ADHD symptoms (WURS) (M = 40.2; SD = 11.0) and the ADHD self-report scale for current symptoms

(M = 30.8; SD = 8.6) [41–44]. In the diagnostic assessment of the 17 individuals with ADHD, 5 individuals met DSM-IV criteria for ADHD – predominantly inattentive type (ADHD-I), 1 patient met criteria for ADHD – hyperactive-impulsive type (ADHD-H) and 11 individuals met criteria for ADHD – combined type (ADHD-C). Moreover, one of the individuals with ADHD reported to suffer from comorbid disorders (anxiety and depression) and was therefore continuously taking antidepressant medication (including the time of the assessment) as prescribed by the attending physician (150 mg per day). Furthermore, four individuals with ADHD were currently treated with methylphenidate and received individually tailored and clinically appropriate doses with a mean dose of 40.5 mg per day, with individual doses ranging from 10 mg to 72 mg. Pharmacological treatment was not discontinued for this study so that the individuals were on their usual prescribed medication at the time of their participation.

Healthy individuals and individuals with ADHD did not differ significantly in either of the demographic variables, including age ($t(98) = 1.778$, $p = .079$), gender (χ^2 $(1) = 0.127$; $p = .721$), body height (t $(98) = 1.072$, $p = .286$), body weight (t $(98) = 0.825$, $p = .411$) and amount of exercise (t $(98) = 0.555$, $p = .580$).

Materials

Self-report Measures of ADHD Symptoms

Two scales of the self-report ADHD Rating Scale (ARS, DSM-IV) were applied, one for current symptoms and one for retrospective symptoms in childhood. The ADHD Rating Scale is a self-report instrument for ADHD symptoms made up of the 18 DSM-IV criteria for ADHD [41,43]. In the Dutch version of the ADHD Rating Scale, five DSM-IV criteria containing double statements were rephrased into two statements, so that the total number of items was 23. In the analysis of the number of fulfilled symptoms, the scores based on the 23 items were recalculated to the original 18 DSM-IV criteria. The items were rated on a 4-point scale (0 = *rarely or never*, 1 = *sometimes*, 2 = *often*, 3 = *very often*) based on participant's behavior in the past six months (scale for current symptoms) or based on the participant's behavior in childhood up to twelve years in age (scale for retrospective symptoms). A symptom was considered to be present, if the answer given to the item was *often* or *very often* (score 2 or 3). There were two dimensions, one for inattentive symptoms (nine criteria) and one for hyperactive-impulsive symptoms (nine criteria). To qualify for a clinical diagnosis of adult ADHD, individuals must have met six or more of the nine DSM-IV criteria of inattention and/or hyperactivity-impulsivity in childhood, and at least five of the nine DSM-IV criteria of inattention and/or hyperactivity-impulsivity in adulthood [43].

Furthermore, two self-report scales were applied in order to quantify ADHD symptomatology currently and retrospectively. Childhood ADHD symptoms were self-rated with the short version of the Wender Utah Rating Scale (WURS). The WURS contains 25 items which are rated on a five-point Likert scale [44,45]. Severity of current ADHD symptoms was self-rated with the ADHD self-report scale [44]. This scale consists of 18 items which correspond to the diagnostic criteria of DSM-IV and which are rated on a four-point Likert scale [44,46]. A sum score was calculated for each rating scale.

Whole Body Vibration

Passive WBV was applied by using a vibrating platform (*Vibe 300,* Tonic Vibe, Nantes, France). A wooden platform (0.5 m×0.9 m) was mounted on the *Vibe 300* to enlarge the platform. On top of the platform, a wooden chair was mounted (Figure 1). Both the wooden platform and the chair were attached to the *Vibe 300* with bolts from underneath the *Vibe 300* in order to keep deviations from the vibrating frequency and amplitude on a minimum. The manufacturer settings of *30 Hz vibration frequency* and *4 mm vibration amplitude* were applied as a previous study showed this setup to be comfortable for the participant as well as efficient [47]. However, the construction of a wooden platform and chair mounted on the vibrating device was assumed to cause some deviations from the manufacturer settings with regard to the vibration frequency and amplitude. The actual vertical displacements (frequency and amplitude) were therefore measured on different locations of the chair (see A, B, C and D in Figure 1) based on acceleration data without a person sitting on the chair. The measured displacements (frequency/amplitude) were 30 Hz/0.44 mm (location A), 30 Hz/0.44 mm (location B), 30 Hz/0.66 mm (location C) and 30 Hz/0.50 mm (location D). The modified *Vibe 300* was located in a quiet laboratory at the Department of Clinical and Developmental Neuropsychology of the University of Groningen, the Netherlands.

Measurement of Attention

To explore the effects of passive WBV on attention, the *Stroop Color-Word Interference task* (Stroop, 1935) was performed. The *Stroop*

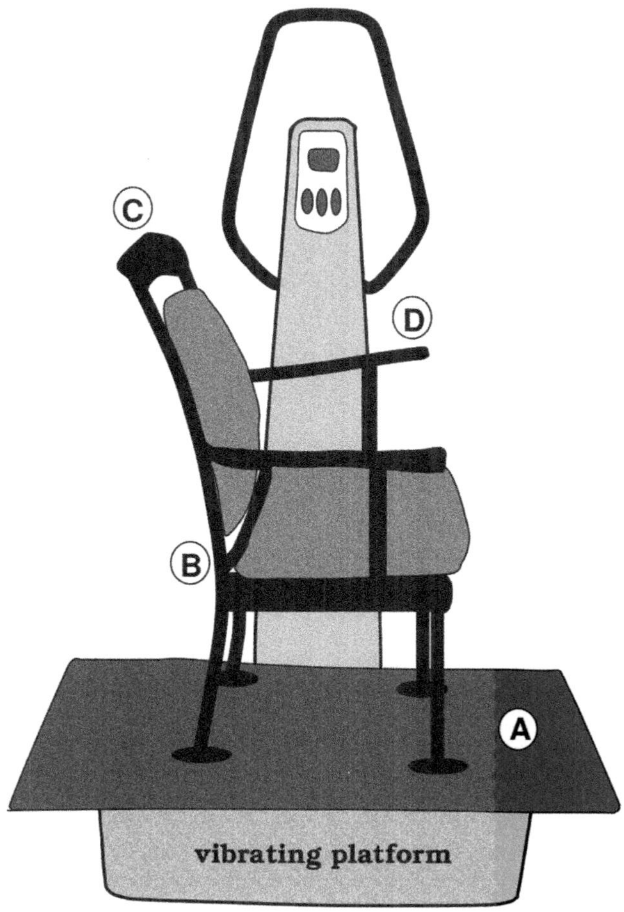

Figure 1. Drawing of the vibrating platform with the mounted wooden platform and chair. Accelerations were measured at location A, B, C and D to determine the actual vibration frequency and amplitude.

Color-Word Interference task measure an aspect of attention, i.e. inhibitory control [9]. In the present study, two conditions of the *Stroop Color-Word Interference task* were applied, the *Color Block Test* and the *Color-Word Interference Test*. In the *Color Block Test*, 20 squares each printed in one of four possible colors (yellow, blue, green or red), were presented on a card. The participant's task was to name the colors of the squares as fast as possible. In the *Color-Word Interference Test*, a list of 52 color names was presented (yellow, blue, green or red). Each word was printed in one of four possible colors (yellow, blue, green or red), however, the color ink of the words was different from the color names (e.g. the word green was printed in blue). The participant was requested to name the ink colors of the words as quickly as possible, thereby ignoring the written color name. In both tests, the time to complete the task was measured. An *interference quotient* was calculated by dividing the time needed for the *Color-Word Interference Test* by the time needed for the *Color Block Test*. The *interference quotient* represented a measure of attention (i.e. inhibitory control), with a larger quotient indicating more problems in inhibitory control. 12 parallel versions (for four practice trials and eight experimental trials) were designed in order to apply the tests in a repeated measure design.

Procedure

At the beginning of the experiment, all participants completed a questionnaire asking for descriptive information including age, sex, body height, body weight, time spent on average per week on exercise as well as red-green color deficiency. Furthermore, participants were asked for any history of psychiatric or neurological diseases as well as pharmacological treatment. For those students who indicated to be diagnosed with ADHD, a psychiatric interview was conducted followed by the completion of four self-report scales of ADHD symptoms. Subsequently, all participants conducted four practice trials of the *Stroop Color-Word Interference task*. For these practice trials, four parallel versions of the task were used, separated by a resting period of three minutes between each time the task was performed. The four practice trials were applied in order to minimize practice effects during the experimental trials.

Prior to the first experimental trial, the participant was requested to take seat on the chair mounted on the *Vibe 300*. The participant was instructed to sit in upright position throughout the whole experiment, the arms on the rest and both feet on the wooden platform. The participant was further instructed to keep body movements to a minimum. The experiment consisted of eight experimental trials. Each trial started with a two-minute period of experimental treatment, either a period of vibration (vibration condition) or a resting period of no vibration (resting condition). Immediately after the experimental treatment, the *Color-Word Interference Test* and the *Color Block Test* of the *Stroop Color-Word Interference task* were performed. The *Color-Word Interference Test* always preceded the *Color Block Test*. Subsequently, a resting period of three minutes followed prior to the beginning of the subsequent experimental trial. The eight experimental trials comprised four trials of vibration and four trials of resting. The sequence of the eight experimental trials followed an ABBA-design in order to balance rank order effects (i.e. practice effects) when comparing the two treatment conditions. A schematic drawing of the procedure of eight experimental trials is presented in Figure 2. The duration of the assessment was about 90 minutes.

Ethics Statement

The study was approved by the Ethical Committee Psychology (ECP) affiliated to the University of Groningen, the Netherlands. All participants signed an informed consent prior to the study and were debriefed after the assessment. All participants were informed that participation was voluntary and that they had the right to refuse or stop participating in the study at any time.

Statistical Analysis

Since the cognitive task were performed repeatedly (eight times) under two different treatment conditions (vibration or resting), mean scores were calculated across the four trials for each treatment condition, separately for healthy individuals and individuals with ADHD. Nonparametric statistical tests (Wilcoxon signed-rank test for dependent samples) were applied in order to compare cognitive performance (mean interference quotient) between the vibration condition and the resting condition, separately for healthy individuals and individuals with ADHD. A significance level of $\alpha = .05$ was applied for all comparisons. Moreover, effect sizes (Cohen's d) were calculated for all comparisons. Following Cohen's guidelines for interpreting effect sizes (Cohen, 1988), negligible effects ($d<0.20$), small effects ($0.20\leq d<0.50$), medium effects ($0.50\leq d<0.80$) and large effects ($d\geq 0.80$) were distinguished [48].

In addition, the effect of WBV on cognition was compared between healthy individuals and individuals with ADHD. For this reason, ipsative scores were calculated for each individual by subtracting the mean interference quotient of vibration conditions per participant from the mean interference quotient of resting conditions per participant. Ipsative scores, which indicated the effect of WBV on cognition, were then compared between healthy individuals and individuals with ADHD by applying a nonparametric statistical test for independent samples (Mann-Whitney-U-Test).

Furthermore, explorative analyses were carried out in order to examine whether the effects of WBV were determined by demographic variables, including age, gender, body height, body weight and amount of active exercise. This was done by correlating ipsative scores of healthy individuals (indicating the effect of WBV on cognition) with their demographic variables (Spearmen rank correlation). According to Cohen [48], negligible effects ($r<0.1$), small effects ($0.1\leq r<0.3$), medium effects ($0.3\leq r< 0.5$) and large effects ($r\geq 0.5$) were distinguished [48]. Finally, gender effects of WBV treatment were analyzed by comparing female and male individuals (Mann-Whitney-U-Test).

Results

Effects of WBV Treatment on Attention

Data analysis revealed that WBV treatment significantly improved attention performance ($M\pm SD$) in both healthy individuals (resting condition: 3.462 ± 0.419; vibration condition: 3.289 ± 0.358; $Z = 4.835$, $p\leq .001$) and individuals with ADHD (resting condition: 3.635 ± 0.373; vibration condition: 3.381 ± 0.419; $Z = 3.243$, $p = .001$). While the difference in healthy individuals was of small size ($d = 0.44$), a medium effect ($d = 0.64$) was found in individuals with ADHD (Figure 3).

A separate exploration of the effects of WBV treatment among different subtypes of ADHD showed beneficial effects in all three groups, including patients of the inattentive subtype ($n = 5$; resting condition: 3.687 ± 0.438; vibration condition: 3.504 ± 0.419), the patient of the hyperactive-impulsive subtype ($n = 1$; resting condition: 3.055; vibration condition: 2.965) and patients of the combined subtype ($n = 11$; resting condition: 3.663 ± 0.331; vibration condition: 3.363 ± 0.398).

A comparison of ipsative scores between healthy individuals ($n = 83$; 0.173 ± 0.293) and the entire group of individuals with

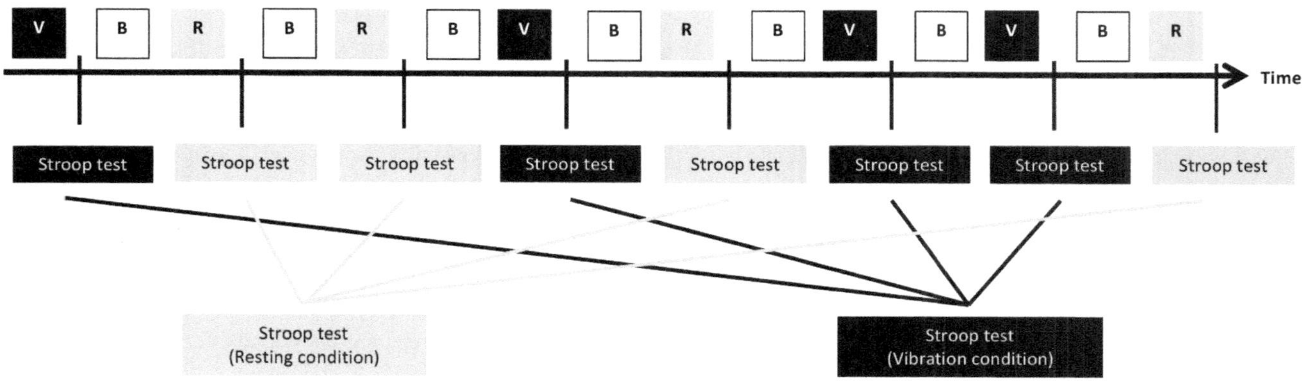

Figure 2. Schematic drawing of the experimental procedure consisting of eight experimental trials. V = Vibration condition: WBV treatment for two minutes; R = Resting condition: No WBV treatment for two minutes; B = Break: Breaks of three minutes (resting); Stroop test = Stroop Color-Word Interference task (Color-Word Interference Test, Color Block Test); For analysis, mean scores were calculated across the four experimental trials for each treatment condition (vibration and resting).

ADHD (n = 17; 0.254±0.218) revealed a non-significant difference of small size (Z = 1.542, p = 0.123, d = 0.31).

Correlations between WBV Treatment Effect and Demographic Variables

Explorative analyses of the association between the effect of WBV treatment and demographic variables in healthy individuals showed that WBV effects were only non-significantly related in small to negligible size to any of the demographic variables including age (r = −.023; p = .836), body height (r = −.178; p = .107), body weight (r = −.091; p = .414) and amount of exercise (r = −.098; p = .380). Female and male individuals did also not differ significantly concerning the effect of WBV treatment as also indicated by a negligible effect size, Z = −1.258; p = .209, d = 0.19.

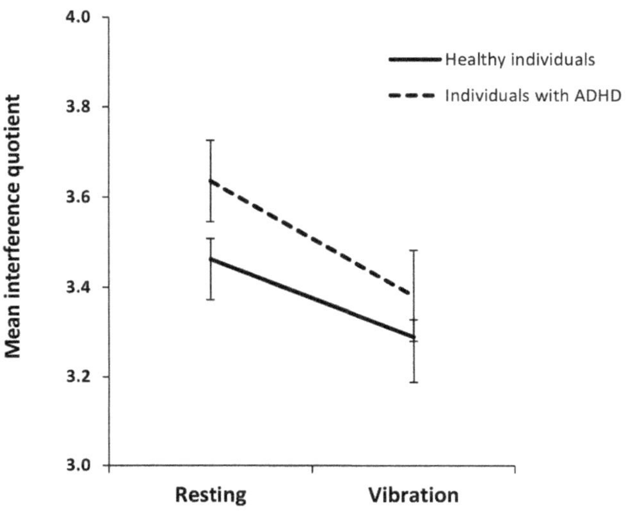

Figure 3. Mean interference quotient for performance of the Stroop Color-Word Interference task following resting and vibration, for both healthy individuals and individuals with ADHD (M±SE).

Discussion

The present study showed in a large sample of healthy young individuals that WBV treatment has a beneficial effect on subsequent cognitive functioning. Already a short interval of two minutes WBV treatment resulted in an acute beneficial effect on attention (i.e. inhibitory control) as measured with the *Stroop Color-Word Interference task*. Even though evidence of long-term beneficial effects of WBV treatment on cognition is still lacking, the present effects of WBV on attention are promising as the treatment period was rather short (two minutes), emphasizing the significance of the effect. Furthermore, it was assumed that there is only little room for exercise related improvements of cognition in early adulthood [49]. Because the sample of the present study represents a homogenous selection of young, physically healthy and mentally high functioning individuals, WBV treatment appears to have the potential to be an effective cognitive enhancer. This is of high relevance as better cognitive functioning is associated with higher academic achievement and socioeconomic status as well as facilitation of social integration [50] and is further assumed to provide a buffer against cognitive impairment (cognitive reserve) as a consequence of the effects of brain pathology or aging [51]. Demographic changes of the society with an increasing number of older people create considerable concerns (e.g. rise of financial burdens in the health sector) and underline the societal interest in maintaining and improving physical health and cognitive abilities of people. If WBV will be proven to have long-term beneficial effects on cognition, WBV treatment might be a suitable approach to contribute in achieving this goal, in particular, because it is inexpensive, non-invasive, easy to apply and safe (especially when applied passively). For example, studies on the musculoskeletal system demonstrated that WBV can be applied safely on children, older individuals and individuals with neurological and psychiatric conditions including individuals with movement disorders [52–57].

In accordance with the studies showing that patients with neurological conditions can benefit from WBV treatment (i.e. in physiological measures, but also cognition) [37], the present study revealed that WBV treatment improves cognitive functioning (i.e. inhibitory control as a measure of attention) of adults diagnosed with ADHD. The effects of WBV treatment on attention in adults with ADHD were of medium size (d = 0.64) and were thus somewhat larger as the effects observed in healthy individuals (d = 0.44). The finding that adults with ADHD benefit more from WBV treatment than healthy individuals cannot be explained by demographic variables since group did not differ in these variables. From a clinical perspective, this finding is very meaningful considering that problems related to attention are common neuropsychological deficits associated with ADHD which has been shown to adversely affect individuals' occupational functioning and quality of life [1,11,58,59]. Since improved cognitive functions may support social integration and occupational functioning and may also lead to an increased quality of life [1,11,58,59], the present findings consequently stress the potential value of WBV in the treatment of cognitive impairments of individuals with ADHD. An exploration of the effects of WBV treatment among different subtypes of ADHD indicated the largest benefit in patients of the combined subtype, even though small sample sizes hamper a reliable comparison of different subtypes of ADHD and therefore requires replication in larger samples. Furthermore, and more importantly in this context, it has to be emphasized that the effects of WBV treatment on subsequent attention performance as shown in the present study are promising but do not yet justify a recommendation for clinical use. Future studies are required examining long-term effects of WBV treatment on cognition by implementing a variety of control conditions (e.g. vibration of specific body parts only or presentation of auditory stimuli) in order to explore the specific mechanism of WBV treatment which causes cognitive enhancement.

Moreover, it has to be emphasized that the present study revealed positive effects of WBV treatment on performance in subsequent cognitive performance and differed in this respect from the majority of previous research in which participants were exposed to WBV at the same time as they performed cognitive tasks [30–35]. These studies reported either no effects or revealed even negative effects of WBV on cognition, which is not surprising considering the distraction that vibratory stimuli may have induced to the simultaneous execution of cognitive tasks. Furthermore, the positive effects of WBV on cognition as shown in the present study on a sample of individuals with ADHD support findings reported by Mueller and colleagues [37], who found positive effects of proprioceptive stimulation (vibration) on cognition and event-related potentials in patients with TBI and thereby suggested that vibratory stimuli may be of potential relevance in a supplementary meaning for the treatment of pathologic cognitive functions.

If cognition enhancing effects of WBV treatment can be replicated in controlled trials, there are several advantages related to a clinical application of WBV treatment emphasizing its value as a novel strategy in the treatment of cognitive dysfunctions of individuals with ADHD. First, WBV does not interfere with other interventions (such as pharmacological treatment) and can thus be applied in addition to conventional interventions. Second, WBV is easy to apply and is (in comparison to other methods) cost effective. A WBV device can be set up in private or institutional settings (e.g. at home, in school or at work) and short periods of WBV treatment of only a few minutes per day might be sufficient to cause clinically relevant effects. In addition, a high compliance rate is expected as this approach requires only little individual effort (e.g. in form of active exercise). Third, no detrimental side effects are currently known by the application of passive WBV. Fourth, and most importantly, WBV was found to have positive acute effects on attention (i.e. inhibitory control), an aspect of cognition which is crucial for everyday life functioning and which has been found to be impaired in both children and adults with ADHD [9,10,13,60,61].

Limitations and Future Directions

The present study must be viewed in the context of some limitations. First, with regard to the conclusions aiming at clinical application of WBV treatment, it has to be taken into consideration that the cognition-enhancing effects of WBV treatment on ADHD were observed in a rather small sample (n = 17) of high functioning individuals diagnosed with ADHD. All individuals with ADHD were college students, implying a relatively high level of cognitive functioning. Furthermore, at the time of the assessment, four individuals with ADHD reported to be treated with stimulant medication which compromises the conclusions drawn upon the effects of WBV treatment on cognition. For this reason, the generalization of the observed effects to the population of adults with ADHD and individuals with other neuropsychological disorders might be questioned. However, assuming that there is only little room for improvement in high functioning individuals (ceiling effects), significant effects of small to medium size revealed in two intellectually high functioning groups of people (healthy college students and college students with ADHD) underline the potential of WBV for the treatment of neuropsychological dysfunctions. A replication of the present findings in a large group of healthy individuals and individuals with neuropsychological dysfunctions appears necessary. Future studies addressing effects of WBV treatment in healthy individuals would benefit from the application of screening instruments for psychiatric disorders (e.g. for depression or ADHD) in order to obtain more homogeneous groups and to exclude individuals with high scores on respective symptom scales suggesting a psychiatric diagnosis.

Second, improvements of attention were measured directly after WBV treatment has been applied (acute effects). To establish WBV as a treatment approach, data showing longer lasting effects of cognitive enhancement are required. Therefore, sustained effects of WBV on cognition needs to be explored and should be subject of future research. Longitudinal studies should also take effects of vibratory stimuli on other domains than cognition into consideration, as it was reported that chronic exposure to WBV (e.g. in the occupational setting) is associated with alterations of mood, including fatigue, depression and anxiety [62].

Third, the present study focused on a single aspect of cognition, i.e. inhibitory control. However, it remains unsolved whether WBV has a selective effect on only particular aspects of cognition or whether a broad range of cognitive functions can benefit from WBV treatment. Hence, future studies should examine which functions are most sensitive to WBV.

Finally, and fourth, so far only little is known about the mechanisms underlying the WBV induced cognitive enhancement, and the present study does not contribute to the understanding of these mechanisms. The present study compared the effects of a two-minute period of WBV treatment with a resting condition in which no vibratory stimuli were applied. The implementation of a variety of control conditions would be necessary in order to explore which elements of WBV treatment are responsible for the cognition enhancing effect. For example, no information was obtained (1) whether it might be efficient enough to stimulate particular body parts (e.g. the hands) of individuals to induce cognition enhancing effects, (2) which settings of vibratory stimuli induce most beneficial effects (i.e. frequency and amplitude) and (3) to which extent the produced noise of the vibrating device contributes to the present results.

It was hypothesized that WBV changes muscle length, leading to stimulation of muscle spindles and a reflex response of the muscle [24]. This may enhance muscle activity, resulting in increased oxygen uptake and heart rate. Furthermore, other mechanoreceptors (such as free nerve endings) might be stimulated which might induce sensory stimulation in cortical brain areas. Despite these findings, the underlying mechanism, determining factors and the neurobiological basis of the effects of WBV on cognition in humans remain however widely unresolved and should be addressed in future research. A series of animal studies (on different mouse strains) has been performed [28,29,63,64] revealing that WBV treatment enhanced cognition (e.g. spatial memory) in young and aged mice compared to non-vibrated control mice. Examinations of brains indicated that WBV activates/increases various mechanisms, including (I) the activity of the cholinergic system in the forebrain, (II) the transportation of glucose across the blood-brain barrier, (III) expression of immediate early genes (which make neurons more responsive), (IV) production of proteins necessary for neuronal plasticity and (V) the neurogenesis (i.e. generating new neurons in the adult brain). Furthermore, following WBV, (VI) an increased concentration of tyrosine hydroxylase has been found, an enzyme responsible for catalyzing the synthesis of a precursor of the neurotransmitter dopamine. Dopamine has been shown to affect movement, motivation and cognition [65–67] and is also assumed to be involved in the pathophysiology of ADHD [68,69].

In addition, it can be speculated that the beneficial effects on cognition are not only the result of the vibratory stimuli, but also of the noise which is produced by the vibrating device. Unfortunately, a condition controlling for noise was not implemented in the present study design. A recent model based on theoretical considerations on brain arousal and stochastic resonance as well as on empirical evidence suggested that auditory stimuli (background white noise) can be beneficial to cognitive performance [70,71]. In these studies, it was argued that whereas auditive noise is detrimental to cognition of healthy individuals, a moderate amount of auditive noise might improve cognitive functions in individuals with hypodopaminergic states, such as individuals with ADHD. With regard to the results of the present study, the beneficial effect of WBV treatment on cognition in adults with ADHD is in line with the prediction of this model. However, as a positive effect of WBV treatment on cognition was also shown in healthy individuals, the model of white noise affecting cognition is not supported and does therefore not appear to be the primary mechanism of the cognitive enhancement found in the present study. However, the present findings in combination with the results of Söderlund and colleagues might indicate that sensory stimulation, independent whether it is auditive noise or mechanic vibration, has the potential to improve cognition in individuals suffering from ADHD.

Author Contributions

Conceived and designed the experiments: ABMF LT JK MJGvH EAvdZ KWL OT. Performed the experiments: ABMF LT. Analyzed the data: ABMF LT JK OT. Contributed reagents/materials/analysis tools: MJGvH EAvdZ OT. Wrote the paper: ABMF LT JK OT.

References

1. Agarwal R, Goldenberg M, Perry R, IsHak WW (2012) The quality of life of adults with attention deficit hyperactivity disorder: A systematic review. Innovations in clinical neuroscience 9: 10–21.
2. Pescosolido BA, Fettes DL, Martin JK, Monahan J, McLeod JD (2007) Perceived dangerousness of children with mental health problems and support for coerced treatment. Psychiatric Services 58: 619–625.
3. Canu WH, Carlson CL (2007) Rejection sensitivity and social outcomes of young adult men with ADHD. Journal of Attention Disorders 10: 261–275.
4. Mueller AK, Fuermaier ABM, Koerts J, Tucha L (2012) Stigma in attention deficit hyperactivity disorder. ADHD Attention Deficit and Hyperactivity Disorders 4: 101–114.
5. Lange KW, Reichl S, Lange KM, Tucha L, Tucha O (2010) The history of attention deficit hyperactivity disorder. ADHD Attention Deficit and Hyperactivity Disorders 2: 241–255.
6. Daley D, Birchwood J (2010) ADHD and academic performance: Why does ADHD impact on academic performance and what can be done to support ADHD children in the classroom? Child Care Health and Development 36: 455–464.
7. Barkley RA (1997) Behavioral inhibition, sustained attention, and executive functions: Constructing a unifying theory of ADHD. Psychol Bull 121: 65–94.
8. Tannock R (1998) Attention deficit hyperactivity disorder: Advances in cognitive, neurobiological, and genetic research. Journal of Child Psychology and Psychiatry 39: 65–99.
9. Boonstra AM, Oosterlaan J, Sergeant JA, Buitelaar JK (2005) Executive functioning in adult ADHD: A meta-analytic review. Psychol Med 35: 1097–1108.
10. Fuermaier ABM, Tucha L, Koerts J, Aschenbrenner S, Westermann C, et al. (2013) Complex prospective memory in adults with attention deficit hyperactivity disorder. PloS ONE 8(3): e58338.
11. Tucha L, Tucha O, Sontag TA, Stasik D, Laufkoetter R, et al. (2011) Differential effects of methylphenidate on problem solving in adults with ADHD. Journal of Attention Disorders 15: 161–173.
12. Tucha O, Mecklinger L, Laufkötter R, Kaunzinger I, Paul GM, et al. (2005) Clustering and switching on verbal and figural fluency functions in adults with attention deficit hyperactivity disorder. Cognitive Neuropsychiatry 10: 231–248.
13. Tucha L, Tucha O, Laufkoetter R, Walitza S, Klein HE, et al. (2008) Neuropsychological assessment of attention in adults with different subtypes of attention-deficit/hyperactivity disorder. J Neural Transm 115: 269–278.
14. Biederman J, Petty CR, Fried R, Black S, Faneuil A, et al. (2008) Discordance between psychometric testing and questionnaire-based definitions of executive function deficits in individuals with ADHD. Journal of Attention Disorders 12: 92–102.
15. Vidal-Estrada R, Bosch-Munso R, Nogueira-Morais M, Casas-Brugue M, Ramos-Quiroga JA (2012) Psychological treatment of attention deficit hyperactivity disorder in adults: A systematic review. Actas Esp Psiquiatr 40: 147–154.
16. Wigal SB (2009) Efficacy and safety limitations of attention-deficit hyperactivity disorder pharmacotherapy in children and adults. Cns Drugs 23: 13–21.
17. Wilens TE, Spencer TJ, Biederman J (2002) A review of the pharmacotherapy of adults with attention-deficit/hyperactivity disorder. Journal of attention disorders 5: 189–202.
18. Sonuga-Barke EJS, Brandeis D, Cortese S, Daley D, Ferrin M, et al. (2013) Nonpharmacological interventions for ADHD: Systematic review and meta-analyses of randomized controlled trials of dietary and psychological treatments. Am J Psychiatry 170: 275–289.
19. Wigal T, Swanson JM, Regino R, Lerner MA, Soliman I, et al. (1999) Stimulant medications for the treatment of ADHD: Efficacy and limitations. Ment Retard Dev Disabil Res Rev 5: 215–224.
20. Adler LA, Spencer T, McGough JJ, Jiang H, Muniz R (2009) Long-term effectiveness and safety of dexmethylphenidate extended-release capsules in adult ADHD. Journal of Attention Disorders 12: 449–459.
21. Tucha O, Mecklinger L, Laufkoetter R, Klein HE, Walitza S, et al. (2006) Methylphenidate-induced improvements of various measures of attention in adults with attention deficit hyperactivity disorder. J Neural Transm 113: 1575–1592.
22. Schoechlin C, Engel RR (2005) Neuropsychological performance in adult attention-deficit hyperactivity disorder: Meta-analysis of empirical data. Archives of Clinical Neuropsychology 20: 727–744.
23. Bogaerts A, Verschueren S, Delecluse C, Claessens AL, Boonen S (2007) Effects of whole body vibration training on postural control in older individuals: A 1 year randomized controlled trial. Gait Posture 26: 309–316.
24. Cardinale M, Bosco C (2003) The use of vibration as an exercise intervention. Exerc Sport Sci Rev 31: 621–624.
25. Cochrane DI, Sartor F, Winwood K, Stannard SR, Narici MV, et al. (2008) A comparison of the physiologic effects of acute whole-body vibration exercise in young and older people. Arch Phys Med Rehabil 89: 815–821.
26. Lam FMH, Lau RWK, Chung RCK, Pang MYC (2012) The effect of whole body vibration on balance, mobility and falls in older adults: A systematic review and meta-analysis. Maturitas 72: 206–213.
27. Stewart JM, Karman C, Montgomery LD, McLeod KJ (2005) Plantar vibration improves leg fluid flow in perimenopausal women. American Journal of Physiology - Regulatory, Integrative and Comparative Physiology 288: 623–629.
28. Keijser N, Piersma D, Postema F, Venema BJ, Luiten PGM, et al. (2011) Improved cognitive performance as a result of whole body stimulation in mice and men. The 9th Dutch Endo-Neuro-Psycho (ENP) Meeting: 125.
29. Van der Zee EA, Riedel G, Rutgers EH, De Vries C, Postema F, et al. (2010) Enhanced neuronal activity in selective brain regions of mice induced by whole body stimulation. Federation of European Neuroscience Societies Abstract 5: 024.49.
30. Ljungberg J, Neely G, Lundstrom R (2004) Cognitive performance and subjective experience during combined exposures to whole-body vibration and noise. Int Arch Occup Environ Health 77: 217–221.

31. Ljungberg JK, Neely G (2007) Stress, subjective experience and cognitive performance during exposure to noise and vibration. J Environ Psychol 27: 44–54.
32. Sandover J, Champion DF (1984) Some effects of a combined noise and vibration environment on a mental arithmetic task. J Sound Vibrat 95: 203–212.
33. Sherwood N, Griffin MJ (1990) Effects of whole-body vibration on short-term-memory. Aviation Space and Environmental Medicine 61: 1092–1097.
34. Sherwood N, Griffin MJ (1992) Evidence of impaired learning during whole-body vibration. Journal of Sound and Vibration 152: 219–225.
35. Costa N, Arezes PM, Melo RB (2012) Effects of vibration exposure on professional drivers: A field test for quantifying visual and cognitive performance. Work - A Journal of Prevention Assessment & Rehabilitation 41: 3039–3042.
36. Poulton EC (1978) Increased vigilance with vertical vibration at 5-Hz - an alerting mechanism. Appl Ergon 9: 73–76.
37. Mueller SV, von Schweder AJ, Frank B, Dengler R, Munte TF, et al. (2002) The effects of proprioceptive stimulation on cognitive processes in patients after traumatic brain injury. Arch Phys Med Rehabil 83: 115–121.
38. Ishihara S (1917) Tests for color-blindness. Tokyo: Hongo Harukicho.
39. Weale RA (1953) Ishihara tables - comparison of the 9th and 10th editions. Br Med J 1: 1148–1148.
40. Barkley RA, Murphy KR (1998) Attention-deficit hyperactivity disorder: A clinical workbook. New York: Guilford.
41. DuPaul GJ, Power TJ, Anastopoulos AD, Reid R (1998) ADHD Rating Scale-IV. Checklists, norms and clinical interpretation. New York: The Guilford Press.
42. Kooij JJS, Boonstra AM, Swinkels SHN, Bekker EM, de Noord I, et al. (2008) Reliability, validity, and utility of instruments for self-report and informant report concerning symptoms of ADHD in adult patients. Journal of Attention Disorders 11: 445–458.
43. Kooij JJS, Buitelaar JK, Van den Oord EJ, Furer JW, Rijnders CAT, et al. (2005) Internal and external validity of attention-deficit hyperactivity disorder in a population-based sample of adults. Psychol Med 35: 817–827.
44. Rösler M, Retz-Junginger P, Retz W, Stieglitz R (2008) Homburger ADHS-Skalen für Erwachsene. Untersuchungsverfahren zur syndromalen und kategorialen Diagnostik der Aufmerksamkeitsdefizit-/Hyperaktivitätsstörung (ADHS) im Erwachsenenalter. Göttingen: Hogrefe.
45. Ward MF, Wender PH, Reimherr FW (1993) The Wender Utah Rating-Scale - an aid in the retrospective diagnosis of childhood attention-deficit hyperactivity disorder. Am J Psychiatry 150: 885–890.
46. American Psychiatric Association, editor. (1994) Diagnostic and statistical manual of mental disorders. Washington, DC: American Psychiatric Press.
47. Regterschot R, van Heuvelen MJG, Zeinstra EB, Fuermaier ABM, Tucha L (*submitted*) Whole body vibration improves cognition in healthy young adults.
48. Cohen J (1988) Statistical power analysis for the behavioral sciences. New Jersey: Hillsdale.
49. Hillman CH, Erickson KI, Kramer AF (2008) Be smart, exercise your heart: Exercise effects on brain and cognition. Nature Reviews Neuroscience 9: 58–65.
50. Heckman JJ (2011) The economics of inequality: The value of early childhood education. American Educator 35: 31–35.
51. Stern Y (2009) Cognitive reserve. Neuropsychologia 47: 2015–2028.
52. del Pozo-Cruz B, Adsuar JC, Parraca JA, del Pozo-Cruz J, Olivares PR, et al. (2012) Using whole-body vibration training in patients affected with common neurological diseases: A systematic literature review. Journal of Alternative and Complementary Medicine 18: 29–41.
53. Kawanabe K, Kawashima A, Sashimoto I, Takeda T, Sato Y, et al. (2007) Effect of whole-body vibration exercise and muscle strengthening, balance, and walking exercises on walking ability in the elderly. Keio J Med 56: 1–10.
54. Santos-Filho SD, Cameron MH, Bernardo-Filho M (2012) Benefits of whole-body vibration with an oscillating platform for people with multiple sclerosis: A systematic review. Multiple sclerosis international. 2012: 274728.
55. Stark C, Nikopoulou-Smyrni P, Stabrey A, Semler O, Schoenau E (2010) Effect of a new physiotherapy concept on bone mineral density, muscle force and gross motor function in children with bilateral cerebral palsy. J Musculoskelet Neuron Interact 10: 151–158.
56. Sitja Rabert M, Rigau Comas D, Fort Vanmeerhaeghe A, Santoyo Medina C, Roque i Figuls M, et al. (2012) Whole-body vibration training for patients with neurodegenerative disease. The Cochrane database of systematic reviews 2: CD009097.
57. King LK, Almeida QJ, Ahonen H. (2009) Short-term effects of vibration therapy on motor impairments in Parkinson's disease. Neurorehabilitation 25: 297–306.
58. Barkley RA, Murphy KR (2010) Impairment in occupational functioning and adult ADHD: The predictive utility of executive function (EF) ratings versus EF tests. Archives of Clinical Neuropsychology 25: 157–173.
59. Boonstra AM, Kooij JJS, Oosterlaan J, Sergeant JA, Buitelaar JK (2010) To act or not to act, that's the problem: Primarily inhibition difficulties in adult ADHD. Neuropsychology 24: 209–221.
60. Tucha O, Walitza S, Mecklinger L, Sontag T-A, Kuebber S, et al. (2006) Attentional functioning in children with ADHD - predominantly hyperactive-impulsive type and children with ADHD - combined type. J Neural Transm 113: 1943–1953.
61. Fuermaier ABM, Tucha L, Koerts J, Aschenbrenner S, Weisbrod M, et al. (2013) Source discrimination in adults with attention deficit hyperactivity disorder. PLoS ONE 8(5): e65134.
62. Abbate C, Micali E, Giorgianni C, Munao F, Brecciaroli R, et al. (2004) Affective correlates of occupational exposure to whole-body vibration - A case-control study. Psychother Psychosom 73: 375–379.
63. Timmer M, Van der Zee EA, Riedel G (2006) Whole body vibration and behavior: Investigation of the role of various neurotransmitter systems. Federation of European Neuroscience Societies Abstract 3: 089.31.
64. Lahr MMH, Postema F, Venema BJ, Luiten PGM, Riedel G, et al. (2009) Whole body stimulation functions as a cognitive enhancer in young and old mice. 8th Dutch Endo-Neuro-Psycho Meeting Abstract 170.
65. Arias-Carrion O, Poeppel E (2007) Dopamine, learning, and reward-seeking behavior. Acta Neurobiol Exp 67: 481–488.
66. Arnsten AFT, Wang MJ, Paspalas CD (2012) Neuromodulation of thought: Flexibilities and vulnerabilities in prefrontal cortical network synapses. Neuron 76: 223–239.
67. Schultz W (2007) Multiple dopamine functions at different time courses. Annu Rev Neurosci 30: 259–288.
68. Tripp G, Wickens JR (2009) Neurobiology of ADHD. Neuropharmacology 57: 579–589.
69. Durston S, Konrad K (2007) Integrating genetic, psychopharmacological and neuroimaging studies: A converging methods approach to understanding the neurobiology of ADHD. Developmental Review 27: 374–395.
70. Söderlund GBW, Sikström S, Loftesnes JM, Sonuga-Barke EJ (2010) The effects of background white noise on memory performance in inattentive school children. Behavioral and Brain Functions 6.
71. Söderlund G, Sikström S, Smart A (2007) Listen to the noise: Noise is beneficial for cognitive performance in ADHD. Journal of Child Psychology and Psychiatry 48: 840–847.

14

Brain Volumetric Correlates of Autism Spectrum Disorder Symptoms in Attention Deficit/Hyperactivity Disorder

Laurence O'Dwyer[1]*, Colby Tanner[2], Eelco V. van Dongen[1], Corina U. Greven[1,3], Janita Bralten[1,4], Marcel P. Zwiers[1], Barbara Franke[4,5], Jaap Oosterlaan[6], Dirk Heslenfeld[6,7], Pieter Hoekstra[8], Catharina A. Hartman[8], Nanda Rommelse[5,9], Jan K. Buitelaar[1,9]

1 Radboud University Medical Center, Donders Institute for Brain, Cognition and Behaviour, Department of Cognitive Neuroscience, Nijmegen, The Netherlands, **2** Department of Ecology and Evolution, University of Lausanne, Lausanne, Switzerland, **3** King's College London, Social, Genetic and Developmental Psychiatry Centre, Institute of Psychiatry, London, United Kingdom, **4** Department of Human Genetics, Radboud University Medical Center, Nijmegen, The Netherlands, **5** Radboud University Medical Center, Donders Institute for Brain, Cognition and Behaviour, Department of Psychiatry, Nijmegen, The Netherlands, **6** Department of Clinical Neuropsychology, Vrije Universiteit, Amsterdam, The Netherlands, **7** Department of Cognitive Psychology, Vrije Universiteit, Amsterdam, The Netherlands, **8** Department of Psychiatry, University Medical Center Groningen, University of Groningen, Groningen, The Netherlands, **9** Karakter Child and Adolescent Psychiatry University Center Nijmegen, Nijmegen, The Netherlands

Abstract

Autism spectrum disorder (ASD) symptoms frequently occur in subjects with attention deficit/hyperactivity disorder (ADHD). While there is evidence that both ADHD and ASD have differential structural correlates, no study to date has investigated these structural correlates within a framework that robustly accounts for the phenotypic overlap between the two disorders. The presence of ASD symptoms was measured by the parent-reported Children's Social and Behavioural Questionnaire (CSBQ) in ADHD subjects (n = 180), their unaffected siblings (n = 118) and healthy controls (n = 146). ADHD symptoms were assessed by a structured interview (K-SADS-PL) and the Conners' ADHD questionnaires. Whole brain T1-weighted MPRAGE images were acquired and the structural MRI correlates of ASD symptom scores were analysed by modelling ASD symptom scores against white matter (WM) and grey matter (GM) volumes using mixed effects models which controlled for ADHD symptom levels. ASD symptoms were significantly elevated in ADHD subjects relative to both controls and unaffected siblings. ASD scores were predicted by the interaction between WM and GM volumes. Increasing ASD score was associated with greater GM volume. Equivocal results from previous structural studies in ADHD and ASD may be due to the fact that comorbidity has not been taken into account in studies to date. The current findings stress the need to account for issues of ASD comorbidity in ADHD.

Editor: Chandan Vaidya, Georgetown University, United States of America

Funding: The NeuroIMAGE study was supported by National Institutes of Health grant R01MH62873 (to Stephen V. Faraone), NWO Large Investment Grant 1750102007010 (to Jan Buitelaar) and matching grants from Radboud University Nijmegen Medical Center, University Medical Center Groningen and Accare, and Vrije Universiteit Amsterdam. The research leading to these results also received support from the European Community's Seventh Framework Programme (FP7/2007–2013) under grant agreement number 278948 (TACTICS), and from the Innovative Medicines Initiative Joint Undertaking (IMI) under grant agreement number 115300-01 (EU-AIMS). CT was supported by a fellowship from the Irish Research Council for Science, Engineering and Technology (IRCSET). The funders had no role in study design, data collection and analysis, decision to publish, or preparation of the manuscript.

Competing Interests: Jan Buitelaar has been a consultant to/member of advisory board of and/or speaker for Janssen Cilag BV, Eli Lilly, Bristol-Myer Squibb, Organon/Shering Plough, UCB, Shire, Medice and Servier. He is not an employee of any of these companies. He is not a stock shareholder of any of these companies. He has no other financial or material support, including expert testimony, patents, royalties. There are no patents, products in development or marketed products to declare. All other authors report no biomedical financial interests or potential conflicts of interest.

* Email: larodwyer@gmail.com

Introduction

Attention-deficit/hyperactivity disorder (ADHD) and autism spectrum disorder (ASD) are both severely impairing, highly heritable neurodevelopmental disorders [1,2]. ASD is characterised by impaired social and communicative skills as well as restricted and repetitive behaviours and interests, whereas ADHD is characterised by severe inattention and/or hyperactivity and impulsivity [3]. Both disorders frequently co-occur with estimates for the presence of ADHD within ASD ranging from 30% to 80%, while the presence of ASD in ADHD is estimated at 20% to 50% [1], [2,4–6]. Deficits in executive function and motor speed have been linked to familial vulnerability for both ASD and ADHD [7–9]. Studies have also documented an overlap of genetic factors that relate to both ASD and ADHD [4]. Overall, these findings suggest that there are shared etiological pathways for ASD and ADHD which need to be studied in more detail.

Quantitative measures that reflect the severity of ASD and ADHD symptoms may be useful to characterise both disorders in terms of a continuous distribution in which clinical disorders represent extreme variants of typical behaviour [10,11]. Studies investigating the continuous distribution of both disorders as well as their overlap, as opposed to an exclusive focus on a categorical diagnosis, may be a fruitful direction for future research [10]. Such an approach may help to better characterise the heterogeneous nature of these disorders as well as the extent to which they overlap [12]. Previously, ASD symptoms have been found to be different in various groupings of ADHD classes, with the class having the most severe ADHD symptoms also having the most severe ASD symptoms [13]. In typically developing people, recent work has found brain regions that are commonly as well as uniquely correlated with ASD and ADHD symptom severity [14]. GM volume in the left inferior frontal gyrus was found to be correlated with symptom severity in both disorders [14]. Volumetric changes in the left posterior cingulate were found to be specific to ASD, while ADHD symptom severity was found to be specifically correlated with the right parietal lobe, right temporal frontal cortex, bilateral thalamus and left hippocampus/amygdala complex [14]. The study by Geurts et al. indicates that ASD and ADHD form a continuum extending into the general population. However, the conclusions were complicated by the fact that the directions of the brain-behaviour relationships were not consistent for all regions compared to clinical studies [14].

Brain volume abnormalities are important indicators of pathophysiological processes that likely reflect disorder etiology. A number of meta-analyses have found reduced brain volume in ADHD in the majority of studies investigated (with ages ranging from ~10–37 years of age) [15], [16,17]. Regional volume reductions in ADHD subjects were robustly localised to the globus pallidus, putamen, caudate nucleus and lentiform gyrus [15], [16,17]. Total brain volume and grey matter volume have both been found to be decreased in ADHD compared with typically developing controls [15,18] [19,20]. However, both increasing age and stimulant medication were also found to be independently associated with more normal GM volumes.

It is of note that the profile of changes in brain volume in ASD is different from that of ADHD, with findings suggesting that the brain undergoes a period of accelerated growth in the first four years of life before reaching a plateau within a normal range by adolescence, which in turn is followed by volume decline in adulthood relative to typically developing controls [21], [22–27]. Importantly, in young children with autism (2–3 years old) WM enlargement has been shown to be greater than GM enlargement (18% more cerebral and 38% more cerebellar WM) [28]. This WM enlargement in young children was then found to be reversed in 12–16 year old children with autism, with WM volume reduced relative to controls [28]. In older individuals with autism, voxel-based methods have also shown less WM intensity than in age-matched controls [29,30]. However, a more recent meta-analysis has indicated consistent increases in WM volume in the right arcuate fasciculus and left inferior frontooccipital and uncinate fasciculi in adults as well as in children and adolescents with ASD [31].

For GM, several studies in adolescents and adults with ASD have reported a 6–12% increase in GM volume relative to controls [32] [31,33,34]. A meta-analysis indicated a small increase in GM volume in the left middle and inferior frontal gyri in ASD [33]. The same meta-analysis also indicated robust reductions in GM in the amygdala-hippocampus complex and medical parietal regions [33]. Overall, the GM findings were found to be more pronounced in adults, but the only statistically significant difference was a greater GM volume reduction in the precuneus in adult compared with adolescent samples [33]. However it is difficult to disentangle whether these effects are due to developmental processes or are secondary to the effects of living with cognitive differences.

Significant age-related improvements in ASD have been documented in adolescents and adults [35]. This also suggests that a selection bias exists in current studies, with older participants possibly having more severe symptoms and thus more likely to have prominent GM abnormalities.

For ADHD, the ontogenetic onset of smaller brain size is not known, but there is some evidence that smaller brain volumes in ADHD persist to the end of adolescence [18]. However, this phenomenon may attenuate in adulthood, with studies noting normal brain size in adults with ADHD [36]. In summary, the most abnormal volumes in ASD generally occur in early childhood, while the most abnormal volumes in ADHD occur in middle to late childhood [15,37,38].

Therefore, while there is evidence that both ADHD and ASD have specific and differential structural correlates, no study to date has investigated these structural correlates within a framework that robustly accounts for the phenotypic overlap between the two disorders. Only one study to date has directly compared brain volumes in ASD and ADHD [39]. The age of all subjects ranged from 10 to 16 years, and no differences were found between the two disorders in terms of total GM and WM volumes [39] Additionally, no differences were found between either disorder and typically developing controls [39]. The relatively small size of the cohort (15 ASD subjects, 15 ADHD subjects, 15 controls) may have contributed to the negative findings.

The present study was based on the premise that the extent to which ASD symptoms occur in ADHD may have a pronounced effect on the profile of structural brain volumes in ADHD. Thus, MRI volumetric correlates of ASD symptoms in a large sample of ADHD probands, their unaffected siblings, as well as healthy controls were investigated. Mixed effects models, which controlled for ADHD symptom levels in the random effects structure of the model, were used to assess the relationship between global WM, GM and autism spectrum symptoms. As previous studies have found raised GM volume [32] in adolescent ASD subjects, we hypothesized that this profile would also be present in ADHD subjects with elevated autistic spectrum symptoms.

Methods

Participants

The study was approved by the Radboud University Medical Centre Research Ethics Committee and was in accordance with the Declaration of Helsinki. All participants over 18 years of age provided informed written consent. For participants under 18 years of age, informed written consent was obtained from the next of kin, caretakers, or guardians on behalf of the participants. This procedure was approved by the Radboud University Medical Centre Research Ethics Committee.

Participants were part of the NeuroIMAGE study. This is a prospective longitudinal MRI study (2009–2012) of the Dutch subsample of the International Multicenter ADHD Genetics (IMAGE) study performed between 2003–2006 [40–42]. All members of ADHD and control families were invited for follow-up measurement, with a mean follow-up period of 5.9 years ($SD = .72$). For the present analyses, subjects were selected from the total data set ($n = 1084$) when the following data was available: a high quality T1-weighted MPRAGE image, complete information from the Children's Social and Behavioural Questionnaire (that provides information on the autism spectrum symptoms), complete information from the Schedule for Affective Disorders and Schizophrenia for School-Age Children - Present and Lifetime Version (K-SADS-PL) [43] and the Conners ADHD questionnaire. IQ information and medication history were also required in order to include subjects in the current study. Subjects with a sub-threshold ADHD diagnosis ($n = 75$), i.e. those with significantly elevated ADHD symptoms but failed to meet the clinical criteria for a diagnosis of ADHD were excluded. Subjects were also excluded if there was inconsistency between the ADHD

Table 1. Demographic and cognitive characteristics of the sample groups.

	ADHD		Unaffected Siblings		Con		AVOVA's	P	Tukey HSD		
	Mean	SD	Mean	SD	Mean	SD			US - Con	ADHD - Con	ADHD - US
Age (years)	16.2	3.7	16.9	4.0	16.8	3.6	F(2,441) = 1.41	0.25			
IQ	98.8	14.9	101.8	14.2	106.6	13.2	F(2,441) = 12.11	<0.0001	0.017	<0.0001	0.19
Social Interest (0–24)	4.3	4.3	1.9	3.4	1.0	1.9	F(2,441) = 40.42	<0.0001	0.12	<0.0001	<0.0001
Understanding (0–14)	5.5	3.7	1.2	1.5	1.2	1.8	F(2,441) = 140.1	<0.0001	0.99	<0.0001	<0.0001
Stereotyped (0–16)	2.1	2.4	0.4	1.0	0.4	1.0	F(2,441) = 50.3	<0.0001	0.99	<0.0001	<0.0001
Resistance to Change (0–6)	1.4	1.7	0.4	0.9	0.4	0.8	F(2,441) = 33.73	<0.0001	0.96	<0.0001	<0.0001
ASD-total (0–60)	13.3	8.9	3.9	5.0	3.0	4.3	F(2,441) = 118	<0.0001	0.54	<0.0001	<0.0001
ADHD-total	13.3	2.9	1.0	1.5	0.4	0.9	F(2,441) = 2008	<0.0001	0.089	<0.0001	<0.0001
Handedness (r/l/a)	152/24/3		101/17/0		126/19/1						

Values are mean ± standard deviation. Significance was set at $p<0.05$. All p-values refer to ANOVAs, except for gender where the p-value refers to a chi-square test. Where ANOVA's returned a significant result, post-hoc Tukey Honest Significant Difference (Tukey HSD) tests were performed. US - Con, refers to a pairwise comparison between unaffected siblings and controls. ADHD-Con, refers to a a pairwise comparison between ADHD and controls. ADHD - US, refers to a pairwise comparison between ADHD and unaffected siblings. Four subscales of the Children's Social and Behavioural Questionnaire (CSBQ) which probe ASD spectrum symptoms are shown in this table: Social Interest, Social Understanding (Understanding), Stereotypy and Resistance to Change. ASD-total is calculated as a sum of these four subscales. ADHD-total scores are calculated according to the algorithm described in detail in the supplementary information (Questionnaire Items S1).

Abbreviations: Gender (m/f), Gender (male/female); Handedness (r/l/a), Handedness (right, left, ambidextrous).

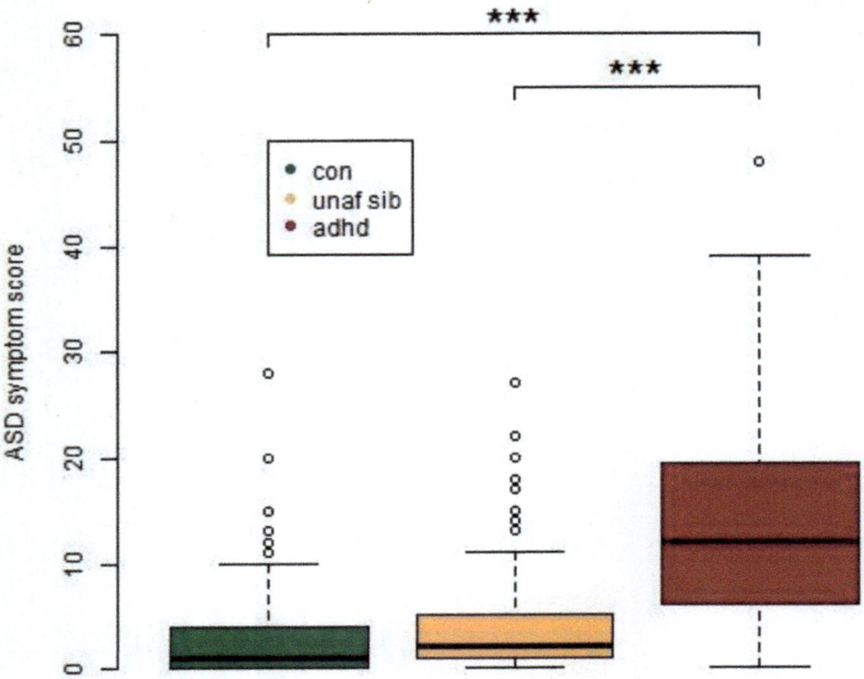

Figure 1. ASD symptoms in healthy controls, unaffected siblings and ADHD. ADHD subjects were found to have significantly higher scores relative to both unaffected siblings and healthy controls. ***$p<0.001$, with post-hoc Tukey test, following an ANOVA. ASD symptom score refers to an aggregate score from the four Children's Social and Behavioural Questionnaire (CSBQ) subscales, (1) social interest, (2) social understanding, (3) stereotypy and (4) resistance to change. Abbreviations: con, Control; unaf sib, Unaffected Siblings, adhd, Attention Deficit Hyperactivity Disorder.

Table 2. Final, generalised mixed-effect model showing fixed effects for ASD score modelled against white matter residual and grey matter volumes.

Fixed Effects	Estimate	Standard Error	t-value	p-value
WM resid	−0.485	0.206	−2.354	0.019
GM	0.013	0.013	0.994	0.321
Unaff. Sib.	−0.538	3.652	−0.147	0.883
ADHD	21.056	3.815	5.519	0.000
Age	0.071	0.177	0.398	0.691
Male	1.847	0.674	2.740	0.006
WM resid×GM	0.001	0.000	2.199	0.028
Unaff. Sib×Age	0.059	0.211	0.279	0.781
ADHD×Age	−0.675	0.207	−3.264	0.001

Formula:

$$ASD\ symptoms \sim WM\ resid * GM + Diagnosis * Age + Gender + (1|Total\ ADHD\ symptoms) + (1|Family) + (1|IQ) + (1|ADHD\ medication) + (1|Scanner\ type);$$

"~" means modelled against, and "(1| factor)" means that a factor is included as a random effect.

A generalised mixed-effect model is run using normalised volumes of grey and white matter as explanatory variables together with age as a random effect. ASD score is set as the response variable. The final model is derived following an iterative model selection procedure that involves comparing successive models using Akaike's Information Criterion (see Methods for detailed description of model selection procedure). ASD score refers to an aggregate score from the four Children's Social and Behavioural Questionnaire (CSBQ) subscales, (1) social interest, (2) social understanding, (3) stereotypy and (4) resistance to change.

Abbreviations: WM, normalised WM volume; GM, normalised GM volume; US, unaffected siblings; WM:GM, WM by GM interaction; US: Age, unaffected sibling by Age interaction; ADHD:Age, ADHD by Age interaction.

Table 3. Final, generalised mixed-effect model showing random effects for ASD score modelled against white matter residual and grey matter volumes.

Random Effects	Variance	S.D.
Family Relatedness	8.765	2.961
IQ	1.098	1.048
Total ADHD Score	5.474	2.340
ADHD medication	0.000	0.000
Scanner Type	0.000	0.000

Formula:

$$ASD\ symptoms \sim WM\ resid * GM + Diagnosis * Age + Gender + (1|Total\ ADHD\ symptoms) + (1|Family) + (1|IQ) + (1|ADHD\ medication) + (1|Scanner\ type)$$

"~" means modelled against, and "(1| factor)" means that a factor is included as a random effect.

A generalised mixed-effect model is run using normalised volumes of grey and white matter as explanatory variables together with age as a random effect. ASD score is set as the response variable. The final model is derived following an iterative model selection procedure that involves comparing successive models using Akaike's Information Criterion (see Methods for detailed description of model selection procedure). ASD score refers to an aggregate score from the four Children's Social and Behavioural Questionnaire (CSBQ) subscales, (1) social interest, (2) social understanding, (3) stereotypy and (4) resistance to change.

Abbreviations: WM, normalised WM volume; GM, normalised GM volume; US, unaffected siblings; WM:GM, WM by GM interaction; US: Age, unaffected sibling by Age interaction; ADHD:Age, ADHD by Age interaction.

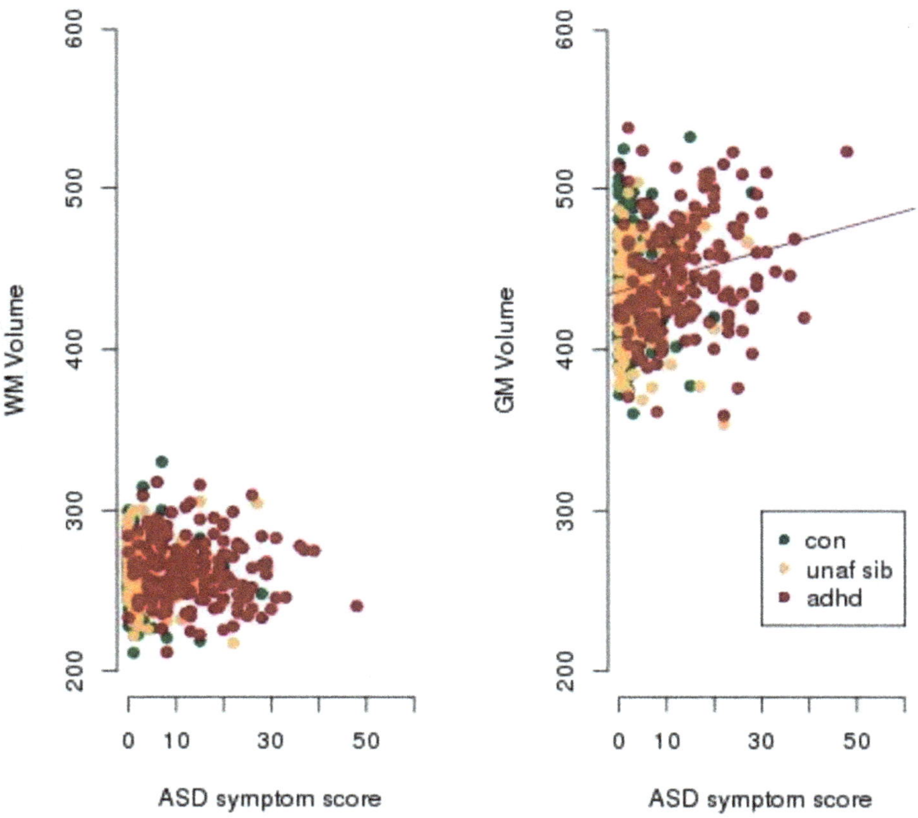

Figure 2. ASD scores are significantly positively correlated with total grey matter volume. The volumes of grey and white matter are normalised for total intracranial volume. A regression line is plotted where the Pearson's product-moment correlation is significant with $p<0.05$. ASD symptom score refers to an aggregate score from the four Children's Social and Behavioural Questionnaire (CSBQ) subscales, (1) social interest, (2) social understanding, (3) stereotypy and (4) resistance to change. Abbreviations: con, Control; unaf sib, Unaffected Siblings, adhd, Attention Deficit Hyperactivity Disorder; ASD, autism spectrum disorder.

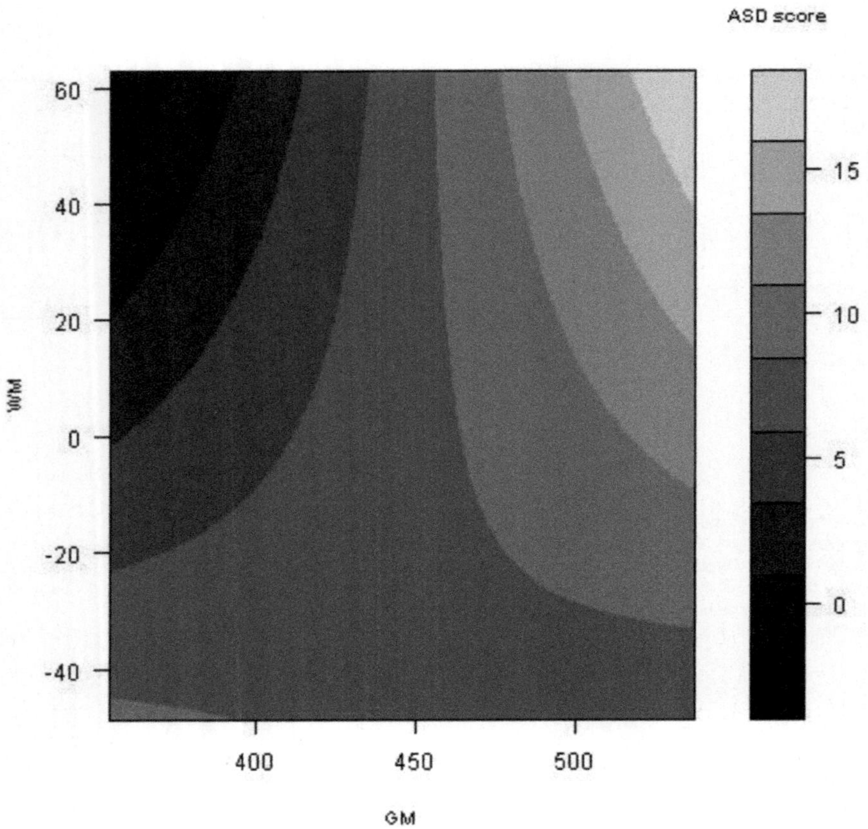

Figure 3. ASD score contour graph for the interaction between WM, GM and ASD scores. The best mixed effects model was converted into a function in R which allowed ASD scores to be extrapolated for a range of GM and WM volumes (see Methods for full description). The best mixed effects model included GM and WM residual terms (see Methods). Volumes are normalised for total intracranial volume. ASD score refers to an aggregate score from the four Children's Social and Behavioural Questionnaire (CSBQ) subscales, (1) social interest, (2) social understanding, (3) stereotypy and (4) resistance to change.

diagnosis derived from the different questionnaires employed (n = 53). The resulting data set was then age- and gender-matched; so that the current study included 90 male and 90 female ADHD subjects, 62 male and 62 female unaffected siblings of ADHD subjects and 70 male and 70 female healthy control children. The age range of participants was 7.4 to 28.5 years. All participants were of European Caucasian descent and had an IQ≥70. Demographic characteristics of each subject group are provided in Table 1. Subjects who were taking ADHD medication stopped medication (both stimulant and non-stimulant) for 48 hours prior to scanning. Regarding medication history, 71 ADHD subjects (39%) were not currently taking ADHD medication, 93 ADHD subjects (52%) were taking one ADHD medication, and 16 ADHD subjects (9%) were currently taking two ADHD medications. A complete overview of medication is provided in Table S1.

ADHD diagnosis and symptom measures

All participants were assessed using a semi-structured diagnostic interview (Dutch translation of the Schedule for Affective Disorders and Schizophrenia for School-Age Children - Present and Lifetime Version (K-SADS-PL) [43] and Conners' ADHD questionnaire to determine ADHD diagnoses. Each child was assessed with a parent-rated questionnaire (Conners' Parent Rating Scale – Revised: Long version (CPRS-R:L) combined with either a teacher-rating (Conners' Teacher Rating Scale – Revised: Long version (CTRS-R:L) applied for children <18 years or a self-report Conners' Adult ADHD Rating Scales – Self-Report: Long version (CAARS-S:L) applied for children ≥18 years. A diagnostic algorithm was applied to combine symptom counts on the K-SADS-PL and Conners' questionnaires. A detailed description of the diagnostic algorithm is provided in the supplementary information (Diagnostic Algorithm S1). This algorithm was used to diagnose subjects and also to provide a continuous score for an overall level of ADHD symptoms that combines both inattentive and hyperactive symptoms. While ASD symptoms were present in the cohort and were significantly elevated in the ADHD group (see Results), a clinical diagnosis of autism or Asperger's syndrome had been an exclusion criterion in the original IMAGE study.

ASD measures

The Children's Social and Behavioural Questionnaire (CSBQ) [44] was used in the current study as it can measure the continuous distribution of autistic symptoms in the general population as well as in clinical groups outside of autism, including ADHD [44,45]. Most instruments for ASD are designed to assess clinical cases and are not suitable for assessing milder ASD symptoms. The CSBQ was originally developed because existing instruments did not capture more subtle social problems found in the milder end of the autism spectrum [44]. The CSBQ has previously been shown to be valuable in measuring subthreshold autistic symptoms [44–49,40]. In the current study, where clinical ASD was an exclusion criterion, but where milder autistic symptoms are expected to be elevated in the ADHD group [2,4–6,50], the CSBQ is ideally suited for the purpose of the study.

The CSBQ contains 49 items on a 3-point Likert scale. It contains items that refer directly to the DSM-IV criteria for autism, but it also captures more subtle symptoms of ASD. Therefore, it is suitable for measuring behavioural problems as seen in children with milder variants of ASD. CSBQ items are grouped into the following six subscales: (1) tuned, (2) social interest, (3) orientation, (4) social understanding, (5) resistance to change, and (6) stereotypy. It was administered in the parent-report form.

All items contained within each subscale are found in the supplemental information (Questionnaire Items S1). The CSBQ has good internal, test-retest, and inter-rater reliability, and demonstrated convergent and divergent validity [44]. The CSBQ appears to differentiate between autism and pervasive developmental disorders - not otherwise specified (PDD-NOS), and can also differentiate between PDD-NOS and ADHD [44,51]. Additionally, to assess the content validity of the CSBQ, it has previously been compared to an autism screening instrument, the Autism Behavior Checklist (ABC) [52]. A strong correlation of 0.75 was found between the total scores of both questionnaires in a large Dutch population sample [45]. The CSBQ has also been compared with the Autism Diagnostic Interview-Revised (ADI-R), Autism Diagnostic Observation Schedule (ADOS), and clinical classification in children with mild and moderate intellectual disability [53]. In that study, the contribution of the CSBQ to a classification of ASD was most specific for the "social" and "stereotypy" subscales, with high coherence with all three classification methods [53].

An aggregate score from the four subscales, (1) social interest, (2) social understanding, (3) stereotypy and (4) resistance to change, was used in the current study to capture the core symptoms of ASD. This aggregate score has been successfully used to selectively probe ASD symptoms in previous studies [47,54]. The remaining two CSBQ subscales (tuned and orientation) probe dysfunctional social behaviours which, although characteristic for ASD, are also related to the ADHD dimensions of hyperactivity/impulsivity and attention problems, respectively [44], and were not considered in the current study for this reason.

High Resolution T1W Structural Image Acquisition and Processing

Whole brain T1 weighted MPRAGE images were acquired at 1.5T using a product 8 channel phased array headcoil on a Siemens Sonata scanner at the Free University in Amsterdam and a 1.5T Siemens Avanto MR scanner at the Donders Institute for Brain, Cognition and Behaviour in Nijmegen. A breakdown of the distribution of subjects scanned at the two sites is included in Table S2. TI/TE/TR = 1000/2.95/2730 ms, imaging matrix 256×256, 176 slices, voxel size $1\times1\times1$ mm^3, GRAPPA acceleration 2. Brain tissue probability maps for white matter (WM), grey matter (GM) and cerebrospinal fluid (CSF) were estimated using the unified

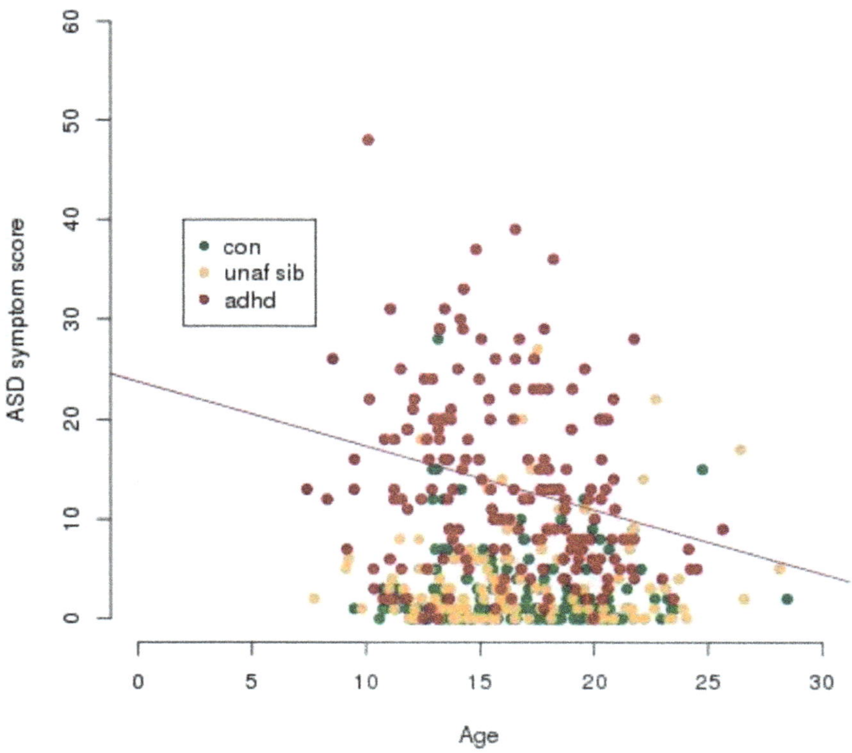

Figure 4. ASD scores decrease significantly with age within the ADHD groups. A regression line is plotted where the Pearson's product-moment correlation is significant with $p<0.05$. ASD score refers to an aggregate score from the four Children's Social and Behavioural Questionnaire (CSBQ) subscales, (1) social interest, (2) social understanding, (3) stereotypy and (4) resistance to change. Abbreviations: con, Control; unaf sib, Unaffected Siblings, ADHD, Attention-deficit/hyperactivity disorder; ASD, autism spectrum disorder.

segmentation algorithm as implemented in the VBM8 toolbox of SPM8 [55]. Total GM, WM and CSF volumes were computed by voxelwise summation of their probability maps. Total intracranial volume (ICV) was then computed as the sum of WM, GM and CSF volume.

The following formula was used to compute normalised volumes of global GM and WM:

total volume of GM (mm^3)/ICV (mm^3)×1000.
total volume of WM (mm^3)/ICV (mm^3)×1000.

Statistics

As ASD scores are influenced by a range of factors, mixed-effects models allow us to consider factors that potentially contribute to the understanding of the data (i.e. fixed factors), while controlling for additional factors associated with the subjects (i.e. random factors).

R statistical software (Version 2.15.1) [56], including the lme4 package [57] was used for all statistical analyses. In the current study, the "glmer" function [57] was used to fit a generalised mixed-effects model using maximum likelihood (ML). As our objective was to determine the extent to which the ASD score is influenced by the diagnosis group (i.e. control, unaffected sibling or ADHD), GM and WM, these three factors were set as fixed effects. Age was also set as a fixed factor. The total ADHD symptom score was set as a random effect, in order to control for differences in ADHD symptoms between participants, thus allowing us to focus specifically on the ASD score. IQ, ADHD medication, scanner type and family relatedness were also set as random effects. The response variable was set as ASD score, calculated as an aggregate of the four CSBQ subscales ('social interest', 'social understanding', 'stereotypy' and 'resistance to change') that probe ASD.

Models were created using normalised WM and GM volumes. Including both WM and GM variables allowed us to determine not only the extent to which GM and WM drive changes in ASD scores, but also the nature of the interactions between the explanatory variables. WM and GM volumes were co-linear (i.e. correlated with each other) and the models developed took this into account by orthogonalizing these regressors relative to each other to isolate the unique contribution of each explanatory variable independent from what is shared between them. A WM residual term was derived from the regression residuals when WM was regressed against GM. This enabled us to use GM together with a WM residual term (WM resid) in our mixed effect model. A model using WM together with a GM residual term (GM resid) was also created. Un-biased analyses and comparisons could then be carried out based on the models.

The models were fitted by maximum likelihood estimation. The starting model using GM resid and WM terms was:

$$\begin{aligned} ASD\ score \sim GM\ resid * WM * Diagnosis * Age * Gender &+ \\ (1|ADHD\ symptoms) &+ \\ (1|Scanner\ type) &+ \\ (1|IQ) &+ \\ (1|Family\ relatedness) &+ \\ (1|ADHD\ medication) & \end{aligned}$$

where "~" means "modelled against"; "(1| factor)" means that factor is included as a random effect, and "Diagnosis" refers to the three diagnostic groups, i.e. control, unaffected siblings and ADHD. "*" means interacting with, and the model assesses interactions among all terms, up to a 5-way interaction among all fixed effects.

The starting model using GM and WM resid terms was:

$$\begin{aligned} ASD\ score \sim WM\ resid * GM * Diagnosis * Age * Gender &+ \\ (1|ADHD\ symptoms) &+ \\ (1|Scanner\ type) &+ \\ (1|IQ) &+ \\ (1|Family\ relatedness) &+ \\ (1|ADHD\ medication) & \end{aligned}$$

We fit the full models as described above and then removed least significant terms in an iterative process, checking for improved fit according to Akaike's Information Criterion (AIC) [58,59] until a final model was obtained [60]. We have previously employed the AIC tool for successful model selection in an MRI and structural volume framework [61]. The models are thus primarily assessing the influence of GM and WM on the ASD scores across all healthy young controls, ADHD subjects and unaffected siblings (Sib) of ADHD subjects.

To determine if the model using GM resid or the WM resid term was a better predictor of ASD symptoms, the fits of the two final models was compared using the "anova" function in R [60].

Contour Plots

The significant interaction between GM and WM was visualized by means of a contour plot. Normalised WM and GM volumes were used for creating this contour plot. ASD scores were modelled as follows: model = lm (ASD score~GM*WM resid); where "~" means modelled against, "*" means interacting with, and, "lm" is used to fit a linear model in R. A matrix was created for the WM and GM volumes, and the function was run from the minimum to the maximum GM value within the matrix, and also from the minimum to the maximum WM value within the matrix. The contour plot enabled changes in ASD scores to be visualised by means of a colour key with darker colours representing lower ASD symptoms and lighter colours representing higher ASD symptoms.

Results

Demographic and Cognitive Characteristics

The demographic characteristics of the cohort are shown in Table 1. ASD scores were significantly different between groups [$F(2,441) = 118$, $p<0.0001$], with ADHD subjects having significantly raised scores relative to both controls ($p<0.0001$) and unaffected siblings ($p<0.0001$), while there was no significant difference between controls and unaffected siblings (Fig. 1; Table 1). ASD scores were found to be significantly positively correlated with ADHD scores in control group ($p = 0.046$, $r = 0.165$; Table S3) and in the ADHD group ($p = 0.254$, $r = 0.001$; Table S3).

Mixed-effects models for ASD symptoms modelled against global grey matter and white matter volumes

Following model simplification based on AIC, the optimal model for ASD symptoms is shown in Table 2 and Table 3. This model used the WM residual term together with GM (WM resid:GM model) and was found to have a lower AIC value than the alternative model that used the GM residual term together with the WM (GM resid:WM model). The alternative model is also shown in Table S4.

For the fixed effects of the WM resid:GM model, the following terms were significant: WM resid ($p = 0.019$); ADHD diagnosis ($p < 0.0001$); male gender ($p = 0.006$); WM resid×GM interaction ($p = 0.028$); ADHD diagnosis×age ($p = 0.001$).

As the range of ASD scores in control and unaffected siblings is limited, a mixed effect model was also developed based on the inclusion of participants with an ASD score of 20 or higher. This model also returned a significant WM resid×GM interaction ($p = 0.0029$; Table S5).

The significant interaction between WM and GM was further visualised with a scatter plot (Fig. 2) and a contour plot (Fig. 3). A significant positive correlation was found between GM volume and ASD scores for the ADHD group ($p = 0.00025$, $r = 0.17$) (Fig. 2). No other significant correlation was found between GM volume and ASD score for control or unaffected siblings. There was also no significant correlation between WM volume and ASD score for any of the groups examined. The best mixed effects model (Table 2 and Table 3) was used to create a contour plot, which further described the interaction between GM and WM. The contour plot developed from the mixed effects model indicates that the lowest ASD scores were found in areas of low GM coupled with high WM (Fig. 3). Increasing ASD score was accompanied by greater GM volume and lower WM volume up to an ASD score on the CSBQ of ~10. For ASD scores greater than ~10, the volumetric profile indicated both raised GM and WM volume (Fig. 3).

As there was a significant interaction found between the ADHD diagnosis and age, this interaction was also visualised with a scatter plot (Fig. 4). ADHD subjects were found to have a significant negative correlation between age and ASD scores ($p < 0.0005$; $r = -0.26$) while there was no correlation between age and ASD scores for unaffected siblings or controls (Fig. 4).

Total Intracranial Volume in Low and High ASD Conditions

Total intracranial volume was plotted for Control, Unaffected Sibling, ADHD with low ASD and ADHD with high ASD scores (Fig. 5). Low ASD score was defined as 20 or lower as per the CSBQ ASD score. A high ASD score was defined as greater than 20. ADHD participants with low ASD scores were found to have significantly lower total intracranial volumes than control subjects ($p < 0.05$). No other significant differences were found.

Discussion

In the current study, ASD symptoms as measured by the CSBQ [44] were found to be significantly elevated in ADHD subjects relative to both controls and unaffected siblings. These findings agree with previous studies that have found elevated levels of ASD symptoms in ADHD subjects [13,62]. There was a non-significant increase in the ASD scores for unaffected siblings relative to controls, which is in line with studies showing moderate increases in ASD symptoms in unaffected siblings of ADHD subjects [40], [63]. For ADHD subjects, the co-morbid ASD symptoms were found to decrease significantly with age.

Structural MRI was used to investigate whether or not raised ASD symptoms would be accompanied by a distinct anatomical profile. When ASD scores were modelled against WM and GM volumes using mixed-effects models that controlled for ADHD symptom levels, a significant WM by GM interaction was found. Investigation of the interaction between WM, GM and ASD scores by means of a contour graph highlighted a specific volumetric landscape with the lowest ASD scores found in areas of low GM coupled with high WM. Increasing ASD scores were accompanied by greater GM volumes and lower WM volumes. While the GM profile constantly increased with greater ASD scores, WM was found to decrease with greater ASD scores but for the highest ASD scores WM volumes were also elevated.

The profile of increased GM volume in subjects with raised ASD symptoms is in line with previous studies that have found GM volume to be significantly increased in adolescent ASD subjects [32]. Globally, decreased brain size has been the predominant finding in ADHD [15,18], while ASD is generally associated with brain overgrowth during infancy followed by a return to normal total brain size in adolescence and possible continued degeneration into middle age [64] [22–27]. Similarly, although the majority of studies have found total brain volume to be reduced in ADHD, some studies have reported no significant differences in total brain volume between ADHD subjects and typically developing controls [36,65–68]. These discrepancies may be partly accounted for by the extent to which ASD symptoms are present in the ADHD sample. The findings in the current paper that ADHD with low ASD score had significantly reduced total intracranial volume compared with control, whereas ADHD with high ASD score showed no significant difference with control, further emphasize the role that ASD symptoms may play in influencing the landscape of brain volumetrics in ADHD subjects.

Meta-analyses suggest that increasing age and medication treatment contribute to a degree of normalisation in brain volumes in ADHD [16,17]. The current findings add to these studies by indicating that ASD comorbidity may be an additional factor that plays an important role in influencing brain volume in ADHD. Decreased GM volume may be more pronounced when ASD symptoms are absent or present only to a minor degree, as was the case in the current study. Conversely, the current findings indicate that elevated ASD symptoms are accompanied by raised GM volume. The WM profile was more complex, with lower volumes found as ASD scores increase, but higher volumes found for the most extreme ASD scores. Previous studies have shown reduced WM volume in adolescent and adult ASD subjects [28], [29,30], while greater WM enlargement has been found in children with ASD [28]. A mixed effects model assessment, based on the same statistical framework as the main analysis, but including only participants with an ASD score of 20 or higher also revealed a significant GM by WM interaction. This supplementary analysis indicates that those with elevated ASD scores in the current cohort have a global volumetric profile similar to that found in ASD studies.

The volumetric landscape for different ASD scores described by the contour plot is not restricted to ADHD subjects but is also applicable to unaffected siblings and healthy controls. No significant interaction between GM, WM and ADHD was found, nor were there significant interactions between GM, WM and unaffected siblings, or between GM, WM and controls.

As ASD scores remained low in both controls and unaffected siblings, their volumetric profiles were constrained to a conjunction of low GM coupled with high WM volume. Conversely, ASD scores for ADHD subjects were more heterogeneous, with a significantly higher mean, as well as greater variance and range. Therefore, ADHD subjects exhibited a wide range of volumetric profiles that were dependent on their ASD spectrum scores.

There was a significant age-related improvement in ASD symptoms in ADHD subjects which is in agreement with previous cross-sectional and longitudinal studies that have also found age-related improvement in ASD [69,70] [71]. Neither WM nor GM volume was found to influence this age-related reduction of ASD

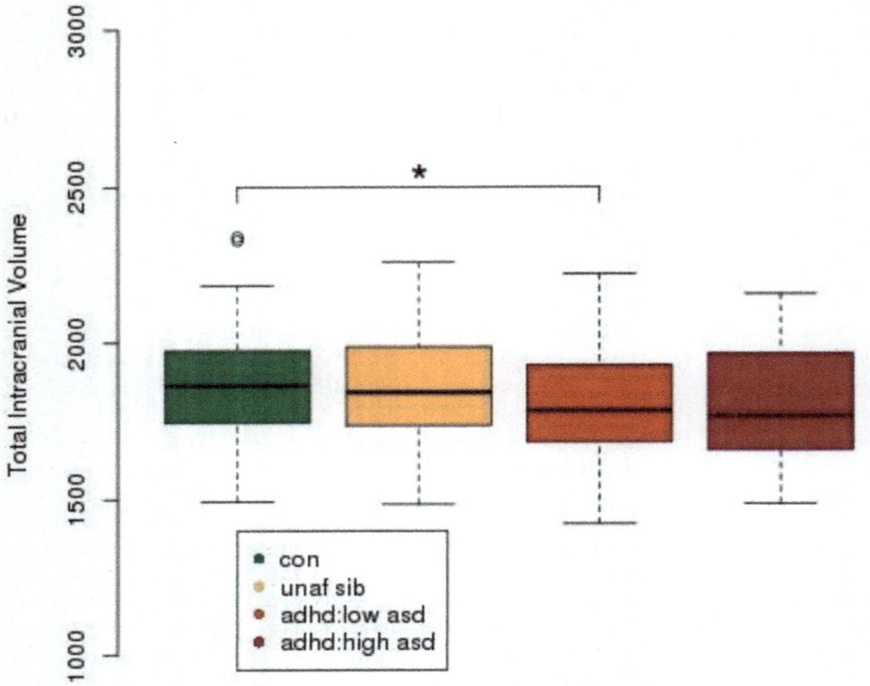

Figure 5. ADHD subjects with low ASD scores have significantly lower total intracranial volume than control subjects ($p<0.05$). ADHD: low ASD is defined as a participant with ADHD and an ASD score of 20 or less. ADHD: high ASD is defined as a participant with ADHD and an ASD score greater than 20.

symptoms in ADHD subjects. Therefore, the neural correlates of this finding remain unknown. Analyses of regional brain volume changes, as well as changes in WM indices of diffusion will be undertaken in a future study and may be able to shed light on this point. One possibility is that while total WM or GM volume may not have an influence on age-related changes in ASD symptoms, subtle regional changes in GM and WM structure changes may lie hidden beneath the global analysis. Structural and functional MRI studies have consistently found the caudate nucleus to be altered in ASD and to be associated with dysfunctions in multiple domains related to ASD, such as repetitive and stereotyped behaviour [72], reward processing [73–75] and executive function [73]. Caudate damage has also been related to reduced cognitive flexibility and perseverative behaviour in a range of species, including monkeys [76], birds [77], rats [78] and cats [79]. Clearly, developmental changes play a crucial role in influencing the trajectories of both disorders. Significant age-related improvements have been noted in restricted and repetitive behaviours [80] and also in overall ASD symptom counts [81]. The significant reduction of ASD scores may be related to a reduction of local short-range circuitry together with a strengthening of long-range connectivity that is seen in adolescent brain development [82]. Normal development is associated with marked changes in WM tracts, with myelination increasing throughout childhood and adolescence [83]. Increasing myelination of fronto-striatal connections during adolescence and early adulthood facilitates top-down executive control of behaviour [84]. Indices of WM integrity such as fractional anisotropy have been found to normalise in ADHD subjects as they progress to adolescence and adulthood [85]. Thus, the apparent improvements in autism symptoms with age as seen in the current study may be associated with improvements in WM integrity. Social adaptation may contribute to a reduction of ASD symptoms with age. Initial studies have also indicated that cognitive behavioural therapy (CBT), when adapted to the special needs of patients with ASD, can offer an effective treatment modality [86], [87,88]. Although there are no pharmacological treatments that specifically target the deficits of ASD, some studies have noted improvement in behavioural symptoms with risperidone [89], while reductions in repetitive behaviours have been found following treatment with oxytocin [90]. Within the current cohort, individuals with low IQ (<70) were excluded, thus an IQ within a normal range may also facilitate compensation or adaptive mechanisms that help ADHD individuals to reduce the overt expression of ASD symptoms.

The current study should be viewed in the context of some limitations. The results are cross-sectional. Future longitudinal studies of MRI-measured developmental trajectories are needed for assessing the impact of age on developing brain structures. The results are also based on global volumetric changes and do not identify specific regional increases or decreases in WM or GM volume. Studies are underway which will assess the current data set in terms of specific regional WM and GM volumetric differences that occur with elevated ASD symptoms. The fact that clinical ASD cases were not included in the cohort is an additional limitation of the study. While the ASD score derived from the aggregate of four sub-scales of the CSBQ questionnaire (social interest, social understanding, stereotypy and resistance to change) has been successfully used to probe ASD symptoms in the past [47,54], caution is needed when interpreting this score as not all social deficits present in ADHD overlap with ASD symptoms [91]. The fact that participants were of European (Caucasian) descent is another limitation, and indicates that results may not be readily generalisable to other communities or ethnicities.

Overall, the current results highlight a specific volumetric profile that is associated with elevated ASD symptoms. This is the first study in a large cohort that robustly accounts for the phenotypic overlap between the ADHD and ASD. Equivocal findings in previous volumetric studies of ADHD and ASD may be due to the fact that issues of comorbidity have generally been ignored in studies to date. Assessing the range of volumetric profiles associated with ADHD coupled with mild ASD symptoms, through to ADHD coupled with severe ASD symptoms, will help to develop a more nuanced understanding of the pathophysiology associated with the continuous distribution and overlap of these two disorders.

Supporting Information

Table S1 Medication Information.

Table S2 Distribution of Scanning over Two Sites.

Table S3 Correlation between ASD score and ADHD symptom levels.

Table S4 Final, generalised mixed-effect model for ASD score modelled against Grey Matter Residual and White Matter Volumes.

Table S5 Final, generalised mixed-effect model for ASD score modelled against Grey Matter and White Matter Volumes using only participants with an ASD score of 20 or higher.

Diagnostic Algorithm S1 Diagnostic algorithm for ADHD in the NeuroIMAGE sample.

Questionnaire Items S1 Children's Social and Behavioural Questionnaire (CSBQ) Summary.

Author Contributions

Conceived and designed the experiments: LOD EVD JKB. Performed the experiments: LOD. Analyzed the data: LOD CT MPZ. Contributed reagents/materials/analysis tools: JKB CT MPZ. Wrote the paper: LOD. Edited the manuscript and contributed conceptual improvements: CUG JB MPZ BF JO DH PH CAH NR JKB.

References

1. Rommelse NNJ, Franke B, Geurts HM, Hartman CA, Buitelaar JK (2010) Shared heritability of attention-deficit/hyperactivity disorder and autism spectrum disorder. Eur Child Adolesc Psychiatry 19: 281–295. doi:10.1007/s00787-010-0092-x.
2. Ronald A, Simonoff E, Kuntsi J, Asherson P, Plomin R (2008) Evidence for overlapping genetic influences on autistic and ADHD behaviours in a community twin sample. J Child Psychol Psychiatry 49: 535–542. doi:10.1111/j.1469-7610.2007.01857.x.
3. Association AP (2000) Diagnostic and Statistical Manual of Mental Disorders, Fourth Edition: DSM-IV-TR. American Psychiatric Pub. 996 p.
4. Ames CS, White SJ (2011) Are ADHD traits dissociable from the autistic profile? Links between cognition and behaviour. J Autism Dev Disord 41: 357–363. doi:10.1007/s10803-010-1049-0.
5. Leyfer OT, Folstein SE, Bacalman S, Davis NO, Dinh E, et al. (2006) Comorbid psychiatric disorders in children with autism: interview development and rates of disorders. J Autism Dev Disord 36: 849–861. doi:10.1007/s10803-006-0123-0.
6. Van Steijn DJ, Richards JS, Oerlemans AM, de Ruiter SW, van Aken MAG, et al. (2012) The co-occurrence of autism spectrum disorder and attention-deficit/hyperactivity disorder symptoms in parents of children with ASD or ASD with ADHD. J Child Psychol Psychiatry 53: 954–963. doi:10.1111/j.1469-7610.2012.02556.x.
7. Corbett BA, Constantine LJ, Hendren R, Rocke D, Ozonoff S (2009) Examining executive functioning in children with autism spectrum disorder, attention deficit hyperactivity disorder and typical development. Psychiatry Res 166: 210–222. doi:10.1016/j.psychres.2008.02.005.
8. Fine JG, Semrud-Clikeman M, Butcher B, Walkowiak J (2008) Brief report: attention effect on a measure of social perception. J Autism Dev Disord 38: 1797–1802. doi:10.1007/s10803-008-0570-x.
9. Booth R, Happé F (2010) "Hunting with a knife and … fork": examining central coherence in autism, attention deficit/hyperactivity disorder, and typical development with a linguistic task. J Exp Child Psychol 107: 377–393. doi:10.1016/j.jecp.2010.06.003.
10. Chabernaud C, Mennes M, Kelly C, Nooner K, Di Martino A, et al. (2012) Dimensional brain-behavior relationships in children with attention-deficit/hyperactivity disorder. Biol Psychiatry 71: 434–442. doi:10.1016/j.biopsych.2011.08.013.
11. Shaw P, Gilliam M, Liverpool M, Weddle C, Malek M, et al. (2011) Cortical development in typically developing children with symptoms of hyperactivity and impulsivity: support for a dimensional view of attention deficit hyperactivity disorder. Am J Psychiatry 168: 143–151. doi:10.1176/appi.ajp.2010.10030385.
12. Castellanos FX, Tannock R (2002) Neuroscience of attention-deficit/hyperactivity disorder: the search for endophenotypes. Nat Rev Neurosci 3: 617–628. doi:10.1038/nrn896.
13. Reiersen AM, Constantino JN, Volk HE, Todd RD (2007) Autistic traits in a population-based ADHD twin sample. J Child Psychol Psychiatry 48: 464–472. doi:10.1111/j.1469-7610.2006.01720.x.
14. Geurts HM, Ridderinkhof KR, Scholte HS (2013) The relationship between grey-matter and ASD and ADHD traits in typical adults. J Autism Dev Disord 43: 1630–1641. doi:10.1007/s10803-012-1708-4.
15. Valera EM, Faraone SV, Murray KE, Seidman LJ (2007) Meta-analysis of structural imaging findings in attention-deficit/hyperactivity disorder. Biol Psychiatry 61: 1361–1369. doi:10.1016/j.biopsych.2006.06.011.
16. Frodl T, Skokauskas N (2012) Meta-analysis of structural MRI studies in children and adults with attention deficit hyperactivity disorder indicates treatment effects. Acta Psychiatr Scand 125: 114–126. doi:10.1111/j.1600-0447.2011.01786.x.
17. Nakao T, Radua J, Rubia K, Mataix-Cols D (2011) Gray matter volume abnormalities in ADHD: voxel-based meta-analysis exploring the effects of age and stimulant medication. Am J Psychiatry 168: 1154–1163. doi:10.1176/appi.ajp.2011.11020281.
18. Seidman LJ, Biederman J, Liang L, Valera EM, Monuteaux MC, et al. (2011) Gray matter alterations in adults with attention-deficit/hyperactivity disorder identified by voxel based morphometry. Biol Psychiatry 69: 857–866. doi:10.1016/j.biopsych.2010.09.053.
19. Carmona S, Vilarroya O, Bielsa A, Trèmols V, Soliva JC, et al. (2005) Global and regional gray matter reductions in ADHD: a voxel-based morphometric study. Neurosci Lett 389: 88–93. doi:10.1016/j.neulet.2005.07.020.
20. Mostofsky SH, Cooper KL, Kates WR, Denckla MB, Kaufmann WE (2002) Smaller prefrontal and premotor volumes in boys with attention-deficit/hyperactivity disorder. Biol Psychiatry 52: 785–794.
21. Shaw P, Gogtay N, Rapoport J (2010) Childhood psychiatric disorders as anomalies in neurodevelopmental trajectories. Hum Brain Mapp 31: 917–925. doi:10.1002/hbm.21028.
22. Courchesne E, Carper R, Akshoomoff N (2003) Evidence of brain overgrowth in the first year of life in autism. JAMA 290: 337–344. doi:10.1001/jama.290.3.337.
23. Redcay E, Courchesne E (2005) When is the brain enlarged in autism? A meta-analysis of all brain size reports. Biol Psychiatry 58: 1–9. doi:10.1016/j.biopsych.2005.03.026.
24. Freitag CM, Luders E, Hulst HE, Narr KL, Thompson PM, et al. (2009) Total brain volume and corpus callosum size in medication-naïve adolescents and young adults with autism spectrum disorder. Biol Psychiatry 66: 316–319. doi:10.1016/j.biopsych.2009.03.011.
25. Herbert MR, Ziegler DA, Deutsch CK, O'Brien LM, Lange N, et al. (2003) Dissociations of cerebral cortex, subcortical and cerebral white matter volumes in autistic boys. Brain 126: 1182–1192.
26. Herbert MR (2005) Large brains in autism: the challenge of pervasive abnormality. Neuroscientist 11: 417–440. doi:10.1177/0091270005278866.
27. Herbert MR, Ziegler DA, Makris N, Filipek PA, Kemper TL, et al. (2004) Localization of white matter volume increase in autism and developmental language disorder. Ann Neurol 55: 530–540. doi:10.1002/ana.20032.
28. Courchesne E, Karns CM, Davis HR, Ziccardi R, Carper RA, et al. (2001) Unusual brain growth patterns in early life in patients with autistic disorder: an MRI study. Neurology 57: 245–254.
29. Chung MK, Dalton KM, Alexander AL, Davidson RJ (2004) Less white matter concentration in autism: 2D voxel-based morphometry. Neuroimage 23: 242–251. doi:10.1016/j.neuroimage.2004.04.037.
30. Waiter GD, Williams JHG, Murray AD, Gilchrist A, Perrett DI, et al. (2005) Structural white matter deficits in high-functioning individuals with autistic

spectrum disorder: a voxel-based investigation. Neuroimage 24: 455–461. doi:10.1016/j.neuroimage.2004.08.049.

31. Radua J, Via E, Catani M, Mataix-Cols D (2011) Voxel-based meta-analysis of regional white-matter volume differences in autism spectrum disorder versus healthy controls. Psychol Med 41: 1539–1550. doi:10.1017/S0033291710002187.
32. Vaccarino FM, Grigorenko EL, Smith KM, Stevens HE (2009) Regulation of cerebral cortical size and neuron number by fibroblast growth factors: implications for autism. J Autism Dev Disord 39: 511–520. doi:10.1007/s10803-008-0653-8.
33. Via E, Radua J, Cardoner N, Happé F, Mataix-Cols D (2011) Meta-analysis of gray matter abnormalities in autism spectrum disorder: should Asperger disorder be subsumed under a broader umbrella of autistic spectrum disorder? Arch Gen Psychiatry 68: 409–418. doi:10.1001/archgenpsychiatry.2011.27.
34. Nickl-Jockschat T, Habel U, Michel TM, Manning J, Laird AR, et al. (2012) Brain structure anomalies in autism spectrum disorder–a meta-analysis of VBM studies using anatomic likelihood estimation. Hum Brain Mapp 33: 1470–1489. doi:10.1002/hbm.21299.
35. Helt M, Kelley E, Kinsbourne M, Pandey J, Boorstein H, et al. (2008) Can children with autism recover? If so, how? Neuropsychol Rev 18: 339–366. doi:10.1007/s11065-008-9075-9.
36. Hesslinger B, Tebartz van Elst L, Thiel T, Haegele K, Hennig J, et al. (2002) Frontoorbital volume reductions in adult patients with attention deficit hyperactivity disorder. Neurosci Lett 328: 319–321.
37. Amaral DG, Schumann CM, Nordahl CW (2008) Neuroanatomy of autism. Trends Neurosci 31: 137–145. doi:10.1016/j.tins.2007.12.005.
38. Piven J, Arndt S, Bailey J, Andreasen N (1996) Regional brain enlargement in autism: a magnetic resonance imaging study. J Am Acad Child Adolesc Psychiatry 35: 530–536. doi:10.1097/00004583-199604000-00020.
39. Brieber S, Neufang S, Bruning N, Kamp-Becker I, Remschmidt H, et al. (2007) Structural brain abnormalities in adolescents with autism spectrum disorder and patients with attention deficit/hyperactivity disorder. J Child Psychol Psychiatry 48: 1251–1258. doi:10.1111/j.1469-7610.2007.01799.x.
40. Nijmeijer JS, Hoekstra PJ, Minderaa RB, Buitelaar JK, Altink ME, et al. (2009) PDD symptoms in ADHD, an independent familial trait? J Abnorm Child Psychol 37: 443–453. doi:10.1007/s10802-008-9282-0.
41. Müller UC, Asherson P, Banaschewski T, Buitelaar JK, Ebstein RP, et al. (2011) The impact of study design and diagnostic approach in a large multi-centre ADHD study. Part 1: ADHD symptom patterns. BMC Psychiatry 11: 54. doi:10.1186/1471-244X-11-54.
42. Müller UC, Asherson P, Banaschewski T, Buitelaar JK, Ebstein RP, et al. (2011) The impact of study design and diagnostic approach in a large multi-centre ADHD study: Part 2: Dimensional measures of psychopathology and intelligence. BMC Psychiatry 11: 55. doi:10.1186/1471-244X-11-55.
43. Kaufman J, Birmaher B, Brent D, Rao U, Flynn C, et al. (1997) Schedule for Affective Disorders and Schizophrenia for School-Age Children-Present and Lifetime Version (K-SADS-PL): initial reliability and validity data. J Am Acad Child Adolesc Psychiatry 36: 980–988. doi:10.1097/00004583-199707000-00021.
44. Hartman CA, Luteijn E, Serra M, Minderaa R (2006) Refinement of the Children's Social Behavior Questionnaire (CSBQ): an instrument that describes the diverse problems seen in milder forms of PDD. J Autism Dev Disord 36: 325–342. doi:10.1007/s10803-005-0072-z.
45. Luteijn EF, Serra M, Jackson S, Steenhuis MP, Althaus M, et al. (2000) How unspecified are disorders of children with a pervasive developmental disorder not otherwise specified? A study of social problems in children with PDD-NOS and ADHD. Eur Child Adolesc Psychiatry 9: 168–179.
46. Nijmeijer JS, Arias-Vásquez A, Rommelse NNJ, Altink ME, Buschgens CJM, et al. (2014) Quantitative Linkage for Autism Spectrum Disorders Symptoms in Attention-Deficit/Hyperactivity Disorder: Significant Locus on Chromosome 7q11. J Autism Dev Disord. doi:10.1007/s10803-014-2039-4.
47. Jaspers M, de Winter AF, Buitelaar JK, Verhulst FC, Reijneveld SA, et al. (2012) Early Childhood Assessments of Community Pediatric Professionals Predict Autism Spectrum and Attention Deficit Hyperactivity Problems. Journal of abnormal child psychology. doi:10.1007/s10802-012-9653-4.
48. Greaves-Lord K, Eussen MLJM, Verhulst FC, Minderaa RB, Mandy W, et al. (2013) Empirically based phenotypic profiles of children with pervasive developmental disorders: interpretation in the light of the DSM-5. J Autism Dev Disord 43: 1784–1797. doi:10.1007/s10803-012-1724-4.
49. Geluk CAML, Jansen LMC, Vermeiren R, Doreleijers TAH, van Domburgh L, et al. (2012) Autistic symptoms in childhood arrestees: longitudinal association with delinquent behavior. J Child Psychol Psychiatry 53: 160–167. doi:10.1111/j.1469-7610.2011.02456.x.
50. Rommelse NNJ, Geurts HM, Franke B, Buitelaar JK, Hartman CA (2011) A review on cognitive and brain endophenotypes that may be common in autism spectrum disorder and attention-deficit/hyperactivity disorder and facilitate the search for pleiotropic genes. Neurosci Biobehav Rev 35: 1363–1396. doi:10.1016/j.neubiorev.2011.02.015.
51. Geurts HM, Luman M, van Meel CS (2008) What's in a game: the effect of social motivation on interference control in boys with ADHD and autism spectrum disorders. J Child Psychol Psychiatry 49: 848–857. doi:10.1111/j.1469-7610.2008.01916.x.
52. Krug DA, Arick J, Almond P (1980) Behavior checklist for identifying severely handicapped individuals with high levels of autistic behavior. J Child Psychol Psychiatry 21: 221–229.
53. De Bildt A, Mulder EJ, Hoekstra PJ, van Lang NDJ, Minderaa RB, et al. (2009) Validity of the Children's Social Behavior Questionnaire (CSBQ) in children with intellectual disability: comparing the CSBQ with ADI-R, ADOS, and clinical DSM-IV-TR classification. J Autism Dev Disord 39: 1464–1470. doi:10.1007/s10803-009-0764-x.
54. 't Hart-Kerkhoffs LA, Jansen LM, Doreleijers TA, Vermeiren R, Minderaa RB, et al. (2009) Autism spectrum disorder symptoms in juvenile suspects of sex offenses. J Clin Psychiatry 70: 266–272.
55. Ashburner J, Friston KJ (2005) Unified segmentation. Neuroimage 26: 839–851. doi:10.1016/j.neuroimage.2005.02.018.
56. R Development Core Team (2010) R: A Language and Environment for Statistical Computing. Vienna, Austria: R Foundation for Statistical Computing. Available: http://www.R-project.org.
57. Bates D, Maechler M, Bolker B (n.d.) lme4: Linear Mixed-Effects Models Using S4 Classes. Available: http://CRAN.R-project.org/package = lme4.
58. Anderson D.R, Burnham K.P. (2002) Model selection and multimodel inference: a practical information-theoretic approach. 2nd Edition. New York, New York, USA: Springer-Verlag. 488 p.
59. Akaike H (1979) A Bayesian extension of the minimum AIC procedure of autoregressive model fitting. Biometrika 66: 237–242. doi:10.1093/biomet/66.2.237.
60. Crawley MJ (2007) The R Book. Available: http://onlinelibrary.wiley.com/book/10.1002/9780470515075. Accessed 31 August 2012.
61. O'Dwyer L, Lamberton F, Matura S, Tanner C, Scheibe M, et al. (2012) Reduced Hippocampal Volume in Healthy Young ApoE4 Carriers: An MRI Study. PLoS ONE 7: e48895. doi:10.1371/journal.pone.0048895.
62. Van der Meer JMJ, Oerlemans AM, van Steijn DJ, Lappenschaar MGA, de Sonneville LMJ, et al. (2012) Are autism spectrum disorder and attention-deficit/hyperactivity disorder different manifestations of one overarching disorder? Cognitive and symptom evidence from a clinical and population-based sample. J Am Acad Child Adolesc Psychiatry 51: 1160–1172.e3. doi:10.1016/j.jaac.2012.08.024.
63. Mulligan A, Anney RJL, O'Regan M, Chen W, Butler L, et al. (2009) Autism symptoms in Attention-Deficit/Hyperactivity Disorder: a familial trait which correlates with conduct, oppositional defiant, language and motor disorders. J Autism Dev Disord 39: 197–209. doi:10.1007/s10803-008-0621-3.
64. Courchesne E, Campbell K, Solso S (2011) Brain growth across the life span in autism: Age-specific changes in anatomical pathology. Brain Research 1380: 138–145. doi:10.1016/j.brainres.2010.09.101.
65. Hynd GW, Semrud-Clikeman M, Lorys AR, Novey ES, Eliopulos D (1990) Brain morphology in developmental dyslexia and attention deficit disorder/hyperactivity. Arch Neurol 47: 919–926.
66. Lyoo IK, Noam GG, Lee CK, Lee HK, Kennedy BP, et al. (1996) The corpus callosum and lateral ventricles in children with attention-deficit hyperactivity disorder: a brain magnetic resonance imaging study. Biol Psychiatry 40: 1060–1063.
67. Bussing R, Grudnik J, Mason D, Wasiak M, Leonard C (2002) ADHD and conduct disorder: an MRI study in a community sample. World J Biol Psychiatry 3: 216–220.
68. Durston S, Hulshoff Pol HE, Schnack HG, Buitelaar JK, Steenhuis MP, et al. (2004) Magnetic resonance imaging of boys with attention-deficit/hyperactivity disorder and their unaffected siblings. J Am Acad Child Adolesc Psychiatry 43: 332–340.
69. Happé F, Booth R, Charlton R, Hughes C (2006) Executive function deficits in autism spectrum disorders and attention-deficit/hyperactivity disorder: examining profiles across domains and ages. Brain Cogn 61: 25–39. doi:10.1016/j.bandc.2006.03.004.
70. Howlin P, Mawhood L, Rutter M (2000) Autism and developmental receptive language disorder–a follow-up comparison in early adult life. II: Social, behavioural, and psychiatric outcomes. J Child Psychol Psychiatry 41: 561–578.
71. Seltzer MM, Shattuck P, Abbeduto L, Greenberg JS (2004) Trajectory of development in adolescents and adults with autism. Mental Retardation and Developmental Disabilities Research Reviews 10: 234–247. doi:10.1002/mrdd.20038.
72. Langen M, Schnack HG, Nederveen H, Bos D, Lahuis BE, et al. (2009) Changes in the developmental trajectories of striatum in autism. Biol Psychiatry 66: 327–333. doi:10.1016/j.biopsych.2009.03.017.
73. Grahn JA, Parkinson JA, Owen AM (2009) The role of the basal ganglia in learning and memory: Neuropsychological studies. Behavioural Brain Research 199: 53–60. doi:10.1016/j.bbr.2008.11.020.
74. Schultz W, Tremblay L, Hollerman JR (2000) Reward processing in primate orbitofrontal cortex and basal ganglia. Cereb Cortex 10: 272–284.
75. Heimer L (2003) A new anatomical framework for neuropsychiatric disorders and drug abuse. Am J Psychiatry 160: 1726–1739.
76. Divac I, Rosvold HE, Szwarcbart MK (1967) Behavioral effects of selective ablation of the caudate nucleus. J Comp Physiol Psychol 63: 184–190.
77. Stettner LJ, Schultz WJ (1967) Brain lesions in birds: effects on discrimination acquisition and reversal. Science 155: 1689–1692.
78. Kirkby RJ (1969) Caudate nucleus lesions and perseverative behavior. Physiology & Behavior 4: 451–454. doi:10.1016/0031-9384(69)90135-8.

79. Thompson RL (1959) Effects of lesions in the caudate nuclei and dorsofrontal cortex on conditioned avoidance behavior in cats. J Comp Physiol Psychol 52: 650–659.
80. Esbensen AJ, Seltzer MM, Lam KSL, Bodfish JW (2009) Age-related differences in restricted repetitive behaviors in autism spectrum disorders. J Autism Dev Disord 39: 57–66. doi:10.1007/s10803-008-0599-x.
81. Taylor JL, Seltzer MM (2010) Changes in the autism behavioral phenotype during the transition to adulthood. J Autism Dev Disord 40: 1431–1446. doi:10.1007/s10803-010-1005-z.
82. Dosenbach NUF, Nardos B, Cohen AL, Fair DA, Power JD, et al. (2010) Prediction of individual brain maturity using fMRI. Science 329: 1358–1361. doi:10.1126/science.1194144.
83. Pfefferbaum A, Mathalon DH, Sullivan EV, Rawles JM, Zipursky RB, et al. (1994) A quantitative magnetic resonance imaging study of changes in brain morphology from infancy to late adulthood. Arch Neurol 51: 874–887.
84. Asato MR, Terwilliger R, Woo J, Luna B (2010) White matter development in adolescence: a DTI study. Cereb Cortex 20: 2122–2131. doi:10.1093/cercor/bhp282.
85. Kleinhans NM, Pauley G, Richards T, Neuhaus E, Martin N, et al. (2012) Age-related abnormalities in white matter microstructure in autism spectrum disorders. Brain Res 1479: 1–16. doi:10.1016/j.brainres.2012.07.056.
86. Dawson G (2008) Early behavioral intervention, brain plasticity, and the prevention of autism spectrum disorder. Development and Psychopathology 20: 775–803. doi:10.1017/S0954579408000370.
87. Scarpa A, Reyes NM (2011) Improving Emotion Regulation with CBT in Young Children with High Functioning Autism Spectrum Disorders: A Pilot Study. Behavioural and Cognitive Psychotherapy 39: 495–500. doi:10.1017/S1352465811000063.
88. Sze KM, Wood JJ (2008) Enhancing CBT for the Treatment of Autism Spectrum Disorders and Concurrent Anxiety. Behavioural and Cognitive Psychotherapy 36. Available: http://www.journals.cambridge.org/abstract_S1352465808004384. Accessed 10 March 2014.
89. Shea S, Turgay A, Carroll A, Schulz M, Orlik H, et al. (2004) Risperidone in the Treatment of Disruptive Behavioral Symptoms in Children With Autistic and Other Pervasive Developmental Disorders. Pediatrics 114: e634–e641. doi:10.1542/peds.2003-0264-F.
90. Hollander E, Novotny S, Hanratty M, Yaffe R, DeCaria CM, et al. (2003) Oxytocin infusion reduces repetitive behaviors in adults with autistic and Asperger's disorders. Neuropsychopharmacology 28: 193–198. doi:10.1038/sj.npp.1300021.
91. Matson JL, Nebel-Schwalm MS (2007) Comorbid psychopathology with autism spectrum disorder in children: an overview. Res Dev Disabil 28: 341–352. doi:10.1016/j.ridd.2005.12.004.

Relative Influence of Genetics and Shared Environment on Child Mental Health Symptoms Depends on Comorbidity

Matthew K. Vendlinski[1◑], Kristin N. Javaras[1◑], Carol A. Van Hulle[1], Kathryn Lemery-Chalfant[2], Rose Maier[3], Richard J. Davidson[1], H. Hill Goldsmith[1*]

1 Department of Psychology and Waisman Center, University of Wisconsin–Madison, Madison, Wisconsin, United States of America, **2** Department of Psychology, Arizona State University, Tempe, Arizona, United States of America, **3** Department of Psychology, University of Oregon, Eugene, Oregon, United States of America

Abstract

Background: Comorbidity among childhood mental health symptoms is common in clinical and community samples and should be accounted for when investigating etiology. We therefore aimed to uncover latent classes of mental health symptoms in middle childhood in a community sample, and to determine the latent genetic and environmental influences on those classes.

Methods: The sample comprised representative cohorts of twins. A questionnaire-based assessment of mental health symptoms was used in latent class analyses. Data on 3223 twins (1578 boys and 1645 girls) with a mean age of 7.5 years were analyzed. The sample was predominantly non-Hispanic Caucasian (92.1%).

Results: Latent class models delineated groups of children according to symptom profiles–not necessarily clinical groups but groups representing the general population, most with scores in the normative range. The best-fitting models suggested 9 classes for both girls and boys. Eight of the classes were very similar across sexes; these classes ranged from a "Low Symptom" class to a "Moderately Internalizing & Severely Externalizing" class. In addition, a "Moderately Anxious" class was identified for girls but not boys, and a "Severely Impulsive & Inattentive" class was identified for boys but not girls. Sex-combined analyses implicated moderate genetic influences for all classes. Shared environmental influences were moderate for the "Low Symptom" and "Moderately Internalizing & Severely Externalizing" classes, and small to zero for other classes.

Conclusions: We conclude that symptom classes are largely similar across sexes in middle childhood. Heritability was moderate for all classes, but shared environment played a greater role for classes in which no one type of symptom predominated.

Editor: Stacey Cherny, University of Hong Kong, Hong Kong

Funding: This work was supported by research grants from the National Institute of Mental Health including R01 MH59785 and R37 MH50560 (to Goldsmith and Lemery-Chalfant), the Wisconsin Center for Affective Science (P50 MH069315), and a Conte Neuroscience Center (P50 MH084051, Center Director, Davidson). Infrastructure support was provided by the Waisman Center via a core grant from the National Institute of Child Health and Human Development (P30 HD03352). The funders had no role in study design, data collection and analysis, decision to publish, or preparation of the manuscript.

Competing Interests: The authors have declared that no competing interests exist.

* Email: hhgoldsm@wisc.edu

◑ These authors contributed equally to this work.

Introduction

Patterns of family resemblance for psychopathology shed important light on its etiology. Although research on family resemblance for child and adolescent psychopathology has lagged behind that for adults, relevant findings regarding the former have recently begun to come into focus. For instance, Burt's (2009) [1] recent meta-analysis of etiological influences on child and adolescent psychopathology allows for some broad generalizations. This meta-analysis included both twin and adoption studies of the etiology of conduct problems, oppositional defiant problems, attention-deficit/hyperactivity disorder (ADHD) symptoms, depression, and anxiety. Across all of these domains of psychopathology, genetic influences account for the largest proportion of variance, followed by unique (to each co-twin) environmental influences, and then shared (by both co-twins) environmental influences, although the limited role for shared environment may be partly an artifact of methodology [2,3]. Notably, the contribution of genetic factors is slightly higher for externalizing problems (i.e., conduct problems, oppositional defiant problems,

ADHD symptoms) than internalizing problems (i.e., depression and anxiety), whereas the contribution of non-shared environmental factors is slightly higher for internalizing problems than externalizing problems. However, one factor that limits these generalizations is the lack of consideration for comorbidity of symptoms from different domains.

Comorbidity between different types of mental health problems is common in childhood and adolescence [4–6]. One meta-analysis examining the comorbidity of depression, overanxiousness, conduct disorder (CD), and ADHD in childhood and adolescence found that every possible two-way combination of these disorders occurred at a rate well above chance [4]. These results derive from population-based samples; rates of comorbidity are typically even higher in clinical samples [7].

Despite the ubiquity of comorbidity, most studies of the latent genetic and environmental influences on childhood mental health symptoms have ignored comorbidity and focused on only one disorder or symptom scale. A few studies have included two disorders or symptom scales [8,9]. Most relevant to our focus here, several studies have examined latent genetic and environmental influences on broadband internalizing/externalizing factors underlying multiple disorders [10–12]. These studies, which examine common (to all disorders or factors) and specific (to one disorder or factor) latent genetic and environmental influences, suggest that the relative contributions of these influences differ depending on whether symptoms/disorders occur in isolation or in combination. For example, these studies found that shared environment was implicated in common but not specific influences on internalizing and externalizing problems in five-year-old twins [11] and in five- to nine-year-old twins [10], although the role of shared environment in comorbid problems may diminish by adolescence [9,10,13]. Similarly, studies of measured genetic [14] and measured environmental [15] influences also suggest that results depend on the presence of comorbidity.

In contrast to the internalizing/externalizing factor approach to addressing comorbidity between multiple symptom domains, latent class analysis (LCA) is a person-centered approach that can be used to identify individuals with similar symptom profiles across multiple symptom domains [16]. Since LCA profiles differ in elevation and shape, LCA makes it possible to investigate etiological influences on different levels, and different combinations, of symptoms. Previous studies using LCA to characterize covariation among common mental health problems uncovered latent classes differentiated by the type and the severity of symptoms [17–19]. When symptoms of depression, anxiety, CD, oppositional defiant disorder (ODD), and ADHD are considered, six to eight latent classes are typically identified, and individual classes rarely map directly onto a single DSM-IV [20] label. For example, one study that used LCA to characterize covariation of ADHD, ODD, CD, and anxiety symptoms identified six common symptom profiles among 4–11 year olds [17]. These symptom profiles included a group of children with very few symptoms; a group with mild symptoms of inattention, ODD, CD, and anxiety; a group with moderate symptoms of inattention, impulsivity, ODD, CD, and anxiety; a group with moderate symptoms of impulsivity, ODD, and CD; a group with severe symptoms of inattention, impulsivity, ODD, CD, and anxiety; and a group with severe symptoms of inattention, impulsivity, ODD, and CD. Although some LCA studies have used twins and have included a range of symptoms (e.g., [18]), few attempted to estimate the heritability of class membership,. Our study moves this body of research forward by characterizing etiological influences on both symptom type and symptom level through genetic/environmental analyses of latent class results. Further, our approach affords the opportunity to estimate genetic and environmental contributions to the absence of psychopathology, as indicated by low symptom levels across multiple symptom domains.

Our aims were twofold. First, we used LCA to characterize typical symptom profiles in middle childhood using symptoms of depression, separation anxiety, overanxiousness, conduct disorder, oppositional defiant disorder, and ADHD. Our aim was *not* to suggest an alternative to current or proposed diagnostic nosology; rather, we sought to examine symptom patterns in the broader population and whether these patterns appear to be similar across boys and girls. Second, we estimated the extent to which latent genetic and environmental influences contributed as sources of variation in these patterns, with equal emphasis on normative and more clinical patterns, the latter of which describe fewer children.

Methods

Participants and Procedure

Data came from a birth-record-based sample of twins born in the state of Wisconsin beginning in 1989 [21,22]. Of families with infant twins, approximately 65% of those we attempted to contact, whether contact was ever made or not, agreed to participate. As twins approached seven years of age, we attempted to recruit all families for the middle childhood phase of data collection, with funding being the only constraint on recruitment (i.e., we did not select twins for follow-up based on their characteristics). Approximately 78% of the families agreed to participate, and caregivers were administered questionnaires over the telephone assessing demographic characteristics, twin zygosity, and child health and behavior. Child health and behavior were assessed using the MacArthur Health and Behavior Questionnaire (HBQ) [23,24], which includes questions assessing DSM-defined symptoms. Parents of the children provided written informed consent following appropriate ethical guidelines, and the protocol was approved by the Social and Behavioral Sciences IRB at the University of Wisconsin–Madison.

We performed latent class analyses on child behavior items (i.e., DSM-defined symptoms) from the HBQ. Concurrent and predictive validity for the LCA results was provided by additional measures (referred to as 'external covariates') administered during ('concurrent') and shortly after ('subsequent') the middle childhood phase. The concurrent external covariates include demographic information and information on impairment from the HBQ. The subsequent external covariates include diagnoses from a diagnostic interview administered to mothers during a follow-up to the middle childhood assessment; the follow-up occurred when children were 8 years old on average (SD = .87 years). By design, 40% of the middle childhood sample participated in the follow-up.

We included 3223 twins (boys = 1578; girls = 1645) with mostly complete HBQ data in latent class analyses because we wanted the classes to be based on as broad a sample of the population as possible. In the LCA sample, the mean age was 7.5 years (SD = .92), and 92.1% of the children were non-Hispanic Caucasian. (Primary caregivers classified the race and ethnicity of children using options provided by study investigators.) Before performing the external covariate and genetic/environmental analyses for the resulting latent classes, we removed 35 boys and 12 girls with developmental disorder diagnoses (primarily autism) or major medical problems (e.g., spina bifida) because behavioral problems in these participants might have a different etiology than in the rest of the sample. Thus, the external covariate analyses included 1543 male and 1633 female twins, although demographics were available for approximately 85–90% and follow-up diagnoses were available only for approximately 40% (mostly by

Table 1. Class descriptions and probabilities of class membership for best-fitting latent class models.

Class	Brief Class Description	Detailed Class Description	Probability of Class Membership
Girls			
G1	Mildly Anxious	Mildly Anxious, Mildly Oppositional, Mildly Impulsive	0.16
G2	Moderately Oppositional	Mildly Anxious, Mildly Impulsive, Moderately Oppositional	0.15
G3	Moderately Impulsive & Inattentive	Mildly Anxious, Moderately Oppositional, Moderately Impulsive, Moderately Inattentive	0.14
G4	Moderately Anxious	Moderately Anxious, Mildly Oppositional, Mildly Impulsive, Mildly Inattentive	0.12
G5	Low Symptom	Low Symptom	0.11
G6	Mildly Oppositional & Impulsive	Mildly Oppositional, Mildly Impulsive, Mildly Inattentive	0.11
G7	Moderately Anxious & non-Conduct Externalizing	Mildly Depressed, Moderately Anxious, Moderately Oppositional, Moderately Impulsive, Moderately Inattentive	0.09
G8	Moderately Externalizing	Mildly Depressed, Mildly Anxious, Moderate Conduct Problems, Severely Oppositional, Moderately Impulsive, Moderately Inattentive	0.08
G9	Moderately Internalizing & Severely Externalizing	Moderately Depressed, Moderately Anxious, Moderate Conduct Problems, Severely Oppositional, Severely Impulsive, Severely Inattentive	0.04
Boys			
B1	Low Symptom	Low Symptom	0.17
B2	Mildly Oppositional & Impulsive	Mildly Oppositional, Mildly Impulsive	0.17
B3	Moderately Impulsive & Inattentive	Mildly Oppositional, Moderately Impulsive, Moderately Inattentive	0.13
B4	Mildly Anxious	Mildly Anxious, Mildly Oppositional, Mildly Impulsive	0.13
B5	Moderately Oppositional	Mildly Anxious, Moderately Oppositional, Moderately Impulsive	0.11
B6	Moderately Anxious & non-Conduct Externalizing	Moderately Anxious, Moderately Oppositional, Moderately Impulsive, Moderately Inattentive	0.10
B7	Moderately Externalizing	Mildly Depressed, Mildly Anxious, Moderate Conduct Problems, Severely Oppositional, Moderately Impulsive, Moderately Inattentive	0.08
B8	Severely Impulsive & Inattentive	Mildly Depressed, Mildly Anxious, Mild Conduct Problems, Moderately Oppositional, Severely Impulsive, Severely Inattentive	0.06
B9	Moderately Internalizing & Severely Externalizing	Moderately Depressed, Moderately Anxious, Moderate Conduct Problems, Severely Oppositional, Severely Impulsive, Severely Inattentive	0.05

design, as described above). In the genetic/environmental analyses, we excluded twins whose zygosity was unclear, as well as twins who did not have a cotwin who could be included (i.e., due to missing data, developmental disorder, or major medical problem). The resulting sample for genetic/environmental analyses included 256 monozygotic (MZ) and 267 dizygotic (DZ) male twin pairs, 318 MZ and 240 DZ female twin pairs, and 479 opposite-sex DZ twin pairs.

Measures

Zygosity. Zygosity was established via the 32-item Zygosity Questionnaire for Young Twins [25], which measures aspects of physical similarity, confusion of twins, and medical information (e.g., chorionicity), and which yields >95% agreement with genotyping [26]. A follow-up with other zygosity determination procedures, including genotyping, was used for a portion of the twins.

Socioeconomic Status. We assessed socioeconomic status (SES) using caregiver report of maternal and paternal educational attainment and gross annual family income. On average, mothers had 14.9 years (SD = 2.3) of education whereas fathers had 14.6 (SD = 2.6) years. The distribution of annual family incomes was as follows: 4.5% below $20,000, 6.5% between $20,001 and $30,000, 23.7% between $30,001 and $50,000, 23.5% between $50,001 and $70,000, 17.4% between $70,001 and $90,000, and 24.4% above $90,001.

Mental Health Problems (Middle Childhood Assessment). Primary caregivers (approximately 98% mothers and 2% fathers) reported child mental health symptoms and associated functional impairment exhibited during the previous six months via the HBQ. Caregivers rated whether statements

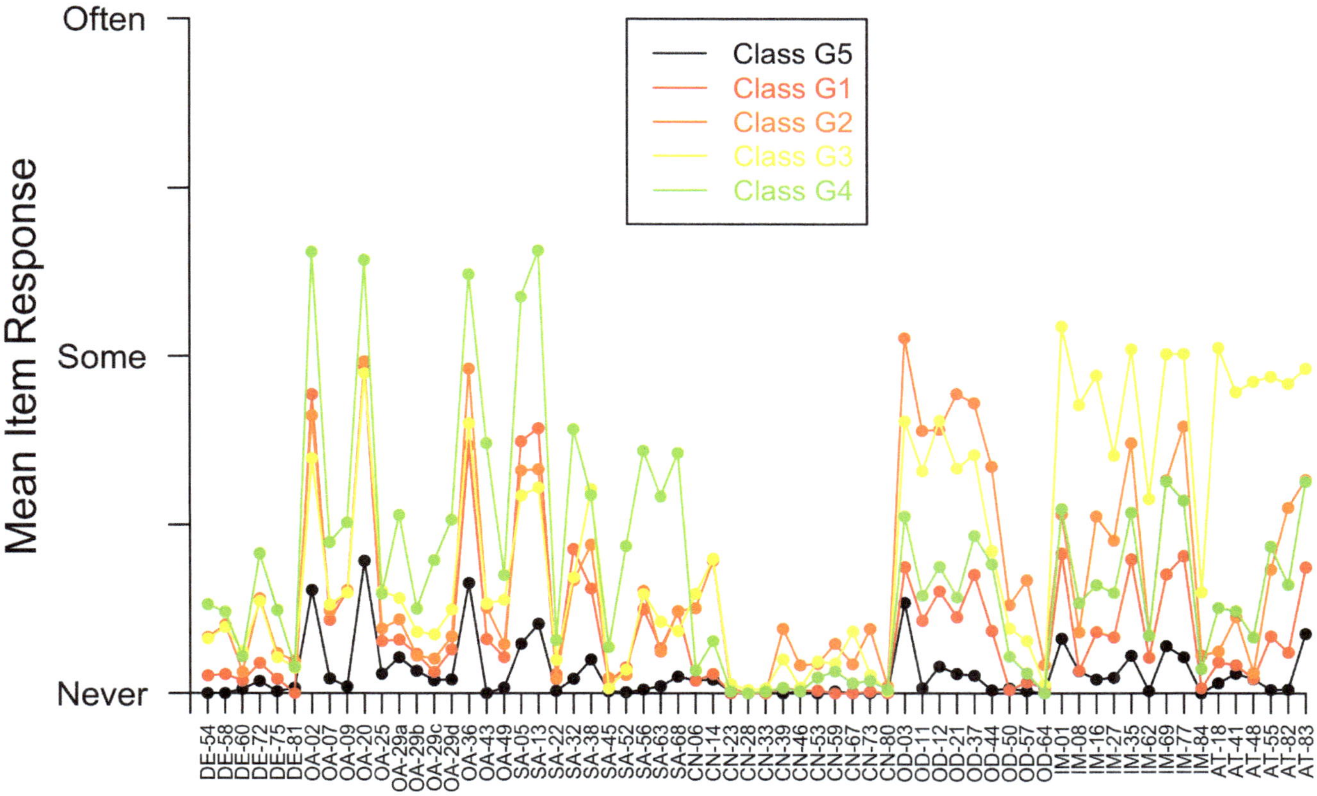
Often
Some
Never
Mean Item Response
Class G5
Class G1
Class G2
Class G3
Class G4
DE-54 DE-58 DE-60 DE-72 DE-75 DE-81 OA-02 OA-07 OA-09 OA-20 OA-25 OA-29a OA-29b OA-29c OA-29d OA-36 OA-43 OA-49 SA-05 SA-13 SA-22 SA-32 SA-38 SA-45 SA-52 SA-56 SA-63 SA-68 CN-06 CN-14 CN-23 CN-28 CN-33 CN-39 CN-46 CN-53 CN-59 CN-67 CN-73 CN-80 OD-03 OD-11 OD-12 OD-21 OD-37 OD-44 OD-50 OD-57 OD-64 IM-01 IM-08 IM-16 IM-27 IM-35 IM-62 IM-69 IM-77 IM-84 AT-18 AT-41 AT-48 AT-55 AT-82 AT-83

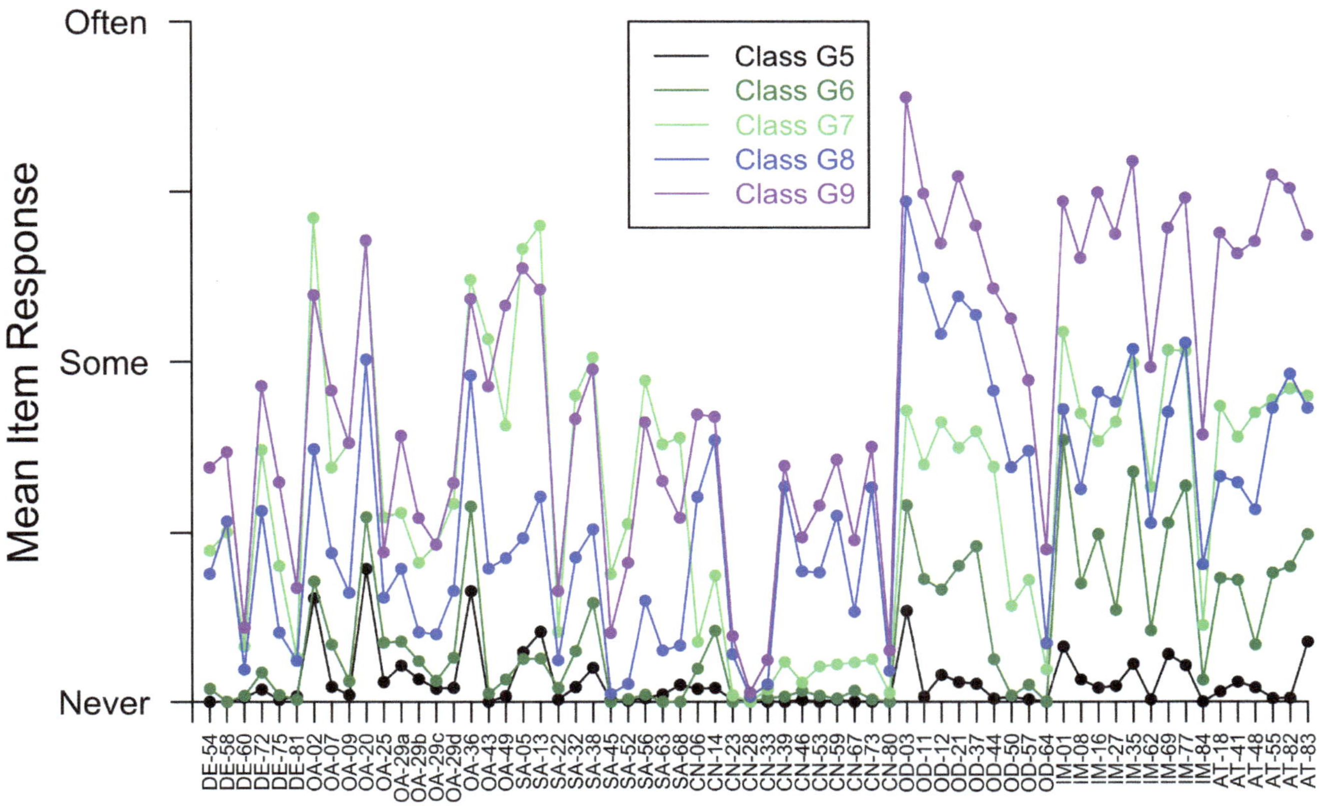
Often
Some
Never
Mean Item Response
Class G5
Class G6
Class G7
Class G8
Class G9
DE-54 DE-58 DE-60 DE-72 DE-75 DE-81 OA-02 OA-07 OA-09 OA-20 OA-25 OA-29a OA-29b OA-29c OA-29d OA-36 OA-43 OA-49 SA-05 SA-13 SA-22 SA-32 SA-38 SA-45 SA-52 SA-56 SA-63 SA-68 CN-06 CN-14 CN-23 CN-28 CN-33 CN-39 CN-46 CN-53 CN-59 CN-67 CN-73 CN-80 OD-03 OD-11 OD-12 OD-21 OD-37 OD-44 OD-50 OD-57 OD-64 IM-01 IM-08 IM-16 IM-27 IM-35 IM-62 IM-69 IM-77 IM-84 AT-18 AT-41 AT-48 AT-55 AT-82 AT-83

Figure 1. Item response plots for girls' latent classes G5 and G1–G4 (upper panel) and girls' latent classes G5 and G6–G9 (lower panel). Abbreviations: DE = Depression; OA = Overanxiousness; SA = Separation Anxiety; CN = Conduct Problems; OD = Oppositional Defiant Problems; IM = Impulsivity; AT = Inattention.

describing DSM-based symptoms were never, somewhat, or often true of their children. Items measuring symptoms of depression (6 items), overanxiousness (12 items), separation anxiety (10 items), conduct problems (12 items), oppositional defiant problems (9 items), impulsivity (9 items), and inattention (6 items) were included in LCA. Caregivers also provided information on the degree to which children were impaired by their symptoms via the Impairment on Self scale (8 items; e.g., "How much trouble has your child had getting along with his/her teacher(s) as a result of the behaviors or behavior problems you identified in the previous section?") and the Impairment on Family scale (8 items); the mean composite scores for these scales were used as external covariates.

Mental Health Problems (Follow-Up to Middle Childhood Assessment). Approximately 6 to 9 months after the middle childhood assessment, DSM-IV diagnoses were obtained for children via caregiver report on the Diagnostic Interview Schedule for Children Version IV (DISC-IV) [27]. Staff administered this fully structured interview during a visit to the family home. We used past year diagnoses generated from the major depressive disorder, generalized anxiety disorder, separation anxiety disorder, conduct disorder, oppositional defiant disorder, and ADHD modules.

Statistical Analysis

We performed LCA, followed by external covariate analyses and genetic/environmental analyses for the best-fitting latent classes. We chose to use LCA–rather than factor mixture models that allow a within-class severity dimension and thus have less restrictive assumptions (e.g., [28,29])–to characterize symptom patterns for conceptual reasons (e.g., patterns with more clinical elevations may not represent merely the extremes of more temperament-based patterns [30]). We conducted LCA separately for boys and girls because previous studies identified important sex differences in the structure of mental health problems [18,31]. Indeed, our own analyses yielded some differences across sexes. We also performed the external covariate analyses separately for boys and girls. However, genetic/environmental analyses were performed after combining boys and girls with similar symptom profiles to increase power. We did not perform genetic/environmental analyses for latent classes that were found for girls only or boys only.

LCA is a type of latent variable modeling that assumes each individual belongs to one of K latent classes, in contrast to latent trait or factor analysis models, which assume that individuals fall along one or more latent continua. In LCA, the manifest variables are also categorical (e.g., ordinal categorical in the case of the HBQ items), and the manifest variables are assumed to be independent within a given class (i.e., assumption of local independence) [32]. The two types of parameters for each latent class are class membership probability, which describes the proportion of individuals falling into that latent class, and item-class parameters characterizing average probabilities of endorsement for each HBQ item for individuals in that latent class. These latter parameters determine the item response (or symptom) profile for the class. Although latent classes in LCA are not assumed to be ordered, finding that the estimated item response profiles for two or more classes have similar patterns differing only in level of endorsement (i.e., severity) suggests those classes are ordered.

To estimate the parameters for each LCA model, we used LatentGOLD software [33], which employs an Expectation Maximization (EM) algorithm [34] to maximize the likelihood for the model. To ensure the EM algorithm found the global maximum of the likelihood for each LCA model, we specified that LatentGold use 1000 sets of random starting values for each fit, and we fitted each model 5 times to ensure that the resulting values of the maximized likelihood were identical. For each sex, we fitted latent class models with K = 1 through K = 11 latent classes. To decide which model fit best for each sex, we selected the model with the lowest Bayesian Information Criterion (BIC) [35]. We also used the bootstrapping function in LatentGOLD to ensure the best-fitting model fit well according to a bootstrapped p-value for the chi-square test because the usual (i.e., non-bootstrapped) p-value may not be valid for data (such as ours) where some combinations of item responses are not observed. Finally, we repeated the procedure just described, but with a family-specific random effect included in each LCA model to account for dependence between cotwins because doing so can give different results regarding the number of classes [36]. For our data, however, BIC results for boys and for girls followed a similar pattern with and without a family-specific random effect. Thus, in all subsequent analyses, we used results from the best-fitting LCA models without a family-specific random effect.

We used item-class parameters for the best-fitting LCA models to plot and describe the item response profiles for each class, for girls and for boys. We describe each class at two levels of detail. To decide on more detailed names, we considered patterns of symptom elevation relative to other classes, in addition to absolute levels. In deciding on less detailed names, which were intended to capture only the most distinctive features of the item response profile for that class, we based names in part on the 10 items with highest endorsement (relative to the "Low Symptom" group) for the class in question. We use the less-detailed names to refer to the classes throughout the text for the sake of brevity.

For the external covariate analyses, we used the probabilities of class membership from the best-fitting LCA models to calculate a weighted average of the external covariates for participants in each class. For each external covariate, we informally compared the various class-specific averages to investigate whether the external covariate varied across the symptom-defined classes as would be expected. For example, we would expect to find the highest levels of self-impairment and family impairment in the moderate and severe symptom classes.

For the genetic/environmental analyses, we used two approaches. In the first approach, we calculated odds ratios (the odds of being in latent class k given that your co-twin is in latent class j divided by the odds of being in latent class k given that your co-twin is not in latent class j) separately for twins of each zygosity, using either the probabilities of class membership for each participant or the modal class assignment (based on the largest probability of class membership for each participant). To calculate the odds ratios and test their significance, we used logistic regression with sex included as a covariate.

In our second approach, we used modal class assignments to fit biometric twin models [37] for membership in each class (but not for cross-class membership). For each class, we used a liability-threshold approach that assumes an unobserved continuous liability for membership in a given class, with membership in

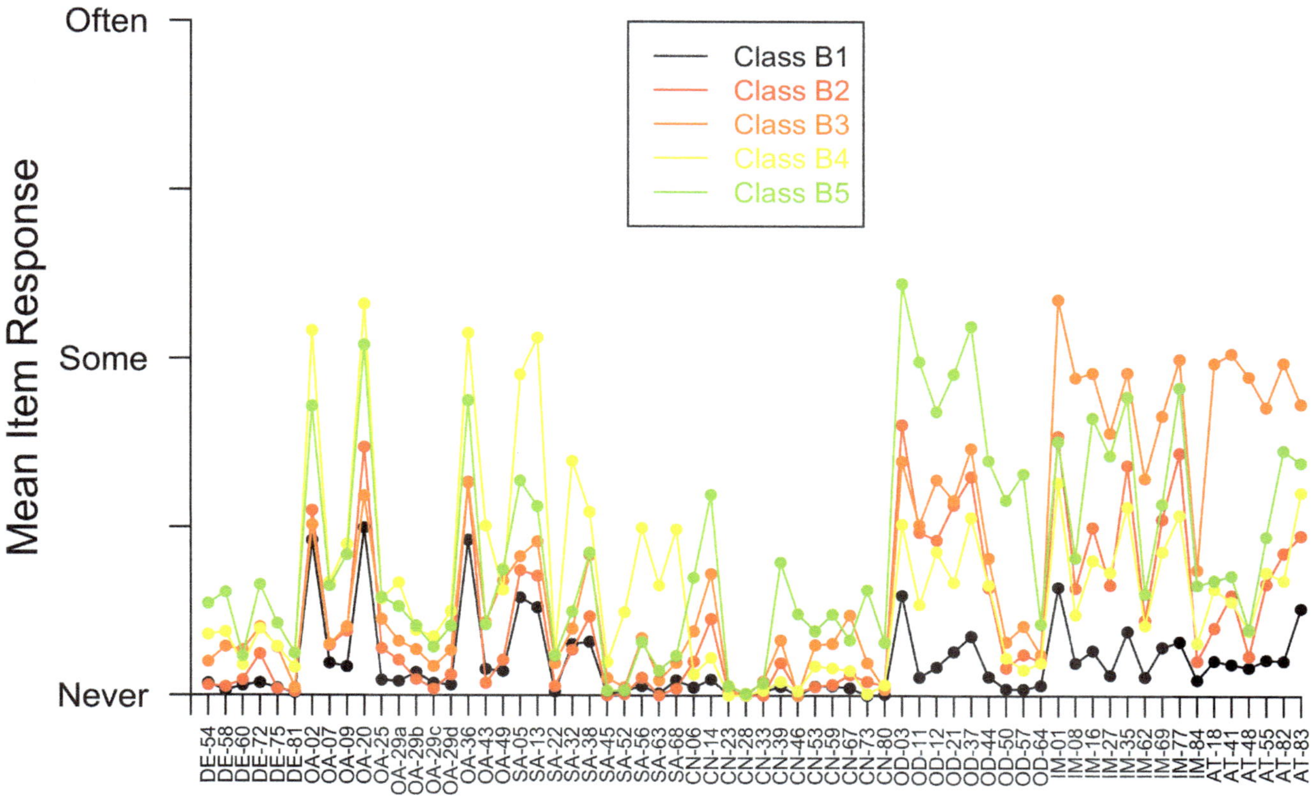
Often
Some
Never
Mean Item Response
Class B1
Class B2
Class B3
Class B4
Class B5
DE-54
DE-58
DE-60
DE-72
DE-75
DE-81
OA-02
OA-07
OA-09
OA-20
OA-25
OA-29a
OA-29b
OA-29c
OA-29d
OA-36
OA-43
OA-49
SA-05
SA-13
SA-22
SA-32
SA-38
SA-45
SA-52
SA-56
SA-63
SA-68
CN-06
CN-14
CN-23
CN-28
CN-33
CN-39
CN-46
CN-53
CN-59
CN-67
CN-73
CN-80
OD-03
OD-11
OD-12
OD-21
OD-37
OD-44
OD-50
OD-57
OD-64
IM-01
IM-08
IM-16
IM-27
IM-35
IM-62
IM-69
IM-77
IM-84
AT-18
AT-41
AT-48
AT-55
AT-82
AT-83

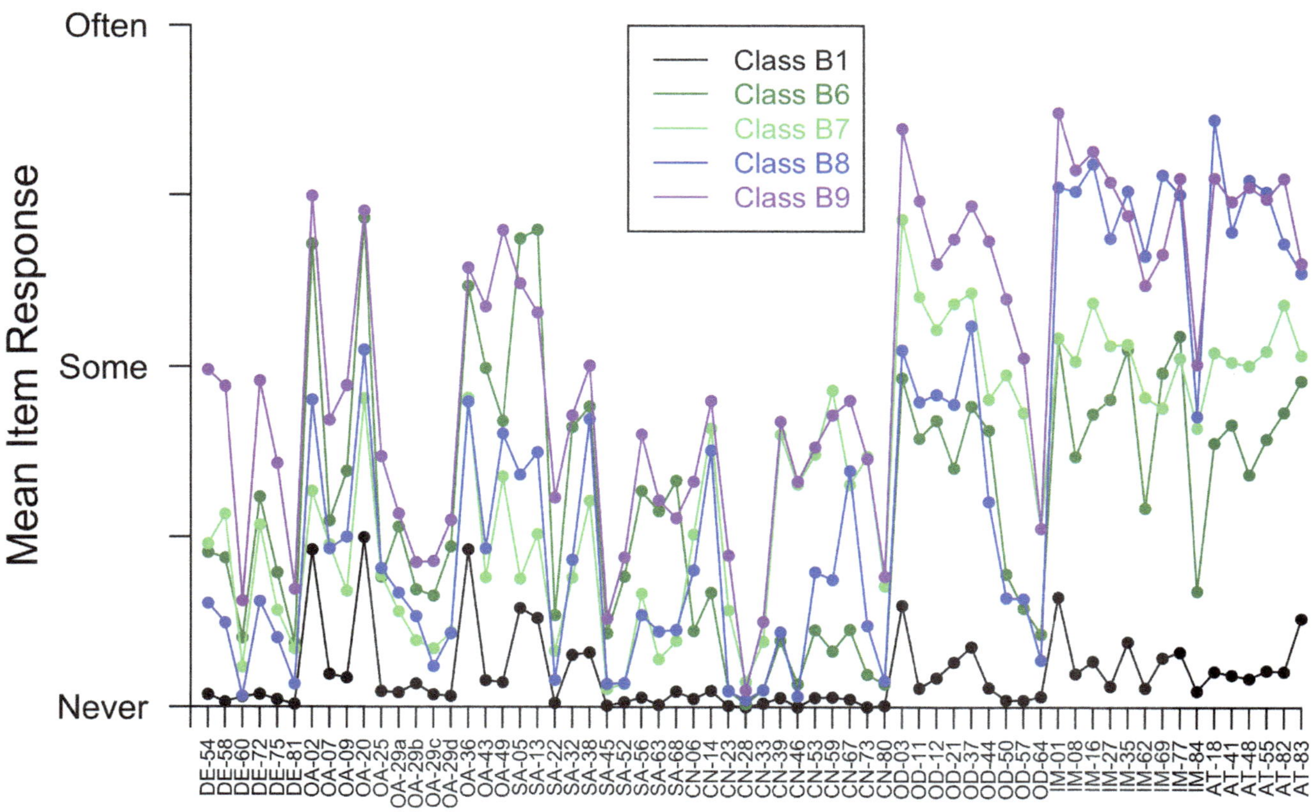
Often
Some
Never
Mean Item Response
Class B1
Class B6
Class B7
Class B8
Class B9
DE-54
DE-58
DE-60
DE-72
DE-75
DE-81
OA-02
OA-07
OA-09
OA-20
OA-25
OA-29a
OA-29b
OA-29c
OA-29d
OA-36
OA-43
OA-49
SA-05
SA-13
SA-22
SA-32
SA-38
SA-45
SA-52
SA-56
SA-63
SA-68
CN-06
CN-14
CN-23
CN-28
CN-33
CN-39
CN-46
CN-53
CN-59
CN-67
CN-73
CN-80
OD-03
OD-11
OD-12
OD-21
OD-37
OD-44
OD-50
OD-57
OD-64
IM-01
IM-08
IM-16
IM-27
IM-35
IM-62
IM-69
IM-77
IM-84
AT-18
AT-41
AT-48
AT-55
AT-82
AT-83

Figure 2. Item response plots for boys' latent classes B1 and B2–B5 (upper panel) and boys' latent classes B1 and B6–B9 (lower panel). Abbreviations: DE = Depression; OA = Overanxiousness; SA = Separation Anxiety; CN = Conduct Problems; OD = Oppositional Defiant Problems; IM = Impulsivity; AT = Inattention.

the class occurring when the liability exceeds a sex-specific threshold corresponding to the prevalence of the class for the relevant sex. To ensure the identification of the model parameters, the liability distribution was assumed to be standard normal [38]. Variation in this liability was decomposed into underlying genetic (A), shared environmental (C), and non-shared environmental (E) variation. Models were fit directly to raw data using the structural equation program Mx [39]. To assess fit of the ACE model for a given latent class, we compared the loglikelihood for the ACE model to the loglikelihood for a saturated model. Under certain conditions, $-2(LL_{ACE}-2LL_{SATURATED})$ follows a chi-square distribution with 2 degrees of freedom.

Results

LCA Results

For girls, BIC was smallest for the 9-class model; further, the bootstrapped p-value from the chi-square test of goodness of fit was 0.35 for the 9-class model, suggesting that this model fit the girls' data well. For boys, BIC was smallest for the 9-class and 10-class models (BIC values for these models were very similar), but we chose the 9-class model for comparability with girls. The bootstrapped p-value from the chi-square test of goodness of fit was 0.33 for the 9-class model, suggesting this model fit the boys' data well. Class names and membership probabilities are presented in Table 1, and symptom profile plots are presented in Figures 1a and 1b for girls and Figures 2a and 2b for boys.

The following 8 classes had remarkably similar profiles across sexes. A "Low Symptom" class, designated G5 for the girls and B1 for the boys in Figures 1a through 2b, showed little elevation across symptoms. Interestingly, this class had the highest probability of class membership for boys (0.17), but the 5th highest for girls (0.11). Two mildly elevated profiles were identified: a "Mildly Anxious" class with slight elevations on overanxiousness and separation anxiety items, and a "Mildly Oppositional & Impulsive" class. Four moderately elevated profiles emerged: a "Moderately Oppositional" class; a "Moderately Impulsive & Inattentive" class; a "Moderately Anxious & non-Conduct Externalizing" class with elevations on overanxiousness, separation anxiety, oppositional, impulsivity, and inattention items; and a "Moderately Externalizing" class with elevations on conduct, oppositional, impulsivity, and inattention items. Finally, a "Moderately Internalizing & Severely Externalizing" class was identified for both sexes. This class showed moderate elevations across depression, overanxiousness, separation anxiety, and conduct items along with more extreme elevations on oppositional, impulsivity, and inattention items. In addition to these 8 classes, a "Moderately Anxious" class was identified in girls but not boys, and a "Severely Impulsive & Inattentive" class was found for boys but not girls. Next, we turn to analyses that expand upon the meaning of these classes.

External Covariates

Class-specific averages of parental education, family income, impairment, and DISC-IV diagnoses are presented in Table 2 (girls) and Table 3 (boys). These averages follow expected patterns, providing external support for the validity of the LCA results. With regard to concurrent validity, self and family impairment scores are highest in the two classes ("Moderately Externalizing" and "Moderately Internalizing & Severely Externalizing") most elevated on externalizing items for both sexes. Similarly, parental education and family income are lowest in theses same two most symptomatic class for both sexes, particularly for classes G9 and B9.

With regard to predictive validity, the proportion of children subsequently diagnosed with conduct disorder was highest in the most symptomatic class. For boys, the three classes with the highest levels of impulsivity and inattention ("Moderately Externalizing," "Severely Impulsive & Inattentive," and "Moderately Internalizing & Severely Externalizing") predict the highest rates of subsequent ADHD diagnoses. For girls, the three classes with the largest elevations on overanxiousness and separation anxiety items ("Moderately Anxious," "Moderately Anxious & non-Conduct Externalizing," and "Moderately Internalizing & Severely Externalizing") are at greatest risk for subsequent separation anxiety diagnoses. Thus, membership in more symptomatic latent classes (based on the HBQ) predicts later diagnoses of a similar nature (based on the DISC-IV).

Genetic/Environmental Analyses

The monozygotic and dizygotic twin odds ratios based on class probabilities (see Table S1 and Table S2) were very similar to those based on modal class assignment (see Table S3 and Table S4). Their similarity suggests fitting biometric twin models to modal class assignments will produce valid estimates of additive genetic (A), shared, or common, environmental (C), and non-shared, or unique, environmental (E) variance, even though modal class assignments ignore some of the information contained in the class probabilities.

Estimates and corresponding confidence intervals for A, C, and E from the biometric twin models are presented in Table 4. The estimates of genetic variance are moderate (approximately 0.30 to 0.50) for all classes. In addition, the estimates of shared environmental variance are moderate for the "Low Symptom" and "Moderately Internalizing & Severely Externalizing" classes, small for the "Moderately Anxious & non-Conduct Externalizing" and "Moderately Externalizing" classes, and zero for the other classes. The width of the confidence intervals suggests that we did not have sufficient power to test whether the variance components differed from zero in some cases, especially for the less prevalent classes.

Discussion

Latent class analyses of common mental health symptoms measured in middle childhood revealed nine distinct profiles of problems for boys and for girls. These profiles reflect symptomatology only, unlike classifications based on DSM-IV diagnoses, which require that symptoms be accompanied by clinically significant impairment. Eight of the profiles were very similar for both sexes. A "Low Symptom" class with almost no problems emerged for both sexes. For the remaining classes, all items were endorsed more frequently than in the "Low Symptom" class, but certain items had more extreme elevations. Two mildly elevated classes were identified: a mildly anxious class and a mildly disruptive class. Four moderately elevated classes were identified: three that encompassed largely disruptive symptoms and one that encompassed both anxious and disruptive symptoms. The mildly

Table 2. Weighted[a] averages of external covariates for girls, by latent class.

		Demographics (Concurrent)			Impairment (Concurrent)		Diagnoses (Subsequent)						
		Maternal Education (yrs)	Paternal Education (yrs)	Family Income Category[b]	Self Impair-Ment[c]	Family Impair-Ment[c]	MDD (%)	GAD (%)	SAD (%)	CD (%)	ODD (%)	ADHD (%)	Any Diag-nosis[d] (%)
G1	Mildly Anxious	14.9	14.9	10.7	0.05	0.05	0.9	0.0	2.9	0.0	3.0	0.0	6.8
G2	Moderately Oppositional	15.1	14.8	10.9	0.17	0.14	0.2	0.0	0.3	2.6	4.7	0.3	8.0
G3	Moderately Impulsive & Inattentive	14.9	14.4	10.4	0.17	0.17	0.0	0.0	2.2	0.1	3.3	16.6	22.1
G4	Moderately Anxious	15.0	14.9	10.4	0.15	0.13	0.0	3.1	9.3	0.0	1.4	0.1	12.3
G5	Low Symptom	14.8	14.8	9.8	0.02	0.01	0.0	0.0	1.0	0.0	1.0	0.0	2.1
G6	Mildly Oppositional & Impulsive	15.2	15.1	10.7	0.07	0.08	1.1	1.1	0.0	0.0	2.4	2.3	4.7
G7	Moderately Anxious & non-Conduct Externalizing	14.3	14.4	10	0.30	0.26	2.4	1.5	20.5	1.5	4.4	6.0	30.4
G8	Moderately Externalizing	15.0	14.7	10.2	0.32	0.31	0.0	0.0	4.7	10.0	19.4	3.9	30.1
G9	Moderately Internalizing & Severely Externalizing	14.2	13.7	8.3	0.59	0.78	3.1	4.5	13.9	11.9	39.2	20.2	62.8

[a]Weighted by class membership probabilities.
[b]Income categories: 8 = \$40,001 to \$45,000; 9 = \$45,001 to \$50,000; 10 = \$50,001 to \$60,000; 11 = \$60,001 to \$70,000; 12 = \$70,001 to \$80,000.
[c]Self Impairment Scale ranges from 0 (no impairment) to 1.9 (highest observed impairment) and Family Impairment Scale ranges from 0 (no impairment) to 2.8 (highest observed impairment).
[d]Any diagnosis refers to a diagnosis of MDD, GAD, SAD, CD, ODD, or ADHD.
Abbreviations: MDD = Major Depressive Disorder; GAD = Generalized Anxiety Disorder; SAD = Separation Anxiety Disorder; CD = Conduct Disorder; ODD = Oppositional Defiant Disorder; ADHD = Attention-Deficit/Hyperactivity Disorder.

Table 3. Weighted[a] averages of external covariates for boys, by latent class.

		Demographics (Concurrent)			Impairment (Concurrent)		Diagnoses (Subsequent)						
		Maternal Education (yrs)	Paternal Education (yrs)	Family Income Category[b]	Self Impairment[c]	Family Impairment[c]	MDD (%)	GAD (%)	SAD (%)	CD (%)	ODD (%)	ADHD (%)	Any Diagnosis[d] (%)
B1	Low Symptom	15.2	15.2	11.0	0.03	0.04	0.0	0.0	0.7	0.6	2.4	1.8	4.9
B2	Mildly Oppositional & Impulsive	15.3	14.9	10.6	0.09	0.10	0.0	0.0	0.1	1.8	3.0	9.0	13.1
B3	Moderately Impulsive & Inattentive	14.9	14.4	10.3	0.19	0.22	0.0	0.0	0.7	3.1	3.6	10.3	16.6
B4	Mildly Anxious	15.0	14.4	10.8	0.11	0.12	0.0	0.0	9.3	3.3	3.7	0.2	16.4
B5	Moderately Oppositional	15.2	14.7	10.8	0.25	0.25	0.0	0.0	1.5	5.8	18.1	8.9	28.6
B6	Moderately Anxious & non-Conduct Externalizing	15.0	14.6	10.2	0.25	0.26	0.0	1.6	13.8	4.6	9.8	16.5	35.4
B7	Moderately Externalizing	14.6	14.0	10.1	0.43	0.52	0.1	0.0	1.8	16	31.4	21.9	49.4
B8	Severely Impulsive & Inattentive	14.6	14.1	10.8	0.31	0.34	3.9	0.0	3.9	5.0	12.7	25.8	39.8
B9	Moderately Internalizing & Severely Externalizing	14.1	13.4	8.4	0.73	0.98	1.9	0.0	11.6	29.3	35.1	21.4	64.3

[a]Weighted by class membership probabilities.
[b]Income categories: 8 = $40,001 to $45,000; 9 = $45,001 to $50,000; 10 = $50,001 to $60,000; 11 = $60,001 to $70,000; 12 = $70,001 to $80,000.
[c]Self Impairment scale ranges from 0 (no impairment) to 1.9 (highest observed impairment) and Family Impairment Scale ranges from 0 (no impairment) to 3.0 (highest observed impairment).
[d]Any diagnosis refers to a diagnosis of MDD, GAD, SAD, CD, ODD, or ADHD.
Abbreviations: MDD = Major Depressive Disorder; GAD = Generalized Anxiety Disorder; SAD = Separation Anxiety Disorder; CD = Conduct Disorder; ODD = Oppositional Defiant Disorder; ADHD = Attention-Deficit/Hyperactivity Disorder.

Table 4. Proportion of variance accounted for (confidence intervals) and model fit of biometric twin models for girls and boys combined.

Girls and Boys Combined	A[a]	C[a]	E[a]	-2LL Sat	-2LL ACE	$\Delta\chi^2$
C1. Mildly Anxious	0.42 (0.07–0.53)	0.0 (0.0–0.25)	0.58 (0.44–0.73)	2578.4	2559.1	19.3***
C2. Moderately Oppositional	0.47 (0.29–0.60)	0.0 (0.0–0.11)	0.53 (0.40–0.68)	2397.2	2377.8	19.4***
C3. Moderately Impulsive & Inattentive	0.51 (0.34–0.64)	0.0 (0.0–0.9)	0.49 (0.36–0.64)	2428.8	2424.7	4.1
C5. Low Symptom	0.29 (0.0–0.54)	0.49 (0.26–0.69)	0.26 (0.16–0.36)	2371.6	2332.7	38.9***
C6. Mildly Oppositional & Impulsive	0.44 (0.02–0.57)	0.01 (0.0–0.33)	0.55 (0.42–0.71)	2446.3	2434.1	12.2**
C7. Moderately Anxious & non-Conduct Externalizing	0.33 (0.0–0.69)	0.22 (0.0–0.53)	0.45 (0.29–0.62)	1881.0	1867.2	13.8**
C8. Moderately Externalizing	0.37 (0.0–0.70)	0.17 (0.0–0.50)	0.46 (0.30–0.65)	1750.8	1732.8	18.0***
C9. Moderately Internalizing & Severely Externalizing	0.40 (0.0–0.79)	0.30 (0.0–0.74)	0.29 (0.16–0.56)	1109.5	1095.5	14.0**

[a]A, C, and E refer to proportion of variance accounted for by additive genetic, shared environment and unique environment, respectively.
Abbreviations: Sat = saturated model; ACE = twin model; LL = log-likelihood; $\Delta\chi^2$ = delta chi square;
*p<.05,
**p<.01,
***p<.001.

elevated classes might be viewed as temperamental variation rather than symptom-based variation in the population, and this temperamental interpretation might partially apply to the moderately elevated classes as well.

The most severe class encompassed comorbid internalizing and externalizing symptoms. The external covariate analyses showed that this was the only class where impairment was substantially elevated and where the majority of children subsequently qualified for DSM-IV diagnoses. This lack of symptom differentiation among the more severely impaired children may be a function of our derivation of classes from a community sample, but may also highlight the notion of a general disposition to more serious but common psychopathology, sometimes called the p-factor [40].

Finally, the two sex-specific classes were a "Moderately Anxious" class in girls only and a "Severely Impulsive & Inattentive" class in boys only. This latter class makes sense, given the sex differences in prevalence of ADHD [5]. Although comparing class prevalence across sexes is not possible because the latent class analyses were performed separately by sex, our pattern of results suggests that the types of problem behavior classes found in boys and girls in middle childhood are generally very similar.

Latent class analyses can inform our understanding of the structure of child mental health symptoms. For instance, the profiles that emerged from our analyses shed light on whether oppositional, impulsive, and inattentive symptoms represent one (oppositional + impulsive + inattentive), two distinct (oppositional + impulsive vs. inattentive), or three distinct (oppositional vs. impulsive vs. inattentive) dimensions of symptoms [31]. Although our approach was not set up to directly test the relative fit of these competing models, the covariation of oppositional, impulsive, and inattentive items across the different latent classes provides important information. In our best-fitting solution, the various class profiles differed in shape for those items. In many classes (e.g., "Moderately Impulsive & Inattentive" and "Moderately Anxious & non-Conduct Externalizing"), the oppositional, impulsivity, and inattention items are similarly elevated. However, in some classes (e.g., "Moderately Oppositional"), the oppositional and impulsivity items are considerably more elevated than the inattention items, and in the "Severely Impulsive & Inattentive" class for boys, the impulsivity and inattention items were more elevated than the oppositional items. These detailed results suggest that oppositional, impulsive, and inattentive symptoms do not reflect a single dimension. In particular, impulsive behaviors can occur alongside oppositional problems, attentional problems, or both, possibly reflecting distinct psychological and biological underlying processes.

Biometric modeling of the genetic and environmental influences on the latent classes for boys and girls combined suggests that genetic variation plays a moderate role in all classes, including the "Low Symptom" class representing the absence of symptoms of psychopathology, which is a novel finding. Another novel finding is that shared environment appears to play a moderate role in only the "Low Symptom" and "Moderately Internalizing & Severely Externalizing" classes, and at most a small role in the other classes. These findings suggest that shared environment plays a larger role in the etiology of profiles with similar elevations (or similar lack of elevations) for internalizing and externalizing symptoms (i.e., profiles with similar levels of comorbid internalizing and externalizing symptoms). Our results are consistent with previous findings of moderate shared environmental correlations between anxiety and conduct problems in two- to four-year-old twins [8] and between internalizing and externalizing symptoms in four- to eleven-year-old twins [12]. Our results are also consistent with previous studies where shared environment was implicated in common but not specific influences on internalizing and externalizing problems in five-year-old twins [11] and in five- to nine-year-old twins [10]. Although these previous studies and ours suggest that shared environmental factors play a moderate role in the etiology of comorbid internalizing and externalizing problems in early and middle childhood, the role of shared environment in comorbid problems may diminish by adolescence [9,10,13].

Our latent class approach allows us to examine genetic and environmental influences on not only mental health symptoms, but also on the lack thereof (i.e., the "Low Symptom" class). Although genetic influences may play a role in membership in the "Low Symptom" class, shared environmental influences play a moderate and statistically significant role. These shared environmental influences may represent the absence of certain familial risk factors for psychopathology (e.g., poverty, domestic violence), but may also represent the presence of certain protective familial factors (e.g., social support).

One limitation of our study is that the latent class analyses were based on mental health symptoms reported via questionnaire by only one informant (the primary caregiver). Thus, we cannot rule out the possibility that the "Low Symptom" classes included children whose primary caregivers were not willing to acknowledge any problem behaviors for either twin, which would lead to inflated estimates of shared environmental influences. However, in analyses using a subset of the LCA sample that had mother, father, and child reports available (results not reported), the latent classes identified and the pattern of genetic and environmental influences on those classes were very similar across informants.

Another potential limitation is our use of a community-based sample. Given that the majority of our sample would not qualify for a psychiatric diagnosis, it is uncertain how well our results would generalize to clinical populations. However, a recent factor analytic study of adults suggests the structure of mental health problems is similar across community and clinical samples [41]. Further, using a community-based sample also increases the representativeness of results and eliminates treatment-seeking biases.

In conclusion, our study identified nine symptom profiles present during middle childhood. Eight profiles are similar across sexes, but a "Moderately Anxious" class only appeared in girls and a "Severely Impulsive & Inattentive" class was found only in boys. We emphasize that these symptoms profiles are not proposed as superior to existing nosology. Rather, they elucidate the patterning of symptoms across the severity range in a general population, with some classes that are virtually free of clinically significant psychopathology. Although genetic influences play a moderate role in the development of all classes, shared environment plays a moderate role in comorbid internalizing and externalizing problems and in the absence of either type of problem. Our findings suggest that accounting for covariation across symptom domains can reveal the impact of shared environment on the development of common mental health problems. The symptom profiles characterized in this study demonstrate that comorbidity is common in childhood and provide clinicians with common patterns to be aware of as they assess children.

Supporting Information

Table S1 Combined-sex probability-based odds ratios (p-values) for monozygotic twins.

Table S2 Combined-sex probability-based odds ratios (p-values) for dizygotic twins.

Table S3 Combined-sex modal-assignment-based odds ratios (p-values) for monozygotic twins.

Table S4 Combined-sex modal-assignment-based odds ratios (p-values) for dizygotic twins.

Acknowledgments

The authors thank Nicole Schmidt, M.S., for providing details on sample characteristics and study design, and Emily Schaefer and Andrew Scrima for editorial assistance.

Author Contributions

Conceived and designed the experiments: MKV KNJ KLC HHG. Performed the experiments: MKV KNJ RM. Analyzed the data: MKV KNJ CVH. Contributed to the writing of the manuscript: MKV KNJ CVH KLC RJD HHG.

References

1. Burt SA (2009) Rethinking environmental contributions to child and adolescent psychopathology: a meta-analysis of shared environmental influences. Psychological Bulletin 135: 608–637.
2. Sullivan PF, Eaves LJ (2002) Evaluation of analyses of univariate discrete twin data. Behavior Genetics 32: 221–227.
3. Wood AC, Buitelaar J, Rijsdijk F, Asherson P, Kuntsi J (2010) Rethinking shared environment as a source of variance underlying attention-deficit/hyperactivity disorder symptoms: Comment on Burt (2009). Psychological Bulletin 136: 331–340.
4. Angold A, Costello EJ, Erkanli A (1999) Comorbidity. Journal of Child Psychology and Psychiatry 40: 57–87.
5. Costello EJ, Mustillo S, Erkanli A, Keeler G, Angold A (2003) Prevalence and development of psychiatric disorders in childhood and adolescence. Archives of General Psychiatry 60: 837–844.
6. Krueger RF, Markon KD (2006) Reinterpreting comorbidity: A model-based approach to understanding and classifying psychopathology. Annual Review of Clinical Psychology 2: 111–133.
7. Jensen PS, Hinshaw SP, Swanson JM, Greenhill LL, Conners CK, et al. (2001) Findings from the NIMH multimodal treatment study of ADHD (MTA): Implications and applications for primary care providers. Journal of Developmental and Behavioral Pediatrics 22: 60–73.
8. Gregory AM, Eley TC, Plomin R (2004) Exploring the association between anxiety and conduct problems in a large sample of twins aged 2–4. Journal of Abnormal Child Psychology 32: 111–122.
9. Subbarao A, Rhee SH, Young SE, Ehringer MA, Corley RP, et al. (2008) Common genetic and environmental influences on major depressive disorder and conduct disorder. Journal of Abnormal Child Psychology 36: 433–444.
10. Gjone H, Stevenson J (1997) The association between internalizing and externalizing behavior in childhood and early adolescence: Genetic or environmental common influences? Journal of Abnormal Child Psychology 25: 277–286.
11. Jaffee SR, Moffitt TE, Caspi A, Taylor A, Arsenault L (2002) Influence of adult domestic violence on children's internalizing and externalizing problems: An environmentally informative twin study. Journal of the American Academy of Child and Adolescent Psychiatry 41: 1095–1103.
12. Schmitz S, Mrazek DA (2001) Genetic and environmental influences on the associations between attention problems and other problem behaviors. Twin Research 4: 453–458.
13. Spatola CAM, Fagnani C, Pesenti-Gritti P, Ogliari A, Stazi M-A, et al. (2007) A general population twin study of the CBCL/6-18 DSM-oriented scales. Journal of the American Academy of Child and Adolescent Psychiatry 46: 619–627.
14. Caspi A, Langley K, Milne B, Moffitt TE, O'Donovan M, et al. (2008) A replicated molecular genetic basis for subtyping antisocial behavior in children with attention-deficit/hyperactivity disorder. Archives of General Psychiatry 65: 203–210.
15. Keiley MK, Lofthouse N, Bates JE, Dodge KA, Pettit GS (2003) Differential risks of covarying and pure components in mother and teacher reports of externalizing and internalizing behavior across ages 5 to 14. Journal of Abnormal Child Psychology 31: 267–283.

16. Magidson J, Vermunt JK (2002) Latent class models for clustering: A comparison with K-means. Canadian Journal of Marketing Research 20: 37–44.
17. Acosta MT, Castellanos FX, Bolton KL, Balog JZ, Eagen P, et al. (2008) Latent class subtyping of attention-deficit/hyperactivity disorder and comorbid conditions. Journal of the American Academy of Child and Adolescent Psychiatry 47: 797–807.
18. Althoff RR, Rettew DC, Faraone SV, Boomsma DI, Hudziak JJ (2006) Latent class analysis shows strong heritability of the Child Behavior Checklist-Juvenile Bipolar Phenotype. Biological Psychiatry 60: 903–911.
19. Ostrander R, Herman K, Sikorski J, Mascendaro P, Lambert S (2008) Patterns of psychopathology in children with ADHD: A latent profile analysis. Journal of Clinical Child & Adolescent Psychology 37: 833–847.
20. American Psychiatric Association (1994) Diagnostic and Statistical Manual of Mental Disorders, 4th ed. Washington, DC: Author.
21. Lemery-Chalfant K, Goldsmith HH, Schmidt NL, Arneson CL, Van Hulle CA (2006) Wisconsin Twin Panel: Current directions and findings. Twin Research and Human Genetics 9: 1030–1037.
22. Schmidt NL, Van Hulle CA, Brooker RJ, Meyer LR, Lemery-Chalfant K, et al. (2013) Wisconsin Twin Research: Early development, childhood psychopathology, autism, and sensory over-responsivity. Twin Research and Human Genetics 16: 376–384.
23. Boyce WT, Essex MJ, Woodward HR, Measelle JR, Ablow JC, et al. (2002) The confluence of mental, physical, social, and academic difficulties in middle childhood. I: Exploring the "headwaters" of early life morbidities. Journal of the American Academy of Child and Adolescent Psychiatry 41: 580–587.
24. Essex MJ, Boyce WT, Goldstein LH, Armstrong JM, Kraemer HC, et al. (2002) The confluence of mental, physical, social, and academic difficulties in middle childhood. II: Developing the MacArthur Health and Behavior Questionnaire. Journal of the American Academy of Child and Adolescent Psychiatry 41: 588–603.
25. Goldsmith HH (1991) A zygosity questionnaire for young twins: A research note. Behavior Genetics 21: 257–269.
26. Price TS, Freeman B, Craig I, Petrill SA, Ebersole L, et al. (2000) Infant zygosity can be assigned by parental report questionnaire data. Twin Research 3: 129–133.
27. Shaffer D, Fisher P, Lucas CP, Dulcan MK, Schwab-Stone ME (2000) NIMH Diagnostic Interview Schedule for Children Version IV (NIMH DISC-IV): Description, differences from previous versions, and reliability of some common diagnoses. Journal of the American Academy of Child and Adolescent Psychiatry 39: 28–38.
28. Muthén B, Asparouhov T, Rebollo I (2006) Advances in behavioral genetics modeling using Mplus: Applications of factor mixture modeling to twin data. Twin Research and Human Genetics 9: 313–324.
29. Uebersax JS (1999) Probit latent class analysis with dichotomous or ordered category measures: Conditional independence/dependence models. Applied Psychological Measurement 23: 283–297.
30. Nigg JT, Goldsmith HH, Sachek J (2004) Temperament and attention deficit hyperactivity disorder: The development of a multiple pathway model. Journal of Clinical Child & Adolescent Psychology 33: 42–53.
31. Lahey BB, Applegate B, Waldman ID, Loft JD, Hankin BL, et al. (2004) The structure of child and adolescent psychopathology: Generating new hypotheses. Journal of Abnormal Psychology 113: 358–385.
32. Goodman LA (1974) The analysis of systems of qualitative variables when some of the variables are unobservable. Part I: A modified latent structure approach. American Journal of Sociology 79: 1179–1259.
33. Vermunt JK, Magidson J (2005) Latent GOLD 4.0 user's guide. Belmont, Massachusetts: Statistical Innovations Inc.
34. Dempster AP, Laird NM, Rubin DB (1977). Maximum likelihood from incomplete data via the EM Algorithm (with discussion). Journal of the Royal Statistical Society, Series B 39: 1–38.
35. Nylund KL, Asparouhov T, Muthén BO (2007) Deciding on the number of classes in latent class analysis and growth mixture modeling: A Monte Carlo simulation study. Structural Equation Modeling 14: 535–569.
36. Muthén BO, Asparouhov T, Rebello I (2006). Advances in behavioral genetics modeling using Mplus: Applications of factor mixture modeling to twin data. Twin Research and Human Genetics 9: 313–324.
37. Neale MC, Cardon LR (1992). Methodology for genetic studies of twins and families. Dordrecht: Kluwer.
38. Neale MC, Eaves LJ, Kendler KS (1994) The power of the classical twin study to resolve variation in threshold traits. Behavior Genetics 24: 239–258.
39. Neale MC, Boker SM, Xie G, Maes HH (2003) Mx statistical modeling, 6th ed. Richmond, Virginia: Department of Psychiatry, Virginia Commonwealth University.
40. Caspi A, Houts RM, Belsky DW, Goldman-Mellor SJ, Harrington H, et al. (2014) The p factor: One general psychopathology factor in the structure of psychiatric disorders? Clinical Psychological Science 2: 119–137.
41. Kotov R, Ruggero CJ, Krueger RF, Watson D, Yuan Q, et al. (2011) New dimensions in the quantitative classification of mental illness. Archives of General Psychiatry 68: 1003–1011.

Attention Deficit/Hyperactivity Disorder Symptoms and Cognitive Abilities in the Late-Life Cohort of the PATH through Life Study

Debjani Das[1]*, Nicolas Cherbuin[2], Simon Easteal[1], Kaarin J. Anstey[2]

1 John Curtin School of Medical Research, The Australian National University, Canberra, Australian Capital Territory, Australia, **2** Centre for Research on Ageing, Health and Wellbeing, The Australian National University, Canberra, Australian Capital Territory, Australia

Abstract

Attention Deficit/Hyperactivity Disorder (ADHD) is a common neuropsychiatric disorder that has not been well studied in older adults. In this study we examined relationships between ADHD symptoms and cognitive ability and compared them between middle-age (MA; 48–52 years) and older-age (OA; 68–74 years) adults sampled from the same population. ADHD, mood disorder symptoms and cognitive abilities were assessed in a large population-based sample (n = 3443; 50% male). We measured current ADHD symptoms using the adult ADHD Self-Report Scale (ASRS), which we found to have the same underlying structure in both cohorts. Older adults reported significantly lower levels of ADHD symptoms and 2.2% of the OA cohort scored equal or above the ASRS cut-off score of 14 (which has been previously associated with ADHD diagnosis) compared with 6.2% of MA adults. Symptom levels were not significantly different between males and females. Using multi-group structural equation modelling we compared ADHD symptom–cognitive performance relationships between the two age groups. Generally higher ADHD symptoms were associated with poorer cognitive performance in the MA cohort. However, higher levels of inattention symptoms were associated with better verbal ability in both cohorts. Surprisingly, greater hyperactivity was associated with better task-switching abilities in older adults. In the OA cohort ADHD symptom–cognition relationships are indirect, mediated largely through the strong association between depression symptoms and cognition. Our results suggest that ADHD symptoms decrease with age and that their relationships with co-occurring mood disorders and cognitive performance also change. Although symptoms of depression are lower in older adults, they are much stronger predictors of cognitive performance and likely mediate the effect of ADHD symptoms on cognition in this age group. These results highlight the need for age-appropriate diagnosis and treatment of comorbid ADHD and mood disorders.

Editor: Karen Lidzba, University Children's Hospital Tuebingen, Germany

Funding: The study was supported by National Health & Medical Research Council (NHMRC) of Australia Unit Grant No. 973302, Program Grant No. 179805, and NHMRC project grant No. 157125. DD is funded by NHMRC Project Grant No. 410215. NC is funded by ARC Future Fellowship No. 120100227. KJA is funded by NHMRC Research Fellowship No. 1002560. The funders had no role in study design, data collection and analysis, decision to publish, or preparation of the manuscript.

Competing Interests: The authors have declared that no competing interests exist.

* E-mail: debjani.das@anu.edu.au

Introduction

Attention Deficit/Hyperactivity Disorder (ADHD) is a neuropsychiatric disorder that develops in childhood and can persist throughout life. It is characterised by age-inappropriate levels of inattention and/or excessive motor activity and impulsivity [1]. In adults inattention is the predominant symptom, which manifests as disorganization, forgetfulness, unreliability, and poor performance in planning, task completion, task shifting and time management. ADHD symptoms affect functioning in multiple life domains often leading to employment and financial difficulties, and interpersonal problems [2,3]. ADHD is associated with cognitive impairment in both children and adults [4–10]. Furthermore, individuals with ADHD are more likely than unaffected individuals to experience comorbid psychiatric disorders [2,11]. The majority of adult with ADHD have at least one lifetime psychiatric comorbidity including anxiety (47%), mood (38%), impulse control (20%) and substance use disorders (15%) [12]. The high level of comorbidity has raised questions about whether the functional impairments in ADHD patients are primarily due to ADHD or the comorbid conditions. Addressing this issue a recent study reported that neuropsychological deficits in ADHD adults go beyond comorbidity [13]. The financial burden of ADHD on families and society is substantial due to direct medical expenses and the indirect costs of workplace productivity loss and accidents [14–18]. Furthermore, the negative impact of ADHD symptoms/impairments on professional, economic, social, and emotional well-being accumulates through life affecting quality of life at late-age [19].

ADHD Prevalence in Late-life

ADHD is a common disorder affecting ~5% of children and 1–7% of adults [20–25]. The prevalence of the disorder is thought to diminish with age [3]. However, very little is known about ADHD in late life since most studies on adult ADHD have focussed on young adults. Kooij et al (2005) [26] estimated the prevalence of

ADHD among older adults (18–75 years) in the Netherlands to be 1–2.5%. The study by Michielsen et al. (2012) [27] reported prevalence rates of 2.8% and 4.2% for syndromatic and symptomatic ADHD, respectively, in adults aged 60–94 years. It is important to note that diagnostic criteria currently used for ADHD were developed for children and adolescents. It is uncertain how well these diagnostic criteria and thresholds apply to adults since the symptom patterns change with age [3]. Following recent recommendations [28], symptom threshold have been lowered for adults in the Diagnostic and Statistical Manual of Mental Disorders (5th ed; DSM-5; [29]). Furthermore, DSM-based diagnosis of adult ADHD requires symptoms to be present in childhood – before 7 years in DSM-IV and before 12 years in DSM-5. Hence, diagnosis of ADHD in adults depends on accurate recall of childhood symptoms, which can be challenging for older adults. Thus, while it is accepted that ADHD persists throughout life, the condition is not well understood in old age and its prevalence is uncertain.

ADHD Dimensionality

Although ADHD remains a categorically distinct clinical condition, there is increasing recognition that clinical ADHD lies at the extreme ends of the distribution of continuous ADHD symptom dimensions. Furthermore, symptoms of ADHD are common and can lead to functional impairment in adults who do not meet all the criteria for clinical diagnosis [2,30]. A dimensional view is supported by evidences from several taxonomic, genetic and neuroimaging studies [31–34]. The majority of these studies are of childhood ADHD, but a recent taxonomic study in a sample of young adults also indicates a dimensional latent structure of ADHD in adults [35]. It is also well-established that ADHD is characterised by two related but distinct dimensions – inattention and hyperactivity [36], which have distinctive brain and cognitive characteristics [37–39]. The specific behavioural and cognitive characteristics of these dimensions are poorly understood. Their relative importance changes with age, with inattention becoming more dominant in adults, which may have an important impact on how the cognitive effects of ADHD change with age.

Cognitive and Functional Consequence of Adult ADHD

Cognitive deficits have been consistently identified in both children and adults with ADHD [4–10]. Compared to unaffected individuals ADHD adults are cognitively different across multiple functional domains, with notable differences in attention, behavioural inhibition and non-executive functional aspects of memory, processing speed and motor speed [40–42]. Meta-analyses have also reported slightly lower IQ in adults with ADHD [40,41,43]. Neuropsychological research in ADHD has focussed primarily on aspects of attention and executive functions with multiple studies demonstrating deficits in vigilance, selective attention, distractibility, divided attention and flexibility, working memory, set shifting and planning [44–49]. Few such studies have been conducted in middle-aged or older adults. From a cross-sectional study of 116 non-medicated ADHD patients 19–55 years of age, Biederman et al. (2011) concluded that the negative impact of ADHD on cognition remains constant across the lifespan [50]. In another study, cognitive test profiles in older adults (62–91 years of age) were found to be associated with reports of childhood ADHD [51]. Using dimensional measures of ADHD symptoms we have previously reported that inattention and hyperactivity symptoms are associated with cognitive performance measures in middle-aged adults (47–54 years) [52]. Symptoms of inattention in particular were associated with poorer performance in this age group. Furthermore, some but not all of the effects of ADHD symptoms on cognition were mediated through co-occurring anxiety and depression symptoms. Thus, a very limited number of studies indicate that ADHD has a negative impact on cognitive functioning in old age, but the extent and nature of the impact is not well understood.

The Present Study

In this study we extend our analyses of ADHD symptoms to a cohort of older adults (68–72 years) in the Personality and Total Health (PATH) Through Life Study, a population-based longitudinal study of mental health and ageing [53]. We focus on the association of ADHD symptoms with cognitive performance measures. To assess ADHD symptoms we used the adult ADHD Self-Report Scale (ASRS) [54], which is a checklist of inattention and hyperactivity symptoms based on the diagnostic criteria outlined in the DSM-IV-Text Revision. The ASRS demonstrated good sensitivity and specificity in clinical validation studies and is recommended for use in epidemiological studies [55]. However, the ASRS has not been validated in older adults. Hence, the first aim of the present study was to test whether the ASRS has the same underlying measurement properties in our middle-age (MA) and older-age (OA) cohorts. The second aim of the study was to examine whether relationships between ASRS latent factors (inattention and hyperactivity) and cognitive performance differ between the age groups. As a part of the second aim we also examined whether co-occurring anxiety and depression symptoms affect ADHD symptom–cognition relationships differently in middle- and older-age cohorts. Based on previous evidence of decrease in ADHD prevalence with age we expected participants in the older cohort to report fewer ADHD symptoms than middle-aged participants. Guided by our previous work on the middle-aged adults [52] we expected cognitive performance to be predominantly associated with symptoms of inattention in older adults.

Methods

Participants

The study sample was drawn from the PATH Through Life Project, a large longitudinal study of mental health and ageing in participants across three age groups (20–24, 40–44, 60–64 years at baseline) with a four-yearly follow-up 'waves' of assessment for up to 20 years [53]. The baseline sample comprised of individuals selected randomly from the electoral roll from the city of Canberra and the adjacent town of Queanbeyan, Australia (which provides a representative population sample because enrolment to vote is a legal requirement for adult Australian citizens).

The present study used data from the third wave of assessment (the ASRS was introduced in this wave) of the MA (40–44 years at baseline) and OA (60–64 years at baseline) cohorts. There were 2182 participants in MA cohort aged 48–52 years (mean age 50.7±1.5 years) and 1973 individuals in the OA cohort aged 68–72 years (mean age 70.6±1.5 years). Twenty-six (1%) and fifty-three participants (2.8%) in the MA and OA cohorts respectively did not complete the ASRS questionnaire and were excluded from further analysis. Being older was associated with increased odds of not completing the questionnaire in the OA cohort. However, non-responders did not differ significantly ($p>0.05$) from responders with respect to gender, total years of education and the levels of anxiety or depression symptoms in either cohort. Participants meeting at least one of the following criteria – history of epilepsy, brain tumour/infection and stroke and with missing data were excluded. Mini Mental State Examination (MMSE) was included in the assessment of the OA cohort to screen for probable dementia. Participants with scores of 23 or less (which is indicative of probable dementia [56]) were also excluded from the analyses. MA adults were not assessed using MMSE since this test was not designed to provide cognitive data on young or middle-aged adults and only presents a challenge for older individuals with significant cognitive difficulties. One MA participant reported taking medically prescribed dexamphetamine (which is used in ADHD treatment) and was excluded since information on dosage, duration of treatment and side effects (such as insomnia and increased anxiety and irritability) was not available, which could potentially affect cognitive performance. A final sample of n = 3443 (50% male) was available for this investigation.

Procedure

Written informed consent for participation in the PATH project was obtained from all participants according to the 'National Statement' guidelines of the National Health and Medical Research Council of Australia and following a protocol approved by the Human Research Ethics Committee of The Australian National University. For wave 3 of the PATH study, on which the present analysis is based, all participants were assessed by trained interviewers to be capable of providing informed consent.

Participants were surveyed once every four years for information on physical and mental health, lifestyle and social factors (for details see [53]). Cognitive assessments were a part of the interview conducted by trained interviewers. The interview lasted for approximately 2 hours although this varied between individuals and was somewhat longer in the older-age group. The assessment was designed to alternate between questionnaire items, psychometric measures, and anthropometrical measures so as to decrease the effects of fatigue and attention lapses. A tea break was also offered in the middle of the assessment. In addition, to minimize the effects of fatigue and attention on sensitive measures, task presenting most difficulty were performed early in the interview.

Measures

The short form of the ASRS was used, which consists of a checklist of six questions regarding symptoms of ADHD based on the diagnostic criteria of DSM-IV [54,55]. The items in the ASRS questionnaire are shown in Table S1 in File S1. Each item requires participants to rate how frequently they experienced a particular symptom of ADHD in the past six months on a five-point response scale from "never" [0] to "very often" [4]. A summary score (ASRS-6 score) with a possible range of 0–24 was obtained as an equally weighted sum of response scores for all questions. Higher scores indicate increased risk of ADHD. This screening tool has performed well in validation studies (sensitivity = 68.7% and specificity = 99.5%) and has high concordance with clinician diagnosis (area under the receiver operator curve of 0.90) [55]. Factor analysis of the ASRS reported previously [57] suggest that the screener is a two-dimensional measure rather than a single unitary measure. Items 1 to 4 relate to inattention symptoms and load on one factor (inattentiveness) and items 5 and 6 load on a second factor (hyperactivity) [57].

Depression and anxiety symptoms were assessed using the Patient Health Questionnaire (PHQ). This is a short version of the patient questionnaire component of the Primary Care Evaluation of Mental Disorders (PRIME-MD) instrument [58,59]. We generated measures of depression and anxiety-related disorders from: 9 items related to depression symptoms [rated on a 4-point scale from "not at all" (1) to "nearly every day" (4)]; 7 items related to anxiety symptoms [rated on a 3-point scale from "not at all" (1) to "more than half the days" (3)]; and 5 items related to panic disorder [rated on a 2-point scale of "no" (1) and "yes" (2)] following the coding algorithm provided in the PHQ instruction manual (available from Patient Health Questionnaire Screeners; http://www.phqscreeners.com/overview.aspx). Variables for panic disorder and other anxiety syndromes were combined to generate a binary categorical variable for anxiety symptoms [both panic disorder and other anxiety syndrome absent (0), either panic disorder or other anxiety syndrome present (1)].

Cognitive Tests

Cognitive data were collected from participants as described previously [52]. The cognitive performance measures used in this study include: the Spot-the-Word Test (STW) which is a measure of verbal ability [60]; the Trail Making Tests A and B (TMT-A and TMT-B) for visual attention and task-switching [61,62]; the Symbol-Digit Modalities Test (SMDT) for information processing speed and attention [63]; immediate and delayed recall of the first trial of the California Verbal Learning Test [64]; the Digits Span Backwards (DSB) task from the Wechsler Memory Scale for verbal working memory [65]; and Simple and Choice Reaction Time (SRT and CRT) [66]. Further details of the cognitive tests are provided in Table S2 in File S1. Percentage of missing data for the cognitive tests were as follows: Spot-the-Word Test (4.2%), Trail Making Test (Part A) (2.6%), Trail Making Test (Part B) (2.9%), Symbol-Digit Modalities Test (2.6%), Immediate Recall (1.7%), Delayed Recall (1.8%), Digits Span Backwards (2.2%), Simple Reaction Time (4.7%) and Choice Reaction Time (4.7%).

Statistical Analysis

All statistical analyses were conducted using SPSS 18 and Amos version 20 (Chicago: SPSS Inc.). Missing data for cognitive measures were imputed using Expectation-Maximization method in SPSS. Means and standard deviations were computed for the ASRS-6 and cognitive test scores. As recommended [54,55], participants were grouped into four strata based on ASRS-6 with the following score ranges: 0–9 (stratum I), 10–13 (stratum II), 14–17 (stratum III) and 18–24 (stratum IV). Comparisons between MA and OA were performed using Student's t-tests and Pearson's Chi-square tests for the continuous and categorical ASRS measures respectively (Table 1). For each cognitive test z-scores were generated. Higher scores on TMT and RT tasks indicate a worse performance, while a higher score on all other tests indicate better cognitive function. Pearson correlations were computed for the ASRS latent factors and cognitive test scores (Tables S3 and S4 in File S1).

We used multi-group structural equation modelling to test cross-group invariance of the ASRS factor structure (Aim 1) and compare ADHD symptom–cognition relationships in MA and OA groups (Aim 2). First, cross-group invariance of the ASRS factor structure was tested using latent factor SEM in the framework of confirmatory factor analysis [67]. Equivalence of ASRS across cohorts was examined according to the procedure outlined in [67]. Once the ASRS factor structures for both cohorts were determined, a second set of SEMs was generated, which included the ASRS latent factors, the cognition variables and covariates to investigate ADHD symptom–cognition relationships. SEMs were fitted using maximum likelihood methods. Standard errors of the regression estimates were calculated from 2000 bootstrap-resampled datasets. Model fit was assessed using goodness-of-fit indices such as tests for chi-square distribution and root-mean square error of approximation (RMSEA; optimal value <0.05 [68]); adjusted goodness of fit index (AGFI; optimal value >0.9 [69]); comparative fit index (CFI; optimal value >0.9 [70]); Akaike information criterion (AIC; [71]); Browne-Cudeck criterion (BCC; [72]). Models with the lowest values for AIC and BCC are

Table 1. Socio-demographic characteristics and measures of ADHD, anxiety and depression symptom and cognitive performance in the sample.

		MA (n = 1907)		OA (n = 1536)				
		Mean (SD)/freq	**Std. Res**	**Mean (SD)/freq**	**Std. Res**	**t/χ^2**	**df**	***p***
Gender						7.365	1	0.007
	Males	907 (47.6%)	−1.3	802 (52.2%)	1.4			
	Females	1000 (52.4%)	1.3	734 (47.8%)	1.4			
Age (years)		50.7 (1.5)		70.6 (1.5)		−386.499	3441	<0.001
Education (years)		14.9 (2.2)		14.1 (2.6)		9.690	3441	<0.001
ASRS-6 score		8.15 (3.40)		6.80 (3.25)		11.824	3441	<0.001
ASRS strata						89.324	3	<0.001
	I	1291 (67.7%)	−3.1	1251 (81.4%)	3.5			
	II	499 (26.2%)	4.1	251 (16.3%)	−4.6			
	III	99 (5.2%)	3.3	29 (1.9%)	−3.7			
	IV	18 (0.9)%	1.5	5 (0.3%)	−1.6			
ASRS score categories						31.203	1	<0.001
	0–13	1790 (93.9%)	−0.8	1502 (97.8%)	0.9			
	14–24	117 (6.1%)	3.6	34 (2.2%)	−4.1			
Depression symptoms present						24.620	1	<0.001
	Yes	258 (13.5%)	3.1	126 (8.2%)	−3.5			
	No	1644 (86.2%)	−1.1	1410 (91.8%)	1.2			
Anxiety symptoms present						19.227	1	<0.001
	Yes	106 (5.6%)	2.9	39 (2.5%)	−3.2			
	No	1801 (94.4%)	−0.6	1497 (97.5%)	0.7			
Spot-the-Word Test[a]		51.77 (4.98)		53.27 (4.92)		−8.800	3441	<0.001
Trail Making Test-A (seconds)[b]		25.78 (7.35)		35.55 (12.34)		−28.813	3441	<0.001
Trail Making Test-B (seconds)[b]		57.40 (20.13)		82.57 (31.83)		−28.230	3441	<0.001
Simple Reaction Time (seconds)[b]		0.24 (0.05)		0.28 (0.07)		−21.618	3441	<0.001
Choice Reaction Time (seconds)[b]		0.30 (0.04)		0.34 (0.05)		−28.206	3441	<0.001
Immediate Recall[a]		8.18 (2.17)		6.70 (2.21)		19.637	3441	<0.001
Delayed Recall[a]		7.38 (2.37)		5.98 (2.32)		17.401	3441	<0.001
Symbol-Digit Modalities Test[a]		59.73 (8.54)		48.58 (8.79)		37.595	3441	<0.001
Digit Span Backwards[a]		5.75 (2.29)		5.17 (2.17)		7.578	3441	<0.001

MA: middle-age cohort; OA: older-age cohort; ASRS: adult ADHD Self-Report Scale; freq: frequency; Std. Res: standardised residuals.
[a]number of correct responses;
[b]time taken to complete.

considered to have the best fit to the data. When sample sizes are large, as in this study, chi-square statistics can be significant even when the differences between the models being compared are small. We therefore also used a range of other goodness-of-fit indices to obtain a broader assessment of model fit.

Analysis of ASRS factor structure: Previous factor analysis has established that ASRS measures two correlated constructs, Inattention and Hyperactivity [57]. We treated these as latent factors in the SEMs, designated as *Inatt* (ASRS Items 1–4, Table S1 in File S1) and *Hyperact* (ASRS Items 5 and 6, Table S1 in File S1), respectively. We first tested the validity of the reported two-factor structure of the ASRS for the MA and OA cohorts individually (Table 2; Models MA and OA). We then examined the equivalence of the two-factor structure in both cohorts simultaneously through a series of models (Table 2; Models 1–6) with different parameters constrained. Model 1 was the baseline model where all parameters were allowed to vary between the two cohorts. For the other models the followings constraints were applied: Model 2– factor loadings (FL); Model 3– FL, variance of both factors (FV) and covariance between factors (FC); Model 4– FL and FC; Model 5a – FL, FC and variance of *Inatt* (V_{Inatt}); Model 5b – FL, FC and variance of *Hyperact* ($V_{Hyperact}$); and Model 6: FL, FC and residual variance (RV) of the ASRS items. Since the more constrained models were nested within the initial model, the Likelihood Ratio Test (difference in Chi-square statistics relative to the change in degrees of freedom) along with other goodness-of-fit indices (see above) was used to select the more parsimonious model.

Analysis of ADHD symptom–cognition relationships: SEMs generated for assessing the effect of ASRS latent factors on cognitive performance included cognitive test scores as dependent variables and *Inatt*, *Hyperact*, sociodemographic variables and mood-disorder symptoms as predictors. A schematic representation of our theoretical model is shown in Figure 1A. Factor

Table 2. Goodness-of-fit statistics from single cohorts (MA, OA) and multi-group (MA+OA) SEMs assessing the ASRS factor structure.

Model	Constraints	χ^2	*df*	RMSEA	AGFI	CFI	AIC	BCC	$\Delta\chi^2$	Δdf	Δp
Individual group analyses											
MA	–	46.386	9	0.047	0.981	0.984	70.386	70.474	–	–	–
OA	–	68.586	9	0.065	0.965	0.958	92.586	92.695	–	–	–
Multi-group analyses											
1	Nil	111.325	18	0.039	0.974	0.975	159.235	159.524	–	–	–
2	FL	112.065	22	0.034	0.979	0.976	152.065	152.231	0.740[a]	4	0.946
3	FL+FV+FC	131.554	25	0.035	0.978	0.972	165.554	165.695	19.489[b]	3	<0.001
4	FL+FC	113.609	23	0.034	0.980	0.976	151.609	151.767	1.544[b]	1	0.214
5a	FL+FC+V_{Inatt}	125.063	24	0.035	0.978	0.973	161.063	161.212	11.454[c]	1	<0.001
5b	FL+FC+$V_{Hyperact}$	119.023	24	0.034	0.979	0.975	155.023	155.172	5.414[c]	1	0.020
6	FL+FC+RV	158.245	28	0.037	0.976	0.966	186.245	186.361	44.636[c]	5	<0.001

MA: middle-age cohort; OA: older-age cohort; FL: Factor loadings of ASRS items on *Inatt* and *Hyperact* latent factors; FV: Factor variance for *Inatt* and *Hyperact*; FC: Covariance between *Inatt* and *Hyperact*; V_{Inatt}: Variance of *Inatt*; $V_{Hyperact}$: Variance of *Hyperact*; RV: Residual Variance of ASRS items.
RMSEA: root-mean square error of approximation (optimal value <0.05); AGFI: adjusted goodness of fit index (optimal value >0.9); CFI: comparative fit index (optimal value >0.9); AIC: Akaike information criterion; BCC: Browne-Cudeck criterion. Models with the lowest values for AIC and BCC are considered to have the best fit to the data.
[a]compared to Model 1;
[b]compared to Model 2;
[c]compared to Model 4.

loadings of the ASRS items on *Inatt* and *Hyperact* and covariance between the factors were constrained to be equal across both groups. All other parameters were estimated freely. To avoid multi-collinearity we used separate models for cognitive variables (Immediate Recall vs. Delayed Recall and Simple Reaction Time vs. Choice Reaction Time) that were highly correlated (r>0.7; Tables S3 and S4 in File S1). Model refinement was guided by comparison of goodness of fit statistics as described above, with non-significant paths (p>0.1) removed to improve the overall parsimony of the models. Only the final, most-parsimonious model and the coefficients of significant paths are reported. Results were considered significant at $p \leq 0.05$.

We also analysed the factor structure of the cognitive tests used in the study. The factor structure that represents the best fit to both cohorts are shown in Figure S1. We generated SEM models with the cognition latent factors as dependent variables using the method outlined above. These results are presented as Table S5 in File S1 and Figure S2.

Results

Demographic characteristics, symptom measures for ADHD, depression and anxiety, and cognitive test scores for both cohorts are presented in Table 1 (Information about access to data is available at: http://crahw.anu.edu.au/research/projects/personality-total-health-path-through-life/data). The OA cohort reported significantly lower levels for ADHD, depression and anxiety. For the ASRS, 2.2% of participants in the OA cohort scored 14 or above, which has previously been identified as indicative of ADHD diagnosis [55], compared with 6.1% in the MA cohort. The OA cohort also has fewer individuals classified in the II, III and IV ASRS strata than the MA cohort. OA participants performed significantly worse than MA participants in all cognitive tests with the exception of the Spot-the-Word Test of verbal ability.

Equivalence of ASRS Instrument in MA and OA Cohorts

The data are well described by models incorporating the proposed two-factor (*Inatt+Hyperact*) ASRS structure in both cohorts individually (Table 2, Models MA and OA). Factor loadings and factor covariance are presented in Figure 1 for MA (panel B) and OA (panel C) adults. The covariance between the latent factors – *Inatt* and *Hyperact* was lower in the OA adults compared to MA adults. The two-factor model also had acceptable goodness-of-fit indices (Table 2) when both cohorts were combined (Table 2: Model 1). When FLs for the OA cohort were constrained to be equal to those estimated for MA adults, the fit indices changed only slightly (Table 2: Model 2). For an increase in 4 degrees of freedom in Model 2 compared to Model 1 the corresponding change in χ^2 was not significant at an alpha level of 0.05. Constraining FLs, FVs and FC to be the same across groups (Table 2: Model 3) also resulted in a well-fitting model. However, the Likelihood Ratio Test indicated that this model was significantly different from Model 2, suggesting that the variance and covariance of the latent factors differed significantly between the age cohorts. To examine this further, we constrained only FC (Table 2: Model 4) and found the model not to be significantly different from Model 2, which suggests that while the covariance between *Inatt* and *Hyperact* was lower in the OA cohort it was not significantly different from the MA cohort. Adding further constraints on the variances of either *Inatt* or *Hyperact* (Table 2: Model 5a and b) or residual variances of the ASRS items (RVs; Table 2: Model 6) caused significant changes in model fit compared to Model 4. This indicates that both the variance of the latent factors and residual variances of the ASRS items differed significantly between the age cohorts. Thus, Model 4 where FLs and FC were constrained to have the same values across cohorts exhibited the best fit to the data for both age groups and hence, only this model was used for subsequent analyses.

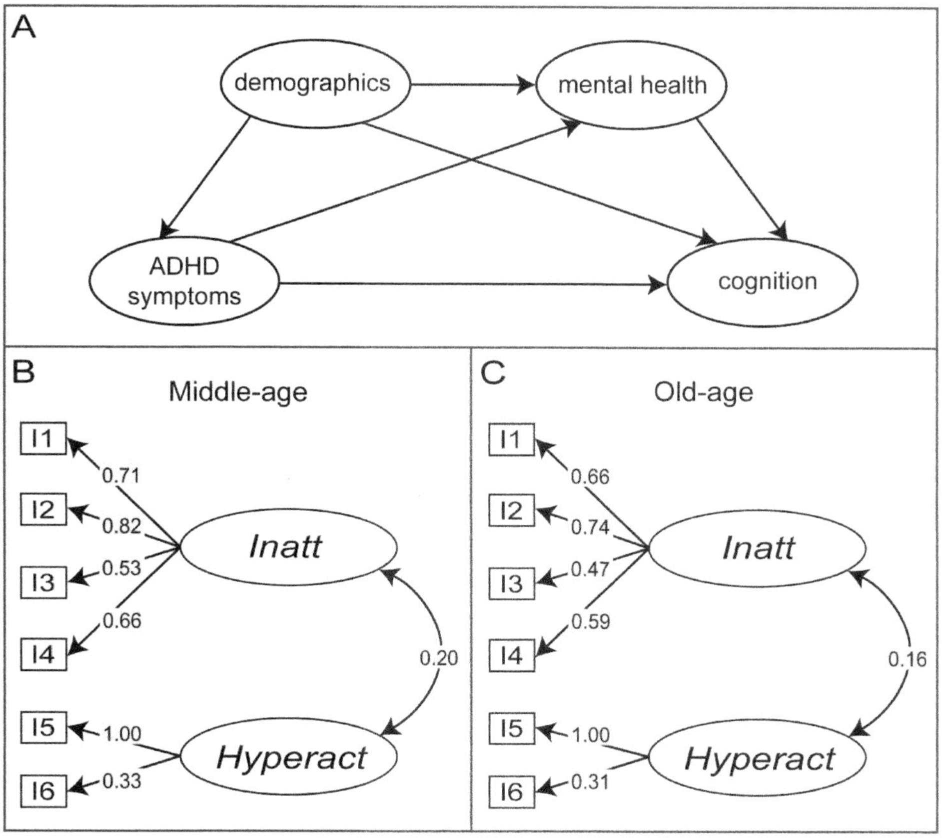

Figure 1. Theoretical model for ADHD symptom–cognition relationships and the factor structure of the ASRS. A) The theoretical model for ADHD symptom–cognition relationships examined in multi-group SEM analysis. Demographic variables include gender, age and education. Anxiety and depression symptom measures are indicated as the mental health variable in the diagram. B) and C) Models representing the ASRS factor structure in MA cohort (B) and OA cohort (C). Standardised factor loadings and covariance between the latent factors – *Inatt* and *Hyperact* are shown. Arrows reflect direction of relationships between variables.

Effect of ADHD Symptoms on Cognitive Performance

Using multi-group SEMs we investigated the effects of ADHD symptoms on cognitive performance, while controlling for sociodemographic variables and mood disorder symptoms (Figure 1A). The ASRS two-factor model (Model 4) described above was included as a measure of ADHD symptoms. The cognitive outcome variables were – Spot-the-Word Test, Trail Making Test, Symbol-Digit Modalities Test, Choice Reaction Time, Delayed Recall and Digits Span Backwards. The baseline model evaluated the theoretical model shown in Figure 1A and had acceptable model fit indices: $\chi^2 = 625.265$, $df = 125$, $p < 0.001$; RMSEA = 0.034; AGFI = 0.947; CFI = 0.955; AIC = 1061.265; BCC = 1066.173. However, coefficients for several paths in the model were not significant. Hence, regression paths with $p > 0.1$ were removed to give a final model with improved overall fit to the data ($\chi^2 = 682.882$, $df = 189$, $p < 0.001$; RMSEA = 0.028; AGFI = 0.961; CFI = 0.956; AIC = 989.882; BCC = 992.342). Significant paths ($p \leq 0.01$) in the final model are shown in Figures 2 and 3 and regression coefficients are presented in Table 3. Models with Immediate-recall and Simple Reaction Time are not reported since they were not significantly associated with the ADHD latent variables in either cohort.

Inatt and *Hyperact* have limited direct effects on cognitive performance. The most notable was a positive association, observed in both cohorts, between *Inatt* and Spot-the-Word Test, implying that higher levels of inattention symptoms are associated with greater verbal intelligence. *Inatt* was also positively associated with Choice Reaction Time, i.e., with slower reaction time in the MA cohort. *Hyperact* was positively associated with the Delayed Recall test (i.e. poor performance) on the MA cohort and Trail Making Test (Part B) (i.e. better performance) in the OA cohort. *Inatt* was associated with depression and anxiety symptoms more strongly in the MA than the OA cohort.

We also investigated the association between ADHD symptoms and latent variables obtained from factor analysis of the cognitive test scores. Factor analysis identified four latent factors (Figure S1) broadly representing: working memory, information processing speed, speed/executive function and verbal memory. The most parsimonious model obtained from the SEM analysis with the cognition latent factors as dependent variables fit the data well for both cohorts (Table S5 in File S1 and Figure S2) and was very similar to the model described in Table 3 and Figures 2 and 3. It is important to note that the cognition tests were included in the PATH study only as indicators of different kinds of cognitive ability and were not designed to measure latent constructs. Hence, cognitive domains represented by these latent factors are both difficult to interpret and would not be considered stable as they have less than three indicators.

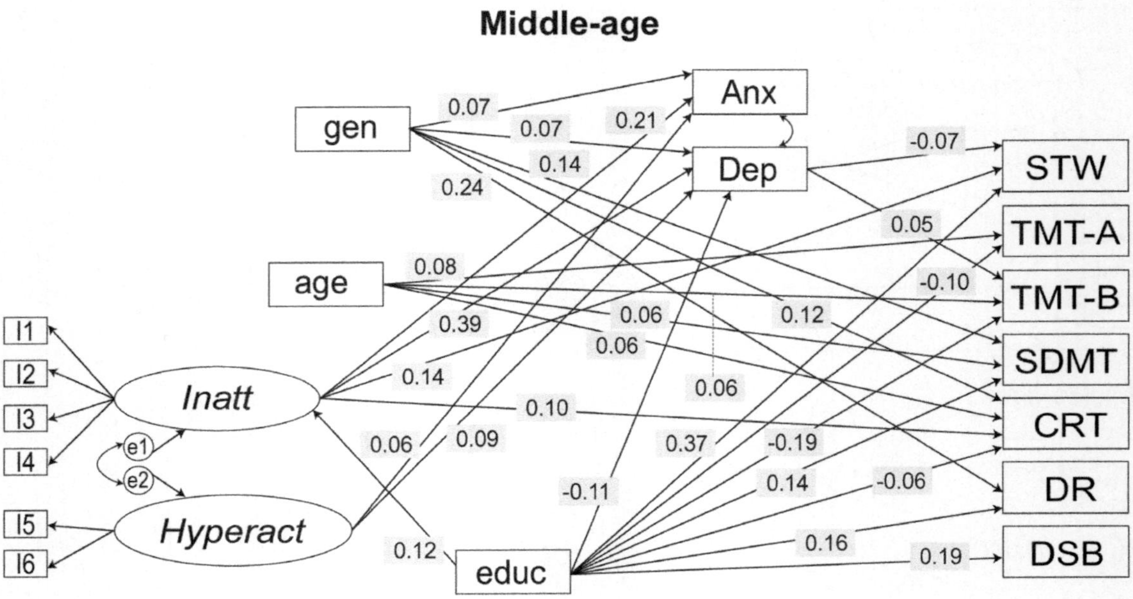

Figure 2. Final model for ADHD symptom–cognition analyses for MA cohort. Only paths significant at $p<0.01$ are shown. Arrows reflect direction of relationships between variables. Standardised regression coefficients are shown. Factor loadings and covariance between the latent factors – *Inatt* and *Hyperact*, which were constrained equal across groups in the analyses, and correlation between cognitive test measures are not shown for the sake of simplicity. I: item; gen: gender; educ: education; *Inatt*: latent factor Inattention; *Hyperact*: latent factor Hyperactivity; DEP: depression symptom measure; ANX: anxiety symptom measure; STW: Spot-the-Word Test; TMT-A: Trail Making Test A; TMT-B: Trail Making Test B; SDMT: Symbol-Digit Modalities Test; CRT: Choice Reaction Time; DR: Delayed Recall; DSB: Digit Span Backwards.

Group Differences in Sociodemographic Variables

The effect of the covariates was similar in the two cohorts, but there were some notable differences. Gender was strongly associated with mood variables and marginally with *Inatt* only in the MA cohort. It had an effect on the Trail Making Test (Part A) in the OA cohort and had no effect on any of the cognitive variables in the MA cohort. Effects of age on the cognitive variables were similar across both cohorts although the effects were stronger in the OA cohort. A point of contrast was the significant effect of age on Delayed Recall test on OA cohort that

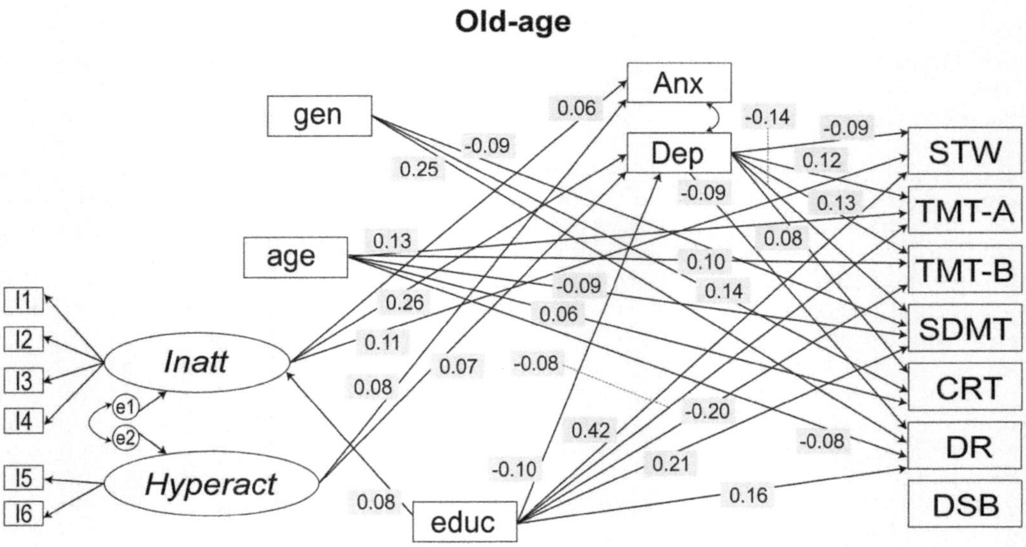

Figure 3. Final model for ADHD symptom–cognition analyses for OA cohort. Only paths significant at $p<0.01$ are shown. Arrows reflect direction of relationships between variables. Standardised regression coefficients are shown. Factor loadings and covariance between the latent factors – *Inatt* and *Hyperact*, which were constrained equal across groups in the analyses, and correlation between cognitive test measures are not shown for the sake of simplicity. I: item; gen: gender; educ: education; *Inatt*: latent factor Inattention; *Hyperact*: latent factor Hyperactivity; DEP: depression symptom measure; ANX: anxiety symptom measure; STW: Spot-the-Word Test; TMT-A: Trail Making Test A; TMT-B: Trail Making Test B; SDMT: Symbol-Digit Modalities Test; CRT: Choice Reaction Time; DR: Delayed Recall; DSB: Digit Span Backwards.

Table 3. Path coefficients from multi-group SEM analyses of ADHD symptom–cognition relationships.

			MA			OA		
			Coefficients[§]	SE[†]	*p*	Coefficients[§]	SE[†]	*p*
age	→	*Hyperact*	–	–	–	−0.034	0.016	0.032
gender	→	*Hyperact*	–	–	–	0.093	0.049	0.056
gender	→	*Inatt*	−0.062	0.032	0.046	–	–	–
education	→	*Inatt*	0.035	0.007	<0.001	0.018	0.007	0.003
gender	→	anxiety	0.031	0.010	0.002	–	–	–
education	→	anxiety	−0.004	0.003	0.080	−0.005	0.002	<0.001
Inatt	→	anxiety	0.077	0.014	<0.001	0.017	0.011	0.056
gender	→	depression	0.565	0.169	0.001	–	–	–
education	→	depression	−0.205	0.040	<0.001	−0.114	0.028	<0.001
Inatt	→	depression	2.463	0.215	<0.001	1.300	0.172	<0.001
education	→	STW	0.154	0.009	<0.001	0.153	0.009	<0.001
Inatt	→	STW	0.198	0.034	<0.001	0.185	0.045	<0.001
depression	→	STW	−0.015	0.005	0.002	−0.030	0.008	<0.001
age	→	TMT-A	0.047	0.013	<0.001	0.060	0.011	<0.001
gender	→	TMT-A	−0.061	0.035	0.085	−0.125	0.032	<0.001
education	→	TMT-A	−0.038	0.009	<0.001	−0.020	0.007	<0.001
Inatt	→	TMT-A	0.062	0.034	0.069	–	–	–
depression	→	TMT-A	0.011	0.005	0.024	0.029	0.007	<0.001
age	→	TMT-B	0.033	0.012	0.006	0.055	0.014	<0.001
education	→	TMT-B	−0.074	0.010	<0.001	−0.064	0.008	<0.001
Hyperact	→	TMT-B	–	–	–	−0.035	0.017	0.034
depression	→	TMT-B	0.012	0.005	0.006	0.039	0.008	<0.001
age	→	SDMT	−0.040	0.013	0.002	−0.053	0.015	<0.001
gender	→	SDMT	0.258	0.037	<0.001	0.170	0.037	<0.001
education	→	SDMT	0.060	0.010	<0.001	0.075	0.009	<0.001
anxiety	→	SDMT	−0.147	0.069	0.063	–	–	–
depression	→	SDMT	–	–	–	−0.045	0.009	<0.001
age	→	CRT	0.028	0.010	0.006	0.036	0.014	0.010
gender	→	CRT	0.172	0.030	<0.001	0.234	0.041	<0.001
education	→	CRT	−0.018	0.008	0.011	–	–	–
Inatt	→	CRT	0.107	0.028	<0.001	–	–	–
depression	→	CRT	–	–	–	0.024	0.008	0.001
age	→	DR	–	–	–	−0.054	0.016	<0.001
gender	→	DR	0.475	0.042	<0.001	0.499	0.047	<0.001
education	→	DR	0.069	0.010	<0.001	0.062	0.009	<0.001
Inatt	→	DR	0.079	0.042	0.059	–	–	–
Hyperact	→	DR	0.045	0.021	0.027	–	–	–
anxiety	→	DR	−0.213	0.112	0.046	–	–	–
depression	→	DR	−0.015	0.007	0.019	−0.031	0.008	<0.001
education	→	DSB	0.084	0.010	<0.001	–	–	–

Coefficients for ASRS items, which were same for both cohorts are not shown.
Only paths significant at $p<0.1$ are shown.
[§]unstandardised estimate.
[†]standard errors were computed from 2000 bootstrap-resampled datasets.
MA: middle-age cohort; OA: older-age cohort; *Inatt*: latent factor Inattention; *Hyperact*: latent factor Hyperactivity; STW: Spot-the-Word test; TMT-A: Trail Making Test A; TMT-B: Trail Making Test B; SDMT: Symbol-Digit Modalities Test; CRT: Choice Reaction Time; DR: Delayed Recall; DSB: Digit Span Backwards.

was absent in the MA cohort. Age was marginally associated with *Hyperact* in older adults only. Education had negative effects on mood variables in both cohorts although the effect on anxiety was much stronger in the OA cohort. The effect of education on *Inatt* was positive in both cohorts and comparatively stronger in the MA cohort, implying that more education is associated with higher levels of inattention. Greater levels of depression symptoms were associated with poorer cognitive performance generally, but the effect is much stronger in the OA cohort. These results did not differ significantly when latent factors underlying the cognition tests were included as dependent variables in the SEM models (Table S5 in File S1 and Figure S2).

Discussion

In this study we investigated ADHD symptoms in a large population-based sample of older adults, focussing on their effects on cognition. Importantly, we established that the underlying construct of the ADHD screener, ASRS, which has been validated in young adults, is similar in middle- and older-aged adults. We could therefore be confident that results obtained using the ASRS related to the same underlying psychological construct in both age groups.

Significant findings from the study are: i) older adults reported fewer/less severe ADHD symptoms compared to middle-aged adults; ii) the effect of ADHD symptoms on cognitive performance was weaker in older adults compared to middle-aged adults; iii) in OA adults the ADHD symptom–cognition relationship was mostly indirect and mediated through the strong association between depression symptoms and cognition.

We found that 2.2% of the OA cohort met the suggested cut-off for the ASRS-6 score that has been linked to clinical diagnosis in previous studies. This estimate falls within the range of 1–2.5% ADHD prevalence reported in the literature for older adults [26,27], and is substantially lower than the estimate for the MA cohort (6.2%). A previous study [27] had found that older elderly adults (71–94 years) reported fewer ADHD symptoms compared to younger elderly adults (60–70 years). Hence, our study replicated previous findings indicating that, when applying the criteria developed for young adults, the prevalence of ADHD symptoms appears to decrease with age. It is important to note that in DSM-5 the symptom threshold for diagnosis of ADHD in adults has been reduced. The impact of this change on the prevalence of ADHD in this age group remains to be investigated.

There may be several reasons for this apparent decline in ADHD symptom levels in old age. The effects of ADHD may become less discernable from other general age-related changes. Thus, even though, as we have demonstrated here, the ASRS appears to measure variation in the same psychological construct in old age, it may do so with lower sensitivity. The relative frequency of people with ADHD in the population will also tend to decline in old age because they have a relatively lower life expectancy [27]. Their relative participation rate may also decline due to the accumulating effects of greater rates of accidents, substance abuse and mood disorders [73,74].

We did not find any significant gender difference in ADHD symptoms in older adults. This result is consistent with our previous observation [75] and that of de Zwaan et al. (2012) [76], but contrary to a previous reports that found significantly higher prevalence of ADHD in males [77]. It is known that gender difference in ADHD prevalence is more extreme in paediatric samples compared to adolescent and adult samples. Since childhood referrals are initiated by parents and teachers, girls without the hyperactivity component of ADHD are less likely to be clinically diagnosed [78]. In contrast, women experience more internalizing problems than men [79], which may lead to higher rates of self-referrals in adulthood. Our results, which are obtained from a general population sample and are free from clinical ascertainment bias, suggest that the relative increase in female ADHD prevalence from childhood to adulthood is not a result of relative over-diagnosis of women.

We replicated the factor structure of the ASRS reported by Hesse et al. (2013) [57] in both MA and OA cohorts. Our results suggest that the ASRS measures similar constructs in both age groups. The latent factors – *Inatt* and *Hyperact* were more strongly correlated in MA than OA adults, however, this difference was not statistically significant. In a previous study of two samples of different age [57], correlation between the latent factors was lower in the sample with a mean age of 35.5 years than the relatively younger sample (mean age 24.6 years). Whether this difference was statistically significant has not been reported. Studies in young and old adults also suggest that among the different ADHD subtypes, the frequency of the combined subtype relative to the other subtypes declines with age [27,80]. Thus, with age, symptoms of inattention and hyperactivity appear both to decrease and to occur less frequently in combination.

In both MA and OA cohorts the Spot-the-Word Test, which measures verbal ability, was positively associated with symptoms of inattention, an effect that we previously reported for the MA cohort [52]. The sizes of the effects were similar and remained significant after controlling for depression symptoms, which were negatively associated with the Spot-the-Word Test, in both cohorts. One possible explanation is suggested by a previous study that found that while ADHD adults performed relatively poorly on verbal learning tests, they did not lose information at a greater rate once it was encoded [81]. In older adults, reaction time was not associated with *Inatt*, in contrast with the MA cohort, suggesting that information processing speed is less affected by symptoms of inattention in older adults.

Surprisingly, in the OA cohort, greater hyperactivity was associated with better task-switching abilities as measured by the Trail Making Test (Part B). However, this association did not reach the more stringent significance threshold of $p<0.01$. This might suggest that hyperactivity symptoms in this age-group are beneficial for certain cognitive activities. It is possible that hyperactivity symptoms in ageing brains make the system noisier at the neuronal level. While noise is generally considered detrimental, under certain circumstances it may aid in processing of weak stimuli through the phenomenon of stochastic resonance [82]. The motor and sensory input associated with hyperactivity could increase noise thus enabling neuronal responses that otherwise would not occur and resulting in improved responses to certain tasks. Such improvements are more likely in older brains since ageing associated neurobiological decline leads to weaker stimuli. The positive association between hyperactivity and cognitive performance in older adults is in contrast to previous reports in younger adults, where ADHD symptoms were related to worse cognitive outcomes [83]. It is important to note that the level of hyperactivity in the OA cohort is much less than that present in younger samples and that the ASRS contains only two items to detect hyperactivity symptoms. Hence, the positive association between symptoms of hyperactivity and task-switching ability in older adults needs to be investigated in future studies.

Our results suggest that the effects of ADHD symptoms are specific to particular cognitive domains, in contrast to a previous study by Biederman et al (2011) [50] that reported consistent poor performance across a neuropsychological battery (assessing executive functions, learning and memory) in non-medicated ADHD patients. This difference may reflect important differences between the two studies. The previous study [50] was based on referred ADHD patients, who were on average younger than our sample. It reported cognitive effects of ADHD diagnosis and did not include comorbid mood disorders. Participants in our study were recruited randomly from the community and were not selected for ADHD. We investigated the effects of the full range of ADHD symptom levels rather clinical diagnosis and we differentiated between symptoms of inattention and hyperactivity and made adjustments for symptoms of anxiety and depression, which are common comorbidities of ADHD.

Our results suggest that inattention symptoms affect cognitive performance indirectly through their effect on depression in the OA cohort. *Inatt* was strongly associated with depression symptoms in both cohorts, and depression symptoms predict worse performance in all cognitive tests in the OA cohort but not in the MA cohort. We also found evidence of statistical mediation of *Inatt* on Symbol-Digit Modalities Test by depression in OA adults since the negative association between *Inatt* and Symbol-Digit Modalities Test became non-significant when depression symptoms were included in the model. Depression symptoms were also significantly associated with Symbol-Digit Modalities Test in OA adults. Thus, our results emphasise the importance of controlling for comorbid mood disorders when investigating ADHD symptom–cognition relationship, especially in older adults.

The strengths of this study are that it was conducted in a large representative population sample, and hence it is likely to be free of the biases that can be associated with clinical and convenience samples. Furthermore, the narrow age range of the sample removes the possible confounding effects of age within each cohort. Consequently, our results are likely to be generalisable to MA and OA populations. Our study included age groups that have not been well studied with respect to ADHD symptoms and thus is a significant addition to the growing literature in this area. We focus on cognitive performance and ADHD symptoms highlighting differences between middle- and old-age, which is important for understanding age-related cognitive change. Finally, we have modelled both direct ADHD symptom-cognition relationships and indirect effects mediated by symptoms of depression, demonstrating age-group differences in these direct and indirect pathways.

Limitations of the study include lack of clinical assessments for ADHD, depression and anxiety. In addition, symptom measures are based on self-reports, which may not be completely accurate (e.g. social desirability and current emotional state could introduce biases [84,85]). However, the assessment instruments we used have been shown to have good sensitivity and specificity and they have been used in a number of previous studies and validated in different cultural settings [55,58,86–88]. Furthermore, we have included appropriate statistical evaluation to ensure that the ASRS measure is equivalent in MA and OA cohorts. A small number of cognitive tests have been analysed in the study. These tests were included in the PATH study as indicators of different abilities and were not designed to measure latent constructs. Hence, detailed analysis on the effect of ADHD symptoms on specific cognitive domains was not possible. Although we found evidence of statistical mediation by symptoms of depression on ADHD symptom–cognition relationships, due to the cross-sectional nature of the study we could not ascertain the causal relation between symptoms of ADHD and depression. Longitudinal follow-up of the cohort may contribute towards understanding the temporal relationships among these factors.

In conclusion, we have shown that although ADHD symptoms persist, they are less common in older compared to middle-aged adults. The relationship between ADHD symptoms and cognitive performance changes with age. While symptoms of depression are lower in older adults, they are much stronger predictors of cognitive performance and appear to mediate the effect of ADHD symptoms on cognition in this age group. Thus, better diagnosis and treatment of comorbid ADHD and mood disorders in older adults is required and might contribute to promoting cognitive health in late-life.

Supporting Information

Figure S1 Models representing the latent structure of the cognitive tests used in the study in the MA (A) and OA (B) cohorts. Standardised factor loadings are shown. IR: Immediate Recall; DR: Delayed Recall; SRT: Simple Reaction Time; CRT: Choice Reaction Time; TMT-A: Trail Making Test A; TMT-B: Trail Making Test B; SDMT: Symbol-Digit Modalities Test; STW: Spot The Word test; DSB: Digit Span Backwards.

Figure S2 Final model for ADHD symptom–cognition analyses for MA (A) and OA (B) cohorts. Only paths significant at $p<0.05$ are shown. Arrows reflect direction of relationships between variables. Standardised regression coefficients are shown. gen: gender; educ: education; *Inatt*: latent factor Inattention; *Hyperact*: latent factor Hyperactivity; DEP: depression symptom measure; ANX: anxiety symptom measure. Indicators of the latent variables are not shown for the sake of clarity.

File S1 Tables S1–S5.

Acknowledgments

The authors are grateful to Anthony Jorm, Bryan Rodgers, Helen Christensen, Andrew Mackinnon, Peter Butterworth, Patricia Jacomb, Karen Maxwell and the PATH interviewers.

Author Contributions

Conceived and designed the experiments: DD KJA. Performed the experiments: DD. Analyzed the data: DD. Contributed reagents/materials/analysis tools: NC SE KJA. Wrote the paper: DD NC SE KJA.

References

1. Biederman J, Faraone SV (2005) Attention-deficit hyperactivity disorder. Lancet 366: 237–248. doi:10.1016/S0140-6736(05)66915-2.
2. Karam RG, Bau CHD, Salgado CAI, Kalil KLS, Victor MM, et al. (2009) Late-onset ADHD in adults: milder, but still dysfunctional. J Psychiatr Res 43: 697–701. doi:10.1016/j.jpsychires.2008.10.001.
3. Barkley RA (2010) Attention Deficit Hyperactivity Disorder in Adults. Sudbury, Massachusetts: Jones & Bartlett Publishers.
4. Berlin L, Bohlin G, Nyberg L, Janols L-O (2004) How well do measures of inhibition and other executive functions discriminate between children with ADHD and controls? Child Neuropsychol 10: 1–13. doi:10.1076/chin.10.1.1.26243.
5. Biederman J, Monuteaux MC, Doyle AE, Seidman LJ, Wilens TE, et al. (2004) Impact of executive function deficits and attention-deficit/hyperactivity disorder (ADHD) on academic outcomes in children. J Consult Clin Psychol 72: 757–766. doi:10.1037/0022-006X.72.5.757.
6. Lambek R, Tannock R, Dalsgaard S, Trillingsgaard A, Damm D, et al. (2011) Executive dysfunction in school-age children with ADHD. J Atten Disord 15: 646–655. doi:10.1177/1087054710370935.
7. Seidman LJ (2006) Neuropsychological functioning in people with ADHD across the lifespan. Clin Psychol Rev 26: 466–485. doi:10.1016/j.cpr.2006.01.004.
8. Adler LA (2010) Monitoring adults with ADHD: a focus on executive and behavioral function. J Clin Psychiatry 71:e18. doi:10.4088/JCP.9066tx3c.
9. Nigg JT (2005) Neuropsychologic theory and findings in attention-deficit/hyperactivity disorder: the state of the field and salient challenges for the coming decade. Biol Psychiatry 57: 1424–1435. doi:10.1016/j.biopsych.2004.11.011.
10. Bálint S, Czobor P, Komlósi S, Mészáros A, Simon V, et al. (2009) Attention deficit hyperactivity disorder (ADHD): gender- and age-related differences in

neurocognition. Psychol Med 39: 1337–1345. doi:10.1017/S0033291708004236.
11. Rösler M, Casas M, Konofal E, Buitelaar J (2010) Attention deficit hyperactivity disorder in adults. World J Biol Psychiatry 11: 684–698. doi:10.3109/15622975.2010.483249.
12. Kessler RC, Adler L, Barkley R, Biederman J, Conners CK, et al. (2006) The prevalence and correlates of adult ADHD in the United States: results from the National Comorbidity Survey Replication. Am J Psychiatry 163: 716–723. doi:10.1176/appi.ajp.163.4.716.
13. Silva KL, Guimaraes-da-Silva PO, Grevet EH, Victor MM, Salgado CAI, et al. (2012) Cognitive Deficits in Adults With ADHD Go Beyond Comorbidity Effects. J Atten Disord. doi:10.1177/1087054711434155.
14. Swensen AR, Birnbaum HG, Secnik K, Marynchenko M, Greenberg P, et al. (2003) Attention-deficit/hyperactivity disorder: increased costs for patients and their families. J Am Acad Child Adolesc Psychiatry 42: 1415–1423. doi:10.1097/00004583-200312000-00008.
15. Secnik K, Swensen A, Lage MJ (2005) Comorbidities and costs of adult patients diagnosed with attention-deficit hyperactivity disorder. Pharmacoeconomics 23: 93–102. doi:10.2165/00019053-200523010-00008.
16. Birnbaum HG, Kessler RC, Lowe SW, Secnik K, Greenberg PE, et al. (2005) Costs of attention deficit-hyperactivity disorder (ADHD) in the US: excess costs of persons with ADHD and their family members in 2000. Curr Med Res Opin 21: 195–206. doi:10.1185/030079904X20303.
17. Matza LS, Paramore C, Prasad M (2005) A review of the economic burden of ADHD. Cost Eff Resour Alloc 3: 5. doi:10.1186/1478-7547-3-5.
18. Bernfort L, Nordfeldt S, Persson J (2008) ADHD from a socio-economic perspective. Acta Paediatr 97: 239–245. doi:10.1111/j.1651-2227.2007.00611.x.
19. Brod M, Schmitt E, Goodwin M, Hodgkins P, Niebler G (2012) ADHD burden of illness in older adults: a life course perspective. Qual Life Res 21: 795–799. doi:10.1007/s11136-011-9981-9.
20. Polanczyk G, de Lima MS, Horta BL, Biederman J, Rohde LA (2007) The worldwide prevalence of ADHD: a systematic review and metaregression analysis. Am J Psychiatry 164: 942–948. doi:10.1176/appi.ajp.164.6.942.
21. Polanczyk G, Rohde LA (2007) Epidemiology of attention-deficit/hyperactivity disorder across the lifespan. Curr Opin Psychiatry 20: 386–392. doi:10.1097/YCO.0b013e3281568d7a.
22. Biederman J, Mick E, Faraone SV (2000) Age-dependent decline of symptoms of attention deficit hyperactivity disorder: impact of remission definition and symptom type. Am J Psychiatry 157: 816–818.
23. Faraone SV, Biederman J, Spencer T, Mick E, Murray K, et al. (2006) Diagnosing adult attention deficit hyperactivity disorder: are late onset and subthreshold diagnoses valid? Am J Psychiatry 163: 1720–1729. doi:10.1176/appi.ajp.163.10.1720.
24. Fayyad J, De Graaf R, Kessler R, Alonso J, Angermeyer M, et al. (2007) Cross-national prevalence and correlates of adult attention-deficit hyperactivity disorder. Br J Psychiatry 190: 402–409. doi:10.1192/bjp.bp.106.034389.
25. Ebejer JL, Medland SE, van der Werf J, Gondro C, Henders AK, et al. (2012) Attention deficit hyperactivity disorder in Australian adults: prevalence, persistence, conduct problems and disadvantage. PLoS ONE 7: e47404. doi:10.1371/journal.pone.0047404.
26. Kooij JJS, Buitelaar JK, Van Den Oord EJ, Furer JW, Rijnders CAT, et al. (2005) Internal and external validity of attention-deficit hyperactivity disorder in a population-based sample of adults. Psychol Med 35: 817–827. doi:10.1017/S003329170400337X.
27. Michielsen M, Semeijn E, Comijs HC, van de Ven P, Beekman ATF, et al. (2012) Prevalence of attention-deficit hyperactivity disorder in older adults in The Netherlands. Br J Psychiatry. doi:10.1192/bjp.bp.111.101196.
28. Solanto MV, Wasserstein J, Marks DJ, Mitchell KJ (2012) Diagnosis of ADHD in Adults: What Is the Appropriate DSM-5 Symptom Threshold for Hyperactivity-Impulsivity? J Atten Disord 16: 631–634. doi:10.1177/1087054711416910.
29. American Psychiatric Association (2013) Diagnostic and Statistical Manual of Mental Disorders. 5 ed. Washington, DC: American Psychiatric Publishing, Incorporated.
30. Arcos-Burgos M, Acosta MT (2007) Tuning major gene variants conditioning human behavior: the anachronism of ADHD. Curr Opin Genet Dev 17: 234–238. doi:10.1016/j.gde.2007.04.011.
31. Hoogman M, Rijpkema M, Janss L, Brunner H, Fernandez G, et al. (2012) Current self-reported symptoms of attention deficit/hyperactivity disorder are associated with total brain volume in healthy adults. PLoS ONE 7: e31273. doi:10.1371/journal.pone.0031273.
32. Lubke GH, Hudziak JJ, Derks EM, van Bijsterveldt TCEM, Boomsma DI (2009) Maternal ratings of attention problems in ADHD: evidence for the existence of a continuum. J Am Acad Child Adolesc Psychiatry 48: 1085–1093. doi:10.1097/CHI.0b013e3181ba3dbb.
33. Nikolas MA, Burt SA (2010) Genetic and environmental influences on ADHD symptom dimensions of inattention and hyperactivity: a meta-analysis. J Abnorm Psychol 119: 1–17. doi:10.1037/a0018010.
34. Shaw P, Gilliam M, Liverpool M, Weddle C, Malek M, et al. (2011) Cortical development in typically developing children with symptoms of hyperactivity and impulsivity: support for a dimensional view of attention deficit hyperactivity disorder. Am J Psychiatry 168: 143–151. doi:10.1176/appi.ajp.2010.10030385.
35. Marcus DK, Norris AL, Coccaro EF (2012) The latent structure of attention deficit/hyperactivity disorder in an adult sample. J Psychiatr Res 46: 782–789. doi:10.1016/j.jpsychires.2012.03.010.
36. American Psychiatric Association (2000) Diagnostic and Statistical Manual of Mental Disorders. 4 ed. Washington, DC: American Psychiatric Publication.
37. Fair DA, Nigg JT, Iyer S, Bathula D, Mills KL, et al. (2012) Distinct neural signatures detected for ADHD subtypes after controlling for micro-movements in resting state functional connectivity MRI data. Front Syst Neurosci 6: 1–31. doi:10.3389/fnsys.2012.00080.
38. Carr L, Henderson J, Nigg JT (2010) Cognitive control and attentional selection in adolescents with ADHD versus ADD. J Clin Child Adolesc Psychol 39: 726–740. doi:10.1080/15374416.2010.517168.
39. Solanto MV, Schulz KP, Fan J, Tang CY, Newcorn JH (2009) Event-related FMRI of inhibitory control in the predominantly inattentive and combined subtypes of ADHD. J Neuroimaging 19: 205–212. doi:10.1111/j.1552-6569.2008.00289.x.
40. Hervey AS, Epstein JN, Curry JF (2004) Neuropsychology of adults with attention-deficit/hyperactivity disorder: a meta-analytic review. Neuropsychology 18: 485–503. doi:10.1037/0894-4105.18.3.485.
41. Schoechlin C, Engel RR (2005) Neuropsychological performance in adult attention-deficit hyperactivity disorder: meta-analysis of empirical data. Arch Clin Neuropsychol 20: 727–744. doi:10.1016/j.acn.2005.04.005.
42. McLean A, Dowson J, Toone B, Young S, Bazanis E, et al. (2004) Characteristic neurocognitive profile associated with adult attention-deficit/hyperactivity disorder. Psychol Med 34: 681–692. doi:10.1017/S0033291703001296.
43. Bridgett DJ, Walker ME (2006) Intellectual functioning in adults with ADHD: a meta-analytic examination of full scale IQ differences between adults with and without ADHD. Psychol Assess 18: 1–14. doi:10.1037/1040-3590.18.1.1.
44. Epstein JN, Johnson DE, Varia IM, Conners CK (2001) Neuropsychological assessment of response inhibition in adults with ADHD. J Clin Exp Neuropsychol 23: 362–371. doi:10.1076/jcen.23.3.362.1186.
45. Tucha L, Tucha O, Walitza S, Sontag TA, Laufkötter R, et al. (2009) Vigilance and sustained attention in children and adults with ADHD. J Atten Disord 12: 410–421. doi:10.1177/1087054708315065.
46. Lange KW, Tucha L, Walitza S, Gerlach M, Linder M, et al. (2007) Interaction of attention and graphomotor functions in children with attention deficit hyperactivity disorder. J Neural Transm Suppl: 249–259.
47. Dinn WM, Robbins NC, Harris CL (2001) Adult attention-deficit/hyperactivity disorder: neuropsychological correlates and clinical presentation. Brain and Cognition 46: 114–121.
48. Boonstra AM, Oosterlann J, Sergeant JA, Buitelaar JK (2005) Executive functioning in adult ADHD: a meta-analytic review. Psychol Med 35: 1097–1108. doi:10.1017/S003329170500499X.
49. Tucha O, Mecklinger L, Laufkötter R, Kaunzinger I, Paul GM, et al. (2005) Clustering and switching on verbal and figural fluency functions in adults with attention deficit hyperactivity disorder. PCNP 10: 231–248. doi:10.1080/13546800444000047.
50. Biederman J, Fried R, Petty CR, Wozniak J, Doyle AE, et al. (2010) Cognitive Development in Adults With Attention-Deficit/Hyperactivity Disorder. J Clin Psychiatry 72: 11–16. doi:10.4088/JCP.09m05420pur.
51. Ivanchak N, Abner EL, Carr SA, Freeman SJ, Seybert A, et al. (2011) Attention-deficit/hyperactivity disorder in childhood is associated with cognitive test profiles in the geriatric population but not with mild cognitive impairment or Alzheimer's disease. J Aging Res 2011: 729801. doi:10.4061/2011/729801.
52. Das D, Cherbuin N, Anstey KJ, Easteal S (2012) ADHD Symptoms and Cognitive Abilities in the Midlife Cohort of the PATH Through Life Study. J Atten Disord. doi:10.1177/1087054712460887.
53. Anstey KJ, Christensen H, Butterworth P, Easteal S, Mackinnon A, et al. (2012) Cohort profile: the PATH through life project. Int J Epidemiol 41: 951–960. doi:10.1093/ije/dyr025.
54. Kessler RC, Adler L, Ames M, Demler O, Faraone S, et al. (2005) The World Health Organization Adult ADHD Self-Report Scale (ASRS): a short screening scale for use in the general population. Psychol Med 35: 245–256. doi:10.1017/S0033291704002892.
55. Kessler RC, Adler LA, Gruber MJ, Sarawate CA, Spencer T, et al. (2007) Validity of the World Health Organization Adult ADHD Self-Report Scale (ASRS) Screener in a representative sample of health plan members. Int J Methods Psychiatr Res 16: 52–65. doi:10.1002/mpr.208.
56. Folstein MF (1983) The Mini-Mental State Examination. Arch Gen Psychiatry 40: 812–812. doi:10.1001/archpsyc.1983.01790060110016.
57. Hesse M (2013) The ASRS-6 Has Two Latent Factors: Attention Deficit and Hyperactivity. J Atten Disord 17: 203–207. doi:10.1177/1087054711430330.
58. Martin A, Rief W, Klaiberg A, Braehler E (2006) Validity of the Brief Patient Health Questionnaire Mood Scale (PHQ-9) in the general population. Gen Hosp Psychiatry 28: 71–77. doi:10.1016/j.genhosppsych.2005.07.003.
59. Spitzer RL, Kroenke K, Williams JB (1999) Validation and utility of a self-report version of PRIME-MD: the PHQ primary care study. Primary Care Evaluation of Mental Disorders. Patient Health Questionnaire. JAMA 282: 1737–1744.
60. Baddeley A, Emslie H, Nimmo-Smith I (1993) The Spot-the-Word test: a robust estimate of verbal intelligence based on lexical decision. Br J Clin Psychol 32: 55–65. doi:10.1111/j.2044-8260.1993.tb01027.x.
61. Sánchez-Cubillo I, Periáñez JA, Adrover-Roig D, Rodríguez-Sánchez JM, Ríos-Lago M, et al. (2009) Construct validity of the Trail Making Test: role of task-switching, working memory, inhibition/interference control, and visuomotor

abilities. J Int Neuropsychol Soc 15: 438–450. doi:10.1017/S1355617709090626.

62. Reitan RM, Wolfson D (1993) The Halstead-Reital Neuropsychology Test Battery: Theory and Clinical Interpretation. Second. Tucson: Neuropsychology Press.
63. Smith A (1982) Symbol Digit Modality Test Manual. Los Angeles: Western Psychological Services.
64. Delis DC, Kramer JH, Kaplan E, Ober BA (1987) California Verbal Learning Test: Adult Version. San Antonio: The Psychological Corporation.
65. Wechsler D (1945) Wechsler memory scale manual. New York : The Psychological Corporation.
66. Welford AT (1988) Reaction time, speed of performance, and age. Ann N Y Acad Sci 515: 1–17.
67. Byrne BM (2004) Testing for Multigroup Invariance Using AMOS Graphics: A Road Less Traveled. Structural Equation Modeling: A Multidisciplinary Journal 11: 272–300. doi:10.1207/s15328007sem1102_8.
68. Browne WM, Cudek R (1993) Alternate ways of assessing model fit. In: Bollen KA, Long JS, editors. Testing Structural Equation Models. Newbury Park: SAGE Publications, Incorporated. 136–162.
69. Joreskog KG, Sorbom D (1984) LISREL VI user's guide. Scientific Software.
70. Bentler PM (1990) Comparative fit indexes in structural models. Psychol Bull 107: 238–246. doi:10.1037/0033-2909.107.2.238.
71. Akaike H (1973) Information Theory and an extension of the maximum likelihood principle. In: Petrov BN, Csaki F, editors. *Proceedings of the 2nd International Symposium on Information Theory*. Budapest: Akademiai Kaido. 267–281.
72. Browne MW, Cudeck R (1989) Single Sample Cross-Validation Indices for Covariance Structures. Multivariate Behavioral Research 24: 445–455. doi:10.1207/s15327906mbr2404_4.
73. Sobanski E (2006) Psychiatric comorbidity in adults with attention-deficit/hyperactivity disorder (ADHD). Eur Arch Psychiatry Clin Neurosci 256 Suppl 1: i26–i31. doi:10.1007/s00406-006-1004-4.
74. Barkley RA, Guevremont DC, Anastopoulos AD, DuPaul GJ, Shelton TL (1993) Driving-related risks and outcomes of attention deficit hyperactivity disorder in adolescents and young adults: a 3- to 5-year follow-up survey. Pediatrics 92: 212–218.
75. Das D, Cherbuin N, Butterworth P, Anstey KJ, Easteal S (2012) A population-based study of attention deficit/hyperactivity disorder symptoms and associated impairment in middle-aged adults. PLoS ONE 7: e31500. doi:10.1371/journal.pone.0031500.
76. de Zwaan M, Gruß B, Müller A, Graap H, Martin A, et al. (2012) The estimated prevalence and correlates of adult ADHD in a German community sample. Eur Arch Psychiatry Clin Neurosci 262: 79–86. doi:10.1007/s00406-011-0211-9.
77. Simon V, Czobor P, Bálint S, Mészáros A, Bitter I (2009) Prevalence and correlates of adult attention-deficit hyperactivity disorder: meta-analysis. Br J Psychiatry 194: 204–211. doi:10.1192/bjp.bp.107.048827.
78. Berry CA, Shaywitz SE, Shaywitz BA (1985) Girls with attention deficit disorder: a silent minority? A report on behavioral and cognitive characteristics. Pediatrics 76: 801–809.
79. Gershon J (2002) A meta-analytic review of gender differences in ADHD. J Atten Disord 5: 143–154. doi:10.1177/108705470200500302.
80. Murphy K, Barkley R (1996) Prevalence of DSM-IV symptoms of ADHD in adult licensed drivers: Implications for clinical diagnosis. J Atten Disord 1: 147–161. doi:10.1177/108705479600100303.
81. Aycicegi-Dinn A, Dervent-Ozbek S, Yazgan Y, Bicer D, Dinn WM (2011) Neurocognitive correlates of adult attention-deficit/hyperactivity disorder in a Turkish sample. Atten Defic Hyperact Disord 3: 41–52. doi:10.1007/s12402-010-0050-y.
82. Moss F, Ward LM, Sannita WG (2004) Stochastic resonance and sensory information processing: a tutorial and review of application. Clin Neurophysiol 115: 267–281.
83. Willcutt EG, Doyle AE, Nigg JT, Faraone SV, Pennington BF (2005) Validity of the executive function theory of attention-deficit/hyperactivity disorder: a meta-analytic review. Biol Psychiatry 57: 1336–1346. doi:10.1016/j.biopsych.2005.02.006.
84. Brewin CR, Andrews B, Gotlib IH (1993) Psychopathology and early experience: A reappraisal of retrospective reports. Psychol Bull 113: 82–98. doi:10.1037/0033-2909.113.1.82.
85. Neugebauer R, Ng S (1990) Differential recall as a source of bias in epidemiologic research. J Clin Epidemiol 43: 1337–1341. doi:10.1016/0895-4356(90)90100-4.
86. Manea L, Gilbody S, McMillan D (2012) Optimal cut-off score for diagnosing depression with the Patient Health Questionnaire (PHQ-9): a meta-analysis. CMAJ 184: E191–E196. doi:10.1503/cmaj.110829.
87. Ramos-Quiroga JA, Daigre C, Valero S, Bosch R, Gómez-Barros N, et al. (2009) Validation of the Spanish version of the attention deficit hyperactivity disorder adult screening scale (ASRS v. 1.1): a novel scoring strategy. Rev Neurol 48: 449–452.
88. Zohar AH, Konfortes H (2010) Diagnosing ADHD in Israeli adults: the psychometric properties of the adult ADHD Self Report Scale (ASRS) in Hebrew. Isr J Psychiatry Relat Sci 47: 308–315.

17

Linguistic Analysis of the Preschool Five Minute Speech Sample: *What* the Parents of Preschool Children with Early Signs of ADHD Say and *How* They Say It?

Elvira Perez[1]*, Melody Turner[1], Anthony Fisher[2], Joanna Lockwood[1], David Daley[1]

1 University of Nottingham, School of Medicine, Nottingham, England, United Kingdom, **2** University of Nottingham, School of English, Nottingham, England, United Kingdom

Abstract

A linguistic analysis was performed on the Preschool Five Minute Speech Sample (PFMSS) of 42 parents. PFMSS is a validated measure for Expressed Emotion (EE) to assess parent-child relationship. Half of these parents (n = 21, clinical group) had preschool children with early symptoms of attention deficit hyperactivity disorder (ADHD), the rest had typically developing children. Early symptoms of ADHD were identified with the Werry-Weiss Peters Rating Scale. The linguistic component of the PFMSS was analysed with keyword and linguistic pattern identification. The results of these two complementary analyses (i.e., EE and linguistic analysis) provided relevant recommendations that may improve the efficacy of psychological treatment for ADHD such as parenting interventions. We discuss the practical implications of these findings.

Editor: Karen Lidzba, University Children's Hospital Tuebingen, Germany

Funding: These authors have no support or funding to report.

Competing Interests: The authors have declared that no competing interests exist.

* Email: elvira.perez@nottingham.ac.uk

Introduction

Attention deficit hyperactivity disorder (ADHD) is a common disorder that affects individuals across the lifespan and it is most frequently diagnosed during the school years [1]. The UK National Institute for Health and Clinical Excellence (NICE) estimated that about 210,000 children aged 5–18 years in England and Wales are affected by ADHD [2] and its core symptoms of hyperactivity, impulsivity, and inattention. The impact of ADHD on self-esteem, interpersonal relationships, and academic achievement is also recognised [3,4]. In the long term, ADHD has also been associated with a significant risk of mental illness and delinquency [5], lower health-related quality of life in all psychosocial areas, and those with comorbidities such as oppositional defiant conduct, internalising, and learning disorders have even greater deficits [6]. In addition to its impact on the daily lives of children, ADHD impacts the health and functioning of families, schools, and the community, creating a substantial burden on families as well as health, social care, and criminal justice systems [7]. Multimodal approaches are recommended for the treatment for ADHD [8], which normally begins during school years. There are multiple evidence-based treatment options, including behaviour therapy and medication. Pharmacological treatments are efficacious [9] and are widely used, however, there are a number of limitations that clinicians, commissioners and service providers should take into account. For example, in a recent systematic review on non-pharmacological interventions for ADHD, Sonuga-Barke and colleagues [10] pointed out that pharmacological treatment efficacy outcomes such as normalisation rates are rare [9]; long-term effectiveness remains to be established [11]; adverse effects on sleep, appetite, and growth, although rarely serious, are common [12]; and some parents and clinicians have reservations about medication use [13] as drug treatment is not recommended for preschool children.

Parents are offered training/education programmes as a first-line treatment [2] and a variety of non-pharmacological interventions are available to treat ADHD symptoms. Evidence for their efficacy has been supported in several systematic reviews and meta-analyses [10,14–18]. Results from a recent meta-analysis [10], however, has shown that the efficacy of behavioural interventions was largely reduced when analysing data from informants who were *probably blind* to treatment status, rather than informants who were involved in treatment delivery (*most proximal*) such as parents. In contrast to the lack of blinded evidence of ADHD symptom reduction, behavioural interventions can have a broader positive impact on a range of other outcomes such as improved parenting (e.g., more positive parenting self-concept [19] and reduced childhood conduct problems [20]. Other studies have shown that the efficacy of well-designed parenting programmes is mediated, however, by successful delivery, implementation, and parent engagement [21]. Parents are primary figures in their children's environment and adverse familial environments are common in ADHD families [22,23].

Whilst unlikely to play a causal role, parenting may be a source of environmental risk involved in the manifestation of ADHD in children with genetic vulnerability [24]. Genetic studies have indicated that ADHD is a highly complex and heterogeneous genetic condition, with multiple genes of very small effect implicated to different degrees across affected individuals. Genes interact with environments so that increased liability for a disorder associated with a gene may be seen more for individuals exposed to particular environmental risks [25]. Accordingly, high levels of conflict and criticism in the families of children with ADHD may moderate the genetic expression for ADHD severity and comorbid conduct problems [26]. Parenting may be related to the development and maintenance of co-morbid disruptive behaviours that commonly occur in children with ADHD [22,23]. There is growing evidence of the significant relationship between parenting and impairments in domains such as academic and social functioning [22] and neuropsychological functioning [27]. Parenting interventions may also be a component of treatment that could be able to target functional impairments often associated with ADHD including, neuropsychological deficits, academic underachievement, maladaptive social and peer functioning, and disruptive behaviour [28].

Parents' interpretation of their child's behaviour may be especially relevant due to the centrality of parent-child relationships for children's optimal attachment and continuous development [29–32]. Parental perceptions of children's ADHD symptomatic behaviour can influence and feed the quality of parent-child relationships. Accordingly, parents' interpretations can aggravate or lessen the impact of ADHD symptoms on parents and parent-child relationships. In a recent study Lench *et al.* [33] assessed the impact of positive interpretations by comparing parents' perceptions of 7–12 years old children with a diagnosis of ADHD and their reports of stressful interactions in three groups of parents: (1) parents of children identified as having ADHD and who use that label, (2) parents of children identified as having ADHD who view their child's ADHD as indicating special abilities (i.e., Indigo Children), and (3) controls (no ADHD diagnosis). Results revealed that parents who perceived symptomatic behaviour as a sign of positive characteristics reported less frequent negative experiences with their child and less intense negative emotions during those experiences. They also view their children as more self-efficacious and as more likely to have a positive future.

For adherence to ADHD treatment to proceed most effectively, professional and lay perceptions also must be reconciled so that the professional expertise of clinicians and researchers, and the personal experiences and beliefs of families jointly determine acceptable and appropriate treatment options [34]. Prior research has documented the importance of understanding *both* physicians' and families' explanatory models of illness as inputs to medical decision making [35]. In order to identify ecological valid outcome measures for the design of effective parenting programmes it is important to comprehend parents' understanding of their child's ADHD early symptoms. Previous studies combining both quantitative and qualitative methodological approaches for the study of ADHD support the need for detail and on-going investigation on how to improve parenting interventions. For example, Bussing *et al.* [36] explored the parental self-care strategies used by the carers of 266 children with ADHD with both questionnaires and open-ended questions. Quantitative findings showed that behaviour modification was the most common strategy amongst these parents, while qualitative analysis pointed out that these parents tried to change their disciplinary action within three domains including changes related to the prevention of disciplinary problems (e.g., time-outs), privilege removal, and parental coping associated with disciplinary problems (e.g., control own emotions, become less judgemental and tolerant and develop more appropriate expectations). Parents' interpretations of their child's ADHD behaviour and the subsequent strategies developed by these parents contain valuable experiential knowledge precious for improving current parenting interventions specifically designed to improve the mental health of both children and carers. Parenting interventions have the potential to also influence parents' perceptions of their child's early ADHD symptoms and therefore maximise treatment efficacy. For example, recognising that it is not the child's fault, may help parents to cope more effectively with challenging behaviours (e.g., fidgeting instead of sitting quietly).

Parents' perspectives have been studied to inform healthcare practitioners and researchers, for example, Hermasen and colleagues [37] conducted a pure phenomenological qualitative study to explore the issues five mothers with children diagnosed with ADHD faced while their children received a non-pharmaceutical intervention (i.e., chiropractic care and the use of an interactive metronome). The themes that emerged were again ecologically relevant to inform about the struggles that carers perceived. Emerging themes from the semi-structured interviews included: medication as their last resort, the importance of family structure, lack of support from the health and educational system and patient satisfaction. Finally, Fiks *et al.* [34] applied freelisting, a standard approach used in anthropology which consists of generating a list of terms to describe perceptions or definitions of a domain. In this mixed methods approach the shared cultural model for the domain is determined from the word choice, order of recall, and modifying terms that are used. Paediatricians and parents of ADHD children systematically explored and shared divergent notions of ADHD. Word lists suggested differing needs and goals for clinicians and parents valuable to foster patient-centred care.

Parental Expressed Emotion

The *Five Minutes Speech Sample* (FMSS) [38] was originally developed as a brief measure to assess expressed emotion (EE) in relatives of adult psychiatric patients. EE is considered a measure of the patient-relative relationship and is a highly valid and reliable predictor of poor clinical outcomes among patients with major psychopathology [39]. The FMSS has been used increasingly to examine the emotional quality of relationships in families with adolescents and children [40,41]. Associations and a range of childhood psychiatric diagnoses, medical conditions and behaviour problems have also been documented [42]. Studies have consistently found that high parental expressed emotion represents a negative family process that is different from other types of family distress and dysfunction [43].

Negative parental EE has been associated with higher levels of ADHD symptoms and conduct problems in children [44]. Likewise, parents express more negative emotions towards their child with an ADHD diagnosis compared with controls [45,46] or unaffected siblings [47]. The relationship between EE and ADHD is still not clear but it is accepted that negative parenting starts as a reaction to the ADHD behaviour in children. Subsequently, negative parenting increases the chances of developing oppositional behaviours in children with ADHD. This in turn may lead to negative parenting, causing a negative spiral of child behaviour affective parenting and so on. However, a recent re-analysis of Cartwright et al [48] has shown that family characteristics play a role in driving negative EE. This study demonstrates that maternal depression and variation in child comorbid symptoms, especially in relation to oppositional and conduct problems rather than ADHD, also influence EE components. These results highlight (1) the value of interventions targeting broader family/siblings and parental mental health in the management of ADHD and (2) the putative role that the family environment may have in ADHD.

In a recent study Richard and colleagues [49] investigated the cross-sectional and longitudinal relationships between conduct problems in children with ADHD and parental EE. Their results showed a negative cross-sectional association between EE (maternal warmth and criticism) and child ADHD symptom severity, and child oppositional and conduct problems. EE was not significantly correlated over time (six years), suggesting that EE is not a predictive measure but rather a snapshot of a momentary state sensitive to contextual and developmental factors. From a developmental psychopathology perspective, each developmental stage comes with specific vulnerabilities that change over time. Parents of preschool children with ADHD may experience different challenges and expectations than those with older children. Because of its sensitivity to developmental phases, EE has the potential to capture parents' perspectives and provide a useful tool to understand parent's perceptions with the objective to maximise the relevancy of early interventions.

The current study applies knowledge from health humanities, such as applied linguistics, to bring new insights and resources for practitioners and researchers interested in developing relevant parenting skills and outcome measures for the assessment of parenting interventions. To our knowledge, linguistic methods have not been used to date. We hypothesise that a deeper understanding of (1) how parents organise language to describe their child's behaviour and (2) how parents linguistically construct images of their child will inform efforts to further understand parents' perceptions, maximise the relevancy and effectiveness of parenting interventions and consequently, improve treatment outcomes and child functioning. To test this hypothesis, the linguistic patterns emerging from the analysis of the speech samples from parents whose pre-school children exhibit early ADHD symptoms and those from matched controls will be compared.

Methods

Setting

Recruitment for the clinical sample was made through radio adverts, posters and referrals from family support workers and healthcare practitioners in Nottingham (UK) and was embedded within a study exploring children at risk of developing ADHD. Recruitment for the control group was made by advertising the study in 40 randomly selected nurseries in Nottingham.

This study has been approved by clinical and non-clinical Medical Research Committee at Nottingham University. Written informed consent was obtained from all participants. All written documentation, including consent forms, will be stored securely in locked filing cabinets at the Division of Psychiatry and Applied Psychology at the Institute of Mental Health, Nottingham University. All participants were assigned an ID number during preparation of transcripts and only members of the research team had access to the participant's contact details. All data has been stored and will be kept for five years in locked filing cabinets prior to being destroyed securely.

Sample

We conducted individual interviews with a purposive sample of 42 parents of children between 2 years 9 months and 4 years 9 months. Half of these parents ($n = 21$) had children who scored ≥20 and the other half ($n = 21$) scored <20 in the WWP activity questionnaire which is a valid tool to discriminate between hyperactive and normally developing children. Participants were informed that the interviews would be audiotaped and used for research purposes. All participants were given the opportunity to decline participation or terminate the interview at any point. The 2.9 to 4.6 year old range was chosen to match that preschool age when ADHD symptoms start to be noticeable and early prevention of later ADHD symptoms. Note ADHD guidelines [2] recommend diagnosis and pharmacological treatment for children ≥6 years of age.

Data collection

In the current study we used an adapted version of the FMSS, the Preschool Five Minutes Speech Sample (PFMSS) [50]. To obtain the Preschool FMSS parents were asked to talk for five minutes and express their thoughts and feeling about their preschool child, what kind of person the child is and how they get along with the child. Monologues were recorded without interruptions. If the parent stopped speaking before the five minutes had elapsed the researcher would wait for 30 seconds and then prompt the parent by saying "Please, tell me anything about (child's name) for a few more minutes". Samples from both groups (clinical and controls) were audio recorded with an *Olympus* digital voice recorder WS-450s and transcribed by three of the authors (M. T., E. P. and J.L.).When recordings were made over the phone researchers used a *Re-Tell* telephone recording connector and a *Polycom SoundPoint IP 331* digital telephone. Content analysis for all transcriptions was done according to Wearder's rating scale [51] to assess the emotional climate of the parent-child relationship. PFMSS yields to three global ratings: initial statement, relationship, and warmth as well as frequency counts of critical comments and positive comments. The PFMSS has demonstrated good code-recode and inter-rater reliability, and adequate test-retest reliability [50]. High or negative EE results from at least one negative or low global category and more critical comments than positive comments. All data collectors were trained using the same collection and coding manual [51].

Transcriptions for all 42 FMSS were completed by M.T. In addition, two other trained coders (E.P. and J.L.) independently transcribed and coded 20% of the audio samples randomly selected to assess inter-rater reliability. Coders E.P. and J.L. were blind to the ADHD status of the children and parent's demographic data. Additional editing was required by J.L. to solve transcription difficulties from participants with strong regional accents.

Participants also completed a child's activity questionnaire, the *Werry-Weiss Peters Rating Scale* (WWP) [52]. This a 27-item questionnaire which identifies the top 15-18% of the population using a score of 20 as cut off [53]. The psychometric properties of the WWP have been reviewed by [54] who reported the discrimination between hyperactive and normally developing children to be good. The inter-parent agreement has also been found to be good ($r = 0.82$) [55]. The WWP takes approximately five minutes to administer and has been shown to have high levels of internal consistency, to correlate with other measures of hyperactivity, and to identify children who have activity problems five years later [56]. This questionnaire includes questions such as 'During meals is the child up and down at the table?' giving three possible answers: 'No, or hardly ever', 'Yes, fairly often' and 'Yes, very often'.

To ensure that both clinical and control groups were matched and to avoid confound factors, parents completed a *demographics* questionnaire that included questions on age, occupation, income, education, relationship status and the child's health a year after birth.

Statistical analysis

SPSS (V.21) software was used to analyse the data. A one-way random Intraclass Correlation Coefficient (ICC) was carried out to check reliability between PFMSS coders. Transcription reliability was calculated as the percentage of agreement within the 20% of the audio samples randomly selected for this purpose using the following formula: Number of linguistic units scored identically divided by total number of units scored and multiplied by 100. A chi square (X^2) statistic was used to calculate whether distributions of categorical variables differed between groups. The Kolmogorov-Smirnov test was used to determine which t-test to use depending on how data was distributed. The Kolmogorov-Smirnov test showed that all scores were normally distributed ($p>0.05$) apart from EE total ($p=0.00$) which required non-parametric statistics (Spearman to calculate correlations and Mann-Whitney U for t-tests). As such Independent Samples T-tests were used to look for significant differences between the two groups. The significance level in this experiment was $p<0.05$. Multivariate analysis of variance controlling for covariates was used to control for demographic differences between participants. Person's correlations were conducted to further explore the associations between child's active behaviour, expressed emotion and socioeconomic status. Cohen's [57] conventions were used to interpret effect size.

Keyword lists were generated using *Wordsmith Tools* and calculated using log-likelihood with a p value of 0.00001.

Data analysis

To interpret the PFMSS we adopted a mixed quantitative and qualitative design. Content analysis or *what* parents said about their children was assessed by measuring parental expressed emotion (EE) which involved quantitative (e.g., counts of positive/negative comments) and qualitative methods (e.g., identifying statements that expressed warmth or concern). To examine *how* parents described their children we used corpus-assisted discourse analysis [58] such as keyword and linguistic pattern identification. Corpus-assisted discourse analysis leads to a more evidence-based approach to uses of language in different contexts and has been facilitated by the development of computer technology and powerful software. The possibilities for corpus research in health care have been relatively under-explored. Some recent studies [59,60,61,62,63] have been successful in exploring how a combined qualitative and quantitative methodology, drawing on tools traditionally used for corpus analysis, can enhance our understanding of a particular context. Keyword lists were generated using *Wordsmith Tools* [64], a digital text analysis software package commonly used in corpus linguistics research. Keywords are those items which occur more frequently in the dataset than they do in a larger reference corpus, to an extent that is statistically significant. Thus, keyword lists differ from word lists in that they provide a measure of *saliency* rather than simple frequency ([65] p. 125). For this study the reference corpus used was the 10 million word spoken sub-corpus of the British National Corpus [66], and the keyword lists were calculated using log-likelihood with a p value of 0.00001.

Once the keyword lists were generated the items in the lists for the two datasets were examined for patterns or tendencies towards particular semantic fields. A relatively high proportion of potentially evaluative words were identified, and so these items were separated into broadly positive and negative categories.

Frequency lists offer an overview of the number of times any word is used in any given text (corpus) relative to other words. The software can also present all occurrences of any key or important word in the text and the language occurring before and after it (i.e., concordance). Here, we can see the context in which words are used. Word frequency lists and concordances can be used as a diagnostic tool to achieve a baseline for determining *what the text is about*, its patterns and regularities of meaning or semantic prosody, and can underpin and support claims of discourse analysis [61].

The transcripts of the forty-two PFMSS were edited to remove interviewer questions, participant IDs, occasional prompts and filled silences before being converted into a text-file (27,892 words). Our analysis involved examining the words and phrases used by parents when describing their preschool children. Using the textual diagnosis as a guide to salient language, the transcriptions were read several times and annotated by the research team to identify patterns and features of discourse that differed between the PFMSS of the control and the clinical sample. The research team comprised three psychologists, a mature medical student and an applied linguist with a research profile in health discourse analysis.

Results

Socioeconomic Status

A total of 42 parents were enrolled in the study. In order to assess how similar both groups were and how generalizable our findings are, variability in socioeconomic status (SES) between the two groups was assessed. There is evidence to support that SES has the potential to heavily influence parent-child relationship [67,68]. Purposive sampling resulted in both parent groups being evenly matched according to age, gender, ethnicity, number of siblings, marital status, and perinatal factors such as type of birth (see Table 1).

The difference between the control and clinical groups' functional income, however, was statistically significant (X^2 (3) = 10.467; $p<.05$). While most of the clinical sample (n = 11) had a weekly functional income of £200 or below, the control group (n = 15) had a weekly income of £301 or above. Efforts to recruit parents of lower income for the control group were made by promoting recruitment within nurseries from less affluent neighbourhoods, unfortunately, recruitment figures were extremely low when compared to nurseries located in more affluent areas. Regarding educational level, results showed that the difference between the control and clinical groups in terms of education was also statistically significant (X^2 (5) = 31.600; $p<0.001$). Most parents from the control (n = 11) group had a professional or postgraduate degree, contrasting with the clinical group, in which a high proportion of participants (n = 6) left school at 16 with no qualifications.

There was a tendency for the clinical group to have larger number of siblings (M = 1.762) than the control (M = 0.952) but this difference was not significant ($p>.05$).

Werry-Weis Peters (WWP) Rating Scale

The WWP Scores of the clinical group (M = 41.714; SD = 8.574) were significantly higher than those of the control group (M = 8.62; SD 4.975; t (20) = 22.295, p = 0.000; Cohen's d = 4.721). This result indicated that the study correctly categorised the preschool children as clinically active or showing typically developing levels of activity. When income and education level differences between groups were controlled, analysis of variance for multiple dependent variables showed that neither education level nor income had an effect on WWP scorings ($p>0.05$).

Table 1. Demographic characteristic of the participants.

	Control group (n = 21)		Clinical group (n = 21)	
Age	18–28	1 (4.8%)	18–28	10 (47.6%)
	29–39	13 (61.9%)	29–39	9 (42.9%)
	40–50	6 (28.6%)	40–50	2 (9.5%)
	51–60	1 (4.8%)	51–60	0
Gender	Male	16 (76.2%)	Male	19 (90.5%)
	Female	5 (23.8%)	Female	2 (9.5%)
Ethnicity	White	19 (90.5%)	White	16 (76.2%)
	Mixed-race	0	Mixed- race	3 (14.3%)
	Afro-Caribbean	0	Afro-Caribbean	2 (9.5%)
	Bangladeshi/Indian	1 (4.8%)	Bangladeshi/Indian	0
	Other	1 (4.8%)	Other	0
Number of Siblings	0	4 (19.1%)	0	5 (23.8%)
	1	14 (66.7%)	1	5 (23.8%)
	2	3 (14.3%)	2	6 (28.6%)
	3+	0	3+	5 (23.8%)
Marital Status	Separated/Divorced	1 (4.8%)	Separated/Divorced	0
	Married/Living with partner	19 (90.4%)	Married/Living with partner	14 (66.7%)
	Single	1 (4.8%)	Single	7 (33.3%)
Type of Birth	Normal	13 (61.9%)	Normal	17 (80.9%)
	Section	5 (23.8%)	Section	3 (14.3%)
	Ventouse	2 (9.5%)	Ventouse	0
	Forceps	1 (4.8%)	Forceps	1 (4.8%)
Weekly Income	£200 or below	2 (9.5%)	£200 or below	11 (52.4%)
	£201–250	4 (19%)	£201–250	3 (14.3%)
	£251–300	16 (76.2%)	£251–300	5 (23.8%)
	£300 or below	0	£300 or below	2 (9.5%)
Educational Level	University	8 (38.1%)	University	2 (9.5%)
	Postgraduate	11 (52.4%)	Postgraduate	0
	College	2 (9.5%)	College	2 (9.5%)
	NVQs	0	NVQs	7 (33.3%)
	GCSE	0	GCSE	4 (19%)
	No qualification	0	No qualification	6 (28.6%)

Expressed Emotion

The components of EE are a rating of warmth, the initial statement the parent makes about the preschool child, and a rating of their relationship. Each component is rated either 1 (positive), 2 (neutral), or 3 (negative). The median EE total for the control group (M = 5.762, SD = 1.300) was lower than the mean EE total for the clinical group (M = 8.619, SD = 0.669). A non-parametric Mann-Whitney U test showed this difference to be significant: U = 14.000; exact $p = 0.01$ (two-tailed). EE was higher for the clinical group indicating that generally those parents expressed a more negative initial statement, showed less warmth, and a worse relationship with their child. This result confirmed that the groups were correctly categorised according to their different emotional relationships with their children. When income and education level differences between groups were controlled as covariates, analysis of variance for multiple dependent variables showed the education level had an effect on EE ratings ($F = 5.42$ (3, 42), $p = 0.02$), however, income did not affect EE scorings ($p > 0.05$).

The positive comments of the clinical group (M = 3.1429; SD 1.681) were significantly lower than those of the control group (M = 9.7619; SD = 3.72699; t (20) = 8.563, $p = .000$; Cohen's $d = 2.891$). This result showed that parents of preschool children with early symptoms of ADHD were more likely to give their child less positive comments than if their child was typically developing. The negative comments of the clinical group (M = 8.9048; SD = 4.20600) were significantly higher than those of the control group (M = 2.0000; SD = 2.21359; t (20) = 9.702, p = .000; Cohen's $d = 3.361$. This result showed that parents whose children had early symptoms of ADHD were more likely to say negative comments to their child than parents with typically developing children. Parents of preschool children with early ADHD symptoms were about three times as likely to say something negative than a positive comment.

Inter-rater reliability was calculated to measure the reliability between all three coders. Results showed a high correlation of 0.97 $p<0.001$ CI 0.877–0.989 for final EE score (i.e., high or low) and also a high correlation for each EE component: initial statement (r = 0.96); warmth (r = 0.68); relationship (r = 0.84); positive comments (r = 0.81); and negative comments (r = 0.89). Percentage of transcription agreement was also high (27822/27892*100 = 99.7%).

Table 2 shows descriptive and between-group comparison data for Expressed Emotion (EE) and Activity questionnaire (WWP) data.

Correlations between WWPS, EE and SES factors per group

Table 3 shows that among the control group, younger parents expressed more warmth, better relationships and more positive initial statements when talking about their children than older parents ($r = -0.47$, $p<.05$). Participants with older partners described their children as less active, obtaining lower scores in the WWP ($r = 0.53$, $p<.05$) than participants with younger partners. Number of siblings was also associated with lower or more positive EE scores as smaller number of siblings was associated with better parent-child relationships, warmth and initial statement ($r = -0.54$, $p<.05$). Age from participant and partner was associated with amount of income ($r = 0.53$ and $r = 0.49$ respectively, $p<.05$). And finally, a small number of siblings was associated with a higher level of participant education ($r = -0.44$, $p<.05$).

In the clinical group we found a strong correlation ($r = 0.637$, $p<.001$) between the EE components (warmth, a positive relationship and a positive initial statement about the pre-school child) and the number of positive comments. The results also indicated a strong positive correlation ($r = 0.580$, $p<.05$) between number of siblings and participant partner age (see Table 4).

Corpus-based Linguistic Analysis

The keyword lists generated in Wordsmith Tools yielded 130 items for the control data, and 112 for the clinical data file. The items on the lists were then grouped together into semantic sets, comprising seven groups of words with related meanings. Table 5 shows the semantic categories identified, the number of different lexical items (types), and the number of actual instances of relevant lexis (tokens) identified within the keyword lists in each category. Full lists of keywords assigned to each category are provided in the analysis to follow.

It must be stressed that the numbers of tokens or actual lexical items observed in the datasets relate only to those items that occur with a frequency that is sufficiently high to be recognized as keywords by the text analysis software ($p\leq0.00001$). Thus, any lexical items with frequencies below the keyword threshold are not counted in the figures provided above. Of course, this is true of both datasets, a circumstance which to some extent must serve to attenuate any exaggeration of observed differences between the clinical and control data. However, it should nevertheless be noted that a comparison of the two datasets based on tokens counted only for those items which appear on keyword lists is necessarily selective.

With this caveat in mind, it is possible to make a number of observations from the results presented in Table 5. Of the seven semantic categories identified, only two, *routines* and *people*, exhibit no significant differences. Attention exclusively to the number of different keywords (types) assigned to each semantic category would suggest that the most marked differences between the clinical and control data pertain to lexis associated with *behaviour, temperament and attitude*, and also *activities*. However, when we consider the actual number of words spoken it becomes apparent that there exist significant differences between the two datasets for each of the five remaining semantic categories. These differences will be considered in more detail below.

Affection

While the control data keyword analysis reveals seven different lexical items belonging to this semantic field, only one is evident in the clinical data (see Table 6).

Items from this semantic field other than *loving* are evident in the clinical data, but only *loving* occurs with a frequency that is statistically significant. This item in fact occurs twice as frequently in the clinical data than in the control data, but there is evidence of qualification in the clinical data that is absent from the control data. In the clinical dataset, *loving* is followed on 4 occasions by lexis referring to negatively evaluative attributes, such as *handful, clingy, bad tempered* and *hyper*. It is also pre-modified by *overly* on one occasion, and on another features as complement in the clause *he can be very loving*. This latter construction occurs some 19 times in the clinical data, where it serves to emphasize capability rather than habitual behaviour.

Enjoyment and positive mood

The most salient item in this category is *likes*, which occurs 105 times in the control data and 38 times in the clinical data (see Table 7).

Of course, insofar as that it is possible to *like* generally undesirable phenomena, this item can be used in a negatively evaluative way, a usage which is apparent in both datasets. But while *like* appears to be used in a negative context only four times in the control data, it is used in this way nine times in the clinical

Table 2. Descriptive and between-group comparison data for Expressed Emotion (EE) and Activity questionnaire (WWP).

	Clinical group	Control group
EE Total score	Median = 5.76 (sd 1.3)*	Median = 8.62 (sd 0.67)*
Initial Statement	N- = 6, N = 10, P = 5 **	N- = 0, N = 1, P = 20**
Relationship	N- = 2, N = 17, P = 2 **	N- = 0, N = 6, P = 15 **
Warmth	N- = 6, N = 13, P = 2 **	N- = 0, N = 1, P = 20 **
Positive comments	M = 3.14 (sd 1.68)**	M = 9.76 (sd 3.72)**
Negative comments	M = 8.9 1 (sd 4.21)**	M = 2.00 (sd 2.21)**
WWP mean score	M = 41.71 (sd 8.574)**	M = 8.62 (sd 4.98)**

Mean values (M); Standard deviation (sd) in brackets; N- = Negative comments; N = Neutral comments; P = positive comments; ** Denotes significant differences between groups ($p\leq0.001$); * Denotes significant differences between groups ($p\leq0.01$).

Table 3. Pearson correlations between Expressed Emotion (EE), Activity questionnaire (WWP[a]) and socio-demographic factors for control group.

Measure	2	3	4	5	6	7	8	9
1. Total WWPS	0.29	0.93	−0.17	0.01	−0.53*	0.05	−0.15	−0.34
2. Total EE	-	−0.14	0.02	−0.47*	−0.26	−0.54*	0.39	−0.08
3. Negative comments		-	−0.05	−0.02	0.01	0.02	0.01	0.05
4. Positive comments			-	−0.29	−0.34	0.16	−0.16	−0.31
5. Age				-	0.54*	0.26	−0.09	0.53*
6. Partner's age					-	0.28	−0.09	0.49*
7. Siblings						-	−0.44*	−0.19
8. Education							-	0.18
9. Income								-

[a]Weiss Werry Peter Scale.
*$p<0.05$.
** $p<0.001$.

Table 4. Correlations between WWPS, EE and socio-demographic factors for the clinical group.

Measure	2	3	4	5	6	7	8	9
1. Total WWPS	−0.29	0.40	−0.21	−0.21	−0.28	0.15	−0.27	−0.15
2. Total EE		−0.33	0.64*	0.88	0.91	0.26	0.37	0.74
3. Negative comments		-	0.16	−0.34	−0.19	0.21	0.28	−0.22
4. Positive comments			-	−0.31	−0.29	−0.28	0.08	0.08
5. Age				-	0.64*	0.31	−0.12	0.34
6. Partner's age					-	0.58*	0.39	0.27
7. Siblings						-	0.23	0.28
8. Education							-	0.32
9. Income								-

*$p<0.05$.
** $p<0.001$.

Table 5. Semantic categories identified distinguishing between the number of different lexical items (types) per participant group, and the number of actual instances of relevant lexis (tokens) identified within the keyword lists in each category.

Semantic Category	Types		Tokens	
	Control	Clinical	Control	Clinical
Affection: *loves, caring, loving, cuddles...*	6	1	29	12
Enjoyment/Positive Mood: *likes, loves, enjoys...*	5	3	179	53
Behaviour/Temperament/Attitude: *inquisitive, cheeky, naughty...*	7	20	45	196
Communication: *interact, talks, listens...*	6	4	28	58
Activities: *playing, play, scooter, toys...*	15	2	110	51
Routines: *nursery, preschool, swimming...*	4	4	55	48
People: *brother, sister, friends...*	4	3	93	106

data, in utterances such as *likes to climb on the table, likes to interrupt*, and *likes to pinch*.

Behaviour, temperament and attitude

Some overlap between the two datasets is clearly evident with regard to lexis relating to *behaviour, temperament and attitude*, specifically the items *naughty* and *tantrum* which appear in the keyword lists for both datasets (see Table 8). Indeed, *tantrum* features with comparable frequency in the clinical and control data, but this seems to be where the similarities end. The most immediately obvious difference between the two keyword lists with regard to this semantic field relates to the number of *types* or different words; the clinical data features some 20 types compared to just seven for the control data. It is also immediately apparent that while all but two of the control group items are positively evaluative, most of those found in the clinical data appear to be negatively evaluative.

The item *difficult* merits further explanation, since of the 25 instances of this item in the clinical data, only six are predicated upon a human agent, as in *X can be very difficult* or *he's quite difficult*. The remaining 13 instances of *difficult* describe situations or circumstances rather than individuals. However, in each of these instances the situations or circumstances described relate, not surprisingly given the topic of discussion, directly to dealing with the child in question. This can be observed in utterances such as *I do find it difficult to communicate with him*, and *X finds it quite difficult to listen sometimes and struggles to gain eye contact*. Thus, even where *difficult* does not describe a quality attributed to the child being discussed, it nevertheless refers to circumstances that relate to the child in some way.

Communication

While the number of *types* relating to communication is slightly greater for the control data, the actual numbers of items (tokens) is far greater for the clinical dataset, with 79 items in all compared to 40 for the control data (see Table 9).

However, while all of these items in the control group data are framed positively, they are more often negated or otherwise problematized in the clinical data. For example, of the 18 instances of *listen* in the clinical data, 11 are directly negated, two framed in terms of difficulty as in *it's difficult for her to listen* and *X finds it difficult to listen*, while all are problematized in some way. Similarly, *understand* is negated in 16 out of 21 instances, while *communicate* is preceded by *difficult* three times and *hard* once, and is problematized in all six occurrences. This suggests that parent-child communication is a more salient topic for the participants in the clinical group, and that the reason for this salience is its problematic nature for these parents.

Activities

While the control group keyword list features 15 items relating to activities, only two such items appear on the keyword list for the clinical dataset (see Table 10).

In fact, a number of other, *non-key* items relating to play and activities can be found in the clinical data, where for example *park* and *telly* each occur six times, *reading* twice and also *playing* 16 times. However, the broader range of items evident in the control data, and the fact that 15 of these items occur with a frequency that is statistically significant compared to only two in the clinical data, provides strong evidence to suggest that talk relating to play and activities is a less salient category in the clinical data than might be expected. The most frequently occurring item in this

Table 6. Lexical items within the category *Affection*.

Control	Clinical
caring (10)	loving (12)
cuddles (4)	
loving (6)	
affectionate (3)	
hugs (3)	
snuggle (3)	

Table 7. Lexical items within category *Enjoyment/Positive Mood.*

Control	Clinical
likes (105)	likes (38)
happy (20)	loves (12)
loves (31)	enjoys (5)
enjoys (10)	
fun (13)	

category for the clinical data is *play*, an item which actually occurs with greater frequency in the clinical than control data at 36 occurrences compared to 29. However, closer analysis reveals important differences in the use of this item in the two datasets. Of the 36 instances of *play* in the clinical data, 16 are either negated or marked as problematic in some sense. These items are presented in context in the concordance output in Appendix S1. No equivalent pattern is observed in the control data, where all instances of *play* are positively evaluative. Of particular interest are lines 2, 3, 5, 8, 11, 12 and 14, all of which problematize an unwillingness or inability to play alone. It is also interesting to consider the item *attention* in the two datasets, an item which appears on the keyword list for clinical data with 35 occurrences, but not on that generated for the control data, in which it occurs just five times. Of the 35 instances of this item in the clinical data, 18 unambiguously relate to a need for parental attention that is framed as excessive.

Mitigating syntax

A prominent pattern observed in both datasets is '*x* can be *y*', where *x* = a proper name or personal pronoun and *y* = an attribute or behaviour (see Table 11). This modal construction is interesting because it places an emphasis on capability or possibility, in this way foregrounding or emphasizing the transitory nature of the behaviour described. Evidence for this interpretation can be found in the 10 million word spoken component of the British National Corpus [66], where the most significant collocate of *can be* + *adjective* is *sometimes*, an adverb typically used to foreground the occasional nature of events or behaviours.

The *x can be y* pattern is more frequent in the clinical data with 19 instances than in the control data with just 12 instances. There are also some interesting differences in the ways in which this phrasing is used in the two datasets (see Appendix S2 for full concordance outputs). The qualities or behaviours referred to in this phrase can be roughly separated into instances that are positively or negatively evaluative, and also a small number which are ambiguous in this regard.

Table 8. Lexical items within category *Behaviour/Temperament/Attitude.*

Control	Clinical
inquisitive (7)	naughty (19)
cheeky (9)	constantly (15)
lively (7)	frustrated (12)
naughty (9)	difficult (25)
excited (6)	behaviour (13)
tantrum (4)	sit (25)
sociable (3)	hyper (6)
	struggles (5)
	tantrum (5)
	hyperactive (4)
	handful (6)
	hitting (7)
	challenging (6)
	handful (6)
	boisterous (4)
	throw (11)
	mardy (3)
	running (about/around/off) (15)
	screaming (5)
	temper (4)

Table 9. Lexical items within category *Communication.*

Control	Clinical
interact (4)	listen (18)
attentive (3)	understand (21)
eloquent (3)	communicate (6)
talks (7)	speech (13)
interaction (4)	
conversations (7)	

Examination of the positively evaluative instances of this phrase is also revealing. In both datasets positive evaluation is contextualized alongside other behaviours which are negatively evaluated, and indeed this seems to be one of the principle functions of this particular phraseology in the data presented here (see Table 12).

However, there appears to be more of a focus on the temporary nature of positively evaluated behaviour in the clinical group; he can be a good lad *sometimes*, she can be good... she can have *really nice moments*, he can be very loving ... *when you get him to sit him down for five minutes*.

Discussion

Analysing *what* parents say about their children and *how* they say it extends and innovates on prior ADHD work by directly comparing and contrasting linguistic data from parents of children at risk of developing ADHD with controls to further understand parents' views and maximise the relevancy of parenting interventions. The general pattern that emerges in the corpus based linguistic analysis can be described in terms of a clear tendency towards negative evaluation in the clinical data. Evidence of positively evaluative language is evident, but this is frequently accompanied by mitigating lexis or syntactic structures. An example of the latter was observed in the modal construction *x can be y*, which was seen to limit the extent of any positive evaluation that might obtain when referring to actions that might normally be subject to such evaluation. The semantic categorisation of keywords made it possible to pin-point specific spheres of activity that are represented by the clinical group as problematic. Significant differences between the two datasets were observed in five of the seven semantic categories identified, suggesting marked differences in the preoccupations and evaluative representations evident in the clinical and control groups. The item *attention* in the two datasets, an item which appears on the keyword list for clinical data with 35 versus five occurrences in the control data provides strong evidence to suggest a general concern with the demands for attention made by the children discussed in the clinical group, while play seems to be an activity in which such demands are particularly salient for these parents.

Regarding the pattern *x can be y*, findings demonstrate that parents from the clinical group produce this mitigating syntax more frequently in negatively evaluative instances than controls. When we compare the negatively evaluative instances of this pattern in the two datasets interesting differences become evident. In both data sets we see evidence of attenuation – in the clinical data a *bit* challenging, *quite* boisterous, *quite* feisty (although it

Table 10. Lexical items within category *Activities.*

Control	Clinical
play (29)	play (36)
playing (30)	toys (15)
scooter (7)	
park (16)	
stories (11)	
swimming (11)	
games (10)	
trampoline (4)	
puzzles (4)	
bedtime (4)	
colouring (5)	
climbing (5)	
watch (15)	
learning (8)	
pirates (3)	
drawing (7)	

Table 11. Mitigating syntax items '*x* can be *y*'.

Control	Clinical
a bit mischievous	a bit challenging
a cheeky monkey	a handful
quite awkward	quite boisterous
quite difficult	really spiteful
trying sometimes	very aggressive
	very challenging
	very difficult (x2)

should be noted that *quite* can function as an intensifier rather than an attenuator). In the control data we see similar patterns – *a bit* mischievous, *a bit* wingey, *quite* awkward, *quite* difficult, trying *sometimes*. However, in the clinical data intensification is also in evidence – *really* spiteful, *very* aggressive, *very* challenging, *very* difficult, while the actual qualities attributed to the subject of the clause– *spiteful, aggressive* and *difficult* compared to *a cheeky monkey, wingey* and *awkward*, are arguably more extreme. When we compare the positively evaluative instances of this pattern, we observed that while negative behaviour is more negative in the clinical data, positive behaviour, when it is referred to, is often framed as a temporary aberration from a more negatively evaluated norm.

Parenting interventions may build upon these linguistic differences to ensure parents' unique experiences, preferences, and goals are met. Our results identify behavioural and emotional aspects important to guide interventions. We will explore the practical implications derived from the five semantic categories exhibiting significant differences between groups.

Affection

Parents from the clinical sample described their children as less affectionate than controls. ADHD symptoms and associated negative and incompliant behaviours [69,70] can lead to parental challenges [71], parental anxiety, and mood problems [72]. On the other hand, parental depression is one of the most well-established risk factors for adverse child development and psychopathology [73] and occurs more often in parents of children with ADHD [74]. Parents with depression engage in more threatening, hostile, and coercive behaviour, are more disengaged and withdrawn during interactions with their child, and are less involved in positive parenting behaviours including displays of praise and affectionate contact [75]. If parental wellbeing has a transactional relationship with difficult behaviour [76], parenting interventions should highlight the importance of praise, positive tone of voice, mutual respect, and physical affection as well as techniques to increase parental wellbeing.

Enjoyment and positive mood

Parents from the clinical sample described their children as enjoying less and having less fun than controls. Previous research has shown that children with ADHD have a different sensitivity to reward [77]. They prefer smaller, immediate rewards over larger later rewards [78] and display greater sensitivity to social rewards [79]. Parenting interventions should be aware of these differences and promote games in which rewards are immediate and frequent, ensuring children engage and participate in playing and fun activities. Behaviour should be reinforced as frequently and immediately as possible and whenever appropriate use 'ear shot' praising techniques. For example, when the child can hear Mum/Dad conversing with another person, Mum/Dad mentions how proud she/he is because the child was affectionate or playing gently with a smaller cousin. The importance of play has already been highlighted by existing parenting interventions [80]. Play supports child development and it can improve the child attention, concentration and listening skills, but it is also a great opportunity to have fun and enjoy parenting.

Table 12. Mitigating syntax used for positive instances.

Control	Clinical
very kind and caring (to his sister, but equally he can push her over)	a good lad (can't he sometimes)
	a really good child
very kind (equally he can be a cheeky monkey)	happy (one minute and flip the next)
	happy playing (he can go into a right mood)
very thoughtful (equally he can be a cheeky monkey)	lovely at times
very thoughtful	really good (she has really nice moments where she can be)
	so nice (one minute)
	very loving (when you get him to sit down for 5 minutes)
	very loving (on the flip side)

Behaviour, temperament and attitude

Parents from the clinical sample described their children as displaying more negative behaviour, temperament and attitude than controls. Effective parenting interventions should emphasise strategies for dealing with temper tantrums and disruptive behaviour. Research has shown that ADHD children may exhibit deficits in temporal processing [81], time discrimination, and reproduction [82] which may explain difficulties in awaiting turns and interruptions. Temporal processing deficits ameliorate with reinforcement in children with ADHD [83]. It may, therefore, be advantageous for parents to routinely set clear instructions about how long a child needs to engage in behaviours in order to receive a reward and use timers. The New Forest Parenting Training (NFPP) [84,85] highlights the importance of practising time management using buzzers, timers, and alarms, and also the use of countdowns and warnings (e.g., 'we are leaving in ten minutes, we are leaving in five minutes, and so on' vs. 'Get your jacket, it's time to go'). For children with ADHD, 'quiet time' has been suggested to be more effective then 'time out'. While 'quiet time' promotes reflection, negotiation, self-regulation, and is not perceived as a punishment, 'time out' is a more extreme measure and should only be used as a last resort when the child's behaviour is unacceptable but distraction, quiet time, presenting the child with choices and other strategies have not worked [85].

Communication

Parents from the clinical sample described their children as displaying more communication problems than controls. Parenting interventions can help both parents and children with their communication skills. For example, the parenting programme '1-2-3 Magic' [86] pays special attention to sympathetic listening (e.g., reflective feelings), while NFPP focuses on more basic communication skills such as active listening (e.g., repeating the message using the same or similar words), making eye contact, and getting the child's attention before giving any instructions. To expand the child language through play, NFPP recommends using descriptive comments and explanations to keep the child interested in carrying on playing while increasing his vocabulary. NFPP also focuses on communication aspects such as voice (e.g., volume and tone), for example, voice should be calm in difficult situations, firm when giving instructions and positive when rewarding and reinforcing behaviour. Parents are also encouraged to give children just two choices to help them decide and also to remember their choice, avoid confrontations, and arguments. The NFPP pays special attention to setting clear goals (e.g., short and simple sentences) and scaffolding which consists on identifying what the child is able to do, extending these abilities by supporting the child in tasks that present moderate challenges and practising them to ensure effective learning. Moreover, positive communication including low levels of criticism and hostility and high levels of warmth and empathy have been shown positively influence the pathogenic mechanism of ADHD [26].

Activities

Parents from the clinical sample described playing time as problematic and also reported less variety of activities. The Incredible Years parenting programme [87] pays special attention to self-directed play to promote positive relationships and encourage parents to pay attention and play with their children for at least 10 minutes every day. '1-2-3- Magic' encourages parents to share one-to-one fun activities with their child to promote bonding. The NFPP also provides support for managing the child outside of the home promoting outdoor activities and skills that facilitate 'teachable moments', for example, asking the child in the supermarket to collect two tins of tomatoes that look the same. Weekly income could affect how much money a parent can invest in their child and therefore it could limit the activities they do together [88]. Even though most of the activities evident only in the control group are inexpensive (e.g., colouring, drawing, and going to the park) and income did not affect EE and WWP ratings, we cannot exclude that economic factors could explain some of the differences observed in the activities reported by both groups.

Mitigating syntax

Parents from the clinical sample evaluated their children more negatively than controls and when they expressed a positive evaluation mitigated it by adding a temporal factor. As discussed above, praise and 'ear shot' techniques are especially relevant for children exhibiting early ADHD symptoms as they are especially sensitive to social reward [85]. Reinforcement is a key component of most parenting interventions and may help to establish target behaviours win children with ADHD, especially those with abnormalities in reward processing. For example, functional Magnetic Resonance Imaging (fMRI) data have shown that reinforcement has a comparable effect on brain function in children with ADHD as medication [89].

Conclusions and Recommendations

The general pattern that emerges in the corpus based linguistic analysis can be described in terms of a clear tendency towards negative evaluation in the clinical data. Evidence of positively evaluative language is evident, but this is frequently accompanied by mitigating lexis or syntactic structures. An example of the latter was observed in the modal construction *x can be y*, which was seen to limit the extent of any positive evaluation that might obtained when referring to actions that might normally be subject to such evaluation. The semantic categorisation of keywords made it possible to pin-point specific spheres of activity that are represented by the control group parents as problematic. Significant differences between the two datasets were observed in five of the seven semantic categories identified, suggesting marked differences in the preoccupations and evaluative representations evident among parents of preschool children with the hyperactive/impulsive subtype of ADHD and control groups.

The findings reported in this article show that corpus-based linguistic analysis is a useful and effective method to further understand parents' unique perceptions of children with ADHD symptoms. Corpus-based linguistic analysis offers new understandings and insights about topics that otherwise may be uncovered. These new insights might help researchers, educators and healthcare professionals to improve the parent-child relationship by strengthening the relevancy and therefore success and acceptability of parenting interventions.

The parents' narratives analysed in this study provide evidence on how parenting programmes should include not just techniques to improve effective behaviour management and communication skills but also strategies that focus on promoting affectionate parent-child relationships, positive perceptions, and activities that facilitate enjoyment and positive mood within the family context. General praise, specific 'ear-shot' praising techniques, positive tone of voice, mutual respect, physical affection, tailored games with immediate and frequent reward, planning activities, and dedicated daily play time are essential aspects that parenting interventions for children with early signs of ADHD should address and weight accordingly.

A future follow-up study could identify those parents from the clinical group that have participated in a parenting programme and compare their post-intervention FMSS with the one collected for the current study (i.e., baseline). These two FMSS measures would allow us to further assess parenting intervention outcomes. Because the way parents describe their children can moderate the relationship between the genetic risk for ADHD and the expression of ADHD symptoms [26], future research should also focus on designing behavioural interventions able to reduce negative Expressed Emotion.

Further studies focusing on family influences and family characteristics are required to establish the direction of causation and extend our understanding of the relationship between Parental Expressed Emotion, ADHD and parenting programmes. A recent meta-analysis on behavioural interventions in ADHD [90] has demonstrated that the value of these interventions does not rest exclusively on the potential effects on child ADHD symptoms but on associated features including child conduct problems, academic performance and social skills. Interestingly, outcomes on parenting functioning and parenting sense of competence were also improved, indicating than when parents successfully engage in behavioural interventions that focus on making parenting more enjoyable, implementing new strategies to manage challenging behaviour, consistency and family routine, those parents report not only an increment on positive parenting but a significant improvement on self-efficacy and self-concept. Behavioural interventions, however, seem to have a limited effect on parental mental health highlighting that the high levels of mental health problems often reported among parents of children with ADHD are not solely the result of issues around parenting, but rather reflect a shared genetic risk for mental health problems within families.

Limitations

Administration of the PFMSS and demographics questionnaire differed between groups. While both measures for the clinical group were collected face-to-face at the parents' home, these measures for the control group were collected over the phone. The WWS was collected over the phone for both groups. Face-to-face and telephone communication does differ, however, research on FMSS collection has shown that this does not affect results [91]. Educational level was an unmatched demographic characteristic that influenced the EE scorings. Interestingly, income could not be matched but did not affect any of the scorings.

Another limitation of this study is the small sample size and the fact that ADHD symptomatology was not assessed in the participating parents.

Acknowledgments

We would like to thank all the parents that participated in this study and the useful comments and corrections provided by two anonymous reviewers.

Author Contributions

Conceived and designed the experiments: EP MT. Performed the experiments: MT AF. Analyzed the data: AF MT EP JL. Contributed reagents/materials/analysis tools: MT AF JL. Contributed to the writing of the manuscript: MT AF AP DD JL.

References

1. Polanczyk G, Rohde LA (2007) Epidemiology of attention-deficit/hyperactivity disorder across the lifespan. Current Opinion Psychiatry, 20,386–392.
2. National Institute for Health and Clinical Excellence (2008) Clinical guideline 672: Attention Deficit Hyperactivity Disorder (ADHD) Full Guideline, London: National Institute of Clinical Excellence. Available: www.nice.org.uk/CG72.
3. Loe IM, Feldman HM (2007) Academic and educational outcomes of children with ADHD. Ambulatory Paediatrics 7: 82–90.
4. Swanson JM, Sergeant JA, Taylor E, Sonuga-Barke EJS, Jensen PS, et al. (1998) Attention-deficit hyperactivity disorder and hyperkinetic disorder. Lancet 351: 429–433.
5. Biederman J, Monuteaux MC, Mick E, Spencer T, Wilens TE, et al. (2006) Psychological Medicine 36: 167–179.
6. Klassen AF, Miller A, Fine S (2004) Health-related quality of life in children and adolescents who have a diagnosis of Attention-Deficit/Hyperactivity Disorder. Paediatrics 114: e541–547.
7. Pelham W, Foster E, Robb J (2007) The economic impact of attention-deficit/hyperactivity disorder in children and adolescent. Journal of Pediatrics Psychology 32,:711–727.
8. Taylor E, Dopfner M, Sergeant J, Asherson P, Banaschewski T,et al. (2004) European clinical guidelines for hyperkinetic disorder: first upgrade. European Child and Adolescent Psychiatry 15: 476–495.
9. Banaschewski T, Coghill D, Santosh P, Zuddas A, Asherson P, et al. (2006) Long-acting medications for the hyperkinetic disorders: a systematic review and European treatment guideline. European Child and Adolescent Psychiatry 15: 476–495.
10. Sonuga-Barke E, Brandeis D, Cortese S, Daley D, Ferrin M, et al. (2013) Nonpharmacological Interventions for ADHD: Systematic Review and Meta-Analyses of Randomized Controlled Trials of Dietary and Psychological Treatments. American Journal of Psychiatry 170(3): 275–289.
11. van de Loo-Neus GH, Rommelse N, Buitelaar JK (2011) To stop or not to stop? How long should medication treatment of attention-deficit hyperactivity disorder be extended? European Neuropsychopharmacology 21: 584–599.
12. Graham J, Banaschewski T, Buitelaar J, Coghill D, Danckaerts M, et al. (2011) European Guidelines Group: European Guidelines on managing adverse effects of medication for ADHD. European Child and Adolescent Psychiatry 20: 17–37.
13. Berger I, Dor T, Nevo Y, Goldzweig G (2008) Attitudes toward attention-deficit hyperactivity disorder (ADHD) treatment: parents' and children's perspectives. Journal of Child Neurology 23: 1036–1042.
14. Nigg JT, Lewis K, Edinger T, Falk M (2012) Meta-analysis of attention-deficit/hyperactivity disorder or attention-deficit/hyperactivity disorder symptoms, restriction diet, and synthetic food color additives. Journal of the American Academy of Child and Adolescent Psychiatry 51: 86–97.
15. Bloch MH, Qawasmi A (2011) Omega-3 fatty acid supplementation for the treatment of children with attention-deficit/hyperactivity disorder symptomatology: systematic review and meta-analysis. Journal of the American Academy of Child and Adolescent Psychiatry 50: 991–1000.
16. Markomichali P, Donnell N, Sonuga-Barke E (2009) Cognitive training for attention, inhibition and working memory deficits: a potential treatment for ADHD? Advances in ADHD 3: 89–96.
17. Arns M, de Ridder S, Strehl U, Breteler M, Coenen A (2009) Efficacy of neurofeedback treatment in ADHD: the effects on innatention, impulsivity, and hyperactivity: a meta-analysis. Clinical Psychology Review 40:180–189.
18. Fabiano GA, Pelham WE Jr, Coles EK, Gnagy EM, Chronis-Tuscano A, et al. (2009) A meta-analysis of behavioural treatments for attention-deficit/hyperactivity disorder. Clin Psyhcol Rev 29: 180–189.
19. Bor W, Sanders M, Markie-Dadds C (2002) The effects of the Triple P-Positive Parenting Programme on preschool children with co-occurring disruptive behavior and attentional/hyperactive difficulties. J Abnorm Child Psycho 30:571–587.
20. Thompson MJ, Laver-Bradbury C, Ayres M, Le Poidevin E, Mead S, et al. (2009) A small-scale randomized controlled trial of the revised New Forest Parenting Package for preschool children with Attention Deficit Hyperactivity Disorder. Eur Child Adolesc Psychiatry 18:605–616.
21. Brown R, Khan L, Parsonage M (2012) A Chance to Change. Delivering effective parenting programmes to transform lives. Annual Report Centre for Mental Health. London.

22. Deault L (2010) A systematic review of parenting in relation to the development of comorbidities and functional impairments in children with attention-deficit/hyperactivity disorder (ADHD). Child Psychiatry Human Development 41(2): 168–192.
23. Johnston C, Mash EJ (2001) Families of children with attention-deficit/hyperactivity disorder: review and recommendations for future research. Clinical Child and Family Psychology Review 4(3): 183–207.
24. Thapar A, Cooper M, Jefferies R, Stergiakouli E (2012) What causes attention deficit hyperactivity disorder? Archives of disease in childhood 97(3): 260–265.
25. Rutter M, Moffitt TE, Caspi A (2006) Gene-environment interplay and psychopathology: multiple varieties but real effects. J Child Psychol Psychiatry 47: 226–261.
26. Sonuga-Barke S, Lasky-Su J, Neale B, Oades R, Chen W, et al. (2008). Does parental expressed emotion moderate genetic effects in ADHD? An exploration using a genome wide association scan. Am J Med Gen 147B, 1359–1368.
27. Hughes C (2011) Changes and challenges in 20 years of research into the development of executive functions. Infant and Child Development 20(3): 251–271.
28. Sonuga-Barke E, Thompson M, Abikoff H, Klein R, Brotman LM (2006) Nonpharmacological interventions for preschoolers with ADHD: the case for specialized parent training. Infants & Young Children 19(2): 142–153.
29. Ainsworth M (1979) Infant-mother attachment. American Psychologist 34: 932–937.
30. Ainsworth M (1989) Attachments beyond infancy. American Psychologist 44:709–716.
31. Shaver P, Mikulincer M (2010) New directions in attachment theory and research. Journal of Social and Personal Relationships 27: 163–172.
32. Simpson J, Rholes W (2010) Attachment and relationships: Milestones and future directions. Journal of Social and Personal Relationships 27: 173–180.
33. Lench H, Levine L, Whalen C (2011) Exasperating or Exceptional? Parent's Interpretations of Their Child's ADHD Behaviour. Journal of Attention Disorders 17(2): 141–151.
34. Fiks A, Gafen A, Hughes C, Hunter K, Barg F (2011) Using freelisting to understand shared decision making in ADHD: Parent's and pediatricians' perspectives. Patient Education Counseling 84: 236–244.
35. Haidet P, O'Malley KJ, Sharf BF, Gladney AP, Greisinger AJ, et al. (2008) Characterizing explanatory models of illness in healthcare: development and validation of the CONNECT instrument. Patient Education Counseling 73: 232–239.
36. Bussing R, Koro-Ljungberg M, Williamson P, Garye F, Wilson C (2006) What "Dr. Mom" ordered: A community-based exploratory study of parental self-care responses to children's ADHD symptoms. Social Science & Medicine 63(4): 871–882.
37. Hermansen M, Miller P (2008) The lived experiences of mothers of ADHD children undergoing chiropractic care: A qualitative study. Clinical Chiropractic 11(4): 182–192.
38. Magana A, Goldstein M, Karno M, Miklowitz D, Jenkins J, et al. (1986) A brief method for assessing expressed emotion in relatives of psychiatric patients. Psychiatry Research 17: 203–212.
39. Hooley J (1985) Expressed emotion: a review of the critical literature. Clinical Psychology Review 5: 119–139.
40. Baker B, Heller T, Henker B (2000) Expressed Emotion, Parenting Stress, and Adjustment in Mothers of Young Children with Behavior Problems. Journal of Child Psychology and Psychiatry 41(7): 907–915.
41. Cartwright KL, Bitsakou P, Daley D, Gramzow RH, Psychogiou L, et al. (2011) Disentangling Child and Family Influences on Maternal Expressed Emotion Toward Children With Attention-Deficit/Hyperactivity Disorder. Journal of the American Academy of Child and Adolescent Psychiatry 50(10): 1042–1053.
42. Stubbe DE, Zahner GEP, Goldstein MJ, Leckman JF (1993) Diagnostic specificity of a brief measure of expressed emotion: a community study of children. Journal of Child Psychology and Psychiatry 34: 139–154.
43. Rogosch FA, Cicchetti D, Toth SL (2004) Expressed emotion in multiple subsystems of the families of toddlers with depressed mothers. Development and Psychopathology 6(3): 689–709.
44. Psychogiou L, Daley D, Thompson M, Sonuga-Barke E (2007) Mother's expressed emotion toward their school-aged sons. Associations with child and maternal symptoms of psychopathology. Eur Child Adolesc Psychiatry 16:458–464.
45. Cussen A, Sciberras E, Ukoumunne O, Efron D (2012) Relationship between symptoms of attention-deficit/hyperactivity disorder and family functioning: a community-based study. Eur J Pediatr 171:271–280.
46. Keown L (2010) Fathering and mothering of pre-school boys with hyperactivity. Int J Behav Dev 35:161–168.
47. Cartwright K, Bitsakou P, Daley D, Gramzow R, Psychogiou L, et al (2011) Disentangling child and family influences on maternal expressed emotion toward children with attention-deficit/hyperactivity disorder. J Am Acad Child Adolesc Psychiatry 50:1042–1053.
48. Sonuga-Barke S, Cartwright K, Tompson M, Brow J, Bitsakou P, et al (2013). Family Characteristics, Expressed Emotion, and ADHD. J Am Acad Child Adolesc Psychiatry 50:547–548.
49. Richards J, Vasquez A, Rommelse N, Oosterlaan J, Hoekstra P, et al. (2014) A Follow-up study on maternal expressed emotion toward children with attention-deficit/hyperactivity disorder (ADHD): Relation with severity and Persistence of ADHD and Comorbidity. J Am Acad Child Adolesc Psychiatry 53: 311–319.
50. Daley D, Sonuga Barker E, Thompson M (2003) Assessing expressed emotion in mothers of preschool AD/HD children: psychometric properties of a modified speech sample. British Journal of Clinical Psychology 42: 53–67.
51. Wearden AJ, Tarrier N, Barrowclough C (2000) A review of expressed emotion research in health care. Clinical Psychology Review 20: 633–666.
52. Routh D (1978) Hyperactivity. In: Magrab P (Ed) Psychological Management of Paediatric Problems. 2nd edition. Baltimore: University Park Press.
53. Thompson M, Stevenson J, Sonuga-Barke, Nott E, Bhatti Z, et al.(1996). The mental health of preschool children and their mothers in a mixed urban/rural population: I. Prevalence and ecological factors. British Journal of Psychiatry 168(1): 16–20.
54. Barkley RA (1988) Attention deficit disorder with hyperactivity. In Mash EJ, Terdal LJ (Eds) Behavioral assessment of childhood disorders (pp. 69–104) New York: Guilford.
55. Mash EJ, Johnson C (1983) Parental perceptions of child behaviour problems, parenting self-esteem, and mothers' reported stress in younger and older hyperactive and normal children. Journal of Consulting and Clinical Psychology 51: 86–99.
56. Sonuga-Barke E, Stevenson J, Thompson M, Viney D (1997) The structure of British pre-school and children's behaviour problems. Psychological Medicine 27: 909–918.
57. Cohen J (1988) Statistical Power Analysis for the Behavioural Sciences (2nd Ed) LEA Publishers. Hillsdale, New Jersey.
58. Partington A, Morley J, Haarman L, Eds. (2004) Corpora and Discourse. Bern: Peter Lang.
59. Crawford P, Brown B, Nerlich B, Koteyko N (2008) The moral careers of microbes and the rise of the matrons: An analysis of UK national press coverage of methicillin resistant staphylococcus aureus (MRSA) 1995–2006. Health, Risk & Society 10(4): 331–347.
60. Crawford P, Gilbert P, Gilbert J, Gale C, Harvey K (2013) The Language of Compassion in Acute Mental Health Care. Qualitative Health Research 23(6), 719–727.
61. Adolphs S, Crawford P, Brown B, Sahota O, Carter RA (2004) Applying Corpus Linguistic in a health care context. International Journal of Applied Linguistics, 1(1), 44–49.
62. Brown B, Crawford P (2009) Post antibiotic apocalypse: Discourses of mutation in narratives of MRSA. Sociology of Health & Illness 31(4): 508–524.
63. Harvey K, Churchill D, Crawford P, Brown B, Mullany L, et al. (2008) Health communication and adolescents: What do their emails tell us? Family Practice 25: 1–8.
64. Scott M (2012) WordSmith Tools. Version 6, Liverpool: Lexical Analysis Software.
65. Baker P (2006) Using Corpora in Discourse Analysis. London: Continuum.
66. British National Corpus (BNC XML Edition v3) Distributed by Oxford University Computing Services on behalf of the BNC Consortium. Available: http://www.natcorp.ox.ac.uk/
67. Bradley HCR (2002) Socioeconomic status and child development. Annual Review of Psychology 53: 371–399.
68. Ermisch JPC (2010) Causal Effects of Parents' Education on Children's education. Institute for Social and Economic Research.
69. Johnston C (1996) Parent characteristics and parent-child interactions in families of non-problem children and ADHD children with higher and lower levels of oppositional-defiant behaviour. Journal of Abnormal Child Psychology 24: 85–104.
70. Johnston C, Murray C, Hinshaw SP, Pelham WE, Hoza B (2002) Responsiveness in interactions of mothers and sons with ADHD: Relations to maternal and child characteristics. Journal of abnormal child psychology 30(1): 77–88.
71. Pelham W, Lang A (1999) Can your children drive you to drink? Stress and parenting in adults interacting with children with ADHD. Alcohol Research and Health 23: 292–298.
72. Gerdes A, Hoza B, Arnold L, Pelham W, Swanson J, et al. (2007) Maternal depressive symptomatology and parenting behaviour: Exploration of possible mediators. Journal of Abnormal Child Psychology 35: 705–714.
73. Goodman SH, Gotlib IH (1999) Risk for psychopathology in the children of depressed mothers: a developmental model for understanding mechanisms of transmission. Psychological Review 106(3): 458.
74. Chronis AM, Lahey BB, Pelham WE, Kipp HL, Baumann BL, et al. (2003) Psychopathology and substance abuse in parents of young children with attention-deficit/hyperactivity disorder. Journal of the American Academy of Child & Adolescent Psychiatry 42: 1424–1432.
75. Lovejoy MC, Graczyk PA, O'Hare E, Neuman G (2000) Maternal depression and parenting behavior: A meta-analytic review. Clinical Psychology Review 20(5): 561–592.
76. Goodman SH, Rouse MH, Connell AM, Broth MR, Hall CM, et al. (2011) Maternal depression and child psychopathology: a meta-analytic review. Clinical Child and Family Psychology Review 14(1): 1–27.
77. Sonuga-Barke E (2011) Editorial: ADHD as a reinforcement disorder: moving from general effects to identifying (six) specific models to test. Journal of Child Psychology and Psychiatry 52(9): 917–918.
78. Sonuga-Barke E, Taylor E, Sembi S, Smith J (1992) Hyperactivity and Delay Aversion—I. The Effect of Delay on Choice. Journal of Child Psychology and Psychiatry 33(2): 387–398.

79. Kohls G, Peltzer J, Herpertz-Dahlmann B, Konrad K (2009) Differential effects of social and non-social reward on response inhibition in children and adolescents. Developmental science 12(4): 614–625.
80. Milteer RM, Ginsburg KR (2012) The Importance of Play in Promoting Healthy Child Development and Maintaining Strong Parent-Child Bond: Focus on Children in Poverty. Pediatrics 129 (1): e204–e213.
81. Toplak ME, Tannock R (2005) Time perception: modality and duration effects in attention-deficit/hyperactivity disorder (ADHD). Journal of abnormal child psychology 33(5): 639–654.
82. Toplak ME, Dockstader C, Tannock R (2006) Temporal information processing in ADHD: findings to date and new methods. Journal of neuroscience methods 151(1): 15–29.
83. van Meel CS, Oosterlaan J, Heslenfeld DJ, Sergeant JA (2005) Motivational effects on motor timing in attention-deficit/hyperactivity disorder. Journal of the American Academy of Child & Adolescent Psychiatry 44(5): 451–460.
84. Sonuga-Barke E, Thompson M, Daley D, Laver-Bradbury C (2004) Parent training for Attention Deficit/Hyperactivity Disorder: Is it as effective when delivered as routine rather than as specialist care? British Journal of Clinical Psychology 43: 449–457.
85. Sonuga-Barke E, Bitsakou P, Thompson M (2010) Beyond the dual pathway model: Evidence for the dissociation of timing, inhibitory, and delay-related impairments in attention-deficit/hyperactivity disorder. Journal of the American Academy of Child & Adolescent Psychiatry 49(4): 345–355.
86. Pelham W (2010) 1-2-3 Magic. Effective discipline for children 2-12. Revised 4th Edition. Quality books Inc. Illinois.
87. Webster-Stratton C, Reid MJ, Beauchaine TP (2012) One-Year Follow-Up of Combined Parent and Child Intervention for Young Children with ADHD. Journal of Clinical Child and Adolescent of Consulting and Clinical Psychology 65: 93–109.
88. Hill M, Duncan G (1987) Parental Family Income and the Socioeconomic Attainment of Children. Social Science Research 16(1): 39–73.
89. Liddle EB, Hollis C, Batty MJ, Groom MJ, Totman JJ, et al. (2011) Task-related default mode network modulation and inhibitory control in ADHD: effects of motivation and methylphenidate. J Child Psychol Psychiatry 52(7): 761–771.
90. Daley D, van der Oord S, Ferrin M, Danckaerts M, Doepfner M, et al. (2014) Behavioral Interventions in Attention-Deficit/Hyperactivity Disorder: A Meta-Analysis of Randomized Controlled Trials across Multiple Outcome Domains. Journal of the American Academy of Child & Adolescent Psychiatry doi: 10.1016/j.jaac.2014.05.013
91. Beck A, Daley D, Hastings RP, Stevenson J (2004) Mothers' expressed emotion towards children with and without intellectual disabilities. Journal of Intellectual Disability Research 48(7): 628–638.

Different Effects of Adding White Noise on Cognitive Performance of Sub-Normal and Super-Attentive School Children

Suzannah K. Helps[1], Susan Bamford[1], Edmund J. S. Sonuga-Barke[1,3]*, Göran B. W. Söderlund[2]*

1 Institute for Disorders of Impulse and Attention, Department of Psychology, University of Southampton, Southampton, United Kingdom, **2** Faculty of Teacher Education and Sports, Sogndal University College, Sogndal, Norway, **3** Department of Experimental Clinical & Health Psychology, University of Ghent, Ghent, Belgium

Abstract

Objectives: Noise often has detrimental effects on performance. However, because of the phenomenon of stochastic resonance (SR), auditory white noise (WN) can alter the "signal to noise" ratio and improve performance. The Moderate Brain Arousal (MBA) model postulates different levels of internal "neural noise" in individuals with different attentional capacities. This in turn determines the particular WN level most beneficial in each individual case–with one level of WN facilitating poor attenders but hindering super-attentive children. The objective of the present study is to find out if added WN affects cognitive performance differently in children that differ in attention ability.

Methods: Participants were teacher-rated super- (N = 25); normal- (N = 29) and sub-attentive (N = 36) children (aged 8 to 10 years). Two non-executive function (EF) tasks (a verbal episodic recall task and a delayed verbal recognition task) and two EF tasks (a visuo-spatial working memory test and a Go-NoGo task) were performed under three WN levels. The non-WN condition was only used to control for potential differences in background noise in the group testing situations.

Results: There were different effects of WN on performance in the three groups-adding moderate WN worsened the performance of super-attentive children for both task types and improved EF performance in sub-attentive children. The normal-attentive children's performance was unaffected by WN exposure. The shift from moderate to high levels of WN had little further effect on performance in any group.

Significance: The predicted differential effect of WN on performance was confirmed. However, the failure to find evidence for an inverted U function challenges current theories. Alternative explanations are discussed. We propose that WN therapy should be further investigated as a possible non-pharmacological treatment for inattention.

Editor: Antonella Gasbarri, University of L'Aquila, Italy

Funding: The work was supported by Wellcome Trust grant reference WT087749MA, http://www.wellcome.ac.uk/. The funder had no role in study design, data collection and analysis, decision to publish, or preparation of the manuscript.

Competing Interests: In the last three years Edmund Sonuga-Barke discloses consultancy, speaker fees, advisory board fees and research grant income from Shire and speaker fees from Janssen Cilag, Qbtech and Medice. Göran Söderlund has founded a company, Smartnoise AB, in collaboration with Sverker Sikström that will utilize the positive effect noise by the development of a noise improvement tool. The company is not yet active and no product is available at the moment.

* Email: goran.soderlund@hisf.no; ejb3@soton.ac.uk

Introduction

Under most circumstances, information processing is disturbed by environmental noise and other non-task compatible distractors [1,2]. Children with attention problems are, under many conditions, especially vulnerable to distraction e.g. [3]. However, researchers have recently reported that under certain circumstances individuals with attention problems appear to benefit from the addition of specific forms of environmental noise. Typically, this facilitative effect has been limited to non-vocal background music on simple arithmetic task performance, [4,5] but Stansfeld et al. [6] found just that under certain conditions even road traffic noise can improve performance on episodic memory tasks, particularly in children at risk of attention problems and academic under-achievement.

Furthermore, Söderlund et al. [7] have demonstrated that adding auditory white noise (WN) to the environment enhanced the memory performance of children with ADHD-type problems but disrupted that of non-ADHD control children. These effects were replicated in a second study for children with sub-clinical attention problems [8]. These results raise two obvious questions. First, how or by what mechanism does WN improve performance? Second, why does the same level of WN have such apparently different effects on children with different levels of attentional problems?

The exact mechanism behind WN benefits is not yet known. It has been proposed that random noise enhances neural communication via the phenomenon of stochastic resonance (SR). The phenomenon of SR is observed when an increase in the level of unpredictable fluctuations, e.g. WN, causes an increase in a metric of the quality of signal transmission or signal detection, or in other words increases the signal-to-noise ratio. SR is usually quantified by plotting signal detection, or in this study cognitive performance, as a function of WN intensity. The SR effect appears highly sensitive to both the intensity of the signal and the noise level; this relationship follows an inverted U-curve function, where performance peaks at moderate noise levels. This means that a moderate level of WN is beneficial for performance whereas too little does not add the power required to bring the signal over the threshold and too much overpowers the signal, leading to a deterioration in attention and performance [9,10]. Signaling in the brain is characterized by noisy inputs and outputs. The task of the central nervous system is to distinguish between the signal, the information-carrying component, and noise (i.e. meaningless neural inputs that interfere with the signal). However, noise is an integral part of interneuronal communication and a sufficient amount of noise may be necessary for the normal functioning of the nervous system [11,12]. This in turn modulates neural synchronization whereby particular brain regions sub-serving specific functions establish transient networks that accomplish perception, cognition, or action [13]. Thus, it has been shown that random noise enhances detection of weak sensory signals like hearing [14], touch [15], vision [16] through SR. "Touch WN" improved vibrotactile sensitivity in healthy young people [15], vibrating soles improved motor performance in elderly [17], in stroke patients [18], and those with Parkinson's disease [19]. High-level performance can also be improved by WN (e.g., face recognition [20] and arithmetic computations (77 dB) [21]). Moreover, SR can work across modalities such that detection of weak visual signals improved considerably when exposed to high levels of auditory noise (75 dB) [22]. To sum up, the concept of SR attempts to explain the paradox that the brain seems to utilize WN to differentiate the signal in the targeted stimuli from non-target noise [23]. WN accordingly improves or increases the signal-to-noise ratio.

How can we explain individual differences in WN effects? Sikström & Söderlund [24] proposed that individual differences arise because each person has a certain level of background "noise" intrinsic to his or her neural system associated with neurotransmitter function. Dopamine was hypothesized to be especially important because it modulates the neural cell's response to the environment and determines the probability that it will fire an action potential following the presentation of salient stimuli [25]. Dopamine function is related to individual differences in attention [26] and cognition [27]. Dysfunction is found among ADHD patients [28]. Stimulant medication, acting via the dopamine system, reduces symptoms of inattention and improves cognitive performance within normal populations [29,30] and in patients with an ADHD diagnosis [31,32]. In the Moderate Brain Arousal Model (MBA); [24] internal neural noise and external WN are hypothesized to act additively in relation to SR. Thus, where there are low levels of neural noise, i.e. low continuous dopamine activity, more external WN is required for SR to occur. The facilitative SR effect is predicted to demand high levels of WN where internal noise levels are low, but where high internal noise levels are present, i.e. high continuous dopamine activity, less external WN will be required. Low accuracy in neural communication is associated with low levels of extracellular dopamine distinguished by neurons firing at random causing inattention and in accordance with Servan-Schreiber et al.'s [25] terminology this is a "low gain" state. From this one can conclude that WN benefit only occurs when a nervous system is not working at its optimum [23,33]. This leads to the prediction that inattentive children will benefit more from higher levels of environmental WN than attentive children, for whom such noise levels will have a detrimental effect on performance. Moreover, the literature describes two kinds of WN facilitation: threshold SR and supra threshold SR (SSR) – differentiated by the nature of the relationship between the strength of the signal and the noise required for SR to occur [23,34]. For example, in auditory threshold SR the signal should be presented just below the hearing threshold (20–35 dB, depending on age and frequency) and the noise should be within the same range (20–35 dB) for SR to occur. In supra threshold SR this will occur when all noises added equal the signal mean amplitude [34,35]. This means that both signal and noise can be far above the hearing threshold. The present study focuses on supra-threshold SR using a lowest WN level of 65 dB.

The goal of the current study was to test the hypothesis that different intensities of WN will exert differential effects on children with different levels of attention-ability through the differential action of SR in a way predicted by the MBA hypothesis. Despite the current categorical approach to the diagnosis of ADHD, attentional problems appear to display a dimensional rather than a categorical structure [36]. This conclusion is supported by taxometric studies that have failed to find evidence for an attention deficit taxon [37,38] as well as behavioral genetic studies that suggest heritability is similar across different ranges of symptom severity [39]. Different severities of inattentiveness, distractibility, and associated academic problems are distributed quasi-normally throughout populations. Children who do not meet the full ADHD criteria may still suffer significant impairment. In fact, there are a number of implications of this conceptualization of attention problems for the current study. In particular it means that the comparison of the moderating effect of attentional abilities on the effects of WN on performance should not be limited to a binary comparison of attentive vs. inattentive or ADHD vs non-ADHD children. From a dimensional perspective the comparison of WN effects across sub-attentive vs. normal attentive vs. super-attentive children would be most appropriate. Assuming that the mechanisms governing the link between attentiveness, internal noise and external WN noise hold across the full range of attentional abilities we would predict different levels of WN being optimal for these different groups of children. Consistent with the MBA hypothesis we predict that the inverted U function of WN is right shifted for sub-attentive children and left-shifted for super-attentive children compared to children with normal attention. The past focus on binary conceptualizations of attention problems has meant that no studies, as far as we are aware, have examined either the neuro-psychological profiles of super-attentive children or the impact of environmental context on performance.

Our specific predictions are as follows: (i) in general, super-attentive children will have superior task performance compared to normal attentive children who will in turn out-perform sub-attentive children; (ii) moderate to high levels of WN will have facilitative effects on attention and related task performance for sub-attentive children but will disrupt performance in super-attentive children with normal attentive children lying somewhere in between. To test these predictions we extended previous studies of WN, attention and performance by: i) comparing children with normal-, sub-, and super- attention ability as defined by teachers; ii) extending the set of signal-to-noise ratios tested by studying multiple WN levels and observing the effect on performance and iii) exploring the generalization of the WN effect across a range of different tasks. Specifically, the original WN studies employed a verbal memory task [7,8]. However, tests of executive functioning (EF) have been more heavily implicated in studies of attention deficits and have been shown to differentiate inattentive from attentive children [40]. Therefore, in addition to the memory task employed in the original study, we include two EF measures in our test battery.

Method

Study recruitment and screening

Ethical approval was obtained from the University of Southampton Psychology Ethics Committee. Written consent was obtained from the school's head teacher on behalf of the children, and written assent was obtained from the children themselves. Prior to the study start, parents were sent information forms about the study and were given the option to opt their children out of the study. Copies of the written consent/assent forms are stored in a locked filing cabinet. This consent procedure was approved by the University of Southampton Psychology Ethics Committee. All children were recruited from a single local junior school; children from school years 4 and 5 (aged 8 to 10 years) and their parents were sent information letters and, in accordance with the head teachers' preferences, were given the option to opt-out of the study. Only one child did so. All remaining year 4 and 5 children (N = 150:58 boys, 92 girls) were screened for levels of attention at school using the teacher-report SWAN rating scale [41]. The SWAN has 18 items probing attention and behavior. On the basis of the teacher-ratings on the attention items of this scale, 36 sub-attentive (bottom 20 percent of scores), 29 average (middle 20 percent), and 25 super-attentive (top 20 percent) children were selected for the study. The groups were matched for age, but were unable to be matched for gender as very few boys were rated in the super-attentive range (only 2 boys out of the 150 screened children were rated as being in the top quintile for attention).

Test Battery

Four laboratory tests, two EF and two non-EF tasks, including the memory task used in the original study [7], were employed. These tasks were presented in a fixed order; participants completed them in small groups (3–4) on individual laptops in a quiet classroom with two experimenters present.

Non-EF verbal memory tasks

i) Verbal episodic memory task (Word recall; 5 minutes; [8]). Lists of nouns were presented to the participants in the auditory mode using a laptop. Participants were asked to remember as many nouns as possible. Two lists of 10 nouns (ISI 5 seconds) were presented in each WN condition: five of these words were low frequency words (frequency <100 per million) and five high frequency words (frequencies >200 per million: as determined by the children's printed word database [42]). Each list was matched for word frequency, word length and syllable number. Immediately after each list, participants were asked to perform a written free recall test. Balanced Latin squares were used to ensure that each word list was equally likely to be heard in each noise condition, and within each list, words were presented in a random order to each child.

ii) Verbal recognition task (Word recognize; 5 minutes). This task tested the recognition of the words presented in the verbal episodic memory task above. The 20 words presented in the verbal episodic memory task and 20 other words (matched to the initial lists on frequency, word length and number of syllables) were presented in the auditory modality via a laptop. Participants were required to indicate whether a word had been presented in the previous task by pressing symbols of either a tick or a cross on computer keyboard. The ISI was 3 seconds and words were presented in a random order for each child.

EF tasks

i) Visuo-spatial working memory test (Spanboard; [43]; 5 minutes). Participants were asked to remember the location of dots that appeared in a 4×4 grid (16 squares) presented on a computer screen and to recall this sequence using the computer mouse to click the correct grid locations. In the first trial, the array consisted of two dots (ISI was 3 seconds, 2250 ms dot exposure, 750 ms pause). On every second successive trial, one dot was added until the participant made an error in both trials on that particular level.

ii) The Go/No-Go Task [44]. The Go/No-Go task required a motor response (pressing the right or left mouse button) to either be selectively executed or inhibited depending on whether a Go (left/right green arrow: 75% trials) or No-Go (double-ended green arrow: 25% trials) stimulus appeared on the computer screen. The inter-stimulus interval (ISI) was 1500 ms: A 100 ms stimulus duration followed by a blank screen for 1400 ms. For the purposes of the current analysis the dependent variable for each of these tasks was the number of correct responses.

Simple two-choice RT task (2-CR RT) [45]. This task was used to validate the attentional ability groupings and so was presented under normal background noise (NBN) condition only. Participants responded to a computer presentation of a green target arrow that pointed left or right. The target arrow was presented in the center of the computer monitor. Participants responded, by pressing a right or left keyboard button, to indicate the direction of each arrow. Each trial lasted 1500 ms (stimulus presentation time 400 ms, inter-stimulus interval 1100 ms). The task duration was 5 minutes and a total of 200 trials were presented. Dependent variables were number of omission and commission errors.

Experimental Design

Each task was performed under three WN levels. Using high quality headphones participants received WN separately in each ear. The WN was mixed in adobe audition and was in phase across ears. Output signal was measured with a standard dB meter. For the two EF tasks these levels were 65 dB, 75 dB and 85 dB. The non-EF tasks were performed under slightly lower WN levels −65 dB, 70 dB and 75 dB. This was necessary as the words were not audible when louder WN levels were used. The order in which noise levels were presented was counterbalanced using a Latin Square. For all tasks the performance was also measured under normal background noise conditions to allow the effect of different levels of background noise on performance, which may vary as a function of time of day and classroom setting, to be controlled in the analyses.

Analytical strategy

All outliers (>2 SD from the group mean score for each condition) and any missing data were replaced with the group mean for that condition. Data was replaced to the following extent: Go/No-Go 3.1% of; Spanboard 2.5%; Word recall 4.9%; and Word recognition 5.8%. Noise in the data set was not caused by individuals and outliers were spread across participants. The SWAN groupings were validated by comparing performance on the four experimental tasks and the simple two choice reaction time tasks in the NBN condition using a one-way ANOVA. We examined the correlations between EF and non-EF measures with a view to combining them to create two dependent variables. Because a different range of WN levels were used for EF and non-

EF tasks we first ran two separate ANOVAs looking at the effects of noise level (65 dB vs 75 dB vs 85 dB for EF tasks; 65 dB vs 70 dB vs 75 dB for non-EF tasks) and group (sub-, vs normal- vs super-attentive) on EF and non-EF performance. We also ran a single three way ANOVA using the two noise levels that were common for tasks: group (sub-vs normal vs super-attentive), noise level (65 dB vs75 dB) and task type (EF vs non-EF) were included as factors. Thereafter we ran separate two-way ANOVAS for all four tasks to control for deviations within the EF and non-EF tasks. In all analyses performance under normal background noise was used as a covariate. This was done because the normal ambient noise at schools was not constant and varied considerably during the day, between test occasions, and between schools, dB values could range from 45–65 dB. The no-noise condition was used as covariate for all separate ANOVA analyses as well. Gender was also added as covariate to control for possible effects of gender on the dependent variable. This did not change data significantly, which is why these figures are not reported in the result section.

Results

Table 1 reports the performance on the five tasks in the normal background noise condition for the three groups. On all tasks there was a large and significant effect of group. More specifically, the sub-attentive group always performed less well than the average attentive group, with the super-attentive group performing the best. The differences between sub- and average/super attentive children were significant for all tasks. The super-attentive children were significantly better than the average attentive children only on the two EF tasks. These effects were unchanged when age, gender and school performance were added as covariates. The correlational analysis supported the combining of the EF ($r = .222$, $p<.001$) and non-EF task pairs ($r = .276$, $p<.001$) to give two measures. These were created using the factor loadings obtained from factor analysis as weights. Factor loadings for each were as follows: GNG.661; Spanboard.558; Word recall.742; Word recognition.723. However, while the correlation only had a moderate strength, the effects of noise levels in all tasks will be presented separately as well.

For non-EF there was a significant effect of group ($F(2,86) = 5.69$, $p<.005$), an effect of WN ($F(2,86) = 3.09$, $p = .048$) and a trend for a significant interaction between group and WN ($F(4,172) = 2.19$, $p = .072$), (see Figure 1). Adding moderate levels of WN had a different effect on the three groups. For the super-attentive there was a significant decline in performance ($F(2,46) = 4.42$, $p = .018$), for the average group there was a small, non-significant decline in performance ($F(2,56) = 1.21$, $p = .305$, *ns*), and for the sub-attentive group there was a small, non-significant increase in performance ($F(2,66) = .385$, $p = .682$, *ns*). This meant that the significant group difference seen at low WN levels (65dB $F(2,86) = 8.18$, $p = .001$) was no longer present at the moderate or the high WN levels (70dB $F(2,86) = 1.88$, $p = .159$, *ns*: 75dB $F(2,86) = .587$, $p = .558$, *ns*), (see Figure 1).

For the EF tasks, although the pattern of performance changes was similar, the patterns of statistical significance were different (see Figure 2). There was only a trend for an effect of group ($F(2,86) = 2.71$, $p = .073$), and no significant effect of WN ($F(2,86) = 1.89$, $p = 154$, *ns*). There was however a significant interaction between group and WN ($F(4,174) = 2.49$, $p = .045$). Again, the shift from low to moderate levels of WN had a different effect on the three groups. The sub-attentive participants displayed a significant improvement in performance ($F(2,66) = 7.39$, $p = .001$), the average attention group showed a small, non-

Table 1. Group characteristics – Sub-attentive (Sub), Normal-attention (Normal) and Super-attentive groups (Super).

	Sub (N = 36) Mean (SD)	*Normal(N = 29) Mean (SD)*	*Super(N = 25) Mean(SD)*	*Test*	*Test statistic*	*p*	*Post-hoc comparisons*
Number girls	11	18	23	$X^2(2)$	22.9	<.001	
Age	9.36 (.64)	9.67 (.59)	9.60 (.53)	F(2,89)	2.4	.096	
Two CR RT task							
Omission errors	8.14 (5.51)	4.21 (3.54)	3.32 (2.72)	F(2,89)	11.4	<.001	Sub<N, Sp
Directional errors	42.72 (17.0)	33.97 (16.37)	29.68(15.33)	F(2,89)	5.10	<.008	Sub<N, Sp
Normal background noise condition							
Span	2.64 (2.37)	3.97 (2.33)	5.32 (2.11)	F(2,89)	10.1	<.001	Sub< N <Sp
Go/No-Go	105.8 (33.1)	143.1 (39.3)	164.2 (27.9)	F(2,89)	22.9	<.001	Sub< N <Sp
Verbal episodic mem.	6.14 (2.63)	8.80 (2.59)	9.44 (2.90)	F(2,89)	13.1	<.001	Sub< N, Sp
Verbal recognition	25.8 (4.62)	28.7(3.64)	31.5 (4.41)	F(2,89)	13.2	<.001	Sub< N, Sp

Note: Post-hoc comparisons are shown where p<.05; Sub = Sub-attentive, N = normal attention, Sp = Super-attentive.

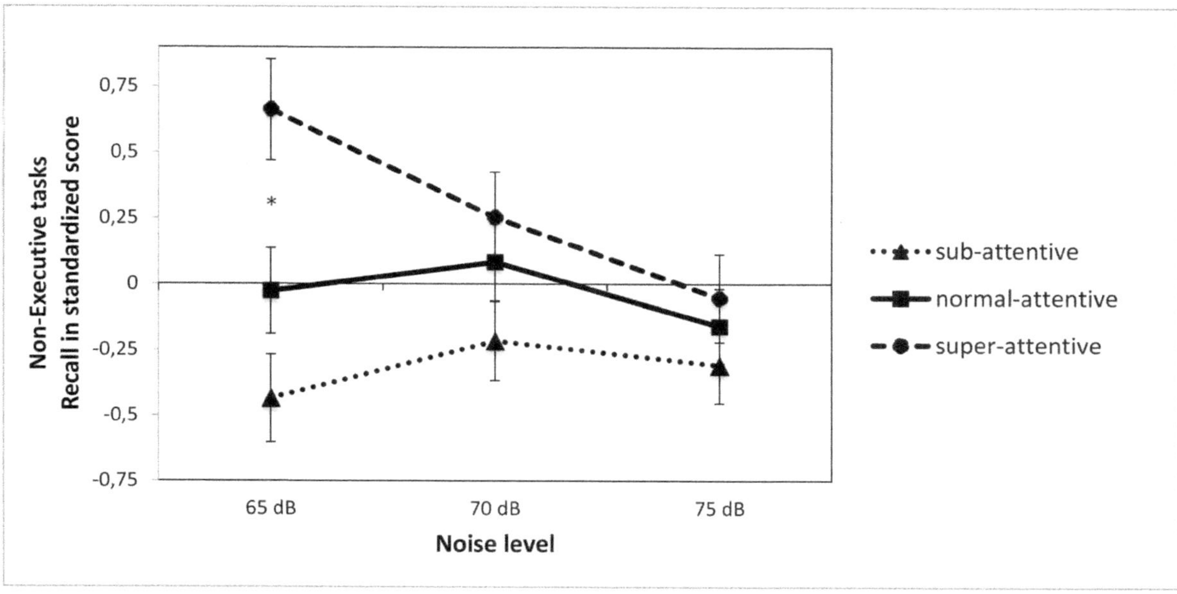

Figure 1. Performance on executive function tasks as a function of attention ability and noise level. *Note: White noise levels were 65, 75, 85 dB; * indicates a significant difference between groups in the 65 dB condition* ($F(2,86) = 6.36$, $p = .003$).

significant improvement in performance ($F(2,56) = .230$, $p = .795$, *ns*), and for the super-attentive group there was a small, non-significant decline in performance ($F(2,46) = .202$, $p = .818$, *ns*). Again, the significant group difference seen at low WN levels was no longer present at the moderate or the high WN levels (65dB $F(2,86) = 6.36$, $p = .003$:75dB $F(2,86) = .490$, $p = .615$, *ns* : 85dB $F(2,86) = .206$, $p = .814$, *ns*), (see Figure 2).

When looking at the tasks separately the non-executive, verbal task data, showed flowingly: In the Word recall task a two-way ANOVA indicated a trend towards an interaction between WM and group ($F(4,172) = 2.12$, $p = .081$) where the sub-attentive group improved their performance and the super-attentive got worse. There was a significant difference between groups ($F(2,86) = 5.12$, $p = .007$). A Bonferroni post hoc test showed a significant difference between the sub- and super-attentive groups in all three noise conditions, (see Figure 3A). In the Word recognition task the pattern was more marked, the difference between the sub- and normal-attentive groups and the super-

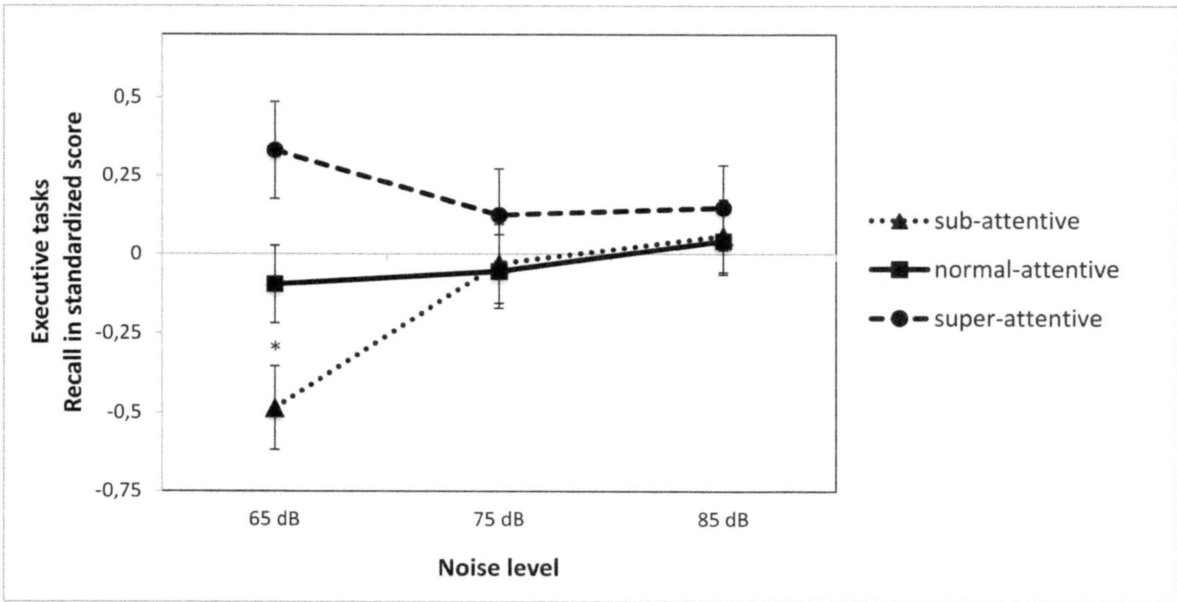

Figure 2. Performance on non-executive function tasks as a function of attention ability and noise level. *Note: White noise levels were 65, 70, 75 dB, speech level ≈ 75 dB; * indicates a significant difference between groups in the 65 dB condition* ($F(2,86) = 8.18$, $p = .001$).

attentive was significant in 65 dB (F(2,87) = 9.47, p<.001) but disappeared in the 70 dB condition (F(2,87) = 0.39, p = .679). A two-way ANOVA revealed a weak interaction between group and WN (F(4,172) = 2.22, p = .069); this interaction became however significant when the highest noise level (75 dB) was excluded (F(2,86) = 4.30, p = .017), (see Figure 3B).

The results for the EF tasks displayed a somewhat different pattern. In the Spanboard task a two-way ANOVA gave away a positive main effect of noise (F(2,85) = 3.57, p = .032 and no interaction between WN and group. Performance levels differed over all noise conditions where the super-attentive group outperformed the other two (F(2,85) = 6.20, p = .003), (see Figure 4A). In the Go/No-Go task, however, the two-way ANOVA indicated a marginal interaction between WN and group (F(4,172) = 2.01, p = .095) but by excluding the normal-attentive group we got a perfect interaction between super- and sub-attentive groups (F(2,114) = 5.17, p = .007). In this task there was no difference in performance level between the groups (over noise conditions; F(2,86) = .224, p = .800), (see Figure 4B).

Notably, when looking at omission errors in the Go/No-Go task there was a large group difference, the sub-attentive group made far more omissions (M = 27,4) as compared to normal- (M = 14,4), and super-attentive groups (F(2,76) = 18.04, p<.001). Moreover, noise did exert a significant effect only on the sub-attentive group who improved considerably by noise exposure. A paired samples t-test gave away significant improvement both from 65 to 75 dB (t(31) = 2.16, p = .38) and from 65 to 85 dB (t(29) = 2,40, p = .023) for the sub attentive group. Noise exposure was however not sufficient to eliminate the differences in omission errors between the groups. No effect at all of noise was found on direction- or commission-errors in the Go/No-Go task for any group.

Table 2 shows the results of the Noise X Group X Task Type repeated measures ANOVA. A significant main effect of Group emerged, and again the super-attentive children performed better than the average attentive children, who outperformed the sub-attentive children (although the difference between the sub-attentive children and the normal attentive children did not reach statistical significance). There was also a significant interaction between WN and Group (Figure 1). The performance of the super-attentive group declined as the WN level increased to 75db (t(24) = 3.744, p = .001); the average attention group was unaffected (t(29) = .369 p = .715) while the sub-attentive group improved (t(34) = −2.247, p = .010).

Discussion

The current paper tested the hypothesis that increasing WN levels will differentially affect children's performance as a function of their attention abilities (as rated by teachers). Based on the MBA model we predicted that high levels of WN will have a facilitative effect on task performance for sub-attentive children but will disrupt performance in super-attentive children. In line with this prediction, when all tasks were combined, adding WN disrupted the performance of the super-attentive group but improved the performance of the sub-attentive group. These findings extend those found in previous studies showing the differential effects of WN on sub- and normal attentive groups [7,8] in a number of ways, including a super attentive group, extending the range of tasks, and extending the noise range.

First, by including a super-attentive group we were able to demonstrate that response to WN varied differentially according to the degree of attentiveness and to show that the children who were rated by their teachers as being the best able to pay attention were generally the most negatively affected by increasing levels of WN. In contrast to those who were least able to pay attention were those that gained the most benefit from increasing levels of WN. This suggests that the mechanisms governing the link between attentiveness, internal noise and external noise operate across the full range of attentional abilities.

Second, by extending the battery of tasks we were able to both: (i) examine the effects of WN on executive and non-executive tasks and (ii) improve the reliability of measurement of the impact of WN. Although there was an overall facilitative effect of moderate WN on sub-attentive children and a disruptive effect on the super-attentive children, the patterns of significance were somewhat different when the effects of EF and non-EF tasks were examined. For the non-EF tasks, the shift from low to moderate levels of WN was characterized by a significant decline in performance in the super-attentive group, whereas for the EF tasks this shift from low to moderate levels of WN was characterized by a significant improvement in performance in the sub-attentive group.

It is possible that the effect of WN on EF tasks is qualitatively different from the effect of WN on non-EF tasks. Thus, on the non-EF tasks moderate levels of WN are generally disruptive, particularly for the super attentive children, but sub-attentive individuals are protected from the disruptive effects of these levels of WN. In contrast, on the EF tasks moderate levels of WN actually have a facilitative effect on the sub-attentive children. However we cannot be certain of this as there are factors other

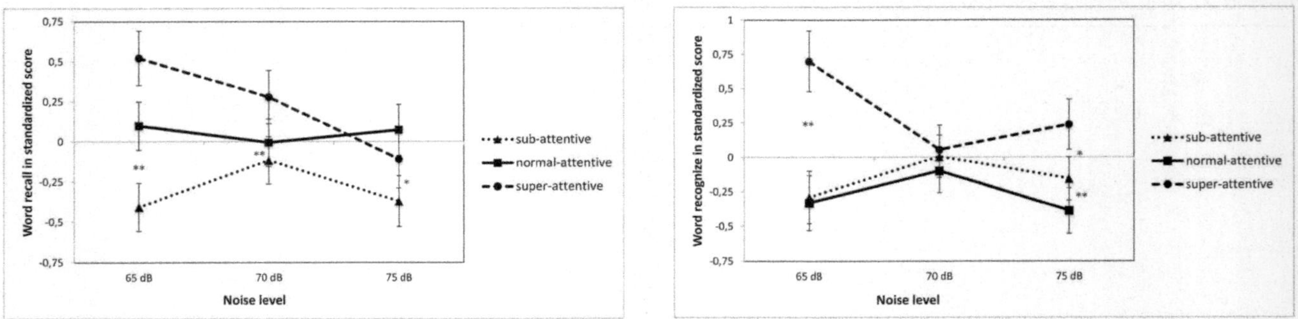

Figure 3. Figure 3A. Performance on Word recall task (non-executive) as a function of attention ability and noise level. *Note: White noise levels were 65, 70, 75 dB, speech level ≈ 75 dB; * (p<.05) and ** (p<.001) indicates significant differences between super- and sub-attentive groups.* **Figure 3B. Performance on Word recognize task (non-executive) as a function of attention ability and noise level.** *Note: White noise levels were 65, 70, 75 dB, speech level ≈ 75 dB; * (p<.05) and ** (p<.001) indicates significant differences between super- and sub, normal-attentive groups in 65 and 75 dB conditions.*

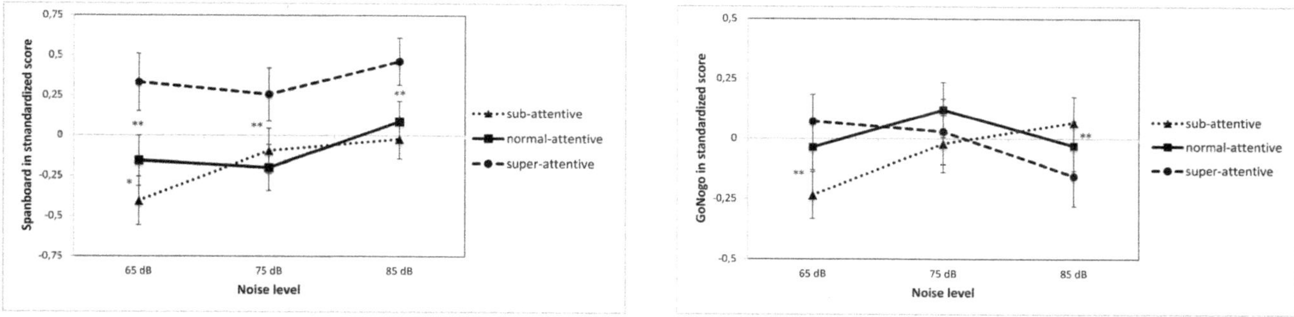

Figure 4. Figure 4A. Performance on Go/No-Go task (executive) as a function of attention ability and noise level. *Note: White noise levels were 65, 75, 85 dB. ** (p<.001) indicates significant differences between super- and sub attentive in 65 and 85 dB conditions.* **Figure 4B. Performance on Spanboard task (executive) as a function of attention ability and noise level.** *Note: White noise levels were 65, 75, 85 dB. * (p<.05) and ** (p<.001) indicates significant differences between groups.*

than the EF/non EF distinction that differ between these two groups: the modality of the tasks (auditory delivered versus visually delivered) and the fact that the tasks were performed under different ranges of WN. It may be that the more fine grained but restricted range of WN levels adopted for the non-EF measures may allow the identification of different aspects of the noise-attention relationship, or that the auditory non-EF tasks were harder to perform under increasing WN levels, as the words became more difficult to hear. Of great importance to note is the cross modal nature of the WN effects seen for the EF tasks: auditory WN exerted an effect on the processing of visual stimuli, which has been shown earlier on signal detection [22] but here, to our knowledge for the first time, on EF as well. In the non-executive tasks noise and signal were exposed within the same modality and results could indicate that lower levels of WN are required for SR to occur within the same modality. Future research replicating these effects in non-auditory modalities, such as in a word recall tasks, in which the words are presented visually, will help to clarify this.

Third, we extended previous research by adding multiple noise levels that gave us more power to both: (i) examine the inverted U function of the effects of WN as predicted by SR models and (ii) identify more subtle differences in the WN-performance relationship and how this might change with increasing noise intensities. In this regard, the following findings were notable. Moving to the highest levels of WN intensity had little effect on the performance of any of the groups. There was little evidence for the inverted WN-performance U-function as predicted by the MBA model, where performance peaks at moderate noise levels but too much noise will cause performance to deteriorate. We further predicted that this inverted U shaped function of performance across different WN intensities would be right-shifted for sub-attentive children and left-shifted for super-attentive children compared to children with normal attention, as inattentive children should require more environmental WN than attentive children for optimal performance in cognitive tasks, and conversely these inattentive children should be able to tolerate greater levels of WN before performance deteriorates. However, the super attentive group showed a general pattern of decline across all three WN levels and the normal attentive group tended to exhibit consistent performance across the three noise levels, with only the sub-attentive group showing an improvement in performance as noise levels increased. In summary, the specific differential patterns of effects of increasing WN levels that we had predicted did not materialize; this could indicate that supra threshold SR acts differently compared to threshold SR [46].

It is not evident that the relation between the noise level and the outcome of high-level cognitive performance depicts an inverted U-curve as in signal detection tasks in threshold SR. When we are dealing with supra threshold SR the pattern might be biphasic

Table 2. Main effects and interactions from a Group X Noise X Task Type repeated measures ANOVA.

	df	*F*	*p*
Main Effects			
Group	(1,85)	5.53	.006*
Noise	(1,85)	1.25	.267
Task Type	(1,85)	.521	.472
Two Way Interactions			
Noise × Group	(2, 85)	4.30	.017*
Task Type × Group	(2, 85)	.016	.984
Task Type × Noise	(2, 85)	4.94	.029*
Three way interactions			
Group × Noise × Task type	(2, 85)	.594	.554

Note. * = *p*<.05.

instead; either there is an effect of noise or there is not. In cross modal SR, auditory noise on visual detection, using similar noise levels as in the present study, responses seems to mimic an inverted U-curve [22]. On the other hand when using stochastic vestibular stimulation to improve balance in healthy adults the effect was either present or not, even if stimulation thresholds differed between individuals [47].

When looking at the EF tasks separately we found that in the Go/No-Go task when inhibition is required there was an interaction between super- and sub attentive children. On the contrary, in the Spanboard task none of the groups was affected negatively by noise exposure and there was a just a positive main effect of noise. The Go/No-Go task put high demands on executive functioning, both the updating of information (inhibition) and maintenance of information, whereas the Spanboard task only put demands on maintenance. From this it can possibly be concluded that the higher the task demands are the more appropriate dopamine levels are required for a high performance [48]. Although noise is not found to increase dopamine levels per se, it looks like external noise in the nervous system acts in a similar fashion as dopamine release [49].

Regarding the two non-EF tasks, Word recall and Word recognition, there were tendencies towards an inverted U-function where performance peaked at 70 dB for the sub-attentive group whereas the super-attentive group got worse when exposed to increased noise levels. Lower levels of WN have to be used to find out if or where a peak would occur for the super-attentive group. The word recognition task represents long-term memory while it has an approximately 30 minutes delay between encoding and recall phases. It is therefore worth mentioning that words that were encoded in a moderately noisy environment were better recalled than the ones that were encoded at lower and higher noise levels for both the sub- and average-attentive groups. This may indicate that the positive effects of noise have not only an acute effect, but also a long-term one. This calls for further investigation.

An alternative explanation to consider is that rather than inducing SR, WN increased arousal in participants, which in turn affected information processing in different ways for the two groups. Such an explanation is consistent with the state regulation deficit model of ADHD [50] derived from cognitive energetic theory [51]. This theory posits that children with attention problems have difficulty modulating their levels of arousal and activation to adjust to changing circumstances and patterns of external stimulation – in particular they have difficulty maintaining arousal levels on challenging and boring tasks. It further predicts that these difficulties are alleviated by the addition of external stimulation. The finding in the current study that the performance of the sub-attentive group improved with moderate levels of WN is consistent with this prediction. Arousal might also offer an alternative explanation for the WN-related deterioration in the super-attentive children's performance. It is possible that arousal levels are optimal for this group at the lowest noise level in the current study and that they become over-aroused by increases in WN. Alternatively it is possible that their performance deteriorates because they just find the noise annoying and distracting. This possibility needs to be investigated in future research using human and animal models, directly measuring known neural and physiological markers of arousal in experiments employing manipulations of alternative factors (event rate or stimulant medication) known to change energetic levels [49,51–62].

Another possible explanation is that WN benefit results from auditory masking, as a masker different from the signal it can facilitate signal detection [63]. It has been shown that if the masker was predictable ADHD participants behave less impulsively [64] and exhibit improved signal detection [65]. Masking effects have been shown in both the visual [66] and tactile modalities [67]. In both SR and in masking, task irrelevant (meaningless) stimulation in different modalities increases the signal-to-noise ratio and thus improves performance on various tasks. To determine the importance of masking it would be useful to compare the effects of WM with sensory noise without sound masking properties like in vestibular noise [20,68,69].

Although our methodology improved on previous studies in a number of ways a number of limitations need to be acknowledged. *First*, we were unable to match the attention groups for sex of participant. Our super attentive group included far more girls (N = 23) than boys (N = 2) and the sub attentive group included more boys (N = 22) than girls (N = 14). We controlled for the effects of gender, using gender as a covariate, in all our analyses but it would be preferable to have the groups matched for gender to detect more clearly if the noise displays any gender differences. All patterns where the same for boys and girls, but we could discern a marginal effect of gender in the non-EF tasks. In the EF tasks using gender as a covariate did not change the noise x attention interaction at all but in the non-EF tasks the interaction got somewhat weaker when the effect of gender was used as a covariate. More statistic power is required to draw any conclusions from this and gender has to be addressed in a separate study for this purpose. Moreover, we screened a high number of children (N = 150) and it may be that preponderance of super-attentive individuals amongst girls is part of the normal variation within the classroom and this is highly interesting per se if it holds for true. *Second*, the experiments were conducted in a classroom setting where participants accomplished tests at their own school in groups of approximately five pupils, which could partly explain the poor results of the sub-attentive group – one might expect that they became more distracted by their class mates than the others. In order to investigate noise benefit in a lower range of WN we need to conduct lab studies where we can hold the ambient noise (NBN) at a constant very low level (<40 dB), as this will give us an opportunity to find out if normal- and super-attentive individuals could benefit from WN. *Third*, we failed to produce an inverted U-curve, as predicted, in any of the participating groups. We cannot rule out the possibility that adding more noise levels, in particular levels with lower intensity (at least 55 and 60 dB) might have produced improvements in the super-attentive group and thus produced an inverted U-curve in this group. SR research, that finds U-curves, is normally done in normal populations, the MBA-model [24] predicting a deviant pattern for inattentive (i.e. low dopamine) subjects. *Fourth*, the three WN levels were determined a-priori and were identical for all participants; it may be that if participants had been able to select their own levels of WN, they would be able to produce an optimal level and thus produce greater WN benefits. Future studies that allow participants to individually adjust the levels of WN exposure may help to clarify this effect further. *Fifth*, there were different patterns of WN effects for the different tasks, EF and non-EF. This may be a modality-related effect. There are few studies that investigate cross modal SR e.g. [22]. There are good reasons to believe that when you present target and noise in the same modality you need less noise to obtain the same SR-effect. For instance in our own data (manuscript in preparation) we find this effect with auditory noise on visual word recall tasks (instead of reading out words they are shown on a computer screen). Future studies should be designed to disentangle the effects of modality and task domains.

The beneficial effects of moderate levels of WN raise the question of its therapeutic potential for children with attention problems. Our data suggest that sub-attentive children benefit from the addition of moderate levels of auditory WN, particularly in tasks that require EFs. If this could be applied in a classroom setting, it may have important practical implications for improving the performance and outcome of children who typically find it difficult to pay attention. It is however unclear whether these effects will also apply to individuals with more extreme problems and clinical diagnoses. Previous research e.g. [4] has shown that background noise can have a beneficial effect on patients with ADHD. Given the fact that the sub-attentive children in the current study were selected because they were in the lowest quintile for attention ability it seems likely that these effects will also apply to clinical populations of patients with ADHD, and might offer an alternative therapy to children who do not respond to stimulant medication [70]. Upcoming research that employs clinical patients with ADHD and compares the efficacy of WN and stimulant medication will elucidate this. It will also be important to carefully tailor and monitor these interventions given the highly heterogeneous nature of ADHD. It is unlikely that all clinical cases will benefit from the same WN intensity, and some cases may not respond to noise at all.

In conclusion, we have demonstrated that adding moderate levels of WN could benefit the performance of sub-attentive children (as rated by their teachers), while similar changes can impair children with already good levels of attention. Increasing WN past moderate levels has little further effect.

Author Contributions

Conceived and designed the experiments: SH GS ESB. Performed the experiments: SH SB. Analyzed the data: GS SH SB. Wrote the paper: SH GS SB ESB. Two revisions and cover letters: GS.

References

1. Broadbent DE (1958) The effects of noise on behaviour. Elmsford, NY, US: Pergamon Press, Inc.
2. Shidara M, Richmond BJ (2005) Effect of visual noise on pattern recognition. Exp Brain Res 163: 239–241.
3. Geffner D, Lucker JR, Koch W (1996) Evaluation of auditory discrimination in children with ADD and without ADD. Child Psychiatry & Human Development 26: 169–180.
4. Abikoff H, Courtney ME, Szeibel PJ, Koplewicz HS (1996) The effects of auditory stimulation on the arithmetic performance of children with ADHD and nondisabled children. Journal of Learning Disabilities 29: 238–246.
5. Gerjets P, Graw T, Heise E, Westermann R, Rothenberger A (2002) Deficits of action control and specific goal intentions in hyperkinetic disorder. II: Empirical results/Handlungskontrolldefizite und störungsspezifische Zielintentionen bei der Hyperkinetischen Störung: II: Empirische Befunde. Zeitschrift für Klinische Psychologie und Psychotherapie: Forschung und Praxis 31: 99–109.
6. Stansfeld S, Berglund B, Clark C, Lopez-Barrio I, Fischer P, et al. (2005) Aircraft and road traffic noise and children's cognition and health: a cross-national study. Lancet 365: 1942–1949.
7. Söderlund GBW, Sikstrom S, Smart A (2007) Listen to the noise: noise is beneficial for cognitive performance in ADHD. Journal of child psychology and psychiatry, and allied disciplines 48: 840–847.
8. Söderlund GBW, Sikström S, Loftesnes JM, Sonuga-Barke E (2010) The effects of background white noise on memory performance in inattentive school children. Behavioral and Brain Functions 6.
9. Moss F, Ward LM, Sannita WG (2004) Stochastic resonance and sensory information processing: a tutorial and review of application. Clinical Neurophysiology 115: 267–281.
10. McDonnell MD, Stocks NG, Abbott D (2007) Optimal stimulus and noise distributions for information transmission via suprathreshold stochastic resonance. Phys Rev E Stat Nonlin Soft Matter Phys 75: 061105.
11. Stein RB, Gossen ER, Jones KE (2005) Neuronal variability: Noise of part of the signal. Nature Reviews Neuroscience 6: 389–397.
12. McDonnell MD (2009) Information capacity of stochastic pooling networks is achieved by discrete inputs. Physical Review E, Statistical, Nonlinear, and Soft Matter Physics 79: 041107.
13. Ward LM, MacLean SE, Kirschner A (2010) Stochastic resonance modulates neural synchronization within and between cortical sources. PloS one 5: e14371.
14. Zeng FG, Fu QJ, Morse R (2000) Human hearing enhanced by noise. Brain Research 869: 251–255.
15. Wells C, Ward LM, Chua R, Timothy Inglis J (2005) Touch noise increases vibrotactile sensitivity in old and young. Psychological Science 16: 313–320.
16. Simonotto E, Spano F, Riani M, Ferrari A, Levero F, et al. (1999) fMRI studies of visual cortical activity during noise stimulation. Neurocomputing: An International Journal Special double volume: Computational neuroscience: Trends in research 1999 26–27: 511–516.
17. Priplata AA, Niemi JB, Harry JD, Lipsitz LA, Collins JJ (2003) Vibrating insoles and balance control in elderly people. Lancet 362: 1123–1124.
18. Priplata AA, Patritti BL, Niemi JB, Hughes R, Gravelle DC, et al. (2006) Noise-enhanced balance control in patients with diabetes and patients with stroke. Ann Neurol 59: 4–12.
19. Novak P, Novak V (2006) Effect of step-synchronized vibration stimulation of soles on gait in Parkinson's disease: a pilot study. J Neuroeng Rehabil 3: 9.
20. Wilkinson D, Nicholls S, Pattenden C, Kilduff P, Milberg W (2008) Galvanic vestibular stimulation speeds visual memory recall. Exp Brain Res 189: 243–248.
21. Usher M, Feingold M (2000) Stochastic resonance in the speed of memory retrieval. Biological Cybernetics 83: L11–16.
22. Manjarrez E, Mendez I, Martinez L, Flores A, Mirasso CR (2007) Effects of auditory noise on the psychophysical detection of visual signals: cross-modal stochastic resonance. Neurosci Lett 415: 231–236.
23. McDonnell MD, Ward LM (2011) The benefits of noise in neural systems: bridging theory and experiment. Nature reviews Neuroscience 12: 415–426.
24. Sikström S, Söderlund GBW (2007) Stimulus-dependent dopamine release in attention-deficit/hyperactivity disorder. Psychological review 114: 1047–1075.
25. Servan-Schreiber D, Printz H, Cohen JD (1990) A network model of catecholamine effects: gain, signal-to-noise ratio, and behavior. Science 249: 892–895.
26. Servan-Schreiber D, Bruno RM, Carter CS, Cohen JD (1998) Dopamine and the mechanisms of cognition: Part I. A neural network model predicting dopamine effects on selective attention. Biological Psychiatry 43: 713–722.
27. Braver TS, Barch DM (2002) A theory of cognitive control, aging cognition, and neuromodulation. Neurosci Biobehav Rev 26: 809–817.
28. Prince J (2008) Catecholamine dysfunction in attention-deficit/hyperactivity disorder: an update. J Clin Psychopharmacol 28: S39–45.
29. Tomasi D, Volkow ND, Wang GJ, Wang R, Telang F, et al. (2011) Methylphenidate enhances brain activation and deactivation responses to visual attention and working memory tasks in healthy controls. Neuroimage 54: 3101–3110.
30. Barch DM, Carter CS (2005) Amphetamine improves cognitive function in medicated individuals with schizophrenia and in healthy volunteers. Schizophrenia research 77: 43–58.
31. Kobel M, Bechtel N, Weber P, Specht K, Klarhofer M, et al. (2009) Effects of methylphenidate on working memory functioning in children with attention deficit/hyperactivity disorder. Eur J Paediatr Neurol 13: 516–523.
32. Biederman J, Seidman LJ, Petty CR, Fried R, Doyle AE, et al. (2008) Effects of stimulant medication on neuropsychological functioning in young adults with attention-deficit/hyperactivity disorder. J Clin Psychiatry 69: 1150–1156.
33. Faisal AA, Selen LP, Wolpert DM (2008) Noise in the nervous system. Nature reviews Neuroscience 9: 292–303.
34. McDonnell MD, Stocks NG, Abbott D (2007) Optimal stimulus and noise distributions for information transmission via suprathreshold stochastic resonance. Physical Review E, Statistical, Nonlinear, and Soft Matter Physics 75.
35. Stocks NG (2000) Suprathreshold stochastic resonance in multilevel threshold systems. Phys Rev Lett 84: 2310–2313.
36. Coghill D, Sonuga-Barke EJ (2012) Annual research review: categories versus dimensions in the classification and conceptualisation of child and adolescent mental disorders-implications of recent empirical study. J Child Psychol Psychiatry 53: 469–489.
37. Frazier TW, Youngstrom EA, Naugle RI, Haggerty KA, Busch RM (2007) The latent structure of cognitive symptom exaggeration on the Victoria Symptom Validity Test. Arch Clin Neuropsychol 22: 197–211.
38. Haslam N, Williams B, Prior M, Haslam R, Graetz B, et al. (2006) The latent structure of attention-deficit/hyperactivity disorder: a taxometric analysis. Aust N Z J Psychiatry 40: 639–647.
39. Levy F, Hay DA, McStephen M, Wood C, Waldman I (1997) Attention-deficit hyperactivity disorder: a category or a continuum? Genetic analysis of a large-scale twin study. J Am Acad Child Adolesc Psychiatry 36: 737–744.
40. Willcutt EG, Doyle AE, Nigg JT, Faraone SV, Pennington BF (2005) Validity of the Executive Function Theory of Attention-Deficit/Hyperactivity Disorder: A Meta-Analytic Review. Biological Psychiatry 57: 1336–1346.
41. Swanson JM, Schuck S, Mann M, Carlson C, Hartman K, et al. (2007) Categorical and dimensional definitions and evaluatios of ADHD: The SNAP and the SWAN rating scales. Retrieved December 2007 from http://wwwADHDnet.
42. Stuart M, Masterson J, Dixon M, Quinlan A (1993) The children's printed word database. http://wwwessexacuk/psychology/cpwd/documents/CPWD manualpdf.
43. Westerberg H, Hirvikoski T, Forssberg H, Klingberg T (2004) Visuo-spatial working memory span: a sensitive measure of cognitive deficits in children with ADHD. Child Neuropsychology 10: 155–161.

44. Bitsakou P, Psychogiou L, Thompson M, Sonuga-Barke EJ (2008) Inhibitory deficits in attention-deficit/hyperactivity disorder are independent of basic processing efficiency and IQ. J Neural Transm 115: 261–268.
45. Hogan AM, Vargha-Khadem F, Kirkham FJ, Baldeweg T (2005) Maturation of action monitoring from adolescence to adulthood: an ERP study. Dev Sci 8: 525–534.
46. McDonnell MD, Stocks NG, Abbott D (2007) Optimal stimulus and noise distributions for information transmission via suprathreshold stochastic resonance. Physical review E, Statistical, nonlinear, and soft matter physics 75: 061105.
47. Mulavara AP, Fiedler MJ, Kofman IS, Wood SJ, Serrador JM, et al. (2011) Improving balance function using vestibular stochastic resonance: optimizing stimulus characteristics. Experimental brain research Experimentelle Hirnforschung Experimentation cerebrale 210: 303–312.
48. Braver TS, Barch DM, Cohen JD (1999) Cognition and control in schizophrenia: a computational model of dopamine and prefrontal function. Biol Psychiatry 46: 312–328.
49. Pålsson E, Söderlund GBW, Klamer D, Bergquist F (2011) Noise benefit in prepulse inhibition of the acoustic startle reflex. Psychopharmacology 214: 675–685.
50. Sonuga-Barke EJ, Bitsakou P, Thompson M (2010) Beyond the dual pathway model: evidence for the dissociation of timing, inhibitory, and delay-related impairments in attention-deficit/hyperactivity disorder. J Am Acad Child Adolesc Psychiatry 49: 345–355.
51. Sergeant JA (2005) Modeling attention-deficit/hyperactivity disorder: a critical appraisal of the cognitive-energetic model. Biological Psychiatry 57: 1248–1255.
52. Sergeant JA (2000) The cognitive-energetic model: an empirical approach to attention-deficit hyperactivity disorder. Neuroscience and Biobehavioral Reviews 24: 7–12.
53. Sonuga-Barke EJ, Taylor E, Heptinstall E (1992) Hyperactivity and delay aversion-II. The effect of self versus externally imposed stimulus presentation periods on memory. Journal of Child Psychology and Psychiatry 33: 399–409.
54. Sonuga-Barke EJ, Taylor E, Sembi S, Smith J (1992) Hyperactivity and delay aversion: I. The effect of delay on choice. Journal of Child Psychology and Psychiatry 33: 387–398.
55. Wiersema R, van der Meere J, Roeyers H, Van Coster R, Baeyens D (2006) Event rate and event-related potentials in ADHD. Journal of Child Psychology and Psychiatry 47: 560–567.
56. van der Meere JJ, Shalev RS, Borger N, Wiersema JR (2009) Methylphenidate, Interstimulus Interval, and Reaction Time Performance of Children with Attention Deficit/Hyperactivity Disorder: A Pilot Study. Child Neuropsychol: 1–13.
57. Knuepfer MM, Printz MP, Stock G (1991) Increased sensitivity to arousal in spontaneously hypertensive rats is partially dependent upon the amygdala. Clin Exp Hypertens A 13: 505–523.
58. Schaefer CF, Brackett DJ, Wilson MF, Gunn CG (1978) Lifelong hyperarousal in the spontaneously hypertensive rat indicated by operant behavior. Pavlov J Biol Sci 13: 217–225.
59. Barry RJ, Clarke AR, Hajos M, McCarthy R, Selikowitz M, et al. (2010) Resting-state EEG gamma activity in children with attention-deficit/hyperactivity disorder. Clin Neurophysiol 121: 1871–1877.
60. Barry RJ, Clarke AR, Johnstone SJ (2003) A review of electrophysiology in attention-deficit/hyperactivity disorder: I. Qualitative and quantitative electroencephalography. Clin Neurophysiol 114: 171–183.
61. Barry RJ, Clarke AR, Johnstone SJ, McCarthy R, Selikowitz M (2009) Electroencephalogram theta/beta ratio and arousal in attention-deficit/hyperactivity disorder: evidence of independent processes. Biol Psychiatry 66: 398–401.
62. Clarke AR, Barry RJ, Dupuy FE, McCarthy R, Selikowitz M, et al. (2013) Excess beta activity in the EEG of children with attention-deficit/hyperactivity disorder: A disorder of arousal? Int J Psychophysiol 89: 314–319.
63. Durlach NI, Mason CR, Shinn-Cunningham BG, Arbogast TL, Colburn HS, et al. (2003) Informational masking: counteracting the effects of stimulus uncertainty by decreasing target-masker similarity. The Journal of the Acoustical Society of America 114: 368–379.
64. Gray LC, Breier JI, Foorman BR, Fletcher JM (2002) Continuum of impulsiveness caused by auditory masking. International Journal of Pediatric Otorhinolaryngology 66: 265–272.
65. Breier JI, Gray LC, Klaas P, Fletcher JM, Foorman B (2002) Dissociation of sensitivity and response bias in children with attention deficit/hyperactivity disorder during central auditory masking. Neuropsychology 16: 28–34.
66. Dawes P, Sirimanna T, Burton M, Vanniasegaram I, Tweedy F, et al. (2009) Temporal auditory and visual motion processing of children diagnosed with auditory processing disorder and dyslexia. Ear Hear 30: 675–686.
67. Tan HZ, Reed CM, Delhorne LA, Durlach NI, Wan N (2003) Temporal masking of multidimensional tactual stimuli. The Journal of the Acoustical Society of America 114: 3295–3308.
68. Wilkinson D, Zubko O, Degutis J, Milberg W, Potter J (2009) Improvement of a figure copying deficit during subsensory galvanic vestibular stimulation. J Neuropsychol.
69. Samoudi G, Nissbrandt H, Dutia MB, Bergquist F (2012) Noisy Galvanic Vestibular Stimulation Promotes GABA Release in the Substantia Nigra and Improves Locomotion in Hemiparkinsonian Rats. PloS one 7: e29308.
70. Graham J, Banaschewski T, Buitelaar J, Coghill D, Danckaerts M, et al. (2011) European guidelines on managing adverse effects of medication for ADHD. European child & adolescent psychiatry 20: 17–37.

Effect of Atomoxetine on Hyperactivity in an Animal Model of Attention-Deficit/Hyperactivity Disorder (ADHD)

Su Jin Moon[1], Chang Ju Kim[2], Yeon Jung Lee[3], Minha Hong[4], Juhee Han[3], Geon Ho Bahn[3]*

1 Department of Psychiatry, Daedong Hospital, Daegu, Korea, **2** Department of Physiology, Kyung Hee University School of Medicine, Seoul, Korea, **3** Department of Psychiatry, Kyung Hee University School of Medicine, Seoul, Korea, **4** Department of Psychiatry, Dankook University Medical College, Cheonan, Korea

Abstract

Background: Hyperactivity related behaviors as well as inattention and impulsivity are regarded as the nuclear symptoms of attention-deficit/hyperactivity disorder (ADHD).

Purpose: To investigate the therapeutic effects of atomoxetine on the motor activity in relation to the expression of the dopamine (DA) D2 receptor based on the hypothesis that DA system hypofunction causes ADHD symptoms, which would correlate with extensive D2 receptor overproduction and a lack of DA synthesis in specific brain regions: prefrontal cortex (PFC), striatum, and hypothalamus.

Methods: Young male spontaneously hypertensive rats (SHR), animal models of ADHD, were randomly divided into four groups according to the daily dosage of atomoxetine and treated for 21 consecutive days. The animals were assessed using an open-field test, and the DA D2 receptor expression was examined.

Results: The motor activity improved continuously in the group treated with atomoxetine at a dose of 1 mg/Kg/day than in the groups treated with atomoxetine at a dose of 0.25 mg/Kg/day or 0.5 mg/Kg/day. With respect to DA D_2 receptor immunohistochemistry, we observed significantly increased DA D_2 receptor expression in the PFC, striatum, and hypothalamus of the SHRs as compared to the WKY rats. Treatment with atomoxetine significantly decreased DA D_2 expression in the PFC, striatum, and hypothalamus of the SHRs, in a dose-dependent manner.

Conclusion: Hyperactivity in young SHRs can be improved by treatment with atomoxetine via the DA D2 pathway.

Editor: Efthimios M. C. Skoulakis, Alexander Fleming Biomedical Sciences Research Center, Greece

Funding: The authors have no support or funding to report.

Competing Interests: The authors have declared that no competing interests exist.

* Email: mompeian@hanmail.net

Introduction

Attention-deficit/hyperactivity disorder (ADHD) is a common childhood and adolescent disorder that affects 5–10% of school-aged children worldwide [1] and can affect 3–5% of the adult population [2]. In spite of the high prevalence of ADHD, its exact pathophysiology has not yet been established. Various biologic factors have been suggested to contribute to the etiology of the disease. The "dopaminergic hypothesis" is the most widely accepted hypothesis by researchers for understanding the ADHD pathophysiology [3]. It is based on dysregulation in dopaminergic neurotransmission causing behavioral alterations in both ADHD and in the spontaneously hypertensive rat (SHR), which has been used as an ADHD animal model [4]. Initial functional MRI studies showed decreased activation of the dopamine (DA) pathway [5] and the DA hypothesis suggested that DA deficits in specific brain regions, such as cortical areas and/or the striatum, could produce ADHD symptoms [6]. DA receptors are the main determinants of the dopamine pathway and are divided into 2 classes [7]. D1-like receptor subtypes, D1 and D5, couple to the G protein Gs and activate adenylyl cyclase. The other receptor subtypes belong to the D2-like subfamily (D2, D3, and D4) and are prototypic of G-protein coupled receptors that inhibit adenylyl cyclase. In particular, the DA D2 receptor is closely associated with neuropsychiatric disorders, including ADHD [8], schizophrenia [9], and depression [10]. The DA D2 receptor belongs to the G protein-coupled receptor family and its activation inhibits synaptogenesis [11]. Enhancement of DA D_2 receptor function, induced by increased expression of the Gi-α protein, accounts for the decreased release of DA in the striatum of SHRs [7]. Further, Bowton et al. [8] demonstrated that dysregulation of dopamine transporters, via DA D2-autoreceptors, triggers an anomalous dopamine efflux associated with ADHD.

It has been known that the cerebral stimulants are closely related to the DA pathway; however, atomoxetine has been identified as a selective inhibitor of norepinephrine transporter that increases the extracellular concentrations of norepinephrine and also dopamine in the prefrontal cortex (PFC) [12]. Although ATX increased DA concentrations in the PFC 3-fold, the selectivity of ATX for NE effects in the PFC was also demonstrated [12]. Therefore, it has been recognized that ATX may have effects on attention, anxiety, and social affect in addition to hyperactivity [13]. Recent studies reported that atomoxetine produced changes in impulsivity via D2/D3 receptors [14].

There are several reports about the effects of atomoxetine on inattention and impulsivity; however, studies on the effect of atomoxetine on hyperactivity, especially via D2 receptors, are very rare [15,16]. The pathological mechanisms of ADHD with respect to DA synthesis, DA receptors, and the effects of atomoxetine on DA synthesis and DA receptors still remain unclear.

Therefore, we investigated the therapeutic effects of atomoxetine on the motor activity in relation to the expression of the DA D_2 receptor in the SHR animal model of ADHD based on the hypothesis that DA system hypofunction causes ADHD symptoms, which would correlate with extensive D_2 receptor overproduction and a lack of DA synthesis in specific brain regions such as PFC, striatum, and hypothalamus.

Materials and Methods

Experimental animals and treatments

The SHR is a valid and currently accepted model for the study of ADHD [17]. The SHRs are known to display hyperactivity, impulsivity, poor sustained attention, and deficits in learning and memory processes in comparison with normotensive Wistar-Kyoto (WKY) rats [4]. Male animals, weighing 180±5 g (6-week-old), were obtained from a commercial breeder (Orient Co., Seoul, Korea): SHRs served as ADHD rats, and WKY rats as controls. Each animal was housed under controlled temperature (23±2°C) and lighting (08:00–20:00) conditions, with food and water made available *ad libitum*. All experimental procedures were performed in accordance with the animal care guidelines of the National Institutes of Health (NIH) and the Korean Academy of Medical Sciences. The protocol was approved by the Ethics Committee of Kyung Hee University and the? Institutional Animal Care and Use Committee (Permit Number: 13-038).

The SHRs were randomly divided into four groups (n = 10 in each group): the untreated SHR group; the 0.25 mg/kg/day atomoxetine-treated SHR group; the 0.5 mg/kg/day atomoxetine-treated SHR group; and the 1 mg/kg/day atomoxetine-treated SHR group. The control group comprised of 10 WKY rats.

The rats in the atomoxetine-treated groups received atomoxetine (Strattera, Eli Lilly Co., Indianapolis, IN, USA) orally once a day for 21 consecutive days, at the respective dosage. The rats in the control group and the untreated SHR group received an equal amount of distilled water for the same duration.

Open-field test

Open-field test has often been used for the assessment of behaviors such as motor activity [18]. Ambulatory and rearing activities in the open field environment were significantly higher in juvenile, stroke-prone SHRs than in WKY rats [19]. The open-field test procedure was performed according to a previous report [20], testing all of the groups four times: one day before the start of the atomoxetine (or water) treatment, one week after the start of treatment, two weeks after the start of treatment, and three weeks after the start of treatment. The open field box was composed of a 100 cm×100 cm×40 cm wooden enclosure, and the field was divided into 25 squares (20×20 cm), defined as 9 central and 16 peripheral squares. Each rat was placed in the central square and allowed to move freely and explore the environment for 1 minute. Next, the number of squares that the rat crossed was recorded for 5 minutes. The entire area was cleaned between tests.

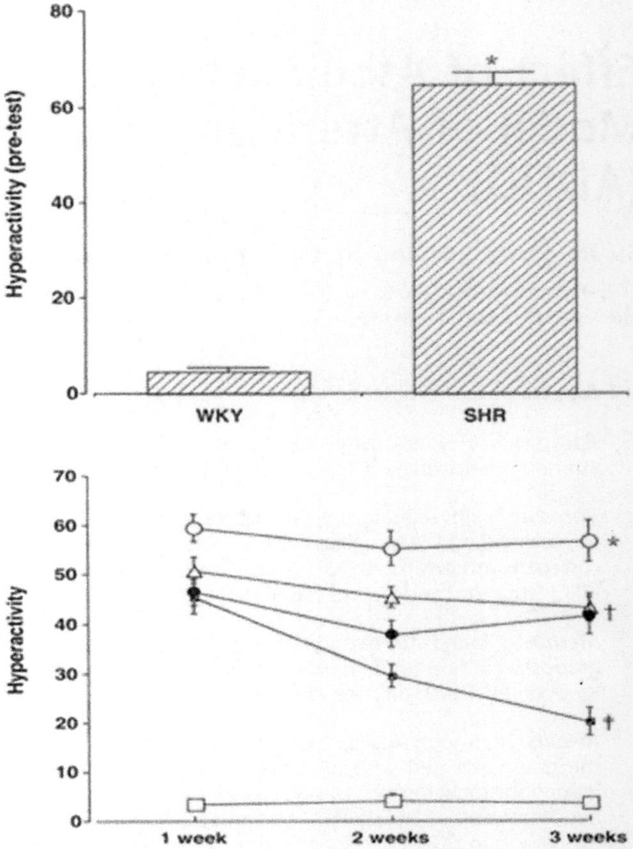

Figure 1. Effect of atomoxetine on hyperactivity in the open field test. Upper: Pre-open field test. Lower: Open field test for experimental periods. (□) Control group, (○) SHR group, (Δ) SHR and 0.25 mg/kg atomoxetine-treatd group, (●) SHR and 0.5 mg/kg atomoxetine-treatd group, (◘) SHR and 1 mg/kg atomoxetine-treatd group. * represents $p<.05$ compared to the control group. † represents $p<.05$ compared to the SHR group. ‡ represents $p<.05$ compared to the SHR and 0.25 mg/kg atomoxetine-treated group.

Tissue preparation

All of the rats were sacrificed at 21 days after the initiation of drug treatment. The animals were anesthetized with Zoletil 50 (10 mg/kg, i.p.; Vibac Laboratories, Carros, France), transcardially perfused with 50 mM phosphate-buffered saline (PBS), and fixed with a freshly-prepared solution of 4% paraformaldehyde in 100 mM phosphate buffer (PB, pH 7.4). Next, the brains were dissected and postfixed in the same fixative overnight, and transferred into a 30% sucrose solution for cryoprotection. Coronal sections of 40 μm thickness were cut with a freezing microtome (Leica, Nussloch, Germany). Ten slice sections were obtained from each rat, with each slice containing the prefrontal cortex (PFC), striatum, and hypothalamus.

DA D2 receptor immunohistochemistry

Immunohistochemistry was performed to immunolabel the DA D_2 receptors in the PFC, striatum, and hypothalamus.

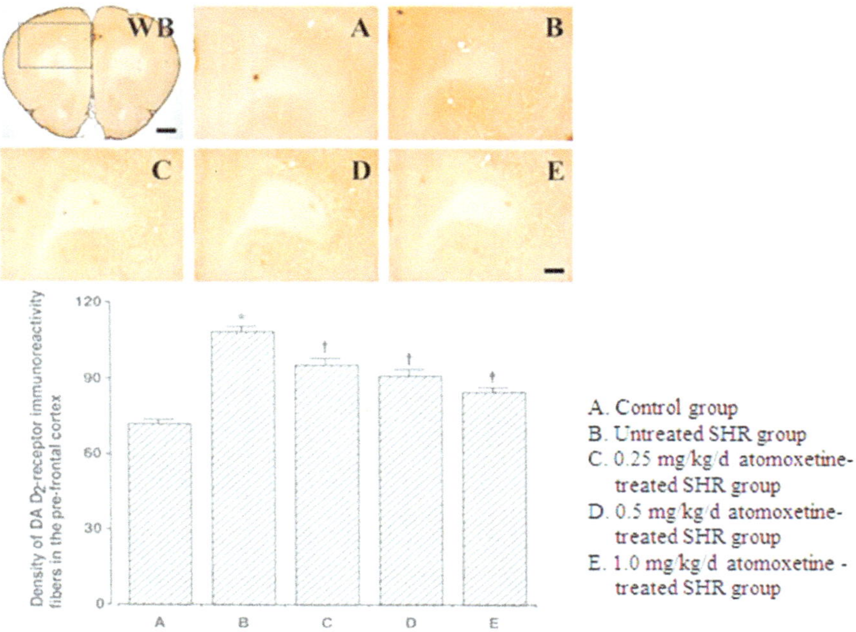

Figure 2. Effect of atomoxetine on DA D_2 receptor expression in the pre-frontal cortex. Upper: Photomicrographs of DA D_2 receptor expression in the pre-frontal cortex. WB: Whole brain. The sections were stained for DA D_2 receptor immunoreactivity (brown). The scale bars represent 50 μm (WB) and 200 μm (A–E). Lower: DA D_2 receptor expression in each group. *$p<0.05$ compared to the control group. †$p<0.05$ compared to the untreated ADHD group.‡$p<0.05$ compared to the untreated ADHD and 0.25 mg/kg/d atomoxetine-treated ADHD groups. The data have been presented as mean ± SEM.

Free-floating tissue sections were incubated overnight with mouse anti-DA D_2 receptor antibody (1:500, Santa Cruz Biotechnology, Santa Cruz, CA, USA) and then incubated for 1 hour with biotinylated anti-mouse secondary antibody (1:200, Vector Laboratories, Burlingame, CA, USA). The sections were subsequently incubated with avidin-biotin-peroxidase complex (Vector Laboratories) for 1 hour at room temperature. To visualize immunoreactivity, the sections were incubated in a solution of 0.05% 3, 3-DAB and 0.01% H_2O_2 in 50 mM Tris-buffer (pH 7.6) for approximately 3 minutes. The sections were then washed three times with PBS and mounted onto gelatin-coated slides. The slides were air-dried overnight at room temperature, and cover slips were mounted using Permount.

We calculated the optical density of DA D_2 receptor-immunoreactive fibers in the PFC, striatum, and hypothalamus in each slice. First, the areas of PFC, striatum, and hypothalamus in each slice were measured using the Image-Pro Plus computer-assisted image analysis system (Media Cybernetics Inc., Silver Spring, MD, USA) attached with a light microscope (Olympus, Tokyo, Japan). Next, the DA D_2 receptor-immunoreactive fiber densities were measured in 100×100 μm square images, of the PFC, striatum, and hypothalamus, using an image analyzer (Multiscan, Fullerton, CA, USA). To estimate the DA D_2 receptor-staining densities, the optical densities were corrected for the nonspecific background density, which was measured in completely denervated areas of the striatum.

Data analysis

Statistical analysis was performed using one-way ANOVA followed by Duncan's post-hoc test, and the results were expressed as the mean ± standard error of the mean (SEM). The limit for statistical significance was set at $p<0.05$.

Results

The open-field tests were carried out one day before the start of atomoxetine and water treatment, one week after the start of atomoxetine and water treatment, two weeks after the start of atomoxetine and water treatment, and three weeks after the start of atomoxetine and water treatment. At one day before the start of treatment, the activity score in controls was 4.60±0.79, and the activity score in SHRs was 64.52±2.37 (Fig. 1). The activity scores at one week after the start of treatment, two weeks after the start of treatment, and three weeks after the start of treatment were 3.60±0.84, 4.30±1.22, and 3.70±0.91, respectively in the control rats; 59.50±2.82, 55.30±3.56, and 56.70±4.18, respectively in the untreated SHR group; 50.90±2.82, 45.50±2.11, and 43.30±2.88, respectively in the 0.25 mg/kg/day atomoxetine-treated SHR group; 46.70±2.81, 38.00±2.69, and 41.70±3.74, respectively in the 0.5 mg/kg/day atomoxetine-treated SHR group; and 45.50±3.47, 29.50±2.28, and 20.10±2.81, respectively in the 1 mg/kg/day atomoxetine-treated SHR group. These results demonstrated that the activity of the SHRs was higher than that of the control rats. Atomoxetine treatment decreased the activity of SHRs in a time- and dose-dependent manner ($F_{(4,45)}=42.178$, $p<0.001$).

The DA D_2 receptor-immunoreactive fiber density in the PFC was 72.20±1.77 in the control group, 108.50±1.72 in the untreated SHR group, 95.00±2.34 in the 0.25 mg/kg/day atomoxetine-treated SHR group, 90.60±2.55 in the 0.5 mg/kg/day atomoxetine-treated SHR group, and 84.40±1.66 in the 1 mg/kg/day atomoxetine-treated SHR group (Fig. 2). These results indicated that the DA D_2 receptor-immunoreactive fiber density in the PFCs of SHRs was significantly higher than that in the PFCs of controls, and atomoxetine treatment significantly and

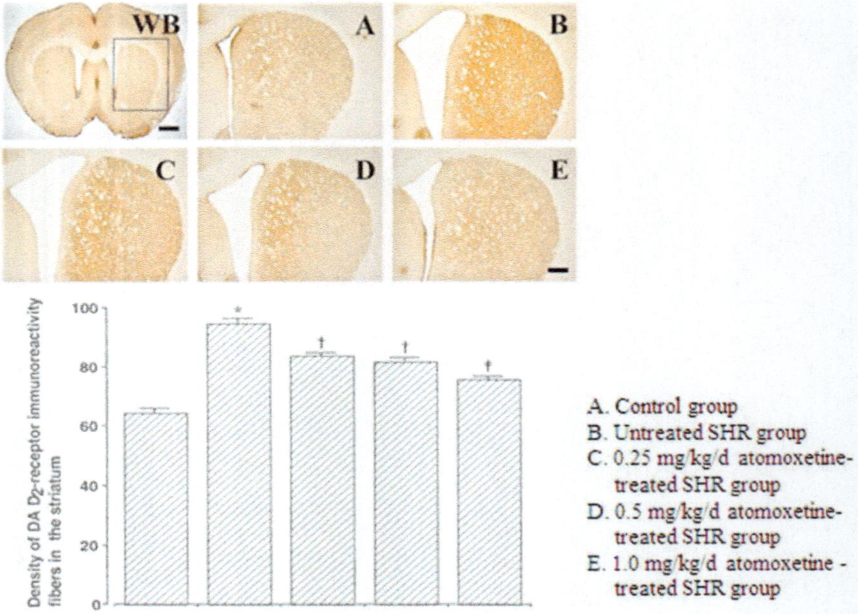

Figure 3. Effect of atomoxetine on DA D_2 receptor expression in the striatum. Upper: Photomicrographs of DA D_2 receptor expression in the striatum. WB: Whole brain. The sections were stained for DA D_2 receptor immunoreactivity (brown). The scale bars represent 50 μm (WB) and 200 μm (A–E). Lower: DA D_2 receptor expression in each group.$*p<0.05$ compared to the control group. $^{\dagger}p<0.05$ compared to the untreated ADHD group. $^{\ddagger}p<0.05$ compared to the untreated ADHD and 0.25 mg/kg/d atomoxetine-treated ADHD groups. The data have been presented as mean ± SEM.

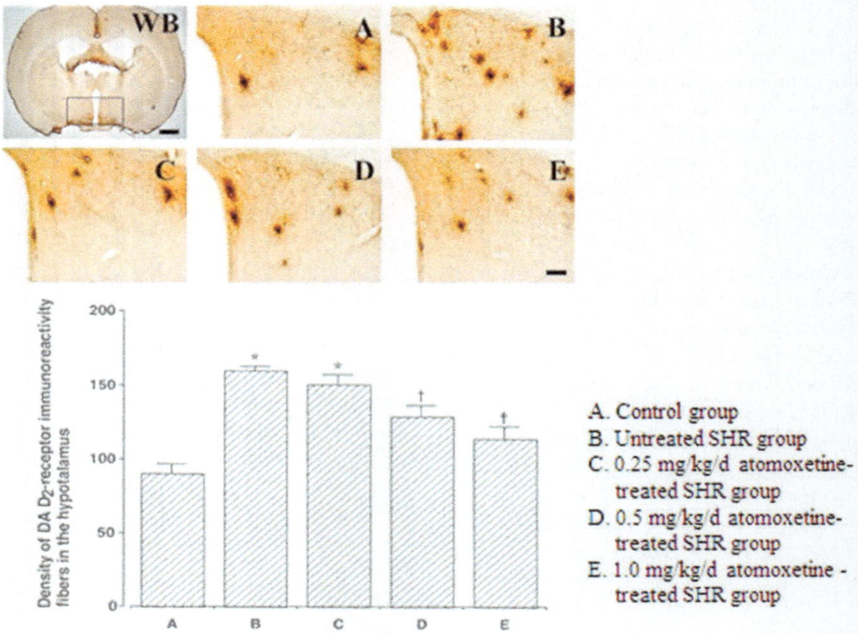

Figure 4. Effect of atomoxetine on DA D_2 receptor expression in the hypothalamus. Upper: Photomicrographs of DA D_2 receptor expression in the hypothalamus. WB: Whole brain. The sections were stained for DA D_2 receptor immunoreactivity (brown). The scale bars represent 50 μm (WB) and 200 μm (A–E). Lower: DA D_2 receptor expression in each group$*p<0.05$ compared to the control group. $^{\dagger}p<0.05$ compared to the untreated ADHD group. $^{\ddagger}p<0.05$ compared to the untreated ADHD and 0.25 mg/kg/d atomoxetine-treated ADHD groups. The data have been presented as mean ±SEM.

dose-dependently decreased the DA D_2 receptor-immunoreactive fiber density in the PFC ($F_{(4,40)} = 44.921$, $p = 0.001$).

The DA D_2 receptor-immunoreactive fiber density in the striatum was 64.40±1.57 in the control group, 94.50±1.92 in the untreated SHR group, 83.60±0.92 in the 0.25 mg/kg/day atomoxetine-treated SHR group, 81.80±1.10 in the 0.5 mg/kg/day atomoxetine-treated SHR group, and 75.70±0.94 in the 1 mg/kg/day atomoxetine-treated SHR group (Fig. 3). These results showed that the DA D_2 receptor-immunoreactive fiber density in the striatum of SHRs was significantly higher than that in the striatum of the controls, and atomoxetine treatment significantly and dose-dependently decreased the DA D_2 receptor-immunoreactive fiber density in the striatum ($F_{(4,40)} = 47.480$, $p<0.001$).

The D_2 receptor-positive cell density in the hypothalamus was 90.00±0.68 in the control group, 160.20±2.35 in the untreated SHR group, 150.20±1.67 in the 0.25 mg/kg atomoxetine-treated SHR group, 120.80±0.74 in the 0.5 mg/kg atomoxetine-treated SHR group, and 114.40±0.77 in the 1 mg/kg atomoxetine-treated SHR group (Fig. 4). These results showed that the D_2 receptor- immunoreactive fiber density in the hypothalamus of SHRs was significantly higher than that in the hypothalamus of controls, and atomoxetine treatment significantly and dose-dependently decreased the number of D_2 receptor-positive cells ($F_{(4,40)} = 65.232$, $p<0.001$).

Discussion

The hyperactive motor activity in the experimental animals improved as the atomoxetine concentration increased: 1 mg/Kg dosage seems to be more accurate than 0.25 mg/Kg or 0.5 mg/Kg. Interestingly, while the improvement in motor activity in the 0.25 mg/Kg and 0.5 mg/Kg groups did not continue after 2 weeks of treatment, the 1 mg/Kg/day group displayed continuous improvement in motor activity even after 2 weeks. This coincides with the clinical findings, demonstrating slower responses to atomoxetine than to cerebral stimulants. In other words, the effects of atomoxetine can be seen after slow titration and optimal dosage. For improving the motor activity in SHRs, these results indicate one of the reasons why pharmacotherapy is less effective than expected, which is inadequate dosage level for treating the symptoms [21].

Current medications for ADHD management mostly aim to control brain levels of dopamine and norepinephrine [2]. The alleviation of ADHD symptoms via atomoxetine treatment probably correlates with changes in NA and DA levels in the PFC, thereby enhancing cognitive function in ADHD patients [22]. In addition, atomoxetine has been demonstrated to increase the expression of tyrosine hydroxylase-positive cells in the PFC and substantia nigra [23]. Atomoxetine treatment has also been reported to suppress DA D_2 receptor density in the striatum and PFC, while NA stimulation increased signaling, by acting preferentially on the DA D_1 receptors in the PFC [23]. Although studies focusing on the relationship between the DA D_2 receptor and ADHD are rare, Bowton et al. [8] emphasized that the DA D_2 receptor acts as a key modulator of DA stimulation in the dopaminergic system. In this experiment, with respect to DA D_2 receptor immunohistochemistry, we observed significantly increased DA D_2 receptor expression in the PFC, striatum, and hypothalamus of the SHRs as compared to the WKY rats. These findings demonstrated that DA D_2 receptor expression was significantly upregulated in the SHRs than in the control rats. That is, the dopamine synthesis in the PFC, striatum, and hypothalamus of the SHRs was lower than that in the PFC, striatum, and hypothalamus of the control rats. However, the experiment with DAT-KO mice treated with atomoxetine by Del'guidice et al. [16] showed amelioration of cognitive performance without change in hyperactivity.

In summary, the motor activity in SHRs was decreased in accordance with the dosage of atomoxetine. This study suggests that atomoxetine increases DA concentrations in the PFC, striatum, and hypothalamus, resulting in downregulation of the DA D_2 receptor expression in SHRs.

Author Contributions

Conceived and designed the experiments: GB CK. Performed the experiments: SM CK. Analyzed the data: CK MH. Contributed reagents/materials/analysis tools: SM YL JH. Contributed to the writing of the manuscript: SM GB MH YL JH.

References

1. Brown RT, Freeman WS, Perrin JM, Stein MT, Amler RW, et al. (2001) Prevalence and assessment of attention-deficit/hyperactivity disorder in primary care settings. Pediatrics 107(3): E43.
2. Dopheide JA, Pliszka SR (2009) Attention-deficit-hyperactivity disorder: an update. Pharmacotherapy 29(6): 656–679.
3. Genro JP, Kieling C, Rohde LA, Hutz MH (2010) Attention-deficit/hyperactivity disorder and the dopaminergic hypothesis. Expert Rev Neurother 10: 587–601.
4. Prediger RD, Pamplona FA, Fernandes D, Takahashi RN (2005) Caffeine improves spatial learning deficits in an animal model of attention deficit hyperactivity disorder (ADHD) the spontaneously hypertensive rat (SHR). Int J Neuropsychopharmacol 8: 583–594.
5. Durston S, Davidson MC, Thomas KM, Worden MS, Tottenham M, et al. (2003) Parametric manipulation of conflict and response competition using rapid mixed-trial event-related fMRI. Neuroimage 20: 2135–2141.
6. Levy F (1991) The dopamine theory of attention deficit hyperactivity disorder (ADHD). Aust NZ J Psychiatry 25: 277–283.
7. Missale C, Nash SR, Robinson SW, Jaber M, Caron MG (1998) Dopamine receptors: from structure to function. Physiol Rev 78(1): 189–225.
8. Bowton E, Saunders C, Erreger K, Sakrikar D, Matthies HJ, et al. (2010) Dysregulation of dopamine transporters via dopamine D_2 autoreceptors triggers anomalous dopamine efflux associated with attention-deficit hyperactivity disorder. J Neurosci 30: 6048–6057.
9. Wang M, Pei L, Fletcher PJ, Kapur S, Seeman P, et al. (2010) Schizophrenia, amphetamine-induced sensitized state and acute amphetamine exposure all show a common alteration: increased dopamine D2 receptor dimerization. Mol Brain 3: 25.
10. Gründer G (2010) Cariprazine, an orally active D_2/D_3 receptor antagonist, for the potential treatment of schizophrenia, bipolar mania and depression. Curr Opin Investig Drugs 11: 823–832.
11. Marcil J, Thibault C, Anand-Srivastava MB (1997) Enhanced expression of Gi-protein precedes the development of blood pressure in spontaneously hypertensive rats. J Mol Cell Cardiol 29: 1009–1022.
12. Bymaster FP, Katner JS, Nelson DL, Hemrick-Luecke SK, Threlkeld PG, et al. (2002) Atomoxetine increases extracellular levels of norepinephrine and dopamine in prefrontal cortex of rat: a potential mechanism for efficacy in attention deficit/hyperactivity disorder. Neuropsychopharmacology 27: 699–711.
13. Levy F (2008) Pharmacological and therapeutic directions in ADHD: Specificity in the PFC. Behav Brain Funct 28(4): 12.
14. Moreno M, Economidou D, Mar AC, López-Granero C, Caprioli D, et al. (2013) Divergent effects of $D_2/_3$ receptor activation in the nucleus accumbens core and shell on impulsivity and locomotor activity in high and low impulsive rats. Psychopharmacology (Berl) 228(1): 19–30
15. Fernando AB, Economidou D, Theobald DE, Zou MF, Newman AH, et al. (2012) Modulation of high impulsivity and attentional performance in rats by selective direct and indirect dopaminergic and noradrenergic receptor agonists. Psychopharmacology (Berl) 219(2): 341–352.
16. Del'guidice T, Lemasson M, Etiévant A, Manta S, Magno LA, et al. (2014) Dissociations between cognitive and motor effects of psychostimulants and atomoxetine in hyperactive DAT-KO mice. Psychopharmacology (Berl) 231(1): 109–122.
17. Davids E, Zhang K, Tarazi FI, Baldessarini RJ (2003) Animal models of attention-deficit hyperactivity disorder. Brain Res Rev 42: 1–21.

18. Wu L, Zhao Q, Zhu X, Peng M, Jia C, et al. (2010) A novel function of microRNA let-7d in regulation of galectin-3 expression in attention deficit hyperactivity disorder rat brain. Brain Pathol 20: 1042–1054.
19. Ueno KI, Togashi H, Mori K, Matsumoto M, Ohashi S, et al. (2002) Behavioral and pharmacological relevance of stroke-prone spontaneously hypertensive rats as an animal model of a developmental disorder. Behav Pharmacol 13: 1–13.
20. Durand M, Berton O, Aguerre S, Edno L, Combourieu I, et al. (1999) Effects of repeated fluoxetine on anxiety-related behaviours, central serotonergic systems, and the corticotropic axis axis in SHR and WKY rats. Neuropharmacology 38(6): 893–907.
21. Scahill L, Oesterheld JR, Martin A (2007) General principles, specific drug treatments, and clinical practice. In: Martin A, Volkmar FR, editors. Lewis's child and adolescent psychiatry: A comprehensive textbook, 4th ed. Philadelphia: Lippincott Williams & Wilkins. 754–756.
22. Stahl SM (2003) Neurotransmission of cognition, part 2. Selective NRIs are smart drugs: exploiting regionally selective actions on both dopamine and norepinephrine to enhance cognition. J Clin Psychiatry 64: 110–111.
23. Levy F (2009) Dopamine vs noradrenaline: inverted-U effects and ADHD theories. Aust N Z J Psychiatry 43: 101–108.

20

Cumulative Risks of Foster Care Placement for Danish Children

Peter Fallesen[1,2]*, Natalia Emanuel[3], Christopher Wildeman[4]

1 Rockwool Foundation Research Unit, Copenhagen, Denmark, **2** Department of Sociology, University of Copenhagen, Copenhagen, Denmark, **3** Department of Economics, Yale University, New Haven, Connecticut, United States of America, **4** Department of Policy Analysis and Management, Cornell University, Ithaca, New York, United States of America

Abstract

Although recent research suggests that the cumulative risk of foster care placement is far higher for American children than originally suspected, little is known about the cumulative risk of foster care placement in other countries, which makes it difficult to gauge the degree to which factor foster care placement is salient in other contexts. In this article, we provide companion estimates to those provided in recent work on the US by using Danish registry data and synthetic cohort life tables to show how high and unequally distributed the cumulative risk of foster care placement is for Danish children. Results suggest that at the beginning of the study period (in 1998) the cumulative risk of foster care placement for Danish children was roughly in line with the risk for American children. Yet, by the end of the study period (2010), the risk had declined to half the risk for American children. Our results also show some variations by parental ethnicity and sex, but these differences are small. Indeed, they appear quite muted relative to racial/ethnic differences in these risks in the United States. Last, though cumulative risks are similar between Danish and American children (especially at the beginning of the study period), the age-specific risk profiles are markedly different, with higher risks for older Danish children than for older American children.

Editor: Guy Brock, University of Louisville, United States of America

Funding: The study was funded by the Rockwool Foundation (http://www.rockwoolfonden.dk/). The funder had no role in study design, data collection and analysis, decision to publish, or preparation of the manuscript.

Competing Interests: The authors have declared that no competing interests exist.

* Email: pf@rff.dk

Introduction

Because foster care placement is such a vital indicator of family instability [1–3], it is important to know how common the risk of foster care placement is and whether the risk differs for various groups. Inequality in the risk of foster care placement between groups is especially relevant if foster care harms children, in which case it might exacerbate social inequality, or helps children, in which case it might ameliorate social inequality by improving the lives of the most marginalized children (for studies attempting to isolate causal effects of foster care placement on children, see [4–9]).

Recent research [10] estimating the cumulative risk of foster care placement for children in the United States from 2000 to 2011 provides two novel insights into how common and unequally distributed this childhood event is. First, the research shows that foster care placement is far more common than previously thought, with four to five percent of children ever experiencing this event by the age of 18. Second, this event is highly unequally distributed by race/ethnicity, with Native American (about 12 percent) and African American (about 10 percent) children far more likely to ever experience foster care placement before age 18 than Hispanic (about 5 percent), white (about 4 percent), and Asian American (about 2 percent) children. These findings extend previous work that studied the cumulative risk of having a maltreatment report [11,12], having a confirmed maltreatment case [13–15], and the cumulative risk of ever being placed in foster care [16]—all in a US context. The existing literature also found substantial rates of reports, confirmed maltreatment, and foster care entry, as well as pronounced differences across race/ethnicity within the US.

However, these estimates neither provide insight into how high these risks are relative to what we might see in other developed democracies nor show how substantial these racial/ethnic disparities are relative to racial/ethnic disparities in other countries. This makes it difficult to ascertain whether the levels of foster care placement and racial/ethnic inequality in risks of foster care placement in the US are exceptional or not. In this

Table 1. Number of Children at Risk of First Foster Care Placement in Denmark by Age (0–17) and Year (1998–2010).

	Year												
Age	**1998**	**1999**	**2000**	**2001**	**2002**	**2003**	**2004**	**2005**	**2006**	**2007**	**2008**	**2009**	**2010**
0	67684	66267	66365	67177	65526	64226	65119	64805	64590	65303	64532	65427	63266
1	68137	67995	66606	66715	67582	65871	64550	65102	65064	64767	65729	64898	65976
2	70825	68329	68158	66815	66904	67702	65884	64600	65157	65072	64980	66068	65203
3	71007	71001	68448	68314	67031	67066	67797	65880	64658	65194	65222	65249	66252
4	68699	71166	71083	68650	68521	67240	67091	67750	65770	64637	65258	65428	65463
5	69268	68837	71257	71201	68885	68706	67279	67060	67677	65758	64710	65429	65543
6	66155	69433	68906	71455	71453	69081	68784	67283	66970	67629	65815	64835	65531
7	65433	66255	69488	69121	71682	71602	69153	68784	67233	66918	67687	65950	64939
8	63395	65665	66357	69661	69307	71853	71714	69227	68736	67178	66938	67760	65981
9	61051	63563	65785	66589	69924	69492	71932	71689	69196	68732	67284	67093	67872
10	58389	61265	63739	66007	66828	70042	69602	71994	71655	69165	68816	67402	67212
11	57808	58559	61392	63940	66257	67063	70169	69687	71966	71674	69272	68986	67535
12	56400	57983	58649	61577	64249	66509	67147	70170	69664	72060	71735	69372	69041
13	54465	56554	58066	58866	61799	64440	66675	67267	70221	69690	72094	71847	69498
14	53370	54696	56735	58323	59148	62049	64587	66765	67256	70298	69793	72334	72022
15	55357	53700	54900	57031	58678	59385	62279	64792	66930	67410	70523	70079	72542
16	55628	55614	53917	55096	57399	58985	59632	62444	64924	67102	67603	70997	70459
17	60194	56208	56182	54606	55844	58056	59652	60284	63010	65459	67636	68230	71290

Source: Statistics Denmark.

Table 2. Number of Children Experiencing First Foster Care Placement in Denmark by Age (0–17) and Year (1998–2010).

	Year												
Age	**1998**	**1999**	**2000**	**2001**	**2002**	**2003**	**2004**	**2005**	**2006**	**2007**	**2008**	**2009**	**2010**
0	157	173	163	192	157	124	143	149	155	165	187	192	144
1	100	96	80	65	65	59	58	59	56	49	52	57	40
2	103	93	78	83	70	46	49	52	54	44	48	49	40
3	112	90	87	94	57	69	58	57	43	59	60	39	40
4	90	102	95	80	82	59	62	45	48	52	43	56	43
5	83	99	92	97	95	63	62	55	60	64	68	45	41
6	104	128	110	100	92	68	67	65	58	56	62	54	45
7	104	135	107	115	100	66	84	75	62	69	79	63	46
8	104	127	131	114	109	78	103	87	71	62	73	70	59
9	112	129	135	141	111	91	82	89	75	79	77	76	45
10	147	156	146	136	110	109	95	100	81	79	80	66	54
11	166	172	172	143	147	134	134	109	88	109	108	92	69
12	163	179	217	187	188	156	156	151	137	159	138	132	70
13	256	244	317	287	274	263	277	280	228	243	244	209	148
14	348	376	426	381	412	357	356	355	301	348	342	329	190
15	399	369	483	435	436	364	378	395	359	385	395	342	219
16	392	383	430	475	459	394	415	424	356	392	374	367	234
17	317	364	402	405	393	355	401	379	303	324	311	288	241

Source: Statistics Denmark.

Table 3. Cumulative Risks of Foster Care Placement from Birth to Age 18 for All Children in Denmark and Native Danish Children, Western Children, and Non-Western Children, 2005.

Age	All Danish Children	Native Danish Children	Western Children	Non-Western Children
0	0.002	0.002	0.001	0.003
1	0.003	0.003	0.001	0.003
2	0.004	0.004	0.001	0.005
3	0.005	0.005	0.001	0.007
4	0.006	0.005	0.001	0.009
5	0.006	0.006	0.003	0.010
6	0.007	0.007	0.004	0.011
7	0.008	0.008	0.009	0.012
8	0.010	0.009	0.009	0.013
9	0.011	0.010	0.010	0.016
10	0.012	0.012	0.016	0.017
11	0.014	0.013	0.017	0.019
12	0.016	0.015	0.020	0.022
13	0.020	0.019	0.032	0.026
14	0.025	0.025	0.041	0.032
15	0.032	0.030	0.050	0.043
16	0.038	0.037	0.055	0.054
17	0.045	0.042	0.062	0.065

Source: Own calculation on data from Statistics Denmark.

article, we provide one set of estimates against which to compare those generated in the US. As the Danish registry data (which will be discussed below) include complete information on the foster care histories of all children, they provide an excellent opportunity to consider the cumulative risk of foster care placement (using the same methods and roughly the same years) in a comparably developed democracy. We do this by using synthetic cohort life tables to estimate the cumulative risk of foster care placement for children in Denmark by (1) sex and (2) race and parental immigrant status, from 1998–2010.

The Danish case is an intriguing comparison to the US because foster care caseloads have long been rather steady in Denmark [17]. The same cannot be said for foster care caseloads in the United States, which increased dramatically from 1985 to 2000 before dropping thereafter [18,19]. Point-in-time estimates show that on any given day roughly 1 percent of all Danish children are in foster care [17]. Yet annual caseloads and point-in-time estimates only present an aggregate of foster care cases, and provide little insight into how prevalent foster care placements are as a childhood experience. By estimating the cumulative risks of entering foster care we can unpack to what extent foster care caseloads and point-in-time estimates describe either (a) a small group of children's somewhat constant placements in foster care or (b) a larger group of Danish children who ever experience foster care placement, with some experiencing short stays, others long ones.

The Danish Foster Care System

The Danish foster care system differs from the US system in a number of noteworthy ways. First, the Danish system relies on a mix of family foster care and institutional care [20,21], whereas the US places more than three quarters of children in family foster care [5]. Especially older children and children with behavioral disorders tend to enter institutional foster care settings in Denmark (see p. 54 in [21]). Second, the Danish system very rarely relies on non-parental family members to serve as foster parents, whereas this practice is quite common in the US [5,20,21]. Finally, the Danish system has historically relied on voluntary and family-oriented interventions [20].

These differences between the Danish and American foster care systems should be kept in mind when comparing the cumulative risks of entering foster care between Denmark and the US. However, recent comparative work has found that across different foster care systems, children who enter foster care exhibit very similar risk factors [22]. So whereas foster care systems differ substantially and children also differ in age at entry (as we will demonstrate in the result section), the children who enter foster care still appear to share risk factors across systems.

Method

Data

In order to estimate the cumulative risk of foster care placement for Danish children, we use administrative data on all first time foster care placements from 1998–2010. Municipal Child Services report all initiated child placements. Through unique individual identification numbers, we link foster care information with information on age, gender, and ethnic origin. Thus, the data we use correspond to the data used by [10] because the data include complete information on all children who entered foster care at any point during the study period. For the denominator, we use aggregate data on the full Danish child population, also obtained from Statistics Denmark.

The data we use come from the same registers that caseworkers use to initiate foster care placements. In addition, all Danish citizens are assigned a unique personal identifier at birth or time of immigration. Thus, the data cover all children in Denmark who

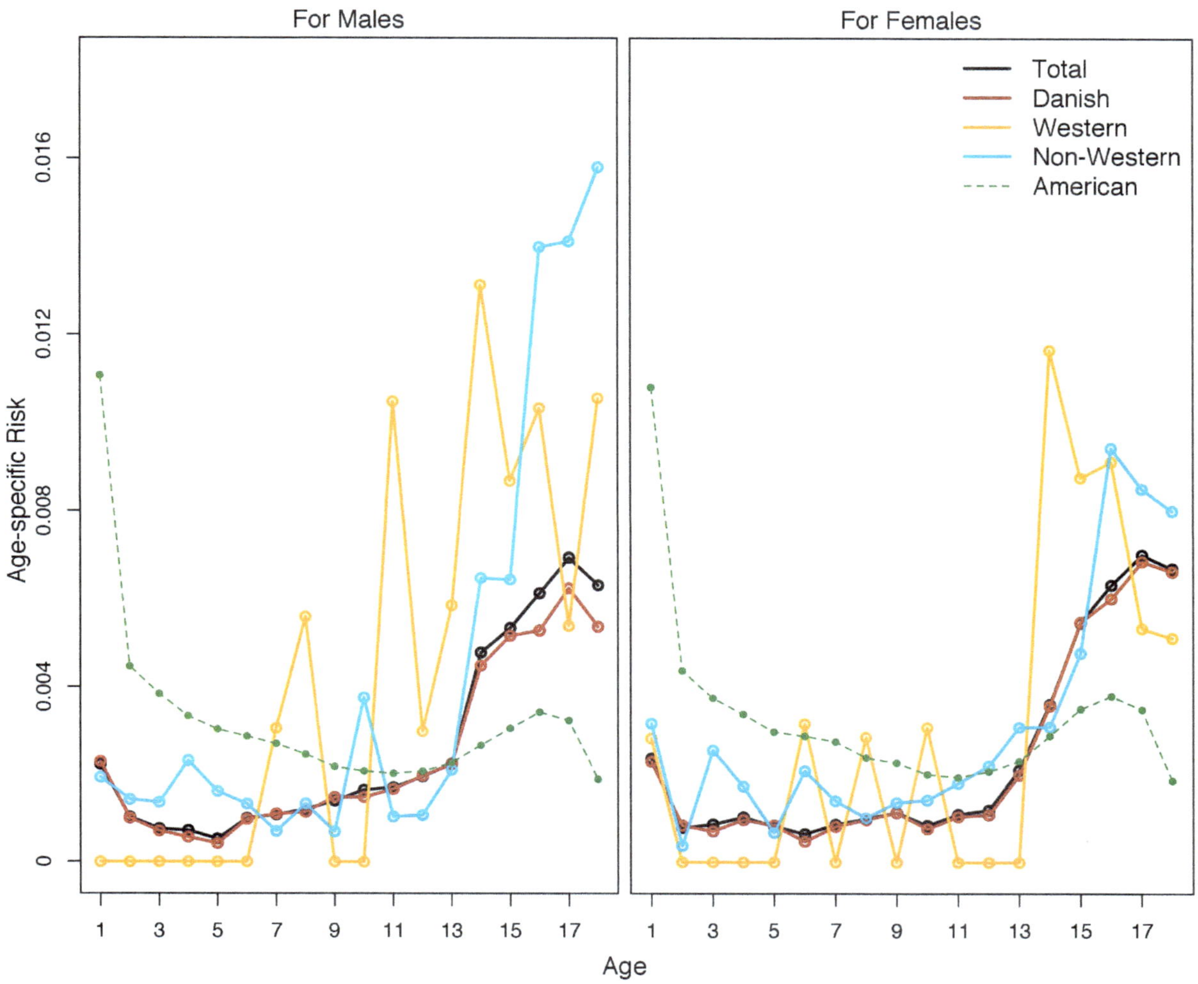

Figure 1. Age-specific Risk of First-time Foster Care Placement in 2005 in Denmark, all Children by Sex and Ethnicity.

enter foster care and do not suffer from retention bias, non-response, or other types of selection issues. Moreover, the data linkage does not rely on probabilistic linkage (as is often the case with linked data), because the unique individual identification numbers are constant across years and administrative datasets.

Statistics Denmark anonymizes and de-identifies the data before making it available to researchers. The data can be accessed through any Danish research institution after signing a terms of use agreement with Statistics Denmark. Because the data are retrospective and de-identified, the Yale University Institutional Review Board (where the second and third authors were when this research was performed) deemed this research exempt. Employees of The Rockwool Foundation Research Unit and University of Copenhagen are allowed to publish on the Danish registry data through a longstanding agreement with Statistics Denmark. Whereas the micro data used in this study cannot be made publicly available because of Statistics Denmark's rules regarding protection of privacy, we have made the aggregate data used to generate the synthetic cohort life tables available as supplementary material online (as File S1). Table 1 records the number of children in Denmark who were at risk of experiencing foster care placement at any given age from 1998–2010; Table 2 records the number of children in Denmark who experienced their first foster care placement at any given age from 1998–2010 (see Table S1, Table S2, Table S3, and Table S4 in File S2 for the two tables by gender). First entrance rates decreased across the study period (with only the most modest of decreases in the population of children over this period), and the decrease was most pronounced amongst older children. Yet we need to estimate the changes in cumulative risk to get a clearer picture of the extent of the decrease.

Measures of Ethnic Origin

Previous US based work has found large racial/ethnic disparities in the cumulative risk of both confirmed maltreatment and entrance into foster care [10,14]. Thus, we also examine whether the cumulative risks for foster care placements differ across ethnicity in Denmark. In our definition of ethnicity, it does not matter whether the child was born in Denmark or outside Denmark; ethnic origin depends on the parents' origin. With this in mind, we define three ethnic groups based on parents' country of origin: (1) children born to at least one Danish parent, (2) children born to parents who originate from a Western country (other than Denmark), and (3) children born to parents who originate from a non-Western country. If both parents were born outside Denmark, but one was born in a Western country and the

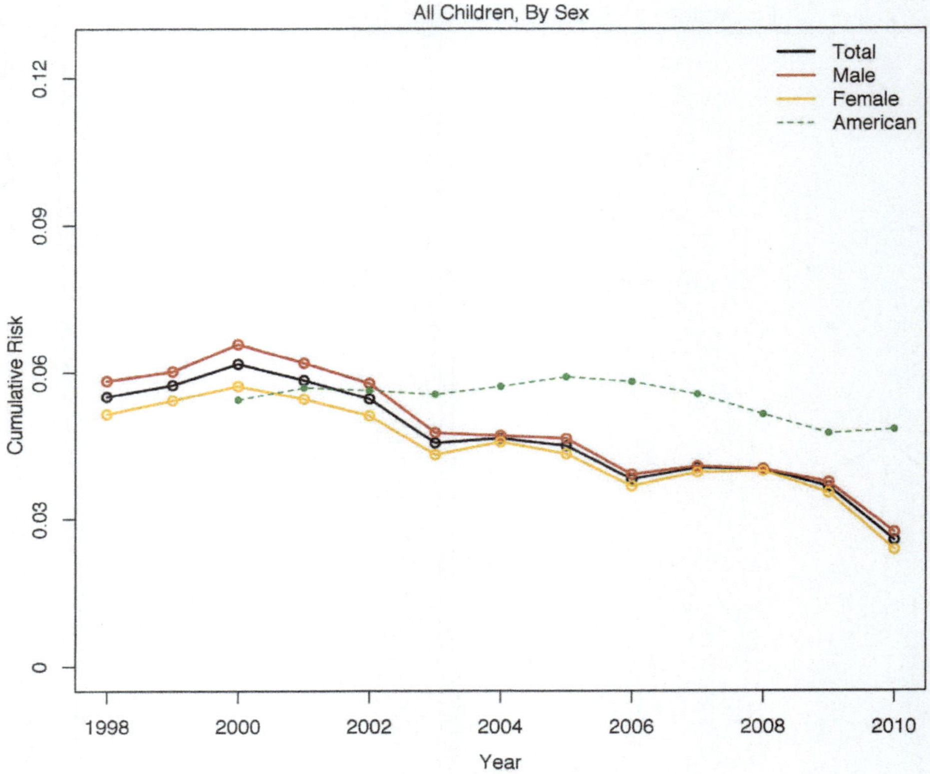

Figure 2. Cumulative Risk of Foster Care Placement by Age 18 in Denmark, all Children by Sex.

other was born in a non-Western, the mother's ethnic origin defines the child's ethnic origin. Statistics Denmark records ethnic origin for all Danish citizens, immigrants, and descendants of immigrants, so we have information for all children who enter foster care and all children in general.

Analytic Method

In order to generate estimates of the cumulative risk of foster care placement, we use synthetic cohort life tables, a method originally used to measure mortality in a population [23]. This method uses first-time incidence rates in the population to estimate the proportion of individuals in a hypothetical cohort subject to those age-specific risks at each age that would be placed in foster care by age 18. By converting the rates ($_nm_x$) to probabilities ($_np_x$), it is possible to create a function of placement for a hypothetical cohort, which can then produce an estimate of how many children could expect to experience foster care placement by age 18. We then use population information on how many individuals are in a given group to determine a cumulative risk figure ($_nc_x$). Life table methods have been widely used in research on the child welfare system in recent years, with some studies adopting only synthetic cohort life table methods [10,13,14], some using only birth cohort life table methods [15], and some using both of them to show robustness [16]. For discussions of the comparative benefits and limitations of synthetic cohort and birth cohort life tables, see [10,16].

Synthetic cohort life tables do, however, have certain limitations. Estimates may be unreliable if the age-specific rates change quickly and the number of synthetic cohorts used is small. Nevertheless, although we do find a substantial decrease in the cumulative risk of foster care placement across the study period, age-specific risks of first entrance decrease gradually and not quickly in our data (with the sole exception being children aged 10 and above in 2010, who did see somewhat large decreases in first entrance rates from the year prior [see Table 2]). Given the large number of years available to us (13), it is also easy to identify years that may have unreliable estimates. In addition, our estimates are similar to birth cohorts estimates found for Danish children born in 1985 [24], indicating both high reliability and robustness (see [16] for discussion of reliability of synthetic cohort estimates when compared to birth cohort estimates).

Comparing with Estimates for the United States

Our estimates of cumulative risks of foster care in Denmark are to a very large extent comparable to the estimates for the United States provided by [10], with one important difference. Whereas [10] use race-, age-, sex- and year-specific population estimates from [25] as the denominator for number at children at risk of entering foster care, we instead rely on full population registers containing demographic information on all individuals living in Denmark January 1 for each year in our study period. Relying on actual population data instead of population estimates makes the estimates for Denmark somewhat less uncertain than those provided by [10]. Yet, the US Census Bureau estimates are still highly accurate when using groups of sizes above county-level [25] and any inaccuracies will only affect the denominator of our analysis, so we expect differences in accuracy to be negligible. The Danish and American data used to calculate the numerator (children entering into care for the first time) are drawn from official registers containing all children in foster care in both countries [26–29]. Thus, these data are judged to be highly reliable and comparable.

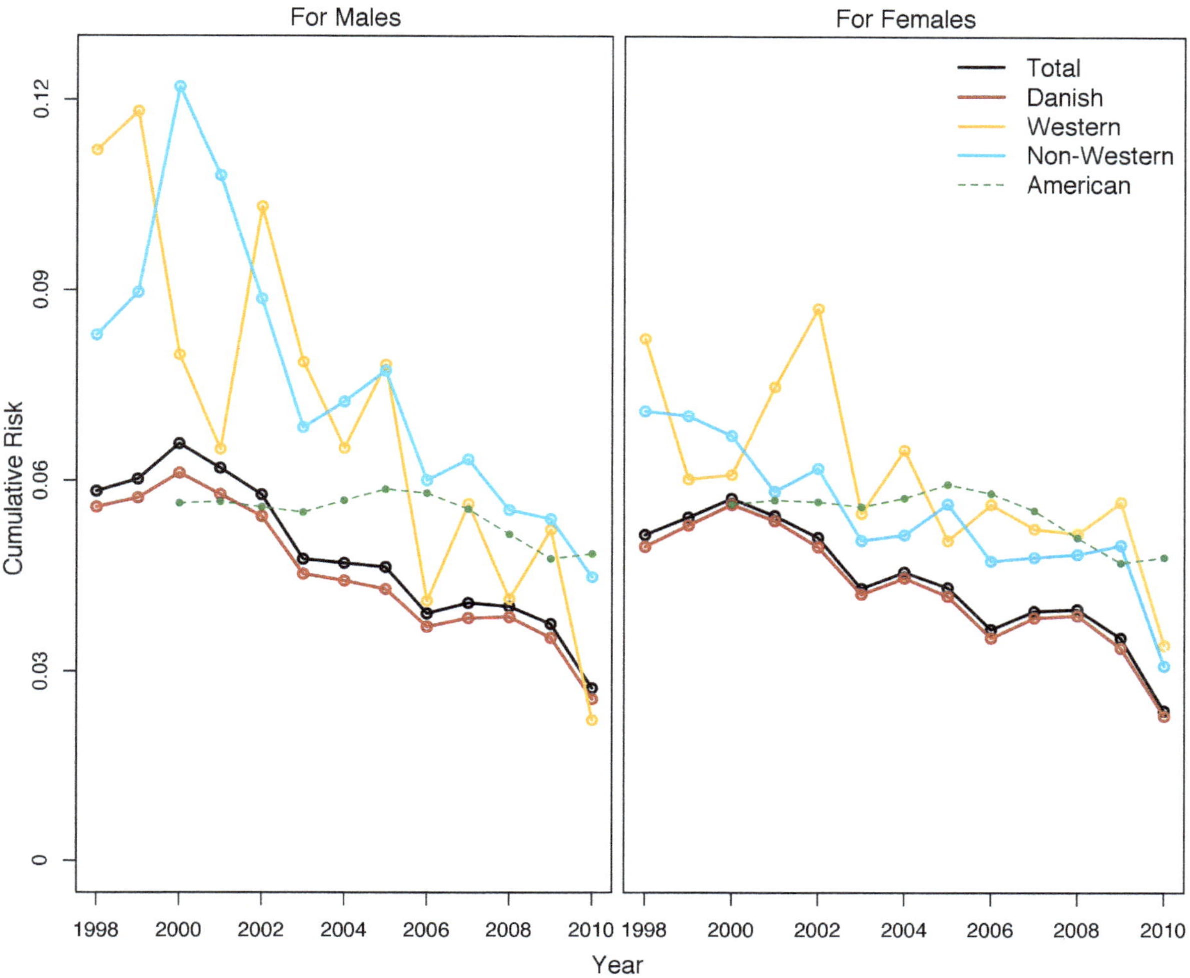

Figure 3. Cumulative Risk of Foster Care Placement by Age 18 in Denmark, by Sex and Ethnicity.

Results

We start by presenting a partial life table for the year 2005 in Table 3 which shows how the cumulative risk of foster care placement accumulates between birth and age 18 for all children in Denmark, native Danish children, Western children, and non-Western children in a sample year. According to the results shown in Table 3, 4.5 percent of all Danish children can expect to ever experience foster care placement at some point in their childhood based on the 2005 first-time admission rates. This is somewhat lower than what is observed in the United States for the same year ([10] reports a risk of 5.9 percent). Both Western children and Non-western children had higher cumulative risks at age 17 than native Danish children, although these differences were not nearly as marked as in the US. As the table also indicates, first-time admissions to foster care are high shortly following the birth and then trail off until the teenage years, at which point they spike dramatically–a finding consistent with trends found in the United States [19]. This teenage spike is, however, especially noteworthy since it is so much greater than the spike for American children [10], suggesting differences in the timing of admissions between Denmark and the US.

Figure 1 further demonstrates just how large this spike is in Denmark relative to the US by showing the age-specific risks for foster care placement across age, gender, and ethnicity. Both boys and girls had high risks of first foster care placement during infancy, then the risk of first placement trailed off until age 13, at which point it increased throughout adolescence to reach its peak around age 16 (although, again, this was the peak only in Denmark, as the US peak occurred in the first year of life, as Figure 1 clearly indicates). When breaking the age-patterning of first placement down by ethnic origin, we see that native Danish children of both sexes and non-Western girl children had similar patterns. In contrast, both Western boys and girls and non-Western boys had different patterns. Both Western groups are numerically small, which explains their less clear pattern. Non-Western boys, however, had increasing age-specific risk across age, with more than 4.4 percent of all non-Western boys entering foster care for the first time after age 14.

Figure 2 shows the trend from 1998 to 2010 in the cumulative risk of foster care placement for male and female children in Denmark relative to the US. The cumulative risk of foster care placement increases slightly until 2000, at which point it then declines until 2005. The cumulative risk remains roughly constant from there until 2008, after which it declines again. Boys have slightly higher risks in the late 1990s and early 2000s than girls have. The sex difference in the cumulative risk of foster care

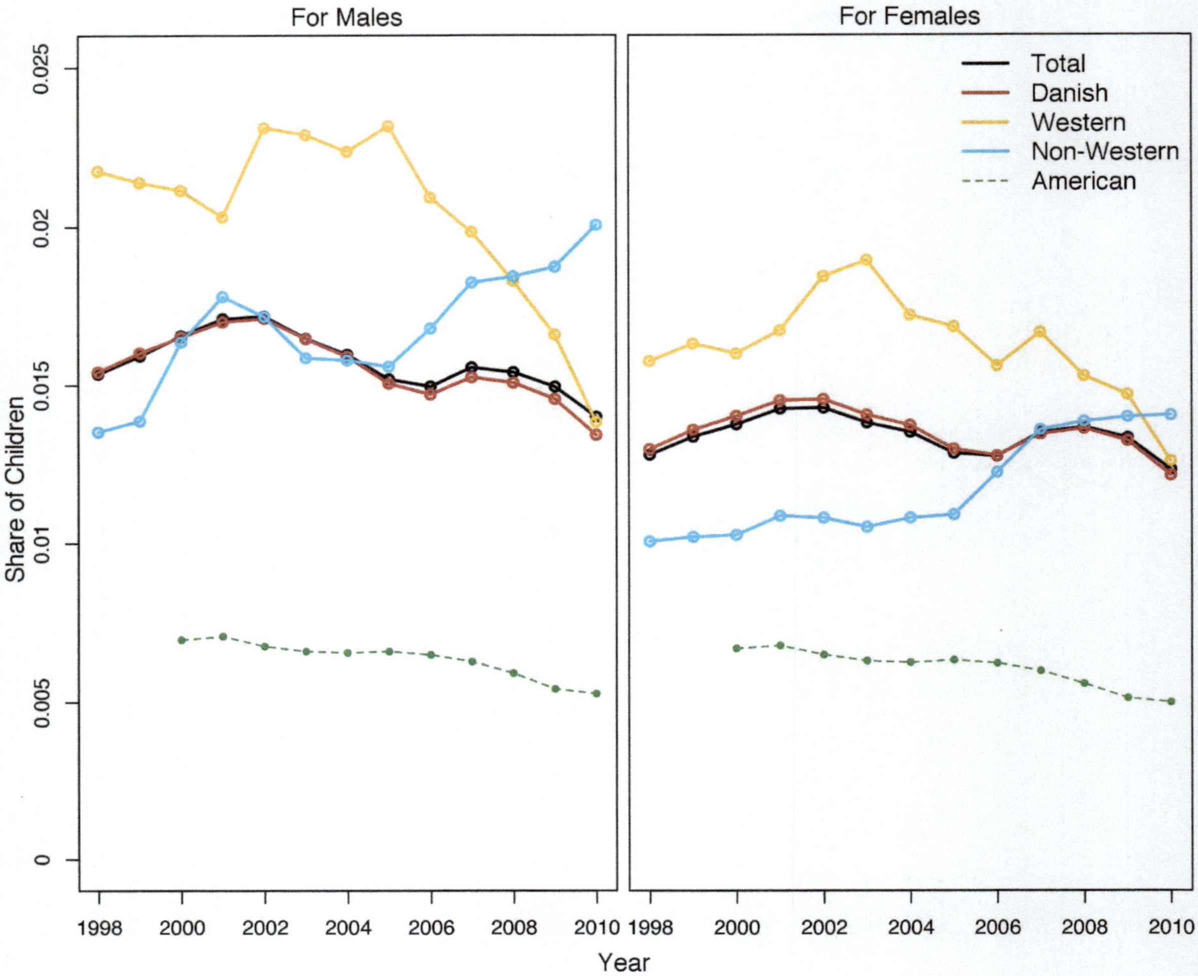

Figure 4. Share of Children in Foster Care at December 31st each Year in Denmark, by Sex and Ethnicity.

placement disappears in the later 2000s and is relatively small until then. Furthermore, the decline in the cumulative risk of foster care placement within Denmark is so dramatic toward the end of the period that by 2010, Danish children had lower cumulative risks of placement than American children had even though their risk early in the period far exceeded the risk for American children.

Figure 3 shows results for the total population, as well as for native Danes, Western immigrants, and non-Western immigrants by sex relative to the US. Although Danish children have lower cumulative risks than do other children, these differences are fairly small—especially when compared to the racial/ethnic disparities shown in the US [10]. Depending on the year, cumulative risks for Western and non-Western immigrants were anywhere from slightly above those of native Danes to about double the risk for native Danes. By 2010, however, cumulative risks are only slightly higher for immigrants than they were for native Danes, with more pronounced disparities for males than for females. Girls of non-Western backgrounds have lower cumulative risks than do girls of Western backgrounds for most years. The reverse is true for boys. Comparing across sexes, we find girls overall to have a somewhat lower risk of placement. For Western and non-Western girls, the cumulative risk starts lower than that of boys of the same ethnic origin. The cumulative risk of placement for non-Western girls remains lower than that for non-Western boys, although the risk for Western boys plummets to below that of Western girls in the later 2000s.

The share of children in care at the end of each year, as shown in Figure 4, does not decline as the cumulative risk does, however. Danish girls retain a constant placement share at around 1.5 percent; Danish boys show a trend of limited decline. The placement shares for non-Western children increase across the period. The share of Western boys in foster care declines dramatically in the second part of the 2000s while the share for Western girls remains rather constant, though with a slight positive bump in the first part of the 2000s and a decline in the end of the 2000s.

The fact that the share of children in foster care remains roughly constant throughout the study period while cumulative risk estimates are declining suggests that while intake levels may have decreased over the study period, the length of stay is probably increasing.

Discussion

Recent research on the cumulative risk of foster care placement in the US provided support for two conclusions [10]. First, far more children will ever be placed in foster care by age 18 than most scholars of American family life would have suspected, with between four and five percent of American children ever experiencing this event by the time they turn 18. Second, this risk is unequally distributed, with up to 15 percent of Native American children and as little as 2 percent of Asian American children ever experiencing this event by age 18 (depending on the year), suggesting potentially important implications for inequality (provided placement has any effects).

The goal of this article was to provide context for these results by examining other developed democracies, using Denmark as a test case. If the Danish estimates roughly correspond with the US results, then that would suggest that the foster care system might merit much more attention from family demographers and scholars of social inequality across the world than it tends to receive. But if the US estimates were dramatically higher than the Danish ones, that might suggest that the foster care system merits greater attention in the US but relatively little attention outside of it. The Danish results we supply here provide tentative support for the idea that foster care is far more common than often thought not just in the US, but also in Denmark, as the cumulative risk of foster care placement at the beginning of the period (in 1998), at around six percent, was higher than estimates over in the same period in the US.

The Danish estimates differed markedly from the earlier American estimates in three key regards. First, the cumulative risk of foster care placement for all Danes plummeted between 1998 and 2010, leading to far lower cumulative risks of foster care placement by the end of the period, with Danish children experiencing a risk of about three percent relative to the five percent risk faced by American children. Second, inequality in the cumulative risk of foster care placement was significantly smaller in Denmark than in the US, suggesting that if foster care placement matters for inequality, it likely does so in the US but not in other developed democracies—or at least not Denmark (or that it matters more for class inequality more than for racial/ethnic inequality, a key alternative to consider). Third, the age-specific risk of first entrance into foster care for Danish children was highest for teenagers, whereas the risk in the US is highest for very youngest children.

A number of explanations for why the cumulative risk of foster care in Denmark decreased in the period 1998–2010 offer themselves. First, one would expect that the financial crisis could have affected the municipal economy, such that there was less budget-room for placing children in foster care in the end of the study-period. However, given that retention rates of children already in foster care were stabile while entrance rates dropped, this does not appear likely. A second possibility is that the study period saw changes in thresholds at which social workers deemed a foster care placement necessary. Some reforms did that take place over the period [20], but their content was not such that we should expect substantial changes in foster care take up.

A third option relates to changes in demand for foster care placement driven by changes in child and parental characteristics. Recent work [30] has shown that a Danish penal reform that lowered the risk of experiencing paternal incarceration led to lower risk of foster care entry for children. Children's characteristics might also have changed during the study period. Children who enter foster care generally displays more behavioral problems that other children, for example ADHD [31]. Previous work has linked untreated ADHD to increased family strain [32] and has also shown that Danish medical treatment rates for ADHD soared in our study period [33]. If medical treatment of ADHD lowers family strain it might also lower the risk of maltreatment, thereby leading to lower risk of foster care entrance—this could be a fruitful avenue for future work.

Supporting Information

File S1 Data Used to Construct Life Tables.

File S2 Number of Children at Risk of First Foster Care Placement and Experiencing First Foster Care Placement in Denmark by Age (0-17), Year (1998-2010), and gender.

Acknowledgments

The authors thank Signe Hald Andersen, Mads Meier Jæger, Signe Frederiksen, Jill Duerr Berrick, and three anonymous reviewers for comments on earlier drafts.

Author Contributions

Analyzed the data: PF NE CW. Contributed reagents/materials/analysis tools: PF NE CW. Wrote the paper: PF NE CW.

References

1. Berger L, Waldfogel J (2004) Out-of-home placement of children and economic factors: An empirical analysis. Review of Economics of the Household 2: 387–411.
2. Lery B (2009) Neighborhood Structures and Foster Care Entry Risk: The Role of Spatial Scale in Defining Neighborhoods. Children and Youth Services Review 31: 331–337.
3. Wildeman C, Waldfogel J (2014) Somebody's children or nobody's children? How the sociological perspective could enliven research on foster care. Annual Review of Sociology: In Press.
4. Berger L, Bruch SK, Johnson EI, James S, Rubin D (2009) Estimating the "impact" of out-of-home placement on child well-being. Approaching the problem of selection bias. Child Development 80: 1856–1876.
5. Doyle JJ (2007) Child protection and child outcomes: measuring the effects of foster care. American Economic Review 97: 1583–1610.
6. Doyle JJ (2008) Child protection and adult crime: using investigator assignment to estimate causal effects of foster care. Journal of Political Economy 116: 1583–1610.
7. Fallesen P (2013) Time well spent: The duration of foster care and early adult labor market, educational, and health outcomes. Journal of Adolescence 36: 1003–1011.
8. Wald MS, Carlsmith JM, Leiderman PH (1988) Protecting Abused and Neglected Children. Stanford: Stanford University Press.
9. Warburton WP, Warburton RN, Sweetman A, Hertzman C (2014) The Impact of Placing Adolescent Males into Foster Care on Education, Income Assistance, and Convictions. Canadian Journal of Economics/Revue canadienne d'économique 47: 35–69.
10. Wildeman C, Emanuel N (2014) Cumulative Risks of Foster Care Placements by Age 18 for American Children by Race/Ethnicity and Sex, 2000-2009. PLOS ONE 9: e92785.
11. Putnam-Hornstein E, Webster D, Needell B, Magruder J (2011) A public health approach to child maltreatment surveillance: Evidence from a data linkage project in the United States. Child Abuse Review 20: 256–273.
12. Wulczyn F (2009) Epidemiological perspectives on maltreatment prevention. The Future of Children 19: 39–66.
13. Sabol W, Coulton C, Polousky E (2004) Measuring child maltreatment risk in communities: A life table approach. Child Abuse & Neglect 28: 967–983.
14. Wildeman C, Emanuel E, Leventhal JM, Putnam-Hornstein E, Waldfogel J, et al (n.d.) The Prevalence of Confirmed Maltreatment Among American Children, 2004–2011. JAMA Pediatrics. In press.
15. Putnam-Hornstein E (2011) Report of maltreatment as a risk factor for injury death: A prospective birth cohort study. Child Maltreatment 16: 163–174.
16. Magruder J, Shaw TV (2008) Children ever in care: an examination of cumulative disproportionality. Child Welfare 87: 169–188.
17. Andersen SH, Ebsen F (2010) Foranstaltninger for udsatte børn i Danmark: Historisk oprindelse og den seneste udvikling. In: Andersen SH, editor. Når man anbringer et barn: Baggrund, stabilitet i anbringelsen og det videre liv København: Syddansk Universitetsforlag. pp. 13–40.

18. Swann C, Sylvester M (2006) The foster care crisis: What caused caseloads to rise. Demography 43: 309–335.
19. U.S. Department of Health and Human Services (2012) Trends in Foster Care and Adoption – FY2002-FY 2011. Available: http://www.acf.hhs.gov/sites/default/files/cb/trends_fostercare_adoption.pdf. Accessed 2013-04-09.
20. Hestbæk A-D (2011) Denmark: A child welfare system under reframing. In: Gilbert N, Parton N, Skivenes M, editors. Child protection systems: International trends and orientations. New York: Oxford University Press. pp. 131–153.
21. Frederiksen S (2012) Empirical essays on placements in outside home care. PhD Thesis, Aarhus University. Available: http://pure.au.dk//portal/files/47873621/Signe_Frederiksen_PhD_Thesis.pdf. Accessed 2014 Jul 8.
22. Simkiss DE, Stallard N, Thorogood M (2013) A systematic literature review of the risk factors associated with children entering public care. Child: Care, Health and Development 39: 628–642.
23. Preston S, Heuveline P, Guillot M (2001) Demography: Measuring and modeling population processes. Oxford, UK: Blackwell.
24. Ejrnæs M, Ejrnæs M, Frederiksen S (2011) Risk factors of entry in out-of-home care: An empirical study of Danish birth cohorts, 1981–2003. Child indicators research 4: 21–44.
25. U.S. Department of Health and Human Services, Centers for Disease Control and Prevention, National Center for Health Statistics, CDC WONDER Online Database (2011) Bridged-Race Population Estimates 1990–2009 Request. Available: http://wonder.cdc.gov/bridged-race-v2009.html. Accessed 2011 Jun 14.
26. Statistics Denmark (2013) Quality Declaration: Assistance to Children and Young People. Available: http://www.dst.dk/en/Statistik/dokumentation/Declarations/assistance-to-children-and-young-people-.aspx. Accessed 2013 Jun 10.
27. U.S. Department of Health and Human Services, Administration for Children and Families, Administration on Children, Youth and Families, Children's Bureau (2012) Federal Reporting Systems: Adoption and Foster Care Analysis and Reporting System (AFCARS). Available: http://www.acf.hhs.gov/programs/cb/resource/about-afcars. Accessed 2013 Jun 10.
28. U.S. Department of Health and Human Services, Administration for Children and Families, Administration on Children, Youth and Families, Children's Bureau (2006) The AFCARS Report: Final Estimates for FY 1998 through FY 2002 (12). Available: http://www.acf.hhs.gov/sites/default/files/cb/afcarsreport12.pdf. Accessed 2013 Jun 10.
29. U.S. Department of Health and Human Services, Administration for Children and Families, Administration on Children, Youth and Families, Children's Bureau (2012) The AFCARS Report: Preliminary FY 2011 Estimates as of July 2012 (No.19). Available: http://www.acf.hhs.gov/sites/default/files/cb/afcarsreport19.pdf. Accessed 2013 Jun 10.
30. Andersen SH, Wildeman C (2014) The Effect of Paternal Incarceration on Children's Risk of Foster Care Placement. Social Forces 93: 269–298.
31. Harman J, Childs G, Kelleher K (2000) Mental health care utilization and expenditures by children in foster care. JAMA Pediatrics 154: 1114–1117.
32. Kvist AP, Nielsen HS, Simonsen M (2013) The importance of children's ADHD for parents' relationship stability and labor supply. Social Science & Medicine 88: 30–38.
33. Dalsgaard S, Nielsen HS, Simonsen M (2013) Five-fold increase in national prevalence rates of attention-deficit/hyperactivity disorder medications for children and adolescents with autism spectrum disorder, attention-deficit/hyperactivity disorder, and other psychiatric disorders: A Danish register-based study. Journal of Child and Adolescent Psychopharmacology 23: 432–439.

21

Prevalence of Psychiatric Disorders among Children and Adolescents in Northeast China

Yang Xiaoli[1], Jiang Chao[2], Pan Wen[1], Xu Wenming[3], Liang Fang[4], Li Ning[1], Mu Huijuan[1], Na Jun[1], Lv Ming[5], An Xiaoxia[6], Yu Chuanyou[7], Fu Zenguo[8], Li Lili[9], Yu Lianzheng[1], Tong Lijuan[10], Pan Guowei[1]*

1 Institute of Chronic Disease, Liaoning Provincial Center for Disease Control and Prevention, Shenyang city, China, **2** Department of Psychiatry, Dalian Medical University, Dalian city, China, **3** Department of Chronic Disease, Panjin Oil Field Center for Disease Control and Prevention, Panjin city, China, **4** Department of Psychiatry, Dalian Municipal Hospital of Psychiatric Disease, Dalian city, China, **5** Department of Chronic Disease, Donggang County Municipal Center for Disease Control and Prevention, Donggang county, Liaoning province, China, **6** Department of Chronic Disease, Benxi Municipal Center for Disease Control and Prevention, Benxi, China, **7** Department of Chronic Disease, Qingyuan County Center for Disease Control and Prevention, Qingyuan county, Liaoning province, Qingyuan, China, **8** Department of Chronic Disease, Zhangwu County Center for Disease Control and Prevention, Zhangwu county, Liaoning province, Zhangwu, China, **9** Department of Psychiatry, the 1st Attached Hospital of China Medical University, Shenyang city, China, **10** Department of Chronic Disease, Panjin Municipal Center for Disease Control and Prevention, Panjin city, China

Abstract

Background: To describe the prevalence of DSM-IV disorders and comorbidity in a large school-based sample of 6–17 year old children and adolescents in northeast China.

Methods: A two-phase cross-sectional study was conducted on 9,806 children. During the screening phase, 8848 children (90.23%) and their mothers and teachers were interviewed using the Strengths and Difficulties Questionnaire (SDQ). During the diagnostic phase, 1129 children with a positive SDQ and 804 randomly selected children with a negative SDQ (11%), and their mothers and teachers, were interviewed using the Development and Well-Being Assessment (DAWBA).

Results: The overall prevalence of DSM-IV disorders was 9.49% (95% CI = 8.10–11.10%). Anxiety disorders were the most common (6.06%, 95% CI = 4.92–7.40), followed by depression (1.32%, 95% CI = 0.91–1.92%), oppositional defiant disorder (1.21%, 95%CI = 0.77–1.87) and attention-deficit hyperactivity disorder (0.84%, 95% CI = 0.52–1.36%). Of the 805 children with a psychiatric disorder, 15.2% had two or more comorbid disorders.

Conclusions: Approximately one in ten Chinese school children has psychiatric disorders involving a level of distress or social impairment likely to warrant treatment. Prevention, early identification and treatment of these disorders are urgently needed and pose a serious challenge in China.

Editor: Katsuaki Suzuki, Hamamatsu University School of Medicine, Japan

Funding: This study was supported by a grant from Science and Technology Department of Liaoning Province (No. 2005225012). The funder had no role in study design, data collection and analysis, decision to publish, or preparation of the manuscript.

Competing Interests: The authors have declared that no competing interests exist.

* Email: panpgw@163.com

Introduction

Psychiatric disorders have a significantly adverse impact on children and adolescents, as well as their parents and families, particularly in relation to quality of life. Accurate estimates of the prevalence for these age groups are essential for setting up adequate services and diminish the consequences of mental disorders on later development and functioning in adulthood. Moreover, valid, reliable, not just of symptoms but also of resultant distress and social impairment, screening and diagnostic measures based on multiple informants can contribute to more precise prevalence estimates [1–2], such as the Strengths and Difficulties Questionnaire (SDQ) [3] and Development and Well-Being Assessment (DAWBA) [4]. Individual, family and socio economic status (SES) characteristics may play a significant role in the onset of psychopathology in this developmental age. A few studies have shown higher prevalence rates of psychiatric disorders in children and adolescents who live in developing countries when compared to their peers from developed countries, probably due to their poor socioeconomic conditions and the higher environmental difficulties faced by the children and adolescents who live in less developed countries [5]. It is reported that the prevalence rate of psychiatric disorders in children and adolescents from developing countries was between 5 and 18% [6], the wide variation in the prevalence of psychiatric disorders between children suggested that it is important to carry out studies in different cultures.

China is the most populous developing country with 197 million schoolchildren (6–18 years old) in 2011. The family planning policy, large scale rural to urban population transmission and rapidly increasing divorce rate, have produced large amount of "one child", "left-behind" and "single-parent family" children in China. The highly competitive education system, high expectation from one-child family, and rapidly changing socioeconomic status has made Chinese schoolchildren face increasing stress [7]. In the past decade, many studies have reported the high detection rates of psychiatric problems in Chinese schoolchildren with different instruments, showing big variations from 10.7% to 27.6% [8–12]. It's estimated that at least 30 million Chinese children and adolescent under 17 years old are troubled with various emotional or behavior problems [13]. However, only two studies have investigated the total prevalence of psychiatric disorders (not just specific disorders or psychiatric problems) in Chinese children and adolescents in Hunan province using a two-phase design [14–15]. A pioneering survey conducted in 1990 reported that 14.89% of 8644 children and adolescents aged 4–16 years had DSM-III-R disorders [14], the second study conducted in 2005 reported 16.22% of 9495 schoolchildren aged 5–17 years had DSM-ãÈ disorders [15]. Both studies have used the screening and diagnostic instruments specifically developed by combing Chinese questionnaire or criteria, such as "Screening Questionnaire for Child Mental Health" [14–15] and "Chinese Classification and Diagnosis Criteria of Psychiatric Disorders" [14], with international standardized questionnaire or criteria, such as Kiddie-Schedule for Affective Disorders and Schizophrenia- Present and Lifetime Version (K-SADS-PL) [15]. Therefore, no study to date has used internationally validated instruments, such as SDQ and DAWBA, for child and adolescent psychiatric epidemiology to evaluate the prevalence of psychiatric disorders among the Chinese children and adolescents. Most studies on the mental health in Chinese children/adolescents employed various questionnaires, e.g., Rutter Questionnaire [11], Child Behavior Checklist/Teacher Report Form (CBCL/TRF) [8,10], Symptom Checklist (SCL-90) [9] or SDQ [12]. Despite their well-established psychometric properties, they are not diagnostic tools and their results do not necessarily map on to formal psychiatric diagnosis. Information on the prevalence of child and adolescent mental health in China is clearly lacking. In this article, we present the first large-scale survey of DSM-IV disorders in China, focusing on prevalence, risk factors, and comorbidity of psychiatric disorders of Chinese schoolchildren.

Materials and Methods

Ethics statement

The study was conducted in accordance with the Declaration of Helsinki on ethical principles for medical research involving human subjects. The ethics committee of Liaoning Provincial Center for Disease Control and Prevention approved of the study. Parents were informed about the study and given an information sheet describing the study. Children were included if their parents had given written informed consent. This was considered to be the most appropriate mode as the study was of a simple, observational design with minimal risk.

Sample

The study was a cross-sectional survey of Chinese schoolchildren aged 6–17 years, attending primary (1st–5th grade), junior (6th–8th grade) and senior schools (9th–11th), and living in three cities (Shenyang, Panjin and Benxi) and three rural counties (Donggang, Zhangwu and Qingyuan) in Liaoning province located in northeast China, which were selected according to areas (urban vs rural) and economic development status. Two–stage sampling was conducted separately at each site by randomly selecting a sample of schools and then by obtaining a random sample of individuals at each selected school. The schools at each site were sampled with stratification by funding source (public/private) and type (banded into key and common schools). The number of schools for each stratum was selected with probabilities proportional in size of the subgroups of students to reflect the public/private ratio, key/common ratio and the neighborhood affluence of the different urban areas. In the first screening phase, the adult version SDQ questionnaire was administered to parents and teachers, and the child version to schoolchildren and adolescent aged 11 and over through the schools in fall 2008.

Figure 1 illustrates the subject flow in the two study phases. Of a total of 9806 students eligible for the screening phase, 434 (4.43%) refused to participate, and 74 did not return the questionnaire. Of the 9298 returned forms, 810 (8.71%) were subsequently excluded because the age of 81 was out of the target range (6–17) and 729 with unqualified SDQ. Therefore, information was collected on 8488 students, comprising completed SDQ from 8055 (86.26%) mothers, 5446 (90.57%) schoolchildren aged 11–17 years and 8418 (89.94%) teachers. Children were defined as screen positives if (1) the emotional and/or conduct section scores was above the 80th percentile cutoff and the impact supplement score was above the 80th percentile cutoff (≥2) for anyone of the three informants; (2) the hyperactivity section score was above the 80th percentile cutoff and the impact supplement score was above the 80th percentile cutoff (≥2) for any two of the three informants. Phase 2 was conducted on all screen-positive participants and on an 11% random sample of screen–negative participants. Of 1129 screen-positive and 804 of 7359 screen-negative schoolchildren, DAWBA face to face interviews were completed for 1824 (94.36%) students, 1535 (79.41%) mothers and 1787 (92.45%) teachers. The mean age of the total sample was 11.0 years (SD 2.3 years), and boys made up 53% of the total sample (662 of 1,251).

Instruments

The socio-demographic form. Demographic information on children and adolescent (gender, age, school attended, academic performance, school bullying, academic performance, repeated grades, domestic violence, life events, parenting style, disease history, birth weight, feeding pattern, number of children) and their parents (educational level, marital status, employment, income, general health status, mental disorders, satisfaction with child, smoking, drinking). Left-behind children is defined as children whose father or mother leave hometown and does not live together for over 12 months.

The Strengths and Difficulties Questionnaire: SDQ

It is a screening questionnaire for mental health problems consisting of 25 items. The items are divided into five subscales with five items each, resulting in scores of emotional symptoms, conduct problems, hyperactive behavior, peer relationships, and prosocial behaviors. All items of the first four scales generate the total difficulties score. An extended version of the questionnaire was used. It contained six extra items assessing the impact of symptoms in terms of suffering, social impairment and burden for relatives, although only five are considered for impact scoring. The Chinese version of SDQ and a computer algorithm, as programmed in SAS version 6.12 (SAS Institute Inc.), is available from the SDQ web site (http://www.sdqinfo.com). The Chinese version of the SDQ has been validated in China [16]. After obtaining written consent forms from parents, an informant-rated version of the SDQ were self-completed by the parents and teachers of the students, while a self-report version of the SDQ was completed by student aged 11–17 year olds themselves, either at school or at home between January and June 2008.

This screening phase allowed children to be divided into "screen positive" and "screen negative" children using by the SDQ algorithm (http://www.iop.kcl.ac.uk/Iop/Departments/ChildPsy/sdq/a1.stm). The original a priori algorithm predicted that a disorder was probably present on the basis that the relevant

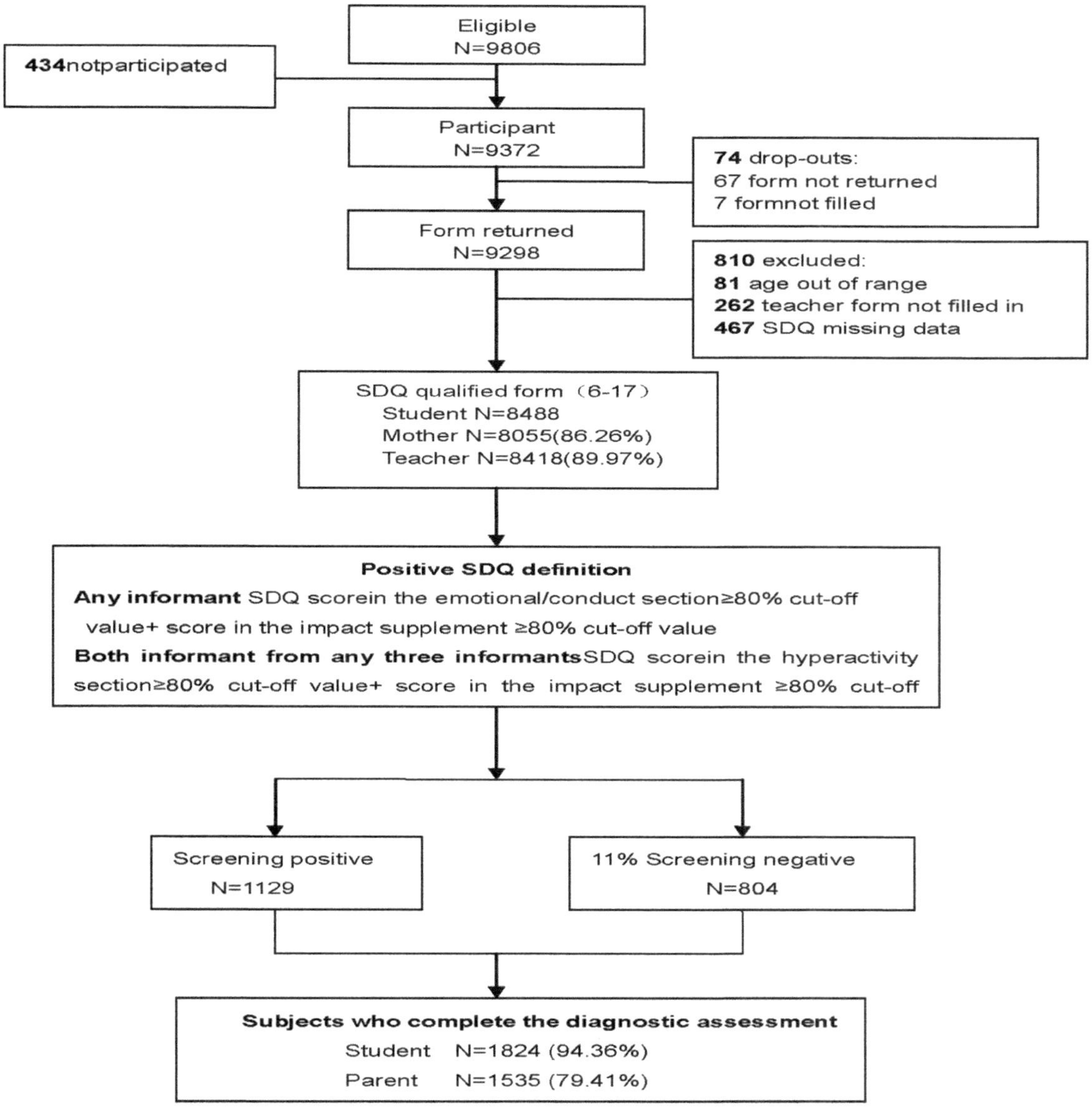

Figure 1. Flowchart showing inclusion criteria for the samples of adolescents in this two-phase design study.

symptom score was above the 95th centile and the impact score was two or more, which previously has been shown to work well in settings as diverse as Britain and Bangladesh [17]. According to the results of a pilot study, we adjusted such a priori criteria to keep the sensitivity of the screening phase and children were taken to be screen positive if (1) they exceeded the 80th percentile of the emotional and/or conduct section scores and the 80th percentile of the impact supplement score for anyone of the three informants; or (2) they exceeded the 80th percentile of the hyperactivity section score and the 80th percentile of the impact supplement score for any two of the three informants. Phase 2 was conducted on all screen-positive participants and on an 11% random sample of screen–negative participants.

Development and wellbeing assessment: DAWBA

Clinical assessment was conducted using the parent and adolescent versions of the DAWBA diagnostic interview [4], which uses a mixture of closed and open questions about child psychiatric symptoms and their impact. The version for parent was used for both the mothers and teachers of all children and adolescents, and the version of adolescent was only used to interview adolescent aged 11–17 years. The Chinese version of DAWBA was provided by the interview's author (Robot Goodman), and a previous study has shown satisfactory validity and reliability [18]. The interviews were administrated by trained layman interviewers who also record verbatim accounts of any problems reported, but not rate them. All the diagnoses were made by two experienced child psychiatrists who had completed the online training available for the DAWBA. The raters reviewed preliminary computer-generated diagnoses by computer algorithm (available at http://www/dawba.com) on the basis of symptom and impairment data independently, using information collected from mothers, teachers and schoolchildren, and then the verbatim transcripts in order to accept or modify the computer-generated diagnoses, and assign not-otherwise-specified (NOS) diagnoses.

When in doubt, the cases were discussed with a senior child and adolescent psychiatrist until a clear consensus was reached. Interrater agreement between the raters was calculated from a random sample of 100 interviewed participants. The kappa coefficient of 0.75 was within the range as the coefficient yielded by the original English version of the interview [18]. To avoid small cell sizes and wide confidence intervals, the specific diagnoses were categorized into internalizing disorders: separation anxiety, specific phobia, social phobia, panic disorder, post-traumatic stress disorder (PTSD), obsessive-compulsive disorder (OCD), generalized anxiety disorder (GAD) and major depressive disorder (MDD); or externalizing disorders: attention deficit and hyperactivity disorder (ADHD), oppositional defiant disorder (ODD) and conduct disorder (CD). Correlates and regression analyses are presented only for "Any DSM-IV diagnosis".

Statistical analysis

We used the SPSS-17 complex sample analysis module (SPSS Inc, Chicago, IL) to calculate the weighted prevalence rates, which uses Taylor series linearization methods to adjust appropriately for sampling weights and clustering within strata in complex surveys designs. The proportions of patients diagnosed in the second phase have been weighted back to allow for the sampling of those screen negatives in the first phase to represent patients originally screened using weights proportional to the inverse of the probability of selection of each subject [19]. Odds ratios (ORs) estimated by logistic regression were used to indicate strength of associations between potential correlates and disorders, as well as the comorbidity between any two of the five major types of disorder (anxiety, depression, ADHD, oppositional defiant, and conduct disorders) while adjusting for the third group.

Results

Table 1 showed that the weighted prevalence of any DSM-IV psychiatric disorder was 9.49% (8.01%–11.10%), internalizing disorders (7.03%, 5.58%–8.46%) were more frequent than externalizing disorders (2.34%, 1.72%–3.18%). Anxiety disorders showed the highest prevalence rate (6.06%), followed by disruptive disorders (1.63%), depressive disorders (1.32%) and ADHD (0.84%). Special phobia (3.59%), oppositional defiant disorder (1.21%), major depression (1.04%), generalized anxiety disorder (1.09) and obsessive-compulsive disorder (1.00%) were the top five individual disorders. 2.51% of the children had two or more disorders.

Table 2 showed significantly higher prevalence of externalizing (RR = 2.89, 95%CI = 1.45–5.68) in male than in female. Rural children showed non-significantly lower prevalence of externalizing disorders (RR = 0.58, 95%CI = 0.29–1.13) than urban counterparts. Younger children (6–10 years) have significantly lower prevalence of any disorders and internalizing disorders than elders ones, children aged 11–14 years have the highest prevalence of internalizing and internalizing disorders. The prevalence of any and internalizing disorders increase significantly with maternal education levels. Children from divorced or low income families have 2–5 fold increased internalizing and externalizing disorders. Children left-behind had significantly elevated externalizing (RR = 3.48, 95%CI = 1.64–7.37) and any disorders (RR = 1.03, 95%CI = 1.03–2.57), but not internalizing disorders. The prevalence of internalizing and externalizing disorders increased significantly with reducing academic performance records of the children. No significant differences were observed between children from families with one or more children.

Comorbidity

Of the 805 children with any DSM-IV psychiatric disorder, 683 (84.8%) had just one type of disorder (anxiety, depression, ADHD, oppositional-conduct disorder, or less common disorder), 117 (14.5%) had two types of disorder, only 3 (0.4%) and 2 (0.2%) had three and four types. Figure 2 illustrates the comorbidity between anxiety disorders, depressive disorders, and disruptive disorders. Children with depression were most likely to have a comorbid diagnosis (36.4%), followed by children with a disruptive disorder (23.5%), while children with an anxiety disorder have the lowest rate (13.7%).

Figure 3 demonstrates the strength of the adjusted associations between the five main categories of disorder, children with anxiety, depression, ADHD, conduct or oppositional disorder all had significantly increased odds of having another major type of disorder, after adjusting for the presence of other disorders, but there was not a significant association between ADHD and either anxiety or depression, between anxiety and conduct disorder, between depression and oppositional defiant disorder

Discussion

The total prevalence of 9.49% is almost the same as 9.48% found in the first study with the DAWBA among 5–15 years old British children [20], higher than Indian children aged 12–16 years (1.81%) [21], Norwegian children aged 8–10 years (7.0%) [22] and Italian schoolchildren aged 10–14 years (8.2%) [23], but lower than Brazilian children and adolescent (10.8%–12.7%) [24], Israeli adolescents aged 14–17 (11.7%) [25], Bangladesh children aged 5–10 years (15.2%) [26], Russian children aged 7–14 years(15.3%) [27], and Yemeni schoolchildren aged 7–10 (15.7%) [28]. Although the overall prevalence rate is somehow lower than that found in the low or middle developed countries [26–28], it is generally in line with previous studies. The prevalence was also lower than previously reported results in Chinese children and adolescents from Hunan province of mainland China (14.9%–16.2%) [14–15], Hong Kong (16.4%) [29] and Taiwan (14.8%–22.7%) [30]. The differences in these studies may reflect the real variations in the prevalence of psychiatric disorders among schoolchildren from different areas in China. Previous studies showed that prevalence rates of mental disorders in children and adolescents may vary greatly, studies using instruments with less restricted criteria for functional impairment have found higher rates [31–32]. It's important to note that the range of disorders covered by the DAWBA is somewhat limited compared with the Youth and Parent versions of DISC-IV (Diagnostic and Statistical Manual of Mental Disorders-4th edition) used in Hunan [15], and the Schedule for Affective Disorders and Schizophrenia for School-Age Children–Epidemiologic Version (K-SADS-E) used in Taiwan [30] and Hong Kong [29], and does not specifically address developmental, somatization, psychotic or substance abuse disorders. The differences in the screening and diagnostic instruments, especially the inclusion of a consideration of impairment in both SDQ and DAWBA, may contribute partly to the lower prevalence in the present study.

Although the rates for any mental disorder are similar in Chinese and Great Britain (9.49%:9.48%), anxiety (6.06%:3.77%) and depression (1.32%:0.92%) disorders prevail in the former whereas behavioral disorder (1.63%:3.67%) and ADHD (0.84%:2.23%) prevail in the latter [20]. The pattern of higher prevalence of internalizing disorders and low prevalence of externalizing disorders (7.03% and 2.34%) was similar to the findings in Israeli adolescents (8.1% and 4.8%) [25]. Previous studies have reported that Chinese/Asian children experience

Table 1. Weighted prevalence (95% CI) for DSM-IV disorder in children aged 6–17.

	Prevalence	95%CI
Any psychatric diagnosis	9.49	8.10–11.10
Internalizing disorder	7.03	5.83–8.46
Anxiety disorders		
Any anxiety disorder	6.06	4.95–7.40
Separation anxiety disorder	0.92	0.57–1.51
Special phobia	3.59	2.70–4.76
Social phobia	0.11	0.10–0.13
PTSD	0.06	0.05–0.08
Obsessive-compulsive disorder	1.00	0.61–1.63
Generalized anxiety disorder	1.09	0.72–1.65
Panic attack	0.34	0.18–0.62
Anxiety NOS	0.91	0.55–1.49
Depressive disorders		
Any depressive disorder	1.32	0.91–1.92
Major depression	1.04	0.71–1.54
Other depressive disorder	0.04	0.03–0.05
Depression NOS	0.39	0.16–0.95
Externalizing disorder	2.34	1.72–3.18
Attention-deficit hyperactivity disorder		
Any ADHD	0.84	0.52–1.36
ADHD combined	0.30	0.27–0.34
ADHD inattentive	0.21	0.08–0.55
ADHD hyperactive	0.37	0.14–0.95
Disruptive disorder		
Any oppositional-conduct disorder	1.63	1.12–2.36
Oppositional defiant disorder	1.21	0.77–1.87
Conduct disorder	0.62	0.39–0.99
Disruptive disorder NOS	0.11	0.02–0.69
Less common disorders	0.97	0.56–1.67
Eating disorders	0.54	0.25–1.14
Tic disorders	0.44	0.20–0.97
Comorbitity		
1	6.87	5.65–8.33
≥2	2.51	1.90–3.31

Note: No subjects were diagnosed with agoraphobia. CI = confidence interval; NOS = not otherwise specified; ADHD = attention-deficit/hyperactivity disorder; less common disorder: tic disorders and eating disorders

more internalizing problems whereas Western children experience more externalizing problems [33–37]. It was reported that the rates of total behavior problems in Chinese preschoolers were largely similar to those in American preschoolers, but Chinese preschoolers scored higher on internalizing problems while American preschoolers scored higher on externalizing problems [35]. In the present study, we found similar mean SDQ subscale scores on the conduct, hyperactivity and inattention problems rated by the parent and teacher between Chinese (data not shown) and British children and adolescents [3], but Chinese parents (0.27±0.87 vs 0.37±0.32) and teachers (0.24±0.78 vs 0.30±0.25) rated significantly lower impact score than their British counterparts, implying that Chinese adults tend to undervalue the impact of such problems. Our results supported the previous speculation that Chinese children subjected to socialization practices that stress self-control, emotional restraint, submissiveness, and dependency on others' opinions are more prone to developing internalizing or over-controlled problems [38–40], as opposed to externalizing or under-controlled problems [41–42].

Furthermore, the Chinese maybe constitutionally less vulnerable to hyperactivity on the basis of a more placid inborn temperament, some evidence has demonstrated ethnic differences between Chinese and American children in their autonomic nervous systems [43]. Despite previous suggestions of cross-cultural differences between Chinese and Western children or their informants on reporting psychopathology [44], a Chinese ethnicity cannot fully explain here our lower prevalence of ADHD, ODD and CD (0.84%, 1.21% 0.62%, respectively), given the higher rates reported in most previous studies in Chinese children and adolescent (3.3–7.5% for ADHD, 1.3–6.8% for

Table 2. Prevalence of psychiatric disorders by socio-demographic and geographic characteristics.

	Any disorder		Internalizing		Externalizing	
	Ratio(95%CI)	RR (95%CI)	Ratio(95%CI)	RR (95%CI)	Ratio(95%CI)	RR (95%CI)
Gender						
Girl	7.99(6.26–10.15)	1.00	6.69(5.11–8.71)	1.00	1.24(0.71–2.16)	1.00
Boy	10.82(8.75–13.30)	1.40(0.98–1.99)	7.17(5.50–9.29)	1.08(0.72–1.61)	3.48(2.40–5.02)	2.89(1.45–5.68)
District						
Urban	9.16(7.32–11.41)	1.00	6.66(5.08–8.68)	1.00	2.93(2.01–4.25)	1.00
Rural	9.62(7.65–12.03)	1.06(0.74–1.50)	7.21(5.55–9.32)	1.09(0.73–1.63)	1.71(0.99–2.94)	0.58(0.29–1.13)
Age						
6–10	4.33(2.87–6.50)	1.00	2.28(1.20–4.29)	1.00	2.45(1.50–3.98)	1.00
11–14	12.75(10.29–15.70)	3.23(1.97–5.28)	9.80(7.65–12.46)	4.66(2.30–9.45)	2.85(1.81–4.45)	1.17(0.59–2.30)
15–17	10.61(7.92–14.06)	2.62(1.53–4.48)	8.45(6.15–11.49)	3.96(1.90–8.28)	1.34(0.56–3.14)	0.54(0.20–1.47)
Maternal education						
≥9	6.60(4.87–8.88)	1.00	4.54(5.16–6.48)	1.00	1.87(1.07–3.25)	1.00
6–9	9.23(7.20–11.76)	1.44(0.95–2.19)	7.15(5.38–9.46)	1.62(1.00–2.63)	1.58(0.93–2.70)	0.84(0.38–1.85)
0–6	12.99(8.99–18.42)	2.11(1.25–3.57)	9.88(6.46–14.82)	2.30(1.27–4.18)	3.29(1.56–6.83)	1.78(0.69–4.62)
Parental marital status						
Married	8.43(7.08–10.01)	1.00	6.52(5.33–7.95)	1.00	1.65(1.16–2.34)	1.00
Divorced/single	18.16(10.99–28.51)	2.41(1.30–4.46)	12.27(6.60–21.68)	2.01(0.98–4.10)	8.23(3.68–17.41)	5.34(2.12–13.48)
Number of children						
1	8.35(6.85–10.15)	1.00	6.12(4.85–7.72)	1.00	1.86(1.27–2.73)	1.00
≥2	9.14(6.53–12.65)	1.08(0.71–1.65)	7.32(5.02–10.56)	1.21(0.75–1.94)	2.25(1.10–4.56)	1.21(0.53–2.77)
Family income						
High	9.00(6.49–12.34)	1.00	7.07(4.87–10.16)	1.00	1.97(1.00–3.85)	1.00
Middle	6.83(5.38–8.64)	0.74(0.48–1.15)	5.15(3.89–6.79)	0.71(0.44–1.17)	1.39(0.89–2.15)	0.70(0.31–1.59)
Low	19.79(14.31–26.71)	2.50(1.47–4.23)	13.92(9.41–20.12)	2.13(1.17–3.85)	7.10(3.98–12.35)	3.80(1.51–9.54)
Left mother or father						
No	8.19(6.74–9.93)	1.00	6.57(5.27–8.18)	1.00	1.42(0.93–2.15)	1.00
Yes	12.69(8.83–17.90)	1.63(1.03–2.57)	8.11(5.13–12.60)	1.26(0.73–2.16)	4.75(2.62–8.47)	3.48(1.64–7.37)
School record						
High	5.13(3.69–7.07)	1.00	4.12(2.85–5.92)	1.00	0.34(0.30–0.40)	1.00
Middle	11.33(8.73–14.57)	2.37(1.51–3.71)	8.62(6.39–11.53)	2.20(1.33–3.62)	2.33(1.29–4.19)	6.90(3.70–12.88)
Low	16.40(12.73–20.88)	3.63(2.31–5.72)	10.87(7.91–14.76)	2.84(1.69–4.77)	7.14(4.79–10.52)	22.22(14.14–34.92)

ODD, 1.41–2.9% for CD) [14–15,29–30]. Several large-scale DSM-IV population surveys also report more conservative prevalence estimates for the total ADHD prevalence (1.3%–2.5%) [20,28,45–47].The differences in methodological issues related to age ranges and diagnostic thresholds, especially the consideration of impairment in both SDQ and DAWBA, may contribute partly to the lower prevalence in the present study. Previous studies using the same diagnostic assessment have also showed big differences in the level and pattern of psychiatric disorders by countries or races, emotional and behavioral disorders are commoner than ADHD, but they have not consistently show that emotional disorders are commoner than behavioral disorders or vice versa [6,18,20,24,27,45], higher rates of emotional than behavioral disorders were also found in Norway [46], Italy [23], Yemen [28] and Israel [25]. Clearly, the possibility of ADHD being less prevalent than previously believed is important to address in future surveys. We detected only one case of autism spectrum disorder (ASD), the low prevalence could be related to the fact that many children with ASD might stay at home or study in the schools specific for the disabled children, and could not be detected in the school-based survey. Another reason could be that the DAWBA could miss some ASD cases because it focuses on present day symptoms [48].

Comorbidity

An overall comorbidity rate of 15.2% in the present study is lower than most reports in youth, ranging from 24% to 29% [20,24,47], but higher than Yemeni children (11.4%) [28]. In comparison with British children with the similar prevalence of any disorders [20], the pattern of lower ADHD (0.84%) and higher anxiety disorders (6.06%) in Chinese children could contribute to the lower level and different structure of comorbid diagnoses. However, we found almost the same pattern of the associations between disorders as British children, although the ORs were about 1/2 lower, supporting that comorbidity is selective, being evident between anxiety and depression, between

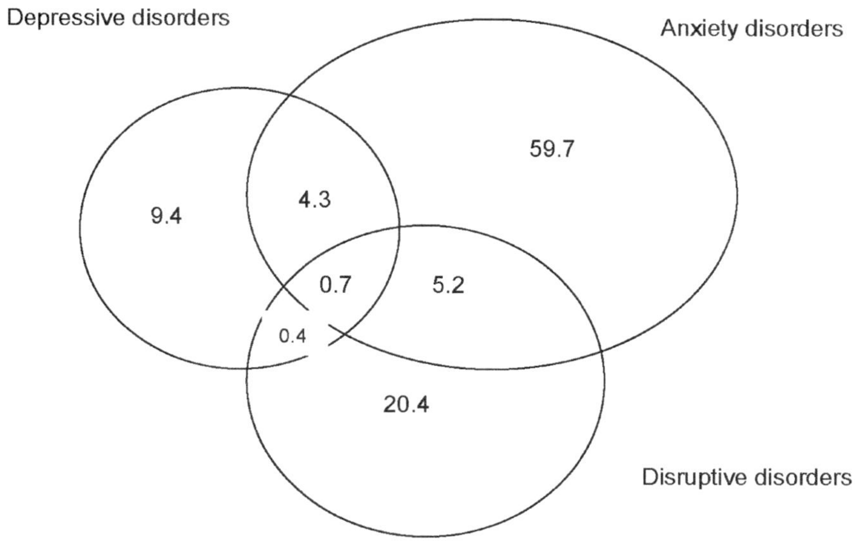

Figure 2. Comorbidity (%) among the 805 children with a psychiatric disorder.

ADHD and behavior disorders, and between depression and some behavior disorders [20]. The striking association between ADHD and behavior disorders and the lack of association between ADHD and emotional disorders corresponds to other surveys in which the association with the third group of disorders was properly controlled for in the analysis [20,24,47].

Distribution by democratic factors

We found that externalizing disorders were much commoner among males than females, while internalizing disorders had a relatively even gender balance, both were associated with learning disabilities, divorced family and low SES, this replicates a well-established pattern found in both developed and developing countries [15,20,22–23,27–28,31,45,47]. Females had insignificantly higher rates of internalizing disorders than males for those aged 6–10 (RR = 1.49, 95%CI = 0.42–5.28) and 15–17 (RR = 1.32, 95%CI = 0.66–2.62), but lower for those aged 11–14 (RR = 0.70, 95%CI = 0.41–1.21). We believe that the absence of gender difference in internalizing disorders could be related to the changing prevalence in school children with different age, similar results have been reported in Yemeni school children [28]. Mental disorders were associated with being elder, rather than younger, for any and internalizing disorders, primarily resulting from the rather lower ADHD in the present study. The higher prevalence of disorder observed for children aged 11–14 could be related to the onset of puberty, especially internalizing disorders [20,23,47]. Many studies have suggested that rural children have fewer mental health problems than urban children [26,28], but the urbanization of previously rural areas can lead to increased mental health problems despite improvements in living conditions, education and physical health [50]. Similar to previous finding in Hunan China [15], the absence of significant urban-rural differences in our study could be the combined effects of complex interactions of multiple factors in a society under rapid urbanization. As expected, the significantly elevated risks of externalizing (RR = 3.48) and total (RR = 1.63) disorders for the left-behind Children (LBC) confirmed previous report that LBC are at higher risk to develop emotional and behavior problems [49]. In the past

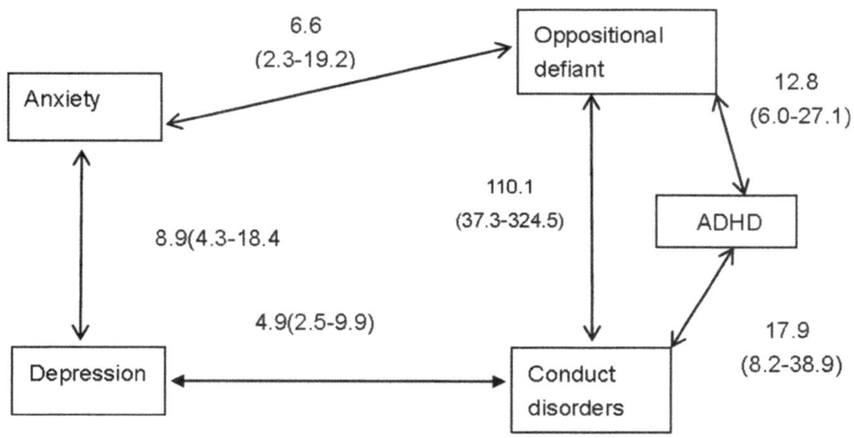

Figure 3. Adjusted odds ratios (95% confidence intervals) for comorbid DSM-IV disorders. ADHD = attention-deficit/hyperactivity disorder.

three decades, millions of Chinese farmers have immigrated to the cities for better life, which is obtained at the expense of family dysfunction and multiple negative impacts on the lives of their children [50–51], further attention is required to improve left-behind children's wellbeing, not only the basic daily care and personal safety, but also parental affection and mental health services.

Limitations

The present results should be viewed in the context of several limitations of the study. First, the survey was conducted among schoolchildren, those children left school because of mental health problem, poor academic achievement or other troubles were not included in the survey. It's therefore conceivable that including all children would have resulted in higher prevalence. Second, the small number of subjects meeting criteria for a diagnosis precluded analysis at the level of individual diagnoses. However, the classification of mental disorders into externalizing and internalizing groups is widely employed and well-validated, and can also contribute to explaining the comorbidity among individual mental disorders. Third, the age and stage of puberty were not assessed, such information could have contributed to elucidate the reasons for the changes in prevalence of mental problems with age. Last, because the teachers have to rate all the students in a class (about 40), they may not have sufficient time to attend to each individual child, it is unclear whether and how this burden may have affected ratings in different sampled areas.

Conclusions

The total prevalence of psychiatric disorder among Chinese schoolchildren was 9.49%, with higher internalizing disorders than externalizing disorders. There was comorbidity between ADHD and behavior disorders, anxiety and depression, emotional disorders and conduct disorder. Given the total number of 208 million students in all the primary and high schools in China, there would be a minimum of 20 million Chinese children and adolescents have significant mental health problems with serious function damage. Family and SES factors are significantly associated to the development of the psychiatric disorders, more attention should be paid to improve the family function and mental health care for the children, early identification and treatment of these problems are an urgent need and a big challenge for China to develop a national mental health policy for the interests of the children, their families and the society as well. Considering the huge, diverse and geographically spread Chinese population, more studies using internationally validated instruments and methodology from different regions are warranted to contribute to the growth of our knowledge on the mental health of Chinese adolescents.

Acknowledgments

The authors thank the schoolmasters, school teachers and parents of school children for their cooperation and support. We thank Dr. Wang Zhe from Liaoning Psychiatric Disorder Hospital and Dr.Xu Junting from Dalian Municipal Hospital of Psychiatric Disease for providing technical support on making DSM-IV diagnosis.

Author Contributions

Conceived and designed the experiments: PG JC. Performed the experiments: YX PW XW LF LN MH NJ LM AX FZ YC LL YL TL. Analyzed the data: YX PW XW NJ PG. Contributed reagents/materials/analysis tools: YX PW XW. Wrote the paper: PG JC YX.

References

1. Roberts RE, Attkinson CC, Rosenblatt A (1998) Prevalence of psychopathology among children and adolescents. Am J Psychiatry 155(6): 715–725.
2. Patel V, Flischer AJ, Hetrick S, McGorry P (2007) Mental health of young people: a global public health challenge. Lancet 369(9569): 1302–1313.
3. Goodman R (2001) Psychometric properties of the strengths and difficulties questionnaire. J Am Acad Child Adolesc Psychiatry 40: 1337–1345.
4. Goodman R, Ford T, Richards H, Gatward R, Meltzer H (2000) The Development and Well-Being Assessment: description and initial validation of an integrated assessment of child and adolescent psychopathology. J Child Psychol Psychiatry 41(5): 645–55.
5. Belfer ML, Rohde LA (2005) Child and adolescent mental health in Latin America and the Caribbean: problems, progress and policy research. Revista Panamericana de Salud Publica 18(4–5): 359–365
6. Mullick MS, Goodman R (2005) The prevalence of psychiatric disorders among 5–10 year olds in rural, urban and slum areas in Bangladesh: an exploratory study. Soc Psychiatry Psychiatr Epidemiol 40: 663–671.
7. Hesketh T, Zhen Y, Lu L, Dong ZX, Jun YX, et al. (2010) Stress and sychosomatic symptoms in Chinese school children: cross-sectional survey. Arch Dis Child 95(2): 136–40.
8. Liu X, Sun Z, Neiderhiser JM, Uchiyama M, Okawa M, et al. (2001) Behavioral and emotional problems in Chinese adolescents: parent and teacher reports. J Am Acad Child Adolesc Psychiatry 40(7): 828–36.
9. Liu H, Zhang JX (2004) Norm of symptoms checklist in Chinese middle school students. Chinese Journal of Epidemiology 15(2): 88–90.
10. Tang GZ, Guo LT, Huang XZ (2005) An epidemiological study on mental problems in adolescents in Chengdu, China. Chinese Journal of Epidemiology 11(26): 878–880.
11. Zhang Y, Wang SQ, Liu SX (2007) Epidemiological survey on psycho- behavior problems of children aged 4-16. Maternal and Child Health Care of China 22(13): 1829–1830.
12. Wang JN, Liu L, Wang L (2013) Prevalence and associated factors of emotional and behavioural problems in Chinese school adolescents: a cross-sectional survey. Child Care Health Dev. In press.
13. Zhang SP (2006) Mental health. In: China Children Center, Children's survival and development in China: Data and analysis. China Women Publishing House. pp. 154–157.
14. Yang ZW, Li YR, Wan GB, Su LY, Luo XR, et al. (1997) Prevalence and status of prevention and treatment of psychiatric disorders for the children and adolescent in Hunan province. Chinese Mental Health Journal 11(5): 260–263.
15. Guan BG, Luo XR, Deng YL, Wei Z, Ye H, et al. (2010) Prevalence of psychiatric disorders in primary and middle school students in Hunan Province. Chinese Journal of Contemporary Pediatrics 12(2): 123–126.
16. Du Y, Kou J, Coghill D (2008) The validity, reliability and normative scores of the parent, teacher and self report versions of the Strengths and Difficulties Questionnaire in China. Child Adolesc Psychiatry Ment Health. 2(1): 8.
17. Goodman R, Renfrew D, Mullick M (2000) Predicting type of psychiatric disorder from Strengths and Difficulties Questionnaire (SDQ) scores in child mental health clinics in London and Dhaka. Eur Child Adolesc Psychiatry 9: 129–134.
18. Zhang GY, Yang YC, Huang YI (2010) Epidemiological investigation on depression among 6~16 years old children and adolescents in Chengdu. Chinese Mental Health Journal 24(3): 211–214.
19. Dunn G, Pickles A, Tansella M, Vazquez Barquero JL (1999) Two phase epidemiological surveys in psychiatric research. Br J Psychiatry 174: 95–100.
20. Ford T, Goodman R, Meltzer H (2003) The British child and adolescent mental health survey 1999: the prevalence of DSMIV disorders. J Am Acad Child Adolesc Psychiatry 42: 1203–1211.
21. Pillai A, Patel V, Cardozo P, Goodman R, Weiss HA, et al. (2008) Non-traditional lifestyles and prevalence of mental disorders in young adolescents in Goa, India. Br J Psychiatry 192: 45–51.
22. Heiervang E, Stormark KM, Lundervold AJ, Heimann M, Goodman R, et al. (2007) Psychiatric disorders in Norwegian 8- to 10-year-olds: an epidemiological survey of prevalence, risk factors, and service use. J Am Acad Child Adolesc Psychiatry 46(4): 438–447.
23. Frigerio A, Rucci P, Goodman R, Ammaniti M, Carlet O, et al. (2009) Prevalence and correlates of mental disorders among adolescents in Italy: the PrISMA study. Eur Child Adolesc Psychiatry. 18(4): 217–26.
24. Fleitlich-Bilyk B, Goodman R (2004) Prevalence of child and adolescent psychiatric disorders in southeast Brazil. J Am Acad Child Adolesc Psychiatry 43(6): 727–734.
25. Steinberg T, Tamir I, Zimmerman-Brenner S, Friling M, Apter A. (2010) Prevalence and correlates of mentaldisorders in Israeli adolescents: results from a national mental health survey. J Child Psychol Psychiatry. 51(5): 630–9.
26. Mullick MS, Goodman R (2005) The prevalence of psychiatric disorders among 5–10 year olds in rural, urban and slum areas in Bangladesh: an exploratory study. Soc Psychiatry Psychiatr Epidemiol 40(8): 663–671.27.
27. Goodman R, Slobodskaya H, Knyazev G (2005) Russian child mental health–a cross-sectional study of prevalence and risk factors. Eur Child Adolesc Psychiatry 14(1): 28–33.

28. Alyahri A, Goodman R (2008) The prevalence of DSM-IV psychiatric disorders among 7–10 year old Yemeni schoolchildren. Soc Psychiatry Psychiatr Epidemiol 43(3): 224–230.
29. Leung PW, Hung SF, Ho TP, Lee CC, Liu WS, et al. (2008) Prevalence of DSM-IV disorders in Chinese adolescents and the effects of an impairment criterion: a pilot community study in Hong Kong. Eur Child Adolesc Psychiatry 17(7): 452–61.
30. Gau SSF, Chong MY, Chen THH, Cheng ATA (2005) A 3-year panel study of mental disorders among adolescents in Taiwan. Am J Psychiatry 162: 1344–1350.
31. Canino G, Shrout PE, Rubio-Stipec M, Bird HR, Bravo M, et al. (2004) The DSM-IV rates of child and adolescent disorders in Puerto Rico: Prevalence, correlates, service use, and the effects of impairment. Archives of General Psychiatry 61: 85–93.
32. Shaffer D, Fisher P, Dulcan MK (1996) The NIMH Diagnostic Interview Schedule for Children, version 2.3 (DISC-2.3): Description, acceptability, prevalence rates, and performance in the MECA study. Journal of the American Academy of Child and Adolescent Psychiatry 35: 865–877.
33. Liu J, Cheng H, Leung PW (2011) The application of the preschool Child Behavior Checklist and the caregiver-teacher report form to Mainland Chinese children: syndrome structure, gender differences, country effects, and inter-informant agreement. J Abnorm Child Psychol 39(2): 251–64.
34. Liu X, Sun Z, Neiderhiser J, Uchiyama M, Okawa M, et al. (2001) Behavioral and emotional problems in Chinese adolescents: parent and teacher reports. Journal of the American Academy of Child & Adolescent Psychiatry 40(7): 828–836.
35. Weine A, Phillips J, Achenbach T (1995) Behavioral and emotional problems among Chinese and American children: parent and teacher reports for ages 6 to 13. Journal of Abnormal Child Psychology 23: 619–639.
36. Yang H, Soong W, Chiang C, Chen W (2000) Competence and behavioral/emotional problems among Taiwanese adolescents as reported by parents and teachers. Journal of the American Academy of Child and Adolescent Psychiatry 39: 232–239.
37. Verhulst FC, Achenbach TM, Ende J, van der Erol N, Lambert MC, et al. (2003) Comparisons of problems reported by youths from seven countries. Am J Psychiatry 160: 1479–1485.
38. Chao R (1995) Chinese and European American cultural models of the self reflected in mothers' child rearing beliefs. Ethos, 23: 328–354.
39. Chen X, Rubin K, Li B (1997) Maternal acceptance and social and school adjustment in Chinese children: a four-year longitudinal study. Merrill-Palmer Quarterly 43: 663–681.
40. Ho D, Kang T(1984) Intergenerational comparisons of child-rearing attitudes and practices in Hong Kong Developmental Psychology 20: 1004–1016.
41. Zahn-Wasler C, Klimes-Dougan B, Slattery M (2000) Internalizing problems of childhood and adolescence: prospects, pitfalls, and progress in understanding the development of anxiety and depression. Development and Psychopathology 12: 443–466.
42. Weisz J, Sigman M, Weiss B, Mosk J (1993) Parent reports of behavioral and emotional problems among children in Kenya, Thailand, and the United States. Child Development 64(1): 98–109.
43. Kagan J, Kearsley R, Zelazo P (1978) Infancy: Its place in human development. Cambridge: Harvard University Press
44. Mann EM, Ikeda Y, Mueller CW, Takahashi A, Tao KT, et al. (1992) Cross-cultural differencesin rating hyperactive-disruptive behaviors in children. Am J Psychiatry 149: 1539–1542.
45. Goodman R, Neves dos Santos D, Robatto Nunes AP, Pereira de Miranda D, Fleitlich-Bilyk B, et al (2005) The Ilha de Mare study: a survey of child mental health problems in a predominantly African-Brazilian rural community. Soc Psychiatry Psychiatr Epidemiol 40: 11–17.
46. Wichstrøm L, Berg-Nielsen TS, Angold A, Egger HL, Solheim E, et al. (2012) Prevalence of psychiatric disorders in preschoolers. J Child Psychol Psychiatry 53(6): 695–705.
47. Costello EJ, Mustillo S, Erkanli A, Keeler G, Angold A (2003) Prevalence and development of psychiatric disorders in childhood and adolescence. Arch Gen Psychiatry 60: 837–844.
48. Posserud M, Lundervold AJ, Lie SA, Gillberg C (2010) The prevalence of autism spectrum disorders: impact of diagnostic instrument and non-response bias. Soc Psychiatry Psychiatr Epidemiol 45(3): 319–27.
49. Fan F, Su L, Gill MK, Birmaher B (2010) Emotional and behavioral problems of Chinese left-behind children: a preliminary study. Soc Psychiatry Psychiatr Epidemiol. 45(6): 655–64.
50. Jingzhong Y, Lu P (2011) Differentiated childhoods: impacts of rural labor migration on left-behind children in China. J Peasant Stud 38(2): 355–77.
51. Rahim SIA, Cederblad M (1986) Effects of rapid urbanization on child behavior and health in a part of Khartoum, Sudan-II. Psycho-social influences on behavior. Soc Sci Med 22: 723–730.

22

Investigation of 15q11-q13, 16p11.2 and 22q13 CNVs in Autism Spectrum Disorder Brazilian Individuals with and without Epilepsy

Danielle P. Moreira[1], Karina Griesi-Oliveira[1], Ana L. Bossolani-Martins[2], Naila C. V. Lourenço[1], Vanessa N. O. Takahashi[1], Kátia M. da Rocha[1], Eloisa S. Moreira[1], Estevão Vadasz[3], Joanna Goes Castro Meira[1], Debora Bertola[1,4], Eoghan O' Halloran[5], Tiago R. Magalhães[5,6], Agnes C. Fett-Conte[2], Maria Rita Passos-Bueno[1]*

1 Centro de Pesquisas sobre o Genoma Humano e Células Tronco, Departamento de Genética e Biologia Evolutiva, Instituto de Biociências, Universidade de São Paulo, São Paulo, Brasil, **2** Departamento de Biologia Molecular, Faculdade de Medicina de São José do Rio Preto, São José do Rio Preto, SP, Brasil, **3** Instituto de Psiquiatria do Hospital das Clínicas, Faculdade de Medicina, Universidade de São Paulo, São Paulo, Brasil, **4** Instituto da Criança da Faculdade de Medicina, Universidade de São Paulo, São Paulo, Brasil, **5** Academic Centre on Rare Diseases, School of Medicine and Medical Science, University College Dublin, Dublin, Ireland, **6** National Children's Research Centre, Our Lady's Children's Hospital, Dublin, Ireland

Abstract

Copy number variations (CNVs) are an important cause of ASD and those located at 15q11-q13, 16p11.2 and 22q13 have been reported as the most frequent. These CNVs exhibit variable clinical expressivity and those at 15q11-q13 and 16p11.2 also show incomplete penetrance. In the present work, through multiplex ligation-dependent probe amplification (MLPA) analysis of 531 ethnically admixed ASD-affected Brazilian individuals, we found that the combined prevalence of the 15q11-q13, 16p11.2 and 22q13 CNVs is 2.1% (11/531). Parental origin could be determined in 8 of the affected individuals, and revealed that 4 of the CNVs represent de novo events. Based on CNV prediction analysis from genome-wide SNP arrays, the size of those CNVs ranged from 206 kb to 2.27 Mb and those at 15q11-q13 were limited to the 15q13.3 region. In addition, this analysis also revealed 6 additional CNVs in 5 out of 11 affected individuals. Finally, we observed that the combined prevalence of CNVs at 15q13.3 and 22q13 in ASD-affected individuals with epilepsy (6.4%) was higher than that in ASD-affected individuals without epilepsy (1.3%; $p<0.014$). Therefore, our data show that the prevalence of CNVs at 15q13.3, 16p11.2 and 22q13 in Brazilian ASD-affected individuals is comparable to that estimated for ASD-affected individuals of pure or predominant European ancestry. Also, it suggests that the likelihood of a greater number of positive MLPA results might be found for the 15q13.3 and 22q13 regions by prioritizing ASD-affected individuals with epilepsy.

Editor: Paulo Lee Ho, Instituto Butantan, Brazil

Funding: Support was provided by FAPESP-INCT - grant number: 2008/57899-7; FAPESP-CEPID - grant number: 2013/08028-1; CNPq [http://www.fapesp.br/]. The funders had no role in study design, data collection and analysis, decision to publish, or preparation of the manuscript.

Competing Interests: The authors have declared that no competing interests exist.

* Email: passos@ib.usp.br

Introduction

Autism Spectrum Disorder (ASD) is a complex genetic disorder characterized by impaired social interaction and communication, and restricted, repetitive and stereotyped behavior patterns. ASD affects about 1% of the world population [1–3] and it occurs four times more commonly in males than in females [4]. In Brazil, a lower prevalence of ASD (0.27%) has been estimated, which was attributed to misdiagnosis [5]. In addition to the core symptoms, over 60% of the ASD-affected individuals can present other clinical conditions, such as epilepsy (~30%), gastrointestinal problems (9–70%), attention deficit and hyperactivity disorder – ADHD – (~30%) and sleep disturbance (~50%) [6–8].

Genome-wide screenings for copy number variations (CNVs) have revealed their occurrence in 10 to 20% of ASD individuals [9–12], in which the great majority of CNVs is usually rare and private. Exceptions to this rule are CNVs at 15q11-q13, 16p11.2 and 22q13, which, combined, have been found in roughly 3 to 5% of ASD-affected individuals [10,13–15]. While most CNVs at 16p11.2 are about 600 kb [14], CNV sizes in the other two regions vary widely. The 15q11-q13 region is particularly complex, with five breakpoint clusters (BP1-BP5) that define chromosome segments more prone to genomic rearrangements. Of these, the most recurrent chromosomal abnormality among ASD-affected individuals is a 15q11-q13 duplication (between BP2 and BP3, and about 4.95 Mb) and CNVs at 15q13.2-q13.3 (between BP4 and BP5 and ranging in size from 500kb to 2 Mb) [16–19]. The size of the 22q13 CNVs ranges from 100 kb to 9 Mb and always involves *SHANK3* [20,21].

CNVs at 15q11-q13, 16p11.2 and 22q13 have also been associated with other neurological conditions, such as epilepsy, schizophrenia and ADHD [22–26]. Apart from the variable clinical expressivity, these CNVs may exhibit incomplete penetrance [11,23,27]. The mechanism underlying the incomplete penetrance and the variable expressivity is not fully understood and it seems to depend on multiple hits [28]. Furthermore, the prevalence of these CNVs in distinct ASD subgroups (for instance, in ASD-affected individuals with epilepsy as compared to those without epilepsy) is unknown. Establishing clinical criteria to increase the likelihood of positive results for these alterations is important to prioritize genetic testing resources.

Whole-genome screening of CNVs in populations around the world have shown that their frequencies vary according to the ethnic background, allowing the distinction of populations of European, African and Asian ancestries [29,30]. Studies of CNVs at 15q11-q13, 16p11.2 and 22q13 have mostly been conducted in populations of pure or predominant European ancestry. It is not known whether they are also prevalent among ASD-affected individuals in populations of other ancestries, such as the Brazilian population, which is tri-hybrid, with important African and Amerindian contributions in addition to the European ancestry [31].

Thus, we conducted the present study to estimate the combined frequency of CNVs at 15q11-q13, 16p11.2 and 22q13 within a group of 531 Brazilian ASD-affected individuals, and we also sought to determine the frequency of CNVs in those regions by taking into account the epileptic and non-epileptic subgroups. Finally, we aimed at investigating whether the individuals with CNVs at the 15q11–13, 16p11.2 and 22q13 regions harbor additional CNVs, through a genome-wide SNP-array analysis.

Materials and Methods

Subjects

This study was approved by the Ethics Committee of the Instituto de Biociencias (IB) – Universidade de Sao Paulo (USP). Written informed consent was obtained from all patients' caregivers upon receiving information about the study.

Five hundred and thirty one Brazilian ASD-affected individuals were recruited for this study and ascertained at the "Centro de Pesquisa sobre o Genoma Humano e Células Tronco" (CEGH-Cel), IB-USP, following previously standardized criteria [32–34], which included a detailed anamnesis – pregnancy history, development history, age at onset, and weight, height and head circumference measurements – and a pedigree analysis. All probands were diagnosed according to Diagnostic and Statistical Manual of Mental Disorders, Fourth Edition (DSM-IV) criteria by psychiatrists from Instituto de Psiquiatria, Hospital das Clinicas - Universidade de Sao Paulo (IPq-USP). Whenever possible, an interview based on Autism Diagnostic Interview-Revised (ADI-R) and Childhood-Autism Rating Scale (CARS) evaluation was applied, as previously reported [32]. Epilepsy diagnosis was based on the occurrence of at least two unprovoked seizure episodes occurring more than 24 hours apart. Whenever possible, additional neurological and laboratorial tests were used to complement the diagnosis.

Blood samples from probands and parents were obtained for genomic DNA isolation, which was performed using the Autopure LS automated workstation, following manufacturer's procedures (Gentra Systems, Minneapolis, US). All the affected boys tested negative for Fragile X Syndrome [35].

Multiplex Ligation-dependent Probe Amplification (MLPA) analysis

MLPA probe sets targeting the chromosomal regions 15q11-q13, 16p11.2 and 22q13, SALSA MLPA kits P343-B1 and P343-C1 that contain 52 probes (9 control probes, 3 covering chr22:51,115,059–51,160,754, 11 covering chr16:28,997,152–30,365,260, and 29 covering chr15:25,297,217–32,988,875). They were purchased from MRC-Holland (Amsterdam, Netherlands) and used according to the manufacturer's protocol. The amplification products were identified and quantified by capillary electrophoresis on an ABI 3730 DNA analyzer (Applied Biosystems, Forster City, CA, US). The data were analyzed using GeneMarker software v1.95 (SoftGenetics, State College, PA, US). Threshold values for the peak height ratio were set at 0.75 and 1.3 for deletions and duplications, respectively.

Microsatellite genotyping

Seven microsatellite markers spanning the 15q11-q13 region were genotyped to identify the parental origin of the duplication of patient 2. The markers D15S1002, D15S1007 and D15S1012, ABI PRISM Linkage Mapping Set version 2.0 (Applied Biosystems, Forster City, CA, US) were genotyped following the manufacturer's protocol. The other primer sequence pairs, D15S1043, D15S976, D15S1031 and D15S1010, were obtained from the UCSC human genome browser (http://genome.ucsc.edu/cgi-bin/hgGateway, Feb 2009 GRCh37/hg19) and a M13 tail was added to the 5′-end of each forward primer [36]. Microsatellite genotyping was performed by means of an ABI DNA Analyzer (Applied Biosystems, Forster City, CA, US). Analysis of the results was performed with the GeneMarker v1.95 software (SoftGenetics, State College, PA, US).

CNV prediction analysis from genome-wide SNP arrays

CNV prediction analysis from genome-wide SNP arrays was carried out using the Affymetrix platform (Affymetrix, Santa Clara, CA, US): GeneChip Human Mapping 100K for ASD-affected individuals 10, as described in [37], and 11, GeneChip Human Mapping 500K Array Set for families of ASD-affected individuals 2 and 3, and Genome-Wide Human SNP Array 6.0 for the remaining ASD-affected individuals and parents. Protocols were performed according to the manufacturer's recommendations.

Data analyses were carried out with Affymetrix Genotyping Console (Affymetrix, Santa Clara, CA, US) and PennCNV (http://www.openbioinformatics.org/penncnv/), using the hg19 assembly (Genome Reference Consortium GRCh37). In both analyses we used the default parameters recommended by the manufacturers. A deletion or duplication was considered for further analyses only when detected by both methods.

We considered a CNV as potentially pathogenic according to two criteria: 1) they contained genes previously associated with ASD and/or other neuropsychiatric and neurological disorders (e.g. ADHD, global developmental delay, intellectual disability, schizophrenia and epilepsy/seizure); and/or 2) they exhibited a minimum overlap of 50% in length with CNVs previously associated with these conditions. For this, we searched Simons Foundation Autism Research Initiative (SFARI – https://gene.sfari.org/autdb/Welcome.do) and Decipher (https://decipher.sanger.ac.uk/) databases. Even though we analyzed, whenever possible, if the CNVs had been inherited, we did not include this information in the classification criteria. The CNVs considered as potentially pathogenic were not found or occurred with a frequency <1% in the Database of Genomic Variants (DGV - http://dgv.tcag.ca/dgv/app/home) [38,39].

Genome-wide SNP-array data are available in the ArrayExpress database (www.ebi.ac.uk/arrayexpress) under accession numbers E-MTAB-2818, E-MTAB-2819, E-MTAB-2820, E-MTAB-2821 and E-MTAB-2823.

Ancestry Analysis

We analyzed the ancestry of 9 out of 11 Brazilian ASD-affected individuals in whom high density genotyping (GeneChip Human Mapping 500K Array Set and Genome-Wide Human SNP Array 6.0) was carried out. The PLINK tool set (http://pngu.mgh.harvard.edu/purcell/plink/) [40] was used to merge the Brazilian dataset with the Human Genome Diversity Project (HGDP) [41] and HapMap project [42] datasets, and to select SNPs with a missing call inferior to 1% (geno option to 0.01), which yielded 84,805 SNPs. Next, we used Ancestry Mapper package from R, to produce AMids [43]. Admixture was used to produce ancestral proportions for each individual [44]. The R statistical language and environment [45] was used in most of the analysis, including the visualization, plotting data and clustering algorithms. Python was used to parse data and in some of the analysis.

Statistical Analysis

To assess the differences in CNV prevalence between the two subgroups, ASD-affected individuals without ($N = 453$) and with epilepsy ($N = 78$), we conducted two-tailed Fisher's exact tests. P-values below 0.05 were considered statistically significant.

Results

Through MLPA analysis, we identified CNVs at 15q11-q13 between BP4 and BP5 (15q13.3), and at 16p11.2 and 22q13, respectively, in three (0.6%), five (0.9%), and three (0.6%) of the 531 (423 boys and 108 girls) Brazilian ASD–affected individuals (Table 1; clinical characteristics in Table S1), which are ethnically admixed (Table S2), with a combined prevalence of 2.1% (11/531). In four of eight of those individuals, whose parents were available for genetic testing, the CNVs were found to be *de novo* (affected individuals 1, 6, 10 and 11). Among the other four individuals (affected individuals 2, 3, 4 and 7), only one CNV was maternally inherited (affected individual 7) (Table 1). The parents of affected individual 2 are consanguineous and both are carriers of the CNV at 15q13.3. The parents share a haplotype at this region, suggesting a common origin of the 15q13.3 duplication. Therefore, they probably inherited the CNV from their mothers, who are sisters, while the proband inherited it from his father (Figure 1A and 1B). None of the carrier parents reported behavioral or neurological issues.

We conducted a CNV prediction analysis from genome-wide SNP arrays in the 11 ASD-affected individuals in whom we detected CNVs at 15q13.3, 16p11.2 and 22q13 regions to determine their sizes as well as to verify whether another potentially pathogenic CNV would be present. The 15q13.3, 16p11.2 and 22q13 CNVs sizes ranged from 206 kb to 2.27 Mb (Table 1). It is worth noting that the two 15q13.3 duplications were about 500 kb and included only the gene *CHRNA7*. Six additional CNVs (3 duplications and 3 deletions) were identified in 5 of those affected individuals (1, 2, 4, 8 and 9), two of the CNVs in individual 4 (Table 1). Four of these CNVs were inherited, while the parents of the other two affected individuals were unavailable for testing (Table 1). The 15q11.2 CNV in affected individual 2 was also present in both consanguineous parents and the maternal copy was transmitted to the affected proband (Figure 1B). Ancestry analysis was conducted in 9 out of 11 ASD-affected individuals (Table S2), which showed that they have the three main ancestral components commonly observed in the Brazilian population.

Next, we evaluated if CNVs at 15q13.3, 16p11.2 and 22q13 occurred more often among ASD-affected individuals with epilepsy. In our total sample, 78 (54 boys and 24 girls) of the 531 ASD-affected individuals had history of epilepsy (Table 2). We observed that 6 of the 453 ASD-affected individuals without epilepsy (1.3%) and 5 of the 78 ASD-affected individuals with epilepsy (6.4%) had CNVs in one of these regions. These frequencies were significantly different ($p = 0.014$; odds ratio = 5.1; 95% CI 1.19–20.55). CNVs at 15q13.3 and 22q13 among ASD-affected individuals with epilepsy were responsible for these differences (Table 2).

Discussion

In the Brazilian sample of ASD-affected patients, the frequencies of CNVs at 15q13.3 (0.6%), 16p11.2 (0.9%), and 22q13 (0.6%) are consistent with those described in the literature [28,38–42]. The Brazilian population is ethnically admixed, with around 56–62% of European contribution [31,46–48]. In ASD-affected individuals positive for CNVs at 15q11-q13, 16p11.2 and 22q13, we observed that the contribution of European ancestry varied from 38 to 98%. This preliminary analysis suggests that the ethnic admixture of our population is not influencing the occurrence of these CNVs.

We identified both inherited and *de novo* CNVs at 15q11-q13 and 16p11.2, as previously described by other groups [49–52]. Indeed, it has been established that maternally and paternally inherited as well as *de novo* 16p11.2 microdeletions and microduplications contribute to the ASD phenotype [51,53–55]. Additionally, 15q13.3 deletions and maternally inherited duplications at 15q11-q13 have been implicated in an increased risk of ASD [28,56,57]. However, the association between the 15q13.3 duplication, involving only *CHRNA7,* and neuropsychiatric disorders is still controversial [24,49,58–60]. In our sample, the two 15q13.3 duplications were inherited from the father, but both maternally and paternally inherited 15q13.3 duplications have been associated with the ASD phenotype [49,58]. Finally, our data on the origin of the 22q13 deletions provide additional support to the hypothesis that they usually represent *de novo* mutations [21,61,62].

The size of the CNVs at 16p11.2 (600kb) and 15q13.3 (500kb or 1.6Mb), are within the range of those previously reported [49,54,57], as expected due to the presence of segmental duplications that flank these regions and mediate rearrangements through non-allelic homologous recombination [49,54,63]. At 22q13 the size of the CNVs were quite variable, but always included *SHANK3*. Loss-of-function mutations involving *SHANK3* cause Phelan-McDermid syndrome, an autosomal dominant condition with full penetrance that presents ASD among other clinical features [21,64]. In addition to the aforementioned CNVs, five ASD-affected individuals also carried at least another CNV with no correlation with the presence of CNVs at 15q13.3, 16p11.2 or 22q13. All those additional CNVs detected by the SNP-array platform overlap partially or completely CNVs previously associated with ASD or other neurological conditions [15,65–74]. Therefore, these additional CNVs, which were found in nearly 50% of our affected individuals, might contribute to the penetrance of the ASD phenotype, in accordance with the two- or multiple hit hypotheses for ASD, that is, these CNVs are not the cause ASD alone and depend on the presence of at least a second mutation [58,75]. Further studies will be necessary for testing their effect and specificity on the phenotype.

Our data suggest that CNVs at 15q13.3 and 22q13 are more prevalent among ASD-affected individuals with epilepsy than among those only with ASD. Indeed, it has been shown that 15q13.3 and 22q13 deletions represent strong genetic risk factors

Table 1. CNVs at the chromosomal regions 15q13.3, 16p11.2 and 22q13 in the Brazilian individuals with ASD.

	MLPA detected CNVs						CNVs detected by SNP-array						
Affected Individual	Region	Position (hg19)	Type	Size (Mb)	N Genes	Inheritance	Region	Position (hg19)	Type	Size (Mb)	Inheritance	Disease association	
												Neurol. Dis.	ASD
1	15q13.2-q13.3	chr15:30,941,572–32,509,926	del	1.56	8	*de novo*	2q13	chr2:110,453,976–111,084,885	dup	0.631	pat	+	+
2*	15q13.3	chr15:32,024,192–32,509,926	dup	0,486	1	pat	15q11.2	chr15:22,410,242–23,222,284	del	0.812	mat	+	+
3	15q13.3	chr15:31,956,036–32,511,581	dup	0,555	1	pat	–	–	–		–		
4	16p11.2	chr16:29,696,973–30,191,907	dup	0,495	25	Pat	4q35.2	chr4:186,934,286–187,137,146	dup	0.203	mat	+	+
							11p11.2	chr11:48,380,903–48,968,027	del	0.587	pat	+	+
5	16p11.2	chr16:29,517,699–30,191,895	dup	0,674	28	father n.a.	–	–	–	–	–		
6	16p11.2	chr16:29,613,495–30,190,030	dup	0,576	27	*de novo*	–	–	–	–	–		
7	16p11.2	chr16:29,402,301–30,226,931	dup	0,824	32	Mat	–	–	–	–	–		
8	16p11.2	chr16:29,517,699–30,191,895	del	0.674	28	father n.a.	7p11.2	chr7:57,260,919–57,882,330	dup	0.621	father n.a.	+	+
9	22q13.3	chr22:51,027,581–51,234,443	del	0.206	6	father n.a.	17q11.2	chr17:25,974,257–26,075,524	del	0.101	father n.a.	–	+
10[¥]	22q13.3	chr22:50,282,986–51,304,566	del	1.02	35	*de novo*	–	–	–	–	–	–	–
11	22q13.3	chr22:49,033,233–51,193,680	del	2.27	37	*de novo*	–	–	–	–	–	–	–

Neurol. Dis. - Neurological Disorder; "–" – not reported in the literature; "**+**" reported in the literature; del – deletion; dup – duplication; n.a. – not available; pat - paternal; mat - maternal;
[¥]- ASD-affected individual 10 was described in [37]; * CNVs at 15q13.3 and 15q11.2 are present in both parents;

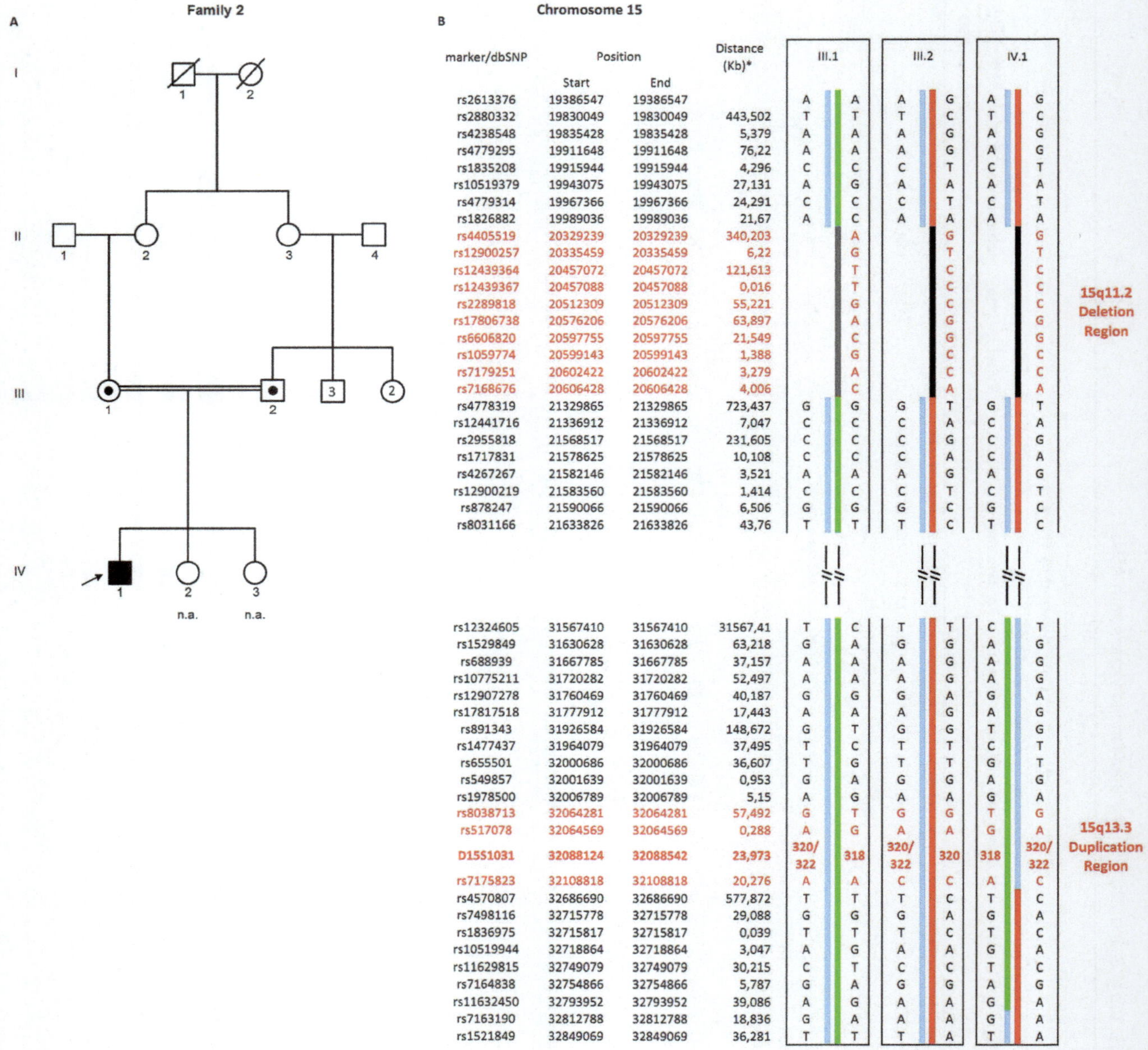

Figure 1. ASD-affected individual 2 pedigree and haplotypes. A) Pedigree of the ASD-affected individual. B) Haplotype analysis of SNPs and microsatellite markers at 15q11-q13. ASD-affected individual – filled symbol; Carriers of 15q13.3 duplication and 15q11.2 deletion – symbols with a black dot in the middle; individuals unavailable or not affected – empty symbols; non-available individuals – n.a. * Distance (in kilobases) from anterior to posterior marker/dbSNP. The other microsatellite markers are not showed.

for ASD and epilepsy [76–79]. However, the contribution of 15q13.3 duplications, particularly those encompassing only *CHRNA7*, to both phenotypes is still uncertain [19,49,58]. Although the 15q13.3 duplication has been implicated in several psychiatric conditions [24,60,80], rare cases presented epilepsy as well [49,81,82]. Within this context, ASD-affected individual 2 deserves special attention: while his 15q13.3 duplication was paternally inherited, his parents, who do not have any history of epilepsy, probably inherited the duplication from their mothers (who are sibs). This individual also harbors a deletion at 15q11.2 (Table 1), which in turn was inherited from his mother, even though both parents carry this 15q11.2 deletion (Figure 1). *De novo* or inherited deletions at 15q11.2 have been associated with both epilepsy and ASD, however the relative risk that this CNV confers to ASD is low [70,83,84]. It is thus possible that CNVs both at 15q11.2 and 15q13.3 are causative factors of ASD and/or epilepsy, supporting the etiologic models that involve multiple genetic alterations in ASD, since both alterations have incomplete penetrance but have already been reported in ASD and other neuropsychiatric diseases.

None of our ASD individuals with epilepsy carry a 16p11.2 CNV. Even though CNVs at 16p11.2 have been associated with epilepsy, this finding is not unexpected, as the phenotype of patients with these CNVs is extremely variable and

Table 2. Main findings in ASD Brazilian individuals with and without epilepsy.

	Total (N = 531)	ASD without epilepsy (N = 453)	ASD with epilepsy (N = 78)
Gender			
Male	423	369	54
Female	108	84	24
Ratio (m:f)	4:1	4.4:1	2.3:1
Mean age, years (mean ± sd)	10.2±6.6	13.2±6.5	9.7±6.5
CNVs at 15q13.3, 16p11.2 and 22q13 (%)	11 (2.1)	6 (1.3)	5 (6.4) *
CNVs at 15q13.3, 22q13 (%)	6 (1.1)	1 (0.02)	5 (6.4)

m - male; f - female; sd, standard deviation; * OR = 5.1; (p-value = 0.014).

the overlap between ASD and epilepsy is not often observed among them [55,85–88].

In summary, this work describes the combined prevalence of CNVs at 15q13.3, 16p11.2 and 22q13 as 2.1% in Brazilian ASD-affected individuals. CNVs at 15q13.3 and 22q13 were significantly more frequent in ASD-affected individuals with epilepsy in our sample; hence, these CNVs should be preferentially screened in ASD-affected individuals if resources are limited. Other potentially pathogenic CNVs were identified in 5 out of 11 ASD-affected individuals studied, thus highlighting the need for understanding how those and other genetic alterations interact to give rise to ASD and other clinical complications.

Supporting Information

Table S1 Phenotypic characteristics of ASD individuals with CNVs at the 15q13.3, 16p11.2 and 22q13 regions.

Table S2 Ancestral Contributions in Brazilian ASD-affected individuals.

Acknowledgments

We are very grateful to the ASD-affected individuals and their family members who participated in this research. We would like to thank Cintia Ribeiro Marques for help in genetic evaluating the families, and MSc Gerson Shigeru Kobayashi for helping with manuscript revision.

Author Contributions

Conceived and designed the experiments: DM MRPB. Performed the experiments: DM ALBM NCVL KMR VNOT. Analyzed the data: DM ALBM NCVL EOH TRM KMR VNOT MRPB. Contributed reagents/materials/analysis tools: EOH TRM. Wrote the paper: DM KGO ALBM ESM ACFC MRPB. Evaluation of patients: EV JGCM DB.

References

1. Kogan MD, Blumberg SJ, Schieve LA, Boyle CA, Perrin JM, et al. (2009) Prevalence of parent-reported diagnosis of autism spectrum disorder among children in the US, 2007. Pediatrics 124: 1395–1403.
2. Lazoff T, Zhong L, Piperni T, Fombonne E (2010) Prevalence of pervasive developmental disorders among children at the English Montreal School Board. Can J Psychiatry 55: 715–720.
3. Brugha TS, McManus S, Bankart J, Scott F, Purdon S, et al. (2011) Epidemiology of Autism Spectrum Disorders in Adults in the Community in England. Arch Gen Psychiatry 68: 459–466.
4. Giarelli E, Wiggins LD, Rice CE, Levy SE, Kirby RS, et al. (2010) Sex differences in the evaluation and diagnosis of autism spectrum disorders among children. Disabil Health J 3: 107–116.
5. Paula C, Ribeiro S, Fombonne E, Mercadante M (2011) Brief report: Prevalence of pervasive developmental disorder in Brazil: A pilot study. J Autism Dev Disord 41: 1738–1742.
6. Gillberg C, Billstedt E (2000) Autism and Asperger syndrome: coexistence with other clinical disorders. Acta Psychiatr Scand 102: 321–330.
7. Simonoff E, Pickles A, Charman T, Chandler S, Loucas T, et al. (2008) Psychiatric disorders in children with autism spectrum disorders: prevalence, comorbidity, and associated factors in a population-derived sample. J Am Acad Child Adolesc Psychiatry 47: 921–929.
8. Xue Ming, Brimacombe M, Chaaban J, Zimmerman-Bier B, Wagner GC (2008) Autism spectrum disorders: concurrent clinical disorders. J Child Neurol 23: 6–13.
9. Sebat J, Lakshmi B, Malhotra D, Troge J, Lese-Martin C, et al. (2007) Strong association of de novo copy number mutations with autism. Science 316: 445–449.
10. Betancur C (2011) Etiological heterogeneity in autism spectrum disorders: more than 100 genetic and genomic disorders and still counting. Brain Res 1380: 42–77.
11. Carter MT, Scherer SW (2013) Autism spectrum disorder in the genetics clinic: a review. Clin Genet 83: 399–407.
12. Pinto D, Delaby E, Merico D, Barbosa M, Merikangas A, et al. (2014) Convergence of Genes and Cellular Pathways Dysregulated in Autism Spectrum Disorders. Am J Hum Genet: 677–694.
13. Walsh KM, Bracken MB (2011) Copy number variation in the dosage-sensitive 16p11.2 interval accounts for only a small proportion of autism incidence: A systematic review and meta-analysis. Genet Med 13: 377–384.
14. Marshall CR, Noor A, Vincent JB, Lionel AC, Feuk L, et al. (2008) Structural variation of chromosomes in autism spectrum disorder. Am J Hum Genet 82: 477–488.
15. Sanders SJ, Ercan-Sencicek AG, Hus V, Luo R, Murtha MT, et al. (2011) Multiple recurrent de novo CNVs, including duplications of the 7q11.23 Williams syndrome region, are strongly associated with autism. Neuron 70: 863–885.
16. Menashe I, Larsen EC, Banerjee-Basu S (2013) Prioritization of Copy Number Variation Loci Associated with Autism from AutDB-An Integrative Multi-Study Genetic Database. PLoS One 8: e66707.
17. Depienne C, Moreno-De-Luca D, Heron D, Bouteiller D, Gennetier A, et al. (2009) Screening for genomic rearrangements and methylation abnormalities of the 15q11-q13 region in autism spectrum disorders. Biol Psychiatry 66: 349–359.
18. Rosenfeld JA, Stephens LE, Coppinger J, Ballif BC, Hoo JJ, et al. (2011) Deletions flanked by breakpoints 3 and 4 on 15q13 may contribute to abnormal phenotypes. Eur J Hum Genet 19: 547–554.
19. Miller DT, Shen Y, Weiss LA, Korn J, Anselm I, et al. (2009) Microdeletion/duplication at 15q13.2q13.3 among individuals with features of autism and other neuropsychiatric disorders. J Med Genet 46: 242–248.
20. Soorya L, Kolevzon A, Zweifach J, Lim T, Dobry Y, et al. (2013) Prospective investigation of autism and genotype-phenotype correlations in 22q13 deletion syndrome and SHANK3 deficiency. Mol Autism 4: 18.
21. Bonaglia MC, Giorda R, Beri S, De Agostini C, Novara F, et al. (2011) Molecular mechanisms generating and stabilizing terminal 22q13 deletions in 44 subjects with Phelan/McDermid syndrome. PLoS Genet 7: e1002173.
22. International T, Consortium S (2008) Rare chromosomal deletions and duplications increase risk of schizophrenia. Nature 455: 237–241.
23. Stefansson H, Meyer-Lindenberg A, Steinberg S, Magnusdottir B, Morgen K, et al. (2014) CNVs conferring risk of autism or schizophrenia affect cognition in controls. Nature 505: 361–366.
24. Williams NM, Franke B, Mick E, Anney RJL, Freitag CM, et al. (2012) Genome-Wide Analysis of Copy Number Variants in Attention Deficit

Hyperactivity Disorder: The Role of Rare Variants and Duplications at 15q13.3. Am J Psychiatry 169: 1–10.
25. Galizia EC, Srikantha M, Palmer R, Waters JJ, Lench N, et al. (2012) Array comparative genomic hybridization: results from an adult population with drug-resistant epilepsy and co-morbidities. Eur J Med Genet 55: 342–348.
26. Striano P, Coppola A, Paravidino R, Malacarne M, Gimelli S, et al. (2012) Clinical significance of rare copy number variations in epilepsy: a case-control survey using microarray-based comparative genomic hybridization. Arch Neurol 69: 322–330.
27. Miles JH (2011) Autism spectrum disorders–a genetics review. Genet Med 13: 278–294.
28. Marshall CR, Scherer SW (2012) Genomic Structural Variants. 838: 115–135.
29. Redon R, Ishikawa S, Fitch KR, Feuk L, Perry GH, et al. (2006) Global variation in copy number in the human genome. Nature 444: 444–454.
30. Jakobsson M, Scholz SW, Scheet P, Gibbs JR, VanLiere JM, et al. (2008) Genotype, haplotype and copy-number variation in worldwide human populations. Nature 451: 998–1003.
31. Giolo SR, Soler JMP, Greenway SC, Almeida MAA, de Andrade M, et al. (2012) Brazilian urban population genetic structure reveals a high degree of admixture. Eur J Hum Genet 20: 111–116.
32. Griesi-Oliveira K, Moreira DP, Davis-Wright N, Sanders S, Mason C, et al. (2012) A complex chromosomal rearrangement involving chromosomes 2, 5, and X in autism spectrum disorder. Am J Med Genet Part B, Neuropsychiatr Genet 159B: 529–536.
33. Griesi-Oliveira K, Sunaga DY, Alvizi L, Vadasz E, Passos-Bueno MR (2013) Stem cells as a good tool to investigate dysregulated biological systems in autism spectrum disorders. Autism Res 6: 354–361.
34. Orabona GM, Griesi-Oliveira K, Vadasz E, Bulcão VLS, Takahashi VNVO, et al. (2009) HTR1B and HTR2C in autism spectrum disorders in Brazilian families. Brain Res 1250: 14–19.
35. Haddad L, Mingroni-Netto R, Vianna-Morgante A, Pena S (1996) A PCR-based test suitable for screening for fragile X syndrome among mentally retarded males. Hum Genet 97: 808–812.
36. Schuelke M (2000) An economic method for the fluorescent labeling of PCR fragments. Nat Biotechnol 18: 233–234.
37. Jehee FS, Takamori JT, Medeiros PFV, Pordeus ACB, Latini FRM, et al. (2011) Using a combination of MLPA kits to detect chromosomal imbalances in patients with multiple congenital anomalies and mental retardation is a valuable choice for developing countries. Eur J Med Genet 54: e425–32.
38. Heil KM, Schaaf CP (2013) The genetics of Autism Spectrum Disorders–a guide for clinicians. Curr Psychiatry Rep 15: 334.
39. Schaefer GB, Mendelsohn NJ (2013) Clinical genetics evaluation in identifying the etiology of autism spectrum disorders: 2013 guideline revisions. Genet Med 15: 399–407.
40. Purcell S, Neale B, Todd-Brown K, Thomas L, Ferreira M a R, et al. (2007) PLINK: a tool set for whole-genome association and population-based linkage analyses. Am J Hum Genet 81: 559–575.
41. Cann HM, de Toma C, Cazes L, Legrand M-F, Morel V, et al. (2002) A Human Genome Diversity Cell Line Panel. Science (80-) 296: 261b–262.
42. Altshuler DM, Gibbs RA, Peltonen L, Dermitzakis E, Schaffner SF, et al. (2010) Integrating common and rare genetic variation in diverse human populations. Nature 467: 52–58.
43. Magalhães TR, Casey JP, Conroy J, Regan R, Fitzpatrick DJ, et al. (2012) HGDP and HapMap analysis by Ancestry Mapper reveals local and global population relationships. PLoS One 7: e49438.
44. Alexander DH, Novembre J, Lange K (2009) Fast model-based estimation of ancestry in unrelated individuals. Genome Res 19: 1655–1664.
45. R Core Team (2013) R: A Language and Environment for Statistical Computing.
46. Santos NPC, Ribeiro-Rodrigues EM, Ribeiro-Dos-Santos AKC, Pereira R, Gusmão L, et al. (2010) Assessing individual interethnic admixture and population substructure using a 48-insertion-deletion (INSEL) ancestry-informative marker (AIM) panel. Hum Mutat 31: 184–190.
47. Brito LA, Cruz LA, Rocha KM, Barbara LK, Silva CBF, et al. (2011) Genetic contribution for non-syndromic cleft lip with or without cleft palate (NS CL/P) in different regions of Brazil and implications for association studies. Am J Med Genet A 155A: 1581–1587.
48. Pena SDJ, Di Pietro G, Fuchshuber-Moraes M, Genro JP, Hutz MH, et al. (2011) The genomic ancestry of individuals from different geographical regions of Brazil is more uniform than expected. PLoS One 6: e17063.
49. Szafranski P, Schaaf CP, Person RE, Gibson IB, Xia Z, et al. (2010) Structures and molecular mechanisms for common 15q13.3 microduplications involving CHRNA7: benign or pathological? Hum Mutat 31: 840–850.
50. Weiss LA, Arking DE, Daly MJ, Chakravarti A (2009) A genome-wide linkage and association scan reveals novel loci for autism. Nature 461: 802–808.
51. Fernandez BA, Roberts W, Chung B, Weksberg R, Meyn S, et al. (2010) Phenotypic spectrum associated with de novo and inherited deletions and duplications at 16p11.2 in individuals ascertained for diagnosis of autism spectrum disorder. J Med Genet 47: 195–203.
52. Pagnamenta AT, Wing K, Sadighi Akha E, Knight SJL, Bölte S, et al. (2009) A 15q13.3 microdeletion segregating with autism. Eur J Hum Genet 17: 687–692.
53. Kumar RA, KaraMohamed S, Sudi J, Conrad DF, Brune C, et al. (2008) Recurrent 16p11.2 microdeletions in autism. Hum Mol Genet 17: 628–638.
54. Weiss LA, Shen Y, Korn JM, Arking DE, Miller DT, et al. (2008) Association between microdeletion and microduplication at 16p11.2 and autism. N Engl J Med 358: 667–675.
55. Ciuladaitė Z, Kasnauskienė J, Cimbalistienė L, Preikšaitienė E, Patsalis PC, et al. (2011) Mental retardation and autism associated with recurrent 16p11.2 microdeletion: incomplete penetrance and variable expressivity. J Appl Genet 52: 443–449.
56. Vorstman J, Staal W, Daalen E, Engeland H, Hochstenbach P, et al. (2006) Identification of novel autism candidate regions through analysis of reported cytogenetic abnormalities associated with autism. Mol Psychiatry 11: 18–28.
57. Ben-Shachar S, Lanpher B, German JR, Qasaymeh M, Potocki L, et al. (2009) Microdeletion 15q13.3: a locus with incomplete penetrance for autism, mental retardation, and psychiatric disorders. J Med Genet 46: 382–388.
58. Leblond CS, Heinrich J, Delorme R, Proepper C, Betancur C, et al. (2012) Genetic and functional analyses of SHANK2 mutations suggest a multiple hit model of autism spectrum disorders. PLoS Genet 8: e1002521.
59. Chilian B, Abdollahpour H, Bierhals T, Haltrich I, Fekete G, et al. (2013) Dysfunction of SHANK2 and CHRNA7 in a patient with intellectual disability and language impairment supports genetic epistasis of the two loci. Clin Genet 3: 9–14.
60. Vu TH, Coccaro EF, Eichler EE, Girirajan S (2011) Genomic architecture of aggression: rare copy number variants in intermittent explosive disorder. Am J Med Genet Part B, Neuropsychiatr Genet 156B: 808–816.
61. Nesslinger NJ, Gorski JL, Kurczynski TW, Shapira SK, Siegel-Bartelt J, et al. (1994) Clinical, cytogenetic, and molecular characterization of seven patients with deletions of chromosome 22q13.3. Am J Hum Genet 54: 464–472.
62. Bonaglia MC, Giorda R, Mani E, Aceti G, Anderlid B-M, et al. (2006) Identification of a recurrent breakpoint within the SHANK3 gene in the 22q13.3 deletion syndrome. J Med Genet 43: 822–828.
63. Lupski JR, Stankiewicz P (2005) Genomic disorders: molecular mechanisms for rearrangements and conveyed phenotypes. PLoS Genet 1: e49.
64. Phelan K, McDermid HE (2011) The 22q13.3 Deletion Syndrome (Phelan-McDermid Syndrome). Mol Syndromol: 186–201.
65. Bisgaard A-M, Kirchhoff M, Nielsen JE, Brandt C, Hove H, et al. (2007) Transmitted cytogenetic abnormalities in patients with mental retardation: pathogenic or normal variants? Eur J Med Genet 50: 243–255.
66. Xu B, Roos JL, Levy S, van Rensburg EJ, Gogos JA, et al. (2008) Strong association of de novo copy number mutations with sporadic schizophrenia. Nat Genet 40: 880–885.
67. Qiao Y, Tyson C, Hrynchak M, Lopez-Rangel E, Hildebrand J, et al. (2013) Clinical application of 2.7M Cytogenetics array for CNV detection in subjects with idiopathic autism and/or intellectual disability. Clin Genet 83: 145–154.
68. Wu DJ, Wang NJ, Driscoll J, Dorrani N, Liu D, et al. (2009) Autistic disorder associated with a paternally derived unbalanced translocation leading to duplication of chromosome 15pter-q13.2: a case report. Mol Cytogenet 2: 27.
69. Kaminsky EB, Kaul V, Paschall J, Church DM, Bunke B, et al. (2011) An evidence-based approach to establish the functional and clinical significance of copy number variants in intellectual and developmental disabilities. Genet Med 13: 777–784.
70. Doornbos M, Sikkema-Raddatz B, Ruijvenkamp CAL, Dijkhuizen T, Bijlsma EK, et al. (2009) Nine patients with a microdeletion 15q11.2 between breakpoints 1 and 2 of the Prader-Willi critical region, possibly associated with behavioural disturbances. Eur J Med Genet 52: 108–115.
71. Girirajan S, Brkanac Z, Coe BP, Baker C, Vives L, et al. (2011) Relative burden of large CNVs on a range of neurodevelopmental phenotypes. PLoS Genet 7: e1002334.
72. Elia J, Gai X, Xie HM, Perin JC, Geiger E, et al. (2010) Rare structural variants found in attention-deficit hyperactivity disorder are preferentially associated with neurodevelopmental genes. Mol Psychiatry 15: 637–646.
73. Rosenfeld JA, Ballif BC, Torchia BS, Sahoo T, Ravnan JB, et al. (2010) Copy number variations associated with autism spectrum disorders contribute to a spectrum of neurodevelopmental disorders. Genet Med 12: 694–702.
74. Wang L, Hranilovic D, Wang K, Lindquist IE, Yurcaba L, et al. (2010) Population-based study of genetic variation in individuals with autism spectrum disorders from Croatia. BMC Med Genet: 9–13.
75. Girirajan S, Rosenfeld JA, Cooper GM, Antonacci F, Siswara P, et al. (2010) A recurrent 16p12.1 microdeletion supports a two-hit model for severe developmental delay. Nat Genet 42: 203–209.
76. Sharp AJ, Mefford HC, Li K, Baker C, Skinner C, et al. (2008) A recurrent 15q13.3 microdeletion syndrome associated with mental retardation and seizures. Nat Genet 40: 322–328.
77. Helbig I, Mefford HC, Sharp AJ, Guipponi M, Fichera M, et al. (2009) 15q13.3 microdeletions increase risk of idiopathic generalized epilepsy. Nat Genet 41: 160–162.
78. Mulley JC, Scheffer IE, Desai T, Bayly MA, Grinton BE, et al. (2011) Investigation of the 15q13.3 CNV as a genetic modifier for familial epilepsies with variable phenotypes. Epilepsia 52: e139–42.
79. Phelan MC, Rogers RC, Saul RA, Stapleton GA, Sweet K, et al. (2001) 22q13 deletion syndrome. Am J Med Genet 101: 91–99.
80. Melchior L, Bertelsen B, Debes NM, Groth C, Skov L, et al. (2013) Microduplication of 15q13.3 and Xq21.31 in a family with tourette syndrome and comorbidities. Am J Med Genet Part B, Neuropsychiatr Genet: 1–7.

81. Beal JC (2013) Case Report: Neuronal Migration Disorder Associated With Chromosome 15q13.3 Duplication in a Boy With Autism and Seizures. J Child Neurol: 13–16.
82. Wiśniowiecka-Kowalnik B, Kastory-Bronowska M, Bartnik M, Derwińska K, Dymczak-Domini W, et al. (2013) Application of custom-designed oligonucleotide array CGH in 145 patients with autistic spectrum disorders. Eur J Hum Genet 21: 620–625.
83. Chaste P, Sanders SJ, Mohan KN, Klei L, Song Y, et al. (2014) Modest impact on risk for autism spectrum disorder of rare copy number variants at 15q11.2, specifically breakpoints 1 to 2. Autism Res 7: 355–362.
84. De Kovel CGF, Trucks H, Helbig I, Mefford HC, Baker C, et al. (2010) Recurrent microdeletions at 15q11.2 and 16p13.11 predispose to idiopathic generalized epilepsies. Brain 133: 23–32.
85. Degenhardt F, Priebe L, Herms S, Mattheisen M, Mühleisen TW, et al. (2012) Association between copy number variants in 16p11.2 and major depressive disorder in a German case-control sample. Am J Med Genet Part B, Neuropsychiatr Genet 159B: 263–273.
86. McCarthy SE, Makarov V, Kirov G, Addington AM, McClellan J, et al. (2009) Microduplications of 16p11.2 are associated with schizophrenia. Nat Genet 41: 1223–1227.
87. Bedoyan JK, Kumar RA, Sudi J, Silverstein F, Ackley T, et al. (2010) Duplication 16p11.2 in a child with infantile seizure disorder. Am J Med Genet A 152A: 1567–1574.
88. Schaaf CP, Goin-Kochel RP, Nowell KP, Hunter JV, Aleck KA, et al. (2011) Expanding the clinical spectrum of the 16p11.2 chromosomal rearrangements: three patients with syringomyelia. Eur J Hum Genet 19: 152–156.

Permissions

All chapters in this book were first published in PLOS ONE, by The Public Library of Science; hereby published with permission under the Creative Commons Attribution License or equivalent. Every chapter published in this book has been scrutinized by our experts. Their significance has been extensively debated. The topics covered herein carry significant findings which will fuel the growth of the discipline. They may even be implemented as practical applications or may be referred to as a beginning point for another development.

The contributors of this book come from diverse backgrounds, making this book a truly international effort. This book will bring forth new frontiers with its revolutionizing research information and detailed analysis of the nascent developments around the world.

We would like to thank all the contributing authors for lending their expertise to make the book truly unique. They have played a crucial role in the development of this book. Without their invaluable contributions this book wouldn't have been possible. They have made vital efforts to compile up to date information on the varied aspects of this subject to make this book a valuable addition to the collection of many professionals and students.

This book was conceptualized with the vision of imparting up-to-date information and advanced data in this field. To ensure the same, a matchless editorial board was set up. Every individual on the board went through rigorous rounds of assessment to prove their worth. After which they invested a large part of their time researching and compiling the most relevant data for our readers.

The editorial board has been involved in producing this book since its inception. They have spent rigorous hours researching and exploring the diverse topics which have resulted in the successful publishing of this book. They have passed on their knowledge of decades through this book. To expedite this challenging task, the publisher supported the team at every step. A small team of assistant editors was also appointed to further simplify the editing procedure and attain best results for the readers.

Apart from the editorial board, the designing team has also invested a significant amount of their time in understanding the subject and creating the most relevant covers. They scrutinized every image to scout for the most suitable representation of the subject and create an appropriate cover for the book.

The publishing team has been an ardent support to the editorial, designing and production team. Their endless efforts to recruit the best for this project, has resulted in the accomplishment of this book. They are a veteran in the field of academics and their pool of knowledge is as vast as their experience in printing. Their expertise and guidance has proved useful at every step. Their uncompromising quality standards have made this book an exceptional effort. Their encouragement from time to time has been an inspiration for everyone.

The publisher and the editorial board hope that this book will prove to be a valuable piece of knowledge for researchers, students, practitioners and scholars across the globe.

List of Contributors

Celeste H. M. Cheung, Philip Asherson, Fruhling Rijsdijk and Jonna Kuntsi
MRC Social, Genetic and Developmental Psychiatry Centre, Institute of Psychiatry, King's College London, London, United Kingdom,

Alexis C. Fazier-Wood
Human Genetics Center, Division of Epidemiology, Human Genetics and Environmental Science, School of Public Health, University of Texas Health Sciences Center at Houston, Houston, Texas, United States of America

Lenard A. Adler
Departments of Psychiatry and Child and Adolescent Psychiatry, New York University, New York, New York, United States of America

David B. Clemow and Todd M. Durell
Lilly USA, LLC, Indianapolis, Indiana, United States of America

David W. Williams
inVentiv Health Clinical, Indianapolis, Indiana, United States of America

Anne Kröger, Katharina Hof, Michael Siniatchkin, Tomasz Jarczok, Christine M. Freitag and Stephan Bender
Department of Child and Adolescent Psychiatry, Psychosomatics, and Psychotherapy, Goethe University Hospital Frankfurt, Frankfurt am Main, Germany

Christoph Krick
Department of Neuroradiology, Saarland University Hospital, Homburg an der Saar, Germany

Sina Kohl, Carolin Wolters, Joachim Klosterkötter and Jens Kuhn
Department for Psychiatry and Psychotherapy, University Hospital of Cologne, Cologne, North Rhine-Westphalia, Germany

Theo O. J. Gruendler
Department for Psychiatry and Psychotherapy, University Hospital of Cologne, Cologne, North Rhine-Westphalia, Germany
Department of Economics, Otto-von-Guericke-University, Magdeburg, Saxony-Anhalt, Germany
Center for Behavioral Brain Sciences, Magdeburg, Saxony-Anhalt, Germany

Kai Vogeley
Department for Psychiatry and Psychotherapy, University Hospital of Cologne, Cologne, North Rhine-Westphalia, Germany
Institute for Neuroscience and Medicine – Cognitive Neuroscience (INM3), Research Center Juelich, Juelich, North Rhine-Westphalia, Germany

Florence T. Bourgeois
Division of Emergency Medicine, Boston Children's Hospital, Boston, Massachusetts, United States of America
Department of Pediatrics, Harvard Medical School, Boston, Boston, Massachusetts, United States of America
Children's Hospital Informatics Program at the Harvard-MIT Division of Health Sciences and Technology, Boston Children's Hospital, Boston, Massachusetts, United States of America

Jeong Min Kim
Faculty of Arts and Sciences, Wellesley College, Wellesley, Massachusetts, United States of America

Kenneth D. Mandl
Division of Emergency Medicine, Boston Children's Hospital, Boston, Massachusetts, United States of America
Department of Pediatrics, Harvard Medical School, Boston, Boston, Massachusetts, United States of America
Children's Hospital Informatics Program at the Harvard-MIT Division of Health Sciences and Technology, Boston Children's Hospital, Boston, Massachusetts, United States of America
Harvard Medical School Center for Biomedical Informatics, Boston, Massachusetts, United States of America

Jingbo Gong
Mental Health Institute of The Second Xiangya Hospital, National Technology Institute of Psychiatry, Key Laboratory of Psychiatry and

Mental Health of Hunan Province, Central South University, Changsha, Hunan, China
Traditional Chinese Medicine University of Hunan, Changsha, Hunan, PR China

Jiajin Yuan
School of Psychology, Southwest University, Chongqing, China

Suhong Wang
Mental Health Institute of The Second Xiangya Hospital, National Technology Institute of Psychiatry, Key Laboratory of Psychiatry and Mental Health of Hunan Province, Central South University, Changsha, Hunan, China
Department of Neuroscience, the Third Affiliated Hospital of Soochow University, Changzhou, China

Lijuan Shi, Xilong Cui and Xuerong Luo
Mental Health Institute of The Second Xiangya Hospital, National Technology Institute of Psychiatry, Key Laboratory of Psychiatry and Mental Health of Hunan Province, Central South University, Changsha, Hunan, China

Regina Boecker, Nathalie E. Holz, Arlette F. Buchmann, Dorothea Blomeyer, Sarah Baumeister and Tobias Banaschewski
Department of Child and Adolescent Psychiatry and Psychotherapy, CIMH Medical Faculty Mannheim/Heidelberg University, Mannheim, Germany

Michael M. Plichta and Andreas Meyer-Lindenberg
Department of Psychiatry and Psychotherapy, CIMH Medical Faculty Mannheim/Heidelberg University, Mannheim, Germany

Isabella Wolf
Department of Child and Adolescent Psychiatry and Psychotherapy, CIMH Medical Faculty Mannheim/Heidelberg University, Mannheim, Germany
Department of Neuroimaging, CIMH Medical Faculty Mannheim/Heidelberg University, Mannheim, Germany

Daniel Brandeis
Department of Child and Adolescent Psychiatry and Psychotherapy, CIMH Medical Faculty Mannheim/Heidelberg University, Mannheim, Germany
Department of Child and Adolescent Psychiatry, University of Zurich, Zurich, Germany
Center for Integrative Human Physiology, University of Zurich, Zurich, Germany
Neuroscience Center Zurich, University of Zurich and ETH Zurich, Zurich, Germany

Manfred Laucht
Department of Child and Adolescent Psychiatry and Psychotherapy, CIMH Medical Faculty Mannheim/Heidelberg University, Mannheim, Germany
Department of Psychology, University of Potsdam, Potsdam, Germany

Amanda Ode, Karin Källén, Lars Rylander, Bo A. G. Jönsson, Christian H. Lindh and Anna Rignell-Hydbom
Division of Occupational and Environmental Medicine, Lund University, Lund, Sweden

Peik Gustafsson
Child and Adolescent Psychiatry Unit, Department of Clinical Sciences, Lund University, Lund, Sweden

Per Olofsson
Obstetrics and Gynecology Unit, Department of Clinical Sciences, Skåne University Hospital, Lund University, Malmö, Sweden

Sten A. Ivarsson
Department of Clinical Sciences, Unit of Pediatric Endocrinology, Lund University/Clinical Research Centre (CRC), Malmö, Sweden

Sharon Levy and William J. Barbaresi
Division of Developmental Medicine, Boston Children's Hospital, Harvard Medical School, Boston, Massachusetts, United States of America

Slavica K. Katusic, Amy L. Weaver and Jill M. Killian
Department of Health Sciences Research, Mayo Clinic, Rochester, Minnesota, United States of America

Robert C. Colligan
Department of Psychiatry and Psychology, Mayo Clinic, Rochester, Minnesota, United States of America

Robert G. Voigt
Department of Pediatrics, Texas Children's Hospital, Baylor College of Medicine, Houston, Texas, United States of America

Natalia Estévez
Institute of Social and Preventive Medicine, Zurich, Switzerland

Department of Neuroradiology, University Hospital Zurich, Zurich, Switzerland

Dominique Eich-Höchli
Psychiatric University Hospital Zurich, Zurich, Switzerland

Michelle Dey and Meichun Mohler-Kuo
Institute of Social and Preventive Medicine, Zurich, Switzerland

Gerhard Gmel and Joseph Studer
Alcohol Treatment Centre, Lausanne University Hospital CHUV, Lausanne, Switzerland

Benito de Celis Alonso
Faculty of Physics and Mathematics, Benemérita Universidad Autónoma de Puebla (BUAP), Puebla, Mexico

Silvia Hidalgo Tobón and Pilar Dies Suarez
Imaging Department, Hospital Infantil de México Federico Gómez, México DF, Mexico

Julio García Flores
Feinberg School of Medicine, Northwestern University, Chicago, Illinois, United States of America

Benito de Celis Carrillo
School of Industrial Engineering, Universidad de León, León, Castilla y León, Spain

Eduardo Barragán Pérez
Neurology Department, Hospital Infantil de México Federico Gómez, México DF, Mexico

Rizan Cassim, Joel B. Talcott and Elisabeth Moores
School of Life and Health Sciences, Aston University, Birmingham, West Midlands, United Kingdom

Anselm B. M. Fuermaier, Lara Tucha, Janneke Koerts and Oliver Tucha
Department of Clinical and Developmental Neuropsychology, University of Groningen, Groningen, the Netherlands

Marieke J. G. van Heuvelen
Center for Human Movement Sciences, University of Groningen, University Medical Center Groningen, Groningen, the Netherlands

Eddy A. van der Zee
Center of Behaviour and Neuroscience, Department of Molecular Neurobiology, University of Groningen, Groningen, the Netherlands

Klaus W. Lange
Department of Experimental Psychology, University of Regensburg, Regensburg, Germany

Laurence O'Dwyer, Eelco V. van Dongen and Marcel P. Zwiers
Radboud University Medical Center, Donders Institute for Brain, Cognition and Behaviour, Department of Cognitive Neuroscience, Nijmegen, The Netherlands

Colby Tanner
Department of Ecology and Evolution, University of Lausanne, Lausanne, Switzerland

Corina U. Greven
Radboud University Medical Center, Donders Institute for Brain, Cognition and Behaviour, Department of Cognitive Neuroscience, Nijmegen, The Netherlands
King's College London, Social, Genetic and Developmental Psychiatry Centre, Institute of Psychiatry, London, United Kingdom

Janita Bralten
Radboud University Medical Center, Donders Institute for Brain, Cognition and Behaviour, Department of Cognitive Neuroscience, Nijmegen, The Netherlands
Department of Human Genetics, Radboud University Medical Center, Nijmegen, The Netherlands

Barbara Franke
Department of Human Genetics, Radboud University Medical Center, Nijmegen, The Netherlands
Radboud University Medical Center, Donders Institute for Brain, Cognition and Behaviour, Department of Psychiatry, Nijmegen, The Netherlands

Jaap Oosterlaan
Department of Clinical Neuropsychology, Vrije Universiteit, Amsterdam, The Netherlands

Dirk Heslenfeld
Department of Clinical Neuropsychology, Vrije Universiteit, Amsterdam, The Netherlands
Department of Cognitive Psychology, Vrije Universiteit, Amsterdam, The Netherlands

Pieter Hoekstra and Catharina A. Hartman
Department of Psychiatry, University Medical Center Groningen, University of Groningen, Groningen, The Netherlands

Nanda Rommelse
Radboud University Medical Center, Donders Institute for Brain, Cognition and Behaviour, Department of Psychiatry, Nijmegen, The Netherlands
Karakter Child and Adolescent Psychiatry University Center Nijmegen, Nijmegen, The Netherlands

Jan K. Buitelaar
Radboud University Medical Center, Donders Institute for Brain, Cognition and Behaviour, Department of Cognitive Neuroscience, Nijmegen, The Netherlands
Karakter Child and Adolescent Psychiatry University Center Nijmegen, Nijmegen, The Netherlands

Matthew K. Vendlinski, Kristin N. Javaras, Carol A. Van Hulle, Richard J. Davidson and H. Hill Goldsmith
Department of Psychology and Waisman Center, University of Wisconsin–Madison, Madison, Wisconsin, United States of America

Kathryn Lemery-Chalfant
Department of Psychology, Arizona State University, Tempe, Arizona, United States of America

Rose Maier
Department of Psychology, University of Oregon, Eugene, Oregon, United States of America

Debjani Das and Simon Easteal
John Curtin School of Medical Research, The Australian National University, Canberra, Australian Capital Territory, Australia

Nicolas Cherbuin and Kaarin J. Anstey
Centre for Research on Ageing, Health and Wellbeing, The Australian National University, Canberra, Australian Capital Territory, Australia

Elvira Perez, Melody Turner, Joanna Lockwood and David Daley
University of Nottingham, School of Medicine, Nottingham, England, United Kingdom

Anthony Fisher
University of Nottingham, School of English, Nottingham, England, United Kingdom

Suzannah K. Helps and Susan Bamford
Institute for Disorders of Impulse and Attention, Department of Psychology, University of Southampton, Southampton, United Kingdom

Edmund J. S. Sonuga-Barke
Institute for Disorders of Impulse and Attention, Department of Psychology, University of Southampton, Southampton, United Kingdom
Department of Experimental Clinical & Health Psychology, University of Ghent, Ghent, Belgium

Göran B. W. Söderlund
Faculty of Teacher Education and Sports, Sogndal University College, Sogndal, Norway

Su Jin Moon
Department of Psychiatry, Daedong Hospital, Daegu, Korea

Chang Ju Kim
Department of Physiology, Kyung Hee University School of Medicine, Seoul, Korea

Yeon Jung Lee, Juhee Han and Geon Ho Bahn
Department of Psychiatry, Kyung Hee University School of Medicine, Seoul, Korea

Minha Hong
Department of Psychiatry, Dankook University Medical College, Cheonan, Korea

Natalia Emanuel
Department of Economics, Yale University, New Haven, Connecticut, United States of America

Christopher Wildeman
Department of Policy Analysis and Management, Cornell University, Ithaca, New York, United States of America

Peter Fallesen
Rockwool Foundation Research Unit, Copenhagen, Denmark
Department of Sociology, University of Copenhagen, Copenhagen, Denmark

Yang Xiaoli, Pan Wen, Li Ning, Mu Huijuan, Na Jun, Yu Lianzheng and Pan Guowei
Institute of Chronic Disease, Liaoning Provincial Center for Disease Control and Prevention, Shenyang city, China

Jiang Chao
Department of Psychiatry, Dalian Medical University, Dalian city, China

Xu Wenming
Department of Chronic Disease, Panjin Oil Field Center for Disease Control and Prevention, Panjin city, China

Liang Fang
Department of Psychiatry, Dalian Municipal Hospital of Psychiatric Disease, Dalian city, China

Lv Ming
Department of Chronic Disease, Donggang County Municipal Center for Disease Control and Prevention, Donggang county, Liaoning province, China

An Xiaoxia
Department of Chronic Disease, Benxi Municipal Center for Disease Control and Prevention, Benxi, China

Yu Chuanyou
Department of Chronic Disease, Qingyuan County Center for Disease Control and Prevention, Qingyuan county, Liaoning province, Qingyuan, China

Fu Zenguo
Department of Chronic Disease, Zhangwu County Center for Disease Control and Prevention, Zhangwu county, Liaoning province, Zhangwu, China

Li Lili
Department of Psychiatry, the 1st Attached Hospital of China Medical University, Shenyang city, China

Tong Lijuan
Department of Chronic Disease, Panjin Municipal Center for Disease Control and Prevention, Panjin city, China

Danielle P. Moreira, Karina Griesi-Oliveira, Naila C. V. Lourenço, Vanessa N. O. Takahashi, Kátia M. da Rocha, Eloisa S. Moreira, Maria Rita Passos-Bueno and Joanna Goes Castro Meira
Centro de Pesquisas sobre o Genoma Humano e Células Tronco, Departamento de Genética e Biologia Evolutiva, Instituto de Biociências, Universidade de São Paulo, São Paulo, Brasil

Ana L. Bossolani-Martins and Agnes C. Fett-Conte
Departamento de Biologia Molecular, Faculdade de Medicina de São José do Rio Preto, São José do Rio Preto, SP, Brasil

Estevão Vadasz
Instituto de Psiquiatria do Hospital das Clínicas, Faculdade de Medicina, Universidade de São Paulo, São Paulo, Brasil

Debora Bertola
Centro de Pesquisas sobre o Genoma Humano e Células Tronco, Departamento de Genética e Biologia Evolutiva, Instituto de Biociências, Universidade de São Paulo, São Paulo, Brasil Instituto da Crianc¸a da Faculdade de Medicina, Universidade de São Paulo, São Paulo, Brasil

Eoghan O' Halloran
Academic Centre on Rare Diseases, School of Medicine and Medical Science, University College Dublin, Dublin, Ireland

Tiago R. Magalhães
Academic Centre on Rare Diseases, School of Medicine and Medical Science, University College Dublin, Dublin, Ireland
National Children's Research Centre, Our Lady's Children's Hospital, Dublin, Ireland

Index